The Epic in Medieval Society
Aesthetic and Moral Values

The Epic in Medieval Society

Aesthetic and Moral Values

Edited by

Harald Scholler

Max Niemeyer Verlag
Tübingen 1977

CIP-Kurztitelaufnahme der Deutschen Bibliothek

The epic in medieval society : aesthet. and moral values / ed. by Harald Scholler. –
1. Aufl. – Tübingen : Niemeyer, 1977.
    ISBN 3-484-60054-3
NE: Scholler , Harald [Hrsg.]

ISBN 3-484-60054-3

Satz und Druck: Bücherdruck Wenzlaff, Kempten. Einband: Heinr. Koch, Tübingen

Dedicated
to
Walter A. Reichart

Inhaltsverzeichnis

Preface

The 23 articles contained in this volume are generally identical with the papers delivered at the Ann Arbor Symposium on medieval epic literature which took place on April 11–14 of 1973. The speakers who gathered on the campus of The University of Michigan came from Canada, Germany, Great Britain, and the United States. They represented eight disciplines and eighteen universities.

The title of the symposium was retained for the publication, with the term »epic« used in a broad sense. Although it was not the explicit task of the participants to question the usage of the English word or its equivalent in other languages, some tacit questioning could hardly be avoided. A renewed and coordinated probing of genre labels might therefore not be unwelcome.

The symposium with its papers and discussions went beyond national boundaries and did not limit itself to the period of the High Middle Ages. Some of its speakers demonstrated approaches to literature which operate, as it were, from opposite directions, that is, those approaches which exclusively treat specific literary aspects of a work, and those which look at a work from a peripherally literary or even extra-literary viewpoint. The contribution on music, it is hoped, will be found useful even though it may be unexpected.

The literatures represented above all include English, French, German, and Scandinavian. Beside the heroic epic it is the courtly epic which has been given special attention. By dealing with works usually not considered central to a treatment of the epic the symposium enlarged the scope of European epic creations considerably as to language, genre or subgenre, geography, and time. The inclusion of the Latin *Waltharius* and *Ruodlieb*, the Dutch beast epic *Reinaert*, the Icelandic sagas, the German *Prosa-Lancelot*, Hartmann's *Armer Heinrich*, Ulrich von

Lichtenstein's *Frauendienst,* and Wittenwiler's comic epic *Der Ring*
provides the reader of this volume with a broad panorama of epic
production.

The works and authors discussed embrace a time-span of roughly a
thousand years, from the days of St. Augustine to around the year
1400. Investigative aspects which received special consideration are
typology, oral tradition, history of early society, history of art, and
philosophy.

We hope that this volume will further the reader's understanding of
ethical and aesthetic concepts of the Middle Ages. He will not hear
much about Aristotle or Homer, being in this respect like the Archpoet
in his vision of 800 years ago (cf. poem IX, »Nocte quadam sabbati«).
But *un*like the Archpoet who claims to consider the opinion of St. Augustine sufficient in the search for truth, the reader does not have to be
content with *one* view only. In a number of instances he will find
differing and even opposing views.

In the discussions during the symposium it became evident that a good
number of the papers had been written with the issues of present day
society in mind. These papers endeavored to show that important
human experiences (successes and failures) as related in literature are
not unique to one particular historical period, and that therefore
present day man might do well to make use of the legacy passed on by
medieval works. The two essays concerning moral values and the generation-gap in the Icelandic saga are good examples of the relevance and
applicability of medieval literature to our time.

The symposium could not have taken place without the generous support of the National Endowment of the Humanities, the American
Council of Learned Societies, The University of Michigan, and the
Deutsche Forschungsgemeinschaft. The editor of this volume and or-
ganizer of the symposium would once again like to thank these institutions and their officers, particularly Dr. Ronald Berman and Dr. David
Wallace, Dr. Frederick Burkhardt, Dr. Donald E. Stokes (then Dean of
the Graduate School of The University of Michigan), and Dr. Claus
Müller-Daehn. Furthermore, sincere appreciation must be conveyed to
the following graduate students who freely gave of their time when
it was needed, especially during the 4 days of the symposium: Astrid
B. Beck, Roswitha A. Lugauer, Daria A. Rothe, Janet A. Spaulding,
Peter Ryan, James R. Wahl, Warren W. Wundt.

Special mention is to be made of the efforts of President Emeritus Har-

Ian H. Hatcher of The University of Michigan and Professor Werner Schröder of the Universität Marburg. Through his kind interest in the project the former contributed much to make this event successful; and the latter, more than any other, was the one who *inpfete daz êrste rîs* out of which this event grew. And then there is Professor Walter A. Reichart whose name has practically been synonymous with that of the Department of Germanic Languages and Literatures at The University of Michigan since 1960. Often unknowingly he was the benevolent motor behind the productive endeavors of the Department. And such is the case with this symposium on medieval epic literature. The published result of it is therefore offered as a tribute to him who for many years has been an esteemed colleague and friend.

Grateful acknowledgment is also made for the financial aid given toward the cost of preparing this conference volume. Without the help of the Deutsche Forschungsgemeinschaft, the Horace H. Rackham School of Graduate Studies of The University of Michigan, and the Frank J. Bedesky Company of Welland, Ontario, Canada, the cost of publication could not have been defrayed. Thanks to the generosity of these patrons it was possible, in spite of the difficulties caused by the economic crisis of 1973 and 1974, to make the core of the symposium available to all interested, even though the publication will not be realized as originally planned. Finally, a word of warm thanks is due to Robert Harsch-Niemeyer of the Max Niemeyer Verlag for his care and understanding shown during the publishing process.

Harald Scholler

Frederick P. Pickering

Historical Thought and Moral Codes in Medieval Epic

It will not cause surprise if in the course of this paper I occasionally let fall the names Augustine and Boethius. For several years now I have been invoking them in an endeavour to draw more accurately the frontier between medieval narrative works written in conformity with a scheme of history going back to the Fathers, Eusebius and S. Augustine himself – Christian »Heilsgeschichte«, and others which take their historical doctrine, still Christian but secular, from Boethius's *De Consolatione Philosophiae*. I expounded this historiographical thesis at considerable length in 1967 in the first volume of an independent study.[1] If reviews are anything to go by I seem to have persuaded some theologians and historians, and indeed some literary historians that I have drawn the dividing line correctly, in such a way for instance as to make Wolfram von Eschenbach's *Parzival* a »Boethian« work.[2] Volume II of the same study is ready to be printed. It presents a chronological documentation of the original thesis, and direct textual evidence, some of which I shall quote from or allude to in this paper.[3] I want none the less to concentrate here on some problems which still require consideration even when the principle of discrimination »according to Augustine« or »according to Boethius« has been accepted. There are for instance, almost obviously one might think, important medieval works written according to *neither* of the masters, for though there are

---

[1] *Augustinus oder Boethius? Geschichtsschreibung und epische Dichtung im Mittelalter – und in der Neuzeit* (Philologische Studien und Quellen, 39), Berlin 1967. The thesis was first openly declared in lecture form in Tübingen, August 1963.
[2] There is no point in the qualification that *Parzival* (and grail romances generally) are »on balance« or »in the last resort« Boethian. An author who invokes »fortune« commits himself to the Boethian scheme, see below.
[3] All the works referred to here are the subject of more or less detailed discussion in Vol. II of *Augustinus oder Boethius*. A reminder in Note 10.

in my opinion no other masters than Augustine and Boethius, there is
a mistress – history itself, »Geschichte schlechthin«. That is my present
argument in a nutshell. I now proceed more slowly and methodically.
In doing so I seek to take account of the »moral codes« which have more
generally been recognized as a preoccupation of medieval narrators
and are scheduled to occupy us during this Conference!

As modern readers and interpreters we should, I think, occasionally
consider in a simpler and more primitive way than is usual in academic
studies, the problems of literary composition involved when »given
story« is retold in a medieval narrative work. By what devices is it
made to conform to, or why must it ignore, established patterns of
history (»Geschichtsbilder«)? Further, though I myself (and I apologize
in advance!) think that a secondary consideration: what control does
the medieval re-narrator gain over his story by interpreting the deeds
of his hero (and the hero's antagonists) in the light of an ideal moral
code? To take this second point first, it is surely a commonplace of
our experience that no major narrative (by that I exclude the *exemplum*) illustrates a *code* of values, for instance the chivalric code, perfectly, and one cannot interpret medieval stories satisfactorily in terms
of an assumed consistent »characterization« invoking those values.
There are all-important actions of the hero (let us keep to heroes!),
essential to his story, which conflict with the code or his »character«.
There are also grave dangers in the so-called »werkimmanent« interpretations now in fashion,[4] for no medieval writer is to that extent
master of the story he tells. It is the hero with his story who is master
(»der âventiure herre«), and the author is his spokesman merely,
commending according to his lights the right decisions of his hero
and glossing over his wrong decisions as he makes them, or offering
little or no comment. He may be an unsatisfactory interpreter of the
deeds of his hero.[5] It is not a purely rhetorical question when the narrator asks: »What will he *do* now?«

The reason for the frequent non-coincidence of heroic action and moral
code, whether the latter is thought of as contemporary with the hero
or with the author, is that history itself (which literature must mirror)

---

[4] Interpretations which seek first to determine the »economy of ideas« present in a
given work, and assume that these will provide a complete gloss on everything said
and done by the chief characters.

[5] Here the textbook example of Eilhart's *Tristan* may suffice. In a fuller statement
one would have to consider whether Hartmann von Aue did indeed always find
»der âventiure meine«.

is not moral in origin, and its course and outcome are not determined by merits. That has always been the teaching of history, which literature cannot flatly deny: that the righteous man or the good cause will not necessarily prosper here on earth. *Virtus* and *fortuna* are not causally connected. It is an occasion for rejoicing (or boasting) when they seem to, for public grief when they patently do not. And so, rationally, evident deserts may have to await their reward in an afterlife. On the whole we vastly prefer for our »entertainment« stories which encourage us in the belief that virtue and the good life have their reward and a »happy ending«, which may be success with the prospect of further activity, or the beatitude of a career or life well completed.

To put all this another way, historians and narrators prefer to deal with merits and qualities systematically in an ethical »code«, and as a matter of major concern only in *digressions* from narrative, in a prologue or epilogue, or when taking formal leave of some character. (Or the author may change genres to write a didactic work, a mirror of knighthood for instance). In terms of story, only a carefully staged and self-contained episode such as that of Job or of Jonah (episodes in God's own story) can illustrate a moral *principle* or a truism of faith. A life lived strictly according to a *code* or creed must be a martyrdom. I shall exclude martyrdoms (whether sacred or profane) from my further remarks, and, despite the reference just made to Job and Jonah, I exclude Biblical story, for by the Middle Ages (say the twelfth century) some five-or-more hundred years of theological exegesis had made all books of the Bible serve the one theology. The exegetes brought Christian story, doctrine and ethic into one register by means no longer available today (except apparently to numerologists, mirror-manipulators and shadow-boxers generally).

But let us press on! Literature concerned with man as a historical being and literature setting forth ideal conceptions of man have little more than language in common. They make different statements. Man's first preoccupation is his destiny. This he understands first and best when it is represented to him in the form of story, in the indicative, not as a list of prescriptions in the imperative. The *sensus historialis* is the first and always the most important sense in which words are used at all. No elevated doctrine, for example of love, and no spiritualizing gloss can annul the facts of »given story«, the fact, for instance, that Tristan is a bed-hopper from first to last. That is his story which no power on earth or in heaven or hell can alter. Being not Biblical – it is not the story of David the adulterer, Solomon the womaniser or Sampson the frequenter of brothels – it is beyond redemption by even the most elastically-minded expositor. Tristan and his Isolde remain memorable adulterers, tricksters. Tristan is to the end »der listenrîche«, the evader of codes, several of them in succession if one takes all the versions of his story into account. These observations may preface the general remark that the more memorable a piece of history or story, the less likely it is that we shall find it illustrative of any *ideal* scheme – of history or of morality.

Let us keep to works of literature in the conventional sense (I shall want to consider historians, below), say *Hildebrandslied, Nibelungen-lied*, the French *Chanson de Roland* and Icelandic sagas. These live and have their being as *story* first, commemorating in whatever refraction »real history«: these things happened in a more or less remote past. Theoderic's army came to Italy at the bidding of »Hunneo truhtin« (or his antecedent), the Burgundian kingdom on the Rhine was wiped out, Charlemagne's campaign against the heathen Saracen ended with the destruction of his rearguard but Christianity was vindicated, *douce France* (according to the German Konrad, the Empire) survived; Iceland was successfully settled. I will refer to these works again.

At the other end of the scale in respect of factual and »real« history is the *Anticlaudianus* (c. 1181–84) of Alan of Lille, a purely intellectual construct with, for all that, a notable »plot« of considerable relevance for anyone seeking the theoretical connection, if any, between ethical codes and history or story. The *Anticlaudianus* is an allegorical epic in which all the characters except one – the hero to be – are personifications of philosophical (or theological) concepts, Natura, Ratio (Fides etc.), or are Virtues or Vices. All are present in a virtually encyclopaedic muster. Concerning the hero in whose interest a momentous enterprise is here set in motion, nothing is more certain than that he, the ideally conceived »new man« to replace in Nature's world the fallen man of an earlier dispensation, is destined to have a *history* – whether he likes it or not, and whether his sponsors want it or not. Ratio is obsessed with the idea of what »should be possible«, Prudencia or Philosophia is slow to assent at all to the project of starting all over again! The Parcae (that is Alan's »antique« name for Providence) have so decreed, and they determine in higher regions what »Fate« shall bring to pass in the world of time. So the new man, having been endowed by God with a soul, must, according to this story, on his descent to earth pass through

Fortune's kingdom.[6] — Alan, it should perhaps be noted, had only recently invoked the Holy Spirit as his Muse, to enable him to treat God's assignment of a soul to the new man. He now reverts to his initial Muse, Apollo, and continues his narrative in a purely Boethian vein. — The new man must now be prepared for his future. This can only be done, one notes, with considerable co-operation from Dame Fortune — whose »realm« Alan describes at quite inordinate length. Alan's fiction is that to avoid the imputation of graceless envy, Fortune will make a special concession: she will for the new man's sake »endeavour to be less arbitrary« and »restrain herself«. That is her contribution. (The Virtues have already undertaken to endow him lavishly with their qualities). He must obviously also be of noble birth. Noble birth is in Fortune's gift through her daughter Nobilitas. What next? It only remains for the new man to *act*. This he does first in alliance with *all* the Virtues against all the Vices in a rather long and tedious *psychomachia*. The Vices and Discord herself are of course routed. Fortune's own waverings and desertion of this »good cause« cannot affect the outcome. What happens after *that* cannot be told within the framework of this allegory. Clearly the new man has nothing more to do until there is a new real world, somehow re-populated, in which he can make use of the qualities bestowed on him. This will require his *decision* to act, and — as the irrational principle governing the outcome of all action — Fortune will be back in business, attending to the new man's *history*.

There appears, therefore, to be no such thing as man without a history, and history of some kind he will make in the exercise of his free-will.[7] Before he acts on his own account he has (the *Anticlaudianus* shows) potentially all the virtues. Thereafter there is history, and there are historians, to record it or not, and to interpret it as they may.

Ranged between the ultimately historical *Nibelungenlied* and the patently pre-historical *Anticlaudianus* we may see the scores of medieval tales which enjoyed the authority of more or less established tradition. These we must for the purposes of this paper consider as being »just as true« as chronicled real history. (We may perhaps be reminded of the

---

6 This is the Boethian solution. Augustine endeavoured to dispense with the idea of »fortune« and to attribute all except the most trivial happenings to »God's will«. He pressed his objection to secular philosophy further: to the point of asking for restraint in the use of the term »fate« for »God's decree«; but this objection could not be sustained, least of all in the context of recent conversion to Christianity, see for instance the Old Saxon *Heliand*.

7 Free-will is common to both schemes, Augustinian and Boethian.

Church's definition of New Testament apocrypha as »non vera sed
credenda«). Parzival, for instance, must win the Grail Kingship after
a failed first attempt, for that is his story, the story is »given«. No
scheme of values by which the hero's actions should be judged is in the
same sense »given«. Any re-narrator of the story is free to impute
motives for Parzival's actions (and his failures to act) according to his
personal prejudices, his social class (etc.). In another context Iwein *must*
pour the water on the slab, give pursuit to the Lord of the Castle and
slay him. In a desperate attempt to gain some kind of »moral« control
of this unfortunate sequence of events Hartmann von Aue will offer
as a personal contribution that Iwein did not remember self-discipline
(»zuht«) when in hot pursuit. That was »wrong« of him, we gather.
And so on! Hartmann's Lord Henry has apparently all the qualities,
including rather strangely an aptitude at Minnesang, required of the
perfect knight or lord. But in respect of the structure of this tale, these
qualities belong to Lord Henry's untold career; they are prehistorical.
It is merely the narrator's historical postulate[8] that he was afflicted
with leprosy as punishment for a moral defect, his arrogance or his
neglect of God. Remoter from any kind of historicity are then such
works of fantasy as Chrétien's *Cligès, Moritz von Craun* or – much
earlier – the *Ruodlieb* romance, the hero of which is from start to finish
Fortune's child.[9] Ruodlieb owes his virtues to the accident of good birth
and native genius (according to some writers genius is in Fortune's gift),
and acquires his experience *ambulando*, through chance encounters
and through a somewhat enigmatic »set« of gnomic precepts, trustingly
followed.
So much for literary works in the accepted sense. I myself should like
for a moment to extend the list of works to be considered to medieval
historians and chroniclers, who are so much more rewarding for the
general-purposes medievalist than at any rate the minor poets. They
range from more or less »objective« chroniclers of events like Gregory
of Tours *via* speculative historians like Bede on the one hand, Regino
of Prüm (see below) on the other, to speculators on history, Otto of
Freising, for instance, who drifts irresponsibly from edited history into

---

8 I treat the »historical postulate« in *Augustinus oder Boethius* II with particular
   reference to the OHG *Ludwigslied:* the assertion in the indicative mood of what
   is a pious hope, in this case a piece of West Frankish progaganda.
9 This does not imply any opposition to Dennis Kratz's interpretation of *Ruodlieb*
   (or of *Waltharius*), see pp. 126–149.

fantastic prognosis in a work conceived on Augustinian lines, the *De Duabus Civitatibus* (c. 1143–46). Then there are exploiters or wilful falsifiers of real history for the purposes of dynastic and political propaganda (Widukind of Corvey and the Archpoet) and vulgarizers of historical fictions of greater or lesser magnitude and complexity: the poet of the *Annolied*, or the slightly later »Kollektiv« of Regensburg clerics responsible for the *Kaiserchronik*. For guidance to the extent to which these last-named works were intended to instruct, to entertain or to propagate a doctrine of Western legitimacy, one must of course consult those modern historians who have thought them worthy of mention, but even Herbert Grundmann was not infallible on the subject of the *Kaiserchronik*, and the historians seem occasionally to show more speed than discretion when they turn to literary works (or the generalizations of literary historians).

And so I return to my starting-point to ask whether the various medieval authors to whom I have alluded so far, see history and story in terms of Augustinian »Heilsgeschichte« or of Boethian secular history: or whether they see history as history pure and simple. I refer now to a number of works in a logical but not chronological order, and as a word of guidance I may mention that the Augustinian scheme of history was known to the Middle Ages from the days of Orosius (c. 400). Its complexities were reduced to memorable form by Isidor of Seville (7th century), and this was transmitted in uninterrupted clerical teaching and preaching. *De Civitate Dei* itself, however, Augustine's own work, was rarely cited or even properly read. Charles the Great certainly did no more than stare at and brood over the few sentences about the *rex justus* and *pacificus* indicated to him by Alcuin's forefinger. (Alcuin pressed his teaching particularly in his correspondence with Charles). Boethius's *De Consolatione Philosophiae* on the other hand was from the time of its completion (c. 525) to about the time of the same Alcuin not known, it was apparently lost to view. Isidor did not know it. Otfrid of Weissenburg (c. 860) on the other hand did, of that I am convinced, but cannot stop to elaborate the point. The first medieval historian to show a full and complete grasp of Boethius's scheme of history with no Augustinian reservations, no illusions about Charlemagne and the Franks, or the *translatio imperii* was Regino of Prüm, c. 900. Regino accepts and *uses* the Boethian philosophy of history at exactly the time when King Alfred of England was *translating* the tract. (This was after Alfred had translated Gregory the

Great's *Cura pastoralis* and »Orosius«, seeking in all cases guidance
on the office of Christian kingship.) Let us bear the date in mind: from
about 900 AD at the latest Western Europe knew *De Consolatione*.
It must have come as a revelation to theologian-advisers of kings,
makers of policy and writers of history. It was a Christian scheme of
history which had the inestimable advantage of according a function to
Fortune as the dispenser (with man) of »history as we know it«. It
afforded respite from the incubus of Augustinian »Heilsgeschichte«.
Western Europe, to the extent that it speculates philosophically on
history at all, is still indebted to Boethius.[10]

Now prior to both Augustine and Boethius in respect of the interpretation of history are, remarkably, the *Nibelungenlied* and the Icelandic sagas. These 13th cent. works recognize no pattern of history
other than that inherent in the events they treat. The poet of the
Nibelungenlied seeks no doubt the »meaning« to him in his day of
the destruction of the Burgundian kingdom. It has clearly nothing to
do with the Fall of Man, the Six Ages or with God's divine dispensation.
It is not Augustinian. More important to the poet are the events themselves and the famous men and women who perished. Their fate is the
history he narrates, not any theodicy – reducing as he may the tempo
of events, retarding the catastrophe which he has nevertheless foretold
in his opening stanzas. But History itself duly negates the poet's efforts
at retardation. It will not let Giselher grow old with the passage of
years, and it destroys the poet's most modern hero Rüdeger, and the
thousands of warriors introduced to delay the final act in what remains
a family or dynastic feud of (vaguely) the Merovingian age. As for
moral codes, that of the *Nibelungenlied* is similarly Merovingian, with
a few »late« chivalric embellishments associated with self-cancelling
cadenzas of action. No City (»civitas«) of this world or the next arises
from the devastation, there is no promise of a better future. Equally
the past glories of Worms are not to be restored, and Etzel's court is in
ashes. There is cause, after the events, for lament (»Klage«) only,
melancholy reflection on the sorrow which must follow happiness.
This is not the Christian cry of *vanitas* or illustration of any doctrine
of the rise and fall of earthly kingdoms. In other words: the history
of the Migrations, elsewhere a story of triumph in battle, conquest and
settlement, is in the case of the Burgundians a story of the decline, fall

---

[10] The evidence for this spate of dogmatic assertions will be found in due course in
Augustinus oder Boethius II, cf. note 3.

and destruction of one people. That is final. The settlement of Iceland on the other hand does not end with the destruction of a people, perhaps here and there of a clan or family. Saga history ends with a present in which a »civitas« of this world *is* established, requiring no remorse, no act of penance from its inheritors. The sagas reflect a conception of history in which a fall, original sin or guilt, redemption and salvation play no role. And so, despite all idealization of man in situations of heroic conflict, despite all accommodation to traditional narrative schemes, what *Nibelungenlied* and the sagas commemorate is memorable history. In that history, Christian institutions may be mentioned. An important encounter may take place before a minster (Worms) or in a stave-church (in Iceland or Norway), and the Christian faith may offer comfort to some characters, or alarm others. It is perhaps significant that in these works Christianity is represented *inter alia* as sustaining swimmers in fjords or saving a parson thrown into the Danube. Christianity is, in these thirteenth century works, still the new religion which, as in sixth-century Europe and Britain, some important people were giving a trial, little more. There can be no question of an Augustinian view of history. As for the Boethian conception of history as the work of God's Providence, Fate, man's Fortune and his free-will – that is equally absent. In *Nibelungenlied* and the sagas Fate is still spoken of in pre-Christian and Germanic, not in Boethian terms.

And now to Regino of Prüm, some passages in whose *Chronicle of the Franks* (c. 900) are, I think, almost as important for students of medieval literature as Walther von der Vogelweide's *Sprüche* in the »Reichston«. It was indeed an essay by Heinz Löwe[11] on Regino's historical thinking on the Carolingians, on the Empire, on Divine Providence, Fate and Fortune, that prompted me to foresake the conventional paths of »Germanistik« a decade ago – to declare my Boethian thesis; for to be reminded by Regino, as Löwe was, of Dante and the historical speculations of the writers of the early Renaissance, is no doubt aesthetically satisfying, – it is historically topsy-turvy! Regino's philosophy of history is (like Dante's) purely Boethian. Furthermore – as Löwe recognized – it involves an abandonment of all ideas of a divine mission of the Franks or any other people. It involves abandonment of the doctrine of a *translatio imperii*. In Regino's day this was surely a

---

11 »Regino von Prüm und das historische Weltbild der Karolingerzeit« (1952), reprinted in *Geschichtsdenken und Geschichtsbild im Mittelalter* (Wege der Forschung, 21), Darmstadt 1961, pp. 91–134.

phenomenal feat of independent historical thinking; he was at least two-hundred years ahead of his time. This the historians have so far only partially recognized. Otto of Freising, who 250 years later exploited Regino's *Chronicle* for its facts, was conceivably converted by it.[12]

I submit now a passage from Regino's *Chronicle* which exemplifies the Boethian mode of history-writing. It is my hope that it will continue to engage the attention of medievalists for many years to come. In the context of our present discussion of »codes« it is also instructive, namely in that in a first self-contained section it treats the »character« of King Karlmann, of whom the historian takes his leave (see above):

a) [880 AD.] Anno dominicae incarnationis DCCCLXXX. Carlomannus rex paralisi dissolutus diem clausit extremum VII. Non. Apr. sepultusque est cum debito honore in Baioariam in loco, qui dicitur Hodingas. Fuit vero iste precellentissimus rex litteris eruditis, christianae religioni deditus, iustus, pacificus et omni morum honestate decoratus; pulchritudo eius corporis insignis, vires quoque in homine admirabiles fuere; nec inferior animi magnitudine. Plurima quippe bella cum patre, pluriora sine patre in regnis Sclavorum gessit semperque victoriae triumphum reportavit; terminos imperii sui ampliando ferro dilatavit; suis mitis, hostibus terribilis apparuit; alloquio blandus, humilitate ornatus, in ordinandis regni negotiis singulari sollertia preditus, prorsus, ut nihil ei deesse regiae maiestatis competens videretur.

(In the year 880 of the divine Incarnation King Karlmann died on the 22nd March, a paralysis of the limbs heralding his collapse. He was buried with due honours in Bavaria at a place there called Ötting. This most excellent king was a man of learning, a devout Christian, just, peace-loving and in every way of distinguished bearing. He was a most handsome man of admirable physique; he was equally high-minded. He conducted many wars in the kingdoms of the Slavs, at first in the following of his father, thereafter still further wars against them alone. He always returned a victor. He extended the confines of his kingdom with the sword. To his enemies he was a man to be feared, to his (friends and allies) he was a lenient lord. In his conversation he was affable but modest; he was extremely efficient and conscientious in the conduct of state business. In short he seemed to lack no quality required of the bearer of the royal title.)

b) Huic ex legitimo matrimonio non est nata soboles propter infecundi-

---

12 This is a literary historian's reading of the evidence, i.e. of the text of Regino's *Chronicle* on the one hand, and Otto's *De Duabus Civitatibus* and *Gesta Frederici* on the other. A more detailed statement will be found in *Augustinus oder Boethius* II. The historians will understandably continue to urge the changed political circumstances as the reason for Otto's (and Rahewin's) more »optimistic« approach in the *Gesta Frederici*.

tatem coniugis, sed ex quadam nobili femina filium elegantissimae speciei suscepit, quem Arnolfum nominari iussit ob recordationem reverentissimi Arnolfi, Metensis ecclesiae episcopi, de cuius sancto germine sua aliorumque regum Francorum prosapia pullulaverat; quod non casu accidisse, sed quodam presagio portentoque futurorum actitatum videtur. Siquidem ab illo genealogia regum *caelitus provisa* per intervalla temporum secundis incrementorum successibus coepit exuberare, quousque in magno Carolo summum imperii fastigium non solum Francorum, verum etiam diversarum gentium regnorumque obtineret. Post cuius decessum *variante fortuna* rerum gloria, quae supra vota fluxerat, eodem, quo accesserat, modo cepit paulatim diffluere, donec deficientibus non modo regnis, sed etiam ipsa regia stirpe partim inmatura aetate pereunte partim sterilitate coniugum marcescente hic solus de tam numerosa regum posteritate idoneus inveniretur, qui imperii Francorum sceptra susciperet; quod in subsequentibus suo in loco lucidius apparebit.

(He had no descendant from his official marriage, his wife being barren, but by a woman of noble birth he had a son of most excellent presence whom he caused to be named Arnolf in memory of the most venerable Arnolf, Bishop of Metz – of whose sacred line his family and the families of other Frankish kings were descended. This seems not to have been a matter of chance, but, as it were, a portent and foreshadowing of things to come. For with Arnolf the royal house began in accordance with *Divine Providence* to ascend by a succession of stages to that eminence which had its final culmination, under Charles the Great, in empire not only over the Franks but over various peoples and kingdoms. After his [Charles's] death *through a change of fortune*, the glory of the empire which had excelled all aspirations began to ebb in the same way as it had once risen, until not only the kingdoms fell away, but the royal line itself was lost through the premature deaths of young princes, the barrenness of wives, and finally there was left only Arnolf worthy to receive the sceptre: this will be shown more clearly in due course, below.) [13]

From this passage and others in Regino's *Chronicle* one can show (that is, Heinz Löwe has shown) that he saw the Imperium itself as subject to Fortune's law, i.e. as a purely historical phenomenon. By 900 AD then, the historical lesson of *De Consolatione* was learnt, and as we shall see in a moment the image of the Wheel of Fortune, for which *De Cons.* Book II is the source, had fixed itself in the mind of historians. (The artists had apparently not yet worked out the iconography of the image, nor evolved the tituli *regnabo, regno, regnavi, sum sine regno*).

---

[13] Quoted from *Quellen zur karolingischen Reichsgeschichte* III, ed. Reinhold Rau, Darmstadt 1966 (= *Ausgewählte Quellen zur deutschen Geschichte des Mittelalters*, Vol. VII, Freiherr vom Stein-Gedächtnisausgabe). My translation of the Latin (ibid. pp. 256 f.).

The lesson was learnt, it is more accurate to say, by *some* writers, unfortunately not by all, not by Rupert of Deutz for instance, but as Rupert of Deutz's fantastic historical projections seem to have had no
discernable influence on secular literature, we may thankfully leave him
out of account and consider for a moment Otto of Freising's treatment
of the passage from Regino of Prüm which we have just quoted. He
reduces the passage to about eight lines, editing out the reference to
Fortune, precisely that! Instead, a page or two later, still taking his
historical facts from Regino, he offers one of his own (innumerable)
short sermons on »mutability«. There is, as we shall see, a world of
difference, not so much in the »mood« of the two writers as in their
modes of expression, their terms of reference.

> »It is remarkable« *(mirum dictu),* he writes, »how Charles the Third, who
> of all the Emperors after Charles the Great enjoyed the greatest power, was
> brought low in such a short space of time. .... How wretched is the lot of
> man! The King, who at the divison of the Eastern Kingdom received the
> smallest portion ... rose at first to such power that he had in his hands the
> Eastern and the Western Kingdom together with the Imperial dignity, but
> finally sank so low that he lacked even bread. Then could he say with Job
> (30,22): ›Thou hast raised me above the clouds and cast me down to the
> ground‹, or with the Psalmist (Ps. 102,11) ›Thou hast raised me up and
> cast me down‹. How otherwise could one refer to earthly glory than under
> the image of a *cloud*? ... or: This miserable game of Fortune, as the philo-
> sophers call it, which like a Wheel turns what has been at the top to the
> bottom (›hic tam miserrimus et iuxta philosophos fortunae in modum
> rotae vertentis ludus‹ etc.) This we call correctly the mutability, willed by
> God, of all earthly things.«[14]

I cannot hope to convince readers at once that this passage in Otto's
De Duabus Civitatibus is one of the most important theoretical statements in all medieval historiography. Otto distinguishes between the
secular view of history represented by his source, Regino, and his own
»correct«view, that of clerical »Heilsgeschichte«. He rejects the Wheel
of Fortune as a »philosopher's« idea.

What will be more readily accepted is that in his next work, the *Gesta
Frederici,* Otto of Freising says not a word[15] about the Six Ages or the
Two Cities, and himself makes dozens of references to Fortune as the

---

[14] Translation from ed. in *Ausgewählte Quellen* (etc., see previous note), Vol. XVI,
p. 446.
[15] I exclude of course the content of »documents« quoted by Otto, and his summaries
of arguments in contemporary theological disputes.

force governing the successful career of Frederick Barbarossa. Otto performs in other words a complete *volte face*. This the historians have always recognized, without of course speaking of a change of »genre« from Augustinian to Boethian historiography.[16] The historians are, however, also surely equally correct in surmising that if Otto had lived to see the Hohenstaufen fall on evil days, namely when Fortuna forsook them and left them with Nemesis and Metanoia, as Barraclough puts it, he would have reverted to his fantastic view of an Age of the Monastic Orders, the last Age before the coming of Antichrist and the Day of Doom.

And that indeed is the real story of »Heilsgeschichte« and its derivatives, that it is in the high Middle Ages an escape from the challenge of factual history, a flight from responsible thought into speculation, the more dangerous in that it was later, as with Joachim of Fiore, quickened with bogus science, the application of numerology and typology to prognostication, millenniarism. One can only be thankful that the secular poets did not allow themselves to be drawn in any significant way into such follies. It is reassuring to know that medieval man did not spend all his days in idle speculation, and that not all medieval men were parsons and monks. »There is a time for everything«, says the Preacher. Charles the Great speculated on the City of God and the office of the *rex justus* in the Winter time. He campaigned in the campaigning season. »Heilsgeschichte« is for Sundays and the Feast Days of the liturgical year, not for weekdays and the great occasions of a well-organized secular life.

With that passing renewed reference to Charles the Great I go on now to a brief consideration of the O. Fr. *Chanson de Roland* (c. 1100) and its German adaptation by Pfaffe Konrad (at the latest c. 1170), a delicate task for an Englishman, and for nothing do I hold my teacher in Breslau, Friedrich Ranke, in greater esteem than for his treatment of this traditional compare-and-contrast exercise. Having spent some two hours characterizing Konrad's »clerical« adaptation, Ranke put it firmly in its place, reminding his German audience of the primacy in every respect of the French national epic: in historical conception, in

---

16 I am grateful to Prof. Peter Munz, the most recent biographer of Barbarossa *(Frederick Barbarossa: a study in medieval politics,* London 1969) for writing to me to state that he thinks my Boethian thesis »proved to the hilt« by the *Gesta Frederici.* This encouraged me to re-read both Otto's works and to venture a more systematic (literary) comparison.

characterization, in poetry. The *Chanson de Roland* is one of the great achievements of Western European literature. What I myself would also stress is the *Chanson's* treatment of Charles as a Christian emperor and his campaigns as those of Christendom against the paynim – indeed also his treatment of Roland as a martyr. One must also bear in mind the vast amplification of the Roland tradition in the lands of Romance language. The Oxford *Roland* is selected for literary study on aesthetic grounds and for convenience. It is but one representative of a rich tradition. It is a gross simplification of German scholarship to say, as is now so fashionable, of Konrad's adaptation: »der Stoff ist in das augustinische Weltbild eingeordnet«, as though an »Augustinian« revision were in itself a meritorious achievement, an advance on the all too modern and national *Chanson!*

I do not wish to belittle Konrad's poem. It is a work in its own right, not merely a testimony to the »influence« or the popularity (»Wirkungsgeschichte«) of the *Chanson*. Given that »douce France« was an idea which a German poet could not sustain, the picture of Charles had to be brought into register with German ideas of Charles, German ideas of a *translatio imperii* to the Carolingians and their historical successors, i.e. with the picture in the *Kaiserchronik*. Charles had to be represented as God's Regent here on earth. This Konrad does most remarkably in his opening passage. Where the *Chanson* says that Charles, having heard matins, conferred with his barons in an orchard, Konrad shows Charles prostrate in a night-long vigil in the presence of God, seeking guidance as to the Divine Will with him. This is the Charles who was to be canonized, albeit by the wrong Pope under strong political pressure. Thereafter Konrad sees the campaign against the Saracen in terms of a swift crusade, the paladins positively hastening to their martyrdom. But this is all the bread-and-butter story of the handbooks.

What I wish to stress is rather that – not for the first time (that was in the *Kaiserchronik*, as I shall mention in a moment) – a historical formula is used by Konrad which persists down to Milton and the poets of the German Baroque: The heathen (or the devilish adversary of the Christian faith), the would-be frustrator of God's purpose, is credited not merely with a ridiculous belief in »Mahmet« or the like, but with a foolish philosophy of history, a belief in »fortune« (*sælde* or *wîlsælde*), and, as *summum bonum,* a »beatitudo« to be found on earth. Germanists will recall that in the *Kaiserchronik* there is a long disquisition on *wîlsælde*, extremely difficult to follow, which clearly taxed to the limit the intelligence of the clerical compilers – who, as Friedrich Ohly has shown, had »lifted« the text bodily from the so-called Cle-mentine *Recognitions*.[17] They were learning from it as they rendered it into German. They were only able to disparage this intellectually demanding *Kairos* doctrine with the help of further liftings. So too, but in much simpler terms, in Konrad's adaptation of the *Chanson* the heathens have a worldly doctrine of *sælde*. It is therefore not merely the bravery in battle and the soldierly code of the heathens, and their decorum in parleys, to which Western writers accord esteem. In any well-organized work of Augustinian conception, the philosophy attrib-uted to the heathen may be based on the best *secular* philosophy avail-able, in Boethius,[18] of which Milton says in *Paradise Lost*, without mentioning Boethius by name, of course, that it affords but »vain Consolation« to the routed hosts of Satan. This becomes, as I have hinted, a commonplace clerical formula. But the German *Rolandslied* is, for all the careful thought which has gone into it, not always a tem-perate and controlled work of adaptation. The author is occasionally carried away by his fervour for the cause of the holy Empire established by Charles, and the martyrdom of his own personal nominees for canonisation. It has often been remarked that Konrad allows his most Christian heroes – knights – to slay the heathen like dogs, »sam die hunte«, or like cattle, »sam daz vihe«, ll. 5421–23. This will have sounded to Konrad's audiences like a reference to procedures in the medieval slaughterhouse – and that was no doubt the intention of the author too, but the idea itself is of course old, and in origin – strange as this may seem – liturgical. The enemies of Christendom, particularly those who beset the just man, the Man of Sorrows in his affliction and Agony, are *canes, vituli, tauri pingues* in the words of the 21st Psalm, the Good Friday Psalm. As such, according to Konrad, they must be slain. The clerical propagandist forgets in other words his training at this point. He risks a misuse of O.T. prophecy, knowing he will not be contradicted. He also shows himself a somewhat crude pragmatist when he allows the most Christian emperor Charles to proceed to the execu-tion of his hostages after the singing of a *Te Deum*. It is at times diffi-

---

17 *Sage und Legende in der Kaiserchronik*, Münster 1940, repr. Darmstadt 1968, pp. 74–84.
18 A heathen form of the »fortune« doctrine can be extracted from *De Consolatione Philosophiae* by omitting reference to Providence and God.

cult to associate the deeds attributed to the heroes in medieval epic, with moral codes.

For all that one may not forget that Western man in his perplexities has always sought comfort in *ideal* schemes and norms. He has reflected on history, »given story«, and on man as he is in his imperfection, to derive some lesson. In my concluding remarks I will now suggest that though modern literary historians may have identified the literary genres for the portrayal of various ideals of life and career, *Vita* and legend for the saint of course, *chanson de geste* for the feudal baron and *âventiure* for the knight, they have been slow to recognize the basic philosophy of history of these latter two secular genres. It is clearly *not* »Heilsgeschichte«, nor any modification of »Heilsgeschichte«. In the context of this conference it is, I think, essential to assert that it has equally little to do with moral codes, which are concerned with character or behaviour but not with action and story itself. The philosophy of history hitherto lacking in our armoury is that of the Christian philosopher Boethius which makes the decisions of mortal men taken in the exercise of their free-will the mainspring of *action*, action followed by consequences, an *eventus* which is the work of fortune *(sælde)*. About that I have written often and talked, perhaps *ad nauseam*. The point I stress now in final reinforcement of the argument is the medieval narrator's concern to deal with mortal man's decisions in their *time context:* the *moment* of time. Man should make his decisions at the right time and in the right frame of mind. He rarely does. He is rarely given the *chance* to act wisely. It remains for us medievalists, in short, to recognize more readily the medieval counterpart of the *Kairos* doctrine of antiquity. It is not enough to make »witty« remarks about Iwein's »Terminschwierigkeiten«, his failure to keep his appointments or the efforts he has to make to catch up with his obligations. Failure to recognize time as a central problem in historical thinking and in narrative technique in the Middle Ages is responsible – for instance – for the hopeless confusion in the mind of »Germanisten« concerning the »guilt« of Hartmann's Gregorius. Gregorius decides to leave the monastery in a fit of youthful rage. He says so himself: he makes his decision in *tumpheit* and *erbolgenheit*.[19] He says he is determined to »give chase to fortune« (he will *sælde erjagen)* and

---

19 ir habet got vil verre / an mir armen geêret / und iuwer heil gemêret, / und nû daz beste vür geleit. / nû ist mir mîn tumpheit / also sêre erbolgen, / si enlât mich iu niht volgen, ll. 1480 ff.

so invites disaster, and has the *metanoia* which must follow from a wilful refusal to accept advice. He follows the call of the blood. His pride
is wounded. He seeks fame and glory, honour and esteem. These are his
values in the moment of decision. His decision in the exercise of Free
Will is wrong, irrational, made at the wrong time. This must be stated
before one can begin to consider the role of *coincidence* in his future
career. Gregorius may spend seventeen years alone on the rock, but the
fatal decision was the work of a moment, and Hartmann's skill as a
time-keeper, stop-watch in hand, at a later point, saves Gregorius from
a final blasphemy when he demands a miracle of God, »or else«. What
he demands as a miracle is however already fact – his tablets have not
been destroyed – and the emissaries from Rome who have come to
lead him to Peter's throne deem that »fortunate«, not an act of grace.[20]
I will however spare readers the ardours of yet another »Nacherzäh-
lung« of *Gregorius*. As for Hartmann's treatment of chivalry and
chivalric values in this story, he has no option but to represent them as
something of which the hero has prior knowledge by virtue of his
princely birth. Hartmann knows that such knowledge is incredible.
He therefore makes it the subject of a completely frivolous passage in
which Gregorius claims not only to know chivalry and horsemanship
but also of the German Knighthood League-Table, Division I.[21] This
is my last example of the priority of story over morality, and on that
note I will abruptly end.

---

[20] weinde sî des jâhen, / diz wære ein sælic man, ll. 3738 f.
[21] The notorious lines »ich enwart nie mit gedanke / ein Beier noch ein Vranke« etc.,
1573 f.

Karl Bosl

Leitbilder und Wertvorstellungen des Adels von der Merowingerzeit bis zur Höhe der feudalen Gesellschaft

Literatur, Epik und Lyrik des hohen Mittelalters ist eine »Sozialgeste«, hat eine gesellschaftliche Funktion, ist aber keine *direkte* und *unmittelbare* Quelle für die Gesellschaftsstruktur der Epoche, obwohl sie ohne den Hintergrund der hochfeudalen Gesellschaft, die zugleich »Aufbruchsepoche« gesamteuropäischer Gesellschaft und Kultur ist, nicht verstanden und interpretiert werden kann. Sie ist gesellschaftliches Phänomen, aber keineswegs bloße Widerspiegelung gesellschaftlicher und historischer Daten. Die Definition von Walter Benjamin, daß Literatur eine »sich objektivierende Handlung unfreier Subjekte« sei, erinnert zwar zu sehr an Hegel oder Marx, sie ist auch zu eng, weil sie den Menschen zu sehr außer acht läßt und nur auf den objektiven Geist anspielt, also normativ wirkt und allein das objektivierte Werk sieht.[1] Ich kann es jedoch nicht unterlassen zu sagen, daß diese Definition, im einfachsten Sinne, aber auch ein heuristisches Deutungsprinzip für die ritterlich-höfische Gesellschaft und für die diesem Kreis zugeordnete Epik und Lyrik ist oder sein kann, mindestens in Deutschland.

Wenn ich heute über Leitbilder und Wertvorstellungen des Adels von der Merowingerzeit bis zur Höhe der Feudalgesellschaft, also vom beginnenden 6. bis zur Mitte des 12. Jahrhunderts spreche, so möchte ich damit eine Kontinuität der politisch führenden und herrschenden Adelsschicht ausdrücken, die sich zwar immer wieder erneuert hat, die aber bis an das Ende der archaischen Epoche um die Mitte des 11. Jahrhunderts und noch bis in das 12. Jahrhundert wesentliche Strukturelemente beibehielt, sich selber aber nicht oder kaum aussprach. Über ihre Mentalité und ihren Geist berichten historische Darstellungen, Legenden, Vitae und dgl., die von Mönchen geschrieben wurden, auch wenn diese

---

1 Nach dieser Theorie ist geschrieben: K. Bertau, *Deutsche Literatur im europäischen Mittelalter*, 2 Bde. (München 1972/73).

von adeliger Herkunft waren, wie Widukind von Corvey oder Hrots-
witha von Gandersheim oder Wipo von Burgund. Adeliges Bewußtsein
war selbstverständlich, ungebrochen, unreflektiert, und adelige Herrschaft wurde von der klerikalen Intellektuellenschicht mit Literatur-
monopol in Latein wie auch von den dienenden und arbeitenden Leibeigenen, die über 90 %% aller Menschen ausmachten, als gegebene und
gottgewollte Tatsache hingenommen.² Die »Constitutio de feudis« Kaiser Konrads II. von 1037 hatte aber schon in Reichsitalien nicht nur ein
starkes wirtschaftliches und gesellschaftliches Gefälle zwischen den großen und den kleinen Lehensträgern, den *capitanei* und den *valvassores*,
erkennen lassen, sondern auch den Herrscher gezwungen, den Rechts-
und Besitzstand der Kleinen gesetzlich abzusichern.³ Der sogenannte
Investiturstreit⁴ und die starke soziale Mobilität, die seither Italien,
Frankreich und Deutschland erfaßte, machten der zahlreichen, aus der
Leibeigenschaft aufsteigenden Schicht der Ministerialen in Deutschland
die Bahn in die politische Führungsschicht des Reiches frei,⁵ die sich auf
diese Weise mit einem *heterogenen* Element ergänzte.

Das Einrücken dieser »adeligen Unfreien« in die Dienstpositionen des
alten Adels beweist nichts besser als die Tatsache, daß sie im 12. Jahrhundert mit dem Wort *ministeriales* bezeichnet wurden, das im 9./10.
Jahrhundert nur auf adelig-geistliche Umgebung des Königs auf höch-
ster Ebene angewandt worden war, daß sie mit den alten Titeln des
Adels wie dominus, nobilis, comes bezeichnet wurden, daß sie sich

---

² K. Bosl, *Die Grundlagen der modernen Gesellschaft im Mittelalter: Eine deutsche
Gesellschaftsgeschichte des Mittelalters*, 2 Bde. (Stuttgart 1972/73). Ders., »Die
gesellschaftliche Entwicklung im Mittelalter 500–1350«, in: Aubin/Zorn, *Handbuch der deutschen Sozial- und Wirtschaftsgeschichte*, I (Stuttgart 1971), 133–168,
226–273. Ders., »Staat, Gesellschaft, Wirtschaft im deutschen Mittelalter«, in: Geb-
hardt/Grundmann, *Handbuch der deutschen Geschichte*, I (Stuttgart, 9. Aufl. 1970),
695–835. Ders., *Frühformen der Gesellschaft im mittelalterlichen Europa* (München
1964). Ders., *Mensch und Gesellschaft in der Geschichte Europas* (München 1972).
Ders., *Die Gesellschaft in der Geschichte des Mittelalters* (Göttingen, 3. Aufl. 1975).
³ *MG Const.* I, Nr. 45, S. 89–91.
⁴ K. Bosl, »Der Investiturstreit und seine Bedeutung für Europa«, in: Bosl, *Mensch
und Gesellschaft*, S. 121–140. Ders., »Gregor VII. und Heinrich IV.«, in: L. Rei-
nisch, *Die Europäer und ihre Geschichte* (München 1961), S. 19–37.
⁵ K. Bosl, *Die Reichsministerialität der Salier und Staufer: Ein Beitrag zur Geschichte des hochmittelalterlichen deutschen Volkes, Staates und Reiches*, 2 Bde.
(2. Aufl. Stuttgart 1969/70). Ders., »Vorstufen der deutschen Königsdienstmann-
schaft«, jetzt *Frühformen* (1964), S. 228–276. Ders., »Das ius ministerialium:
Dienstrecht und Lehenrecht im deutschen Mittelalter«, *Frühformen*, S. 277–325.
Ders., »Castes, ordres et classes en Allemagne«, in: R. Mounier, *Problèmes de
stratification sociale* (= Actes du colloque de 1966) (Paris), S. 15–23.

korporativ zusammenschlossen, brutal ihre Forderungen durchsetzten, auch durch den Mord an ihren Herren, daß der alte Adel sich *liber* = »edel = frei« in den Zeugenreihen der Urkunden nannte, was soviel wie »freigeboren« meinte. König und Adel sahen sich gezwungen, diese breite Schicht von politisch arrivierten »newcomers« auch in ihren adeligen Gesellschaftskreis als »junior partners« aufzunehmen, sie an die Festtafel zu bitten und ihnen neben den Amtsfunktionen der Hofdienste auch ein Forum für die Darstellung ihrer Bewußtseinsinhalte und Leitvorstellungen zu bieten oder besser sie in den altadeligen Geist zu integrieren und zu neuen Kündern alter Leitbilder und Wertvorstellungen in einer neuen Sprache zu machen. Das geschah rechtlich dadurch, daß die unfreien Dienstmannen in zunehmendem Maße *echte* Lehen erhielten, womit sie besitzrechtlich sich dem alten Adel anglichen. Politisch nahmen sie nicht nur in Reichsitalien, sondern auch in Deutschland in der 2. Hälfte des 12. Jahrhunderts alle Amtspositionen des alten Adels ein.

Aus diesen Kreisen aber stammten in Deutschland fast alle geistig-schöpferischen Kräfte, die in gewandelten alten Stoffen, aber in neuer Sprache in potenzierter Form die Mentalité des alten Adels übernahmen und verwandelten. Ich nenne Wolfram von Eschenbach, Hartmann von Aue, Walther v. d. Vogelweide, den ich in das fränkische Feuchtwangen erstmals mit Sachargumenten lokalisiert habe.[6] Daß diese Parvenus ihre eigene Auffassung vom Leben hatten, daß sie kritisch zur alten Adelsgesellschaft standen und sich sogar in zunehmendem Maße haeretisch zur reichen Macht- und Herrschaftskirche stellten, das scheint mir mehr als gewiß. Sie standen zwar der alten Kultur des Adels schon lange nahe und mochten sich auch teilweise damit identifizieren, aber sie mußten sich diese erst selber geistig und ethisch aneignen und sie taten dies aus Gründen gesellschaftlicher Adaptation. Genauso wie beim homme de lettre und beim Bildungsphilister in Deutschland (vor 180 Jahren) wurde dabei Adelskultur für den Dienstmann zur gesellschaftlichen Angelegenheit, zur Sache des Sozialprestiges und des Strebens nach dem Höheren, das eben jenes Höhere gesellschaftlich verwertete und damit *ent*wertete.

Der homme de lettre und der Bildungsphilister waren übrigens auch in den Adelssalons des 18. Jahrhunderts groß geworden. Es war aber ein erster Ausverkauf adeliger Werte, der damit begann, daß die Ministe-

---

[6] K. Bosl, »Feuchtwangen und Walther von der Vogelweide«, in: *Zs. f. Bayerische Landesgeschichte* 32 (München 1969), 832–849.

rialität den Wert der Adelskultur entdeckte, indem sie diese bewußt machte und sie literarisch in *Werte* transformierte. Wir sprechen von Massenkultur und vergessen zu oft, daß sie das Ergebnis der Vergesellschaftung einer Kultur ist, die aus den Adelssalons des 18. Jahrhunderts kam. Dieser Prozeß bemächtigte sich zuerst der oberen Klassen und Stände, er begann erstmals im höfisch-ritterlichen Gesellschaftskreis bei den deutschen Ministerialen; im 19./20. Jahrhundert erfaßte er alle Schichten und wurde ein *Massenphänomen*. Es klingt fast wie ein Witz, daß alle die Eigenschaften, die die Massenpsychologie inzwischen am Massenmenschen entdeckt hat, erst einmal in der elitären »Massengesellschaft« des 18. Jahrhunderts vorkamen. Ich meine Verlassenheit, die weder mit Isoliertheit noch Einsamkeit identisch ist, da sie mit größter Anpassungsfähigkeit gepaart erscheint, weiters Erregbarkeit und Haltlosigkeit, außerordentliche Konsumierungsfähigkeit bei völliger Unfähigkeit, Qualitäten zu beurteilen oder zu unterscheiden, vor allem Egozentrik und eine verhängnisvolle Weltentfremdung, die als Selbstentfremdung mißverstanden wird. Die ersten »Massenmenschen« sind so wenig eine Masse im Sinne der Quantität, daß sie sich sogar als Elite fühlen konnten. Diese waren der deutsche Bildungsphilister, der englische Snob, der amerikanische High-Brow-Intellektuelle, der aber eine echte Reaktion auf die amerikanische Massengesellschaft war, der französische bien-pensant mit esprit sérieux. Sie taten im Grunde dasselbe, was die leibeigenen Ministerialen in der ritterlich-höfischen Gesellschaft taten, sie ergriffen das Kulturelle als Kulturwert, sicherten sich damit eine höhere gesellschaftliche Position, höher, als es ihnen von Natur oder von Geburt zuzukommen selber dünkte.

Kulturwerte waren hier wie dort Tauschwerte und die damit automatisch verbundene Entwertung lag darin, daß Kultur für gesellschaftliche Zwecke gebraucht wurde. Kulturwerte ergriffen die Menschen nicht mehr, sondern wurden von ihnen ergriffen. Aber diese zu Werten veränderten Kulturdinge wurden nicht verzehrt und konsumiert, wie im Lebensprozeß des Vergnügens die modernen Konsumgüter verzehrt werden. Meiner These kurzer Sinn ist der, daß gerade in Deutschland seit dem Aufstieg der Ministerialität in die höfisch-ritterliche Gesellschaft und bei der Ergreifung der alten archaischen Adelskultur und ihrer Werte durch newcomers und Arrivierte in der Bewußtwerdung der höfischen Epik und Literatur alte Leitbilder und Vorstellungswerte vergesellschaftlicht wurden und diese ihnen so eine höhere Stellung sicherten. Um die Wende vom 11. zum 12. Jahrhundert, d. h. mit der

Aufbruchsepoche, vollzog sich in Deutschland, wenigstens auf der konkreten Ebene der feudalen Gesellschaft, ein Wandel der Leitbilder und
Werte, deren Erscheinungsbilder in der Literatur zu analysieren die
Aufgabe des Literarhistorikers ist. Dem Gesellschaftshistoriker ist es
aufgegeben, den realen Hintergrund mit den Daten sowie die allgemeine Struktur zu entfalten. Das versuche ich nun.

Seit den Anfängen der Merowingerherrschaft war *Besitz von Land und
Leuten* eine entscheidende Grundlage adeliger Herrschaft. Beispiele aus
Gregor v. Tours' Frankengeschichte zeigen aber auch, daß Reichtum
allein nicht genügte, um die Zugehörigkeit eines aus den Unterschichten
aufgestiegenen Mannes zum Kreise der Adeligen von Geburt zu begründen. Adelige Herkunft und Reichtum an Land und Leuten standen
in einem Verhältnis gegenseitiger Abhängigkeit, wobei Herkunft wohl
Priorität hatte. Die fränkischen Könige griffen von Anfang an bei der
Wahl ihrer engsten Mitarbeiter und bei der Vergabe von Ämtern auf
den grundbesitzenden Adel zurück, wie später das Edikt von Paris von
614[7] vorschrieb. Die Anfänge fränkisch-adeliger Grundherrschaft gehen
schon in das 5. Jahrhundert zurück. Chlodwig hat nicht den fränkischen
Adel schlechthin ausgerottet; er konnte nicht allein mit der gallorömi-
schen Senatorenaristokratie Gallien regieren, sondern brauchte zur Eroberung wie zur Beherrschung Galliens gerade den fränkischen Er-
obereradel, der schon bei der Eroberung mit reichem Besitz ausgestattet
wurde, wie der außerordentliche Beigabenreichtum der Adelsgräber der
Chlodwigzeit bezeugt. Herrschaft über Grund und Boden und Herrschaft über abhängige Leute flossen in der Hausherrschaft zusammen,
in der königliche und adelige Herrschaft ihre Wurzel haben. Die Her-
rengewalt, die über die engere Hausherrschaft hinausging, war in fränkischer Zeit vermutlich Gefolgschaftsherrschaft. Es ist zu erweisen, daß
der merowingische Adelige eine Gefolgschaft hatte, die einen Treueeid
leistete, auf jeden Fall Dienstmannschaften, wo der Aspekt des Dienstes,
nicht der der Treue im Vordergrund stand. Herrschaft über Land und
Leute übte nicht nur der fränkische Adel, sondern auch die gallorömische
Senatorenaristokratie Südwestgalliens etwa; ein besonderes Element
der Herrschaftsorganisation war anfänglich zumeist beim romanischen
Adel allein der befestigte Herrensitz bzw. die Burg (*castrum*), d.h.
eine stärkere landschaftliche Bindung.

Wirtschaftliche Macht und Herrschaft über abhängige Leute erklären

---

7 *MG* Cap. I (Boretius, Neudruck 1960), 21 ff.

aber nicht eine dauerhafte Anerkennung des adeligen Führungs-
anspruchs in der archaischen (= frühmittelalterlichen) Gesellschaft.
Die repräsentative Rolle des Adels, seine Funktion als Elite, vor allem
seine Potenz, jenseits aller übertragenen oder usurpierten Befugnisse
beispielhaft und richtungweisend zu wirken, müssen einen tieferen
Grund haben. Es muß dieser Gruppe in irgendeiner Form ein religiös
gedachtes Charisma zuerkannt worden sein. So entspricht es auch dem
Wesen archaischen Denkens und archaischer Totalität.[8] Religion war
Bindemittel archaischer Staatlichkeit, Gesellschaft, Kultur, archaischen
Rechts. Handfest belegen kann man dies dadurch, daß die Hagiographen des 7.–9. Jahrhunderts, die z. T. selber Adelige waren, mindestens
unbewußt ein neues adeliges Heiligenideal schufen und damit eine
Rechtfertigung der herrenständischen Ordnung lieferten.[9] F. Prinz
meint sogar, freilich ohne Beleg, daß die Hagiographie der durch den
Glaubenswechsel erschütterten heidnisch-charismatischen Adelsherrschaft des Frankenreiches eine neue religiöse, *christliche* Sanktion geboten habe.[10] Die Heiligenlegenden messen der Darstellung adeliger
Abstammung, der politisch-herrschaftlichen Funktion und den fami-
liären Beziehungen übergroßen Wert bei, wie man es bei dieser Lite-
raturgattung nicht erwartet. F. Graus verweist darauf, daß in den Vitae
bei Heiraten großer Wert auf Ebenburt gelegt wurde und daß der Adel
dem Mönchsideal folgte, weil von »Adelskloster« und »adeligem Hei-
ligengrab« die Rede ist.[11] Die Hagiographen stellen übereinstimmend
typische Formen, Inhalte und Symbole adeligen Lebens dar. Wie recht
aber Prinz mit seiner Rede von der politischen »Instinkthandlung« des
fränkischen Adels beim Glaubenswechsel, und von einer Art »Selbst-
heiligung« in der Legende und einer Legitimierung der Adelsherrschaft
hatte, zeigt uns der Prolog zur Vita Gertruds v. Nivelles,[12] der sagt,

---

[8] G. Schmidt, »Religion, Mythos, Liturgie und Herrschaft im frühen Mittelalter: Zum
Verständnis des Archaischen in der Geschichte«, in: *Zs. f. Bayerische Landesgeschichte* 34 (1971), 15–84.

[9] K. Bosl, »Der Adelsheilige: Ideal und Wirklichkeit, Gesellschaft und Kultur im
merowingischen Bayern des 7. und 8. Jahrhunderts«, in: *Speculum Historiale*, =
Festschr. J. Spörl (1966), 167–183. F. Prinz, »Zur geistigen Kultur des Mönchtums
im spätantiken Gallien und im Merowingerreich«, in: *Zs. f. Bayer. Landesgeschichte* 26 (1963), 29–102.

[10] F. Prinz, *Frühes Mönchtum im Frankenreich: Kultur und Gesellschaft in Gallien,
den Rheinlanden und Bayern am Beispiel der monastischen Entwicklung (4. bis
8. Jahrhundert),* (München–Wien 1965).

[11] F. Graus, *Volk, Herrscher und Heiliger im Reich der Merowinger: Studien zur
Hagiographie der Merowingerzeit* (Praha 1965).

[12] *SS RM* II, p. 454.

daß der Verfasser nicht nur das Andenken der Heiligen bewahren, sondern an Heil, Heiligkeit und *virtutes* der Hausheiligen Gertrud die Größe und das Prestige der arnulfingisch-karolingischen Familie zeichnen wollte. In der Vita des zweiten karolingischen Hausheiligen und Stammvaters Arnulf von Metz aber wird gezeigt, daß Heiligkeit und Segen des Ahnen Arnulf die Karolinger mit der höheren Geblütsweihe eines echten Königshauses versehen haben und daß die Übertragung der Königsherrschaft eine Folge des von Arnulf erwirkten Heiles war.[13]
In seiner nach 1071 verfaßten 3. Vita des Hl. Lambert zählt Sigibert von Gembloux die Faktoren auf, die Pippin des Mittleren königsgleiche Stellung im Frankenreich begründeten.[14] *Ruhm* begründet durch siegreiche Schlachten, *Virtus* = Kraft (nicht eine Einzeltugend) gesteigert durch *Adel* und *Heiligkeit* seiner Vorfahren von Vater- und Mutterseite; dabei werden aufgezählt die sanctitas seiner matertera Gertrud, seines Onkels (patruus) Chlodulf, Bischofs v. Metz, seiner Mutter Begga und seines Großvaters, Bischofs Arnulf von Metz, der eine »Wundergestalt« im Leben und im Tode war (mirabilis fuit); deshalb kann Sigibert zusammenfassen, daß Pippin »nihil *gloriae,* nihil *potentiae* vel *felicitatis* deesset« = daß er über *Ruhm, Macht, Heil* verfügte. Das sind objektive Grundwerte adeligen Lebens, die von anderen festgestellt werden, und das noch im 11. Jahrhundert am Ende der archaischen Epoche. Die gloria ist Folge der crebri victoriarum tytuli, also einer kriegerisch-schwerttragenden Herrenschicht; die potentia geht zurück auf die nobilitas der Vorfahren, die große Herren über Land und Leute waren und Ämter innehatten; die felicitas (= Glück und Heil) war begründet in den monimenta sanctitatis, in der segenspendenden Heiligkeit. Das alles macht das *Führungscharisma* des Adels aus.
Der letzte antike Enzyklopädist Isidor von Sevilla definiert als *nobilis* den »cuius et nomen et genus scitur«.[15] Familie und Name machen den Adel aus. »Nomen« ist in der merowingischen Hagiographie Inbegriff des hohen gesellschaftlichen Prestiges eines Adeligen. Wenn man Namen und Herkunft eines Mannes nicht nennt, will man ihn tief herabsetzen. Die Zusätze in der Fredegar-Chronik zu Individuen wie genere francus, Romanus, Burgundionum meinen nicht allein Stammeszugehörigkeit, sondern Mitglied der höchsten Adelsschicht. Nach der Vorstellung des

---

13 *SS RM* II, p. 433.
14 III Vita Landberti ep. Traiectensis, cap. 26 = *SS RM* VI,397.
15 Isidor v. Sevilla, *Etymologiae* X 185, p. 386 (vgl. X 147, p. 382) (ed. F. Arevalo, Migne *PL* 82).

Mittelalters übernahm und überkam man mit dem Namen bestimmte Eigenschaften, ja das Heil des früheren Trägers eines bestimmten Namens. Genus und nomen sollen ebenso übereinstimmen wie genus und mores (fortuna et mores bei Konrad I. Designation Heinrichs I.). Die adelige Geburt verpflichtet dazu, die qualifizierte Herkunft durch *vita nobilis* und *actio sublimis* zu bestätigen und zur persönlichen oder individuellen nobilitas zu steigern. Ein zu vita nobilis und actio sublimis verwandtes Paar ist nobilitas et virtus (= actio). Damit sind Normen und Werte adeliger actio und virtus in der Merowingerzeit angesprochen.[16]

P. Bodmer,[17] J. M. Wallace-Hadrill[18] und F. Irsigler[19] haben darauf hingewiesen, daß als eine Art Oberbegriff der oft genannten Eigenschaften virilis, sagax, efficax, strenuus, elegans opere, versutus usw. immer wieder die Bezeichnung *utilis* auftaucht. Wallace-Hadrill[20] meint, daß Gregor mit utilitas einen »aspect of barbarian virility« bezeichnet habe; doch bedeute es mehr als »plain violence« (= nackte Gewalttätigkeit, Brutalität). Beda Ven. verwendet dieses Wort auch für die angelsächsischen Könige. Utilitas war jedenfalls nach Gregor die ideale Eigenschaft des merowingischen Königs. Utilitas ist nicht nur Tüchtigkeit, sondern auch felicitas und virtus, Heil und Eignung (vielleicht auch idoneitas); utilitas als Inbegriff von Heil und Eignung gilt für König und Adel gleichermaßen. Die archaische und hochfeudale Hochform der Herrschaft gerade in Deutschland war immer und ist von wenigen Situationen abgesehen die *»Aristokratie mit monarchischer Spitze«.* Als sich 603 (nach Fredegar) in Orleans der austrasische Hausmeier Bertoald und der neustrische Hausmeier Landerich an der Spitze ihrer Gefolgschaftshaufen gegenübertraten, wurde Landerich von Bertoald zum Zweikampf herausgefordert, um ein größeres Blutvergießen zu vermeiden und um ein Gottesurteil zu erzwingen, aber auch um Heil und Eignung eines von ihnen zu erproben (ibique tua et mea utilitas adparebit). Die Adressaten in fränkischen Königsurkunden des 7. Jahr-

---

16 K. Bosl, »Reges ex nobilitate, duces ex virtute sumunt (Tacitus, Germania c. 7)«, in: *Frühformen*, S. 631–642.

17 P. Bodmer, *Der Krieger in der Merowingerzeit und seine Welt: Eine Studie über Kriegertum als Form der menschlichen Existenz im Frühmittelalter* (Zürich 1957).

18 J. M. Wallace-Hadrill, »The work of Gregory of Tours in the light of modern research«, in: *Transact. of Hist. Soc. London* (1951). Ders., *The longhaired kings and other studies in Frankish history* (London 1962).

19 F. Irsigler, *Untersuchungen zur Geschichte des frühfränkischen Adels* (Bonn 1969). Eine ausgezeichnete Studie mit wichtigen Ergebnissen.

20 Wallace-Hadrill, ebd., S. 62.

hunderts werden angesprochen mit »magnetudo seu utilitas vestra«
oder »magnetudo seu nobilitas vestra«. Utilitas ist demnach eindeutig
Adelsprädikat, das die Qualität der Eignung mitausdrückt. In der Lex
Alam (35,1) kann der alemannische dux die utilitas regis nur dann erfüllen (implere), wenn er sein exercitum gubernare und sein equum
ascendere kann, und vom bayerischen dux (tit 2,9) wird verlangt, daß
er imstande ist, »iudicio contendere, in exercitu ambulare, populum
iudicare, equum viriliter ascendere, arma sua viraciter baiulare«; außerdem sollte er weder stumm noch blind sein. Diese beiden süddeutschen
Stammesrechte sind fränkisches Königsrecht und beruhen auf römischem
Recht, wie ich in der Festschrift für Luitpold Wallach gezeigt habe.
Damit habe ich einen Katalog von Führungseigenschaften aufgezählt,
der damals für den Adel galt, Fähigkeit Recht zu sprechen und durch-
zusetzen (Richteramt), Eignung zum Heerführer, Gewandtheit im Rei-
ten, Geschicklichkeit im Gebrauch der Waffen, körperliche Unversehrt-
heit. Das waren die unabdingbaren Voraussetzungen für die standes-
gemäße Lebensführung des Adeligen.
Doch war dieses fränkische Adelsleitbild nicht nur germanisch, wie
Schlesinger[21] und Buchner[22] meinen, und der fränkische Adel war nicht
nur von diesen Wertvorstellungen und besonderen Tätigkeiten geprägt.
E. Zöllner[23] bezeichnet zwar die Eigenschaften, die der längere Prolog
der Lex Salica = 100 Titel Text[24] der gens inclita francorum zuschreibt,
nämlich »fortis in arma ... profunda in consilio, corporea nobilis ...
forma egregia, audax, velox et aspera«, als stärkstes Dokument fränkischen Selbstbewußtseins, aber wir haben Belege dafür, daß der fränkische Adel *auch* literarisch interessiert war, daß ein Teil der fränkischen
Aristokratie nach dem Beispiel Arbogasts von Trier und dem Zeugnis
des Apollinaris Sidonius die Feder ebensogut wie das Schwert führte.
In der 2. Hälfte des 6. Jahrhunderts betonte Venantius Fortunatus bei
der adeligen Oberschicht der Franken die zum Adelsideal der Zeit ge-
hörende literarische Bildung, während Gregor von Tours diese fast
nur seinen gallorömisch-senatorischen Standesgenossen zuerkennt.[25]

---

[21] W. Schlesinger, »Über germanisches Heerkönigtum«, in: Schlesinger, *Beiträge zur
deutschen Verfassungsgeschichte des Mittelalters* 1 (1962), 53–87, bes. S. 82.
[22] R. Buchner, »Das merowingische Königtum«, in: Th. Mayer, *Das Königtum*, =
Vortr. u. Forschungen 3 (Konstanz 1956), 143–154, bes. S. 145.
[23] E. Zöllner, *Die politische Stellung der Völker im Frankenreich* (Wien 1950), S. 68.
[24] Editio K. A. Eckhardt, S. 82.
[25] Venantius Fortunatus, *Carm. Lib.* VI,2 (vgl. II,26; VII,8; IX,16) = MG AA IV,1
(1885, ed. L. Leo).

Bezzola[26] und Wallace-Hadrill haben gezeigt, daß Fortunat darin den eigentlichen Inhalt der »noblesse de caractère« sah, ein wirkliches Standessymbol, das einen hohen Rang zuwies. Er hebt Gogo, den Erzieher König Childeberts II. hervor und vergleicht ihn mit Cicero; Gogo war der Leiter der Palastschule zu Paris. Das starke Interesse fränkischer Adeliger an den Werten römischer Bildung und die engen Kontakte zwischen gallorömischem und fränkischem Adel besonders im Zeichen der gemeinsamen spätantiken Rhetorenschule reichen schon in die 1. Hälfte des 6. Jahrhunderts zurück. Das zeugt nicht nur für die lebendig weiterwirkende Kraft der antiken Tradition, sondern auch vom hohen Niveau und geistig-kulturellen Anspruch der fränkischen Aristokratie. Trotzdem diesem Bildungsinteresse Leitbildcharakter zukommt, muß man sagen, daß diese gebildeten Leute auf den (austrasischen) Hof beschränkt waren und auch innerhalb des Hofadels nur eine kleine Elitegruppe bildeten. Die Merkmale des Venantius sind also von den hohen Würdenträgern abgeleitet.

Über charakteristische Elemente, Symbole und Formen adeligen Lebens und daraus folgernd über die aristokratische Struktur der archaischen Gesellschaft berichten am ausführlichsten die hagiographischen Quellen, und zwar für das 7. Jahrhundert. Man muß dabei ihre topische Gebundenheit in Rechnung stellen. Sie sind darum eine gute Quelle, weil sie uns einen Wandel von Wertvorstellungen erkennen lassen; das Heiligenideal und die hagiographische Umwelt der Heiligen haben sich im Verlaufe des 7./8. Jahrhunderts grundlegend gewandelt. Wir stellen einen Übergang der spätgallischen Zeit zum Typ des »Adelsheiligen« im 7. und 8. Jahrhundert fest. Adelige Lebensart enthält im Sinne der Hagiographie typische Züge der vita saecularis und stand so in direktem Gegensatz zur echten Askese. Bodmers Untersuchung[27] sprach von einer Form hochstehenden aristokratischen Kriegertums. Die Heiligenviten schätzen die kriegerische Tätigkeit, aber sie kennen den Typ des hl. Kriegsmannes nicht. Aber seit dem 7. und im 8. Jahrhundert treten im Idealbild des merowingischen Heiligen, vor allem seit der zeitgenössischen Vita des Arnulf von Metz Tapferkeit und Waffenglück als rechter Hintergrund für den »athleta Christi« hervor; der weiß mit den Waffen des Glaubens ebenso zu fechten, wie vorher mit Schild und Schwert. Neben dem Kampf wird die Jagd als genuine Form standes-

---

[26] R. R. Bezzola, *Les origines et la formation de la littérature courtoise en Occident (500–1200)*, I (Paris 1958), bes. 41 ff.
[27] S. Anm. 17.

gemäßen adeligen Lebens im Frankenreich geschildert; gegenüber der
idealen sanctitas erscheint sie freilich als vanitas saecularis. Und ein drit-
tes Merkmal adeliger Lebensart ist die adelige Tischgemeinschaft. Der
Aufnahme Adeliger in die *Tischgemeinschaft* kam eine ganz große gesellschaftliche Bedeutung zu.[28] Die adelige Tischgemeinschaft hatte eine
rangzuweisende Funktion, war ein Element der Friedewahrung und ein
Instrument, Treuebindungen zwischen Gleichgesinnten zu schaffen und
Treuepflichten zu festigen. Friedensschlüsse und Verträge, politische
Abmachungen untereinander, Friedensschluß nach einer Fehde, Abschluß einer Schwurfreundschaft bekräftigten König und Adel durch
ein gemeinsames Mahl. Übrigens war die aristokratisch bestimmte
Herrschafts- und Gesellschaftsordnung des weltlichen Bereichs in den
merowingischen Klöstern nicht aufgehoben. In der Darstellung Arbeos
von Freising freute sich Corbinian, der Adelsheilige, an Schmuck und
wertvollen Kleidern, hatte sein Vergnügen an sportlicher Leistung und
Wohlgeratenheit, war unbekümmert, ja schroff im Anordnen und Herr-
schen und war ein ausgezeichneter Kenner edler Pferde, kurz ein voll-
endeter Aristokrat. Die schrittweise Angleichung an das Adelsideal der
Zeit, gleichbedeutend mit »Säkularisierung« des Heiligenadels war notwendig, damit keine zu große Divergenz zwischen Heiligenideal und
Wirklichkeit eintrat, um keine Einbuße an Wirkung und Anziehung als
Modell und Leitbild für die alles bestimmende adelige Oberschicht zu
erleiden.

Doch fragen wir uns in einem zweiten Schritt nach dem Fortleben dieses
Adelsleitbildes und der damit verbundenen Wertvorstellung zwischen
8./9. Jahrhundert und der Schwelle des 12. Jahrhunderts. Handbücher
der Literaturgeschichte schweigen sich über die Probleme adeliger Lebensart, Leitbilder, Kultur vor dem Zeitalter der höfisch-ritterlichen
Dichtung (1160–1250) meist aus. Man interessiert sich für die Entstehung der literarischen Gattung des Heldenliedes und seiner Stoffe.
Da es kaum eine deutschsprachige weltliche Literatur vor dem 12. Jahrhundert gibt und die lateinische Literatur, die für unser Thema aussage-
kräftig wäre, ebenso wenig wie eine deutsche unter gesellschaftsgeschicht-
lichem Aspekt beschrieben ist, hat die Forschung bislang den Anteil
adeliger Überlieferung und adeligen Einfluß auf die vorstaufische Literatur recht gering eingeschätzt. Für die Merowingerzeit sind wir heute

---

[28] Fritze, »Die fränkische Schwurfreundschaft der Merowingerzeit: Ihr Wesen und
ihre politische Funktion«, in: *ZRG, GA* 71 (1954), 74–125. W. Grönbech, *Kultur
und Religion der Germanen,* 2 Bde. (Stuttgart, 5. Aufl. 1954).

schon besser informiert, auch für die ottonisch-frühsalische Zeit.[29] Es ist primär Aufgabe des germanistischen Philologen und Literarhistorikers, die Einflüsse adeliger Mentalität auf die literarischen Leistungen zu analysieren; aber es ist die Aufgabe des Historikers, die adelige Mentalität und ihr Ethos zu zeigen. Diese versuche ich nun vom 10.–12. Jahrhundert kurz zu skizzieren.

In der historischen Literatur der Zeit, in Annalen und Chroniken herrscht bis zur Mitte des 11. Jahrhunderts der Standpunkt des Königs vor; erst später wird der Standpunkt des Adels entscheidend; trotzdem erfahren wir daraus relativ viel, wenn auch tendenziös, von den Verhaltensnormen des Adels. Abgesehen vom Wert der nobilitas (carnis) wird ein vielschichtiger *Ehrbegriff* als Zentralproblem adeligen Ethos und adeliger Mentalität immer wieder in den Quellen sichtbar. Der Adelige reagiert auf jede Ehrverletzung, die standesgemäß mit den Waffen gerächt wird; mit der Ehre des einzelnen ist die Ehre der Familie verbunden. Dadurch wurden das aristokratische Ehrproblem und damit Rache und Fehde zu einem starken Unsicherheitsfaktor in Gesellschaft und Staat und Reich.[30] Zentralbegriff blieb die nobilitas carnis = das Bewußtsein von der Sonderstellung im Gesellschaftsgefüge, die religiös mit einem heilskräftigen, außergewöhnlichen Verhältnis zu Gott begründet wurde. Damit verbunden waren Pflege des Ahnenbewußtseins und der Traditionen der Ahnen, deren elitäre Kraft sich durch Glück und Heil öffentlich erwies. Neben vornehmer Abstammung stand weiter virtus = persönliche Bewährung als integrierender Bestandteil des Adelsethos. Deshalb strebte der einzelne nach höchstem Ruhm auf dem Felde der Politik und des Krieges. Ruhm und Ansehen werden weiter gesteigert durch die *largitas* des adeligen Herrn, dessen Reichtum die Möglichkeit bot, ein großes Gefolge zu halten. Auch in der vasallitischen Treuebindung an den Herrn will der Adelige seine »Freiheit« gewahrt wissen. Pflicht und Recht des freien adeligen Vasallen (miles) waren Rat und Hilfe und Zustimmung im politischen Bereich. Wird seine Freiheit, sein Rechtsstand bedroht, nimmt er das Widerstandsrecht gegen den tyrannisch-vertragsbrüchigen König und Adelsgenossen in Anspruch; dieses beruht auf der Entscheidung seines persönlich-

---

[29] H. Kallfelz, *Das Standesethos des Adels im 10. und 11. Jahrhundert* (Würzburg 1970). K. Hauck, »Haus- und sippengebundene Literatur mittelalterlicher Adelsgeschlechter, von Adelssatiren des 11. und 12. Jahrhunderts her erläutert«, in: *MIÖG* 62 (1954), 121–145.

[30] O. Brunner, *Land und Herrschaft: Grundfragen der territorialen Verfassungsgeschichte Südostdeutschlands im Mittelalter* (Baden b. Wien, 1. Aufl. 1939).

individuellen Gewinns. In den Augen des Königs hat das Adelsethos
nicht immer positive Züge. Das eifersüchtige Wachen und Pochen auf
das eigene Ansehen und die Freiheit, der verschwenderische Haushalt,
die starren Zwänge von Ehre und Rache machten die adelige Führungsschicht des Reiches damals zu einem Unruheherd der Gesamtherrschaft
im Großreich. Königstreue Autoren äußern sich darum kritisch über die
aemulatio des Adels, über seine permanente Forderung nach *aequalitas,*
die keinen anderen hochkommen lassen wollte. Die historischen Quellen
berichten wenig über den Alltag des Adels. Historiker und Dichter sahen
das als Selbstverständlichkeit an. Diese Nichterwähnung darf nicht vergessen lassen, daß es auch in der Adelswelt Höhepunkte und Glanz-
punkte von außerordentlichem Charakter gab, nicht nur am Hof und in
der Königswelt.[31]
Mehr als die Geschichtsschreibung des 9.–11. Jahrhunderts berichten
uns Viten und die nichthistorisch-literarische Produktion dieser archaischen Endepoche. Hier finden wir die Zeugnisse adeliger Mentalität.
Ich nenne hier als adeliges Selbstzeugnis modellhaft das sogenannte
Manuale der Dhuoda, Gemahlin des berühmten Bernhard v. Septi-
manien und Schwiegertochter des in den chansons de geste gefeierten
Wilhelm von Gellone.[32] Dhuoda verfaßte ca. 842 dieses Familienalbum
für ihren Sohn Bernhard. In den Belehrungen steht der Vater nach Gott
an erster Stelle, auch vor dem König, d. h. der Sohn hat dem Vater mehr
zu gehorchen als dem König. Wir ersehen weiter die besondere Obsorge
für das Familien- und Ahnengrab. Im Pflichtenkatalog des Adeligen
steht obenan das servitium für Gott und darnach das servitium für den
weltlichen Herrn, den König. Das Königtum bewertet die im Kloster
erzogene und theologisch gebildete Dhuoda ganz besonders hoch. Der
Königshof ist für sie schlechthin das gesellschaftliche Zentrum, an dem
sich ihr Sohn alle virtutes aneignen kann. Zweihundert Jahre später
beurteilt der *Ruodlieb* die Rolle des Königshofes ebenso hoch wie
Dhuoda. Die *Königsnähe* ist also ein zentrales Anliegen des empor-
strebenden und vom Prestigedenken getriebenen Adels. Noch in der
höfischen Literatur des 12./13. Jahrhunderts ist die Tafelrunde des Kö-

---

31 Über den Adel hat zuletzt umfassend aus den Quellen gearbeitet: W. Störmer,
   Früher Adel: Studien zur politischen Führungsschicht im fränkisch-deutschen Reich
   vom 8. bis zum 11. Jahrhundert (= Monographien zur Geschichte des Mittelalters VI, 1 u. 2, 1973). Ders., »König Artus als aristokratisches Leitbild des spä-
   teren Mittelalters«, *Zs. f. Bayer. Landesgeschichte* 35 (1972), 946–971.
32 W. Wollasch, *Eine adelige Familie des frühen Mittelalters: Ihr Selbstverständnis*
   und ihre Wirklichkeit (1957), 169 ff.

nigs Artus (= der König) das Zentrum der adelig-ritterlichen Welt. Die Emanzipation des Adels vom König beginnt im 11. Jahrhundert und hat den Aufstieg der Ministerialität in Deutschland gebracht. Wenn die Königspfalz der Standort des Adels ist, dann wird die Struktur des Adels davon maßgeblich beeinflußt.[33] Zweifellos steht das Selbstbewußtsein der reichsaristokratischen Führungsschicht besonders im Karolingerreich (aber auch schon bei den Merowingern) in direktem Zusammenhang mit dem Königshof. Da alle deutschen Klöster vor 1050 Reichs- und Königsklöster waren, berichten ihre fundationes immer wieder von der Verwandtschaft ihrer adeligen Gründer mit dem König. Nicht das adelige Haus, die Burg, sondern der Königshof war zunächst der Kristallisationspunkt dieses Selbstbewußtseins. Der mächtige Adel hatte damals kein eigenes festes Zentrum, sondern nur verstreute curtes, die in vielen Landschaften lagen; sie lebten fortwährend auf Wanderschaft wie der König auch. Adelsleben stand damals im Gegensatz zum seßhaften Leben des schollegebundenen Bauern.

Der archaische Adel kennt ein prinzipiell von ihm abgesetztes Königtum nicht. Die in der archaischen Adelsgesellschaft herrschenden Auffassungen von Ehre und Mannestugend, die dort geltenden ethischen Normen umschließen König und Adel. Für beide sind hohe Abstammung, Ahnenbewußtsein, Ahnenstolz, Zugehörigkeit zu einem »Geschlecht« Grundtatsachen des Adelsethos. Das Geschlecht ist schon vorher da, es gibt den *agnatischen* neben dem *kognatischen* Verband; seit dem 11. Jahrhundert wird das Geschlecht endgültig ein scharf abgegrenzter *agnatischer* Familienverband, der Träger einer an einen festen Sitz, die Burg, gebundenen Herrschaft war; nach dieser Burg benennen sich diese adeligen Familien, Geschlechter, Häuser; diese Burg ist die certa habitatio, das praedium libertatis = Hantgemal, an dem ihre Adelsqualität lokal und sachenrechtlich hing; kein germanisches, sondern ein römischrechtliches Symbol und Rechtswahrzeichen. Bis zum 10./11. Jahrhundert besaß für das Geschlechtsbewußtsein die kognatische Seite = die Verwandtschaft der Frau, Mutter, Großmutter eine ausschlaggebende Bedeutung, besonders wenn der vornehmere Adel, das leuchtendere Beispiel, der größere Einfluß auf der Seite der Mutter lag.

---

[33] K. Bosl, »Pfalzen und Forsten«, in: H. Heimpel (Hg.), *Deutsche Königspfalzen: Beiträge zu ihrer historischen und archäologischen Erforschung* 1 (Göttingen 1963), 1–29. K. Bosl, »Pfalzen, Klöster, Forste in Bayern«, in: *Verhandlungen d. Hist. Vereins f. Oberpfalz und Regensburg* 106 (1966), 43–62.

Nobilitas carnis = blutmäßig hohe Abstammung garantierte nicht jedem einzelnen Sippen- und Familienglied Qualität. Deshalb unterschieden die Quellen seit dem 10./11. Jahrhundert zwischen genius und persona, zwischen nobilitas mentis (animi) und nobilitas carnis, ohne daß letztere zunächst im Werte gemindert erschiene. Doch kam einmal der Tag, da die nobilitas mentis gegen das reine Geblüt ausgespielt wurde; das 13. Jahrhundert stellte dann fest, daß es ohne nobilitas mentis keine nobilitas carnis geben könne. Trotzdem widersetzte sich der Geblütsadel mit Erfolg der Entwertung der nobilitas carnis bis zur Auflösung der aristokratischen Ordnung im 18./19. Jahrhundert. Er kompensierte seinen biologischen Schwund durch Neuaufnahmen ganzer Schichten wie der Ministerialität zuerst in die höfisch-ritterliche Gesellschaft und in den Niederadel. Das Einsetzen rationalen Denkens, der ersten europäischen Aufklärung im theologisch-philosophischen Raum der Scholastik, die Trennung von Weltlichem und Geistlichem, von Natur und Übernatur, deren magisch-kultische Verbundenheit einen Wesenszug des Archaischen, die Totalität des Denkens darstellte, machte die nobilitas carnis ebenso fragwürdig wie die archaische Spitzen- und Mittlerstellung von König und Adel. Fragwürdig mußte sie vor allem dem Ministerialen sein, dem das Geblüt fehlte, um adelig zu sein. Doch setzte er sich durch Bewährung in höchsten Stellen, durch kriegerische, politische, geistige, schöpferische, literarische Leistung, durch den Erweis einer überragenden geistigen Qualität, einer nobilitas mentis in Ritterepos, Heldenepos, Minnesang ebenbürtig neben Adel und Klerus, an die Seite des Königs gegen den Papst. Er häufte reichen Besitz an, seine Spitzenfiguren waren ebenso reich und mächtig wie der vollfreie hohe Adel; sie glichen auch durch eigene Traditionsbildung im Familienverband den Makel des fehlenden Blutes aus, wurden dann in den Gesellschaftskreis des hohen Adels in die Ritterkultur aufgenommen und konnten nach dem Aussterben der alten Dynastengeschlechter im 11., 12. und 13. Jahrhundert in deren politische und gesellschaftliche Positionen einrücken.

Der adelige Herr muß aus dem vollen leben können, muß Aufwand und Pracht entfalten, muß große Feste feiern und kann es auch, weil die große Masse der Unterschichten[34] für ihn arbeitete, ihm ein Leben in Freiheit und Ungebundenheit möglich machte. Armut entehrte in dieser

---

[34] Den Unterschied zwischen Ober- und Unterschichten hat theoretisch und praktisch am feinsten analysiert: Th. Vjeblen, *The leisure class*, 1960. (Deutsch: *Die Theorie der feinen Leute.*)

aristokratisch-feudalen Gesellschaft ebenso wie Arbeit. Das ist die Gegenseite des Adelsideals. Der adelige Herr hatte zahlreiche Gefolgs-leute und dann viele Vasallen, die von seiner liberalitas = Freigebigkeit lebten. Magnificentia = großartiges Auftreten, also Macht, Reichtum, Pomp, Luxus, Überfluß steht neben liberalitas. Der Adel förderte zu *seiner* Ehre und Verherrlichung Kunst und Literatur, stattete seine Herrensitze und Eigenklöster prächtig aus, arrangierte große Ritter-feste, auf denen die Dichter und Sänger ihre Epen und Minnelieder vor-trugen, in der Provence und in Nordfrankreich, zu Paris und Orleans, in Deutschland zu Mainz, Regensburg, Wien, auf der Wartburg. Die Andechs-Meranier auf dem Bischofstuhl zu Bamberg ließen durch deut-sche und französische Baumeister den ragenden spätromanischen Dom des 13. Jahrhunderts errichten, einmalig in Deutschland durch Skulp-turen, Portale, Raumgliederung.[35] Adeliges Leben war Herrendasein, Machtausübung, Gewaltanwendung. Das Schwert war nicht nur seine Waffe, sondern auch sein Ornat und seine Zier. Durch Übergabe des Schwertes wurde der junge Adelige für mündig erklärt, wurden Alt-adeliger und Ministerialer im höfischen Kreis zum Ritter geschlagen. Körperliche Tüchtigkeit war ein selbstverständlicher Bestandteil des adeligen Mannesideals, Draufgängertum und ungebändigte Vitalität, Tapferkeit, Mut, Kühnheit, Unerschrockenheit, Ausdauer, Beständig-keit, Vorsicht, kluges Ratfinden in Gefahr machten den vollendeten Aristokraten aus. Wesentlich für das adelige Leitbild war die constantia = der Abscheu vor dem Schwanken, vor der Schwachheit gegenüber allen möglichen Einflüssen, die Abneigung gegen Neuerung und Wech-sel, kurz der »konservative« Grundzug dieser aristokratischen Herren-schicht, die sich über Masse und Bürgertum, anfänglich auch über die Ministerialen erhaben fühlte, weil für diese instabilis, avidus, rerum novarum cupidus, vulgus intemperans gilt, d. h. weil sie schwankende, leicht verführbare, kopflose Masse oder Parvenus sind, die nicht die Schranken kennen, die in dieser aristokratisch-königlichen Welt dem Untertanenvolk, dem nichtherrschaftsfähigen »pauper«[36] durch adelige Herrschaft, Sitte und Lebensform gesetzt sind. Der Adel nannte sich vor

---

[35] K. Bosl, »Europäischer Adel im 12./13. Jahrhundert: Die internationalen Verflech-tungen des bayerischen Hochadelsgeschlechtes der Andechs-Meranier«, in: *Zs. f. Bayer. Landesgeschichte* 30 (1967), 20–52.

[36] K. Bosl, »Potens und Pauper: Begriffsgeschichtliche Studien zur gesellschaftlichen Differenzierung im frühen Mittelalter und zum ›Pauperismus‹ des Hochmittel-alters«, in: *Frühformen*, 106–134. Ders., »Dominati e dominanti nella società Ger-manica medievale«, in: *Pensiero Politico* 1 (1937), 61–73.

dem 12. Jahrhundert kaum und selten »frei«. Er tat es erst von dem
Augenblick an, da die unfreien Dienstmannen einen Platz an seiner
Seite forderten; in den Zeugenreihen der Urkunden des 12. Jahrhun-
derts stehen darum liberi vor den ministeriales; liber bedeutet hier edel-
frei = vollfrei, adeligen Geblüts, hochadelig, weil der Ministeriale
Leibeigener von Geburt ist.

Edle Geburt, echte Tat der Persönlichkeit, in der sich die Standes-
tugenden bewähren, Ruhm und Ehre, Macht und Herrschaft waren
Höchstwerte im adeligen Selbstverständnis; darnach bemaß sich bis
über das 12. Jahrhundert hinaus in der archaischen wie in der Aufbruchsepoche das adelige Leitbild.

Der geistige und gesellschaftliche Umbruch seit der Mitte des 11. Jahrhunderts hat das Adelsideal erstmals erschüttert. Die Wirkung sehen
wir im Jahrzehnt nach der Mitte des 12. Jahrhunderts im literarischen
Werk Heinrichs von Melk.[37] Er zeichnet ein Gegenbild der Adelswelt
und des adeligen Leitbildes. Die Ritterschaft erscheint hier offenbar
schon als die Gesellschaft der Adeligen *und* Ministerialen; deren Sitten
und Gebräuche schildert er kritisch und ausführlich. Er wirft ihnen
Prahlerei über sexuelle Ausschweifungen und Mordtaten vor, dazu
Gruppenzwang und Solidarität im Schlechten. Das kriegerische und
kämpferische Leitbild dieser Schicht wird desillusioniert und entwertet
durch die Feststellung, daß bei diesen Leuten nur der ein ganzer Kerl
ist, der viele erschlagen hat. Der verrohte Lebensstil des Rittertums
trägt in seinen Augen wesentliche Schuld am Verderben der unvollkommenen Welt. Er prangert die Treulosigkeit der Herren und Knechte
untereinander an. In der Welt Heinrichs von Melk kann sich nur der
Pragmatiker mit brutalem Selbsterhaltungstrieb durchsetzen. Im Gegensatz zu der im Minnesang und Epos sooft apostrophierten »mâze« herr-
schen Maßlosigkeit und Genußsucht in allen Gesellschaftsschichten.
Schweigert[38] hat aus dem Wortschatz und der Mentalität des Dichters
geschlossen, daß Heinrich selber der ritterlichen Gesellschaft und den
führenden Laienschichten angehörte; denn Rittertum, ritterlicher Ehrbegriff, Ausrüstung, Besitz, Minne, das Kämpferische schlechthin prä-
gen sein Sinnen und Denken. Seine Gedichte haben einen starken Er-
lebnishintergrund und stellen vermutlich Satiren dar; Heinrich leidet an
den offenbaren Widersprüchen seiner Zeit und Gesellschaft; er geißelt

---

[37] Kritische Ausgabe von R. Heinzel (1867).
[38] E. Schweigert, »Studien zu Heinrich von Melk« (Phil. Diss., München 1952).

wie der große zeitgenössische Zeitkritiker Gerhoh von Reichersberg[39] superbia und avaritia als Hauptübel der Gesellschaft. Für Heinrichs Welteinsicht war das vampirhafte Sexualwesen der Frau der Motor der herrschenden Verderbnis.

Kein Zweifel, die Satire Heinrichs von Melk steht in krassem Gegensatz zur höfischen Dichtung und zum Adelsleitbild des 12. Jahrhunderts, ist keineswegs aus der Luft gegriffen. Dieselben Motive zeigt die Vagantenlyrik unter einem rein weltlichen Aspekt. Heinrich wählte im Gegensatz zu Gerhoh die Volkssprache und konnte so einen breiteren Kreis von Hörern mit seiner Gesellschaftskritik ansprechen. Die gängigen Leitbilder blieben also nicht mehr unangefochten, auch wenn in den unmittelbar folgenden Jahrzehnten der Glanz der feudalen Adelswelt in der höfischen Dichtung einen Höhepunkt seiner Darstellung fand. Dafür gilt aber die Feststellung von Karl Hauck, daß trotz starker Fortdauer der Unschriftlichkeit der Adelskultur man von einer Adelsliteratur vom 9.–12. Jahrhundert sprechen muß, die gesellschaftlich zentriert war um Haus, Sippe, Klosterfamilie und um vergleichbare weltliche und geistliche Gemeinschaften. Die kritische Dichtung Heinrichs von Melk ist Gegenstück zu der besten romanhaften Zeichnung der adelig-königlichen Laienwelt im *Ruodlieb* des 11. Jahrhunderts, deren Gegenbild aber schon der freche, verschlagene, verlogene, brutale und anmaßende Rotkopf war, in dem der Ministeriale getroffen werden sollte, gegen den sich der alte Adel mit allen Mitteln wehrte.[40]

Seit dem Beginn des europäischen Aufbruchs nach der Mitte des 11. Jahrhunderts, vorab seit der großen kirchlichen Reformwelle gerieten die Werte, die der »homo nobilis et clarus« verkörperte, in Gefahr, als unkirchlich, unethisch, unnütz entlarvt und abgewürdigt zu werden. Bei Heinrich von Melk geschah das. Den adeligen Laien mußte das Gefühl ergreifen, daß er sich zwischen zwei Wertwelten bewegte, wenn er seine Eigenständigkeit, seine »werlde« mit »êre« und ihrem »lône« hochhalten wollte. Die Adelskultur lebte in der Spannung zwischen werlde und gotes hulde. Wenn die Scheidung in geistliche und weltliche Sittlichkeit noch nicht bewußt wurde und man das ethische Denken der höfisch-

---

[39] A. Lazzarino del Grosso, »Povertà e richezza nel Pensiero di Gerhochi di Reichersberg«, *Annali della Facoltà di Giurisprudenza* VIII (Milano 1969), 146–193; X (1971), 65–122; X (1971), 361–431. (Deutsch: *Armut und Reichtum im Denken G. v. R.*, 1973.)

[40] W. Braun, *Studien zum Ruodlieb: Ritterideal, Erzählstruktur und Darstellungsstil* (Berlin 1962). F. Brunhölzl, »Zum Ruodlieb«, in: *DVj* 39 (1965), 506–522.

ritterlichen Gesellschaft noch für vereinbar hielt mit dem Ideal des vollkommenen Christen, so begannen sich Gott-Jenseits und Welt-Diesseits
trotzdem auseinander zu bewegen, auch im Bereich der virtutes = Tugenden. Walther v. d. Vogelweide ahnte schon, daß sich beide Bereiche
in seiner Seele nicht mehr vereinen ließen. Die archaische Adelskultur,
die die Ministerialen ergriffen und vergesellschafteten, wurde damit
zwangsweise entwertet und elitär »vermaßt«.

Kenneth L. Schmitz

Shapes of Evil in Medieval Epics: A Philosophical Analysis

Evil assumes various shapes in medieval epics. Each shape corresponds to its own form of conflict. The present essay will attempt a philosophical analysis of some shapes of epic evil. The analysis, however, is obliged to take the poems seriously and must not simply employ a conception of evil drawn up beforehand from non-poetic sources. A philosophical analysis of the poetic presentation of evil will fail, if it avoids the very poems to which it intends to contribute an interpretation; and it will shatter, if it proceeds against the evidence of the poems themselves. Moreover, it must take into account the scholarly and critical work on the poems. Nevertheless, a philosophical analysis must pursue its own interests. Now, the present analysis intends to examine the action of several poems, seen against their background and horizon; to select salient events which provoke a crisis in our understanding of the action; and to thereby articulate the manner in which an epic poem may be said to have its own mode of existence as a concrete totality of meaning. In pursuit of this interest, evil will be taken as the theme, because it illuminates the tension between the action of an epic and its horizon.

I. *An antecedent philosophical account of evil.* Philosophy has its history, and so, before turning to the poems, we will take our bearings from a late classical consideration of evil. Among the theological and philosophical authors with whom most medieval epic poets in western Europe might have been at least indirectly familiar, we must place St. Augustine and Boethius. While St. Augustine located human evil in the misuse man has made of his God-given free will, he did not view Adam's fall as simply a human act of restricted importance. He was fully sensitive to the pervasive economy of evil. It was, however, Boethius who provided the Latin middle ages with a sustained philosophical account of the origin, nature and effects of evil. In the *Consolation of Philosophy* he first accounts for moral evil as due to a deficiency in knowledge, that is, to our ignorance and folly. He then passes on to evil as lodged in the restless inconstancy of things; this cosmic transiency by which nothing abides is called melancholy fortune or chance. Finally, he proposes his most basic account of evil: it is the absence of due order, a lack of being that should be there. Boethius thus provides an anthropological interpretation of evil inasmuch as it lurks in the misguided mind and will of man, a cosmological interpretation inasmuch as it moves in the shiftiness of things, and an ontological interpretation inasmuch as it withdraws into the deprivation of being. Taken together, these comprise the massive fact of evil, and they provide the ground for the complicity of man and world in the many shapes of evil. Boethius, too, realizes how deeply evil is embedded in the web of man and things, for he concedes that it is not so much an infliction (from without) as a deep-set infection.[1] Nevertheless, his rational reflection attempts to dissipate the power of evil by unmasking its illusory nature. The epic poet, on the other hand, takes a less ultimate view, and depicts evil in its immediate power, so that the course of events seems neither so rational nor so benign. For reasons philosophical and otherwise, many philosophers today are wary of Boethius' translation of such a theme into purely abstract conceptual terms. The thematic of evil is notoriously ready to escape a purely rational account such as Boethius gives it in the prose passages of the *Consolation*. By attending to concrete poetic presentations of evil, the philosopher may be able to say something about the way in which a poetic presentation exists and about the character of evil – something which Boethius did not say.

On the other hand, Boethius did not merely dissipate the power of evil. He provided both philosopher and poet with a compass by which they might locate it initially. Indeed, F. P. Pickering[2] has argued that the *Consolation* offers the only schema which medieval authors of history and fiction knew. It is a four-fold schema: there is God's immutable plan, *Divine Providence;* there is the divine order as it unfolds in mutable things, *Fate;* there is man's freedom to act, *Human Will;* and

---

1 *The Consolation of Philosophy* IV,3 (tr. E. V. Watts, Penguin, 1969, p. 125).
2 *Literature and Art in the Middle Ages*, Macmillan, 1970, pp. 177–84 (tr. of *Literatur und darstellende Kunst im Mittelalter*, Berlin 1966). For Boethius, see *Consolation*, esp. IV,6.

finally, there is that which seems irrational and arbitrary in fate, that is, *Chance* or *Fortune*. What interests the poet in this scheme is how »fate becomes event in the moment when man acts«, for it is just then that evil may become actual and an evil fate may then »befall« a man. It is, adds Pickering, just this »befalls«, this fortune within fate, that is the highest power with which the poet deals. It is the chance event brought into actuality in accordance with fate through man's free act. For Boethius, of course, fortune, fate and freedom are grounded in the unchanging simplicity and goodness of Providence. The simplest chance or mischance, therefore – if we could but read its meaning –, would be fully comprehensible as a sign of the well-ordered scheme of things.[3] In such a four-fold scheme the fortune embedded in the fate of events is a token of God's providential plan, and thereby carries us to the centre and circumference of reality. The medieval epic poet, as we have already indicated, does not always find such a transparent window upon the fundamental meaning of conflict and evil.

II. *The poem as a totality of existence and meaning.* To see how the epic poet develops the theme of evil we must begin by respecting the poem as a whole; for the source of evil must be situated and its promiscuity traced out within the poem as a whole, if we are to take the measure of the significance of the poem and its evil. Now an individual poem is a totality in several senses. It is, first of all, an individual artistic work: Béroul's *version* of Tristan differs from Gottfried's. But Béroul's poem also differs in *story* from the legend of Roland, and in *genre* from the lyrical »Tristrant« of Heinrich von Veldeke. Even more, as an instance of poetic *discourse*, the poem differs from all non-poetic discourse. And finally, as included within the totality of life, the poem differs from all non-linguistic *enterprises*. As a totality, then, Béroul's poem is version, story, type, discourse and enterprise. Among these various modes of totality, the context will indicate the appropriate sense, but they are all ingredient in the somewhat indeterminate differentiating principle of a particular epic which sets it apart from its fellows and from everything else. The paramount intent of this analysis is to achieve an understanding of the way in which a narrative poem, and principally certain medieval epics, may be said to exist in and through the presentation of evil.[4]

---

[3] C. S. Lewis, *The Discarded Image*, Cambridge, 1964, p. 87.
[4] Despite its philosophical character, the present analysis does not seek to arrive at

It is common enough to speak of the »world« of an epic, and to mean
by it either the social milieu of the audience for which it was intended
or the dramatic ensemble of characters and events. In this latter sense,
the term designates a certain fundamental and all-inclusive unity within
which the characters move and understand themselves. In this sense,
a well-made poem is a world in itself, because it presents itself as having
everything needed to sustain the action. The poetic suspension creates
the dramatic space and time in which the story is to be sung or told,
and lays open the opportunity for it to unfold. The characters and
events may be said to »belong« to the particular world of the poem.
Before an event appears, it waits in the wings, so to speak, and when it
has played out its dramatic power, it comes to rest as the sedimented
past of the action. It does not remain in the foreground space of the
action, for that is crowded with the new event. It survives, so to speak,
at the »edge« of the poem, belonging to it as to its past. As the event
withdraws from the foreground, it is received again by the horizon.
These provisional metaphors are simply initial attempts to underline
the cohesion of characters and events within the unity of the poem.
Such a unity may be more or less loose. Indeed, medieval epic poems are
often episodic in structure, for they were intended to be heard at court
in short passages over an extended period of time. Nevertheless, whatever unity the poem has is achieved through a cohesive principle which
we must now make clearer.

As a world of its own a poem is bounded by its own »horizon«.[5] The
non-technical sense of the term indicates the spatial limits of visual
perception, but by transference to philosophy it comes to mean the
limiting principle of all perceptual experience. In that experience we

---

a well-formed definition of the medieval epic. Such a definition would state its
essential features and would exclude cognate poetic forms such as the romance.
Instead, I shall subsequently use the Tristan story, even though it is not an epic
in the strict sense of the word. What I seek to elucidate here is the thematic of evil
in several narrative poems in the light of their mode of existence as poetic total-
ities. For this purpose the important differences between epic heroes and tragic
lovers are not germane.

5 The term has been made philosophically current largely by Edmund Husserl. See,
for example, his late work, *The Crisis of European Sciences and Transcendental
Phenomenology*, No. 37–8, Northwestern, Evanston, 1970, pp. 142–47 (tr. from
Die Krisis ..., hg. v. W. Biemel, Nijhoff, den Haag, 1954). Cf. also the interesting work of H.-G. Gadamer, *Wahrheit und Methode*, 2. Aufl., Mohr, Tübingen,
1965, esp. pp. 285–86 and the first note to p. 232 in which the term is linked to
W. James' term »fringes«.

encounter individuals which appear and have significance as members of a totality. As a perceiver shifts his position and his perspective his horizon also shifts, but the ultimate horizon of such perceptual experience is the world-horizon. This all-inclusive principle englobes the things, qualities, processes, persons, actions and goals of all perceptual experience. Such a universal principle is temporal as well as spatial. There are two characteristics of such an ultimate principle that are of use for us. First, the world-horizon is not given directly in any perception, but is rather given *along with* every perception; it is already there in every presentation of a thing or situation. The world with its limiting principle, the world-horizon, does not itself appear, for it is not an individual entity. Indeed, the world is there uniquely, but neither as an abstract universal conception nor as a particular instance. So, too, the world-horizon is there as a certain unicity which is prior to every singular or plural; but it is not there separately from them. It is there as their co-present foundation. For that reason, it never appears itself, though it may be said to manifest itself in and through the entities which do appear. Secondly, the world-horizon is not a limiting principle in the manner of a container which encloses the things of the world. It exercizes its limitation, rather, as a discipline and as a demand for a radical sort of compatibility among all perceptual objects. This mute demand enters into all our validation of experience, for by it we continually monitor the correctness and truth of our perceptual judgments. Every new perception must meet the demand of such a principle even if the perception expands or transforms the perceptual horizon, since a too radical break would pass beyond perceptual consciousness. Such an occurrence would bring with it no consciousness of the past and would no longer be temporal or perceptual.

The term »horizon« can be modified in order to indicate the ultimate limiting principle of other modes of consciousness, such as the limits of conceptual thought or of projected action. In a contracted and derivative sense it can also designate a poem as a totality, as when we might speak of the »horizon« of a particular epic poem and mean to indicate thereby the somewhat indeterminate differentiating principle which, in giving a particular epic poem its unity, also sets it apart both from other poems and from all other enterprises. In using the term to designate the principle of poetic totality we mean to underline the two features just mentioned: first, that the horizon functions as the fundamental presupposition for the action of the poem; and second, that it advances a demand for radical compatibility among the elements of the poem. Taken together these features of the horizon secure the unity of the poem and the manner in which it exists.

The first feature: The poetic horizon provides the fundamental presupposition for the characters and action of the poem. The poem, taken as a totality or world, is not apprehended in the same way as are the characters and events which appear within the poem. The horizon itself never appears, just because it is the foundation upon which the characters and events make *their* appearance. As the principle of totality, the horizon can never be made wholly explicit within the poem. But neither can it be left wholly implicit, for although it cannot appear, it must be able to be apprehended *in some fashion* by the hearer of the poem. Characters and incidents are no more able to sustain themselves alone than are the hearers able to sustain their own lives without their supporting world and its horizon. If events were to occur baldly, they would be without that context which prepares the hearer and enables him to place them in their fuller and more powerful meaning. And this brings us to the second feature: the demand for radical compatibility. The poetic imagination must indicate the horizon as that wherein the characters may fittingly act, think and feel. The characters live out their poetic career, or part of it, within the horizon of the poem. In many epics and adventures they may reappear and reference may be made to the reputation they have already gained in other poetic exploits; but they fall under the exigency of the poem at hand, whose need for focus, relevance, coherence and dramatic power directs the possibility of their employment. The horizon may be more or less open to shifts and transformations, but they must be neither discontinuous nor too radical.[6]

The question of aesthetic »fit« requires a consideration of the action of the poem in order to see how its incidents and characters conform to

---

[6] An instructive example of the openness of horizon may be seen in M. O'C. Walshe's contribution to the present volume in which non-trivial developments in both Gottfried's *Tristan* and Wolfram's *Parzival* are traced to their artistic rivalry. In his contribution to the present volume, Hans-Erich Keller suggests that a change in the literary climate brought about a shift in the »ideological axis« of the *Song of Roland*. Such alterations put stress upon the unity of a poem and may even sacrifice a certain aesthetic coherence to achieve non-aesthetic values, such as social relevance, political persuasion, etc. If the latter portion of the *Song of Roland* underwent changes in the interests of Suger's monarchist propaganda, this may tell us why the Baligant episode was put into the poem, but it does not tell us why it does or does not fit. Such a reason can only be poetic.

the prevailing principle of unity and totality. Now such a principle is not simply to be identified with the theme or story, nor with the arrangement or economy of the elements, nor with the background or setting of the poem, nor with its mood or emotional burden. On the contrary, these are all expressions of a principle which never appears in such determinate forms. Or rather, they are ways in and through which the horizon is manifested, for although it never appears in itself and is never articulated in itself, it must be sensed by poet and audience, and perhaps also by the performer. In setting out the theme, striking the mood and sketching the setting, certain limits of possibility are suggested, for some alternatives and developments are already excluded as incompatible with what has been suggested. The question of aesthetic fit may be put this way: If the characters were, so to speak, to fall out of the poem in disarray, or to wander over its »edge« into incoherence, the poem would lose that power it has begun to accumulate. Now such a principle of coherence or compatibility must not be thought of as a merely formal tautology, as though it were to insist merely that all characters and events within the poem must be components of the poem, must be linguistic expressions, must be adjacent to or connected with one another, etc. Such a merely formal principle of unity would be like Kant's analytic *a priori* principles. The horizon functions, rather, in the manner of a Kantian synthetic *a priori* principle. It is *a priori*, not because it is given in itself before any characters or events are presented, but because it is given along with them as their ground. And it is synthetic, because it furthers and promotes the unity, validity and power of the poem, even as a synthetic *a priori* principle, according to Kant, anticipates experience.[7] The elements of the poem »belong« to it inasmuch as they appear in relation to its horizon. Such a principle of coherence or compatibility, then functions as a restraining discipline upon the mutual possibilities of characters and events, and is more than a simple »edge« which holds in the characters. It enters into the very process by which the central action of the story is supported, heightened in colour or mood, and even advanced, as we shall try to show. The horizon is a principle which secures aesthetic fitness, sometimes by reinforcement, sometimes by balance, sometimes by prolepsis. More precisely, the horizon does not *do* anything, but it is the measure which also anticipates. When the horizon is skillfully indicated, it suggests the

---

[7] Immanuel Kant, *Critique of Pure Reason*, A6B10–A10B14, B14–B18, A150B189–A158B197, A166B207–A176B218 *inter alia*.

direction of events in an indeterminate way. By grounding the action, the horizon reinforces it and promotes its credibility. At the same time, in marking off the limits of the poem, the horizon joins it to other enterprises by an odd sort of referral; but this suggests another term.

A poem is an individual of a rather special sort, and its horizon is a sort of »boundary« which marks off the poetic »extension« of the poem. Now to have recognized a boundary is to already have placed oneself on both sides of it; for in distinguishing two domains, a boundary is also a meeting-place and a passage-way from one into the other.[8] The internal domain houses the elements of the poem, whereas the external domain contains everything else. Now, while the boundary is a limiting principle for the characters, it is precisely where poet, hearer and critic must place themselves. They must not only be »at« the boundary of the poem, but must also pass into and out of it in order to realize their undertakings as poet, hearer or critic. They recognize the boundary as the defining principle which must be able to be occupied on both sides. It is for this reason that the janus-faced *limes* is the source for the being of the poem, that is, for the limits and possibilities of its action, and also for the source of its meaning, that is, for the intentionality which carries it towards its own completion and refers it to the larger context of life itself.

The epic poet brings his materials to the border of the poem which he is in the process of making. These materials lie outside the poem itself and consist of the stuff of life – experience and history –, and of the stuff of art – myths, legends, other versions of the epic story –, and these stuffs carry within them a certain social value and cultural weight. He transforms these materials under the discipline of poetic imagination. The horizon, then, is the poet's power objectified into the contours and dimensions of the poem as it borders all other existences. It is the poetic imagination viewed from the perspective of the poem as a work coming into being, rather than from the perspective of the poet's psyche. It belongs to the ontology of the poem rather than to the psychology of the poet. Often the epic poet and his hearers have already met the matters which are to be recast in a new rendering of a familiar story. The tale, its characters, setting, events and outcome have already existed in other poems, and in more fragmentary fashion in the speech and

---

8 G. W. F. Hegel, *The Science of Logic* (tr. A. V. Miller), George, Allen and Unwin, London, 1969, pp. 122–33. [*Wissenschaft der Logik,* hg. v. G. Lasson, F. Meiner, Hamburg (1934) 1967, pp. 110–21].

imagination of a people. In fashioning a new existence, then, the epic poet has had to reckon with other modes of existence which the materials have previously acquired. The matters may have been more or less firmly embedded within the horizons of complete poems, or they may have floated as fragments in a poetic tradition. The problem of the poet was, in any event, to make the action appear to arise from within the horizon of his poem; it was the problem of assimilation, transformation and poetic coherence, of bringing the incidents into credible interplay within a horizon. That horizon had to be launched early in the poem in the very act by which he announced the theme. He had to create the horizon in the very act by which he disengaged it from the epic tradition in which he had found the story and also from the more general cultural horizon.

The hearer or reader must also take his place »at« the horizon, for he finds there the passage-way which permits him to appreciate the poem. His response cannot take place wholly within the space and time of the poem itself. If he were wholly within the poem, he would have become a character within it and would lack the distance needed for aesthetic appreciation. Unable to get out of the poem, he would be unable to relate it to the rest of his life. On the other hand, if he remained simply outside the poem, he would never be able to enter into its spirit in order to apprehend its meaning and power. Nor can he adequately retrieve the power and meaning of the poem by translating what goes on within its borders into a set of literal propositions belonging simply to the external side of the boundary. At the boundary, however, he is able to mediate the sense of the poem with the sense of his own experience, so that they penetrate and modify each other. He can then articulate the meaning of the poem as an irreducible tension between what lies on both sides of its border.

The critic, of course, attempts to thematize the poem, and to render explicit its structure. His interpretation tests the qualities of the poem in the light of the principles of his poetic criticism and with the knowledge of the history and tradition of epic poetry. In recovering the poetic unity of the epic, recent criticsm has quite rightly turned away from an excessive non-poetic preoccupation with the supposed historical sources lying outside the epic itself. It would, however, be almost as unsatisfactory to transliterate the poem into a system of social and ethical values. For the poetic horizon of the poem is no more identical with its socio-ethical horizon than are the poetic materials identical with prior historical events and personages. Historical events and personages may be appropriate materials for an epic poem, and socio-cultural value-systems may provide a general context. Moreover, history is undoubtedly more pliant in being bent to epic use, whereas the poetic imagination is more firmly guided by prevailing socio-cultural values. Nevertheless, the considerations which lead the poet to appropriate materials and to indicate values are poetic and aesthetic ones, and arise out of the demand for the unity of horizon with action in the poem being made. The critic is always tempted to provide an interpretation of the poem which grounds it simply, directly and literally in some non-poetic context of meaning – if not in historical realities, then in social systems. The larger significance of the poem, however, remains non-literal, for it consists in the irreducible tension between what exists within the poem and what exists outside it. Its meaning is dialectical, if we mean by that the *coincidentia oppositorum,* in which a unity of meaning is achieved in and through the opposition of different modes of existence.

The poet with his materials and his poetic intention, the hearer with his experience and aesthetic expectation, and the critic with his principles and interpretive task start their journeys from the horizon or boundary, because it is the essential condition for access to the poem itself and is even the condition for the poem being more than a series of contingent events.

III. *The poetic problem of indicating a horizon.* The horizon of an epic sets the mood and tone of the poem, as weather, wind and light give a landscape its dynamic setting. Indeed, the play of light and dark is perhaps the oldest and most significant of all images. Boethius used it continually in counterpoise to his rational analysis of good and evil:[9]

> The night was put to flight, the darkness fled . . .
> Like when the wild west wind accumulates
> Black clouds and stormy darkness fills the sky:
> The sun lies hid . . . [But then]
> Out shines the sun with sudden light suffused
> And dazzles with its rays the blinking eye.

C. S. Lewis[10] places the medieval Christian »at the bottom of a stair whose top is invisible with light«. The natural cosmic symbol of God

---

[9] *Consolation* I,2 (Penguin, p. 38).
[10] *The Discarded Image,* pp. 73–4.

was the transforming radiance, the Divine Splendour *(illustratio)* of
which Dionysius wrote. C. S. Baldwin remarks that [11]

> a hundred images of light, suggestions of dawn, noon, stars, the ordinary
> lamp, the candle in the church, lead not to individual emotion, but to the
> poetry of theology. In every light is the light of the world. The night light
> *(vigil lucerna)* leads up to the giver of light *(ignis creator igneus)*. Poetry
> discerns a new earth because of a new heaven, and finds both one.

There can be no doubt that the Christian liturgy was the mother of
many poetic images, but the symbolism of light and dark was undoubtedly present in still more ancient rites, feelings and language. As explicit
paganism became more remote, a diffused religious attitude towards the
symbolism of light and dark would receive more or less specifically
Christian sense in one or another epic, depending upon the poetic intention, the audience and its milieu and even the theme itself.[12]
It is a religious as well as an Iberian light that surrounds the *Poem of
the Cid* with a firm clear horizon. It has been described as a sun-
drenched poem,[13] because although it begins with a harsh exile[14] its
mood is essentially happy.[15] Even without consulting the chronicles, the
reason for the Cid's exile seems intelligible primarily because of the
way in which he accepts it and seeks to win back favour with his king.
The most striking instance of evil occurs with the beating of his daughters; but if the insult had not been so grave, the incident would have
had aspects of the ludicrous, not because of the Cid who was injured
or his daughters who were wronged, but because of the paltry characters
of the sons-in-law. The clouds of evil on the horizon, while not simply
summer clouds, are storm clouds that are blown away, letting the sun
break through again. The Cid wins fame, fortune and his good name
by his own efforts and by the judgment of God. In speaking of a religious light, I do not mean to suggest that religious or specifically

---

11 *Medieval Rhetoric and Poetic*, Macmillan, 1928, p. 124; cf. pp. 203–04, 239–41.
   Cf. also Marie P. Hamilton, »The Religious Principle in Beowulf«, in *An Anthology of Beowulf Criticism* (ed. L. E. Nicholson), Notre Dame, 1963, p. 105.
12 Cf., for example, the discussion in this volume by C. Donahue, »Social Function
   and Literary Value in *Beowulf*«.
13 See Lesley Bird Simpson, *The Poem of the Cid*, Berkeley, 1970, p. XVI.
14 See Colin Smith (ed.), *Poema de mio Cid*, Oxford, 1972, p. LXII.
15 G. T. Northrup, *An Introduction to Spanish Literature*, Chicago, 1925, p. 47: »The
   tone is as austerely grave as the landscape of Old Castille«. But it is not tragic
   nor even unhappy. The mention of magic and miracle that follow are made by
   Northrup, *ibid.*

Christian considerations provide explicit and primary motives. There is little use of religious miracle and no use of magic at all. In the un-medieval words of a modern editor, the action takes place on »a credible human and social plane«.[16] Nevertheless, the Cid does acknowledge Christ as his Lord, and the action is set »firmly in a divinely ordered universe«.[17] The setting indicates a stable horizon which sponsors the value of the Cid's action, frames the response of the hearer and guides the interpretation of the critic. The horizon resembles in poetic fashion the intellectual confidence which led Boethius to link once-blind fate with all-seeing Providence.

Setting, mood and arrangement are preferred poetic indicators of an epic horizon. It is important, of course, to continue to distinguish between the ultimate principle of poetic unity and totality, viz. the horizon or boundary, and the more determinate signs of that totality, such as the setting, mood and arrangement. The setting of the *Song of Roland* is as stark as that of the *Cid*, but its mood is more sombre. Nevertheless, the horizon within which the characters act, and the light which illuminates their action is also stable. Firm, clear and reassuring signs abound: The king dreams visions, angels come to the aid of the Franks, and the very sun stops for their revenge. Moreover, the dark earth trembles in grief or anger at Roland's death. In addition, the dark valleys of the mountain landscape harbour no monsters such as roam the wild moors of *Beowulf*. Instead, monsters are sublimated into the king's visions or transformed into emblems and ciphers. The self-understanding of the chief protagonists of the poem is couched in a Christian belief in the providential and moral nature of the world. The Frankish people have a clear sense of divine mission. There is sorrow at Roland's death, to be sure, but there is celebration too, for as he lifts up his glove to his Lord and God,[18] we see the confident transmission of an epic hero into eternity. The praise and honour which Roland so »unashamedly« seeks[19] is taken up into the mystery of clear light which surrounds the poem with a divine glory. The tears remain – for friends lost and honour lost and the future yet to be won. Indeed, nothing stops the Em-

---

[16] Smith, *Poema*, p. LXVII.
[17] Smith, *Poema*, p. LXI.
[18] R. Harrison (tr.), *The Song of Roland*, Mentor, New York, 1970, p. 24. This translation is based largely upon the »Oxford ms.«, as are others (D. D. R. Owen, D. Sayers), either more or less directly or through reliance upon the modern editions by J. Bédier and others.
[19] C. S. Lewis, *The Discarded Image*, pp. 80–81.

peror's tears.[20] It is as though the king's great grief and the mountain valleys frame the action of the poem. Setting and mood: the mountain valleys stand at the centre of the principal action, and the grief touches even the outer limits of the poem, reechoing in its closing stanza. Setting, mood and light: W. P. Ker[21] has noticed that the light at Roncesvalles is more majestic than the »grey light« of Maldon's battlefield, and that it is conveyed by a mysterious half-lyrical refrain which resounds throughout the tale of the battle:

High are the mountains and dark the valleys.

There is, he adds,

> the impersonal power of the scene, the strength of the hills under which the fight goes on ... There is a vastness and vagueness throughout, coming partly from the numbers of the hosts engaged, partly from the author's sense of the mystery of the Pyrenean valleys, and, in a very large measure, from the heavenly aid accorded to the champion of Christendom.

A more intense light seems to play about the king in the latter part of the poem, a light which emanates from his mission and his burden, and therefore from the horizon of the poem itself as from its totality. The light embodies a poetically transformed meaning which derives in large measure from a concrete and situated apprehension of the great themes of Christian revelation, that is, from faith in Divine Providence, from fear before the lingering mystery of evil and from the hope of the final triumph over evil in and through death.[22] Such a conception is rooted in religious, scriptural and theological bases, its mystery is rooted in an excess of light, and its power is manifested by a firm control of fate and fortune.[23] Here again, it is important to distinguish. The epic horizon is not simply the Christian theology of Providence, although that is operative on both sides of the boundary. It is, rather, that Christian faith seems to inspire a confidence which enters into and is transformed by the poetic imagination so that this faith becomes both a constituent of the epic horizon and an ingredient in the action itself.[24]

---

[20] For other suggestions, see G. Fenwick Jones, *The Ethos of the Song of Roland*, Johns Hopkins, Baltimore, 1963, pp. 144–45.

[21] *Epic and Romance*, London (1896) 1931, p. 56.

[22] W. T. H. Jackson, *The Literature of the Middle Ages*, Columbia, 1960, p. 165–68.

[23] Harrison, *Roland*, p. 25, 45–7.

[24] In an otherwise useful work, G. F. Jones, *Ethos*, generally fails to appreciate the actual conditions which make human acceptance of the Gospel, in every age *including our own*, never adequate to the full measure of the Gospel. On these

IV. *The form of conflict and the shape of evil in Beowulf.* Perhaps
in no medieval epic is the struggle of evil and good so closely wedded
to the imagery of light and dark as in *Beowulf.* In the mead hall there
is laughter and mirth, a flood of golden light and sweet song singing of
earth, »a bright field fair«; and when the friendly dawn comes it is
welcomed as »light from the east ... bright signal of God«. Outside,
the monstrous Grendel rages, »who dwelt in darkness«, in lonely pain,
the »dark death shadow«, lord of a domain of misshapen, misbegotten
things, ogres, giants and malign elementals, banished from the light and
favour of God.[25] The horizon of the poem shifts with a peculiar light
and darkness as it calls for the depiction of evil in numinous form.[26]
The dark meres lying on the edge of the action are cradles of evil, form-
less shapes. The monsters are neither allegories of evil-in-general,[27] nor
mere personifications of it.[28] They are personalities in their own right.
This is the source of their power. Nor does their fearful power reside in
the vagueness of their poetic description,[29] but in the formlessness and
malformedness of their poetic being. Their evil does not strike us as
mere imprecision, nor as simple reduction to unindividuated type.[30]
It rises, rather, in our throat with the sense of being overwhelmed by
a presence confined within no ordinary bounds. Normal weapons are
of no avail, for the power of the monsters lies in their numinous, and
therefore in their extraordinary, character. Grendel does not only dwell
in the darkness; his very being is a shadowy formlessness, so that the
darkness on which he lives and feeds becomes one with the mode of his
being.[31] The darkness does not only cover him and his mother; it fuses

---

grounds, no age or literature could ever be called »Christian«. Moreover, his
conception of what it is to be »Christian« is so exclusively moral that it simply
ignores traditional aspects that have been important for both Latin and Greek
Christians, such as ecclesiastical offices, liturgical rites, religious dogma and the
like.

[25] The quoted phrases are from the translation by E. Talbot Donaldson (based upon
F. Klaeber's 3rd edition) in *The Norton Anthology of English Literature* (rev.),
Norton, 1968, pp. 8–17.

[26] W. T. H. Jackson, *Literature of the Middle Ages*, pp. 188–89.

[27] Jackson, *op. cit.*, p. 184. See M. P. Hamilton, »The Religious Principle ...«, in
An Anthology of Beowulf Criticism, p. 135.

[28] W. T. H. Jackson, *Medieval Literature*, Collier, 1966, p. 32.

[29] Jackson, *Literature of the Middle Ages*, p. 189; *Medieval Literature*, p. 32.

[30] Ker, *Epic and Romance*, p. 165.

[31] J. R. R. Tolkien, »Beowulf: The Monsters and the Critics« (1936), in *An Anthology of Beowulf Criticism*, p. 90 links the darkness of the night with that of Death
and Hell.

with them to become their very substance, so that the darkness itself is more than night-fall; it is the fall of powers and strange wills into malignancy. Conflict becomes confrontation between hero and alien personal powers.[32] The horizon which bounds the poem prepares us for just such shadowy otherness. The strangeness of Scyld's treasure-laden, pilotless boat, and his funeral barge of which no men can say who received its cargo, and the smoke which heaven receives from Beowulf's own funeral pyre – these seem to suggest an indeterminate but numinous horizon, and even another world.[33] Indeed, the janus-like nature of the horizon is appropriated and brought within the poem itself as the horizon of life and death. Within such a horizon, the struggle against evil is not simply reducible to its moral dimensions, but calls forth our deepest fears and revulsion. The monsters intensify and deepen the power of the struggle by lending it a numinous quality which the struggles between men in the *Cid,* and even in the *Roland,* do not.[34] Moreover, although *Wyrd* (Fate) seems to conform to God's will, this identification is neither so clear nor so straightforwardly manifest as in the *Cid* and the *Roland.*

V. *The form of conflict and the shape of evil in Nibelungenlied.* The *Nibelungenlied* begins with a brightly polished picture of the lovely maiden Kriemhild and the young prince Siegfried; and the first half of the poem has a sort of hard brightness that has led some critics to question its compatibility with the terrible second half.[35] Nevertheless, the doom is announced in the first adventure (st. 2):[35a]

Well favoured was the damsel, and by reason of her died many warriors.

Moreover, in the opening stanzas she dreams a foreboding dream of

---

[32] Tolkien, »Beowulf«, p. 85, 87.

[33] H. R. Patch, *The Other World,* Harvard, 1950, p. 242.

[34] Although the latter has a somewhat numinous quality. Cf. Tolkien, »Beowulf«, p. 77. Kemp Malone, »Beowulf«, in *An Anthology of Beowulf Criticism,* p. 148 writes: »The poet, pious Christian that he was, found spiritual values in Beowulf's monster-quelling which he could not find in Offa's man-quelling.« It would be more precise to say that his »religious«, rather than his specifically Christian, sensibilities find expression here, though they may have come to the same, since traditional Christianity includes a dimension of the numinous.

[35] Jan de Vries, *Heroic Song and Heroic Legend* (Dutch 1959), London, 1963, p. 61 ff. Jackson, *Medieval Literature,* p. 142.

[35a] The quotations from the poem are in the transl. by M. Armour (*The Nibelungenlied,* Heritage, New York 1961). The stanza numbers correspond to those of the *NL* ed. by U. Pretzel (S. Hirzel, Stuttgart 1973).

a falcon wrested from her hands, as Siegfried was to be murdered by her kin:

> and bitter was her vengeance on her kinsmen that slew him, and by reason of his death died many a mother's son.   (cf. 6)

From the third adventure on, the doom of the treasure lowers on the horizon. It gradually envelopes everyone, until only Dietrich and Etzel remain alive. Associated with the treasure[36] are strange accessories: dwarfs and giants as guardians, the invincible sword Balmung, the cloak of invisibility *(Tarnkappe)*, and perhaps even the dragon whose blood confers upon Siegfried all but complete invulnerability.[37] It is a magical and legendary world, and the accessories reinforce the strangeness of the treasure and its curse. Moreover, its mysterious power is enhanced because its role is never made explicit. Unlike the mystery of excessive light, it is a dark mystery. All the principals are so wealthy that they scarcely need the treasure.[38] When Kriemhild does use it to buy support for her revenge, it never seems to diminish appreciably. Even this, its one brief use throughout the poem, is an attempt to buy not praise but doom, and perhaps honour without praise.[39] When Hagen seizes it from her, instead of spending it as one would ordinary wealth, he sinks it in the Rhine, beyond human reach. That is far from the end of the treasure, however, for it lies like a heavy magnet upon the headlong rush of events, and it infects every major character with its poison. Indeed, in and through its accessories it enters into every major action in the poem: the cloak of invisibility makes possible Siegfried's indiscreet boast, which through Kriemhild's pride becomes Brunhild's shame and Gunther's dishonour. From the quarrel between the queens every tragic event follows: Siegfried's death, Hagen's theft, the fall of the Nibelungs. When the Burgundians arrive at Etzel's court, Kriemhild's greeting is a question: Where is the treasure? Why did you not bring it to me? Some critics ask: Can this she-devil have once been the tender maid and wife? And does she mourn her husband's death or her loss of the treasure? They allege a rift in her character and an ambiguity in her motive.[40] However, if Siegfried's death is inseparable

---

[36] G. F. Jones, *Honor in German Literature*, Chapel Hill, p. 19, underlines its uncanny power. Cf. *Beowulf:* »The great princes who had put it [the treasure] there had laid on it so deep a curse until doomsday.«

[37] M. O'C. Walshe, *Medieval German Literature: A Survey*, London, 1962, pp. 222–23.

[38] Jackson, *Medieval Literature*, p. 145; *Literature of the Middle Ages*, p. 211.

[39] Jones, *Honor*, p. 95.

[40] Jackson, *Literature of the Middle Ages*, p. 212; de Vries, *Heroic Song*, p. 61 ff.

from the treasure, then in seeking to recover the honour which she has lost through his death, Kriemhild seeks revenge *and* the treasure. Far from being two conflicting or ambiguous motives, they are one and the same. And the treasure embedded in her motive is also the underlying presence throughout those actions by which she is transformed from proud wife into she-devil. When her brother Gunther seems to obstruct her from reclaiming the treasure, she carries his head to Hagen, who loses his because he refuses to tell her where the treasure is, even though it lies beyond human reach in the river Rhine. What drives her is no ordinary greed, but shame and revenge for honour lost, honour that had been won in part through the possession of the treasure. And beyond her shame is felt the magnetism of the cursed treasure. In turn she dies, Nibelung's sword in hand:

> Now all whom Fate had doomed were dead ... Joy turns to sorrow in the
> end ... This is the fall of the Nibelungs.[42]   (2315)

The shape of evil in the *Nibelunglied* is far removed from the parapersonal confrontation which it assumes in *Beowulf*. The battle is heroic in scale but no monsters fight in it, only men under the spell of doom. In shedding its gloom, the malignant presence of the treasure spreads evil not by confrontation but by infection.[43] Indeed, the peculiar quality of despair in the *Nibelungenlied* is grounded in the impossibility of *confronting* evil. Whereas Beowulf wins victory and death with honour, the individual is hapless before an evil which rages like an unchecked disease. The plight of Rüdeger illustrates the impossibility of victory or honour in resolving the conflict. Unable to confront the evil which undermines him, he tries to retrieve some good – not victory, but at least his honour (if that is possible without victory) –, and he seeks to retrieve some solace by *divestment* of all that he has received.

His fourfold plaint begins. Etzel and Kriemhild ask his help, quite properly, for he is Etzel's vassal and holds from him lands, castles and red gold enough. Moreover, Kriemhild reminds him that he has already sworn to risk both his honour and his life to avenge her injury. Indeed, he had sworn his special vow to her as Etzel's ambassador and vassal.

---

[41] Jones, *Honor*, p. 95.

[42] The centrality of Hagen (see Jackson, *Literature of the Middle Ages*, p. 211) or of Kriemhild (see Walshe, *Medieval German Literature*, p. 229) is a capital issue for interpretation. I have favoured the latter.

[43] Cf. Paul Ricoeur, *The Symbolism of Evil* (tr. E. Buchanan), Harper and Row, New York, 1967, Part 1, chapter 1.

But across the vows of vassalage there cuts a vow more ancient yet and holier. He accepted responsibility for the Burgundians as their host and protector. Indeed, he had also undertaken that vow of hospitality as Etzel's vassal. No conflict would have arisen in these intertwined vows, had it not been for Kriemhild's revenge and the treasure's doom. The »entertainment« at Bechlaren had been no mere »idyllic episode«,[44] however, by which the poet playfully lightened the shadow of impending disaster. It was also the scene of the inexorable weaving of fate by which Rüdeger was bound more closely to the general ruin through the vow of hospitality:

> How can I do it? [he cries] I bade them to my house and home; I set meat and drink before them, and gave them my gifts. Shall I also smite them dead? (2096)

But everything sane and normal is coming unhinged, and Kriemhild seizes her opportunity to cry out:

> Most noble Rüdeger, take pity on us both. Bethink thee that never host had guests like these. (2099)

What is more, out of those festivities had come the betrothal of his daughter to Giselher, the charming Burgundian prince. And so, to his vows of vassal and host he has added another, that of kinship with the Burgundians. Finally, although he has mortgaged his life and honour to his queen, he protests that he »swore no oath that [he] would lose his soul«. This implies an obligation before God.[45] Caught in the toils, he cries out that God has forsaken him; and conscious of his vanishing honour, he realizes that the whole world will reproach him, whether he acts on one side or the other or not at all. The shout to God is to be taken

---

44 Jackson, *Literature of the Middle Ages,* p. 206–07.

45 Jones, *Honor,* p. 119, sees the reference to God as a reflection of the clerical attitude in contrast to the lay. This seems to me to be a confusion of considerations which threatens to see nothing more in the incident than a clash of theoretical categories, viz. the clerical and secular. Whatever the value of the remark as a sociological analysis of medieval society at that time, these sociological categories can be taken at most as indicators in a general sense of systems of value-priorities, but certainly not as prisons for a great poet's feeling in the face of a deeply human conflict. Even if we did concede some meaning to the remark, we should still have to go on to interpret *Rüdeger's* plight, not simply as the clash of two ideologies, but as the compulsion to act in circumstances in which the individual must divest himself of every normal incentive to act, of every normal support and reward for acting. His concern for his soul simply intensifies and radicalizes the plight, which already exists in the clash of his vows as vassal, host and kinsman. For a discussion of recent views on Rüdeger, see J. Splett, *Rüdiger von Bechlaren,* C. Winter, Heidelberg 1968.

seriously, I think, but it does not indicate an opening towards a possible resolution or new light on the horizon. It is rather meant to underline and intensify the dark desperation of the conflict.

Rüdeger's futile gestures articulate the hopeless trap in which he is caught. He had first appealed to Dietrich to mediate the quarrel. When this failed, he had tried to give back to Etzel the wealth which bound him to Etzel, hoping to go again into exile as a poor man. When Etzel refuses to release him, Rüdeger begs to God to let him die right then and there. When both impoverished exile and innocent death are denied to him, he prepares to honour his vows as a vassal, but he laments:

> Whether I do this thing, or do it not, I sin.   (2091)

To his erstwhile friends and kin he calls:

> I would have helped you [but must] now renounce my loyalty to you.   (2112)

In anguish he cries out that he cannot but be false to their friendship and trust. He wishes that he could have served them well, wishes that they were now safe back in their homeland and he dead with honour. Instead, his new kinsmen remind him of his pledge as kinsman and host, complain that he is about to make his daughter too soon a widow, and remind him that he has given them many gifts, including the sword which is to kill him. As a last gesture to his broken vow as host, protector and gift-giver, he throws his own shield to Hagen who had asked for it in need. It is as though Rüdeger has divested himself of all his previous gains: his fiefs, his family whom he gives over to the care of Etzel, his shield, and at last his life. But he has shed them all without retaining his honour.[46] Gernot calls out:

> I will turn thy gift [the sword] against thee, for thou hast taken many friends from me . . .   (2154)

Whereupon the poet laments:

> So rich a gift was never worse requited. So they fell in the strife, slain by each other's hand.   (2158)

VI. *The form of conflict and the shape of evil in Tristan and Isolde.* As a narrative poem, more properly a romance than an epic, *Tristan and Isolde* in its several versions [47] offers still another form of

---

46 Jones, *Honor*, pp. 75–6.
47 For Englished versions, see *Gottfried von Strassburg: Tristan. With the Surviving Fragments of the Tristan of Thomas* (tr. A. T. Hatto, from the text of R. Ranke

conflict and another shape assumed by evil. At first, evil seems to take
the not unfamiliar shape of adulterous love and betrayed loyalties.[48]
But the course of their love from the magical potion through exile and
ordeal to their death runs an extraordinary career.[49] Their love feeds
wholly upon itself, or upon the mysterious power inherent in the love-
drink. Their *minne* knows »no other goal ... no ethical measure and
law than its own«.[50] It is the assertive »right of passion«,[51] before which
»everything must yield ... all rights and duties vanish«.[52] At the end
of the middle ages, Calvalcanti was to complain that love's

> judgment is without regard for well-being ... [that] its power often results
> in death ... [and that] desire becomes so great that it surpasses the norm
> of nature.[53]

Unless we sentimentalize their love into a sublime and mystical affair,[54]
or trivialize it into a pretty story of private lovers hounded by society,[55]
we must share the lovers' sense of their own misfortune. For their tragedy vanishes if we do not take seriously the nature of their conflict: it
is not simply of two against the world. Their well-being is divided by a
conflict rooted deeply in their own needs. For they have needs as social
beings along with that noble need for *minne* of which Gottfried speaks,
»love which is no longer an obscure instinct but a profound and nostalgic need for the whole human being«.[56] Torn between this *minne* and

---

(1930) for Gottfried and from the editions of J. Bédier (1902, 1905) and B. H. Wind
(1950) for Thomas), Penguin, rev. 1967; and *Beroul: The Romance of Tristan*
(tr. A. S. Fedrick, from the edition of A. Ewert, 1938), Penguin, 1970. Hatto and
Fedrick discuss the versions briefly, respectively on pp. 8–9 and p. 11 fn. Bédier
details the sources of his lovely but modern reconstruction in a note to Gaston
Paris' Preface in *Le Roman de Tristan et Iseut*, Paris, n.d., pp. XII–XIII (tr. by
H. Belloc). W. Golther attempts a reconstruction of the »Ur-Tristan« in *Tristan
und Isolde*, Leipzig, 1929. See also Gertrude Schoepperle, *Tristan and Isolt*, 2 vols.,
London, 1913.

48 Schoepperle (*Tristan* II, pp. 401–08, 456), cited by Myrrha Lot-Borodine, *De
l'amour profane à l'amour sacré*, Paris, 1961, p. 54.

49 E. Gilson in the preface to Lot-Borodine, *De l'amour*, p. VIII.

50 Bodo Mergell, *Tristan und Isolde*, Mainz, 1949, p. 124.

51 Gaston Paris, *Poèmes et Légendes du Moyen-Age*, Paris, 1900, p. 175.

52 Aldo Scaglione, *Nature and Love in the Late Middle Ages*, Berkeley, 1963, p. 22.

53 J. E. Shaw, *Guido Cavalcanti's Theory of Love*, Toronto, 1949, pp. 99–100.

54 Thus Mergell, *Tristan*, p. 178; but see Lot-Borodine, *De l'amour*, p. 54.

55 See some recent treatments of the story in Maurice Halperin, *Le Roman de Tristan
et Iseut dans la littérature anglo-américaine aux XIXe et au XXe siècles*, Paris,
1931.

56 Lot-Borodine, *De l'amour*, p. 53, said of Gottfried's version in distinction from
some of the earlier cruder and the later degenerate versions.

their positions in the world which marks their honour, they lament that they have abandonned the world and it them.[57] Their final refuge is found, not in clandestine meetings or in woodland exile, but in death itself. It is a chill solace, however, for there is in the medieval versions no Wagnerian love of death as that which dissolves the pain of individual existence.

On that warm day when the thirsty young pair drank their death unknowingly, the power of the love philtre entered their lives. There are questions to be raised about the nature of the magical potion, and the poetic tradition itself is unstable and various concerning it. Were the lovers, or at least the impressionable Isolde, in love before that fateful drink? Did the potion simply ratify what nature had already begun?[58] Was the potion permanent in its effect or did its power disappear or diminish? And was its effect confined to the lovers, or did it affect King Mark as well?[59] I shall consider the potion to be permanent in its effect, confined to the lovers, and to be more than a mere sign of a love already grounded in their consent. Surely de Rougemont is out of touch with the poem when he dismisses the potion as an »alibi«, a device for self-deception and a poetic retreat before unbridled passion.[60] This suggests that the problem resides in the lovers' refusal to recognize their true condition and in their reluctance to do something about it, as though they *could* do something. Whether or not there were the beginnings of affection prior to the drink, the potion is more than simply a sign of their love; it is their fortune. Before the drink, none of the tragic conflict and consequences were fixed – loss of honour, betrayal of friendship, disloyalty, adultery, deception, outlawry and death. The drink does not merely indicate their love. Like a dark sacrament, it binds them to one another with indissoluble bonds.[61]

We might further ask, what kind of universe is this, in which inanimate things can wreak such havoc with human wills, and hold to their own magical power independent of a clear and deliberate human intention?

---

[57] Lot-Borodine, *De l'amour*, p. 55.

[58] Mergell, *Tristan*, p. 165. Cf. Wagner's version as discussed in Halperin, *Le Roman*, p. 18.

[59] Golther's »Ur-Tristan«, *Tristan*, has an impermanent potion and no *Gottesurteil*. For permanent potions, Schoepperle, *Tristan* I, p. 21, 72, and Jackson, *Medieval Literature*, p. 93, 136.

[60] *Love in the Western World*, New York, 1940 (1939), p. 41.

[61] There is in Gottfried the suggestion of the disintegration of their love; see Hatto, *Gottfried von Strassburg: Tristan*, p. 25 and also »Isolde of the White Hands«, pp. 284–297.

After all, the love potion had been intended for Mark and his bride. The hearer might protest that two persons ought to be left to work out their own relationships without resort to magical power. Obviously, the queen mother had feared that such a natural course might have led to a dutiful but unpassionate Isolde or a Mark who accepted her merely as a dynastic pledge. In any event, even though medieval penitential books indict magic, the poem gives no hint of such disapproval. Of course, when a third thing is interposed between two persons in the hope of uniting them, there enters the risk of unpredictable misalliance.

The love-potion, then, is a thing used to cement two wills into one love by a compulsion that transcends the ordinary power of instruments. To invoke magic is to invoke an indeterminate power, »a blind force of destiny«, so that destiny finds its way into reality by a chance event, a mischance which slips away from the original intent in using it. It pounces upon mischance. It *happened* to be hot, the young pair were *naturally* thirsty, their lady-in-waiting *chanced* to be away, the servant *noticed* the philtre, and so on. The horizon of the poem, then, must accommodate the blind power lodged in things, which, pouncing upon ignorance, change and privation, compels two wills beyond their powers. Had they confessed to Mark at the outset and suffered shame, or had they been killed on the journey to Cornwall, the consequences would have been shorter-lived. These possibilities represent the modicum of freedom still operative under the compulsion of the drink, for their fortune is just this meeting of their freedom with their fate.[62] The match is so uneven, however, that with the drinking of the potion, they are lifted outside human law and plunged into a rarefied atmosphere, though not without penalty. The way is prepared to make them outlaws.[63] The form of conflict is just this contradiction between their love and their honour, and the shape which evil takes is disloyalty to Mark, dishonour to themselves, outlawry and death.[64] The cause of the evil lies in the fatal and mysterious power of the potion to induce a passion which places the lovers, not wholly outside their society, nor in a state of rebellion against it, but at its outer limits and just beyond it.[65]

---

[62] Lot-Borodine, *De l'amour*, p. 44.

[63] Lot-Borodine, *De l'amour*, p. 52.

[64] The less brutal a version depicts Mark the more poignant is that version of his injury. See note 68 below.

[65] Erich O. Köhler, *Ideal und Wirklichkeit in der höfischen Epik*, Tübingen, 1956, p. 150, 158.

It is not easy to determine the limits of possibility in the poem, if only because the horizon of the poem must include that boundary which is the lovers' own self-division, the boundary between their passion and their honour. Their suffering arises out of that force which drives them out of the one world without carrying them into another. Their exile begins well, but – for whatever reason, physical and spiritual emaciation, or shame over lost honour – they seek to return to the only world they have.[66] Their wound is self-destructive because their relation is constituted in and through the flaw whose source is the wild, irresponsible power of the potion, which cares neither for society nor for the lovers. The horizon of the poem is not simply the social values of their courtly world, for then the appropriate response would be either indignation at or mere pity for the lovers. The honour which they have lost certainly counts for something, but so too does their love. It is tempting to think that their entrapment by mischance completely exonerates them in a straightforward manner, but it does not seem to.[67] Nor can the poem tolerate such simple innocence. For if they are absolved of all wrong-doing, then Mark is not aggrieved but only vindictive,[68] and the conflict is merely an unjustified persecution. If, however, their loss of honour and Mark's shame is an objective fact, then it is not so easy to talk about absolving the lovers of all wrong.

It is interesting, therefore, to consider Isolde's ambiguous oath and successful ordeal by fire. Previously Tristan had leapt to almost certain death and was preserved unharmed. We may see here an informal judgment of God rendered in his favour.[69] Isolde's formal oath over the relics of St. Hilary[70] is meant to witness to her innocence, and the fire into which she plunges her hands without injury is taken to be God's

---

[66] The return out of woodland exile seems clearly so motivated, though in the hands of Thomas, Tristan's marriage seems rooted at least partly in lust. See Hatto, *Gottfried von Strassburg: Tristan*, p. 361.

[67] Fedrick's discussion in *Beroul: Tristan*, p. 20 is too simple.

[68] Indeed, Mark's character is as unstable in the poetic tradition as is the potion, although his character shows a certain refinement in most of the later versions. In others, especially in the early versions, he is crudely vengeful, and to that extent all but loses his moral and legal rights. It is important to realize that he did not have firm legal grounds for proceeding against the lovers; see Fedrick, *Beroul: Tristan*, p. 21 note. Also see note 75 below (Riedl).

[69] Schoepperle, *Tristan* I, pp. 284–85. Nor is this the first divine intervention in Gottfried's version, for in episode 3 God commands a storm in order to free Tristan from his captors.

[70] Pierre Jonin, *Les Personnages Féminins dans les Romans Français de Tristan au XIIe siècle*, Aix-en-Provence, 1958, pp. 344–46. Cf. Stephen G. Nichols, Jr., »Ethi-

vindication of the truth of her oath.[71] Her oath is worded in an ambiguous way, but its intention is clearly to deceive her husband while appearing to (but not actually) denying her adultery. In so swearing, Isolde presumed not a little upon her »Maker's courtesy«,[72] even though a medieval tradition praises God for his mercy towards lovers.[73] It may be true that trial by combat was not originally concerned with the question of *moral* right and wrong,[74] and that the outcome of the trial determined the »fact« of guilt or innocence for the first time.[75] Furthermore, it may be argued that God, in preserving Isolde, has only acted in accordance with the *prima facie* terms of the oath. Nevertheless, in sustaining Isolde's verbal fraud, even a courtly and casuistical God, who was willing to overlook their adultery,[76] may be expected to have balked at declaring the guilty innocent and the injured unwronged. Isolde herself doesn't seem to have been that confident. Of course, if the honour at stake – Isolde's, Tristan's *and* Mark's – was something not yet internalized as a noble sentiment in our modern sense of moral righteousness, and if instead it was an objective status of respect which could be given to someone by society or by God, then the ordeal as a judgment of God could be understood as the preservation by God of their mutual honour. Still, a courtly God is a socially conscious one, and the problem stubbornly remains: How can a God sensible of the importance of honour, justice and true speech become the major and indispensable accomplice in a verbal fraud? Certainly, God was not himself taken in by the deception.[77] Finally, in some versions the pair has been unable to repent when urged by the hermit who speaks out of a religious concern for their souls.[78] It is enough to trouble even the poets.[79] S. G. Nichols, Jr. explains the tension between the illusion

  cal Criticism and Medieval Literature«, in W. Mathews (ed.), *Medieval Secular Literature*, Berkeley, 1965, pp. 85–86.

71 Jones, *Honor*, p. 43.

72 Schoepperle, *Tristan* I, p. 246.

73 Jonin, *Les Personnages*, p. 340.

74 Jones, *Honor*, p. 19 cites Hans Kuhn.

75 Schoepperle, *Tristan* I, p. 284 cites Bédier. Cf. F. Carl Riedl, *Crime and Punishment in the Old French Romances*, Columbia, 1938, pp. 29–34.

76 Jones, *Honor*, p. 96.

77 Despite the suggestion by Jackson, *Medieval Literature*, p. 93.

78 Lot-Borodine, *De l'amour*, p. 56; Fedrick, *Beroul: Tristan*, p. 20. Cf. Tristan and Ogrin in the Belloc translation of the modern Bédier version, *The Romance of Tristan and Iseult*, Heritage, New York, 1960 (1945), p. 76.

79 And scholars, too. Hatto, *Gottfried von Strassburg: Tristan*, p. 19, finds light

sustained by the false oath and the reality of their love as the boundary between art and reality.[80] But this seems doubly unsatisfactory, for it confuses a particular illusion wrought by a character within the horizon of the poem with the boundary-line between the poetic and non-poetic; and in any event, it identifies art with illusion. Perhaps it is better with Köhler[81] to describe the tension as rooted in the vain attempt to pass beyond social reality *(Wirklichkeit, Einpassung)* into an ideal relation between two isolated individuals *(Ideal, Isolierung)*. But this does not help us to understand the ordeal and Isolde's vindication therein.

It would be extravagant to base too much upon God's intervention on Isolde's behalf, but its importance may lie in a less partisan disclosure. In contrast to the horizon of the *Cid* and the *Roland,* the religious perspective in this romance is less determinate, and is occasional and unclear. Nevertheless, if we take the intervention seriously, we may discover a modest but important sense in which the sacred in the ordeal takes the measure of the magic in the potion, and in which the fate of two individuals is set in balance with the weight of society. There remains throughout, of course, the solid assurance of a standard by which actions can be assessed and found objectively good or evil, honourable or dishonourable, loyal or disloyal, true or false. Yet, in the ordeal, we see that, while this objective standard remains undisputed in ordinary affairs, it is here suspended in some way by the intervention of God. That intervention does not only protect Isolde from being burnt by fire and dishonoured by injury, it also becomes *constitutive of the ultimate meaning of their love.* It is an intervention which discloses the depth of their conflict. But, while the vindication is certainly not a condemnation of their guilt, neither is it a straightforward declaration of their innocence. Padraic Colum comes near to the mark when he says that »the lovers are guilty, yet they may not be judged«.[82] For they return to the illicit love which they had never intended to give up, and they suffer and die because of it. Nevertheless, there are three elements within the ordeal: their love, their social responsibility and the divine judgment upon this conflict. The intervention of God, then, is not so much an interpretation which resolves the conflict, for that re-

---

irony in the poet's treatment of religion, whereas Mergell, *Tristan,* pp. 177–78, finds in the same passage proof of Gottfried's deep and even mystical piety.
[80] »Ethical Criticism . . .«, in Mathews, *Medieval Secular Literature,* p. 89.
[81] *Ideal,* p. 150, 158.
[82] In his preface to Belloc's translation (see note 78 above), pp. IX–X.

mains. It is, rather, a restraint upon us, which prevents us from interpreting the conflict of private love and public duty from either an
asocial viewpoint or a social one. It is a sort of divine reservation upon
our interpretation, a »nevertheless ... « There is the clash of opposites:
fateful potion and impotent freedom, passion and honour, love and
loyalty. God intervenes and restores the sense of a larger horizon within
whose perspective alone the final verdict will be given, but which remains beyond human reach. Now it is just this suspension which the poet
needs, for he will have lost the tension which constitutes his tragic theme
if we side with private passion and pass over into irresponsible and
trivial sentiment, or equally if we side with public duty and pass over
into indignant condemnation. As for the lovers, their fate awaits them.
That is enough. We leave the rest to death – and God.

VII. *Epos: totum et individuum.* An epic poem is both a totality and
an individual of a rather odd sort. Because it is a totality its limiting
principle of unity functions as its horizon, and because it is an individual that same limiting principle functions as a boundary. In order to
uncover its mode of being and meaning, a philosophical reflection must
use concrete means of analysis. And so, in addition to formal and abstract considerations of meaning in strictly conceptual form, philosophy must also proceed in a manner that is open to poetic modes of
meaning, that is, to dialectical, symbolic and metaphorical expression.
For their philosophical completion, of course, such analyses need to be
anchored in a broader theory which accommodates *all* modes of meaning, including those found, for example, in religious myth, as well as
the more conceptual modes found, for example, in much of science.[83]
The thematic of evil was chosen for the present analysis because evil
can provoke a crisis that illuminates the significance of the poem as a
whole. Indeed, in the three poems chiefly considered, evil appears as the
power of injury which lies ultimately beyond human control. Even in
the *Roland* the solution to evil lies in the hands of God. And, if the
Cid's own efforts are rewarded, still we must not forget that they are
safeguarded by the divinely ordered dimensions of a moral world. In
Beowulf evil appears as a challenge from and confrontation with malignant wills lying beyond ordinary human power. Their defeat is accomplished only by heroic effort, with numinous weapons, and only for

---

[83] K. L. Schmitz, »Philosophy of Religion and the Redefinition of Philosophy«, *Man
and World*, Vol. 3, no. 2, May 1970, pp. 54–82.

a brief time, a certain place and a particular people. Ultimately (i.e. in Boewulf's fight with the dragon), victory is won only at the cost of his life. In the *Nibelungenlied* evil appears as a contagion which spreads beyond the power of human wills to stop its poison. Such endemic evil seduces mutually supporting values into a destructive war among themselves, and its victims are humans who cannot come to grips with the anonymous shape of evil. Even the desperate attempt to be absolved through divestment fails. In *Tristan* evil appears as a circumstance which induces a compulsion and brings about a contradiction or cleavage within the principal characters themselves. In all of these, death is the ultimate result. In *Beowulf* with honour, but in the latter two without it.

My purpose in the present essay has not been to provide a definitive interpretation of the main actions of these poems, but to deliberately »shake« each poem by an eccentric reading of it. Such displacement is meant to complement and enter into an over-all interpretation of the main action. The »eccentricity« of these meditations lies in their uncovering for thought what does not appear, in bringing to the foreground what is background, and in focusing upon incidents which are either partial (Grendel), ancillary (Rüdeger) or ambiguous (Isolde's ordeal). I have used these incidents in order to mediate between the main action of each poem and its horizon-boundary, so that a nonliteral tension may be sustained as the proper mode of epic meaning. The epic presentation of evil illustrates this tension, for it provokes a crisis whose issue is important. How the struggle is resolved is vital for the characters within the poem: whether the struggle is between men or with something more or less than human; whether it is undertaken with human strength alone or with the aid of some other power; whether that power is personal, para-personal, sub-personal or anonymous; and what the outcome is for the well-being of the protagonists. These considerations are also important for the hearer and critic, because the fate of the characters determines a further outcome, namely, just how the poem exists, among other things, as a thing of meaning.

Werner Schröder

Zum Typologie-Begriff und Typologie-Verständnis in der mediävistischen Literaturwissenschaft

I

Auf ›Typologisches in mittelalterlicher Dichtung‹ hat schon vor einem halben Jahrhundert Julius Schwietering in seinem so überschriebenen Beitrag zur Festgabe für Gustav Ehrismann (›*Vom Werden des deutschen Geistes*‹, Berlin u. Leipzig 1925, S. 40–55) die Aufmerksamkeit der deutschen Philologen gelenkt. »Wie alttestamentliche Zyklen der Verheißung neutestamentlichen der Erfüllung«, heißt es da, so »treten einzelne Dichtungen oder Episoden vor allem des antiken Sagenkreises höfischer Artusepik gegenüber«, und es könne kein Zweifel sein, »daß wir das Verhältnis der Titurelszene zur Laviniaepisode, des Gahmuretepos zur ›*Eneide*‹ in eben diesem typologischen Sinne deuten dürfen«. Denn »es müßte geradezu auffallend erscheinen, wenn sich diese auf Typus und Antitypus gestellte Tektonik nicht auch außerhalb des biblischen Bilderkreises und ebenso wie in der Bild- auch in der Wortkunst fände« (S. 48).
Ein solches ›typologisches‹ Verhältnis wurde von Schwietering nicht bloß zwischen vorhöfischer und höfischer Dichtung, sondern auch innerhalb eines höfischen Werkes beobachtet, indem – wie in der Rezension von Gottfried Webers ›*Parzival: Ringen und Vollendung*‹ (Oberursel 1948) *AfdA* 64, 1948/50, 14–20 ausgeführt ist – in Wolframs ›*Parzival*‹ »höfisches Rittertum von bedingter Geltung und Vorbildlichkeit« »als Typus der Verheißung« »vom Antitypus der Gralritterschaft seinen Sinn« erhalte (S. 18). Daß heilsgeschichtliche, ›typologische Sicht‹, »durch Schriftauslegung und Laienunterweisung tief eingewurzelt«, »an der dichterischen Vision der Gralritterschaft wesentlich mitbeteiligt« sei (ebd.), stand für ihn außer Frage.
Inzwischen hatte sein Schüler Friedrich Ohly ›*Sage und Legende in der Kaiserchronik*‹ (Münster 1940) in ›typologische‹ Beziehung gesetzt und »Typologie als Formprinzip mittelalterlicher Dichtung« proklamiert.

Obwohl er sie recht präzise als »den in der Spannung zwischen alttestamentlicher Präfiguration und neutestamentlicher Erfüllung wal-
tenden Sinnbezug gegenseitiger Bedeutsamkeit zweier oder mehrerer
biblischer Geschehnisse ...«[1] (S. 26) definierte, sah er wie Schwietering
die »Typologie als spezifisch mittelalterliche Denkform« (ebd.) von
vornherein »nicht an den Bereich der Bibel gebunden, sondern auf die
verschiedensten Bezugsverhältnisse anwendbar«, und postulierte »auch
halbbiblische und außerbiblische typologische Beziehungen« (S. 27).
»Die Möglichkeit einer Übertragung der Denkform der Typologie auf
Außerbiblisches haben Schwietering und Auerbach gesehen und nach-
gewiesen«, wiederholte er noch in dem Kölner Vortrag ›Synagoge und
Ecclesia: Typologisches in mittelalterlicher Dichtung‹ (*Miscellanea
Mediaevalia*, ed. P. Wilpert, Bd. 4, Berlin 1966, S. 350–369; hier S. 353).
Allerdings, liest man weiter, würden die halb- und außerbiblischen
Spielarten »von der Theologie meist außer Betracht gelassen«: um so
mehr habe »der Kunst- und Literaturhistoriker ... sie zu seinem Gegen-
stand zu machen« (S. 364).
Der mittelalterliche Dichter denke nämlich »oft typologisch, ohne laut
zu denken, wenn er die typologische Beziehung in Form und Sinn des
Werks geheimnisvoll erscheinen läßt« (S. 354). Überall, »wo die
Denkform der Typologie den Raum der Theologie verläßt«, werde
man um ihre Grenzen »weniger streng bemüht sein müssen, da die
Künste freier sind als die Verkündigung der Kirche« (S. 364). Wie in
der ›*Kaiserchronik*‹ das Verhältnis von römischer Heldensage und
christlicher Heiligenlegende so sei in Priester Wernhers ›*Marienleben*‹,
in Hartmanns ›*Gregorius*‹, Wolframs ›*Parzival*‹ und Gottfrieds ›*Tristan*‹ das Verhältnis von »Elternvorgeschichte und Hauptgeschichte
typologischer Natur« (S. 365). »Typologisches Denken« stimuliere »die
dichterische Erfindung aus dem Bezug auf einen zu überwindenden, aus
einem neuen Geist zu erfüllenden Typus«: das Leben des Gregorius
werde »begreiflich als das Gegenleben« des Judas; und es dürfe gefragt
werden, »inwiefern Gyburg in Wolframs ›*Willehalm*‹ eine gesteigerte
Helena« sei (S. 366). »Das Dichtergebet um Inspiration ist keine christliche Variation des Musenanrufs, sondern überhöht ihn typologisch«
(S. 367): auch die dichterischen Formen ließen sich als »antitypische
Überhöhung« antiker (S. 368) begreifen.
Vom vorgegebenen biblischen Ort (S. 357) aller typologischen Exegese

---

[1] Den unkorrekten Zusatz »oder Worte« habe ich ausgelassen.

liegt das nachgerade ziemlich weit ab. Ihr (S. 358 unterstrichener) »christozentrischer« Charakter ist ebenso preisgegeben wie die konstitutive Basis heilsgeschichtlicher Fakten. Nur das Prinzip der Steigerung ist geblieben – aber reicht das aus, um die behaupteten Anwendungsfälle aus biblischer Typologie abzuleiten? Bevor die Möglichkeit einer Übertragung per analogiam erwogen werden kann, müßte geklärt sein, was unverzichtbar zu ihr gehört. Je weiter ein Begriff wird, desto nichtssagender ist er, desto manipulierbarer werden seine Inhalte.

Während nach Schwieterings Ansicht die mittelalterlichen Anverwandler von Vergils ›Aeneis‹ das antike Gedicht nur partiell mit mittelalterlichem Sinngehalt zu erfüllen vermochten, indem Veldeke sowohl wie der französische Anonymus der »religiös sittlichen und nationalen« Konzeption des Römers nur ein »durch wesensfremde Züge der Überlieferung getrübtes höfisches Ideal gegenüberzustellen« hatten (Ehrismann-Festgabe, S. 40), hat unlängst Marie-Luise Dittrich (in ihrem Buch ›Die ›Eneide‹ Heinrichs von Veldeke, I. Teil‹, Wiesbaden 1966; voraus ging der Aufsatz ›gote und got in Heinrichs von Veldeke Eneide‹, ZfdA 90, 1960/61, 85–122, 198–240, 274–302) an Hand des Wortgebrauchs von *gote* und *got* nachzuweisen versucht, daß Veldeke seinen Helden als Antitypus zu demjenigen Vergils verstanden habe und somit schon zwischen ›Aeneis‹ und ›Eneit‹ jener ›typologische‹ Bezug bestehe, den Schwietering erst in freieren Phantasiegebilden keltischer oder byzantinischer Herkunft, »die die straffe Formung klassischer Antike nicht durchliefen« (Ehrismann-Festgabe, S. 41), verwirklicht sah.[2]

Auch M.-L. Dittrich operiert mit unausgesprochenen ›typologischen‹ Beziehungen, und die öffnen willkürlicher Textauslegung Tür und Tor. Zum Wesen biblischer Typologie gehört aber gerade, daß sie explizit gemacht werden muß: *Sicut enim fuit Jonas in ventre ceti tribus diebus et tribus noctibus, sic erit Filius hominis in corde terrae tribus diebus et tribus noctibus. . . . Et ecce plus quam Jonas hic* (Mt. 12, 40 f.). Die frühmittelhochdeutschen geistlichen Dichter haben sich daran gehalten. In den Vorauer Büchern Moses (ed. Diemer) heißt es von Mose: *einen slangen er frumen began / uzze kopher unde uzer ere: / daz bezeichenet Crist den herren* (62,8–10). Veldeke dagegen hat mit keiner Silbe angedeutet, sein Held Eneas sei bestimmt, das antike Muster christlich zu überhöhen. Seine Interpretin hat das nicht gestört.

---

2 Vgl. Vf., ›Veldeke-Studien‹, Berlin 1969, S. 60–103.

»Daß beide, Typ und Antityp, im Werk gestaltet gegenwärtig sind«, ist auch nach Ohly nicht erforderlich: »Der Antitypus kann Gestalt und Sinn des Typs voraussetzen in schöpferischem Sich-darauf-Beziehen« (*Misc. Mediaev.* 4, S. 354). »Einzelne Epochen, Gattungen oder Dichtungen stellen sich mit ihrer antitypischen Eigengestalt in typologischen Bezug zu einer andersartigen typischen Eigengestalt, sie begreifen sich selbst nur als den einen positiven Pol typologischer Spannung, während der negative Pol nur unausgesprochen im Prozesse dichterischen Schaffens wirksam insofern hindurchscheint, als er die besondere antitypische Ausprägung bedingt« (›*Sage und Legende*‹, S. 29). Ob aber die Dichter und gar die Epochen wirklich gewollt und getan haben, was ihnen da unterstellt wird, dafür brauchte man unwiderlegliche Zeugnisse. Daß die Theologen sich gegen solche Ausweitung biblischer Typologie skeptisch verhalten haben, wird man nicht unbegreiflich finden können.

II

Strenger gefaßt erscheint das gleiche Denk- und Interpretationsschema bei Erich Auerbach, der von romanistischer Seite neben und unabhängig von Schwietering und auf anderen Wegen ebenfalls zu der Überzeugung gelangte, »daß die typologische Exegese ... das eigentliche Lebenselement der christlich-mittelalterlichen Dichtung bildet«. Der zitierte Satz aus einem Vortrag im Kölner Petrarca-Institut, ›Typologische Motive in der mittelalterlichen Literatur‹ betitelt (Krefeld 1953; hier S. 16 f.), zieht das Fazit aus früheren Arbeiten, besonders dem großen ›Figura‹-Aufsatz im *Archivum Romanicum* (22, 1938, 436–489). *figura* ist das dem griechischen τύπος entsprechende lateinische und deshalb bei den lateinischen Kirchenvätern ungleich häufigere Wort für den realprophetischen Sachverhalt, den Tertullian zumeist mit *figuram implere* bezeichnet hat. *Pascha figura Christi* meint, daß sich das alttestamentliche Ereignis zum neutestamentlichen wie *umbra* und *veritas*, *praefiguratio* und Erfüllung verhalten.

Auerbachs ›Figuraldeutung‹ ist im Ansatz nach Tertullian ›Realprophetie‹: »vorausdeutende Gestalt des Zukünftigen; *figura* ist etwas Wirkliches, Geschichtliches, welches etwas anderes, ebenfalls Wirkliches und Geschichtliches darstellt und ankündigt« (*Arch. Rom.* 22, 451). Moses ist als *umbra* Christi genauso historisch und konkret wie dieser als

veritas. In der Folgezeit ist das auf Realprophetie gegründete herme-
neutische Verfahren nicht immer rein bewahrt worden. Es hat sich mit
der Lehre vom vierfachen Schriftsinn *(sensus historicus; allegoricus,
tropologicus, anagogicus)* gekreuzt, und es hat bei Augustinus eine drei-
stufige Gestalt angenommen, indem die Inkarnation Christi zugleich als
›antitypische‹ Erfüllung des Gesetzes und als ›typische‹ Verheißung des
Gottesreiches erschien.

So versteht sie auch Auerbach bis und bei Dante: »Die Geschichte ist das
Erlösungsdrama: der Sündenfall zu Beginn, Inkarnation und Passion
als mittlerer Wendepunkt, und das Jüngste Gericht mit dem erfüllten
Gottesreich am Ende. Die Zeiten vor dem Gesetz und unter dem Gesetz
bis zur Fleischwerdung Gottes sind Erwartung und Vordeutung, die
Zeiten zwischen Inkarnation und Weltende sind Nachahmung und Er-
werb der Gnade« (›Typol. Motive‹, S. 13 f.). Obwohl noch ein Unterschied gemacht wird zwischen ›Vordeutung‹ *ante legem* und *sub lege*
und ›Nachahmung‹ *sub gratia*, kündigt sich da eine verunklärende Er-
weiterung der Figuraldeutung an, »die das konkrete Ereignis, so vollständig es auch erhalten bleibt, als *figura* aus der Zeit heraus und in die
Perspektive der Jederzeitlichkeit und Ewigkeit versetzt« *(Arch. Rom.
22, 459).* Um so entschiedener ist im Hinblick auf die behauptete mittelalterliche Sprengung des biblischen Rahmens festzuhalten, und das hat
Auerbach selbst betont, daß sie von Hause aus »einen Zusammenhang
zwischen zwei Geschehnissen oder Personen herstellt, in dem eines von
ihnen nicht nur sich selbst, sondern auch das andere bedeutet, das andere
hingegen das eine einschließt oder erfüllt. Beide Pole der Figur sind
zeitlich getrennt, liegen aber beide, als wirkliche Vorgänge oder Gestalten, innerhalb der Zeit« (S. 468).

Obgleich sie nicht immer klar von ihr geschieden wurde und wird, ist
die Figuraldeutung von der allegorischen Auslegung streng zu scheiden.
Auerbach hat das mit Nachdruck gefordert (S. 476) und trotzdem selbst
nicht immer genügend beachtet. Die historische Einmaligkeit von ver-
hüllter Figur und enthüllter Erfüllung ist in Gefahr, wenn sie als »Pro-
phetien eines jederzeit Bestehenden« (S. 473), nämlich »in der Vorsehung Gottes, in der kein Unterschied der Zeiten ist« (S. 474) angesehen werden. Der biblische Boden ist schon verlassen, wenn gefragt
wird, ob »die Legende der Maria Aegyptiaca ... nicht eine Figur des
aus Aegypten ziehenden Volkes Israel sein« sollte (S. 476); er ist obsolet
geworden, wenn sogar ästhetischen Vorstellungen figurale Bestimmung
zugeschrieben und gefragt wird: »wie weit also das Kunstwerk als

figura einer noch unerreichbaren Erfüllungswirklichkeit aufgefaßt
wird« (S. 476 f.).

Daß »schon sehr früh ... auch profane und heidnische Stoffe figural gedeutet« werden (S. 478), hält Auerbach wie Schwietering für erwiesen
und exemplifiziert es an Dante, der im ›Purgatorio‹ Catos Freitod um
der irdischen politischen Freiheit willen als *figura* der ewigen Freiheit
der Kinder Gottes verwendet habe: Dieser »Cato ist ohne Zweifel eine
figura ...«, und zwar eine erfüllte, bereits Wahrheit gewordene Figur«
(S. 481) – ein Antitypus also zu seinem bloß vorgestellten Typus. Und
die ›*Divina comedia*‹ »ist eine Vision, die die figurale Wahrheit als schon
erfüllt sieht und verkündet, und eben dies ist das Eigentümliche an ihr,
daß sie die in der Vision geschaute Wahrheit ganz im Sinne der Figuraldeutung auf eine genaue und konkrete Weise mit den irdisch-geschicht-
lichen Vorgängen verbindet« (ebd.).

Hier spätestens ist Skepsis geboten: der gerechtfertigte Selbstmörder aus
Utica im Jenseits ist weder eine geschichtliche noch eine von dem be-
wunderten Römer abhebbare Gestalt, auf die dieser realprophetisch
verwiesen hätte, wie typologische Deutung es fordert. Und für Dantes
Vergil gilt dasselbe: eine durch sich selbst erfüllte, in sich selbst gesteigerte *figura* ist eine contradictio in adjecto. Wo wirkliche Personen und
Ereignisse nicht auf ebenso wirkliche spätere, sie übertreffende bezogen,
sondern als »*umbra* und *figura* des Eigentlichen, Zukünftigen, Endgül-
tigen und Wahren« (S. 485) gedeutet werden, ist allegorisch-anagogische
Auslegung im mittelalterlichen Sinne, nicht Typologie am Werk.

Der Dante-Interpret setzt sich in Widerspruch zu seiner eigenen, aus
Bibel und Patristik abgeleiteten Definition, wonach die typologische
Exegese »zwei zeitlich und kausal weit voneinander entfernte Ereignisse ... durch einen beiden gemeinsamen Sinn« verknüpft (›Typol.
Motive‹, S. 13), und zwar »in ihrer reinen Form ein wirklich vorgefal-
lenes historisches Ereignis als reale Prophetie eines anderen wirklich
vorgefallenen oder als wirklich vorfallend erwarteten historischen Er-
eignisses deutet, also etwa das Opfer Isaacs als Figur des Opfers Christi« (S. 10). Der Antitypus ist nichts Vorläufiges wie der Typus: die
Inkarnation i s t die Erfüllung, nicht »Prophetie eines jederzeit oder
zeitlos Bestehenden, welches nur die Menschen noch verhüllt sehen«
(S. 15). Typologie im strengen Sinne ist christozentrisch. Schon die Einbeziehung von Ereignissen *sub gratia* und erst recht die Jederzeitlichkeit
des Bezuges auf ein (platonisches) Urbild schaffen Einbruchsstellen der
allegorischen Auslegung und werden zur Quelle jedweder ›Misch-

formen‹. Zu ihnen zählen wohl auch die angeblich »unzähligen typologischen Gedankengänge und Anspielungen in der mittelalterlichen Epik und bei den Chronisten« (S. 7), für deren Figuralcharakter man gern schlüssige Beweise hätte.

III

Einen Versuch, die schon bei den Kirchenvätern nicht immer säuberlich geschiedenen Verfahrensweisen typologischer Deutung und allegorischer Auslegung nach dem vierfachen Schriftsinn, die in der mittelalterlichen Theologie und dem von ihr bestimmten Schrifttum mannigfache Mischungen eingegangen sind, systematisch zu sondern, hat am Material der frühmittelhochdeutschen geistlichen Dichtung Heinz Jantsch in seinen ›*Studien zum Symbolischen in frühmittelhochdeutscher Literatur*‹ (Tübingen 1959) unternommen. Von vornherein fernzuhalten ist die Allegorie als ästhetische Kategorie, die »ihre Grotten auf eine beabsichtigte Aussage hin allererst selbst baut« (S. 351) und Gedankliches mit Hilfe erfundener poetischer Bilder veranschaulicht. Allegorische Auslegung in heilsgeschichtlicher Absicht entschlüsselt in Dingen, Personen, Ereignissen angelegten verborgenen Sinn, denn *álso íst uerhólan díu spiritualis intelligentia in historica narratione*, wie Williram von Ebersberg in seiner ›*Expositio in cantica canticorum*‹ (ed. Seemüller, 66,7 f.) sagt. Sie »versteht sich als inspiriertes Erschließen eines den Dingen der Welt und besonders den heilsgeschichtlichen Motiven ante Christum mitgegebenen Verweisauftrags« (S. 388). Das Ausgangsmaterial ist auch hier die Heilige Schrift, und es ist die Meinung, daß jede Textstelle außer dem bloß literalen einen eigentlichen, allegorischen Sinn habe, der je nachdem mystice, tropologice oder anagogice erschlossen werden kann und muß. Dieser hebt das historische Faktum nicht auf, ist vielmehr die geistliche Dimension, auf die es verweist, die im *signum* erscheinende *res*: der Auszug der Israeliten aus Ägypten *bezeichenet* unsere Heimkehr aus dem *ellende* der Welt: *Nu sule wir besuchen / mit michelen ruchen, / wa uns daz dinc anege, / ob der uerte iht beste. / Wir sin ellende / uon deme himelisken lande. / so wir in allen gahen / zerganclichev dinc uirsmahen / unde wir unsere sinne / rihten zu gestlichen dingen, / wir suchen unser erbe: / daz lant ist da ze himele, / daz uns got geheizen hat / ... / daz bezeichenet daz here: / so uare wir gerastet an daz mere* (›Vor. Bücher Moses‹, ed. Diemer, 49,3–18).

Die Typologie erscheint in Jantschs etwas überzogener Systematik als ein Spezialfall allegorischer Auslegung, der überall dort gegeben sei, wo der Ton »auf dem heilsgeschichtlichen Gefälle vom Alten (*umbra*) zum Neuen (*veritas*)« liegt (S. 2). Sie »ist ein spezifischer Modus der exegetischen Bemühung um das AT« (S. 5): denn »typologisch ist diejenige Auffassung, die das Alte als Präfiguration des Neuen erkennt« (S. 8). Während »die Geschichtlichkeit des Berichteten und damit der Wortsinn des Textes ... für die Allegorie gleichgültig« sind, sind sie »für die Typologie Grundlage« (S. 15). »Gegenstand typologischer Deutung können nur geschichtliche Fakten, d. h. Personen, Handlungen, Ereignisse und Einrichtungen sein« (S. 17). Typen und Antitypen sind heilsgeschichtlich aufeinander bezogen »im Sinne von Vorbereitung und Erfüllung, die ihrerseits wieder neue Verheißung ist« (ebd.). Da taucht auch bei Jantsch die augustinische Dreistufigkeit auf. Jedoch, wenn für echte Typologie Historizität und Steigerung konstitutiv sind, welcher Art könnten sie über die antitypische Erfüllung in Christus hinaus noch sein?

Den Verlust an Geschichte in Auerbachs Figuralinterpretation hat Jantsch wohl bemerkt: sie scheine »charakteristisch anders nuanciert zu sein als eigentliche ursprüngliche biblische Typologie«: wenn im *figura*-Begriff »ein f a k t i s c h e r Sachverhalt einen anderen insinuiert«, rücke »das Figurale gegenüber der stark zeiteingebundenen ursprünglichen Typologie mehr in die Nähe des jederzeitlich-achronisch überhaupt Andeutenden, ja bildhaft Umschreibenden« (S. 37). Der Typus ist geschichtlich fixiert, Auerbachs *figura* kann jederzeitlich sein und gedeutet werden – und eben das scheint er für die eigentlich mittelalterliche Verfahrensweise zu halten. Von Typologie im biblischen Sinne wäre dabei dann nicht zu sprechen, wenn anders das Feststellen »einer vorausweisfähigen Qualität eines atl. Faktums, bei gleichzeitiger Erwägung des heilsgeschichtlich verschiedenen Ortes von Typus einerseits und Antitypus andererseits« deren »spezifischen Ansatz« (S. 43) ausmacht.

Gerade, weil »sich in der Auslegung allegorische und typologische mit noch anderen Elementen« mischen, müsse man »das Grundsätzliche zu trennen versuchen« (S. 13). Das geschieht in nochmaligem Anlauf auf Grund der Interpretation frühmittelhochdeutscher Texte, welche die Ergebnisse der seitherigen Bibelexegese popularisieren. Der entscheidende Unterschied sei dieser: Die typologische Methode realisiere die alttestamentlichen Motive »in ihrem historisch-faktischen Gestaltsinn (z. B. Passah als ›Opfer‹)«, und diese Fakten »p r ä f i g u r i e r e n das

Spätere, Christliche, im Rahmen der zeitlich verlaufenden Heilsgeschichte« (S. 320); demgegenüber ist allegorische Auslegung »eine
Art der Sinnfindung« (S. 321), »ein Erschließen der von Gott in die
Dinge gelegten Verweisfunktionen« (S. 299). Realprophetie in der Zeit
ist etwas anderes als »das allenthalben Figuriertsein des Geistlichen
überhaupt« (S. 347), denn da »verweisen prä-figurierende Fakten
vorausabbildend auf das Kommende« (S. 387). Das bedeute, daß Typologie »ihrem Wesen nach, wennschon nicht streng ›innerbiblisch‹ so doch
›innerheilsgeschichtlich‹« (S. 389) sei. Achronisch-jederzeitlich verweis-
trächtige Dinge besitzen »die Möglichkeit typologischen Verweisens«
nicht (S. 391).
»Auch das Zitieren von Instanzen ist keine Typologie« (S. 392).
Wolframs Erinnerung an die Wiederbelebung des Stiers durch Silvester
und die Erweckung des Lazarus gelegentlich der Heilung des Anfortas
im ›Parzival‹ (ed. Lachmann):

> der durch sant Silvestern einen stier / Von tode lebendec dan hiez gen, /
> unt der Lazarum bat uf sten, / der selbe half daz Anfortas / wart gesunt
> unt wol genas (795,30 ff.),

begründet keine typologische Beziehung, sondern vergleicht lediglich
parallele Fälle göttlicher Hilfe und gehört zur ›Exemplarik‹, die Jantsch
als »darbietende Erarbeitung der von der Heilsgeschichte her verpflich-
tenden Muster für uns« (S. 397) definiert.
Innerhalb eines immer noch weitgefaßten Begriffs vom Typologischen
werden am Ende vier Nuancen unterschieden:
1. »die eigentlich heilsgeschichtliche« Typologie von der Art Passah-
   Christus;
2. »jederzeitliche Figuralität« wie Judith-Christus: *quod haec vidua
   vicit tyrannum, significat quod caro Christi vicit diabolum* (Honorius Augustodunensis, ›Speculum Ecclesiae‹, Migne PL 172, 1070 C);
3. »die Vorstellungs- und Aussageform der ›Waage‹: Adam-Christus«
   für den »heilsgeschichtlichen Descensus und Ascensus« (S. 394);
4. »antithetische Typologie«, d. h. »Linien, die (meist moraliter) unmittelbar zu uns führen« (S. 396).

Zuvor hatte Jantsch erwogen, die Figuralinterpretation ihres »insinuie-
renden Charakters« wegen »zwischen dem streng zeitbezogenen Typus
und dem mehr allgemein demonstrierenden Exempel« (S. 393) einzu-
ordnen, dann jedoch nicht darauf beharrt, weil man »vorerst nichts anderes tun« könne, »als den Nuancen der konkreten Erscheinungen nach-

zulauschen« (ebd.). Sein erklärtes Ziel, »einer terminologischen Misere«
(S. XVI) zu steuern, scheint da am Ende wieder preisgegeben, angesichts
der in entscheidenden Punkten erreichten Klärung im Grunde ohne Not.
Zweierlei bleibt festzuhalten: Außerbiblische Typologien sind per defi-
nitionem ausgeschlossen (S. 210[1]); und wo ein typologischer Bezug
intendiert ist, muß er ausgesprochen werden: »Die Typologie lebt
aus der expliziten Beziehung. Typologie mit ›unausgesproche-
ner Sinnmitte‹ ist eine contradictio in se« (S. 213).

IV

Die mangelnde Übereinstimmung in der Beurteilung und Anwendung
eines Denkschemas, das von nicht wenigen als grundlegend für das Verständnis mittelalterlicher Dichtung erachtet wird, ist in den interpreta-
torischen Bemühungen um diese allenthalben spürbar. Was die einen
als Schlüssel zu mittelaltergemäßer Deutung ansehen, ist in den Augen
anderer mit Unsicherheiten belastet, die an der Mittelaltergemäßheit
des hermeneutischen Ansatzes zweifeln lassen. Daß das durch und durch
christlich und geistlich imprägnierte Mittelalter gar nicht anders ge-
konnt habe, als das aus der Bibelexegese vertraute Schema von alttestamentlicher Präfiguration und neutestamentlicher Erfüllung bewußt oder
unbewußt auch auf außerbiblische Verhältnisse, zumal auf die Rezep-
tion der Antike, auszudehnen, muß so lange eine Hypothese bleiben, als
die Möglichkeit einer Übertragung und ihre Bedingungen nicht geklärt
sind. Offensichtlich ist die biblische Typologie in den Händen der Literaturhistoriker mehr und mehr verfremdet und den gewagtesten Inter-
pretationen dienstbar gemacht worden. Im Falle von Veldekes ›Eneit‹
würde die Annahme einer – auch sonst geübten – naiven christlichen
Einfärbung dem Sachverhalt zweifellos besser gerecht als die Unter-
stellung eines historisch adäquaten Vergilverständnisses, das die Voraussetzung für eine spezifische ›typologische‹ Überhöhung wäre, wie sie
M. L. Dittrich behauptet hat; und daß sich Gahmuret zu Parzival oder
Gawan zu Parzival in irgendeiner Beziehung wie der Typus Jonas zum
Antitypus Christus verhielten, kann niemand glauben.
Daß das berechtigte Verlangen nach mehr begrifflicher Klarheit auf
semasiologischem Wege nicht zu befriedigen ist, hat schon Auerbach
gezeigt und Jantsch bestätigt. Die Kirchenväter bevorzugen für das
paulinische τύπος *figura* vor den Fremdwörtern *typus* und *allegoria;*

daneben begegnen *umbra, imago* u. a. Das Wort für den Antitypus ist
in der Regel *veritas*. Im Mittelalter überwiegt das vieldeutige *allegoria*
typus und *figura*. Für die exegetische Praxis mittelalterlicher Theologie
ist das Vorbild der Väter verbindlich, und von den geistlichen Dichtern
sind eigenmächtige Grenzüberschreitungen erst recht nicht zu erwarten.
Sie reproduzieren nur Vorgedachtes und Approbiertes. Was bei Hörern
und Lesern an ›typologischem‹ Verständnis vorausgesetzt wurde, müßte
in volkssprachigen Predigten und anderer religiöser Unterweisung von
Laien auffindbar und nachweisbar sein. Als geeignete Untersuchungs-
objekte boten sich das dem 12. Jahrhundert angehörende ›*Predigtbuch*
des Priesters Konrad‹ und die ›*Biblia Pauperum*‹ vom Ende des 13. Jahrhunderts an.

Mit der letztgenannten hat sich die Dissertation Hartmut Hoefers
›*Typologie im Mittelalter: Zur Übertragbarkeit typologischer Inter-*
pretation auf weltliche Dichtung‹ (Marburg 1969 = GAG 54, Göppingen 1971) beschäftigt. Der weitgefaßte Titel rechtfertigt sich durch
den Rückgriff auf die Patristik, zu der im Anschluß an Mignes ›*Patro-*
logia Latina‹ die gesamte theologische Literatur bis gegen 1200 gerech-
net wird. Daß der Befund der Armenbibel um 1300 noch immer zu ihrer
mehr oder weniger streng biblisch determinierten Auffassung von typologischer Auslegung stimmt, wird als »Hinweis auf die Stabilität der
mittelalterlichen Vorstellung von Typologie in Theologie und Bild-
kunst« (S. 49) gewertet und weckt den Verdacht, daß die angebliche
weite Verbreitung ›typologischen‹ Denkens im Mittelalter möglicherweise nur dem allzu weiten Begriff zu verdanken ist, den sich die mediä-
vistische Literaturwissenschaft davon gemacht hat.

Was die spätantike und mittelalterliche Theologie unter dem von uns
als Typologie bezeichneten exegetischen Verfahren versteht, entnimmt
Hoefer hauptsächlich dem Lehrgespräch ›*Instituta regularia divinae*
legis‹ (ed. H. Kihn, Freiburg 1880) des in der ersten Hälfte des 6. Jahrhunderts am Hofe Justinians I. schreibenden Junilius Africanus. Diese
Schrift erschien deshalb besonders geeignet und unverdächtig, weil sie in
systematisierender Absicht die Möglichkeiten und Grenzen typologischer
Exegese so weit wie irgend möglich gesteckt hat. Junilius erwägt und
hält für zulässig, daß Typus und Antitypus auch gleichzeitig sein können, ja daß der zweite dem ersten voraufgehen kann. Seine Antwort auf
die Frage: *Quid est ergo typus sive figura?* lautet: *Praesentium aut*
praeteritarum aut futurarum rerum ignotarum per opera, secundum
id quod opera sunt, manifestatio (Lib. II c. 16, S. 45). Typologie ist Real-

prophetie: die *manifestatio* geschieht in ihr nicht durch das Wort, sondern durch ein *opus*.

Die Einbeziehung von Gegenwärtigem und Vergangenem entspricht, wie Hoefer zeigt, der auch mittelalterlichen Vorstellung von *prophetia* als *manifestatio* jeder *res latens* oder, mit Thomas von Aquino, alles dessen, *quae procul a nostra cognitione sunt* (›*Summa theologica*‹, 2–2 Qu. 171, *De prophetia*, Art. III). Damit und dadurch, daß Junilius auch Typen *sub gratia* kennt, würde der von Ohly für konstitutiv gehaltene »Zeitensprung in Christus« (*Misc. Mediaev.* 4, S. 353) hinfällig. Berücksichtigt man außerdem, daß die Überbietung des Typus durch den Antitypus nicht, wie im NT, ausdrücklich zur Bedingung gemacht ist, ergibt sich die folgende allgemeine Definition Hoefers als »weitester Rahmen ..., in dem von Typologie gesprochen werden kann«: »Typologie ist eine Deutungsweise, die davon ausgeht, daß zwei historisch reale Ereignisse aus der Heiligen Schrift und aus dem Leben der Gemeinde, soweit es sich im Religiösen bewegt, bis hin zur Zeit nach dem Jüngsten Tag, so in Verbindung stehen, daß das eine Ereignis das andere vorabbildet. Beide Ereignisse bleiben historisch real. Ihre spirituelle Beziehung kann in Parallelität *(similitudo)* oder Antithese *(antiphrasis)* begründet sein« (S. 113).

Es ist aber sehr die Frage, ob dieser weiteste Begriff von Typologie jemals historisch wirksam geworden ist. Die Beispiele des Junilius für gleichzeitige oder rückwärts gerichtete Realprophetie »taugen nicht viel«, »sie lassen sich auch unter dem Begriff der *manifestatio futurarum rerum* fassen« (S. 90), und diese »hat für die Typologie des Mittelalters ... die entscheidende Bedeutung erhalten« (S. 95). Daß ein Typus *sub gratia* gewählt wird, kommt kaum vor: das einzige Beispiel des Junilius, der in Demut vor Gott mit bedecktem Kopf ins Taufwasser steigende Täufling als *typus* Adams, der sich nach dem Sündenfall aus Furcht vor Gott versteckte (Gen. 3,10), hat Hoefer sonst nirgends gefunden. Der typologische Bezug wäre besser umzukehren: Adam als *forma futuri* und *figura* des Täuflings, d. h. als *manifestatio futurarum rerum.* Typen *ante legem* und *sub lege* überwiegen weitaus: »die temporale, auf Geschichte bezogene Variante der Realprophetie, deren Typus alttestamentlich ist, wird deutlich bevorzugt« (S. 109). Schon bei Junilius wird sie »fast absolut gesetzt« (S. 113), *Quia veteris quidem testamenti figurae ad novum intentione respiciunt, novum autem futurae vitae beatitudinem repromittit, et sic omnia ad futuri saeculi spem ex ipsa intentione concurrunt* (Lib. II c. 17, S. 48). Mit dem »ausdrücklich

heilsgeschichtlich bezogenen Aspekt« (S. 113) stellt sich auch das Prinzip
der Steigerung ein, die Überbietung des unvollkommenen Typus durch
den vollkommenen Antitypus. Der weitere Typologie-Begriff hat allenfalls theoretische Bedeutung; in der Praxis herrscht der engere, und der
hat in aller Regel »die Überbietung eines Geschehens *sub lege* oder *ante
legem* durch eines, das sich *sub gratia* ereignet hat« (S. 42) zum Inhalt.
Die typologische Darstellung des Lebens Jesu auf dem von Nicolaus
von Verdun 1181 geschaffenen Klosterneuburger Altar entspricht dem
genau, indem je eine Präfiguration *ante legem* oben und eine *sub lege*
unten den zentralen neutestamentlichen Antitypus einrahmen. Im Cod.
Vindob. 1198 der ›*Biblia Pauperum*‹ (um 1330) ist das im Prinzip nicht
anders. Die zulässigen Aussagemöglichkeiten der typologischen Motive,
über die die Theologen verfügten, werden nirgends überschritten. Sie
bis ins Detail zu verstehen, dürfte jedoch auch einem mittelalterlichen
Laien schwergefallen sein. Um so problematischer erscheine es, bei weltlichen Dichtern »einen gar vom festen Typenbestand losgelösten freien
Umgang mit typologischem Denken annehmen zu wollen« (S. 175).
In der ›*Biblia Pauperum*‹ stellt jede typologische Gruppe einen bildlich
und sprachlich (durch *tituli* und Lektionen) explizit gemachten figuralen
Vorgang dar. Hoefer hat aus dem Cod. Vindob. 1198, aus Ms. 31 des
Konstanzer Rosgartenmuseums und aus der Blockbuchfassung sämtliche
die typologische Beziehung verdeutlichenden Bezeichnungen (*significat,
praefigurat, adimpletum est, sicut-ita* etc.) gesammelt und festgestellt,
»daß überall und ausnahmslos ein solches sprachliches Signalement vorliegt« (S. 189). Rund 400 patristische Belege beweisen, daß auch bei den
Kirchenvätern »die sprachliche Nennung des typologischen Vorgangs
regelmäßig vorhanden« ist (S. 190). Daraus folgt: »das sprachliche Signal, das den Bezug zwischen den beiden Ereignissen als typologisch
ausweist, gehört zur literarischen Darstellung der Typologie hinzu«
(S. 191 f.). »Eine unausgesprochene Evidenz gibt es in der Typologie
des Mittelalters nicht. Ihre Eindeutigkeit muß sprachlich vermittelt
werden«; »fehlt das sprachliche Signal, kann man füglich nicht von
Typologie reden« (S. 198).
Wir nehmen als Ergebnis mit, daß »auch im Mittelalter ... Typologie
sachlich und formal eindeutig bestimmt« war (S. 194). Sie darf »nicht
abgelöst von ihrem Gebrauch im Neuen Testament als ein speziell mit-
telalterliches Instrument der Exegese verstanden werden« (S. 99). Zu
den Bedingungen ihrer Möglichkeit als Realprophetie gehören gemein-
hin: biblische Historizität, heilsgeschichtliche Steigerung sowie explizite

sprachliche (oder bildliche) Vermittlung. Sollen diese Kriterien gelten, verboten und verbieten sich außerbiblische Typologien. Hoefer läßt daran keinen Zweifel: »Von Typologie als Darstellungsprinzip von Dichtung zu sprechen und deshalb die Übertragung typologischer Interpretation auf weltliche Dichtung zu verlangen, heißt, den mittelalterlichen Begriff und die Erscheinungsform echter Typologie zu übergehen« (S. 200). Man kann sich auch schwer vorstellen, daß ausgerechnet die weltlichen Poeten jene Grenzüberschreitung gewagt haben sollten, der sich die Theologen auf Dauer versagt haben. Vielmehr scheint es so, als ob »die Erscheinungsform der Typologie so fest geprägt ist, daß man nur mit der Übernahme einzelner festgeformter typologischer Motive wird rechnen dürfen« (S. 128).

V

Das Fazit von Hoefers Untersuchung, daß von Theorie und Praxis typologischer Bibelexegese in der patristischen und mittelalterlichen Theologie kein gangbarer Weg zu Schwieterings und Auerbachs mittelalterlicher ›Typologie‹ als Strukturprinzip weltlicher Dichtung führt, bestätigt den von Jantsch und anderen an frühmittelhochdeutscher geistlicher Dichtung erhobenen Befund, wonach typologische Motive in ihr nur Zitatcharakter tragen wie die überwiegende allegorische Schriftauslegung auch. Die geistlichen Dichter folgen darin dem Beispiel der Predigt, die ihnen nicht selten hauptberuflich oblag. Von ihr sind daher am ehesten Auskünfte darüber zu erwarten, wieviel Theologie den Laien zugetraut, mit welchen exegetischen Methoden und Inhalten sie konfrontiert wurden und für welche Verständnis bei ihnen vorausgesetzt wurde. Predigtsammlungen spiegeln die auf diesem Felde herrschende Vielfalt noch ungleich besser und breiter wider als die auf eine geschlossene Demonstration biblischer Typologie abzielende ›Biblia Pauperum‹.

In dem sog. ›Predigtbuch des Priesters Konrad‹ (ed. Schönbach, ›Altdeutsche Predigten III‹) sind, wie Peter Jentzmik in einer derjenigen Hoefers parallelen Marburger Dissertation ›Zu Möglichkeiten und Grenzen typologischer Exegese in mittelalterlicher Predigt und Dichtung‹ (1972) gezeigt hat, die allegorischen Auslegungen (im Sinne von Jantsch) viel zahlreicher als die Typologien, und beide sind nicht immer säuberlich auseinanderzuhalten. Die von Augustinus gegebene Definition von *allegoria* als *tropus ubi ex alio aliud intellegitur* (›De trinitate‹, CC 50A, 481) oder noch allgemeiner mit Hugo von St. Victor: *aliud dicitur et aliud significatur* (›De scripturis et scriptoribus sacris‹, PL 175, 12B) gilt für allegorisches und typologisches Verfahren gleichermaßen: was sie trennt, ist (mit Hoefer, S. 56), daß »für die Allegorie die Zeit als Vorgang keine Bedeutung hat, während die Typologie gerade den Ablauf der Zeit bedenkt«. Der allegorische Sinn ist in der jeweiligen *res* immer schon enthalten und bedarf nicht der erneuten geschichtlichen Konkretisierung, wie sie der präfigurierende Typus in dem ihn über-höhenden Antitypus erfährt. Die geistliche Allegorese ist nicht auf histo-rische oder für historisch gehaltene Personen und Fakten eingeengt: die Edelsteine sind ihr ebenso zugänglich wie die Physiologus-Tiere, und der ihnen beigelegte *sensus mysticus* ist denn auch oft gesucht und will-kürlich genug. Hier stand ein außerordentlich dehnbares Instrument zu umfassender Vergeistlichung der Welt zur Verfügung. Die Dichtung des Mittelalters ist voll von ihr, aber ›typologisch‹ kann sie nicht heißen.

Das ist nicht ein Streit um Worte. Es macht einen Unterschied, ob Per-sonen und Geschehen einer Erzählung von Fall zu Fall *mystice* gedeutet werden – wie das Leben Jesu in Otfrids ›*Liber evangeliorum*‹ –, oder ob die Personen und Geschehnisse in ihr ›typologisch‹ aufeinander be-zogen sind und das ganze Gedicht als einen vorgegebenen Typus über-bietender Antitypus verstanden werden will. Gerade dies, die Prokla-mierung der nachweisbaren biblischen Typologie zum unausgesproche-nen Strukturprinzip weltlicher Dichtung war Schwieterings und Auer-bachs zündender Gedanke. Die Hypothese bedurfte der Verifizierung. Daß sie nicht längst erfolgt ist, nährt den Verdacht, daß der Nachweis mit Hilfe des verfügbaren Materials nicht zu erbringen war. Der Gegen-beweis ließe sich eher führen, und das ist auch schon hier und da ansatz-weise geschehen. Man hat es nur nicht zur Kenntnis genommen, weil man sich von einer nachgerade liebgewordenen Vorstellung und Inter-pretationspraxis nicht trennen wollte. Ehrliche Eingeständnisse wie das des Danteforschers Johan Chydenius, daß »as a rule, the theologians of the Middle Ages were of the opinion that typology is to be found only in Scripture« (›*The Typological Problem in Dante: A Study in the History of Medieval Ideas*‹, Helsingfors 1958, S. 41), sind selten. Und auch Chydenius sucht und findet dann noch einen Ausweg, die ›*Divina comedia*‹ ›typologisch‹ zu deuten, weil sie Vorgänge beschreibe, »which are endowed by God with a signification other than their own« (S. 43).

Jentzmik hält sich von solchen Manipulationen fern. Alle biblische Typologie – und eine andere gebe es nicht – ziele auf Christus: er stelle den »heilsgeschichtlich antitypischen Endpunkt« (S. 24) dar. Antitypen neben und nach Christus könne es nicht geben: »Christus ist in theologischer Sicht der erste Antitypus und gleichzeitig der letzte; als solchen weissagen ihn die Propheten und als solchen bezeugen ihn die Apostel« (S. 26).[3] Die Geschichte nach Christus sei typologischer Deutung ebensowenig zugänglich wie das himmlische Jerusalem samt der dreistufigen Heilsgeschichte: »Da es sich ... bei der biblischen Typologie um die heilsgeschichtliche Beziehung zweier geschichtlicher Fakten handelt, die im Verhältnis der Steigerung zueinander stehen, und im geschichtlichen Jesus die Geschichte endgültig heilsgeschichtlich erfüllt ist, gibt es in der auf Christus folgenden Zeit keine größere heilsgeschichtliche Erfüllung der Geschichte; der historische Jesus existiert als der pneumatische Christus fort, die Erfüllung verlagert sich aus der Geschichte in den Bereich des Jenseits, der Ewigkeit, und wird zur tropologischen und anagogischen Erfüllung, die nur in der Nachfolge Christi und nicht mehr durch antitypische Vervollkommnung des Heilswerkes Christi erreicht werden kann« (S. 31 f.). Der christozentrische Charakter der biblischen Typologie schließt ihre Übertragbarkeit aus. »Typologische Beziehungen im strengen Sinne«, schrieb bereits Karl Stackmann in seinem Buch ›Der Spruchdichter Heinrich von Mügeln‹ (Heidelberg 1958; hier S. 112 f.), »gibt es nur im Bereich der biblischen Schriften. Denn dort allein trat dem mittelalterlichen Betrachter eine deutliche Zweiteilung des Geschichtsablaufs in eine Periode der Verheißung und eine der Erfüllung entgegen, welche die unerläßliche Voraussetzung eines typologischen Denkens bildet.« Um diesen strengen Sinn geht es, und auf ihn hätte ganz besonders bedacht sein müssen, wer sich dieser spezifisch biblischen Exegese auf außerbiblischen Feldern bediente.

Grenzüberschreitungen wären eher einem Gottesgelehrten und Prediger zuzutrauen. In dem ›Predigtbuch des Priesters Konrad‹ (ed. A. E. Schönbach), einer um 1170 entstandenen Sammlung von Musterpredigten, die nach den Untersuchungen von Volker Mertens (›Das Predigtbuch des Priesters Konrad: Überlieferung, Gestalt, Gehalt und Texte‹, München 1971) »trotz der unterschiedlichen Herkunft der einzelnen Stücke«

---

[3] Jentzmik kann sich dabei auf das grundlegende Werk von theologischer Seite: Leonhard Goppelt, ›Typos: Die typologische Deutung des Alten Testaments im Neuen‹ (Gütersloh 1939), S. 139 berufen: »Es gibt keine Typologie an Christus vorbei, er ist der Antityp des AT schlechthin«.

»als ein im wesentlichen einheitliches Ganzes« (a.a.O., S. 90) anzusehen
ist, hat Jentzmik keine entdecken können. Im Gegenteil: »so extensiv
Konrad von der Allegorie Gebrauch macht, so zurückhaltend verfährt
er mit der Typologie« (S. 176). Die wenigen von ihm beigezogenen
Typologien sind streng biblisch und traditionell: Als *typus Christi* werden Adam, Isaak, das Passahlamm, Moses, Gideon, Salomon und Johannes der Täufer begriffen; sie genügen allesamt Jentzmiks Definition,
die »Steigerung zwischen Präfiguration und Erfüllung« und »Christo-
zentrizität« (ebd.) verlangt.

Konrad selbst scheint etwas weniger rigoros und bezieht auch Personen
und Vorgänge um Christus durchaus mit ein. Wie der brennende und
doch nicht verbrennende Dornbusch (Ex. 3,2) präfiguriert Gideons Vlies
die unbefleckte Empfängnis: *der schæpær der da betouwet was der bezeichent die heren maigt, únser vrouwen s. Marien; wan als daz tou von
himel an den schæpær viel, dem schæpær unschædelich, also wart och
diu here maigt swanger unde perhaft des heiligen Christes von dem
heren tou unde von [dem] súzen trore des heiligen geistes an aller
slahte mail* (III 10,33–38). Jentzmik zwar hält es für theologisch un-
erlaubt, Gideons Vlies als Typus zum Antitypus Maria zu verstehen,
und beruft sich auf den differenzierten Sprachgebrauch der patristischen
Quellen; aber warum können nicht beide Formulierungen Hrabans:
(auf Gideon bezogen) *figuram nimirum Christi gestabat* (PL 108,
1157D) und *vellus est virgo Maria* (PL 112,1073B) heilsgeschichtlich-
typologisch gemeint sein?[4] Konrad macht da keinen Unterschied: *der
schæpær bezeichent* Maria wie *Gedeon, der gotes herzoge ... den heiligen Christum ... bezeichent* (III 11,6–11)! Daß er auch im ersten Falle
eine Typologie im Sinne hatte, ergibt sich weiterhin daraus, daß er ihr
noch eine allegorische Auslegung folgen läßt: das betaute Vlies (Maria,
die den Gottessohn trug) korrespondiert der dürren und unerlösten, das
trockene Vlies einer durch Christi Leiden und Sterben betauten und
erlösten Welt. Die typologische Beziehung zwischen Rotem Meer und
christlicher Taufe wird genauso hergestellt und ausgedrückt, und die
läßt Jentzmik gelten: *daz rote mere daz bezeichent die heilige toufe,
wan daz ist daz wazer unde der rote swaiz der da floz uz des heiligen
Christes siten, wan da hat er alle iwer vint, daz sint alle iwer sunde,
inne ertrenchet* (III 195,16–19). Die historischen oder für historisch ge-
haltenen Ereignisse um Christi Geburt waren als Erfüllung messiani-

---

4 Wie *esse* in lateinischen Texten begegnet bei Konrad *sîn* neben *bezeichenen* als
sprachliches Zeichen für eine beabsichtigte typologische Verknüpfung.

scher Hoffnungen und prophetischer Weissagungen für typologische Deutung geradezu prädestiniert. Auch heilsgeschichtliches Geschehen, das den Erlöser nur indirekt betraf, darf christozentrisch heißen und konnte antitypisch begriffen werden. Jentzmiks Typologie-Begriff ist in diesem Punkte zu eng.

Um so überraschender ist, daß er sogar eine ›halbbiblische Typologie‹ im Sinne Ohlys mindestens erwogen hat. In der Weihnachtspredigt über Lukas 2,1–7 vergleicht Konrad Christus mit Augustus: *der geweltige cheiser den ûnser herre got in der zit da ze Rome geordent hete, do er an dise welte geborn wolt werden, der bezæichent in selben, wan er von rehte ist ein cheiser unde chûnic ob allen chûnigen; wan alsam der heidensche chûnc die welt alle mit sim gewalt dar zuo betwûngen hæte daz im diu elliu zinshaft was, alsam hat och er vil lieber herre mit der ladunge des heiligen glouben in sinen dienst braht alle cristæn zungen. Ipse est pax vera. der grozze vride der ouch da was do er geborn wart, der bezeichent daz daz er selbe ist der ware vrideman der mit siner heiligen geburt die alten unminne da versônet hat diu da entzwischen dem almæhtigen got was unde allem manchûnne* (III 8,34–9,6). Nach Ansicht des Exegeten verweist die auctoritas des Weltherrschers Augustus auf die des Himmelskönigs Christus, die pax Augustana auf die pax christiana, aber nicht realprophetisch als heilsgeschichtliche Präfiguration, sondern kraft allegorischer Auslegung, der Tatsachen der Geschichte ebenso zugänglich sind wie Erscheinungen der Natur. Augustus ist nicht *typus Christi* wie Moses oder Gideon, und seine Befriedung der von Rom beherrschten Welt verhält sich zu dem Frieden, den Christus gebracht hat, nicht wie Verheißung und Erfüllung. Vielmehr bestand diese darin, *daz iuch der ware chûnic, der heilige Christus, von disem ellende mit im wider hain hat geladen zuo dem iuwern alten erbe, zuo dem heiligen paradis da iuwer altvordern Adam unde Eva inne warn unde da si von des tievels untriuwen uz verstozen wurden* (III 9,11–14), d. h. im Widerruf der Verstoßung, in der Umkehr des descensus in den ascensus; sie gehört letztlich zur Adam-Christus-Typologie.

Leider hat Konrad wenig getan (seine patristischen Gewährsleute allerdings auch nicht mehr), seine hermeneutischen Kategorien terminologisch abzugrenzen. Wie *typus, figura, allegoria* werden *bezeichenen, sîn* u. a. gleichermaßen für Typologisches und für allegorische Auslegung verwendet. Die Signalwörter sind somit als Kriterium ungeeignet und nur insofern relevant, als sie auch bei typologischen Sachverhalten nicht fehlen dürfen, wie schon Hoefer festgestellt hatte.

VI

Zum Abschluß dieser Überlegungen seien noch ein paar Anwendungs-fälle der zum Strukturprinzip mittelalterlicher Dichtung erklärten quasi-typologischen Denkform besprochen. Charakteristisch für sie alle ist, daß sie die biblische Basis weit hinter sich lassen, gleichwohl aber behaupten, daß heilsgeschichtliche Erfüllung und Überhöhung inten-diert sei. Auch die Übertragung einer exegetischen Methode per analo-giam – die für die typologische im Mittelalter weder theoretisch gerecht-fertigt noch praktisch geübt worden zu sein scheint – müßte wenigstens den formalen Bedingungen ihrer ursprünglichen Konzeption genügen! Sie müßte in der Lage sein, solche historischen oder für historisch gehal-tenen Fakten steigernd aufeinander zu beziehen, die einem einheitlichen, teleologisch verstandenen Geschichtsablauf angehören, und sie müßte den beabsichtigten Bezug in jedem Falle explizit machen. Erwogene ›Typologien‹ wie Odysseus als *figura* Christi oder Gregorius als Anti-typus zu Judas genügen diesen Minimalanforderungen offenbar nicht.

Die ›*Kaiserchronik*‹ bietet – aufgehängt an den Viten historischer oder unhistorischer Kaiser – *exempla* richtiger und falscher Handlungsweise des Menschen in heidnischer und christlicher Zeit. Lucretia ist in An-sehung des für sie geltenden Wertesystems nicht weniger vorbildlich als Crescentia im Rahmen des ihren. Ein unausgesprochenes Bezogen-sein beider ist um so weniger zu konstruieren, als ihre jeweilige Lage gründlich verschieden und kein gemeinsamer Bezugspunkt auszumachen ist: Crescentia steht gar nicht vor der Frage, ob sie als Geschändete weiterleben will, und für Lucretia gibt es kein göttliches Gebot, das ihr den Freitod verwehrte. In den Augen des Verfassers der ›*Kaiserchronik*‹ (ed. E. Schröder) ist das Verhalten b e i d e r Frauen *uns armen gesaget ad exemplum* (v. 11339). Genauso wie das des Kaisers Heraclius, von dem es ausdrücklich gesagt ist, weil er *parvuoz* (v. 11334), *mit grozer deumuote* (v. 11343) in Jerusalem einzog. Daß er damit den Kaiser Hadrian überboten habe, ist mit keiner Silbe angedeutet. Dessen Ver-dienste um den Wiederaufbau Jerusalems: *er begunde di stat ze lieben, / harte wol zieren, / er äverte wider die stat, / also man hiute wol chiesen mach* (v. 7222–7225) waren eher größer, und er erschien dem Dichter nur darum tadelnswert, weil er der Stadt seinen Namen oktroyieren wollte. Aber ihm war auch kein Engel erschienen, wie Heraclius, der ihn an der unbewußten Hybris gehindert hätte. Wiederum ist die Situation beider im Grunde unvergleichbar, da von offenem Ungehorsam Hadrians keine Rede und Heraclius nicht aus eigenem Antrieb demütig ist. Der Autor führt zwei *exempla* kaiserlichen Verhaltens im Rahmen seines heilsgeschichtlich begriffenen Ablaufs der Geschichte vor, die beide auf ihre Weise vorbildlich sind, im Vergleich etwa mit *ainem gotes widerwarten* (v. 5559) wie Domitian oder Nero, *dem aller wirsisten man, / der von muoter in dise werlt ie bekom* (v. 4085 f.): auf diese Konfrontation von Bösen und Guten kommt es ihm letztlich an, und die war unüberhörbar.

Um Nachahmung, *imitatio*, handelt es sich, wenn in mittelalterlicher Legendendichtung das Leben des Heiligen analog zum Erdenwege Jesu stilisiert und z. T. mit wörtlichen Zitaten aus seiner biblischen Lebens- und Leidensgeschichte erzählt wird. Fritz Tschirch (›Der heilige Georg als *figura Christi*‹, Festschrift Helmut de Boor zum 75. Geburtstag, Tübingen 1966, S. 1–19) hat auch deren fiktiven Nachvollzug im Martyrium eines Heiligen unter den Begriff der ›Typologisierung‹ gefaßt und als ›postfigurale‹ »Überhöhung des Lebens Christi« (S. 14) bezeichnet. Der Gorio des althochdeutschen ›Georgsliedes‹ (ed. Braune, ›Althochdeutsches Lesebuch‹, Nr. XXXV) sei ein »postfigural überhöhter Christus« (ebd.). »Der Verweischarakter der gesamten Darstellung« erfahre »nicht zuletzt dadurch eine starke Unterstreichung, daß sie aus jedem Zusammenhang mit Ort und Zeit gelöst ist« (S. 15), obwohl das Lied »nirgendwo eigens den Hörer auf den überall gemeinten heilsgeschichtlichen Symbolbezug« stößt (S. 11). Der Hinweis »unterbleibt« auch »für gewöhnlich« (S. 2) in dem hilfsweise beigezogenen Volksbuch 15. Jahrhunderts (ed. Bachmann, BLV 185, S. 259–328), während in dem ›Heiligen Georg‹ Reinbots von Durne (ed. C. v. Kraus) der ›postfigurale‹ Charakter des Helden erst »aus dem Panzer der säkularisierten Weltanschauung und Lebensführung des höfischen Rittertums« (S. 15) befreit werden müsse.

Tschirchs unscharfer, zwischen »imitatio Christi« (S. 14) und »typologischer Bedeutsamkeit« (S. 15) schwankender Sprachgebrauch verschleiert den in der behaupteten ›postfiguralen Überhöhung‹ liegenden Widersinn. Auch die postulierte Identifizierung, die »Aufhöhung des heiligen Ritters zum Ebenbild Christi« (S. 10) wäre blasphemisch, und die Parallelisierung von Heiligenleben und Christusleben, wo sie gewollt ist, kann im Falle Georgs schon wegen seiner bis in das Volksbuch festgehaltenen Zuordnung zu den sog. ›Märtyrern vom unzerstörbaren Leben‹ nicht aufgehen. Der unglückliche Begriff der ›Postfiguration‹ könnte nichts anderes als eine angesichts der unaufhebbaren fragilitas humanae conditionis unvollkommene *imitatio* meinen und ermangelt wegen der Beliebigkeit des jederzeitlichen Bezuges der konstitutiven heilsgeschichtlichen Notwendigkeit. Mit Typologie im biblischen und mittelalterlichen Sinne hat das alles nichts zu tun.

Petrus Tax hat in ›Studien zum Symbolischen in Hartmanns Erec‹ (*ZfdPh* 82, 1963, 29–44) – wenigstens in einer Fußnote – offen eingestanden, daß er »den Begriff der Typologie ... insofern in einem gegenüber der ursprünglichen Verwendungsweise (Verhältnis AT/NT) erweiterten Sinn« gebrauche, »als einerseits auch die heidnische Antike als Typus fungieren, andererseits der Antitypus die ganze christliche Zeit *sub gratia* umfassen kann« (S. 37[29]). Dieser erweiterten »typologischen Denkform« (S. 37) soll sich Hartmann von Aue im ›Erec‹ (ed. Leitzmann-Wolff) bei der Schilderung von Enites Pferd bedient haben. Indem Enite auf Sattel und Sattelkissen sitzend zu denken sei, werde ihre wiederhergestellte Ehe mit Erec ›typologisch‹ über die darauf abgebildeten »antiken Liebespaare als Vertreter der Liebesleidenschaft«: Eneas und Dido, Piramus und Tispe erhöht. Ihrer *concupiscentia* hätte sich das Paar zuvor ebenfalls schuldig gemacht und »damit ... der Gewalt des Teufels ergeben« (S. 43). Und indem ihre Satteldecke mit dem *lachen* verglichen werde, *daz Jupiter ze decke truoc / und diu gotinne Juno* (v. 7659 f.) bei ihrer Vermählung, erscheine Enite, weil »über der Satteldecke gedacht«, »in typologischer Sicht als Antitypus der heidnischen Ehegöttin«, die »unter ihrem *lachen*« vorgestellt sei (S. 40). »Erst das symbolische Verständnis der Schilderung von Enites Pferd« erschließe so »die wirkliche, ethisch-religiöse Bedeutung von Erecs und Enites früherer Schuld« (S. 43).

Das Halsbrecherische dieser Folgerung mag hier auf sich beruhen. Auch der mißliche Umstand, daß den auf dem kostbaren *gereite* abgebildeten antiken Typenpaaren Enite allein gegenübergestellt werden muß, weil Pferd und Sattel nun einmal für sie allein eingerichtet sind, braucht uns nicht weiter zu beschäftigen. Aber will der Verfasser uns allen Ernstes glauben machen, der Dichter habe Jupiter und Juno als Präfigurationen seines höfischen Heldenpaares eingeführt? Augustinus, den er zum Kronzeugen für seinen ›erweiterten‹ Typologiebegriff erkoren hat, wäre darob vermutlich nicht weniger verwundert gewesen als Hartmann.

Man könnte den mißlungenen Versuch, »mittelaltergemäß zu denken und zu empfinden« (S. 44), auf sich beruhen lassen, wenn der freizügige Umgang mit anderweit festgelegten Begriffen nicht auch sonst anzutreffen wäre. Die weitherzige Supponierung des Schemas von alttestamentlicher Präfiguration und neutestamentlicher Erfüllung bringt, wie immer abgewandelt, durch den (beabsichtigten) Anklang an seinen biblischen Ort und heilsgeschichtlichen Sinn, gewollt oder ungewollt, einen falschen Zungenschlag in die Interpretation mittelalterlicher Dichtung und gefährdet durch voreilige und oft willkürliche Spiritualisierung das buchstäbliche Verständnis der Texte, das dem Philologen vor allem aufgegeben ist.

Es müßten wohl überzeugendere Analogie-Fälle beigebracht werden, bevor die vorausgesetzte stillschweigende Übertragung biblisch-typologischer Exegese auf weltliche Dichtung durch deren Autoren und das korrespondierende, für selbstverständlich gehaltene Verstehen auf seiten des Publikums als wahrscheinlich und glaubhaft angesehen werden könnten.

Franz H. Bäuml

The Unmaking of the Hero:
Some Critical Implications of the Transition
from Oral to Written Epic

Every art historian is acquainted with that pithy advice which reflects
the wisdom of generations of his colleagues: if you want to prove anything, don't illustrate it. Perhaps as a medievalist I am far too realistic
to expect to prove anything, I do not intend to follow this advice.
But before I illustrate some of my contentions, it will be necessary to
traverse, first, a small plot of methodological ground, and second, a
somewhat larger theoretical stretch.
We are all familiar with the view that the interpretation of a work of
art is akin to the solution of a problem: the so-called meaning of the
work is somehow hidden, and one must find the key. We are likewise
familiar with some of the strange attempts to explain the fact that the
door doesn't open when such keys are turned in their keyholes, such as
the contention that »the *Nibelungenlied* was little understood at the
time« of its composition.[1] In order to transcend the impasse of traditional, naive »interpretation«, it is essential to realize that, in the words
of Fredric Jameson, »In matters of art, and particularly of artistic
perception, ... it is wrong to want to *decide,* to want to *resolve* a difficulty: what is wanted is a kind of mental procedure which suddenly
shifts gears, which throws everything in an inextricable tangle one floor
higher and turns the very problem itself ... into its own solution ... by
widening its frame in such a way that it now takes in its own mental
processes as well as the object of those processes«.[2] In short, »every com-

---

1 D. G. Mowatt and Hugh Sacker, *The Nibelungenlied: An Interpretative Commentary* (Toronto and Buffalo, 1967), p. 26; H. de Boor, *Geschichte der deutschen
Literatur* (München, 1964) II, p. 167; H. Bekker, *The Nibelungenlied: A Literary
Analysis* (Toronto and Buffalo, 1971), p. 4.
2 Fredric Jameson, »Metacommentary«, *PMLA* 86 (1971), 9–18.

mentary must be at the same time a metacommentary«. Let me begin, however, with a few bald assertions.

Neither the so-called »Spielmannsepen«, nor the *Nibelungenlied,* nor the *Kudrun* can be viewed any longer as they could still be viewed not many years ago. The combination of *Orendel, St. Oswald, König Rother,* and *Salman und Morolf* in one genre has become all but untenable.[3] And it is not too much to say that Andreas Heusler's theory of evolution of the *Nibelungenlied* must now also be regarded as not conforming to the probable facts.[4]

But what are the probable facts? The researches of Milman Parry and Albert B. Lord in the area of the South Slavic oral epic enable us to see the evolution of the Middle High German so-called heroic epics in an entirely new light.[5] We now know that Heusler's neatly economical system of precisely five ancestral incarnations of the *Nibelungenlied* is as untenable as Lachmann's twenty so-called original songs. The same can be said of any other reconstruction of a stable »original« text of the *Nibelungenlied* or, for that matter, of the so-called »Spielmannsepen«. The Parry-Lord theory of oral epic transmission is not without its own internal problems and several of its components are certainly not beyond criticism.[6] My present purpose, however, is not to criticize this or that aspect of the Parry-Lord theory, but rather to confront the transmitted text of the *Nibelungenlied,* of *Orendel,* and by implication the *Kudrun,* with the mode of existence of oral epic poetry.

The illiterate poet of epic poems does not memorize a text. This is the basic fact of life of oral epic poetry.[7] Memorization of a text presupposes the existence of a text in fixed form, i.e. in written form. It is dependent on retention of fixed components of that which is to be memorized, i.e. words. Whether the claim of Lord, that the illiterate poet doesn't know what a word is since he has never seen one, is universally valid, is beside the point. It is a fact that the oral poet com-

---

[3] Michael Curschmann, »*Spielmannsepik*«: *Wege und Ergebnisse der Forschung von 1907–1965* [Erweiterter Sonderdruck aus *DVj* 40 (1966)] (Stuttgart, 1968).

[4] Franz H. Bäuml and Donald J. Ward, »Zur mündlichen Überlieferung des Nibelungenliedes«, *DVj* 41 (1967), 352–390.

[5] Albert B. Lord, *The Singer of Tales* (Cambridge, Mass., 1960).

[6] Franz H. Bäuml and Agnes M. Bruno, »Weiteres zur mündlichen Überlieferung des Nibelungenliedes«, *DVj* 46 (1972), 479–493, and Franz H. Bäuml and Edda Spielmann, »From Illiteracy to Literacy: Prolegomena to a Study of the *Nibelungenlied*«, *FMLS* 10 (1974), 248–259, and *Oral Literature,* ed. J. J. Duggan (Edinburgh and London, 1975), 62–63.

[7] Lord, pp. 22, 24, 124–138.

poses with segments larger than words, i.e. formulae and themes. The reason could very well be that a relatively large semantic segment which is metrically organized makes instantaneous oral composition easier. At any rate, these formulae – these »groups of words ... regularly employed under the same metrical conditions to express a given essential idea« as Parry and Lord define them,[8] are part of the tradition of oral epic poetry. The apprentice poet learns them not by memorizing them, but by hearing them perform their function in many different oral epics. These formulae are, moreover, not static – for this too would presuppose a fixed text. They are lexically variable – the metric structure of a formula can be filled in many different ways and semantically adapted to the context. The facility with which such adaptations are performed marks the caliber of the oral poet.[9]

The larger narrative elements, the so-called epic »themes« of which the formulae are the lexical expression, are likewise traditionally determined. Like the formulae, they are protean and adaptable to the demands of the context. Robert Scholes and Robert Kellogg have very aptly compared their function to that of topoi in written compositions dependent on rhetorical tradition.[10]

Since the oral poet composes his poem by means of formulae and themes each time he recites it, rather than merely reproducing a stable text by memorization, each recitation of the same poem is different from each other recitation, even if the poet is the same. There is, therefore, in the oral tradition, no such thing as an »Urtext«, since every recitation is an original. To apply concepts such as »archetype«, or »descent« to oral epic poetry is to view it through the spectacles of literacy.[11]

The basic determinant of the *modus operandi* of the oral poet and of the functions of his tools is illiteracy – his own and that of his audience. It is, however, false to conclude that illiteracy is invariable, no matter when or where it occurs. The characteristics of illiteracy are subject to change no less than those of literacy. The society of Homeric Greece, for instance, was a functionally illiterate society, i.e. its laws, beliefs, all that characterized it as a society, was not transmitted in writing.

---

8 Milman Parry, *Studies in the Epic Technique of Oral Verse-Making I,* in *Harvard Studies in Classical Philology* 41 (1930), p. 80, and Lord, p. 30.
9 Lord, pp. 49–65.
10 Robert Scholes and Robert Kellogg, *The Nature of Narrative* (New York, 1966), p. 26.
11 Lord, pp. 49–65.

Linear B served a different purpose altogether. The repositories of learning, of the knowledge necessary for the preservation of the fabric of society, were the epic poets, who, as Eric Havelock has shown, transmitted this knowledge in their poems to an illiterate society.[12] When writing became the accepted method for the transmission of knowledge, the function of poetry shifted: it ceased to be predominantly didactic and became predominantly aesthetic. The leading classes of society looked to the written word, and no longer to oral poetry, as transmitting the cement of their society. When a society becomes literate in this basically modern sense, oral poetry *sinks* to the illiterate, i.e. the *disadvantaged* in such a society. We are therefore on solid ground in this respect, when we apply the criteria of oral epic poetry as observed by Parry and Lord in Yugoslavia during the 1930's and 1950's to certain types of epic poetry of the twelfth or the thirteenth century: in both cases oral poetry was the poetry, not of an illiterate or pre-literate society, but of illiterates within a literate society – literate, that is, in the sense that it relied upon the written word for the transmission of all that constitutes the identity of a society. It must be emphasized in this respect that I am not concerned here with the »literacy« or »illiteracy« of individuals, but rather with their perceptual orientation. It is not necessary for an individual to be able to read and write himself to be a member of the »literate« stratum of society. He needs merely rely on the individual literacy of others for his acquisition of culturally necessary knowledge.

The poems under discussion – the *Nibelungenlied*, the *Kudrun*, and *Orendel* – exhibit all the characteristics of oral composition as posited by the Parry-Lord theory: the use of formulae, oral themes, and a paucity of enjambement. This does not mean, however, that these poems are therefore oral epic poems. If a written record of an oral performance is analyzed for its formula-content, that content will be relatively even in density throughout the poem. This density will, of course, depend on the distance of the written record from the oral performance: the more written intermediaries, the lower the formulaic density. An analysis of the formulaic content of the *Nibelungenlied*, for example, shows very pronounced fluctuations in formulaic density: some passages are upwards of 75 % formulaic, others a mere 25 % or less. Since markedly high formulaic density presupposes oral composi-

---

12 Eric Havelock, *Preface to Plato* (Cambridge, Mass., 1963), pp. 36–60.

tion and low density argues for written composition, it appears logical
to conclude that the *Nibelungenlied* – and certainly *Orendel* and probably the *Kudrun* also – was once an oral composition, orally transmitted, which then was not merely recorded and transmitted in writing
as such, but adapted, in the case of the *Nibelungenlied* and the *Kudrun,*
by a literate poet for an audience with concerns and interests quite
different from those of the audience of the oral poet. In the case of
Orendel the situation, as I shall point out, appears to be somewhat
different.

We have now arrived at the crux of the matter: the perception of the
text by the contemporary audience. In this respect there is a basic
distinction between the perception of the recitation of an oral poem
and the perception of a written text, even if that text is read aloud by a
reciter, or is recited from memory. It is essential, however, to emphasize
at this point, that my subsequent remarks are intended to be understood
as a hypothesis, a model. There is much that, at the present state of our
knowledge, cannot be »proven«. Perhaps some aspects of my hypothesis
will be shown to be invalid; yet no validity or invalidity can be established without a model, the construction of which is in this instance
required by the empirical findings of Parry and Lord and their implications.

In the recitation of an oral poem, the reciter is the poet, and the personal pronoun first person singular within the text refers to him. His
name need not be given, for he stands before the audience, and he is not
distinct from the »narrator« in his poem. In short, the oral poet = the
reciter = the narrator = the text, all of which are perceived directly
and on the same level by the audience. Not so with the reciter of a
written text – and, of course, not with the direct perception of the
written text. It is obvious to the perceiver that the reciter of a written
text is not the poet, and that the »narrator« is therefore also a separate
entity from the reciter and, of course, from the poet. That this awareness of the distinction between poet and »narrator« can be posited for
the thirteenth century is borne out by Wolfram von Eschenbach, whose
narrator claims that he »kan deheinen buochstap« (*Parzival* II,115.27),[13]
and by the *Nibelungenlied*, whose generally omniscient narrator, for
instance, claims ignorance of Siegfried's motivation in taking Brünhild's belt. The equation of the oral recitative situation is clearly illus-

---

[13] Scholes and Kellog, pp. 55–56.

trated in the first stanza of the *Nibelungenlied:* with the words »uns ist in alten mæren wunders vil geseit« the poet-reciter-narrator places himself along with his audience (»uns«) into line as recipient of the narrative tradition. With the last half-line of the stanza »muget ir nu wunder hœren sagen« he separates himself from his audience (»ir«) as the vehicle for the transmission of the narrative tradition. Soon, however, the narrator's stance separates him also from the text, – as, for instance, in his claim that the Burgundian court contains all sorts of knights »des ich genennen niene kan« (10,4). When the narrator comments on the text – and the narrator's words »Dar zuo nam er ir gürtel, daz was ein porte guot. / ine weiz ob er daz tæte durh sînen hôhen muot« (680,1.2) are nothing if not a comment –, it is clear that someone not present at the recitation is responsible for this commentary, i.e. the poet, who, consequently, is also not the reciter. Whereas in an oral performance the audience perceives poet, reciter, narrator, and text equally and immediately since they are identical, the audience of a reading of a poem perceives only the reciter and the text. All elements, poet, reciter, narrator, and text are entities separate from one another. Therefore, the poet can use the narrator to comment on the text, and the reciter, in turn, can use his function for such commentary on a text which is not his own, by inflection of his voice, gesture, etc. Both the poet and the reciter can therefore take a stance toward the text, i.e. the tradition, which it is impossible for the oral poet-reciter-narrator to take: they can take issue with the text, and to the extent that the narrative matter embodied by the text is traditional, they can challenge the tradition which – unlike the oral poet – they do not embody. If, as can be asserted with some justice, the *Kudrun* is indeed an anti-*Nibelungenlied,* this is exactly what the poet of the *Kudrun* has done.

But what of the *Nibelungenlied* itself? I have observed that the narrator of the *Nibelungenlied* functions as a commentator; he can participate in the text – »von schulden si dô klageten: des gie in wærlîche nôt« (70,4) – or stand apart and comment upon it: »von ir vil hôhen werdekeit und von ir ritterscaft, / der di herren pflâgen mit vröuden al ir leben, / des enkunde iu ze wâre niemen gar ein ende geben« (12,2–4). But beyond this he can also assume that most literate of narrative guises – the guise of the ironical narrator. Of course, the role of textual and dramatic irony in the *Nibelungenlied* is obvious: Siegfried sets out to conquer Kriemhild by force (59,1), arrives at Worms and forgets all about her while he attempts to provoke the Burgundians into a fight.

The irony of the situation is compounded by the fact that the self-discipline of his opponents gives him the opportunity to remember why he came: »›Daz sol ich eine wenden‹, sprach aber Gêrnôt. / allen sînen degenen reden er verbôt / iht mit übermüete des im wære leit. / dô gedâhte ouch Sîvrit an die hêrlîchen meit« (123). The most famous example of textual irony, the episode of Gunther's wedding night, in which Brünhild »truoc in z'einem nagele unt hienc in an die want« (637,2) is not dependent upon literacy for its perception, since it is basically burlesque.

Perhaps the most ignored item of irony in the poem is Hagen's assertion to Kriemhild that »jâ hân ich des gesworn, / daz ich den hort iht zeige die wîle daz si leben, / deheiner mîner herren, sô sol ich in niemene geben« (2368,2–4), thus immediately causing the murder of his king – a curious accomplishment for one who, throughout, »was den Nibelungen ein helflîcher trôst«. The perception of irony hinges on double participation: one participator in an ironic action or situation participates or perceives without understanding, the other participates or perceives with an understanding of the situation as well as of the lack of understanding of the other participator. This is particularly obvious in forms of dramatic irony, with which the *Nibelungenlied* abounds. The first example which comes to mind is, of course, Kriemhild's reply to her mother's interpretation of her dream: »›Die rede lât belîben‹, sprach si, ›frouwe mîn. / ez ist an manegen wîben vil dicke worden scîn / wie liebe mit leide ze jungest lônen kan. / ich sol si mîden beide, sone kan mir nimmer missegân‹« (17).

The improbability of the operation of irony in oral poetry becomes obvious when we consider the function of the narrative matter of a heroic epic which originated in the oral tradition. The narrative matter, being »heroic«, glorifies a »hero« through his actions. This very glorification is the point of the whole epic, the whole myth of the hero. There is little we can say about the historical causes of »heroic ages« from which emanate the tales about heroes. We do know something, however, about the psychological »causes« of such »heroic ages« in the perception of posterity. Cecil Bowra lists four of these:[14] (1) conquest (e.g. the Welsh memories of a »heroic age« were stimulated by the loss of Welsh lands to the Angles and Saxons), (2) movement of a people from its homeland and a consequent glorification of it, (3) disinte-

---

[14] Cecil M. Bowra, *In General and in Particular* (London, 1964), pp. 73–78.

gration of an apparently reliable political system (e.g. the Carolingian empire under Charlemagne), (4) attempts at suppression of a heroic vision by a priestly caste and its defiant survival. The heroism of a »heroic age« is to be sought not in the historical reality of that age itself – a reality largely lost upon posterity –, but in the manner in which posterity views it and in the reasons for that view. The view of a »heroic age« as »heroic«, as embodied in the actions of an admired »hero«, and an ironic view of such a hero, are therefore mutually exclusive. A hero ironized is no hero, for those who ironize him no longer admire him, but judge him and find him wanting. Purely from the standpoint of the narrative itself, then, it is far less likely that an illiterate and therefore disadvantaged subgroup of a literate society should take an ironic stance toward traditional »heroic« material than that the privileged, literate, leading class representing a culture no longer that of the hero should view such material ironically. But there are other reasons as well, which argue for the improbability of irony on the oral and its probability on the literate level.

The listener to a reading of the *Nibelungenlied* or to a recitation from memory has the necessary advantage over the listener to an oral performance of being able to predict as well as look back upon the narrative matter being recited. The existence of thirty-four manuscripts, all but one of which agree in most of two groups of readings, testifies to the fact that the narrative was viewed as a stable, i.e. written text, and that therefore the listeners at any given reading – or, for that matter, any recitation from memory – can be assumed to have a knowledge of this inert narrative from other readings or memorized recitations. The listener to an oral performance has no such firm basis of necessary comparison. This does not mean that these ironical situations cannot be present in oral poetry, but merely that the conditions of recitation and perception of oral poetry prevent them from being perceived as ironic. At the moment when traditional epic epithets are perceived to imply one thing, and the actions of the denoted hero are perceived to imply another, the traditional hero is ironized. This process, which theoretically is not dependent at all on lexical change, but merely on the perception of a text, can be most clearly illustrated by considering the functional changes brought about by literate perception of formulae and by noting the consequences of a change in social context which a former oral poem undergoes when it becomes »literate« and thereby changes audiences.

The illiterate listener to an oral poem perceives meaning not through
words, but through traditional formulae. Such formulae as »ein ûz
erwelter degen«, »ein sneller degen guot«, »ein degen küen' unde balt«,
function as epic epithets in the oral tradition. They, and dozens like
them, are the only means by which a hero or king can be mentioned at
all in oral poetry. In a written text – or to a literate audience, i.e. an
audience accustomed to the written word and therefore perceiving a
text in terms of literacy – such formulae no longer function as traditional epithets, as in themselves necessary denotations. What was formerly an oral formula is now a series of words, stable lexical components of a text and therefore verifyable – and the »ûz erwelter
degen«, taken »literally«, is now juxtaposed to the action he performs.
The oral formula, the epic epithet, has become a characterization, and
the characterization may or may not fit the action of the hero which
characterizes him no less – and if it does not fit, it is perceived to function ironically.
The irony resulting from the change in perception from formula to
word, from epic epithet to characterization is exemplified, among other
instances, by st. 435 of the *Nibelungenlied*. The scene is Îsenstein;
Dancwart and Hagen are worried about Gunther's chances of getting
away with his life in the forthcoming athletic contest with Brünhild;
Siegfried has slipped away to the ship to get his magic cloak; and Brünhild approaches, armed to the teeth:

> Dô kom ir gesinde. die truogen dar ze hant / von alrôtem golde einen
> schildes rant, / mit stahelherten spangen, vil michel unde breit, / dar under
> spilen wolde diu vil minneclîche meit.   (435)

»Diu vil minneclîche meit« is a formula, and as such can denote any
female protagonist not depicted like Kundrie in *Parzival*. But the
literate audience perceives words, not formulae. As a series of words,
this former formula functions as partial characterization, which is at
variance with its context, and therefore constitutes an instance of irony.
The fact is further borne out by the diametrically opposite characterization four stanzas later. The scene is the same: Brünhild's retainers are
bringing her shield:

> Alsô der starke Hagene den schilt dar tragen sach, / mit grimmigem muote
> der helt von Tronege sprach: / ›wâ nu, künic Gunther? wie vliesen wir den
> lîp! / der ir dâ gert ze minnen, diu ist des tiuveles wîp.‹   (438)

But it is not only the first of the two elements, epitheton and action, which undergoes a perceptional change with the charge from orality to literacy. It is well known that pre-literate cultures are homoeostatic. They are provided with cultural amnesia: whatever of the past does not apply to the present is eliminated or changed to a form which renders it relevant.[15] Oral poetry, the preeminent didactic vehicle in pre-literate societies, therefore exhibits no consciousness of the past as past, but constantly adapts traditional narrative matter and renders it familiar within the context of the present. It is noteworthy in this connection, that some of the so-called »courtly« passages of the *Nibelungenlied* are heavily formulaic. When oral poetry flourishes in a literate society, it addresses itself to an illiterate, disadvantaged segment of that society. It is now very easy for such poetry to change audiences, i.e. to enter the realm of literacy. However, when originally oral poetry is perceived by the literate segment of society, it also changes social levels. Both as traditional narrative matter, and, as such, as a class-distinguished form of expression, the components which rendered it functional in pre- or illiterate society will be perceived as anachronistic by a literate audience. An action, for instance, which is perceived as heroic in traditional terms by the illiterate stratum of a literate society will not necessarily be seen in the same light by literate perceivers.

This change can likewise give rise to irony: Siegfried's behavior at his arrival at Worms, Brünhild's petite bourgeoise worry that Gunther's »kamerære mir wil der mînen wât lâzen niht belîben« (517) are cases in point. Hagen's murder of Siegfried, a »grôze missewende«, was perceivable as such by an illiterate audience. Once the line into literacy – and another social class – was crossed, however, the inappropriateness of the weapon used lends an ironic dimension to the deed.

---

15 One example of many: The state of Gonja in Northern Ghana is divided into a number of chiefdoms, certain of which are recognized as providing in turn the ruler of the whole nation. When asked to explain their system, the Gonja recount how the founder of the state enthroned himself as chief and his sons as rulers of its territorial divisions. After his death, each divisional chief succeeded to paramountcy in turn. When the story was first recorded at the turn of this century, the founder of the state was said to have had seven sons. This corresponded to the number of divisions whose chiefs were eligible for the supreme office. But when the British arrived, two of the seven divisions disappeared, one being incorporated in a neighboring division, and another because of some boundary changes made by the British administration. Sixty years later, when the myths of state were again recorded, the founding chief was credited with only five sons. The founders of the two divisions which had since disappeared from the map had also disappeared from the myth. Cf. Jack Goody and Ian Watt, »The Consequences of Literacy«, *Comparative Studies in Society and History*, 5 (1963), 310.

In its shift sometime around 1200 from its oral existence among an illiterate social substratum to a written existence among a stratum of society which perceived it as a fixed, written text, the *Nibelungenlied*, in changing modes of existence and modes of perception, therefore, also changed modes of possible »meaning«.

A literate society, or the literate stratum of a society, is by definition not homoeostatic in its historical perception. The written word is the basis of its knowledge, and once a word is written, a fact or opinion recorded, that record is fixed. It cannot be made non-existent by the mere act of forgetting, for the written record has an existence separate from that of human memory. It is clear then, that that which can be called »meaning« is not only perceived differently, but also functions in totally different ways in the two types of society. If the so-called meaning of a text is conditioned by the perception of the relationship of the content of that text to the world around it, then the characteristics of illiterate perception as I have outlined them can only permit such a text to be »understood« as a representation of the world around it. Literate perception, however, by virtue of its cognition of the various forms of irony and of concepts, can embrace not only representation, which in written literature takes the form of historical or biographical writing, but also commentary on or elucidation of that which oral poetry can only attempt to represent, i.e. some aspect of the world external to the text. Elucidative literature, or illustrative literature in the terms of Scholes and Kellogg, achieves its purest state in allegory. Unlike representation, elucidation has no need for adherence to natural consecutiveness, or for the observation of the law of cause and effect in the world external to the text, since it is concerned with commentary, not depiction. Hence the incongruities of the *Nibelungenlied:* from Siegfried's two youths, the courtly and the mythological, to Dietrich's extremely odd behavior at the end.[16] An incongruity to perception conditioned by representation is not necessarily an incongruity to perception conditioned by elucidative literature.

It would be wrong to conclude, however, that the movement of narrative matter from orality to literacy as illustrated by the *Nibelungenlied,* was typical. *Orendel* is an example of development in the opposite direction. The poem as a whole is densely formulaic. The character of the formulae, however, varies. Formulaic systems, i.e. adaptations of

---

[16] Cf. the review by Hans Kuhn, *AfdA* 76 (1965), 1–18.

formulae, can be traced throughout the Bride-episodes, but in those episodes devoted primarily to the seamless cloak of Christ the recurrence of formulae is predominantly verbatim. It appears to be logical, therefore, to conclude that those episodes have been concocted by a literate poet, possibly a cleric charged with propagandizing Trier as a place of pilgrimage. In short, *Orendel* in its transmitted form is an example of an oral poem, which has been adapted by a literate poet, but not for a literate audience. The adaptations indicate that it was destined to return to the oral realm and there find favor in its familiar formulaic form, but with a new message: the story of Orendel and Bride, but the seamless cloak by which Orendel came to be known is now, after many adventures, at Trier.

To return now to our methodological starting-point and the strictures of metacommentary: to ascribe discrepancies to the incompetence of the poet, to assert that the contemporaneous audience – however it is conceived – did not »understand« this or that work, – all this is tantamount to having formed one's own opinion about a text and then comparing the text to that opinion. The difference between one's own opinion and the text is then either the fault of the author or of the contemporaneous audience. This is all very reassuring, but it amounts to little more than writing one's own *Nibelungenlied*, and comparing the transmitted text with it. Both attitudes, of course, reflect certain phases in the history of criticism: the first, the ascription of textual characteristics to an intention of the author which they either do or do not »successfully« embody, is the view of romantic criticism of the nineteenth century, which regarded the poem as symptom of the emotions and intentions of the poet; the second standpoint, the assertion that the contemporaneous audience failed to understand a given work, is a logical consequence of textual analysis *in vacuo* based on the ahistorical stance of the »new criticism« – a stance which is defensible in the context of a relatively ahistorical process such as textual analysis, but which is absurd when the attempt is made to give historical validity to the results of the analysis by regarding them as eternally valid and merely not achievable by the audience for which the work was created.

A work of art is its effect, and its »meaning« is the perception of that meaning. This is by no means as relativistic as it sounds. Effects and perceptions are to a great extent culturally conditioned variables. The traditional concern with the work of art as either the result of a development or as an isolated object is, at best, an approach to only half the problem. An approach to the other half of the problem – the perception of a work of art by a given type of audience – can perhaps demonstrate the necessity for metacommentary most clearly. The perception of a work of art by an audience must, in order to be described, be perceived by the critic. What the critic describes is therefore not something which objectively existed, but something which is modified by his own perceptions and the factors which modify them, – and here, I think, we are going beyond Jauss' *Literaturgeschichte als Provokation*. Throughout the nineteenth and far into the twentieth century the text of the *Nibelungenlied* was read and analyzed in terms of a representation of external »reality«. It is only in the last fifteen years that the *Nibelungenlied* has begun to be viewed as an elucidative work. The same change, of course, also characterized the study of the courtly epic during the same period: compare, for instance, any nineteenth century positivist with Reto Bezzola. The modifications in our perceptions which brought about those changes either emanated from, or at least are evident in our perception of modern works of art. The elucidative function dominates all modern art – or at least our perception of it, just as it now appears to have dominated medieval art. In applying this perception to an analysis of the perceptions of medieval works by medieval audiences we must, of course, seek the support of textual, historical, sociological, and anthropological facts, – for otherwise we can hope to practice nothing more than what Frederick C. Crews called »anaesthetic criticism«.[17] But simultaneously it must be kept in mind that »the process of criticism is not so much an interpretation of content as it is a revealing of it, a laying bare, a restoration of the original experience, beneath the distortions of the censor: and this revelation takes the form of an explanation why the content was so distorted; it is inseparable from a description of the mechanism of censorship itself«.[18] It is irresponsible to attempt a »critical analysis« of a work of art without a methodological basis which takes into account the mode of existence of the work of art at a given time and in a given social context, and the effects of changes in its modes of existence upon its perception. What is wanted is not, on the one hand, the »problem« solved, the work interpreted for all eternity, nor on the other hand the relativism of sub-

[17] Frederick C. Crews, »Anaesthetic Criticism«, *The New York Review* 14 (Feb. 26, 1970), 31–35, and No. 15 (March 12, 1970), 49–52.
[18] Jameson, *PMLA* 86 (1971), 16.

jectivity, but an approach which takes into account the work of art and the forces which shape it and its perception as well as those which shape the critic and his vision. The fact that the critic and his vision are not eternal verities is a historical fact which justifies the constant renewal of this approach. Only in this manner can one hope to come to terms with the problem central to all criticism: how does a work of art function?

M. Alison Stones

Sacred and Profane Art:
Secular and Liturgical Book-Illumination
in the Thirteenth Century

The eleventh to thirteenth centuries mark the emergence of new directions in medieval thought which found their reflection in the development of a secular tradition in literature and in art. The flowering of
new literary genres – epic, romance, and poetry – in France and Germany in the late eleventh and twelfth centuries bears witness to this and
the popularity of the new material continued into the thirteenth century and beyond, in the translations and prose versions of poems relating the deeds of the great heroes like Roland, William, and Arthur.
There is much in the stories and legends of these figures that reflects
the Christian ethic; the cult of Charlemagne arose at the end of the
twelfth century,[1] Roland became a popular saint although he was never
officially canonised[2] as was William,[3] while the quest for the Holy
Grail is permeated with christological symbolism.[4] The illustration of
this new textual material likewise marks a new development in medieval book-production, and in many ways the illuminators, like the
authors of the texts, relied to a large degree on patterns already familiar
from liturgical illumination.
At the same time it becomes apparent in thirteenth-century book-illu-
mination that cross-fertilisation is at work; in the first half of the cen-

---

[1] It seems that popular devotion to Charlemagne began in Germany at the time of
the quarrel between Frederick Barbarossa and the pope. The title of »Blessed«
was conferred upon Charlemagne by Benedict XIV. See *Acta Sanctorum*, III,3,
pp. 490–507, January 28.

[2] Despite the fact he was never canonised, Roland is represented among a group of
martyrs in the sculpture of the south door jambs of the cathedral of Chartres
(see R. Lejeune and J. Stiennon, *La Légende de Roland dans l'art du moyen âge*,
Brussels 1966, II, pp. 192–203), and in the glass of Chartres he is shown with a
halo (*ibid*. pp. 203–07).

[3] Canonised in 1066. See *Acta Sanctorum*, XIX,6, pp. 798–817, May 28.

[4] See in particular the description of the Grail liturgy in *La Queste del saint Graal*,
ed. A. Pauphilet, Paris, 1923, pp. 269–70.

tury the illumination of secular texts[5] is still rare and their quality is often inferior in scope and in execution to their liturgical counterparts, while the illuminators adapt liturgical themes to meet the requirements of their secular texts. By the end of the century, however, the best workshops not only made splendid MSS of secular content as well as religious books, but the decorative layout of the latter reflect the secular content of the former, while the motifs themselves take on an independence of the context of the text they illustrate, whether it be sacred or profane in nature.

It is the purpose of this paper to examine the kinds of change that take place during the thirteenth century, drawing examples from the illustration of epic, romance, and poetry, and setting them in relation to religious illumination. Since it is in France that the sequence of secular illumination may best be followed, most of the material here selected for discussion is French. The relations between picture, text, and model will be considered first, followed by an analysis of secular and liturgical products of the same shop.

The earliest illustrations in secular texts tend to rely heavily on generalised types without rendering the complexities of the situations their texts narrate. One of the earliest secular MSS to contain a cycle of pictures is the *Ruolantesliet* Heidelberg, Universitätsbibliothek, MS cod. pal. germ. 112.[6] (fig. 1) In combat scenes, pagans are not visually distinct from christians; the illuminators use *topoi* such as could have been adapted from such sources as, for instance, *Psychomachia* illustration, of which there are eleventh and twelfth-century illuminated copies,[7] or a scene drawn from biblical illumination from a book such as Kings or Maccabees.

---

[5] In art, as in literature, the distinction between the »secular« and the »liturgical« is not an easy one to make, nor would the difference between what we would now term the »sacred« and the »profane« necessarily have occurred to the medieval mind. In terms of book-production one may reasonably distinguish between different types of book on the basis of the need for which the book was created. Thus »liturgical« is here understood to refer to books created for use in the liturgy of the church, interpreted in the broadest sense to include the Bible as well as Psalters, Breviaries, Missals etc., while »secular« refers to books made to be read and looked at for general enjoyment and entertainment. We are concerned in the present inquiry with the degree to which »sacred« and »profane« elements overlap from a »liturgical« to a »secular« context or vice versa.

[6] Facsimile Wiesbaden, 1970. Lejeune and Stiennon, *op. cit.* I, pp. 111–138.

[7] See H. Woodruff, *The Illustrated Manuscripts of Prudentius*, Cambridge Mass. 1930. Cf. also the *Psychomachia* illustrations in the *Hortus Deliciarum* of Herrad of Landsberg (A. Straub, *Hortus Deliciarum*, Straßburg, 1879–99).

This famous late twelfth-century *Ruolantesliet* in many ways stands at the beginning of secular illumination used for texts written in the vernacular; its illustrations form a sharp contrast to later representations of the Roland story such as the Chartres window of c. 1220[8] or the *Karl der Große* MS of c. 1300, St. Gall, Biblioteca Vadiana 302.[9] (figs. 2 and 3) Both MSS contain scenes of Roland's death, showing the hero breaking his sword on the rock and blowing his oliphant. In each case, the representation conveys a great deal of the narrative detail of the text version they illustrate, showing that at some stage in the planning of the illumination, either the artist himself, or the person in charge of the illustrative layout of the book or window, must have read the text and based pictorial compositions directly on its verbal description.

Another method of text-illustration found in thirteenth-century secular MSS shows that the artist's imagination might also be aided by familiar prototypes in a manner somewhat akin to the use of generalised scenes in the *Ruolantesliet* MS dicussed above. An example of this is the illustration of an episode from the *Queste* section of the French prose *Lancelot*.[10] The story describes how Lancelot falls asleep beneath a cross, whereupon the Grail appears. Lancelot, since he is asleep, does not see the Grail, but the latter is seen by a lame man on a bier, whom Lancelot has just rescued. Only six *Queste* MSS contain an illustration of this episode.[11] In B.N. fr. 342 (fig. 4) the Grail is not represented at all in the miniature; but in the other MSS it is represented as a chalice (figs. 5–7). The illuminators make use of a well-established liturgical object in their depiction of this important life-giving symbol, which the French prose version of the text describes as a *vessel*. The liturgy of the Grail as described in *Queste* refers to the presence in the Grail of a

---

8 See above, note 2. The iconography of this window is assumed to represent scenes from a now lost version of the Roland story. See, in addition to Lejeune and Stiennon, D. J. A. Ross, »The Iconography of *Roland*«, *Medium Aevum* XXXVII (1968), pp. 46–65.

9 Lejeune and Stiennon, *op. cit.* I, pp. 226–238, pl. XXIV–VI.

10 *Queste*, ed. Pauphilet, pp. 57–62.

11 This episode is illustrated in Paris, B.N. fr. 342, written in 1274; Bonn 526, written in 1286; London B.M. Add. 10294 and Roy. 14. E. III; Manchester, Rylands French 1, the last three MSS all come from the same workshop and were made c. 1315–25; Paris, Ars. 5218, although it contains no miniature for this particular episode, does include a unique representation of the Grail liturgy whose iconography is of great interest to the present discussion. It was written and illuminated in 1351 by Piérart dou Tielt. See H. Martin, »Un caricaturiste au temps du roi Jean, Piérart dou Tielt«, *Gazette des Beaux-Arts* 2 (1909), pp. 89–102.

bleeding figure, a concept no doubt inspired by the concept of the real presence of Christ in the Eucharistic Host, which, as the doctrine of Transubstantiation, became official dogma at the fourth Lateran Council in 1215. Two of the *Queste* illustrations reflect this concept, as manifested not only in the text which they illustrate, but also in the doctrine of the church and in liturgical illumination. In Bonn 526, the chalice contains a cross; this motif is not used in the text in the verbal description of the Grail, either at the point in the text when it appears before Lancelot, or later, in the Grail liturgy. That the motif in the *Queste* illustration is derived from liturgical sources is suggested by the appearance of the same motif in the illustration of the Moralised Bibles[12] (fig. 8) in representations concerning the consecration of the sacred elements. The representation of the Grail liturgy in Ars. 5218 shows the Grail as a chalice containing a human figure that is bleeding. While it is possible to point to parallels in liturgical illumination for the consecrated host with a human figure emerging from it, there appear to be no parallels for a chalice containing a figure, far less a figure that is bleeding (Paris, Musée de Cluny, S. Martin embroidery). It would therefore appear that we witness in this mid-fourteenth-century MS a return to the direct method of deriving picture from text that is evident more than a century earlier in the Chartres window.

Secular text illustration, then, employs no single method in selecting models, but may equally well adapt a model from a liturgical context or invent one on the basis of the words of the text concerned. A consideration of secular MSS in relation to the workshops that produced them leads to other kinds of parallels between secular and liturgical illumination. There is evidence that both types of book were illuminated by the same illuminators, although in the thirteenth century

---

[12] The original Moralised Bible was commissioned in all probability by Saint Louis, king of France, since his portrait, along with that of his mother, Blanche of Castille, appears in the frontispiece illustration in the New York section of the Toledo Bible. The thirteenth century Moralised Bible MSS are: 1) New York, Morgan Library MS 280 and Toledo Cathedral Library; 2) Paris, B.N. lat. 11560; London, B.M. Harley 1526–7; Oxford, Bodleian Library Bod. 270b; 3) Vienna, Ö.N.B. 1179; 4) Vienna Ö.N.B. 2554. For the Oxford/Paris/London MS see A. Laborde, *La bible moralisée illustrée*, Paris, 1911–27. A facsimile of the Vienna 2554 MS and a book on the Moralised Bibles are being prepared by Prof. Dr. R. Haussherr. See also R. Haussherr, »Tempel Salomonis und Ecclesia Christi«, *Zeitschrift für Kunstgeschichte*, 1968, pp. 101–121, and »*Sensus litteralis* und *sensus spiritualis* in der Bible moralisée«, *Frühmittelalterliche Studien* VI (1972), pp. 356–80.

we are still in a period in which comparatively little is known about the exact circumstances of book-production because of the scarcity of documents, unlike the fifteenth century, when it is possible to follow in detail the work of different scribes, decorators, and illuminators in different books and to trace their movements as they shifted from one workshop to another.[13]

For the first half of the thirteenth century our concept of the artistic workshop is based largely on similarity of style and motif; there is also some evidence from tax records, in particular for Paris, to show that book-production was by and large a commercial enterprise operating in towns rather than in monasteries, and that the work was on the whole done by lay craftsmen.[14] This applies not only to secular books but also to liturgical ones including the Bible. As far as documentary evidence is concerned, there is far more material extant from the late thirteenth century, both from the Paris tax rolls of the decade of the 1290s and also from the tax records and town plans of the north-eastern French and Belgian commercial centres like Arras, Cambrai and Tournai, showing that scribes, illuminators, parchment makers, bookbinders and book-dealers all had their shops in neighbouring streets and that their operations were closely interrelated.[15]

A comparison between the secular and liturgical products of some workshops from the mid-thirteenth to the early fourteenth centuries indicates the kinds of changes that occur in the course of that period in relation to the layout or type of illustration selected for each kind of text and the relative quality of each, as well as shedding further light on the question of dependence or independence of illustration on text.

---

[13] See in particular the exhibition catalogue by the late L. M. J. Delaissé, *Le Mécénat de Philippe le Bon*, Brussels, 1959, which pioneered study in this area.

[14] R. Branner, »Manuscript makers in thirteenth-century Paris«, *Art Bulletin*, 1966, pp. 65–7; H. Géraud, *Paris sous Philippe le Bel d'après des documents originaux et d'après un document contenant le rôle de la taille imposée sur les habitants de Paris en 1292*, Paris, 1837; K. Michaëlsson, »Le Livre de la taille de Paris, 1313«, *Acta Universitatis Gothoburgensis*, Göteborg, 1951, also for 1296 (*ibid.* 1958) and 1297 (*ibid.* 1961). This tax roll also includes records for 1298, 1299 and 1300 which are still incompletely edited. See, however, F. Baron, »Les peintres, enlumineurs et imagiers parisiens«, *Bulletin de la Société française d'archéologie*, 1968, pp. 1–49, which includes material from all the rolls.

[15] C. Dehaisnes, *Documents et extraits divers concernant l'histoire de l'art dans la Flandre, l'Artois et le Hainaut avant le XVe siècle*, Lille, 1886; id., *L'Art à Douai dans la vie privée des bourgeois*, Paris, 1864; J. Lestocquoy, *Études d'histoire urbaine, villes et abbayes: Arras au moyen âge*, Arras, 1966.

Few of the secular MSS made around the middle of the thirteenth century in France contain illumination that is comparable either in quality of execution or in complexity of layout and design to that of the major Bibles of the period. Apart from the Moralised Bibles mentioned above, the most spectacular collection of illustrative bible material surviving from this period must surely be the Old Testament Picture Bible, New York, Pierpont Morgan Library MS 638. It contains a full-page sequence of illustrations starting with Genesis and ending with the end of the book of Kings.[16] The number of pictures per biblical episode, the emphasis on dramatic narrative, and the attention to detail make this sequence of Old Testament illustrations unique[17] while puzzles also remain as to the original patron, the provenance, and the date of the MS. There is certainly no secular epic or romance that contains so full a cycle of pictures depicting battles, cruelty or heroism, nor indeed does any secular illustration of the period rival the wealth of narrative detail that characterise the work of this illuminator. One is struck not only by the realistic brutality of the scenes of combat but also by the different types of arms and armour here represented, showing different varieties of helmet, kettle-hat and helm, mail coifs, plate greaves for Goliath (fig. 9), shield straps and sword belts. Particularly noticeable in the representations of armour are the padded gambesons and coudières (fig. 10), an in the battle equipment most striking are the elaborate mechanisms of war.[18] In a broad sense this wealth of detail must have been observed from life and may be seen as a reflection of the general move towards naturalism which found other manifestations in thir-

---

[16] Facsimile New York/London, 1969.

[17] Harvey Stahl is working on the iconography of this MS. As regards its elaborate sequence of full-page miniatures, the MS stands out not only among bible illustration but also in relation to secular illumination, where the full-page miniature as such is comparatively infrequent. Despite the fact that full-page pictures are the rule in much of the German secular illumination of the thirteenth century (e.g. *Eneit*, Berlin germ. fol. 282, *Tristan*, Munich cgm 19; *Parzival*, Munich cgm 51; and the *Karl der Große* cited above, S. Gall, Vadiana 302) the most common form for secular illumination in France is small miniatures, or, more occasionally, historiated initials, scattered in the text (see below). Comparatively few MSS contain even a few full-page miniatures in the thirteenth and turn of the fourteenth centuries. They are: B.N. fr. 1610 (see F. Saxl, »The Troy romance in French and Italian art«, *Lectures*, I, London, 1951, pp. 125–138, and H. Buchthal, *Historia Troiana*, London, 1971); B.N. fr. 12558 and 12559, *Cygne;* B.N. fr. 2186, *Poire;* Berlin Kupferstichkabinett 78.C.1, Brussels B.R. 11040 and London B.M. Harley 4979, *Alexander;* Paris B.N. fr. 1433, *Yvain;* and Paris, B.N. fr. 142, *Fauvel.*

[18] See especially facsimile plates 74 (fol. 10ᵛ), 150 (fol. 23ᵛ) and 215–6 (fol. 35ᵛ).

teenth-century France such as the sculpted foliage of the capitals and the interior west wall of the cathedral of Reims.[19] However, unlike the sculpture of Reims, for which one can find parallels at the Sainte-Chapelle[20] or at the cathedral of Southwell in England,[21] no parallels have so far been found for the treatment of arms, armour, and battle equipment in this MS.

It is largely on the basis of the use of similar details that a secular MS may now, I believe, be attributed to the same workshop as the Bible. It is the *Chevalier au cygne* MS Paris, Ars. 3139.[22] Superficially there is very little resemblance between the illustrations of this MS and the Bible. The *Cygne* MS (fig. 11) is in very poor condition and the miniatures are badly preserved; and then the scope of the illustration is modest by contrast with the Bible. Instead of a continuous sequence of full-page miniatures, the illustration is confined to a limited number of narrow rectangles the length of two text-columns, with coloured borders and wavy-lined motifs, quite different from the gold frames of the Bible and the architectural canopies that divide the scenes. Similarly the complex structure of the scenes in the Bible, the variety of action and movement, and the overwhelming abundance of detail, find hardly any reflection in the illuminations of the *Cygne* MS. Nevertheless some of the more unusual motifs found in the Bible do reappear in *Cygne*, in particular the padded gambesons and coudières. These are motifs that are so rare in the thirteenth century, not only in manuscript illumination but also in monumental painting and sculpture, that their appearance in the *Cygne* MS must indicate that the relation between it and the Bible is very close.[23] I suggest that these motifs were part of the stock repertoire of the workshop to which the Bible illuminator or illuminators belonged, and that they were motifs which could therefore be reproduced by minor illuminators of the same shop – in this case the

19 See W. Sauerländer, *Gothic Sculpture in France*, Munich, 1970.
20 See L. Grodecki, *La Sainte-Chapelle*, Paris, 1968.
21 See N. Pevsner, *The Leaves of Southwell*, London, 1949.
22 Written in 1268. H. Martin and P. Lauer, *Les principaux MSS à peintures de la Bibliothèque de l'Arsenal à Paris*, Paris, 1929, pl. X.
23 There were many opportunities for thirteenth-century illuminators to represent scenes of battle and combat to illustrate not only in bibles the books of Kings and Maccabees, but also in the many secular epics, romances, and historical texts like William of Tyre's crusading history (on which see the forthcoming study by Dr. J. Folda) where such scenes were required. Despite the large body of illustrated battle scenes that do exist I have found no other examples of the use of padded gambesons or coudières.

illuminator of the *Cygne* MS, who, I believe, was a lesser employee of the shop, set to work on a less important text than the Bible, and one whose illumination was correspondingly done on a much less lavish scale. That the artists were, however, closely related, may be seen not only in the details of battle dress but also more generally in elements like the treatment of hair, faces, and drapery, allowing of course for the fact that one illuminator is a supreme master of his craft while the other is endowed with considerably less talent. The relative value placed on each type of book and its illumination seems to me to find its reflection in the selection of the major artist to work on the Bible pictures and the minor one to work on the secular book, despite the intrinsic similarity of the illustrative materials required for both texts.[24] This scale of values changes towàrds the end of the thirteenth century.[25] Crucial to that change is the emerging personality of the illuminator whose imagination begins, in part at least, to assume an independence from liturgical models and also from the words of the text he illustrates.

---

[24] Through its association with the Arsenal *Cygne* MS of 1268, the Old Testament Picture Bible may now be related to a large group of MSS made in the 1260s in the area of Arras, Douai, Tournai, Cambrai, or Lille. See G. von Vitzthum, *Die Pariser Miniaturmalerei zur Zeit des heiligen Ludwigs,* Leipzig, 1907, pp. 117–124; E. J. Beer, »Das Scriptorium des Johannes Philomena und seine Illuminatoren«, *Scriptorium xxiii* (1969), pp. 24–38; H. Stahl, »Le Bestiaire de Douai«, *Revue de l'art* viii (1970), pp. 6–15; M. A. Stones, »Le Missel de Tournai«, *Trésors sacrés* exhibition catalogue, Tournai, 1971, pp. 51–3; R. Branner, »A cutting from a thirteenth-century French Bible«, *The Bulletin of the Cleveland Museum of Art* lviii (1971), pp. 219–227; E. J. Beer, »Liller Bibelcodices, Tournai und die Scriptorien der Stadt Arras«, *Aachener Kunstblätter,* 1973, pp. 190–226. Further unnoticed MSS that belong to this group are the *Chansonnier* London, B.M. Egerton 274; the Bible, New York Public Library MS 4; and the Pontifical of Cambrai in the Cathedral Library at Toledo. An article on these MSS is announced by the present author. The Toledo Pontifical provides the best comparison for the figure style of the Morgan Picture Bible. Other comparisons for the Bible style have been suggested by O. Pächt and J. J. G. Alexander in their *Illuminated Manuscripts in the Bodleian Library,* I, Oxford, 1966, as Douce 381 ff., 122–24 (cat. no. 536) and Douce 50, Psalter (cat. no. 535). They further connect the Bible, less convincingly in my view, with the *Poire* MS Paris, B.N. fr. 2186, and with the Missal of Saint Louis at San Francesco, Assisi. There is still a great deal of work to be done on the precise stylistic relations between the MSS of this large group. It is likely that we may be dealing not only with the work of numerous illuminators of varying quality but also with the work of itinerant illuminators who contributed to the output of different ateliers.

[25] The change, it must be admitted, is not altogether absolute. Of the secular MSS produced by Master Honoré and the shop to which he belonged, for instance, there are very few which can rival the best of the liturgical books the shop produced, like the David page of the Breviary of Philippe le Bel or the Death of the

From an important workshop dating from the last quarter of the thirteenth century and located in north-eastern France there survive few
liturgical books in relation to the secular output of the shop. The best-
known MS of this group is the *Lancelot* Bonn 526, whose Grail illustration was discussed above.[26] Its illumination takes the form of small
square miniatures set in one text column and this arrangement is followed by the other secular MSS made in the shop,[27] while the liturgical
books use historiated initials as is more usual for the bulk of liturgical
illumination in the thirteenth century. Two complete prose *Lancelots*
have survived from the group, Bonn 526 and Paris, B.N. fr. 110. Both
employ a special arrangement for the opening pages (fig. 12), with
two or more miniatures and a border supporting animals or figures.
The use of a border of this kind is uncommon before the end of the thirteenth century in secular MSS, while in liturgical books on the other
hand it was a method of illustration established since the 1260s and
continued in the liturgical MSS made in the workshop under discussion.[28] The illuminators of these *Lancelots* adapt an established pattern
from a liturgical context to a secular one.

Virgin page of the Nürnberg Breviary (Paris, B.N. lat. 1023, Breviary of Philippe
le Bel, and Nürnberg Solger 4°, 4, Breviary). One such, however, may have been
the opening miniature of the Brunetto Latini *Trésor*, Florence, Laurenziana MS
Ash. 122, before it was defaced. Traces of exceptionally good drapery modelling
can still be seen.

[26] R. S. and L. H. Loomis, *Arthurian Legends in Medieval Art*, New York, 1938,
pp. 94–6, figs. 217–223. This is one of the few MSS that contain the complete prose
Lancelot cycle in French. For a list of *Lancelot* MSS see B. Woledge, *Bibliographie
des romans et nouvelles en prose française*, Geneva, 1954.

[27] For a detailed study of the MSS of this group see M. A. Stones, »The Illustrations
of the French prose Lancelot in Belgium, Flanders, and Paris, 1250–1340«, unpublished diss., University of London, 1970, pp. 208–224 and 451–461. The related
MSS are, in order of stylistic similarity: London, Sion College Arc. L. 40 2/L 28,
Bestiary; Boulogne-sur-Mer 192, *Cycle de Guillaume d'Orange;* Paris, B.N. fr. 110,
prose *Lancelot;* London, B.M. Add. 5474, *Tristan;* S. Omer 5, Bible; Douai 193,
Psalter; Arras Musée Diocésain 47, Psalter-Hours; Oxford Bod. Douce 24, Psalter;
New York, Morgan 79, Psalter; Cambrai 153–4, Missals; Paris B.N. fr. 19162 and
fr. 24394, *Lancelot;* Paris Sainte-Geneviève 2200, *Bestiary;* London B.M. Yates
Thompson 43, Psalter. Dated MSS are: Y.T. 43, 1277; Bonn 526, 1286; Bou-
logne 192, 1295.

[28] See in particular the MSS mentioned above, note 24, especially, within that group,
Cambrai 189–90 and the Toledo Cathedral Pontifical. There is also one marginal
illumination without a border in Ars. 3139; cf. also the Psalter of Isabella, Cambridge, Fitzwilliam 300, facsimile ed. S. C. Cockerell, 1905, and E. J. Beer, »Zum
Problem der Biblia Porta«, *Festschrift für Hans R. Hahnloser*, Basel, 1961,
pp. 271–86.

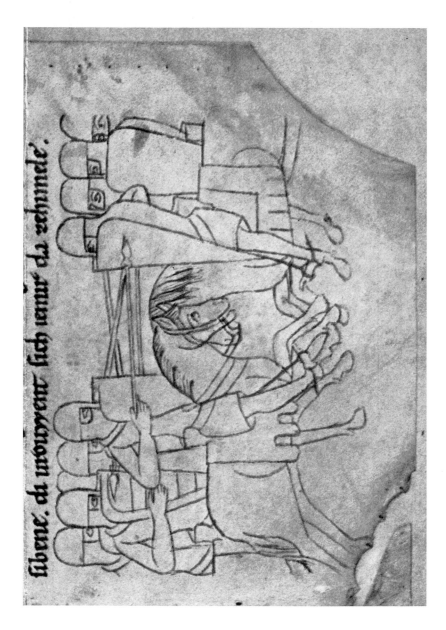

Fig. 1: Heidelberg, cod. pal. germ. 112, fol. 63, *Ruolantesliet*, combat between pagans and christians (Photo after facsimile)

Svr reine vnd also lobelich·   vil michel lob vñ ere bi
warr solancec ende·   Nv horet wa von daz quam
d o got von siner heude   daz man die warheit vnam
den hemrelnich selbe nennen hiez·   waz si sprachen vnd taten
vnt in vor rode wizzen liez   swaz si begangen haten
daz er gote war ein lieber knecht·   dazu mohtens selbe niht gesagen·
der ist ovch billich vnd recht·   si wrden allesamt erslagen·

Fig. 2: St. Gall, Vadiana 302, fol. 52ᵛ, Der Stricker's *Karl der Große,* death of Roland
(Photo after Lejeune and Stiennon)

Fig. 3: Chartres Cathedral, Roland window, death of Roland (Photo after Lejeune and Stiennon)

Fig. 4: Paris, B.N. fr. 342, fol. 77, prose *Lancelot*, *Queste*, Lancelot asleep as the Grail appears (Photo Bibliothèque Nationale)

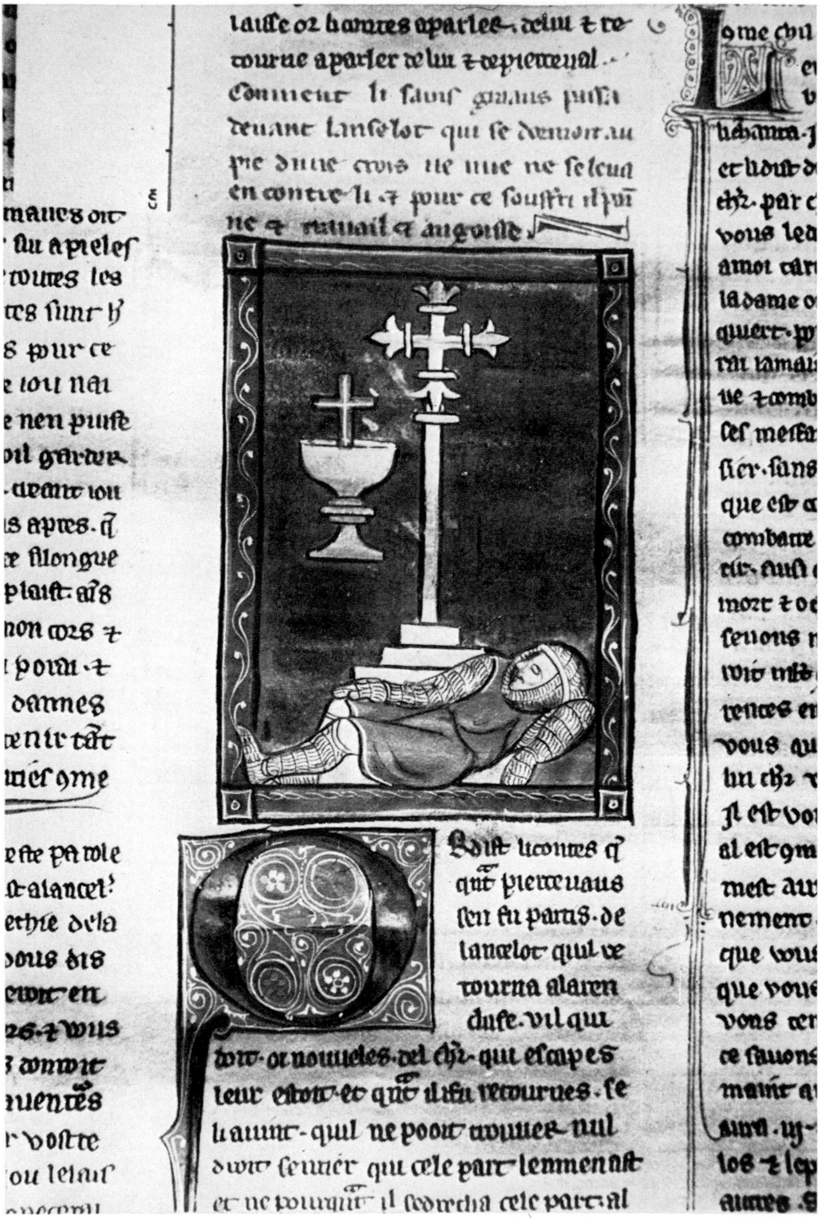

Fig. 5: Bonn, 526, fol. 426, prose *Lancelot*, *Queste*, Lancelot asleep as the Grail appears (Photo Alison Stones)

Fig. 6: Manchester, Rylands French 1, fol. 195ᵛ, *Lancelot, Queste,* Lancelot asleep as the Grail appears (Photo Rylands Library)

Fig. 7: Paris, Ars. 5218, fol. 88, *Lancelot, Queste,* the Grail liturgy (Photo Bibliothèque Nationale)

Fig. 8: Oxford, Bodleian, Bod. 270b, fol. 50, Moralised Bible (Photo after Laborde)

Fig. 9: New York, Morgan 638, fol. 28ᵛ, Old Testament Picture Bible, David and Goliath (Photo after facsimile)

Fig. 10: New York, Morgan 638, fol. 43ᵛ, Old Testament Picture Bible, The Rescue of Lot (Photo after facsimile)

Fig. 11: Paris, Ars. 3139, fol. 109, *Cygne*, siege of Nicea (Photo Alison Stones)

Fig. 12: Bonn, 526, fol. 1, *Lancelot, Estoire*, scenes from the life of Joseph of Arimathea (Photo Alison Stones)

le sirecourne aprsler del roi nantre de
garlot. Et nouf content licontes q
ment tinstmessages li uint dire que
li saisne li ardoient et destruioient tou
te sa terre.

Q dist li contes que qui
liroue nantes uit quil a
uoit perdu son fil galescin.
sienfu mlt dolaus et mlt
courreces. Et dist degrosses proles a lase
me et lenblasme mlt durement et en
fu tant courreces quil neprrla ati de
bien ne demal si fu passes .i. mois en
tiers. Lors auint .i. roesdi au son en
autril cinis messages li uint duo et con
ter la grant destrution ou liroit agui
cant auoit esbe. et comment li saisne

Fig. 13: Bonn, 526, fol. 97ᵛ, *Lancelot, Estoire*, battle between the king of Nantes and the Saxons (Photo Alison Stones)

Fig. 14: Boulogne, 192, fol. 272, *Cycle de Guillaume d'Orange*, combat between Guillaume and pagan (Photo Alison Stones)

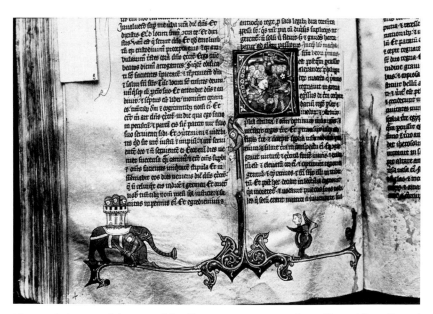

Fig. 15: S. Omer, 5, fol. 145ᵛ, Bible, illustrations to I Maccabees (Photo Alison Stones)

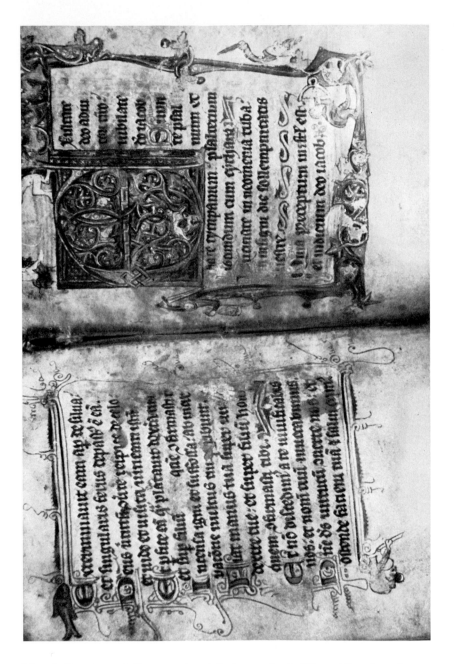

Fig. 16: Douai, 193, folios unnumbered, Psalter, psalm 80 (Photo Alison Stones)

Fig. 17: S. Omer, 5, fol. 62, Bible, illustrations to Jeremiah (Photo Alison Stones)

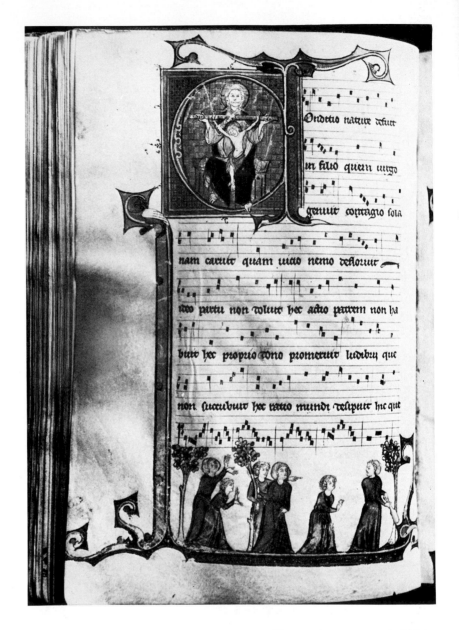

Fig. 18: Montpellier, Fac. Méd. H 196, fol. 87ᵛ, *Chansonnier*, poem to the Trinity
(Photo Alison Stones)

Fig. 19: Montpellier, Fac. Méd. H 196, fol. 88, *Chansonnier*, poem to the Trinity
(Photo Alison Stones)

Fig. 20: Verdun, 107, fol. 1, Breviary of Renaud de Bar, Psalm 1 (Photo Alison Stones)

Further similarities, this time of motif, between the various MSS of this group bear witness to cross-fertilisation between the secular and the liturgical. In all these MSS the battle scenes are generalised, so that the same moduli or patterns can be and are used for different episodes and between different protagonists. In the case of the secular MSS, captions explain to the reader who the protagonists are. In figs. 13–15, not only are the mail convention and helmets similarly treated, but the same motif of a falling horse appears in each. Of particular interest in the Bible Saint-Omer MS 5 is a detail of the initial terminal which shows a knight holding a severed head. In this case the detail is related in a general way to the context of the historiated initial, which illustrates the book of Maccabees, but it is also a stock motif of this workshop and reappears in the Psalter Douai 193 (fig. 16). In a context like this one, the motif of a knight and severed head may originally have been invented as an allusion to David and Goliath, but, while such a theme is in general relevant to psalm illustration it does not reflect the content of this particular psalm, whose visual accompaniment is usually David playing bells.[29] Furthermore, the severed head, in this instance, is female and so could not possibly refer to Goliath. Perhaps this motif was originally made up for a David and Goliath context, but once part of the repertoire of a shop could be taken out of a pattern book, adapted, and used in a context in which it had no connection with the text.[30] What is still unknown about the process of using model books is who decided what motif was relevant to what context. It becomes evident in the last decade of the thirteenth and the early fourteenth centuries that clear-cut distinctions of relevance and irrelevance or secular and liturgical, sacred and profane, become blurred. Some of the border scenes in S. Omer 5 are based on the text; such a case is the killing of an elephant on the Maccabees page, whose source is an incident in the battle of Bethzechariah, in which Eleazar crawls under the elephant and kills it with his sword, whereupon he himself is crushed as the

---

[29] See the tables in G. Haseloff, *Die Psalterillustration im 13. Jahrhundert*, Kiel, 1938. That the actual words of the psalms were frequently taken up by illuminators has been demonstrated by F. P. Pickering, *Art and Literature in the Middle Ages*, London, 1970, pp. 273–85. I do not think, however, that this was the method employed in the instance under discussion.

[30] R. Scheller, *A Survey of Medieval Model-Books*, Haarlem, 1963, provides the best overview. See also D. J. A. Ross, »A late twelfth-century artist's pattern sheet«, *Journal of Warburg and Courtauld Institutes* xxv (1962), pp. 119–28. No pattern-sheets or books relating to the material under discussion have survived.

animal falls on him (fig. 15) (I Maccabees 6,45–47). Other marginal
motifs, however, are used without relation to the text. In S. Omer 5 is
a figure of a man throwing a stone. This motif, like the knight and
severed head, is one of many patterns that appear several times within
the products of this shop, each time used in a different, and equally
irrelevant, context. The stone-throwing man is also found on the border
of the *Lancelot* B.N. fr. 110, where it has nothing to do with the text;
in the Bible it appears in the border of the Jeremiah page. This particular motif, again like the knight with the severed head, may have been
invented to fit a particular context – in this case no doubt a scene of the
martyrdom of Saint Stephen.[31] (fig. 17)

The use of motifs derived from biblical (David) or sacred (St. Stephen)
sources in secular border decoration parallels the use of comparable
motifs in the main miniatures or historiated initials in both types of
book. What is more interesting, however, is the fact that, while the
Bible of this group includes other irrelevant material, and contains a
highly decorated border on every illuminated page, the secular MSS
rarely employ borders at all, and such borders as do appear are very
sparsely decorated.[32] It might seem that the use of motifs out of context
might be more admissible in a secular book, and yet, in the last decade

---

31 However, it is interesting to note in this context that a scene of martyrdom by
   stoning is used for the historiated initial to the book of Jeremiah in a group of
   Franco/Flemish 13th century bibles: MSS B.N. lat. 16719–22; Basel, Öffentliche
   Kunstsammlung U. IX.30; Lille 835–8; New York, Kraus Collection, Marquette
   Bible; Arras 1–3; Brussels, B.R. II.2523. See E. J. Beer, »Liller Bibelcodices, Tournai und die Scriptorien der Stadt Arras«, *Aachener Kunstblätter*, 1973, pp. 190–226.
   To Beer's list one may add MSS Boulogne 4 and London, B.M. Yates Thompson 22.
   A convenient list of other motifs is found in L. Randall, *Images in the Margins
   of Gothic Manuscripts*, Berkeley/Los Angeles, 1966. Another example in S. Omer 5
   that is probably based on a scene of martyrdom again used out of context is the
   marginal illustration to the Epistle of James (fol. 267) which shows a mitred figure
   being thrown from the roof of a church by a knight. This does not refer to the
   martyrdom of James, who was martyred by the sword, but is probably based on
   an illustration to the martyrdom of Saint Clement. A comparable example, though
   not from the same workshop, is in the *Martyrology* Valenciennes 838, fol. 124.

32 There is an added dimension in the border illustration to S. Omer 5; while much
   of it, as we have seen, is derived from non-biblical sources and seems irrelevant
   to the text on the page, there are also many cases where the border illustration
   of an Old Testament book contains an illustration from a New Testament scene,
   thus illustrating medieval ideas on the typological relationship between the Old
   and New Testaments. This arrangement is, however, most unusual. For yet another
   type of border illustration, but one that does not apply to the present material,
   see L. Randall, »Exempla as a source of gothic marginal illumination«, *Art Bulletin*
   57 (1957), pp. 97–107.

of the thirteenth century, it is in liturgical books that the illuminators' imagination is given freer rein.

Ten years or so later there is more of a balance between the mingling of the sacred and the profane in secular and liturgical, or at least sacred, illumination. The well-known Montpellier *Chansonnier* MS Fac. Méd. H. 196 provides ample illustration of this.[33] The MS includes poems that are both sacred and profane in content; and while the historiated initials of each reflect the content of the poem they illustrate, the illuminators matched secular themes in the border with sacred themes in the historiated initial and the poem (figs. 18 and 19). At the same time a parallel development is witnessed in the outstanding liturgical books of the period like the Verdun Breviary[34] (fig. 20) in which the borders contain scenes that are essentially secular in nature.

The interpretation of this mingling of levels in late thirteenth-century French illumination is not easy. Even when we know who the patrons of illuminated MSS were, as in the case of the Verdun Breviary, we lack evidence to show the extent to which a patron might dictate in detail the designs and motifs used to decorate his book. Similarly, our knowledge of workshop structure and administration is insufficient to show whether an illuminated page is the result of careful planning by the

---

[33] Facsimile ed. Y. Rockseth, Paris, 1935–9. Only one of the illuminators who worked on this MS uses the borders to present scenes. Few stylistic parallels have been suggested for his work. Closely related to this hand are the first two illuminated pages of the Bible Paris, Mazarine 34, made for Anthony Bec, bishop of Durham under Edward I (identification of Bec's coat of arms by Dr. Adelaide Bennett). Although the illumination of this as yet unpublished MS is English, I do not think it is necessary to assume that this hand of the *Chansonnier* was also English. Another MS related by less direct stylistic connection to the *Chansonnier* is a bible in the University Library at Santa Barbara; see L. Ayres, »The Miniatures of the Santa Barbara Bible: A Preliminary Report«, *Soundings* III (1971), pp. 5–21.

[34] Verdun 107 and London, B.M. Yates Thompson 8. The workshop of the Bar Breviary has not yet received the detailed study deserved by its exceptional quality. There are two main styles, both of which appear in Verdun 107, where the work of both is incomplete. Related to the second hand of Verdun 107 are Y.T. 8; the Metz Pontifical, Cambridge, Fitzwilliam 298 (also incomplete), facsimile ed. E. S. Dewick, Roxburgh Club, 1902; *Grandes Chroniques de France*, Paris, Sainte-Geneviève 782; and a Book of Hours, Paris, Arsenal 288, to which my attention was kindly drawn by M. F. Avril. There is nothing that is of comparable quality to the first hand of Verdun 107 and in the same style; hitherto unnoticed lesser MSS by an inferior hand of the same workshop are a Book of Hours, Paris, B.N. lat. 1361, and fragments of a *Legenda Aurea*, London, Victoria and Albert Museum, MS 706–16. I believe that the well-known *Tournoi de Chauvency* MS, Oxford, Bodleian Library, Douce 308, text ed. M. Delbouille, Liège/Paris, 1931, was also a product of this *atelier*.

head of the shop or whether the whim of an individual may not also have played a part in it. Liturgical and secular traditions were never very far apart as far as their artistic expression is concerned; the adaptation of the liturgical to suit the secular is something that characterises twelfth and thirteenth-century literary as well as artistic works. While there are undoubtedly changes in the relative value placed upon secular as against liturgical books during the course of the thirteenth century, which result in the equalising of the aesthetic merit of both, what emerges most strikingly is the detachment of motif from context, whether it be sacred or profane, that characterises the last decade of the thirteenth century. Perhaps what we are really witnessing here is, after all, the emergence of the independent artistic personality which is free to choose motifs at will – art for art's sake, rather than art subordinated either to the sacred or to the secular?

David Crawford

Secular Songs in Mid-Fifteenth Century Continental Masses

One of the most significant developments in fifteenth century music was the increasing use of polyphony for the Mass Ordinary, those major items of the Mass which remain constant whenever a Mass is celebrated. By the middle of the century, composers frequently provided cycles of polyphony for those texts, and the cyclic Mass stands as the longest sustained effort in written composition until the invention of opera around 1600. There was one other category of performance where time was such an imposing enemy: the musical performance of epic poetry. But historical methodology for studying the role of music there breaks down quickly, for whatever the performers did seems to have been rooted in an oral tradition. Their melodies were only rarely preserved in notation and those few examples of music for the *chanson de geste* which we do know are simple and brief melodic formulas, merely a basis for musical elaboration. Of all the medieval music theorists, only one, Grocheo, mentions *cantus gestualis*. But he merely confirms that such things existed; his discussion is far too vague to enable us to reconstruct an actual performance. So, even though the epic musician-poet and the Mass composer share the problem of a large-scale performance, they worked within different creative traditions. Furthermore, the poet can call upon his literary inventiveness, an element not available to the Mass composer. The poet-musician gives a performance, story-oriented, accompanied by his own music which was to some extent spontaneously conceived. But Masses are completed compositions, awaiting performers to realize the composer's instructions. The problem for the Mass composer is that he must rely upon his musical skill to provide aesthetic interest and stimulation for a long period of time, and yet observe some structure so the listener is not plunged into an irrational chaos.

A common solution was to quote a Gregorian chant, repeating the same chant in the tenor during each section of the Mass. In these tenor Masses, the selected chant was normally not part of the Ordinary; it was taken from a Proper for some specific feast. The resulting Mass was often named after the borrowed chant, such as *Missa Alma Redemptoris Mater,* and musical content, as well as the title, makes the Mass more appropriate for some feasts than for others. But sometimes secular tunes, rather than Gregorian chant, were quoted in those tenors. This secular current was established near the beginning of the epoch of the tenor Mass and it flourished for about 100 years. Since music composition and performances of epic poetry were not reconcilable traditions,[1] the surviving examples of secular tenors employ the shorter lyrical forms.

As the decades passed, the popularity of secular materials in the Mass increased. Josquin des Prez, for example, has left us 20 complete Masses, only six of those possessing identified liturgical origins. The secular practice was so widespread at the time of Josquin that one of his contemporaries, Erasmus of Rotterdam, wrote the following attack:

> We have brought into the sacred edifices a certain elaborate and theatrical music, a confused interplay of diverse sounds, such as I do not believe was ever heard in Greek or Roman theatres. ... Amorous and shameful songs are heard, the kind to which harlots and mimes dance. People flock to church as to a theatre for aural delight. ... I ask you to consider how many paupers, dying in want, could be supported on the salaries of singers.[2]

A few others shared Erasmus' views, but obviously these were not the attitudes of practicing musicians or their patrons. The borrowing of secular melodies did diminish during the Counter Reformation. An illustrative composer here would be Palestrina, who composed over 100 Masses during the second half of the sixteenth century. Only eight of those bear secular titles.

To be sure, this secularization within ritual at the end of the Middle Ages has caught the attention of modern scholars.[3] Our explanations

---

1 About seventy compositions by sixteenth-century Spanish composers seem, at first glance, to be exceptions, since they are settings of romance texts. But these, too, are short works and they quote only one or several stanzas of poetry, thereby confirming composers' unwillingness to notate a genuine epic performance.

2 Quoted in Clement Miller, »Erasmus on Music«, *The Musical Quarterly,* 52 (1966), 339.

3 See, for example, Donald Grout, *A History of Western Music,* 2nd edition (New York, 1972), pp. 198–199; Paul Henry Lang, *Music in Western Civilization* (New

have been that it illustrates a breakdown of liturgical propriety, a triumph of art-for-art's sake, or a composer's mischievous prank upon non-musicians. Some conventional views about humanism and its secular attitudes do invite such interpretations. However, certain recent Renaissance studies emphasize the fervent sense of piety which often accompanied humanism. For example, in the Foreword to his book on humanistic philosophies, Charles Trinkaus offers this sentence:

> Instead of viewing the secular, non-religious or even anti-religious aspects of the Renaissance period as typical and central to the culture, these are seen as incorporated into a new religious vision of *Homo triumphans* that found its inspiration in the patristic Christian tradition brilliantly combined with the non-rational aspects of the ancient rhetorical tradition and its ethics.[4]

Such attitudes should encourage us to reconsider the use of secular tunes in the Mass, and my contention is that they can be justified within a serious and influential theological framework.

In the first place, there was nothing secretive about the quotation of the secular tunes. The tune usually gave the Mass its title, and in many cases those titles appeared in the manuscripts of the period. Often the secular text incipit was copied under the tenor voice, raising some possibility of singing that text along with the Mass text in the other voices. Clerics, aristocrats, and courtiers held knowledge of music to be a point of honor; the use of well-known secular songs in the Mass could not have escaped their attention. Furthermore, the composers during this 100-year span were, almost without exception, trained in ecclesiastically supervised choir schools; there is no reason to think that their sincerity lagged when they continued to participate in church music as adults. Music theorists, as well as manuscript makers, put the »secular« and the sacred Masses side-by-side and treated them with equal respect without any special comment.

First let us review several illustrations of secular tenors used in cyclic Masses. One case is an anonymous *Missa Esclave*, composed about 1440, and found in a manuscript at Trent, Italy.[5] Its tenor proves to be the tenor of a rondeau by Binchois; the full text is available in other manuscripts and it reads as follows:

York, 1941), pp. 186–189; Edgar Sparks, *Cantus Firmus in Mass and Motet* (Berkeley and Los Angeles, 1963), pp. 96–98; Peter Wagner, *Geschichte der Messe, I. Teil; Bis 1600* (Leipzig, 1913), pp. 59–65.
4 Charles Trinkaus, *In Our Image and Likeness,* I (Chicago, 1970), pp. xx–xxi.
5 Trent, Castello del Buon Consiglio, MS 88, ff. 388'-399.

Esclave puist yl devenir / En une galée sur mer, / Qui monstera samblant
d'amer / S'il ne le veult par maintenir. / Che seroit pour amans trahir /
Qui de tels tours vouldroit user. / Esclave puist ... / Or mette chascun son
plaisir / A servir une sans amer / Et cellui d'honneur desarmer / Qui ne
veut che chemin tenir / Esclave puist ...[6]

All movements of the Mass cycle quote this same tenor, the normal
Mass texts being supplied for the other voices. But in the manuscript
a Latin motet follows the Agnus Dei, and it is based upon the same
French tenor. Recently published research by Robert Snow has shown
that the motet forms part of the Mass and that this is one of six known
Mass-motet cycles.[7] The text of the motet is a Responsory for Matins
for the feast of Assumption, so this cycle was probably meant to be performed at the Assumption of the Blessed Virgin Mary and throughout
its octave.

With this in mind we can return to Binchois' rondeau and read into it
an appropriate meaning. The worshipper who engages in transient love
deserves servitude; satisfaction should be achieved by serving one lady.
When contemplated at Mass on the feast of Assumption, this text identifies Mary as the recipient of ideal devotion, and the threat of punishment for the faithless evokes the Day of Judgment. Binchois' rondeau
is no longer a trifle in the long tradition of French love lyrics; it becomes
a call to serve Mary eternally, thus taking on a new meaning which
enhances the spiritual value of the Mass. This example demonstrates
the necessity for remaining sensitive to a central feature about quotation – material quoted may assume a far different meaning in its new
context. The rondeau, at one time a stylized divertissement for a Burgundian court, becomes quite a different thing when contemplated as
part of the feast of Assumption. Now it becomes clear why this Mass-
motet cycle offers an appropriate starting point for our study; it was
the motet which held the clue to interpreting the secular tenor. Unfortunately, only three other Masses based upon secular tenors are
known to have motets appended to them in this manner.

---

6 May he become a slave In a galley on the sea, Who makes a show of loving If he
   does it not for keeps. Anyone who used such tricks Would do that to betray lovers.
   May he become. ... Now let each one his pleasure find In serving one lady
   without love And in the way of disarming honor, He who does not wish to go
   this road, May he become. ...
7 Robert J. Snow, »The Mass-Motet Cycle; A Mid-Fifteenth-Century Experiment«,
   Essays in Musicology in Honor of Dragan Plamenac on his 70th Birthday (Pittsburgh, 1969), pp. 301–320.

Another Mass-motet cycle, *Missa Soyez aprantiz* by W. de Rouge, is based upon Walter Frye's English ballade *So ys emprentid*.[8] One continental manuscript source of the ballade gives the French incipit used by Rouge and that source also includes other French expressions in the text. The English version, although incomplete in our sources, was probably the authentic one. It reads as follows:

> So ys emprentid in my remembrace / Your womanhede your yowght ... / Your goodly port, your frenly continance, / Your prysid byaulte with your ... / That that lorde alle wot tak y to witnesse / That walky, slepey, or wat thing y do, / In wele, in wo, in joye ore heuenesse, / Myn hert ys with yow, go wey that ye go.

The text of the appended motet, *Stella coeli extirpavit,* is a prayer to Mary *tempore pestilentiae*.[9] Since Frye's ballade pledges allegiance to a lady regardless of good or ill fortune, it can be sung appropriately as part of a Marian Mass in time of plague.

The third Mass-motet cycle is a *Missa Hilf und gib rat* ascribed to Philipus, with a Marian motet as its conclusion.[10] Snow discovered that the text and music of the first phrase of the tenor also appear as the tenor's fourth phrase of a quodlibet in the *Glogauer Liederbuch*.[11] But the complete *Lied* has not been located. Although this Mass-motet cycle does illustrate a mixture of vernacular and Latin materials, no case can be made for the symbolic intermingling of secular and sacred elements; the full text of the original *Lied* may have been sacred.

The final Mass-motet cycle is an anonymous *Missa O rosa bella*.[12] Its secular tenor is borrowed from John Dunstable's setting of a well-known ballata text, presumably by Leonardo Giustiniani, which reads as follows:

> O rosa bella, o dolce anima mia / Non mi lassar morire in cortesia. / Ay lasso mi dolente, dezo finire / Per ben servire e lialment amare. / O dio

---

8 The Mass appears in Trent, Castello del Buon Consiglio, MS 90, ff. 310'–318, and the motet on the same tenor in Trent 88, ff. 11'–13. Frye's ballade is edited by Sylvia Kenney in *Walter Frye, Collected Works, Corpus Mensurabilis Musicae 19* (1960), 5–6.

9 Clemens Blume, *Analecta Hymnica Medii Aevi,* XXXI (Leipzig, 1898), 210.

10 This cycle is preserved in Prague, Památník Národního Písemnictvi, MS D.G. IV.47 (Strahov), ff. 105'–114.

11 Snow, p. 306. The quodlibet is published in Heribert Ringemann, ed., *Das Glogauer Liederbuch,* I, *Das Erbe Deutscher Musik,* Band 4 (Kassel, 1954), 40–41.

12 Preserved in Strahov, ff. 152–161; Modena, Biblioteca Estense, MS 456, No. 9; and Trent, Castello del Buon Consiglio, MS 89, ff. 330'–339.

d'amor, che pena è questa amare. / Vedi ch'io moro tutt' ora per questa giudea / Soccorremi ormai del mio languire. / Cor del corpo mio, non mi lassar morire.[13]

The motet associated with this text is no help in this case, for its liturgical role, if any, remains unidentified. But the Mass also possesses another important feature: the Kyrie contains the *Rex virginum* trope, a traditional trope for Marian feasts.[14] The presence of this trope establishes the Marian nature of the Mass, and the O *rosa bella* tenor points strongly to the same interpretation, for the rose was commonly associated with the Virgin Mary. The festal implication of the motet's text is vague, not contradicting this conclusion. Two other anonymous Masses based upon O *rosa bella* also survive,[15] and they, too, can be designated Marian Masses.

By now we have exhausted the repertory of applicable Mass-motet cycles and we have seen some illustrations of interpreting the secular tenors. A few precedents for related secular procedures in continental Masses do exist, one being the earliest of the complete Mass Ordinaries, the anonymous Tournai Mass[16] of about 1330. At the very end, on the words *Ite, missa est,* the composer has written a conventional medieval motet. The tenor part quotes a traditional chant for that text, the voice above it sings a moralizing Latin poem, and simultaneously the highest voice sings a French love poem. The Latin advises the mighty to love their fellow countrymen while the French text advises the disappointed lover to accept a wise renunciation. These texts seem not to identify a particular feast, but they do complement each other rather nicely. The Latin text is for those of good fortune and the vernacular love song, although purely secular, comforts the humble or distressed. Compositions constructed like this one were popular in France throughout the

---

13 O beautiful rose, O my sweet soul, Do not let me die in courtliness. Ah, woe is me, must I end Sorrowing for having served well and loyally loved? O god of love, how anguishing is this love. See that I die repeatedly for your decision. Help me now in my languishing. Heart of my body, do not let me die.
   Concerning the original form of the text, see John Dunstable, *Complete Works,* ed. Manfred Bukofzer, *Musica Brittanica,* 8 (London, 1953), 186, and Gustave Reese, *Music in the Renaissance* (New York, 1954), p. 30. The remarkable popularity of O *rosa bella* among musicians is documented in Victor Lederer, *Über Heimat und Ursprung der mehrstimmigen Tonkunst* (Leipzig, 1906), 219–222.
14 Blume, XLVII (Leipzig, 1905), 205.
15 Trent 88, ff. 363'–372, and Trent 90, ff. 420'–430.
16 *Missa Tornacensis,* ed. Charles Van den Borren, *Corpus Mensurabilis Musicae 13* (1957).

fourteenth century and they show that an integration of sacred and secular elements was common. But the tenors of those other motets derive from portions of the liturgy outside the Mass Ordinary. Since no other illustrations have survived for passages within Mass Ordinaries, this promising beginning for the polyphonic Mass with secular elements reaches a dead end.

The scene is quite different in Italy. Around the middle of the fourteenth century Italian composers had developed a flourishing school, one of special interest because its style was largely independent of French traditions and Gregorian chant. These composers concentrated almost exclusively upon settings of contemporary Italian poetry, but some polyphony for the Mass Ordinary has survived, occasionally showing interesting relationships to secular repertories. In a few cases, the texts of secular pieces were simply replaced by texts for the Mass. This was an expedient way to acquire Mass music when the majority of available pieces was secular, and it shows that nothing inhibited these musicians from using purely secular compositions in the Mass.[17] Of special interest is an extraordinary Sanctus, copied around 1400, in a manuscript perhaps of Florentine origin.[18] This anonymous composition quotes the Sanctus text in its tenor, but the upper two parts sing an Italian trope, beginning, *Cantano gli angioletti Sanctus*. The trope is a sacred text, but it illustrates the use of vernacular and a secular influence is beyond question, because it falls into the lyric form of the contemporaneous madrigal. Even though few settings of Mass Ordinaries survive in Italian repertories, secular elements are present in the *contrafacta* and in the form of this vernacular trope. Musicians reflecting French or Italian traditions seem to account for the only continental Mass composers until around 1450.

England sported a thriving group of composers in the early fifteenth century, a school which participated vividly in composing Mass Ordinaries. Many works by these musicians are preserved in continental manuscripts and there is no question of their deep influence upon continental musicians. Complete Mass cycles based upon recurring tenors

---

[17] The practice is described, with bibliographical details, in Kurt von Fischer, »Kontrafakturen und Parodien italienischer Werke des Trecento und frühen Quattrocento«, *Annales Musicologiques*, I (1957), 43–59.

[18] London, British Museum, Additional MS 29987, ff. 36'–38. See Gilbert Reaney, *The Manuscript London, British Museum, Additional 29987, A Facsimile Edition with an Introduction*, in *Musicological Studies and Documents 13* (1965).

seem to have been their invention, with works attributed to John Dunstable and Leonel Power apparently predating any by continental composers. However, English repertories copied in England contain no identified secular materials. Continental composers such as Dufay were quick to seize upon the tenor Mass concept and, within about a decade after its invention, the continental musicians were openly quoting widespread secular tunes in place of the chant. Even though they drew heavily upon English practices, the continental composers seem to have been responsible for the earliest uses of secular tunes in the Mass. Bedingham's *Missa Dueil angouisseux*[19] is nearly an exception. But this work is preserved only in continental sources and it borrows from a chanson by Binchois. Even though the Mass composer is English, the secular material can be explained as a reflection of continental, not English, practices. The view, based upon Masses bearing attributions, that English composers generally eschewed secular tenors is further confirmed by anonymous English Masses in continental manuscripts. Charles Hamm's catalogue of those works which agree with the known traits of English composers contains 49 Mass movements, 5 Mass pairs, and 15 Mass cycles. Although tenor Mass construction obtains in many of those works, none of the tenors can be identified as secular.[20]

We have traced the several secular elements in Masses up to the early fifteenth century and we have seen that the secular tenor Mass was flourishing by about 1450. A manuscript at Bologna, copied around 1430, enters into consideration at this point.[21] BL is a major manuscript containing music by internationally esteemed composers who invoked French, Italian, and English practices. The first 17 gatherings contain 140 Mass sections; this in itself signals an essential landmark, showing that polyphony for the Mass Ordinary is now more popular than ever before on the continent. The Mass repertory observes a general plan, falling into layers as follows: Layer I, Composite Masses; Layer II, Gloria-Credo pairs; Layer III, two interpolated signatures of Masses; Layer IV, Composite Masses and Liturgical Fragments.

---

[19] Trent 88, ff. 26'–30', and Trent 90, ff. 386'–395.

[20] Charles Hamm, »A Catalogue of Anonymous English Music in Fifteenth-Century Continental Manuscripts«, *Musica Disciplina*, XXII (1968), 47–76. It should be remembered, though, that his appendix of »works with some strong English characteristics, but other features atypical of English music« does include two Masses based upon French tenors.

[21] Bologna, Civico Museo Bibliografico Musicale, MS Q 15 (*olim* MS 37). Hereafter referred to by its traditional *siglum*, BL.

Frequently the scribe also grouped together works by composer or nationality and often he juxtaposed two different Mass movements which the composer had conceived as one interrelated Mass pair. The secular traits noted in earlier continental Masses also survive here: a Mass pair by Dufay (ff. 33'–38) contains vernacular tropes, and the scribe grouped together four Mass movements which are *contrafacta* of vernacular models (ff. 66'–76), titling them according to their models.

Of special interest in this manuscript is the fact that the scribe interspersed eleven French songs throughout Layer I. In five cases it is reasonably certain that the French song has no musical relationship to the surrounding Mass movements. In the other six cases some relationships do exist (most notably, corresponding clefs and mensurations), but they are tenuous ones, perhaps coincidental. The strongest existing relationships appear on ff. 41'–44, where we find three works attributed to Ar. de Lantins: a Gloria, a Credo, and then a rondeau, *Chanter ne sçay ce poise moy*. All three compositions are cast in the same modality, clefs, and conflicting signature. Although the rondeau seems not to share actual melodies with the Mass pair, the scribe may have been observing the composer's intentions when he grouped the three works together. But this remains only a possibility, and most of the French songs in this layer require a simpler solution. All of the songs are brief and, in nine of the eleven instances, they simply fill empty space on an opening after the end of a Mass section. The scribe may have merely decided to fill up the empty space with an available short piece. But even if the composers had little or nothing to do with this juxtaposition of Mass and secular music, the importance of the act still remains. First of all, the scribe saw nothing inappropriate about combining Masses and secular pieces. Secondly, a reader or user of this manuscript observes a Mass text and then his eye falls upon a secular one. It is easy, almost inevitable, to concoct some conceptual explanation for such a series of thoughts. Even if the scribe had no plan in mind, the user of the book is likely to perceive one.

In the decades following 1450 some composers of other nationalities gradually adopted secular tenors. Those early works are rare, however, and the few surviving examples resist solutions. One such composition is an anonymous *Missa Grüne linden*, based upon a *Lied* which seems to have enjoyed several centuries of popularity. But the tenor has come down to us with a variety of texts, and it cannot be established that the

Mass composer had a secular poem in mind.[22] Another German tenor is quoted in an anonymous *Missa Sig säld und heil*,[23] but a full text for this tenor has not been located. At least one Spanish musician, Johannes Cornago, composed a Mass on a vernacular tenor, *Ayo iusto*, and it bears the colorful title *La Missa de la mapa mundi apud Neapolim et la nostra donna Sancta Maria*. But even the language of the tenor's text has not been established with certainty, much less whether it is sacred or secular.[24] Quite possibly some anonymous Masses on French and Italian tenors are, in fact, composed by German or Spanish musicians, but this problem lies outside the scope of the present study.

Let us return from these exceptional problems to the mainstream of Mass composers, where we can identify the trends observed by the later musicians of the High Renaissance. The leading composer of the Burgundian School, a man who held prestigious positions in Italy and the Lowlands, and who mastered all the musical genres of his era, was Guillaume Dufay. He, too, composed tenor Masses and his first effort in this category was probably one based upon a secular tenor.[25] It was his *Missa Se la face*, with a tenor borrowed from a popular ballade which he had composed. The ballade was so popular that only four other compositions by Dufay appear more frequently in manuscripts of the period. The song was composed between 1433 and about 1455 and its text reads as follows:

> Se la face ay pale, / La cause est amer. / C'est la principale, / Et tant m'est amer / Amer, qu'en la mer / Me voldroye voir. / Or scet bien de voir / La belle a qui suis, / Que nul bien avoir / Sans elle ne puis.[26]

---

[22] The Mass is preserved in Trent 88, ff. 375'–384. For an edition and informative introduction to the Mass, see *Denkmäler der Tonkunst in Oesterreich*, Jg. XIX, 38. Band, *Sechs Trienter Codices* (Vienna, 1910), xxx–xxxii and 159–173.

[23] The Mass is found in Trent, Castello del Buon Consiglio, MS 91, ff. 216'–225. The tenor matches *Sig seld und heil*, No. 229 in the *Buxheimer Orgelbuch*, ed. by Bertha Wallner, *Das Erbe Deutscher Musik*, 38, 286. The opening phrase also appears in the *Glogauer Liederbuch*, No. 66, as phrase 10 of a tenor quodlibet. This quodlibet is published in Ringmann, pp. 40–41, and it supplies one more phrase of the text: *Sig seld und heil, im herzen geil.*

[24] Compare Reese, p. 576, and Higinio Anglès, »Cornago, Frater Johannes«, in *Die Musik in Geschichte und Gegenwart*, II (Kassel, 1952), col. 1681.

[25] All statements in this paper which refer to the chronology of Dufay's compositions rely upon Charles Hamm, *A Chronology of the Works of Guillaume Dufay Based on a Study of Mensural Practice* (Princeton, 1964).

[26] If my face is pale, The cause of it is love. And so bitter is it for me To love, that in the sea I'd rather see myself. Now, it is right well known To that beauteous one whom I follow That without her I can have No reward.

The text is a love song, although it seems not to specify a certain feast. But helpful evidence is supplied in a Sistine manuscript where the Mass is preserved.[27]

This manuscript begins with two Kyries for Easter and then continues with three Marian Masses, followed by Dufay's *Missa Se la face*. The organization of the manuscript, then, suggests that Dufay's Mass was also intended for Mary. Secondly, an illuminator decorated the beginning of the Mass with a portrayal of Venus Marina.[28] The earlier three Marian Masses are embellished by Marian scenes, so the illuminations are symbolically meaningful, not to be dismissed as sheer art-for-art's sake. That the illuminator intended for Venus to symbolize Mary is made clear later in the manuscript, where he uses the same image to introduce Dufay's *Missa Ecce ancilla Domini*, a Mass based upon an antiphon for the Annunciation, BVM. Venus frequently appeared as a symbol for the Virgin Mary, Botticelli's *The Birth of Venus* and *La Primavera* being several of the best known examples. When viewed as a Marian text, Dufay's ballade observes that devotion to Mary requires great courage, but Mary is the only means to salvation. Venus Marina was a clever choice for the illuminator. Dufay's ballade mentions the sea, and plays upon the words for »sea« and »love« are common. (Note lines 4 and 5 of Dufay's ballade and also lines 2 and 3 of Binchois' *Esclave puist*.) Puns relating »Mary« to »sea« were also common in vocabularies derived from Latin. A widely known illustration is the beginning of the Marian hymn, *Ave maris stella;* here only one letter distinguishes the incipit from the salutation *Ave Maria.*

Allegory such as that of Botticelli or the Sistine illuminator was common among the humanist scholars, for they had to reconcile their beloved classical literature with their Christian consciences.[29] Neoplatonic art and literature fostered allegorical interpretations of secular topics, and the era of Neoplatonic allegory corresponds neatly with the rise and decline of the »secular« Mass. But the musician who wished to engage in allegory could not look to antiquity for his materials. The

---

[27] Vatican, Biblioteca Apostolica Vaticana, Cappella Sistina, MS 14, ff. 27'–38.

[28] I had originally identified the figure as Venus, based upon its obvious similarity to Botticelli's *The Birth of Venus*. This more specific identification was kindly brought to my attention by Professor F. P. Pickering.

[29] See Trinkaus, II, 683–721, a chapter entitled »From *Theologia Poetica* to *Theologia Platonica*«, and also E. H. Gombrich, »Botticelli's Mythologies, a Study in the Neoplatonic Symbolism of his Circle«, *Journal of the Warburg and Courtauld Institute*, VIII (1945), 7–69.

oldest music available to him was that handed down through the
Church; this was inappropriate material because its Christian meaning
was already established. If a musician wished to exercise an allegorical
facility, his only recourse was to the contemporary secular melodies
around him.

One of the influential Neoplatonists whose career intersected with
artists and musicians was Marsilio Ficino. He claimed that all revelation, whether from Plato, mythology, or God, actually descended from
one divine source. Hence Venus, a pagan goddess of love, can be used
interchangeably with the source of divine love, the Virgin Mary. And
to Ficino, divine love is realized through the cognition of beauty, a
process which takes place in the mind of the beholder. Although Ficino
did not develop a complete theory of aesthetics, he was a practicing
musician and he produced a treatise about music. He wrote with conviction on the psychological powers of music, stating that it originates
in the soul of the musician and that it can cause the soul of the listener
to rise into the realm of celestial harmony.[30] Perhaps some truth lies
in the thought that any Mass of the period which stimulates a cognition
of beauty was therefore ecclesiastically justified, but this would be a
vague solution, and it provides no specific rationale for the secular
materials.

More constructive is the fact that most secular songs used in Masses
are love songs. The frequent use of Venus as an analogue for Mary
demonstrates a Renaissance view relating mortal to divine love. This
is carefully illustrated in another famous example, Titian's *Sacred and
Profane Love*, where two attractive and complementary aspects of love
are depicted. Of special interest is the conclusion that the woman
embodying Sacred Love is actually Venus.[31] Fifteenth-century writers
gave much attention to the topic of love, often elevating it to a spiritual
value. Lorenzo Valla, for example, saw love as an active and gratifying
experience which unifies all of man's other activities and pleasures.
When relating its affects to Christianity, he asserts,

> Pleasure itself is love but what makes pleasure is God. The recipient loves,
> the received is loved; loving is delight itself, or pleasure, or beatitude, or

---

[30] P. O. Kristeller, *Il Pensiero Filosofico di Marsilio Ficino* (Florence, 1953),
pp. 331–332.
[31] R. Frehan, »The Evolution of the Caritas Figure in the Thirteenth and Fourteenth
Centuries«, *Journal of the Warburg and Courtauld Institute*, XI (1948), 85–86.

happiness, or charity, which is the ultimate end and on account of which all other things are made.[32]

Castiglione later took up the topic, and in an extensive discourse he described the progress toward an ideal spiritual state as a climb up the ladder of love.[33] This was the exercise which many Masses of the period afforded.

---

[32] Quoted and discussed in Trinkaus, I, 138.
[33] Baldassare Castiglione, *Il Libro del Cortegiano*, Book IV, written between 1509 and about 1518. Numerous editions are readily available.

Dennis M. Kratz

Quid Waltharius Ruodliebque cum Christo?

I. Introduction

No Classical poet exerted greater influence on Christian Latin literature
than Vergil; nor was any Classical genre more imitated than the epic.
Yet, while the *Aeneid* and its Classical successors inspired the production of many Christian heroic narratives, the authors of these works
were compelled to face the inherent conflict between the pagan concept of heroism and the standards of Christian ethics. In this essay,
I will discuss two Medieval epic poems, the *Waltharius* and the *Ruodlieb*, in terms of their response to this conflict, and the ways in which
their authors have adapted a non-Christian literary tradition to the
expression of Christian values.[1]

II. O saeva cupido: the Christian Theme of the Waltharius

The *Waltharius* was composed around the middle of the ninth century
by a German monk, probably the same Gerald whose 22-verse dedica-
tion precedes the narrative in several manuscripts.[2] In 1456 hexameters,
which fall into three main parts roughly equal in length, it tells the
following tale.

> Part 1: As the army of Attila sweeps through Europe, three kings ransom
> their kingdoms with tribute and hostages. The hostages are Walter of
> Aquitaine, his betrothed Hiltgunt, and the warrior Hagen (sent in place
> of the young prince Gunther). In time, all three hostages rise to positions of
> prominence in Attila's court, especially Walter, the greatest of Attila's

---

1 I wish to express my gratitude to Professors Carl C. Schlam and Gordon B. Ford, Jr.,
  for their valuable suggestions to me during the preparation of this essay.
2 For a survey of *Waltharius* criticism, see Otto Schumann, »Waltharius-Literatur
  seit 1926«, *AfdA* 65 (1951–52), pp. 13–41; Wolfram von den Steinen, »Der Waltharius und sein Dichter«, *ZfdA* 84 (1952), pp. 1–47.

soldiers and now the commander of his army. Then Hagen escapes after learning that Gunther has become king and abrogated his father's treaty with the Huns. Later, Walter and Hiltgunt also flee. Walter's successful plan of escape involves inviting the Huns to a banquet, and fleeing during the night while they are deep in drunken sleep. The plan includes in addition the theft of two large boxes crammed with treasure.

Part 2: Walter and Hiltgunt eventually pass through Gunther's territory. Hagen is delighted that his friend has escaped, but Gunther thinks only of capturing the treasure which the fugitives are carrying. Despite Hagen's objections, Gunther gathers eleven warriors (including Hagen, who, however, refuses to join the actual assault against Walter) and sets out. Walter takes his stand in a mountain pass whose narrowness allows the men to approach only one at a time. In a series of individual combats, he kills each warrior who dares to attack him, until only Gunther and Hagen remain.

Part 3: Hagen now joins the battle in order to avenge his nephew, one of Gunther's vassals killed by Walter. He and Gunther attack Walter. In the ensuing fight, each man is grievously wounded. Walter cuts off Gunther's leg, then attacks Hagen; but his sword shatters on Hagen's helmet. When the frustrated Walter throws away the useless hilt, Hagen cuts off his outstretched right hand. With his left hand, Walter grabs a short sword and puts out Hagen's right eye as well as six of his teeth. The men now lay down their weapons, drink wine, enjoy some rather cruel jokes at their wounds, and depart. The poet mentions that Walter will reach home, marry Hiltgunt, and rule happily in Aquitaine for thirty years.

That the *Waltharius* is conceived as part of the continuum of the Latin epic tradition is undeniable. In language, form, and content it harks back to two Classical epics, Vergil's *Aeneid* and the *Thebaid* of Statius. The author was strongly influenced also by a fourth century allegorical epic, Prudentius' *Psychomachia*, which recounts a series of battles in which Christian Virtues conquer personified Sins.

The poet's style reflects his desire to create a work within the bounds of the Latin epic genre. The simile, for example, is an important part of the traditional epic style. Eight similes, ranging in length from a few words (585,899) to seven lines (1337–1343), appear in the *Waltharius*. The similes are representative of the poet's use of earlier works. Each has an identifiable Classical model, but none is taken verbatim from its source.

For example, the poem's longest simile compares Walter to a cornered bear (1337–1343):[3]

---

[3] Quotations from the *Waltharius* are from *MGH*, *PLAC*, Vol. 6, Part 1 ed. K. Strecker (Weimar, 1951), pp. 1–83; for Gerald's Prologue, see K. Strecker, ed., *Waltharius* (Berlin, 1947). The English translations are my own.

Haud aliter, Numidus quam dum venabitur ursus
Et canibus circumdatus astat et artubus horret
Et caput occultans submurmurat ac propiantes
Amplexans Umbros miserum mutire coartat,
– Tum rabidi circumlatrant hinc inde Molossi
Comminus ac dirae metuunt accedere belvae –,
Taliter in nonam conflictus fluxerat horam.

(As when a Numidian bear is being hunted and,
surrounded by dogs, makes a stand and threatens
with its claws and, hiding its head, growls and,
grabbing the approaching dogs, compels them to
howl wretchedly – then the angry Molossian hounds
bark at it from every side, and yet they are afraid
to attack the fierce beast: thus the battle raged
into the ninth hour.)

The apparent source for this simile is Vergil's extended comparison of
Mezentius, not to a bear, but to a boar (*Aeneid* X.707–715). In each
description, the wild animal is being chased by dogs:

... ursus
Et canibus circumdatus ...   (*Waltharius* 1337–1338)

... ille canum morsu de montibus altis
Actus ... (*Aeneid* X. 707–708).

But no dog dares venture too near:

Comminus ac dirae metuunt accedere belvae.   (*Waltharius* 1342)

Nec cuiquam irasci propiusque accedere virtus.   (*Aeneid* X.713).

In choosing this simile, the *Waltharius* poet seems also to have had two
passages from the *Thebaid* in mind. In Statius' epic, a woman in a
Bacchic frenzy sees a vision of two bulls fighting to the death, a vision
which she interprets as an omen of the impending battle between Eteoc-
les and Polynices (*Thebaid* IV.396–400). Both brothers do eventually
perish in a battle which Statius describes with a simile that makes use
of the animal imagery of the woman's vision (*Thebaid* XI.530–535).
The same pattern occurs in the *Waltharius;* for there too the animal
image of the simile serves to fulfill the symbolic language of a prophecy.
That prophecy is a dream in which Hagen sees a bear rip out his eye
and some teeth after having bitten off Gunther's leg (617–627). Thus
we see the poet borrowing his image and language primarily from Vergil, but reflecting the *Thebaid* in the narrative function of the particular
image.

Similes and Prophecy are but two of the epic conventions imitated in the *Waltharius*. Others include the Banquet and the Battle. In the battle descriptions, the poet includes such traditional motifs as *aristeiai* and a Catalogue. He draws his language now from Vergil, now from Statius, now subtly interweaves allusions to both Classical poets. He is careful, moreover, to incorporate into his scenes the various topoi out of which Classical epic battles are largely composed.[4]

Whereas the battle descriptions reveal a broad based approach to imitation, the banquet scene in the *Waltharius* has a specific exemplar, the banquet given by Dido in honor of Aeneas (*Aeneid* I.637–756). The ninth century version includes both verbal echoes and the inclusion of particular motifs, such as the description of a goblet on which are sculpted the heroic deeds of the host's ancestors (*Waltharius* 308–309, *Aeneid* I.640–642). At one point, Walter proposes a toast whose ironic use of *laetanter ... laetificetis* (305 ... 307) recalls the similar irony of the *laetum diem ... laetitiae* (*Aeneid* I.731 ... 735) of Dido's toast. The wine brings no joy certainly to Attila, who the next morning will bitterly lament not only Walter's departure but also his own hangover.

Granted, then the *Waltharius* represents a careful and skilled recreation of the Classical epic genre. On this issue, there is no longer serious disagreement. But there remains a more important issue, concerning which no general agreement is to be found. To what extent, if at all, was the poet able to take pagan German legend, and the Classical epic tradition, and transform his material into a work which is Christian in spirit? Answers to this question have varied. Some (Brinkmann, Schumann, von den Steinen) find the poem to be essentially, even totally Christian. Others have labelled its Christian elements inconsequential (Grimm), or defined the ethos of the *Waltharius* as hardly Christian at all (Jones).[5]

---

4 For a discussion of these topoi, consult Pierre-Jean Miniconi, *Index des thèmes »guerriers« de la poésie épique latine* (Paris, 1951); for the *Waltharius* poet's use of Vergilian reminiscences, Hans Wagner, »Ekkehard und Vergil«, *Quellen und Studien zur Geschichte und Kultur des Altertums und des Mittelalters*, Reihe D, 9 (Heidelberg, 1939); on the general question of the poet's use of Classical models, an important work is Karl Stackmann, »Antike Elemente im Waltharius«, *Euphorion* 45 (1950), pp. 231–248.

5 Hennig Brinkmann, »Ekkehards Waltharius als Kunstwerk«, *Zeitschrift für deutsche Bildung* 43 (1928), pp. 625–636; Schumann, »Zum Waltharius«, *ZfdA* 83 (1951), pp. 12–40; von den Steinen, *op. cit.*; Jacob Grimm and Andreas Schmeller, *Lateinische Gedichte des X. und XI. Jahrhunderts* (Göttingen, 1838), pp. 57–64; George F. Jones, »The Ethos of the *Waltharius*«, *Middle Ages, Reformation,*

Diverse as these judgments have been, they have shared the common assumption that the key to the meaning of the poem is the issue of whether or not its central figure, Walter, can be regarded as a Christian hero. The question has been argued largely in terms of whether Walter's behavior reflects Christian values.[6] However, this very emphasis on Walter, I believe, has obscured the poem's actual thematic design, of which Walter's portrait is but one part in a carefully integrated whole.

I suggest that the *Waltharius* is indeed a Christian epic, with an unmistakably Christian theme; but that this Christian theme is not exemplified in a positive way by Walter – or, for that matter, by any single character in the narrative. The *Waltharius* is an epic which has no hero; for the poet has taken the traditional function of epic, the celebration of heroic excellence, and inverted it to emphasize instead the *vitia* which prevent Walter, Hagen, and Gunther from being Christian heroes. Specifically, it is the condemnation of *avaritia*, not the characterization of Walter, which underlies the poem's thematic design.

A study of the epic's three main characters should help illustrate the nature of the poet's narrative technique and the influence of Christian sources on that technique. The Bible and the *Psychomachia* are especially important to a proper understanding of the symbolic meaning of the *Waltharius*.

The behavior of King Gunther is, by any measure, unheroic. He is a coward. His performance in the final battle is so unimpressive (1415: *Martis opus tepide atque enerviter egit*) that afterwards there is no question in Walter's mind, as he distributes the wine, which combatant should drink last. Gunther is also described as stupid (1228, 1304, 1332),

---

Volkskunde: Festschrift for John G. Kunstmann (Chapel Hill, North Carolina, 1959), pp. 1–20.

6 Cf. the contradictory opinions of von den Steinen, *op. cit.*, p. 20: »Walther ist durchaus ein idealer Held und soll es sein: aber nicht einem klassischen Helden wie Aeneas nachgeprägt und auch nicht vom Schnitt germanischer Sagenkönige, sondern eine Gestalt, wie sie erst seit Karl dem Großen geträumt werden konnte, bei aller Schwertgewalt christlichuntadlig und wiederum bei aller Gewissenhaftigkeit unbefangen von den kirchlichen Formen gelöst«, and Jones, *op. cit.*, p. 6: »There is evidence that Christianity is only skin-deep in the *Waltharius*. Walther asks divine forgiveness for boasting (561), yet he continues to boast thereafter without further apology ... Even though Walther crosses himself (225) and invokes and thanks God, he shows no Christian mercy to his defenseless and imploring victims ... In other words, Christianity is not strong enough to interfere with literary tradition or secular custom.«

greedy (cf. 470–472, 640–643), and arrogant (468, 720). The epithet *superbus* seems to cling to him. In two instances, the poet depicts Gunther in language which echoes the personification of *Superbia* in the *Psychomachia*. When he sees Walter's footprints in the dust, Gunther rejoices (513–515):

> Ast ubi Guntharius vestigia pulvere vidit,
> Cornipedem rapidum saevis calcaribus urget,
> Exultansque animis frustra sic fatur ad auras.

> (But when Gunther saw the tracks in the dust, he
> goads his swift horse with cruel spurs, and rejoicing
> in vain, thus speaks.)

This passage recalls Prudentius' description of *Superbia* just before she is defeated (*Psychomachia* 253–256)[7]:

> Talia vociferans rapidum calcaribus urget
> Cornipedem laxisque volat temeraria frenis
> Hostem humilem cupiens inpulsu umbonis equini
> Sternere deiectampue supercalcare ruinam.

> Thus exclaiming she spurs on her swift charger,
> and flies wildly along with loose rein, eager to upset
> her lowly enemy with the shock of her horse-hide
> shield and trample on her fallen body.)[8]

But above all else, Gunther is an avaricious man; and we must remember that it is precisely his obsessive desire for the treasure which Walter is carrying which precipitates the assault that leads to so much death and destruction.

This negative portrait of Gunther is balanced somewhat by the poet's description of Hagen. A noble man plagued by dual loyalties, he opposes the greed-motivated enterprise against his friend. For a while he even withdraws from the scene of the fighting. Hagen is drawn into the final assault on Walter only to avenge the death of his nephew Batavrid, one of the warriors sent to his doom by the greedy Gunther. When Hagen sees Batavrid advancing toward Walter, he delivers an impassioned address (857–872):

> O vortex mundi, fames insatiatus habendi,
> Gurges avaritiae, cunctorum fibra malorum!

---

[7] Latin quotations and English translations for Prudentius are taken from H. J. Thomson, ed., *Prudentius* I (Loeb Classical Library: Cambridge, Mass., 1969).

[8] See also *Waltharius* 530–531 and *Psychomachia* 203–205.

O utinam solum gluttires dira metallum
Divitiasque alias, homines impune remittens!
Sed tu nunc homines perverso numine perflans
Incendis nullique suum iam sufficit. ecce
Non trepidant mortem pro lucro incurrere turpem.
Quanto plus retinent, tanto sitis ardet habendi.
Externis modo vi modo furtive potiunter
Et, quod plus renovat gemitus lacrimasque ciebit,
Caeligenas animas Erebi fornace retrudunt.
Ecce ego dilectum nequeo revocare nepotem,
Instimulatus enim de te est, o saeva cupido.
En caecus mortem properat gustare nefandam.
Et vili pro laude cupit descendere ad umbras.
Heu, mihi care nepos, quid matri, perdite, mandas?

(O whirlpool of the world, insatiable hunger for
having, abyss of avarice, source of all evils! Dire
one, if only you devoured only metal, leaving men alone.
But now, inspiring men with your perverse power, cou
set them on fire, and his own is not enough for anyone.
Behold! They are not afraid to incur a shameful death
for wealth. The more they own, the more the thirst for
having burnst their throats. They get others' goods now
by force, now by theft, and [a fact which provokes
greater sighs and tears] they thrust heaven-born souls
into the pit of Hell. Behold! I cannot call back my
beloved nephew, for he is goaded on by you, cruel greed.
Yes, blind he hurries to taste infamous death and, for
vile praise, he desires to descend to the shades below.
Alas, my dear nephew, what message, lost one, do you send
to your mother?)

It is significant that the poet has chosen the moment of this decisive battle – the result of which will impel a revenge-seeking Hagen to attack and wound Walter – to interrupt the narrative and have Hagen condemn *avaritia* at such length. Hagen's words emphasize the centrality of the *avaritia* theme; for they can be applied not only to his nephew, but also to Walter's original greed in stealing the treasure, and to Gunther's insane lust to seize it.

Yet the subject of the harangue is at first a surprise, since the poet states clearly that Batavrid was seeking not gold but glory (854: *Arsit enim venis laudem captare cupiscens*). But at the end of his speech Hagen makes the connection by implying that the desire for praise is in fact a kind of greed (868–871).

This connection later proves relevant to Hagen himself. When he agrees to join Gunther in attacking Walter, he gives Walter the following justification for his decision (1275–1279):

> Haec res est, pactum qua irritasti prior almum,
> Iccircoque gazam cupio pro foedere nullam.
> Sitne tibi soli virtus, volo discere in armis,
> Deque tuis manibus caedem perquiro nepotis.
> En aut oppeto sive aliquid memorabile faxo.

> (This is how [by killing Batavrid] you first broke our
> pact of friendship. Therefore I desire no payment in
> return for a truce. I wish to learn in battle whether
> you have courage; and from your hands I seek vengeance
> for the death of my nephew. Yes, either I will die or
> I will perform some memorable deed.)

Hagen states clearly that he is motivated by a desire for revenge. However, although he disclaims any wish for treasure, nonetheless when he expresses a concern about glory (1279: *aliquid memorabile faxo*), he involves himself with the taint of *avaritia* as a result of his own earlier equation of the desire for glory with that sin.

Finally, Walter. Is he intended as a portrait of an idealized Christian hero? I think not, even though he does exhibit many noble qualities. He is, to be sure, a brave, even awesome, warrior. In other respects, he is a good man by Christian standards. During the many days, and nights, of the flight from Attila, Walter refrains from sexual intercourse with Hiltgunt, and for his continence earns the poet's praise (426–427). When he utters an arrogant boast just prior to the first attack by a vassal of Gunther, he interrupts himself and begs God's forgiveness for what he has been saying (559–565).

Moreover, in the interval of time between his conquest of the ten warriors sent against him by Gunther and the climactic confrontation with Hagen and the king himself, strong feelings of compassion and remorse well up in Walter. Searching out the trunks of the four soldiers whom he has decapitated, Walter joins their severed heads to their bodies. He contemplates his victory with remorse rather than joy and, falling to the ground, prays for the salvation of his enemies and himself (1150–1167).

This passage has been cited in efforts to prove that Walter is a new kind of hero, one who reflects Christian rather than pagan values. But it must be admitted that Walter's compassion, like his rather macabre acts of kindness, comes too late. The men are, after all, dead. Nor do these feelings keep Walter from immediately reentering the fray in order – in his own words – that his right hand may not have slain many enemies in vain, that he may avoid dishonor, and that he may hold on to his possessions (1214–1218).

His avarice prevents Walter from being a model of Christian virtue. When he explains his escape plan to Hiltgunt, he instructs her first to get armor, then to fill two boxes with treasure. Only then does he think of such travel necessities as shoes and fish hooks. The poet calls our attention to the stolen treasure when Walter and Hiltgunt set out on their journey (326–330). Indeed, once he has stolen the treasure, it defines for Walter his view of right action. He fights to keep it and to avoid the shame of losing it. When one defeated adversary begs for mercy, Walter first taunts then kills him (750–753). He kills another man to prevent him from boasting that he cut off two locks from his hair (976–981); and tells another to report to his friends in the Underworld his failure to avenge Walter's murder of them (1056–1058). In the heat of battle Walter's mercy and compassion melt away; and the values which remain bear little resemblance to an idealized Christian ethic.

Yet the poet has managed to create a Christian poem. In the epic's final scene, he employs direct moralizing combined with purposeful allusions to the Bible and the *Psychomachia* to draw together the disparate threads of the preceding narrative and underline his basic theme. The Christian references are used to cast a mocking light on the heroic motifs.

This final portion of the epic contains two episodes. In the first occurs the disfigurement of the three warriors; in the second, they desist from the feud and refresh themselves. The wounds which they suffer have symbolic meaning. What, after all, motivated Hagen at last to join the assault against Walter? Revenge. How appropriate, therefore, his wounds – the loss of his right eye and six teeth – appear to be when we call to mind (as the poem's intended audience of monks surely would have done) the Biblical injunction »an eye for an eye, a tooth for a tooth« (Exodus 21:22–25).

The poet himself intrudes into the narrative to make his own moral position explicit, immediately after having described the wounds suffered by each man. The passage reads (1401–1404):

> Postquam finis adest, insignia quemque notabant:
> Illic Guntharii regis pes, palma iacebat
> Waltharii nec non tremulus Haganonis ocellus.
> Sic sic armillas partiti sunt Avarenses!
>
> (After the end of the battle has come, distinctive marks
> branded each man; there was lying King Gunther's foot,
> Walter's hand, and Hagen's twitching eye. Thus, thus
> they divided the treasure of the Huns!)

It is worth noting that in this list of injuries the poet fails to mention Hagen's missing teeth. Moreover, although Walter had hacked off Gunther's whole leg with the knee up to the thigh (1369: *crus cum poplite adusque femur*), the poet in the same catalogue mentions only the amputated foot. These apparent errors are most unusual lapses on the part of a craftsman who, as Brinkmann first showed, prides himself on attention to accuracy in even minor details. But they are not lapses. The omission and the change serve to turn the list into another unmistakable scriptural reference (Mark 9:42–48):

> And if your hand causes you to sin, cut it off; it is better for you to enter life maimed than with two hands to go to hell, to the unquenchable fire. And if your foot causes you to sin, cut it off; it is better for you to enter life lame than with two feet to be thrown into hell. And if your eye causes you to sin, pluck it out; it is better for you to enter the kingdom of God with one eye than with two eyes to be thrown into hell, where the worm does not die, and the fire is not quenched.[9]

The Biblical allusion made by the list of wounds in the *Waltharius* suggests that they are meant to be viewed as punishments suffered by the three men for yielding to temptation. Walter and Gunther have yielded directly to avarice; Hagen, indirectly, by yielding to his desire for vengeance.[10]

The particular case of Walter's wound recalls a corresponding passage in Matthew which refers to the cutting off of one's *right* hand (Matthew 5:30):

> And if your right hand causes you to sin, cut it off and throw it away; it is better that you lose one of your members than that your whole body go into hell.

---

[9] For other statements of this theme, see also Matthew 18:7–9 and Deuteronomy 19:21.

[10] In the light of the preceding discussion, we can now recognize that the expression *armillas Avarenses* (1404) is surely intended as a pun on *avaritia*.

When we remember Walter's earlier avowed faith in his right hand to protect his possessions, the loss of that hand seems immediately appropriate. But the poet intends an even more precise connection between Walter's wound and punishment for his greed. To understand fully the link between the Biblical allusion and the poem's basic theme, we must turn to the *Psychomachia,* and to Prudentius' description of the dire fiend *Avaritia* (*Psychomachia* 459–463):

> [Avaritia] iuvat infercire cruminis
> turpe lucrum et gravidos furtis distendere fiscos,
> quos laeva celante tegit laterisque sinistri
> velat opermento; velox nam dextra rapinas
> abradit spoliisque ungues exercet aenos.

> (Avarice delights to stuff her filthy gain in
> money-bags, and to cram full of her theft purses,
> which she hides with her left hand; for her swift
> right hand is scraping up spoils with fingernails
> hard as brass.)

It is with her right hand that *Avaritia* is pictured as grabbing plunder; hence, it is proper, indeed inevitable, that Walter lose the grasping right hand as punishment for the *avaritia* that led him to stuff treasure chests full of *armillae Avarenses*.

One final correlation of this concluding scene with the *Psychomachia* emphasizes the Christian message of the *Waltharius.* In Prudentius' epic, after *Avaritia* has been killed, victorious *Operatio* announces that now is the time for the Virtues to rest and refresh themselves (*Psychomachia* 606–608):

> Solvite procinctum, iusti, et discedite ab armis!
> causa mali tanti iacet interfecta; lucrandi
> ingluvie pereunte licet requiescere sanctis.

> (Doff your armour, ye upright, and lay your weapons
> aside. The cause of all our ill lies slain. Now that
> the lust of gain is dead, the pure may rest.)

This episode (*Psychomachia* 603–663) provides the model for the drinking which ends the *Waltharius;* for *avaritia* has been, if not conquered, at least justly rewarded.

Puzzlement has been expressed concerning the ending of the *Waltharius.*[11] Why does Hagen fail to kill Walter after amputating his right

---

11 See von den Steinen, *op. cit.,* p. 19; Jones, *op. cit.,* p. 18, speaks of the »trick ending« of the poem.

hand? Why do the warriors so quickly give up the fighting? Why is there
no further mention of the treasure for which they were so recently
fighting with such bitterness? All these seeming inconsistencies are dis-
solved, however, once we accept that the *Waltharius* poet's intention is
not the realistic portrayal of action or human psychology – not, at least,
according to twentieth century assumptions of realism – but rather the
narrative exemplification of his theme. That theme is the condemnation
of avarice; and in this context the conclusion of the poem is neither
puzzling nor inconsistent.

The *Waltharius*, then, while utilizing the trappings of epic, turns the
genre to a new purpose. It resolves the problem of welding Christian
content to Classical form by attacking the values of at first glance heroic
figures and rendering them, in essence, ridiculous. In this sense, we
might even venture to call the *Waltharius* a mock epic. But we should
not forget that sin is the source of the humor, and the ridicule of sin is
subordinate to the poem's serious Christian spirit.

III. The Ruodlieb and Christian Heroism

The *Ruodlieb* [12] takes a radically different approach to the creation of
a poem which is at once Christian in spirit and yet a part of the Latin
epic tradition. This Latin narrative was composed in southern Germany
in the mid-eleventh century, some two hundred years after the *Waltharius.*

> The manuscript is incomplete, but the 2300 verses which have survived
> clearly recount the adventures of a young knight who leaves home to better
> his fortunes. He first distinguishes himself – as hunter, warrior, and diplo-
> mat – at the court of a foreign king, whose rewards to the hero include both
> gnomic counsels and a generous supply of treasure. A letter from his
> mother, who reports that all his enemies have been eliminated, prompts
> Ruodlieb to leave the court and return home. The journey homeward
> includes episodes demonstrating the wisdom of several of the king's coun-
> sels, particularly one admonishing against red-headed men. Later, the hero
> stops at the castle of a widow, and there arranges the marriage of her
> daughter with his nephew. At home, Ruodlieb gains great honors; and a
> dream which appears to his mother foretells more successes. The next scene
> describes Ruodlieb's conquest of a dwarf, who promises to reveal to the
> hero the location of a great treasure. The narrative breaks off abruptly at
> this point.

---

[12] I have treated the *Ruodlieb* by itself in »Ruodlieb: Christian Epic Hero«, *Classical
Folia* 27, Number 2 (1973), pp. 252–266.

Unlike the *Waltharius*, the *Ruodlieb* is not widely accepted as a part of the Latin epic tradition. It has been variously labelled as the first courtly romance (Wilmotte), the earliest courtly novel (Zeydel), the first realistic novel (Gamer), and a romantic epic (Raby). Others have associated it wholly or in part with Greek romances (Burdach) or the entertainments of mime-players (Winterfeld). It has even been called a totally individualistic work divorced from any literary tradition (Manitius).[13]

Three critical essays published since 1962 have addressed the nagging question of the relationship of the *Ruodlieb* to the epic genre.[14] Braun emphatically denies that the poem has any relationship at all to Classical epic. Brunhölzl, on the other hand, argues for the *Aeneid* as the *Ruodlieb's* model, and concludes that the poem is an attempt, clumsy and utterly unsuccessful, at a Vergilian epic. Brunhölzl's harsh judgment concerning the failure of the *Ruodlieb* needs to be understood in the context of his own bias, that any deviation in language or form from Vergil is a flaw. If the *Ruodlieb* poet does not imitate his Classical model precisely, it is a confession of incompetence, since he certainly would have imitated more closely had he been able.

The fallaciousness of this viewpoint need not detain us here, especially since it has already been attacked eloquently by Gamer and more recently by Dronke.[15] In his essay, Dronke argues that the *Ruodlieb*

---

13 Maurice Wilmotte, »Le Ruodlieb, notre premier roman courtois«, *Romania* 44 (1915–1917), pp. 373–406; Edwin Zeydel, *Ruodlieb: The Earliest Courtly Novel* (Chapel Hill, N. C., 1959); Helena Gamer, »The *Ruodlieb* and Tradition«, *ARV: Journal of Scandinavian Folklore* 11 (1955), pp. 65–103; F. J. E. Raby, *A History of Secular Latin Poetry* I (Oxford, 1957²), pp. 395–399; Konrad Burdach, *Vorspiel, Gesammelte Schriften zur Geschichte des deutschen Geistes* I (Halle, 1925), pp. 153–157; Paul von Winterfeld and Hermann Reich, *Deutsche Dichter des lateinischen Mittelalters* (Munich, 1922), pp. 491–502; Max Manitius, *Geschichte der lateinischen Literatur des Mittelalters* II (Munich, 1923), pp. 547–555.

14 Werner Braun, *Studien zum Ruodlieb* (Berlin, 1962); Franz Brunhölzl, »Zum Ruodlieb«, *DVj* 39 (1965), no. 4, pp. 506–522; Peter Dronke, »*Ruodlieb*: The Emergence of Romance«, *Poetic Individuality in the Middle Ages* (Oxford, 1970), pp. 33–65.

15 Gamer, *op. cit.*, p. 68 (speaking generally): »Two equally fallacious tendencies have been widespread, first, an inclination to size up the stature of a mediaeval writer by determining the faithfulness with which he renders Classical themes, motifs, and stories; second, to judge the author's language and style by the standards of Classical Latin. Both tendencies emanate from the assumption that the mediaeval Latin works are decadent products of a long and honorable ancient lineage, and thus pass over the vital questions of the growth of a language and a literature and the originality of an author. These lines of thought overlook the

should be regarded as an experiment in poetic narrative, and emphasizes approaching the poem on its own terms rather than in terms of sources or analogues. He pays particular attention to the poet's ability to achieve characterization through dialogue and to his use of realistic detail to enhance the meaning of specific scenes. Dronke's illuminating study is a major contribution to our understanding of the poet's artistry, but it is deficient in its consideration of the problem of genre. Dronke refers to the *Ruodlieb* at one point as the first Medieval verse romance. Elsewhere, he labels it an epic romance, but qualifies this assertion by saying, like Braun, that in themes and conception it owes almost nothing to ancient epic.

All these earlier discussions of the genre and literary heritage of the *Ruodlieb* seem to me to miss the mark. My suggestion is to reassert the poem's epic character, but in a revised sense; for an examination of the text reveals the *Ruodlieb* poet to have made far more use of the conventions of Classical epic than has previously been suspected. The *Ruodlieb* is intended as an imitation and a rival of the *Aeneid*. In this sense of the term, it is an epic poem.

The poet's choice of Latin hexameters to narrate the adventures of a central heroic figure is the first indication of his epic intent. At the very beginning of the work, several allusions to the *Aeneid* announce that intent. The first strokes of the portrait of Ruodlieb bear unmistakable resemblances to Vergil's Aeneas. The opening line of each poem introduces its hero simply as *vir*. Ruodlieb, like Aeneas, is an exile from his native land who, suffering many hardships, travels through foreign lands (I.15–17)[16]:

> Nusquam secure se sperans vivere posse,
> Rebus dispositis cunctis matrique subactis,
> Tandem de patria pergens petit extera regna.

---

fact that borrowed matter may be used, on the one hand, ›accurately‹ and at the same time badly, and, on the other, quite freely, and with a high degree of poetic perfection – as indeed a Shakespeare and a Dante employed traditional materials.« Dronke, *op. cit.*, pp. 63–64 (rebutting Brunhölzl directly): »Brunhölzl's suggestion that this poet would have liked to imitate classical diction but could not has, quite simply, no foundation in the text. To speak as he does of this poet's ›unlateinische Ausdrucksweise‹ is to set up arbitrarily a particular norm of Latin as if this were valid for every age and every artistic purpose.«

16 Quotations from the *Ruodlieb* are taken from Gordon B. Ford, Jr., *The Ruodlieb: Linguistic Introduction, Latin Text, and Glossary* (Leiden, 1966). English translations are from Ford, *The Ruodlieb: The First Medieval Epic of Chivalry from eleventh century Germany* (Leiden, 1965).

> (Realizing that he could live nowhere securely,
> with his affairs put in order and entrusted to his
> mother, at last leaving his homeland, he seeks foreign
> lands.)

The phrase *petit extera regna* calls to mind Vergil's expression, applied
to Aeneas, *extera quaerere regna* (*Aeneid* IV.350). Later in the *Ruodlieb,* the hero is described as having endured many labors (V.235:
sustinuisse labores), an echo of Vergil's description of Aeneas as a man
compelled to undergo labors (*Aeneid* I.10: *adire labores*). Moreover,
Ruodlieb, like Aeneas, is prone to tears. The first reference to this
characteristic is made in connection with the hero's departure from
home (I.49):

> Perfusa lacrimis facie dabat oscula cunctis.

> (His face moistened with tears, he kissed everybody.)

This line contains an adaptation of Vergil's *lacrimis ... perfusa genas*
(*Aeneid* XII.64–65). One final Vergilian reference occurs in a description of Ruodlieb's mother immediately after the departure of her
son (I.56–59):

> Detersis lacrimis qui tunc lotis faciebus
> Consolaturi dominam subeunt cito cuncti,
> Quae simulando spem premit altum corde dolorem.
> Consolatur eos, male dum se cernit habere.

> (After all of them had wiped off their tears and
> washed their faces, they went quickly to console their
> mistress. Feigning hope, she suppressed her sorrow
> deep in her heart and consoled them when she saw that
> they were suffering.)

Simulando spem reworks Vergil's phrase *spem vultu simulat* (*Aeneid*
I.209), while *premit altum corde dolorem* is an exact borrowing from
the same line in the *Aeneid*. When we consider the real paucity in the
Ruodlieb of identifiable references to Classical literature, this complex
of allusions is all the more arresting.

One method, then, by which the poet attempts to link his narrative
with the *Aeneid* and hence Latin epic is the comparison of Ruodlieb
with Aeneas. In addition, he has incorporated into his narrative specific themes found in the *Aeneid*. The Hunt is one such theme. In the
Ruodlieb we find one hunting episode (I.27–48), and two other episodes
in which the hero displays his skill as a fisherman (II.1–26; X.1–49).

In the second fishing scene, there occurs an epic Catalogue – of fish (X.38–48). Prophecy, another standard feature of Vergilian epic, appears in the dream of Ruodlieb's mother (XVII.88–128). The poet is also fond of Ekphrasis; and one extended description (of an embossed goblet) occurs as part of a Banquet (VII.1–25), still another stock epic scene.

The description of the goblet (VII.12–16) provides an insight into the poet's relation to his Classical model. The stimulus for this description is undoubtedly the goblet which appears in Dido's banquet (*Aeneid* I.640–642). However, in the *Ruodlieb* the embossing does not, as it does in the *Waltharius*, repeat Vergil's motif of the deeds of ancestors. Rather, on the bowl there are the Christian motifs of the four rivers of paradise and the right hand of God. The filling of a Classical convention with a Christian content is analogous to the poet's use of the epic genre for the expression of a basically Christian tale.

The *Ruodlieb*, then, makes use of many elements of the epic genre. Of the important conventions, only the Battle and its apparatus are missing from the poem – an omission which is in fact an integral part of the poem's overall thematic structure. The poem was not created in a literary vacuum, nor is it the isolated phenomenon that has been proposed. The author may indeed have been influenced by a variety of literary and folk traditions. But in giving form to his story, he chose to imitate the Latin epic. Whatever affinities this intriguing work may have with other genres, or however unique it may seem, it has an identifiable literary model in the *Aeneid*.

I have dwelt on the issue of the genre of the *Ruodlieb*, because the poet's artistry can be properly appreciated only with reference to the tradition of the Latin epic, and its limitations as a vehicle for the expression of Christian values; for the poet's intention is to take the Latin epic form and fill it with Christian content. The *Ruodlieb* is essentially different from the *Aeneid*, not because its author was incapable of more precise imitation, but because he was trying to create, within the epic framework, a poem different in spirit. Though the innovations which the *Ruodlieb* poet introduced into the epic genre are many, I will restrict my remarks to what I consider his boldest and most significant departure from his Classical model: his attempt to forge, in the person of Ruodlieb, a new Christian exemplar of epic heroism.

The narrative itself is the record of Ruodlieb's growth toward Christian heroic excellence. It begins with the following description of the young knight (I.1–10):

> Quidam prosapia vir progenitus generosa
> Moribus ingenitam decorabat nobilitatem,
> Qui dominos plures habuisse datur locupletes,
> Saepius ad libitum quibus is famulans et honorum
> Nil deservisse potuit, putat ut meruisse.
> Quicquid et illorum sibi quis commisit herorum
> Aut ulciscendum causaeque suae peragendum
> Non prolongabat, quam strennuiter peragebat.
> Saepius in mortem se pro dominis dat eisdem
> Seu bello seu venatu seu quolibet actu.

> (A certain man, born of a noble family, adorned his
> inherited nobility with his character. He is said to
> have had many wealthy lords. Although he served them
> often according to their wishes, he was unable to obtain
> any of the honors which he thought that he deserved.
> He did not put off whatever any of these lords
> entrusted to him – whether it was to avenge them or to
> transact their business – but he accomplished it as
> energetically as possible. Often he risked his life
> for these same lords in war and in hunting and in every
> type of action.)

Several aspects of this passage deserve attention. First, the hero is pictured as already having attained excellence as a hunter and a soldier. Second, he has been unfortunate in serving unworthy lords who have cheated him of his rightful *honores*. Finally, he cannot yet be called a truly Christian hero because of his willingness to serve his lords as an avenger (I.7: *ulciscendum*), in contrast to the teaching of Christ with regard to vengeance (Matthew 5:38–42).

Ruodlieb's travels take him to a foreign court, whose lord – called the Rex Maior – is both just and generous. The hero first impresses the Rex Maior with his skill as a hunter and fisherman. Then the poet shifts the narrative emphasis to a war which has erupted between Ruodlieb's new lord and a neighboring ruler. Now the opportunity beckons to display the hero's aforementioned prowess as a soldier in an epic Battle. However, even though Ruodlieb is in fact the commander of the army which defeats the invaders, no battle is described. The poet's interest lies elsewhere. We learn only of the war's outcome, through the brief report of a messenger. On the other hand, the peace negotiations which follow the war, and Ruodlieb's effective performance as a diplomat, are treated in detail.

In the role of diplomat, Ruodlieb strongly condemns the foolish pride (III.2: *stulta superbia*) and desire for self-glorification which motivated the leader of the defeated force. That man, he declares, deserves to be hanged from a tree by the calves of his legs. Now the soldiers all shout their agreement, asking why indeed Ruodlieb hesitates to do just this. But Ruodlieb has changed his opinion concerning retribution. Citing the orders of the Rex Maior, he now contends that there is no honor in vengeance. Ruodlieb instead proposes a new concept of revenge, to spare one's wrath (III.7–14):

> Princeps respondit: »rex noster non ita iussit,
> Aut se dedentem vel captum perdere quemquam,
> Sed, si possemus, captivos erueremus
> Cum praeda pariter, quae fecimus ambo decenter.
> Vincere victorem, maiorem vult quis honorem?
> Sis leo pugnando par ulciscendo sed agno!
> Non honor est vobis, ulcisci damna doloris.
> Magnum vindictae genus est, si parcitis irae.«

> (The commander answered: »Our king did not order us
> to destroy anyone who either surrendered or was
> captured but, if we could, to rescue the prisoners
> together with the booty. Both of these things we have
> done properly. Who wishes greater honor than to vanquish
> a victor? Be a lion in battle but like a lamb when
> taking vengeance! It is not honorable to you to avenge
> grievous losses. The best kind of vengeance is when
> you spare your wrath.«)

The reference to the lamb which Ruodlieb employs (III.12: *par ulciscendo sed agno*) underscores the Christian basis of the teaching, the lamb being of course a common figura for Christ. The repetition of the gerundive form of *ulcisci* recalls I.7 and the hero's ethos, as it were, at the beginning of the narrative.

The Rex Maior is the source not just for Ruodlieb's disavowal of vengeance. He is in fact a general model of proper Christian behavior. In sharp contrast to Ruodlieb's former lords, the Rex Maior is a fair and compassionate man whose behavior reflects *virtus, sophia, pietas*, and *clementia*. The king demonstrates these noble qualities most clearly in his treatment of his vanquished enemies, with whom he deals in a spirit of forgiveness. He expresses his philosophy in this manner (V.42):

Nam mala malo bono quam reddere vincere pravo.

(I prefer to return good for evil, rather than to conquer
with injustice.)

When the defeated king, known as the Rex Minor, praises the Rex
Maior for his noble behavior, the summation of the lesser king's praise
is that the Rex Maior, through his possession of the qualities *virtus,
sophia, pietas,* and *clementia* (IV.137–147), is the earthly representative
of Christ (IV.154: *columen nostri tu solus es in vice Christi*).

The encomium of the Rex Minor represents just one way in which the
poet establishes the Rex Maior as the model of an excellence which is
specifically Christian. Ruodlieb, we recall, when citing the Rex Maior's
injunction against vengeance, used the Christian image of the lamb.
Elsewhere, the Rex Maior praises Ruodlieb's ability as a peacemaker
by saying that the young knight rendered him, whenever he became
angry, »gentle as a lamb« (V.407: *irascentem me mitem reddit ut
agnum*). The poet ties together these Christian images in the speech
Ruodlieb delivers when he is about to leave the Rex Maior's court
(V.303–307):

Quod tibi servivi, mihi quam bene retribuisti.
Huc postquam veni, pie rex, tibi meque subegi,
Pascha fuit tecum mihi semper cottidianum,
Semper habens multum vel honorum sive bonorum
A te non solum sed ab unoquoque tuorum.

(How well you have rewarded me for serving you! After
I came here, gracious king, and made myself your
subject, every day with you has always been Easter to
me. I have always had many honors and good things not
only from you but from every one of your people.)

The Easter reference (V.305: *Pascha*) restates the Rex Maior's role as
man *in vice Christi*. Ruodlieb's words also indicate, it should be noted,
his belief that his original quest has been successful. He left home, we
recall, because he had not received fitting *honores*. He now reveals his
conviction that he has in fact been amply honored.

Ruodlieb, as we have seen, learns *clementia* from the Rex Maior. The
king is also the source of *sophia* for the young knight. When Ruodlieb
announces his desire to return home to his mother, the king offers him
a choice between two final rewards for his service. The two possibilities
are wealth and wisdom. In a long speech (V.425–445), Ruodlieb replies
that pious wisdom (V.431: *pia ... sophia*), which gives a man inner

strength, is what he desires. This choice leads to Ruodlieb's receiving both wisdom and wealth. The wealth is in the form of a generous supply of gold and jewels hidden in loaves of bread which the king instructs him not to break open until he reaches home. The wisdom takes the form of a series of twelve maxims to guide Ruodlieb in his future life (V.449–526).[17]

Now the time has come for Ruodlieb to depart. The Rex Maior dismisses the hero with these words (V.532–533):

> Rex ait: »ito domum cunctorum plenus honorum
> Atque vide matrem totamque tuam pariter rem.«

> (The king said: »Go home, full of every honor, and see
> both your mother and all your possessions.«)

This statement, of course, articulates the actual success which Ruodlieb earlier believed that he had attained. He is now in fact *plenus honorum*.

Ruodlieb begins his journey home. One of the king's maxims had warned him against associating with any red-headed man (V.451–456):

> Non tibi sit rufus umquam specialis amicus!
> Si fit is iratus, non est fidei memoratus;
> Nam vehemens dira sibi stat durabilis ira.
> Tam bonus haut fuerit, aliqua fraus quin in eo sit,
> Quam vitare nequis, quin ex hac commaculeris;
> Nam tangendo picem vix expurgaris ad unguem.

> (Never let a redheaded man be a special friend of yours!
> If he becomes angry, he will not be mindful of loyalty,
> for violent, dreadful, and enduring is his wrath. He
> will not be so good that there will be no deceit in him,
> by which you cannot help being defiled. For if you
> touch pitch, you can scarcely be cleansed to the nail.)

Unfortunately, almost immediately after he leaves the court of the Rex Maior, Ruodlieb is joined by a red-headed man whose rash actions, and their disastrous consequences, form a major sub-plot of the epic. The red-headed man precipitates his own woe when he seeks lodging for the

---

[17] These pieces of advice may originally have been intended by the poet as a framework for the rest of his narrative. The episode which follows does illustrate the correctness of the first three counsels. However, although other counsels are relevant to the story as it unfolds, the poet seems to abandon this framework and lets the narrative proceed in a different fashion. Concerning the folk origin of such a counsel framework, see Friedrich Seiler, *Ruodlieb* (Halle, 1882), pp. 45–74.

night in the home of an old man with a young wife. This act is contrary
to another maxim offered Ruodlieb by the Rex Maior (V.461–467),
one which the hero wisely follows. At the moment the red-headed man
inquires about such lodgings, the poet describes him as »vain and very
arrogant« (VII.117: *vanus nimiumque superbus*). The husband, it turns
out, is not only old but also exceedingly ugly. His face is so bristly with
hair that the only feature visible on it is a long nose full of veins. The
wife is not only young but also promiscuous. Seduction follows, and
the lovers, when discovered by the husband, murder him. The two are
brought to trial; and, although the portion of the text relating the red-
head's fate is missing, we can assume that his *superbia* is severely
punished.

As the Rex Maior's function in the poem is to serve as a positive model
for Ruodlieb, so the red-head is a negative model. His role is not unlike
that of Gunther in the *Waltharius;* for each man represents the *superbia*
which the Christian hero must subdue in himself.

Meanwhile, Ruodlieb continues on his journey. When at last he reaches
home, he discovers the treasure secreted by the Rex Maior in the loaves
of bread which were parting gifts. Ruodlieb, whose *pietas* has been
emphasized throughout the poem (cf. I.69–71; III.27–30), immediately
gives thanks to God (XIII.56). Then, falling to his knees, he pours forth
a long prayer. (XIII.64–77):

> Miles humi dat se terram premit oreque saepe,
> Ceu se pro regis pedibus domini daret eius.
> Tunc nimium plorans faciem lacrimando tingens
> Orabat: »domine, num par tibi quis valet esse,
> Qui clemens illum miserum dignaris homullum
> Sic locupletare vel honoribus amplificare,
> Eius nec vitiis reminiscere quod patereris?
> Nunc mihi des, domine, quo non moriar, precor, ante
> Quam rursus videam, quem pauper egensque petebam,
> Qui mandante te clementer suscipiens me
> Fecit tantarum consortem deliciarum
> Et miserum denos secum retinendo per annos
> Amplificavit me, queo quod posthac sat honeste
> Vivere fidenter, haec si tracto sapienter.«

> (The knight cast himself to the ground and again and
> again pressed the earth with his lips as if he were
> throwing himself before the feet of the King, his Lord.
> Then weeping a lot and wetting his face with tears,
> he prayed: »O Lord, who can be equal to You, who

> mercifully deign thus to enrich and to increase with
> honors a poor little man such as I, but not to remember
> that You have suffered on account of my sins? Now, O
> Lord, I pray, grant to me that I will not die before I
> see again the king to whom I came poor and needy and
> who received me kindly at Your request and made me a
> participant in such great delights. Keeping me, a
> poor man, with him for ten years, he enriched me so that
> now I can live very honorably and confidently if I
> manage these things wisely.«)

This prayer, itself a reflection of Ruodlieb's *pietas*, continues the epic's other major themes of *clementia* (XIII.68: *clemens*), *sophia* (XIII.77: *haec si tracto sapienter*), and *honores* as the reward for excellence (XIII.69: *locupletare vel honoribus amplificare*).

In the episodes which follow, the poet emphasizes the hero's relationship with his mother and her role in helping him gain his greatest honors. In so doing, the poet returns to the perspective from which he began his tale. At the beginning of the epic, he had focused on the mother's intense grief at her son's departure. Now she sees her grief turned to joy. Moreover, Ruodlieb's respectful treatment of her provides another example of his excellence. We should remember that, happy though he was at the court of the Rex Maior, the hero rushed home when she summoned him. Later, remembering another of the Rex Maior's gnomic counsels (V.485–497), Ruodlieb defers to his mother's wishes by seeking a bride. The woman, unfortunately, proves less than desirable, for she is in the midst of a clandestine affair with a cleric. There is no marriage; nevertheless, Ruodlieb's reward for his filial devotion in this and other instances is God's favor (XVI.32–34).

God's favor is soon to be translated into further *honores*. And it is Ruodlieb's mother who is instrumental in his gaining them (XVII.85–88). God reveals the imminence of these honors to her when in a dream she sees Ruodlieb kill two boars and a herd of sows which are threatening her. Next she beholds her son sitting in a linden tree, where a white dove flies to him and places a crown on his head.[18] The mother interprets this vision as a portent of successes to come to her son in the future and says to him (XVII.123):

---

[18] For the relation of this dream to other literature, consult Paul Schach, »Some Parallels to the Tree Dream in *Ruodlieb*«, *Monatshefte für deutschen Unterricht* 46 (1954), pp. 353–364; consult also Gamer, *op. cit.*, pp. 99–101 for other possible sources of the dream motif.

> Nunc scio, maiores nacturus eris quod honores.

> (Now I know that you will obtain greater honors.)

The following scene, the last of the epic, is intended, I believe, to illustrate the correctness of the mother's interpretation of her dream. For when the poem breaks off suddenly, Ruodlieb has just captured a dwarf whom he spares in return for being told the whereabouts of a large treasure.[19]

Thus the poem ends. The picture of Ruodlieb is completed, and its clarity seems to refute those critics who would judge the poet incapable of organizing his subject matter into a coherent, meaningful whole. Ruodlieb is a Christian hero, a man of peace. He embodies the four qualities of *virtus, pietas, clementia,* and *sophia.* Two of these qualities, *clementia* and *sophia,* he acquires through his relationship with the Rex Maior. From the king, God's representative on earth, he first receives the *honores* of which he had previously been unjustly deprived in his homeland. At the conclusion of the epic, he has returned home, where, because of his own noble actions (and those of his mother), he is now granted even greater honors by God himself.

It can be seen that this portrait of a heroic life, based on Christian values, contrasts sharply with the pattern of heroic behavior found in the *Aeneid.* The poet's determination to stress forgiveness and peacemaking as central to the definition of heroism led him to omit from his narrative the battle scenes traditionally associated with epic. In turn, the emphasis on *clementia* and peace introduce a vital new dimension into the concept of the epic hero. The poet of the *Ruodlieb* did not invent a new literary genre any more than the *Waltharius* poet did. His achievement was in creating a new kind of epic poem.

IV. Summation

The authors of the *Waltharius* and the *Ruodlieb* were both striving to extend the capabilities of Latin epic by exploring ways of making it a suitable vehicle for the expression of Christian values. The *Waltharius*

---

19 There have been many guesses, none of which is convincing, as to why the poet did not complete the *Ruodlieb.* The most attractive hypothesis is that by Ford, who proposes (*Ruodlieb: The First Medieval Epic,* pp. 4–5) that »the poet intentionally ended his work at this point and desired to leave Ruodlieb's future crowning and marriage to the reader's imagination«.

is a mock epic, whose basic Christian theme, the condemnation of *avaritia,* is inextricably bound up with a denial of Classical standards of heroic action. The key to the poet's mocking attack on Walter, Hagen, and Gunther is our recognition of the symbolic meaning – based on allusions to the Bible and the *Psychomachia* – of the narrative's final episode, particularly the wounds suffered by each man. The *Ruodlieb,* on the other hand, attempts to provide a new definition of heroism – emphasizing the Christian virtues of *pietas, clementia,* and *sophia* – in the person of Ruodlieb. The epic is the account of Ruodlieb's growth toward Christian excellence. The turning point for him is his association with the Rex Maior, from whom he learns wisdom and the renunciation of vengeance, and from whom he first receives worldly rewards *(honores)* for his excellence.

Despite their different approaches to the creation of Christian epic, the two poets seem to share much the same moral and esthetic outlook. Each seeks to be innovative within a context of established literary tradition. Each condemns the destructive power of *superbia* and of vengeance as a response to injury. Each, in adapting the epic genre to his Christian purpose, focuses attention specifically on the incompatability of the Classical heroic code with his own Christian values. In articulating their responses to this conflict, the two poets produced works which must be ranked among the high points of Christian Latin narrative. They also created two of the most striking figures in the history of Latin epic: Walter of Aquitaine, personified warning against avarice; and Ruodlieb, Christian alternative to Aeneas.

Hans-Erich Keller

Changes in Old French Epic Poetry and Changes in the Taste of its Audience

About one hundred years after the battle of Hastings, the Norman chronicler Wace gives the following account:

>»Taillefer, that splendid singer, riding on his swift steed, rode before the duke singing of Charlemagne, of Roland, of Oliver and the vassals who died at Roncevaux. As they were approaching the English, Taillefer said: ›Sire, I beg of you! I have served you long; all this you owe to me. Today, may it please you, repay me. As my only reward, I ask and do most earnestly beseech you to grant me – for I shall not fail – the first blow of the battle.‹ The duke replied: ›Indeed I grant it.‹ Then Taillefer spurred out in front of all the rest, struck an Englishman and killed him dead. Beneath his breast, straight through his belly, did he drive his lance. Flat on the ground he knocked him. Then drawing his sword he struck another and cried out: ›Come on, come on! What are you doing? Strike, strike!‹ Then, at his second blow, the English surrounded him. Lo, the growing noise and shouts, as those on both sides rush in! The Normans want to attack and the English make good defense. The first strike, the others hit. So bold are they, they fear each other not. Behold the battle is joined whose fame endures today.«[1]

---

[1] Wace, *Roman de Rou*, III, ll. 8013–8048 (ed. A. J. Holden): »Taillefer, qui mult bien chantout, / sor un cheval qui tost alout, / devant le duc alout chantant / de Karlemaigne e de Rollant, / e d'Oliver e des vassals / qui morurent en Rencevals. / Quant il orent chevalchié tant / qu'as Engleis vindrent apreismant, / ›Sire‹, dist Taillefer, ›merci! / Jo vos ai longuement servi, / tot mon servise me devez, / hui, se vos plaist, le me rendez; / por toz guerredon vos requier, / e si vos voil forment preier, / otreiez mei, que jo n'i faille, / le premier colp de la bataille‹. / Li dus respont: ›E jo l'otrei‹. / E Taillefer point a desrei, / devant toz les altres se mist, / un Engleis feri, si l'ocist, / desoz le piez, parmié la pance / li fist passer ultre la lance; / a terre estendu l'abati, / pois traist l'espee, aultre feri; / pois a crié: ›Venez, venez! / Que faites vos? Ferez, ferez!‹ / Donc l'ont Engleis avironé / al segont colp qu'il out doné. / Eis vos noise levé e cri, / d'ambes parz poplë estormi; / Normant a assaillir entendent / e li Engleis bien se deffendent, / li un fierent, li altre botent, / tant sunt hardi ne s'entredotent; / eis vos la bataille assemblee / donc encor est grant renomee.« This text was translated into English by my friend and colleague, Professor David A. Griffin, to whom I would also express my sincere thanks for revising the style of this paper.

It is quite possible that the figure of the juggler, Taillefer, is historic, for in 1067, only a year after Hastings, the bishop Guy of Amiens mentions him in his *De Hastingae Proëlio*.[2] Moreover, ten years later, on the Tapestry of Bayeux,[3] being exhibited, probably for the first time, on the 14th of July 1077, we find a horseman who had killed one Englishman with his lance and another with his sword. The scene is very suggestive of this high deed of courage and devotion.[4] But it is difficult to imagine that a man on horseback could have time to think about singing of Roland, Oliver, and the Twelve Peers, his head covered with

---

[2] ll. 389–407 (ed. C. Morton and H. Muntz): »Interea, dubio pendent dum prelia Marte, / Eminet et telis mortis amara lues, / Histrio, cor audax nimium quem nobilitabat, / Agmina precedens innumerosa ducis, / Hortatur Gallos uerbis et territat Anglos: / Alte proiciens ludit et ense suo. / Anglorum quidam, cum de tot milibus unum / Ludentem gladio cernit abire procul, / Milicie, cordis tactus feruore decenti, / Viuere postponens, prosilit ire mori. / Incisorferri mimus cognomine dictus, / Vt fuerat captus, pungit equum stimulis. / Angligene scutum telo transfudit acuto; / Corpore prostrato distulit ense caput. / Lumina conuertens sociis hec gaudia profert, / Belli principium monstrat et esse suum. / Omnes letantur, Dominum pariter uenerantur; / Exultant ictus quod prior extat eis, / Et tremor et feruor per corda uirilia currunt, / Festinantque simul iungere scuta uiri.« (Meantime, while the battle hung in ominous suspense and the dread scourge of death in war was pending, a player, whom his most valiant soul greatly ennobled, rode out before the countless army of the duke. He heartened the men of France and terrified the English, and, tossing his sword high, he sported with it. A certain Englishman, when he saw a lone man out of so many thousands move off at a distance, juggling with his sword, was fired with the ardour proper to a soldier's heart – heedless of life, he sprang forward to meet his death. The nummer, surnamed Taillefer, as soon as he had been reached, pricked his horse with the spurs; he pierced the Englishman's shield with his keen lance and hewed the head from the prostrate body with his sword. Turning his eyes on his comrades, he displayed this trophy and showed that the beginning of the battle favoured them. All rejoiced and at the same time called upon the Lord. They exulted that the first blow was theirs, both a tremor and a thrill ran through brave hearts and at once the men hastened to close shields.) – A number of works relating to Taillefer are cited by E. Faral, *Les Jongleurs en France au moyen âge* (Paris, 1910), p. 57 n. 2, p. 275 f., but the significance of his story in the *Carmen* for the understanding of the battle of Hastings was first noted by C. Morton and H. Muntz in *The Carmen de Hastingae Proelio of Guy bishop of Amiens*, p. 81 f.

[3] S. Bertrand, *La tapisserie de Bayeux et la manière de vivre au onzième siècle* (Bayeux, 1966), pl. 120.

[4] Even an Anglo-Saxon origin of the Tapistry, as suggested by F. Sidney Walls, *The Bayeux Tapistry: Its Sources and Influence* (Scripta Humanistica Kentuckiana. Supplement to the Kentucky Foreign Language Quarterly, 6, Lexington, 1962), does not contradict this hypothesis, because Geffrei Gaimar, *L'Estoire des Engleis* (ca. 1139), the only chronicler who relates the battle of Hastings from the English side, even augments the juggler's feats (ll. 5265–5300, ed. A. Bell): »Un des Franceis dunc se hastat, / Devant les autres chevalchat, / Taillifer ert cil apelez, /

chain-mail, his helmet with a long nose-piece stretching down over his mouth, as he holds both his shield and the reins of his horse in his left hand and wields his lance or his sword in his right.[5] Wace's source here, William of Malmesbury (ca. 1125), was more circumspect when he simply told posterity: »Then, beginning the *Song of Roland* so that the war-like example of that man might stimulate the soldiers, and calling on God for assistance, the battle commenced on both sides.«[6] That indeed the *Song of Roland* was sung before the battle of Hastings is not impossible given the fact that the Normans had camped for more than two weeks near Hastings before the battle took place. While it seems likely that both, the *Song of Roland* and Taillefer, were involved at Hastings, the combination of these two elements is the innovation of

---

Juglere [estait] ardiz asez, / Armes aveit e bon cheval, / Si ert hardi e noble vassal. / Devant les autres cil se mist, / Devant Engleis merveilles fist. / Sa lance prist par le [tüet], / Si cum co fust un bastunet, / Encuntremunt halt le geta / E par le fer rec[e]u l'a. / Treis feiz getad issi sa lance, / La quarte feiz mult pres s'avance, / Entre les Engleis la lançat, / Parmi le cors un en navrat. / Puis trait l'espee, ariere vint, / Getat l'espee qu'il tint / Encuntremun[t], [puis] le receit. / L'un dit a l'autre qui ço veit / Que ço esteit enchantement / Que cil faiseit devant la gent. / Quant treis feiz ot geté l'espee, / Le cheval [od] gule baiee / vers les Engleis vint esleissié; / Alquant quident estre mangié / Pur le cheval que si baiot; / Le jugleür apris lui ot. / De l'[espee] fiert un Engleis, / Le puin li fait voler maneis, / Altre en fiert tant cum il pot, / Mal gueredon le jur en ot / Kar les Engleis de tutes parz / Li lancent gavelocs e darz, / Lui ocistrent e sun destrier. / Mar demanda le cop premier.«

5 It is true that Rodulfus Tortarius, monk at Fleury (1065?–1114?), reports in the prose portion of his *Miracula s. Benedicti* that a gang of robbers, in their war against the inhabitants of Châtillon-sur-Loire, were so confident in their number that they asked a minstrel to precede them and to sing of the exploits of their Burgundian ancestors, accompanied by a musical instrument (»[...], ut scurram se praecedere facerent, qui musico instrumento res fortiter gestas et priorum bella praecineret«, *Recueil des Historiens des Gaules et de la France*, nouv. éd., p.p. L. Deslisle, vol. XI, Paris: V. Palmé, 1876, p. 489); it is also true that, according to Saxo Grammaticus, *Gesta Danorum*, book XIV (beg. 13th cent.), a minstrel incited Waldemar the Great's army in the battle of Grathehede (23 of October 1157) against king Sweyns by singing of Sweyns' murder of king Canute (»Medius acies interequitabat cantor, qui parricidalem Suenonis perfidima famoso carmine prosequendo, Waldemari milites per summam vindictae exhortationem in bellum accenderet«, ed. Frankfurt, 1576, p. 252). But Edmond Faral, *op. cit.*, p. 56, is certainly right when he calls attention to the fact that these deeds must be quite isolated and exceptional in order to be recorded, and in both instances the minstrels do not take an active part in the battle, at least not in an exceptional way.
6 *Willelmi Malmesberiensis Monachi De Gestis Regum Anglorum libri quinque*, ed. William Stubbs (London, 1889), II, 302: »Tunc cantilena Rollandi inchoata, ut martium viri exemplum pugnaturos accenderet, inclamatoque Dei auxilio, praelium consertum, bellatumque acriter, neutris in multam diei horam cedentibus.«

Wace, an innovation which seemed unlikely even to his contemporaries. Benedict of Sainte-Maure, for instance, does not pick it up again in his *Chronicle of the Dukes of Normandy* (ca. 1175).[7] Indeed, we may consider Wace's way of looking at the recitation of a *chanson de geste* as Romantic before the fact. In any case, it is clear that, from the time of Eleanor and Henry II, there was already a misconception of this literary genre, although it was still cultivated and new songs were even composed on the model of the old ones, much in the same way as Romanesque churches were still being built along with the new style Gothic cathedrals.

Wace, then, clearly bears witness to the decline of a literary genre which found its apogee in the second half of the eleventh century. Although direct attestations are few, those that we do possess point to that period as the most propitious hour for the flourishing of the heroic epic. Our evidence consists of the following facts: (1) the list of brothers baptised with the names Oliver and Roland (later in the order Roland and Oliver) attested from about 1020; (2) the numerous mentions of Oliver, a literary name, first in the South and later in the North of France from about the year 1000 and still later in Catalonia and Italy; (3) the Latin prose version of a poetic fragment composed in hexameters in which Charlemagne and four other heroes of the William of Orange cycle are seen laying siege to a hostile city (a fragment dating from between 980 and 1030 and presently preserved in the Royal Library at The Hague); (4) a short note in Latin written on a manuscript of the third quarter of the eleventh century belonging to the monastery of San Millán de la Cogolla in Spain which gives a precise résumé of the theme of Roland and Roncevaux; (5) a Latin prose narrative of the *Conversio Othgerii militis*, composed about 1070–1080, revealing how the illustrious warrior Ogier the Dane, second only to Charlemagne in the Empire, took the Benedictine habit at the abbey of St. Faron at Meaux; (6) a diploma falsified about 1090 at the abbey of St. Yrieux in the Limousin and which the monks wished to give a solemn character by having it authenticated by Charlemagne himself in the presence of the

---

7 »Benoît [*Chronique des ducs de Normandie*, ed. C. Fahlin, Uppsala, 1951/1954, ll. 39725 ff.] singles out Taillefer as one of those who did the enemy most harm that day, and represents him as taking great prizes, riding coolly in among the press of the English and fighting still more gallantly when mortally wounded. »The poet declares that he is following an earlier account (vv. 39732 ff.), but his version answers to none of those that survive.« (C. Morton and H. Muntz, *op. cit.*, p. 82.)

Twelve Peers at the very moment when they were setting out on their
Spanish expedition.

We have little else from a period which marks a turning point in medieval history.[8] It is a time when Christian Europe, so long assailed
by pagan and Moslem forces, once again took the offensive that had
been lost since Charlemagne. The Normans had been Christian for a
century, the Hungarians since the year 1000. Only the Moslems remained, against whom all the potential of the Christian world would
be mobilized.

> »The eleventh century«, wrote Bédier,[9] »opens with the letter whereby
> Sylvester II, the French pope, for the first time calls the Christians to arms
> against the Infidel; it closes with the preaching of the French pope Urban II,
> *Ite praedicabiles per Orbem milites; eat Francorum virtus!* ... In the mean-
> time, expeditions arose against the Moslems of Europe, expeditions which
> set the scene for the crusade to the Holy Land: the Norman campaign of
> Roger of Toëny in 1018; the Burgundian campaign of 1063 led by Odilon,
> abbot of Cluny; the campaign of Guy-Geoffrey, duke of Aquitaine, in
> 1963; of Eble, count of Roucy and of Reims, in 1073; and of Hugh, duke
> of Burgundy, in 1078. These were not peaceful processions of pilgrims who
> rode toward the Pyrenees, toward Roncevaux, but rather troups or armed
> legions ordinarily accompanied by monks from Cluny, who were the great
> instigators of these enterprises, since Cluny possessed rich domains in
> Spain.«

The ruling class in France was changing fast. According to Philippe
Wolff,[10] it was the nobles who reaped the benefit of agricultural progress. The rents paid by their tenants and the profits from the sale of
surplus products piled up in their coffers. All the same, occasions to
spend money were also multiplying rapidly. By the end of the eleventh
century, there were many lords who had served their time as Crusaders
in defense of the Holy Land or in fighting against the Infidel in Spain.

---

8 I am translating, in the following passage, a historical sketch of the period by
   A. Burger in *Romania* 70 (1948–49), 466. – I am most happy to discover that
   most of my own observations concerning the Latin character of the poems preceding the *chansons de geste* in the vernacular were already expressed by the
   eminent medievalist emeritus of the University of Geneva in his article »La Légende de Roncevaux avant la *Chanson de Roland*«, *Romania* 70 (1948–49),
   433–473, especially p. 468 ff., where he defended Bédier's views on this problem
   but also corrected them on important details.

9 »Les Chansons de geste«, *Histoire de la Nation française*, dir. by G. Hanotaux,
   t. XII: *Histoire des Lettres*, I: *Des Origines à Ronsard* (Paris: Plon-Nourrit, 1921),
   p. 205.

10 *The Awakening of Europe* (The Pelican History of European Thought, 1, 1968),
   p. 203 f.

There they came into contact with more refined civilizations, and those who did not die or settle in distant lands came home with a broader range of experience and higher standards of comfort. Among the best of the nobility, this increasing refinement of life was accompanied by both moral and intellectual progress. With good reason the Church had directed their warlike ferocity against the Infidel, and regularly blessed the sword of a new-made knight, holding up to him the ideal of protector of the weak and righter of wrongs. These lords were no longer satisfied to fill their leisure hours with hunting and tournaments. They began to show an interest in culture and education. They took a fancy to the poetry sung by travelling minstrels who accompanied themselves on a variety of instruments. A number of feudal courts became centers of literary activity.

In this climate lived, for example, Berenger, the father of Abelard, who, although only a humble knight, was able to boast of a fairly broad education and who was anxious to pass this on to his children as well. And it was in this climate that Hugh of Avranches, earl of Chester, lived. According to Orderic Vitalis, he was noted for his »huge household, full of the noise of swarms of boys of both high and humble birth. A number of honourable men, clerks and knights, were also of his company, and he gladly shared with them his riches no less than his labours.«[11] Serving in his chapel was a cleric from Avranches, Gerold son of Reginald de Breone, who had come to England in the reign of William I and had attached himself to Earl Hugh, who had him ordained as his chaplain by Wulfstan bishop of Worcester. Gerold was remarkable for his piety and good character and deep learning.

>To great lords, simple knights, and noble boys alike he gave salutary counsel; and he made a great collection of tales of the combats of holy knights, drawn from the Old Testament and more recent records of Christian achievements, for them to imitate. He told them vivid stories of the conflicts of Demetrius and George, of Theodore and Sebastian, of the Theban legion and Maurice its leader, and of Eustace, supreme commander of the army and his companions, who won the crown of martyrdom in heaven. He also told them of the holy champion, William, who after long service in war renounced the world and fought gloriously for the Lord under the

---

11 *The Ecclesiastical History of Orderic Vitalis,* ed. and transl. by M. Chibnall, III (Oxford: Clarendon Press, 1972), Books V and VI, pp. 216–17: »Huic maxima semper adherebat familia, in quibus nobilium ignobiliumque puerorum numerosa perstrepebat copia. Cum eodem consule commorabantur uiri honorabiles clerici et milites quos tam laborum quam diutiarium gratulabatur esse suarum participes.«

monastic rule. And many profited from his exhortations, for he brought them from the wide ocean of the world to the safe harbour of life under the Rule.«[12]

In this way, the clerics adapted their exhortations to suit the bellicose tastes of the feudal class of the times. Exploits of holy warriors who had fought for the faith became of prime interest. First came the exploits of the martyrs of early Christianity; later, from a more recent period and from their own country, the exploits of heroes such as Saint William, the famous William of Orange. We may conclude from the above mentioned chronicle that in Orderic's time, that is to say, in the first half of the twelfth century, there were in circulation various versions – indeed two are still extant – of the epic poem *Moniage Guillaume*. In fact, Orderic Vitalis confirms that the minstrels spread one version of the song but that he himself preferred what he thought was the more authentic account, carefully composed by the learned clergy and read with reverence by assiduous *lectores* in the community of brothers. He inserts a detailed summary of this *relatio autentica* in his chronicle.[13]

But this passage from Orderic's *Historia Ecclesiastica* tells us also that it was not a jongleur who extolled the prowess of St. William of Gellone to the noble knights, but a cleric. According to Orderic, this took place at the court of a count who was fond of worldly display, an aspect of life which he regarded as the richest part of the human beatitudes. Orderic tells us that this count was »always in the forefront in battle, lavish to the point of prodigality, a lover of games and luxuries, actors, horses, and dogs and other vanities of the same kind.«[14] So, jongleurs were relegated to the company of horses and dogs. But the story of St. William is put on the same level as that of St. George or St. Eustace and consequently was not considered appropriate for jongleurs.

From this we may see that the *chanson de geste* had been but a partic-

---

12 *Loc. cit.*: »Praecipuis baronibus et modestis militibus puerisque nobilibus salutares monitus promebat, et de ueteri testamento nouisque Christianorum gestis imitanda sanctorum militum tirocinia ubertim coaceruabat. Luculenter enim enarrabat conflictus Demetrii et Georgii, Teodori et Sebastiani, Mauricii ducis et Thebeae legionis, et Eustachii precelsi magistri militum cum sociis suis, qui per martirium coronari meruerunt in coelis. Addebat etiam *de sancto athleta Guillelmo*, qui post longam militiam abnunciauit seculo, et sub monachili regula gloriose militauit Domino. Multis igitur profuit eius exhortatio, quos ad tutam regularis uitae stationem e mundiali protraxit pelago.«

13 *Ed. cit.*, book VI, 3 (p. 218 ff.).

14 *Ed. cit.*, p. 216: »Erat enim in militia promptus in dando nimis prodigus, gaudens ludis et luxibus, *mimis,* equis et canibus, aliisque huiusmodi uanitatibus.«

ular type of hagiographic song, essentially the same as the one example of the hagiographic genre remaining from this period, *The Life of Saint Alexis,* doubtless written around 1050 at Rouen. In his treatise *De Musica* from about 1300, Johannes de Grocheo, subsumed hagiographic narratives and epics under the same term, *cantus gestualis,* and even gives a literary and musical description of them. Ever since the famous *Tu Autem* composed around 1096–1099 at the abbey of St. Martial in Limoges, we have known the musical scheme of these hagiographic narratives. And from the thirteenth century, we also have specimens of the music of three *chansons de geste,* doubtless preserved without change, since the second half of the eleventh century.[15]

This intimate relationship between the hagiographic genre and the epic is a well-known fact and is not limited to French literature. Albert B. Lord, in his entry »Narrative Poetry« in the *Encyclopedia of Poetry and Poetics,* shows parallels in both English and German literature. »In other words«, he concludes, »both religious and secular epic are written in vernacular style during this period.«[16] Paul Zumthor, in his article »From the universal to the particular in medieval poetry«, clearly stated the reason for this when he writes that »although creation as such is indubitably individual, the medieval literary work appears less as an individual creation, as grasping a particular quality of its object, than as a mimetic activity, derived from a need for collective participation, comparable to a choral song or dance«.[17] This is well confirmed by Orderic Vitalis when he tells us that the cleric Gerold elegantly narrated the story of the martyr Eustace and of William of Orange before Earl Hugh and his court. »The poet«, says Professor Zumthor, »produces his own personal language, by means of patterns transmitted to him by the community. It is the community which confers their motivations on the signs constituting the poem. The individual being is rooted in the social group, and, if he is a poet, he justifies his belonging to it by giving in his work a new structure of his own to the cultural, already well-elaborated elements with which this group has provided him.«[18]

It is evident that the clerics themselves took great pleasure in these epic stories. They were not too far from the time when Alcuin addressed

---

[15] Cf. J. Chailley, *L'École musicale de Saint-Martial de Limoges jusqu'à la fin du XIe siècle* (Paris, 1960), p. 352, pp. 357–58.
[16] Princeton: University Press, 1965, p. 546b.
[17] *Modern Language Notes* 85 (1970), 816.
[18] *Op. cit.,* pp. 816–17.

a letter to bishop Speratus of Lindisfarne, in which he wrote: »The
work of God should be read at meals of bishops and priests. There, it
is more suitable to listen to the *lector* and not to the minstrel, to the
sermons of the fathers, not to the songs of the heathen. For what has
Ingeld the Dane to do with the Christ? The house is small; both do not
fit in it.«[19]

At least Alcuin's efforts to establish the Latin language in the Carolingian schools and the introduction of the Trivium and the Quadrivium
had borne some fruit: the clerics and monks of the eleventh century
wrote their heroic poems in Medieval Latin. The audience for these
texts was to be found in clerical circles, mainly in the abbeys, as Orderic
Vitalis shows by telling us that he learned about the *Moniage Guillaume*
from a monk of Winchester during the visit of this monk to Orderic's
abbey at St. Evroult. Stories like that of St. William must have inspired
the monks to compose new songs centering around the exploits of a
hero who had become legendary in the particular monastery where the
song was composed. Without a doubt, the model of the *Girart de Roussillon*, for instance, was composed at the abbey of Vézelay in Burgundy
where Girart was a legendary figure. In the same way, the abbey of
Gellone in Languedoc perpetuated the memory of William of Orange
(and for this reason is now called Saint-Guilhem-le-Desert). Likewise
in Picardy, the abbey of St. Riquier kept alive the memory of Isembart.

There does not seem to be any doubt that these songs were composed
in Latin, and Orderic Vitalis bears witness to the fact that they were
circulated over a wide area, for it is attested that a copy of the *Vita
Sancti Wilhelmi* from Gellone in Languedoc was found in Winchester
in England before 1120. From there the monk Anthony took it to the
abbey of St. Evroult in Normandy where Orderic hastened to make a
résumé of it.[20] Another proof of the wide dissemination of these songs
is the epic *Waltharius manufortis*, which has as its subject a Visigothic
hero, attested in Aquitaine (*Waltarius vocor, ex Aquitanis sum gene-
ratus*) and to whom the *Nibelungenlied* alludes, calling him *von Spânje*

---

[19] Passage published by O. Jänicke in *ZfdA* 15 (1872), 314: »Verba Dei legantur in
sacerdotali convivio. Ibi decet lectorem audiri, non citharistam; sermones patrum,
non carmina gentilium. Quid enim Hinieldus cum Christo? Angusta est domus,
utrosque tenere non poterit. Non vult rex celestis cum paganis et perditis nome-
tenus regibus communionem habere, quia rex ille aeternus regnat in caelis; ille
paganus perditus plangit in inferno.«

[20] Cf. *ed. cit.*, pp. 218–19.

Walther. This Latin poem has come down to us in no less than 29 manuscripts scattered across Europe. It is, then, not at all surprising to find Gautier, Waltarius if you will, in the *Song of Roland,* where he appears in his native Aquitania as guardian of the passes in the Pyrenees.[21] Another indication is furnished by *The Hague Fragment* cited above, in which a portion of the Latin poem, composed in very polished and emphatic hexameters, appears in Latin prose in order to facilitate reading the poem.[22] Moreover, we have already mentioned another Latin prose version, the *Conversio Othgerii militis,* composed around 1070–1080 at the abbey of St. Faron at Meaux in the Ile-de-France.

Therefore, we are hardly astonished by the statement that in the second half of the eleventh century the clerics attached to the feudal courts in the North of France and in England and spurred on by the growing cultural and political awareness of the feudal class, did not limit themselves to the lives of saints. As Orderic Vitalis reports,[23] they passed from the narratives of martyrs and of the holy warriors of the Old Testament to the exploits of the heroes of the Merovingian and Carolingian dynasties and to epic material even closer to their own times.

There is every indication that these stories were first read in Latin and then explicated to the non-learned public by the clerics, just as they were accustomed to do with religious texts. But there came a time when the clergy was given the task of translating the Latin poems, probably at the request of the cultured laity. Sometimes, a cleric was merely the translator of a Latin poem, at other times he was the author as well. Such was the case with the incredible epic voyage of St. Brendan from the beginning of the twelfth century which Queen Adelaide, wife of Henry I of England, asked its author, a certain Benedict, to translate from Latin into the vernacular. Unfortunately, we do not know of any author who was also the translator of a Latin heroic epic poem, with the exception, perhaps, of the priest Conrad, who tells us in the epilogue of his *Ruolantes liet* that he is also the author of a Latin version of the *Song of Roland.*[24] But this testimony is from the second half of the

---

21 Cf. R. Lejeune, »La composition du personnage de Gautier del Hum dans la *Chanson de Roland«, La Technique littéraire des chansons de geste* (Paris: Les Belles Lettres, 1959), pp. 237–269.

22 Cf. P. Aebischer, »Le Fragment de La Haye. Les problèmes qu'il pose et les enseignements qu'il donne«, *ZfrPh* 73 (1957), 26–7 (article reprinted in *Rolandiana et Oliveriana: Recueil d'études sur les chansons de geste.* Genève: Droz, 1967, p. 24).

23 Cf. n. 12.

24 ll. 9080–83: »also iz an dem buche gescribin stat / in franczischer zungen, / so

twelfth century and therefore no longer typical of the literary genre
under discussion, one of the characteristic features of which was precisely the anonymity of its authors. That is hardly surprising. In his
previously mentioned article, Professor Zumthor rightly insists on the
fact that

> »most medieval works are anonymous. When we are able to detect some-
> thing of an author's personality, our information seldom reaches further
> than his name, roughly his chronological position, and supposed cultural
> environment. This fact is not totally accidental or without general signifi-
> cance. We hardly distinguish the part played by the individual in the in-
> formation of the literary work; probably it had little value in the opinion
> of medieval people. The work is entirely ›objectified‹; its ›subject‹ (the
> author's subjectivity) has dissolved in the course of time, not only because
> time has slipped away, but because in some way the author's individuality
> was not an essential factor of the work.«[25]

In the most refined circles, the clerics took over the role of the popular
story-tellers, from whom they not only borrowed subject matter but
style as well.[26] This explains, too, the phenomenon which we arbitrarily
call »formulas«, movable clusters of words for which we can refer the
reader to the fine interpretation of the phenomenon by Professor Edward
A. Heinemann in his paper »Network of Narrative Details: The Motif

---

han ich iz in die latine bedwngin, / danne in di tutiske gekeret.« (*Das Rolandslied
des Pfaffen Konrad*, hg. von C. Wesle. 2. Aufl. besorgt von P. Wapnewski. Altdeutsche Textbibliothek Nr. 69. Tübingen: Niemeyer, 1967, p. 318). – For more on
this problem see note 58.

25 *Op. cit.*, p. 817.

26 About the transition from oral to written epic cf. especially Professor Franz
H. Bäuml's paper read at this Conference, »The Unmaking of the Hero: Some
Critical Implications of the Transition from Oral to Written Epic«, as well as,
by the same author, »Zur mündlichen Überlieferung des Nibelungenliedes«, *DVj*
41 (1967), 351–90 (together with Donald J. Ward), and »Weiteres zur mündlichen
Überlieferung des Nibelungenliedes«, *DVj* 46 (1972), 479–493 (together with
Agnes M. Bruno), especially pp. 483–488 and note 17, wherein the remark about
the *Heliand* is also applicable to the oldest Old French epics: »Der Formel-
reichtum des Heliand sowie seine von Rathofer festgestellten strukturellen Eigenschaften könnten wohl damit erklärt werden, daß er das Werk eines schreibenden,
gelehrten Dichters ist, der die Mittel der mündlichen Dichtung benützte, nicht weil
er sie unbedingt zum Kompositionsakt nötig hatte, sondern weil er sein Gedicht
stilistisch sowie in manchen inhaltlichen Aspekten dem noch kulturell heidnischen,
analphabetischen und an formelhafte mündliche Dichtung gewöhnten Publikum
verständlich machen mußte. Das Verfahren des Dichters ist also als ›schriftlich‹,
weil ›schreibend‹, zu bezeichnen. Seine Kompositionsmittel sind aber die der
›mündlichen‹ Dichtung. Sein Gebrauch dieser Mittel ist der eines ›schreibenden‹
Dichters, da er sie zur Komposition nicht unbedingt nötig hatte.«

of the Journey in the *Chanson de Geste*«, also read at this Conference. It seems clear that the popular story-tellers used these formulas together with others to generate a descriptive whole which would suggest to the audience a given motif, like that of the journey studied by Professor Heinemann or that of the killing of a Saracen by a Christian, studied in Eugene Vance's brilliant chapter »Formulaic Language and Heroic Warfare«.[27] Quoting from Adam Parry's »Language of Achilles«[28] a passage to the effect that »the style of Homer emphasizes constantly the accepted attitude toward each thing in the world, and this makes for a great unity of experience«, Vance concludes[29] that

> »this ›unity of experience‹, which is a function of the conventionality in the poem's language, would seem to create difficulties for a poet who wishes to isolate what is *particular* about a given individual; yet he may overcome this dilemma by making *quantitative*, rather than *qualitative*, distinctions between his character's actions. Fatally wounded, for example, Archbishop Turpin delivers more than a thousand blows (CLIV); the *Roland* distinguished its heroes by magnifying them, just as a Romanesque sculptor (such as the master of Vézelay) will make his Christ twice as big as the lesser spiritual heroes around him. Physical dimensions and God-given force are measures of spiritual virtue in Romanesque art.«[30]

The clerics transformed existing epic poems – as well as the stories that they themselves invented – into poems which exalted the virile virtues in the service of Christianity and at the same time censured excess and *démesure*. Just as Romanesque art does not have any perspective of space, so too the organizing perspective of time, any futurity, is absent in these poems.[31] This is particularly true of the fragment of *Gormont et Isembart*, which represents probably the oldest epic poem which has come down to us.[32] The military spirit of the feudal class of the eleventh

---

[27] E. Vance, *Reading the »Song of Roland«*, Englewood Cliffs, N.J.: Prentice-Hall, Inc., 1970, pp. 21–38.

[28] *Transactions and Proceedings of the American Philological Association* 87 (1956), p. 3.

[29] p. 25.

[30] Vance writes »measures of spiritual virtue in twelfth-century art«, but it is obvious that the spirit he is describing is that of an earlier period, although the narthex of the abbatial church of the Madeleine at Vézelay was not finished until 1150, at the very decline of Romanesque and the rise of Gothic art.

[31] This is an adaptation of a sentence by E. Vance, *op. cit.*, p. 11.

[32] The chronicle of the abbey of St. Riquier near Abbeville, written by the monk Hariulf in 1088 and revised in 1104, mentions it (»[...] non solum historiis, sed etiam patriensium memoria quotidie recolitur et cantatur, [...]«); cf. E. C. Southward, in *Romania* 59 (1946–47), 104.

century is completely evident in this work recounting the somber drama
of a renegade, Isembart, who mobilized the aid of the pagan army of
Gormont in England and then returns to ravage his own domain, the
coast of Picardy. He burns, among other things, the abbey of S. Riquier,
until finally King Louis takes the field and puts down the pagan, and
Isembart, before he dies, returns to the Christian faith. Although the
poet depicts the renegade sympathetically, with a basically French and
Christian feeling, his main interest lies in the figure of the king, Louis,
who is described as an ideal heroic prince who fulfills the duties of king
in an exemplary fashion. In the end he dies not only unvanquished like
Roland but victorious, for when he had dealt his mighty and fatal
blow to the Saracen king Gormont, Louis himself had to struggle to
remain in the saddle. In so doing, he ruptures his midriff, a wound from
which he will die several weeks later. *Gormont et Isembart,* which
marks the beginning of heroic poetry in French literature, is the poem
of the holy king who triumphs over an enemy religion.[33] Isembart,
combining the *démesure* of Roland and the revolt of Ganelon, represents a revolt against Divine harmony. It is totally different from the
German *Ludwigslied,* written in 881 or 882 and praising the same king
and the same victory. For in the latter Louis is only God's instrument;
God brought him up, God orders him to fight, the Norman invasion
is God's punishment, God himself decides who will die in this battle,
and the poem ends in a general lyric eleison.

The concept of man in the French poem clearly reflects the influence of
the philosophical school known as »Exaggerated Realism«, dominant
precisely toward the end of the eleventh century. According to this
view, which is already implied in the teaching of John Scotus Eriugena,
man is the substantial unity of many individuals *(Homo est multorum
hominum substantialis unitas).*[34] Thus, individual men differ only
accidentally from each other. This concept of the individual hero leads
to a completely static view of characters with predetermined identities,
as in laisse XII of the *Song of Roland,* when the principal actors make
their entry into the poem. »Along with the others came Count Roland

---

[33] Cf. also K.-H. Bender, *König und Vasall. Untersuchungen zur Chanson de Geste
des XII. Jahrhunderts* (Studia Romanica, 13. Heft. Heidelberg: Winter, 1967),
pp. 43–45: »Die vorbildliche Ludwigsgestalt der Frühzeit«.

[34] Cf. Fr. Copleston, *A History of Philosophy,* vol. II: *Mediaeval Philosophy,* part 2:
From Augustine to Bonaventure (A Doubleday Image Book, Garden City, N.Y.,
1962), p. 162.

and Oliver, one bold, the other noble; there were more than a thousand Franks; Ganelon came, who committed the treason. Now begins the council which brought evil.«[35] As Professor Vance[36] observed, characters already describable in such terms bring into the poem with them a basic framework of causality from which the action must derive. The mere mention of specific names is evidently enough by this time to guarantee a tale of a certain type, a type complete in the minds of both poet and audience before the action even occurs. It is not surprising to find such a strong influence of the »Exaggerated Realism« in the first part of the *Song of Roland* because this philosophical theory was held particularly by the School of Chartres, which preserved, even in the twelfth century, a certain conservative spirit and flavor, as is shown in its Platonist tradition, especially in its devotion to the *Timaeus* of Plato and also to the more Platonical writings of Aristotle.[37]

For some time now, on the other hand, it has been the general consensus that the *Song of Roland*, such as we read it today in the Oxford manuscript, is traceable, especially through the principal characteristics of its first part, back to a poem composed around 1090 somewhere between Paris and Orleans in the vicinity of Chartres.[38] Because this poem strongly influenced the oldest vernacular work of the William of Orange cycle, the same conception of characters, the same literary technique and the same oral style are found in the *Song of William,* which certain scholars have dated later than 1150. With an almost baroque and Shakespearian richness of contrasts, only with difficulty held within a common framework, one notes a certain preponderance of battle honor and virile ruggedness over Christian pathos and love of country. But in the first and clearly older part, the figure of King Louis keeps the same traits as the loyal liege lord of *Gormont et Isembart*.[39] We discover here, however, still another aspect of feudal society of the close of the eleventh century, that is to say, the glorification of

---

[35] ll. 175–9: »Ensembl'od els li quens Rollant i vint, / E Oliver, li proz e li gentilz. / Des Francs de France en i ad plus de mil. / Guenes i vint, ki la traïsun fist. / Des or cumencet le cunseill que mal prist.« (*La Chanson de Roland,* ed. C. Segre. Documenti di Filologia, 16; Milano-Napoli: Ricciardi, 1971, p. 30 f.). The English translation is that of E. Vance, *op. cit.,* p. 10.

[36] *Op. cit.,* p. 10.

[37] Cf. Fr. Copleston, *op. cit.,* p. 191.

[38] Cf. M. Delbouille, *Sur la Genèse de la »Chanson de Roland« (Travaux récents – Propositions nouvelles). Essai critique.* Bruxelles: Palais des Académies, 1954, p. 96.

[39] See also K.-H. Bender, *op. cit.,* p. 46 f.

the battle tradition of a great feudal family in defense of the country against the invaders.

The poet of the *Song of William* confines the number of heroes to a small group. In the *Song of Roland* the abundance of names is there to give us the impression of the quantity of individuals which make up the community. But in the *William* we find a counter-meaning. There exists neither a larger community nor a comradeship of the Twelve Peers. There is only lineage. From this conception of lineage comes the role attributed to Guiborc, the wife of William, who excites his courage by exalting the glory of the family.

> »This first powerful feminine figure in French epic literature«, writes Professor Bezzola,[40] »in no way foreshadows the lady of the *roman courtois*. We are still far from the *société courtoise* of the second half of the twelfth century where every exploit is done for love of the lady who pushes the hero towards individual adventure, the only means of attaining a common ideal. We are still completely involved in a sacred community, as in the case of the *Song of Roland,* with the exception that here the great feudal family, lineage, has replaced the empire. In this sacred community of lineage, the wife is called on to play a role of the first order. She is not the coveted object of a distant love, the lady whom it is necessary to conquer or serve, but the symbol of the home that is to be defended against the invader.«

This is the spirit which reflects the demands of feudal society upon the feudal king. In the case of the big barons, however, this spirit remains invisible. They have to struggle on their own against aggressors. This was especially true, indeed, for the barons in the South – I am thinking particularly of the counts of Barcelona who appear linked to the legend of William of Orange already in the so-called *Nota Emilianense* found in the abbey San Millán de la Cogolla as mentioned above.

But the idea of empire, as Bezzola sees it in his comparison of the *Song of Roland* and the *Song of William,* is developed in the former only in the Baligant episode.[41] We hear for the first time of Baligant, the emir of Babylonia, in laisse CLXXXVIII, when we suddenly learn that Marsile has been imploring Baligant for aid during the seven years of Charlemagne's campaign in Spain but that Baligant only now has

---

40 Reto R. Bezzola, *Les Origines et la Formation de la littérature courtoise en Occident (500–1200).* Deuxième partie: *La Société féodale et la transformation de la littérature de cour,* t. II (Bibl. de l'École des Hautes Études. Sciences historiques et philologiques, fasc. 313. Paris: Champion, 1960), p. 503.

41 It is significant that the word *empire* occurs only in the epilogue of the *Chanson;* cf. C. Segre, *ed. cit.,* l. 3994.

decided to rally to the support of his defeated ally. »Occupying more than a quarter of the total of the *Roland* text«, writes Professor Vance,[42] »the so-called ›Baligant episode‹ includes a long chronicle-like list of battle-corps from both sides (the French have ten, the Saracens no less than thirty), a rather pale description of a combat between them and a compressed narration of a duel between Charlemagne and Baligant, which can be described as little more than epic shorthand.« As Vance points out, the story of blind temerity could doubtless still appeal to an eleventh century audience as a monument to a glorious age still within memory and considered as a model to follow, but »as an expression of contemporary needs ... [it] challenged the poet to an extension«.[43] Unfortunately, Professor Vance does not specify which »contemporary« period he is thinking of, but everything he says here is doubtless quite correct. Before continuing, we should recall the following passage from his book:

> »... the Baligant episode and the trial of Ganelon [...] may both be re-
> garded as responses to cultural attitudes in Capetian France which inspired
> men to emphasize those aspects of legendary history that could enhance
> the hope of achieving some kind of political stability in the world. Even
> though Roland's death is already avenged before the Baligant episode, the
> poet probably wished to revive an image of Charlemagne enjoying the full
> prestige that his memory could still evoke [...] Accordingly, a need arose
> in the poem for an antagonist of Charlemagne's own stature, one who could
> pretend to the same universalism as Charlemagne's himself. With the ar-
> rival of Baligant, the ideological axis of the poem no longer involves just
> France and Moslem Spain, but East and West.«[44]

This last statement needs some modification, as we shall see, but the rest would appear to fit the expectations of an audience of the middle of the 12th century very well. Such an atmosphere did indeed prevail in 1147, 1148 and 1149, when King Louis VII was participating in the Second Crusade. It has long been noted[45] that, despite the confrontation between East and West depicted in the Baligant episode, the author of this expansion had no intention of inciting the Christians to undertake a crusade, although he is entirely pervaded by the ideas which inspired them to do so and is living in the moral sphere which had given rise

---

[42] *Op. cit.*, p. 73.
[43] *Op. cit.*, p. 73.
[44] *Loc. cit.*
[45] J. Horrent, *La Chanson de Roland dans les littératures française et espagnole au moyen âge* (Paris: Les Belles Lettres, 1951), p. 319.

to such military expeditions. This was exactly the case of the abbot
Suger of St. Denis, regent during Louis' absence in the Orient. Suger had
not favored his king's project of going on a crusade and tried to per-
suade him not to abandon the kingdom, the throne of which many
barons were only too ready to occupy in view of the lack of male descendants. And he was perfectly right: as soon as the king's army had
left France in the summer of 1147, disorders broke out and within a
very short time there was complete anarchy: churches were ransacked,
clercs and merchants robbed, counts occupied the free cities and drove
out the officers of the king, candidates for certain episcopal sees mobilized the mob and terrorized the electoral colleges. In short, the whole
effort of more than twenty years to pacify the country and to improve
its situation seemed to be ruined within months. But with the help of a
few very powerful barons, who were also his personal friends, especially with the help of Geoffrey Plantagenet (1113–1151), duke of
Normandy and count of Anjou and Maine, and that of count Thierry
of Flanders (died in 1168), Suger managed little by little to restore
order.[46] As I have shown in an article to be published in the Festschrift
for Erhard Lommatzsch, the two barons and many others of Suger's
circle are named as being among the knights of Charlemagne's army
against Baligant. Among other points, we may here merely mention,
for example, that Geoffrey and Thierry are among the four barons who
help to revive Charlemagne after he had fainted at Roncevaux on finding his dead nephew and the other barons, an allegoric gesture quite
typical of Suger's style.

Gefreid d'Anjou even bears the royal banner, the same one which King
Louis had taken from the main altar at the abbey of St. Denis where it
had been kept, and which had now been consecrated for the crusade by
Pope Eugene III. The mention of the royal banner in the Baligant episode proves once again that the author of this continuation of the old
Song of Roland must have belonged to the circle of the regent and was
writing for his cause and that of the king. This allusion to the banner
is now introduced into the poem with considerable discretion, as though
its appearance were simply another traditional element. But we know,
of course, that up to this time there had been no such practice. In reality
the banner in question had been that of the counts of Vexin, until in

---

[46] Cf. O. Cartellieri, *Abt Suger von Saint-Denis, 1081–1151* (Historische Studien
veröffentlicht von E. Ebering, Heft XI. Berlin, 1898), p. 53; M. Aubert, *Suger*
(Abbaye S. Wandrille, 1950), p. 101.

1077, or 1081,[47] after the death of the last count, King Philip I seized the Vexin because of its strategic importance in the struggle against the duke of Normandy, who was now also king of England. But the king of France had no other interest in the Vexin, until Suger, abbot of St. Denis since 1122, turned the attention of King Louis VI the Fat to it in 1124, when an Anglo-German invasion threatened France, and the German emperor, Henry V, at the head of a large army, was preparing to invade France and march on Reims. In this serious situation, Suger persuaded the king to invoke publicly the aid of his patron saint, saint Dennis, and to have the reliquary of the martyr raised up on the altar, a moving symbolic ceremony – again, much as Suger liked – and which, done in time of danger to the kingdom, recalled an old Merovingian tradition. He then offered the old *vexillum* of the counts of the Vexin to his king, in order to rally the support of the valiant barons of the county behind the king, and the king took it with him for the first time on a military campaign. Fortunately, the German invasion was called off for political reasons and the banner returned to St. Denis, not to leave it again until 1147 in an even more solemn ceremony arranged by the same Suger.

It is, indeed, the spirit of Suger which we can detect in the Baligant episode, for, as Erwin Panofsky points out,[48] the mighty abbot of St. Denis placed his superior gifts of organization and political feeling at the service of two ambitions; he wanted to strengthen the power of the Crown of France, and he wanted to glorify the abbey of St. Denis and extend its influence. To Suger, these ambitions did not conflict with each other. On the contrary, they appeared to him as aspects of but one ideal which he believed to correspond both to natural law and to Divine will. For he was convinced that »a king, and most particularly the king of France, was a ›vicar of God‹, ›bearing God's image in his person and bringing it to life‹«. But this fact, far from implying that the king could do no wrong, entailed the postulate that the king *must* do no wrong (»it disgraces a king«, Suger writes, »to transgress the law, for the king and the law – *rex et lex* – are receptacles of the same supreme power of government«, as is demonstrated, for example, in the trial of Ganelon). Secondly, any king of France, but quite especially Suger's beloved mas-

---

47 About the question of the Vexin cf. R. Barroux, »L'Abbé Suger et la vassalité du Vexin en 1124«, *Le Moyen Age* 64 (1958), 1–26, especially 1–15.
48 *Abbot Suger on the Abbey of St.-Denis and its Art Treasures* (Princeton: University Press, 1946), p. 2.

ter, Louis the Fat, who at his coronation in 1108 had divested himself
of the secular sword and had been girded with the spiritual sword »for
defense of the Church and the poor«, had both »the right and the sacred
duty to subdue all forces conducive to internal strife and obstructive
to his central authority«.

There is no doubt in my mind that the *Song of Roland* was reworked
in the years of Suger's regency (1147–1149) and that the poet was also
a monk at St. Denis.[49] It is to him that we owe the combination of the
old Song of the battle of Roncevaux with the revenge of Roland in the
trial of Ganelon.[50] But he is also the author of a third ingredient based
on contemporary historical events – the arrival of Baligant in Spain
itself[51] –, thus creating a new episode which serves as political propaganda for the central power of the French king.

The effect of this new version of the poem on the feudal audience must
have been tremendous, for we can witness a mushrooming of epics concerning a particular hero's struggle with the central power and especially with the abuses of its prerogatives. William of Orange, Ogier the
Dane, Girart of Roussillon, Renaut of Montauban, the barons of the
Lorraine, etc. have each their poem which tells the story of the hero,
victim of an injustice – or so they believed – on the part of the kings
of France, Charles Martel, Charlemagne, Charles the Bald, or a certain

---

[49] The iconographic evidence does not contradict this dating. It is true that art
historians date from ca. 1120–1130 the famous lintel of the Angoulême cathedral
in which scenes of the *Song of Roland* are depicted, but these scenes all represent
episodes of the old (ca. 1090?) song of the battle at Roncevaux, cf. R. Lejeune and
J. Stiennon, *La Légende de Roland dans l'art du moyen âge* (Bruxelles, 1967),
p. 36.

[50] J. Halverson, »Ganelon's Trial«, *Speculum* 42 (1967), 668, too, places the composition of this episode in the 12th century.

[51] Recently, J. Poncet, »La Chanson de Roland à la lumière de l'histoire: vérité de
Baligant«, *Revue de l'Occident musulman et de la Méditerrannée* 1970, pp. 125–139,
succeeded in identifying even Baligant, »l'amiraill de Babilonie«, himself. The name
goes back to two sons of Ali Ghâniya, namely Yahya and Mohammed *Ben Ali
Ghâniya*, whom the Christians may already have known when they were generals
of the Moslem armies of the Levant from 1126 on, but particularly after their
arrival in Spain, where they fought mainly in Aragon and in Cerdagne (which
explains certain geographical incongruities and contradictions of the *Song of Roland*) and became famous in the whole Christian world by their victory in 1134
at Fraga over King Alphonso I (El Batallador) of Aragon, who died of the wounds
of this battle, the same king who in 1118 had conquered Saragossa from the Saracens and had made it the capital of his kingdom, which had been confined to the
Pyrenees until Alphonso's conquest of the Ebro valley.

Louis.[52] What is striking about these heroic epics after 1150 is the fact that they all focus on the psychological evolution of the hero. This is best demonstrated by the story of the most famous, but also the most terrible, epic of this type, *Raoul of Cambrai,* which, besides the attack on the central power of the king, depicts the human tragedy of Raoul's vassal Bernier, who is bound by the ties of allegiance to his lord, while the latter commits crime after crime in order to avenge what he considers an injustice on the part of the king. Bernier, whose family supports the cause of the king and who recognizes the ill-founded reasons of Raoul's wars, has no right to free himself from these ties, even when Raoul burns down the monastery of which his mother is abbess, thus causing her to be burned alive together with all the other nuns. It is only when Raoul hits him on the head so that his blood flows that he is free to become the instrument of the monster's destruction.[53]

But this tragedy of individuals was composed at the end of the 12th century, at least in the form in which we read it today. At that moment, the description of intimate dramas and of individual conscience had already been present in the *chanson de geste* for some time. If we are not mistaken, it is again the *Song of Roland* which attests to it first, not in the version inspired by Suger, but in the reworked Anglo-Norman text of which the manuscript of the Bodleian Library at Oxford is a close copy. In this text, which could be by the Turoldus mentioned in the last line, one finds, besides other minor changes, the purpose of which was to make the poem more contemporary, a more relevant one: an additional laisse dedicated to the conversion at Aachen of the queen of the Saracens, Bramimonde. The Anglo-Norman poet obviously took great interest in the spiritual welfare of the lady. She already plays a very active role in the version inspired by Suger, where she expresses aloud her doubts concerning the power of the pagan gods (l. 2600: »Our gods committed an act of treason«). The Anglo-Norman poet wanted to complete the portrait of the charming lady by bringing her entirely within the pale of the Christian Church: »In my palace, there is a noble prisoner«, says Charlemagne. »She hears so many sermons and edifying

---

[52] Cf. J. Bédier, »Les Chansons de geste«, *op. cit.,* pp. 226–30.

[53] For a fine literary analysis of this powerful poem, see I. Siciliano, *Les Chansons de geste et l'épopée, Mythes – Histoire – Poèmes* (Biblioteca di Studi Francesi, 3. Turin: Società Editrice Internazionale, 1968), pp. 395–416. Some good observations, although unfortunately dispersed throughout the text, can also be found in William C. Calin, *The Old French Epic of Revolt: Raoul de Cambrai, Renaud de Montauban, Gormond et Isembard.* Geneva: Droz/Paris: Minard, 1962.

tales that she wants to believe in God and asks for the Christian faith.«[54]
And, concluding the episode, the poet insists again on the queen's own
initiative in her conversion by saying (l. 3987): »She is Christian
through knowledge of the true faith.«

This attitude supposes a completely different audience than that which
had applauded those fabulous blows in the battle at Roncevaux. This
audience was interested in the salvation of a noble pagan lady who was
to be brought to Christianity not by force, not by persuasion, but
through her own inner motivation. We are reminded here of Peter the
Venerable's fervent conviction that the Moslems were not to be approached, »as our people often do, by arms, but by words; not by force,
but by reason; not in hatred, but in love«.[55] But Peter the Venerable,
»by his insistence, on the familiar grounds of the Gospels and patristic
tradition, that the Moslems of his day were as specifically intended as
any of the Gentiles to participate in Christian salvation, [...] was in
fact a pioneer«.[56] His treatise *Liber contra sectam sive Haeresim Sar-
acenorum* does not seem to have had a great influence in his own period, preoccupied as it was with the Second Crusade. Nevertheless, he
must be considered as a forerunner of an evolution which was to gain
momentum rapidly. Peter died on Christmas 1156, and the most likely
date for the manuscript of the Oxford *Roland* is about 1170.[57] In a few
years, the attitude of the nobility must have changed considerably so
that it could accept the fact that Turoldus nearly ended his poem with
the story of an individual conversion of a noble lady.

This new spirit is not characteristic of the England of the Plantagenet
alone, but also, for instance, of the Saxony of Henry the Lion, as is
shown by the priest Conrad, whose *Ruolantes liet* was probably written
at the court of Brunswick between 1186 and 1189.[58] Conrad is the only

---

[54] ll. 3978–3980: »En ma maisun ad une caitive franche; / Tant ad oït e sermuns e
essamples, / Creire voelt Deu, chrestïentét demandet.« *(ed. cit.,* p. 672).

[55] »Non ut nostri sepe faciunt armis sed uerbis, non ui sed ratione, non odio sed
amore«, quoted from J. Kritzeck, *Peter the Venerable and Islam* (Princeton Orien-
tal Studies, 23. Princeton: University Press, 1964), p. 47 n. 155.

[56] J. Kritzeck, *op. cit.,* p. 24.

[57] We too adopt this practical and »parlant« date proposed by Gaston Paris and
accepted, among others, by Joseph Bédier. For a detailed discussion of this date
and the others proposed see J. Horrent, *op. cit.,* pp. 32–42, especially p. 32 f.,
where Horrent lists all the proposals, before proceeding to a linguistic analysis of
the text, which leads him to the conclusion: »Ceci nous situe dans la deuxième
moitié du XIIe siècle plutôt que dans la première« (p. 42).

[58] For the text of this note see p. 174.

other poet in the whole of preserved Roland literature to report Bramimonde's conversion. But that he should do so is not surprising given the fact that the duchess Mathilda, Henry the Lion's wife, was a daughter of Henry II and Eleonor of Aquitania, and iconographic evidence has established beyond doubt that Conrad's French model must have been written in England.[59] It is even likely that Henry the Lion brought it back from his stay in exile (spring 1182 – fall 1185) at the court of the Plantagenet. Still more significant is the careful description Conrad gives of Brechmunda's religious evolution: she is already a Christian in her heart when Marsilie is dying at Saragossa, as is evidenced not so much by her cursing the pagan gods aloud and violently, as she does in Turoldus' poem, but in her ethics. Weeping, she says to her husband: »Could I but purify you! I would give in exchange all that I ever saw. Your misfortune touches me. Never will I be able to redeem you. You will burn in hell.«[60] Conrad is so eager to save this soul that he even changes the plot to have Brechmunda ask for the Christian faith upon opening the gates of Saragossa to Charlemagne: »I am consoled by your coming, for I know the truth you bring. Take me into Christendom. I believe in my Lord, and I shall do your bidding!«[61] But this is not enough: after her conversion, she gets still further attention from our poet. After the conquest of Saragossa, the Emperor bewails the dead warriors on the battlefield, according to the customs of his ancestors. Brechmunda cannot tolerate this lamentation and says: »May God forbid that, my Lord! It is my belief that, because they died for the just cause, they live for ever before God. Now, I heard you say, my Lord, that one must not bewail the just, for their death is a true Christian one. There are the avowed sinners who die the ultimate death. The holy men here will obtain the grace of God for us.«[62] The Emperor marvels at her wise words and indeed stops mourning.

---

[59] Cf. R. Lejeune and J. Stiennon, *op. cit.*, p. 135 f.

[60] ll. 8599–8604: »si sprach: ›macht ich dich geraine, / da ware umbe uaile / aldaz ich ie gesach. / uil lait ist mir din ungemach. / nune mac dich niemen wider gewinnen: / in der helle mustu brinnen.‹« (*ed. cit.*, p. 297).

[61] ll. 8626–8630: »du bist mir zetroste chom. / ich erkenne wol dine warhait: / hilf du mir zu der christinhait! / ich geloube an mínín trechtin: / swi du gebiutest so wil ich sin.« (*ed. cit.*, p. 298 f.).

[62] ll. 8646–8656: »›daz uerbietiu, herre, min trechtin‹, / sprach di frouwe, / ›daz ist de min geloube, / want si durh daz rechte sint gelegen, / daz sie uor gote iemir leben. / nu hort ich dich, herre, sagen: / die rechten scol man nicht chlagen / (ir tot ist geware), / sunt offen suntare, / di totliche ersterben. / dise heiligin sculen uns gotes hulde erweruen.‹« (*ed. cit.*, p. 300).

There is no more striking proof of the rapid change in taste of the audience than a comparison of this episode with the literary »climate« at the battle of Roncevaux in the French *Song of Roland,* where we read repeatedly: »The Frenchmen strike, then multiply their blows. Some of the pagans die, while others faint. The archbishop says, ›Blessed be our barons!‹«[63] There the Christians get the blessing of the Church for slaughtering the Saracens like animals,[64] here the highest secular representative of Christianity takes theological advice from, and admires the wisdom of, a lady recently converted from paganism of her own free will. One could not have a better illustration of how far the heroic epic in the second half of the 12th century has come from the uniform, collective passions depicted by the poets of those earlier *chansons de geste* based on the tastes of audiences in the second half of the 11th century. It is true that Conrad's *Ruolantes liet* was never intended as an heroic epic *per se,* but it is characteristic of this period when the individual and his problems were beginning to emerge in literature that Conrad could find these elements in his Anglo-Norman model.

Does this surprise us, however, if we remember that, at the time when Turoldus wrote his version of the *Song of Roland,* on the other side of the Channel another great poet at Troyes was already writing masterworks in the literary genre of the *roman,* with its innumerable individual adventures of body and soul? Indeed, from the second half of the 12th century on, it is no longer possible to distinguish between the tastes of the audience for the *chansons de geste* and those of audiences more concerned with other literary productions in the vernacular, especially as audiences were not now composed so much of listeners – at least not in high society – as of readers, whether those who merely read for themselves or to a small audience in place of the *clerc lisant.* Let us recall the nice scene in *Yvain* where Chrestien describes a family gathering at which the daughter reads aloud to others who are illiterate:

---

[63] ll. 1347–9: »E li Franceis i fierent e si caplent. / Moerent paien e alquanz en i pasment. / Dist l'arcevesque: ›Ben ait nostre barnage!‹« (*ed. cit.,* p. 240 f.).

[64] Professor F. P. Pickering, in the discussion of my paper at the Ann Arbor symposium, called attention to ll. 5418–23 of the *Ruolantes liet:* »fluchte si si noten / mit ir scarphen swerten, / daz si sich zeiungist nine werten. / si [the Saracens] uielen sam daz uihe zetal, / si slugen si uon dem wal / rechte sam di hunte.« (*ed. cit.,* p. 208 f.). But it is obvious to me that an adapter like Conrad could not escape the influence of his model, although he was able to give another meaning to the poem; let us not forget that in this passage Conrad was reworking the oldest part of the *Song of Roland,* the battle of Roncevaux, composed probably between 1086 and 1095.

»[Yvain] saw a rich man stretched out on a silken cloth and resting on his elbow. In front of him a young girl was reading some story or other. In order to listen to her, a fine lady had come in and rested on her elbow too; it was her mother, and the gentleman her father. They could, indeed, rejoice at seeing her and listening to her.«[65]

It is clear that after 1150, although the *chanson de geste* will still remain alive for another century at least, it had lost its intrinsic function, namely, the appeal to the *sainte mellee* (the holy medley) and to the perpetual military pilgrimage in the cause of Christendom. The tastes of the audience now required that the poet praise not so much heroes with extraordinary physical force and endurance in the service of France and Christianity but heroes without ties with their own period, incorporating the virtues defined by the new type of knight of courtly society.

Now, it was precisely for this society that Wace evoked the spirit of the battle of Roncevaux,[66] and in such an atmosphere it is not surprising that he should have failed to grasp the original social function of the *chanson de geste*.

---

[65] ll. 5356–5366: »voit apoié desor son cote / un riche home qui se gisoit / sor un drap de soie; et lisoit / une pucele devant lui / en un romans, ne sai de cui; / et por le romans escoter / s'i estoit venue acoter / une dame; et s'estoit sa mere, / e li sires estoit ses pere; / si se porent molt esjoïr / de li bien veoir et oïr. / [. . .]« (*Les Romans de Chrétien de Troyes*. IV: *Le Chevalier au Lion (Yvain)*, p.p. M. Roques. Les Classiques français du moyen âge, 89. Paris: Champion, 1960, p. 163). Despite this direct testimony, it is still a mystery to me how the medieval reader succeeded in reading fluently, often aloud to listeners, as here in *Yvain*, manuscripts which sometimes present considerable difficulties even to well-trained modern paleographers. It is possible that the daughter of the chatelain of Pesme-Aventure knew the story already when she read it to her parents, but how did she learn it? Was it read to her by the person who brought her the manuscript or gave her an opportunity to transcribe it? Or did the copyist of her manuscript first read it to her?

[66] For Wace, the high deeds of heroes must no longer be remembered for a moral or political purpose, but rather to prevent them from sinking into oblivion, in other words, they are not different from the exciting exploits of an Arthurian hero told in a captivating way in a romance; cf. the beginning of the Third Part of his *Roman de Rou* (ll. 1–10, ed. Holden, vol. 1, p. 161): »Pur remembrer des ancesurs / les feiz e les diz e les murs, / les felunies des feluns / e les barnages des baruns, / deit l'um les livres e les gestes / e les estoires lire a festes. / Si escripture ne fust feite / e puis par clers litte e retraite, / mult fussent choses ubliees / ki de viez tens sunt trespassees.« (In order to remember the exploits and the sayings and the customs of ancestors, the misdeeds of felons and the high deeds of barons, one must read books and chronicles and stories at festivals. If they had not been written down and then read and told by clerics, many things which happened a long time ago would have been forgotten.)

Note 58 of p. 170

R. Lejeune and J. Stiennon, *La légende de Roland dans l'art du moyen âge* (Bruxelles: Arcade, 1967), p. 119, write »entre 1180 et 1195«, but Henry was in the most troubled period of his life between 1174 and 1182 and then went into exile for more than three years, and again after Easter 1189; after his return in October of the same year, the last struggle, against Henry VI, entirely absorbed his attention, and from his last days (1193–1195), the chronicles report his exclusive concern with religious matters; besides, the duchess Mathilda died June 28, 1189.

The last scholar who studied the epilogue of Conrad's poem, Chr. Gellinek, »The Epilogue of Konrad's Rolandslied: Commission and dating«, *Modern Language Notes* 83 (1968), 390–405, brings interesting arguments in favor of another duke Henry, namely Henry »Jasomirgott« of Babenberg, who in 1184 married Theodora, the niece of Manuel Comnenus Emperor of Byzantium, a highly educated woman of exquisite literary taste and mother of Leopold V of Babenberg, Reinmar of Hagenau's and Walther of the Vogelweide's maecenas. But Henry already lost Bavaria in 1156 to Henry the Lion, and the chronicles make it very clear that Bavaria – and especially Regensburg – had no sympathies whatsoever for the Babenberger; cf. M. Philippson, *Heinrich der Löwe, Herzog von Bayern und Sachsen. Sein Leben und seine Zeit.* 2nd ed., Leipzig: O. Leiner, 1918, p. 53. But there is more: although E. Fr. Ohly, »Zum Reichsgedanken des deutschen Rolandsliedes«, *ZfdA* 77 (1940), 189–217, rejected Helmut Röhr's theory (»Die politische Umwelt des deutschen Rolandsliedes«, *PBB* 64, 1940, 1–39) which identified the lion in Roland's shield with Henry the Welf's insignia and maintained rather that it was suggested by the *Song of Rolands's* comparison of Roland with a lion, it is nevertheless highly interesting to note that Roland bears a lion in his shield (»Roland der milte, / ain lewen furt er an sinem schilte, / uzer golde ergrabin.« ll. 3985–7), because it was a fairly recent practice to have shields bearing other elements than just stripes. This new mode was developed by the Plantagenet and is attested for the first time in 1127, when an official act by Henri I of England attests that in knighting his son-in-law Geoffrey of Anjou he presented him with a blue shield bearing six small golden lions, which became Geoffrey's distinctive insignia throughout his lifetime; upon his death the insignia were adopted by Henry II and successive generations, and they became the first known example of true heraldry (cf. M. H. Pakula, *Heraldry and Armor of the Middle Ages*, South Brunswick/New York: Barnes, 1972, p. 20). In Germany the mode was introduced with the Norman longshield in the middle of the 12th cent., where the vassals of the emperor had the right to bear the imperial eagle on their shield, e.g. Henry of Babenberg (»Jasomirgott«) as duke of Austria. But »Heinrich der Löwe [führt] bis zur Absetzung 1180 im Schilde seines Reitersiegels *kein* Wappenbild; bei seiner bekannten Gegenstellung zum Kaiser *wollte* er nicht den Adler tragen. Später als *Allodialherr* von Braunschweig und Lüneburg *durfte* er den *Lehns*adler nicht in sein Wappen stellen, deshalb führte er auch kein Reitersiegel mehr, sondern frei im Felde einen Löwen, dem er seinen Beinamen verdankt.« (E. Gritzner, »Heraldik«, *Grundriss der Geschichtswissenschaft*, hg. A. Meister, vol. I, Part 4. 2nd ed., Leipzig/Berlin: Teubner, 1912, p. 68). Thus, before 1180 no poet could possibly speak of a shield bearing a lion!

In Mulagir, »das beste sachs«, which duke Naimes gave »Karle sinem herren«, who in turn presented Genelun with it, but who lost it to the Saracens, a deed which caused so many Christians to suffer, it is possible, moreover, to see an allusion to the fact that Henry was forced to renounce the title of duke of Bavaria in 1180. »Swa er sich uirsumet hat, / ze gerichte er im nu stat: / an dem iungistin tag / da got sin gerichte habe, / daz er in ze gerichte nine uordere, / sundir er in ordine / zu den ewigin gnaden, / dar umbe rufe wir alle AMEN!« (ll. 9069–9076), with its reference to wrong done in the past by Henry and to the concentration on the conciliation of God, is equally characteristic of the period of *poenitentia cottidiana* (R. Seeberg), when Henry the Lion was reduced to the possessions of his mother after his humiliation by the Emperor but when he was still interested in worldly matters and especially in the arts and literature.

It is the period when he and Mathilda were particularly active in the construction of the Saint Blasius cathedral at Brunswick, when most objects of the famous treasure were assembled and when poets were still entertaining the court of the duke. We mention only Eilhart of Oberge, whose *Tristrant unde Isalde* was probably composed for the court of Brunswick – the Rhenish influences which can be detected in the fragments, e.g. influences of the so-called *Alexander of Strasburg*, are easy to understand, for Henry the Lion's relations with Cologne were very close, politically (archbishop Philip of Heinsberg was one of his staunchest supporters) and in the arts (e.g. the enamel pieces of his treasure are inspired by the Cologne school).

The duke's artistic interests were very strong, as is shown by his personal intervention in the editing of the *Große Lucidarius,* also written in the same period; cf. from the prologue: »Diz buch heizet Lucidarius, / und ist durch recht geheizen sus, / wan ez ist ein luhtere. / Swer gerne vremede mere / von der schrift vernemen will, / der mach hie wunders horen vil / in deseme cleinen buche. / Man soldez verne suche(n) / ê man ez vunde ensamt geschreben. / Got hat ime den sin gegeben, / *dem herzogen der ez schriben liez:* / sine capellane er hiez / die rede suchen an den schriften, / und bat sie daz *sie ez dihten* / *ane rimen wolden.* / Wande sie en solden / niht schriben wan die warheit, / *als ez ze latine steit.* / Daz daden sie willecliche / *dem herzogen Heinriche,* / der ez in gebot unde bat: / *ze Bruneswich in der stat* / wart ez gedihtet und geschreben. / *Der herzoge wolde,* / daz man ez hize da / »Aurea Gemma« / do duhte ez dem meister besser sus, / daz ez hieze Lucidarius / wan ez ein luhtere ist. / Man vindet uz maneger schrifte / ein deil geschrieben dor inne.« (ap. Fr. Philippi, »Heinrich der Löwe als Beförderer von Kunst und Wissenschaft«, *Historische Zeitschrift* 127 (1923), p. 62). With such a personal intervention into the creative process of a literary work, it seems not unlikely that the duke also intervened in the edition of the *Rolandslied,* as can be seen from the ll. 9031–4: »daz si [the duke and the duchess] sin [of the *Song of Roland*] gedachten, / daz man iz fur brachte / intutische zungin gekeret, / da ist daz riche wol mit geret«, a passage not unlikely to the prologue quoted above (concerning the interpretation of l. 9034, cf. D. Kartschoke, *Die Datierung des deutschen Rolandsliedes,* Stuttgart: Metzler, 1965, pp. 14–16).

The personal interest of the duke also adds weight to the explanation of the curious fact that Conrad translated first into Latin and subsequently into German, as it is given by M. Lintzel, »Zur Datierung des deutschen Rolandsliedes«, *ZfdPh* 51 (1926), p. 17, although Professor Gellinek certainly has a point when he doubts that Conrad would translate the matter of Roland into an uncommissioned language (*op. cit.,* p. 395): given the fact that even in the 13th century the literary activity in Latin was so great in Saxony that *Herzog Ernst* and Hartmann's *Gregorius* were translated into Latin (according to D. Kartschoke, *op. cit.,* p. 36), it is not surprising that Conrad was commissioned first with an adaptation of the *Song of Roland* into Latin and subsequently for another one into German, for a less educated but probably more chivalric audience, which he based equally on his French model, contrary to the conclusion reached by Ch. Gellinek (*op. cit.,* p. 405); the two verbs, *bedwingen* and *keren* are obviously synonymous in this passage (ll. 9080–3: »also iz an dem bûche gescribin stat / in franczischer zungen, / so han ich iz in die latine *bedwngin*, / danne in die tutiske *gekeret*«).

Given Henri the Lion's great interest in the letters and the arts, it is not surprising to find also Bavarian artists at his court in Brunswick, especially as the loyalty of Bavaria, and of Regensburg in particular, to the cause of the Welfs is a well-known fact (see, for instance, how Henry »Jasomirgott« of Babenberg was treated in 1138 by the citizens of Regensburg). Conrad, even if he is identical with the *Chuonrat plebanus* discovered by Professor von Mandach in a necrology of the abbey of Obermünster at Regensburg (cf. A. von Mandach, *Naissance et développement de la Chanson de geste en Europe*. I: *La Geste de Charlemagne et de Roland*, Geneva/Paris: Droz/Minard, 1961, p. 206 f.), was a parish priest and therefore could very well stay at the ducal court in Brunswick. This is the more likely as the presence of other Bavarian artists in Saxony is attested in this period. The famous Gospelbook of Henry the Lion and his wife Mathilda, the so-called Gmunden-Gospels, which is a copy of a manuscript executed at St. Albans in England (cf. Otto Pächt, *The Rise of pictural narrative in Twelfth-century England*, Oxford: Clarendon Press, 1962, p. 46), was illustrated by the illuminators of Helmars-hausen in Upper Saxony (cf. F. Jansen, *Die Helmarshausener Buchmalerei zur Zeit Heinrichs des Löwen*, Hildesheim, 1933, p. 83). The illuminations of the Heidelberg manuscript and of the two preserved ones of the Strasburg Fragments of Conrad's *Ruolantes liet* show strong similarities with those of the Gmunden-Gospels, although they principally belong to the style of the school of Regensburg-Prüfening (cf. J. Stiennon, in R. Lejeune and J. Stiennon, *op. cit.*, p. 135 f.). Thus, illuminators trained at Regensburg-Prüfening must have been at work in Helmars-hausen during Henry the Lion's patronage. As a matter of fact, the poem itself does not contain any indication that Conrad was actually working at Regensburg (*Regensburch*, in l. 1602, refers only to the legendary smith Madelger, maker of Duke Naimes' sword Mulagir).

Nor do I think that it is only by accident that most of the fragments of manu-scripts of the *Ruolantes liet* are preserved in places which were in some kind of relationship with the state of Henry the Lion. Although Mecklenburg, conquered in 1160 by Henry, became an imperial fief in 1181, Henry's relations with the bishops of Schwerin remained cordial until his death. Therefore it is quite under-standable why the Fragment of Schwerin of the poem bears such a strong resem-blance with the oldest preserved text, the manuscript of Heidelberg. Arnstadt in Thuringia, south of Erfurt, was an important and very old place (mentioned al-ready in 704) in Henry the Lion's state and particularly active in cultural affairs (cf. J. Bühring, *Geschichte der Stadt Arnstadt*, 1904); it is then not surprising that a copy of the *Ruolantes liet* is found there as early as the end of the 12th century. The relationship of Erfurt with Henry the Lion is well-known because of his sub-mission to the emperor in this town in 1180; although this fragment seems to post-date by some decades the manuscript of Heidelberg and the Arnstadt Fragment, it proves quite well that Conrad's poem circulated first in the regions of Henry's strongest influence. The Fragments of Strasburg alone escape a direct influence of the court of Brunswick; at least, it seems so, but as they are preserved today only in a copy made by Johann Georg Scherz in the second volume of Johann Schilter's *Thesaurus Antiquitatum Teutonicarum* of 1727, it will never be possible to know anything about their provenience. Finally, the only complete manuscript of Conrad's poem, preserved in the cod. germ. 112 of the ancient library of the Elector Palatine is itself the best proof that the poem originated at the court of the duke of Saxony. For not only do the illuminations plead for a strong relationship between Henry's artists with those of England (cf. T. S. R. Boase, *English Art*,

1100–1216, Oxford: Clarendon Press, 1953, p. 192), but the manuscript, which dates from the late 12th century and was certainly among the oldest copies of the poem, must have been in the possession of the Elector Palatine for centuries, because the old inventories of the university library at Heidelberg do not mention its acquisition before its fusion with the ducal library in the 16th century (cf. F. Wilken, *Geschichte der Bildung, Beraubung und Vernichtung der alten Heidelbergischen Büchersammlungen*, Heidelberg, 1817). Thus, it is quite likely that it belonged to the dukes of the Palatinate since the time of Henry the Lion's son Henry, the son-in-law of the first duke and his successor, who may have inherited the manuscript from his father's estate.

Henry the Lion's strong interest in Roland, and especially in the figure of Charlemagne, finds its explanation in the fact that the family of the Welfs prided itself on direct descendancy from Eticho, a supposed brother (in reality perhaps a nephew) of the empress Judith, second wife of Louis the Pious: Henry the Lion was thus a relative of Charlemagne's family (cf. »Historia Welforum Weingartensis«, *Monumenta Germaniae Historica. Scriptores*, 21 (Hannover: A. Hahn, 1868), 458 f.; written between 1169 and 1181). Cf. also R. Folz, *Le Souvenir et la légende de Charlemagne dans l'Empire germanique médiéval*. Publications de l'Université de Dijon, 7 (Paris: Les Belles Lettres, 1950), p. 250: »Les efforts du prêtre Conrad ne sont d'ailleurs pas isolés: une tendance générale existe, qui rattache le duc de Saxe à la tradition carolingienne et qu'illustrent d'autres témoignages encore: voici Brunswick, appelée à tenir la place d'Aix-la-Chapelle pour l'Allemagne nouvelle de l'Est; le château de Dankwarderode, sis tout à côté de la cathédrale, est une réplique du palais d'Aix qu'une galerie reliait à la chapelle.« Fr. Philippi, *op. cit.*, p. 53 f., interprets even the famous lion in bronze in front of his palace (erected in 1066) as inspired by the so-called wolf in front of Charlemagne's cathedral at Aachen.

Edward A. Heinemann

Network of Narrative Details:
The Motif of the Journey in the *Chanson de Geste*

The subject of my paper is conventionality and the extent to which it may have been exploited artistically in the *chanson de geste*. That this genre is highly »stereotyped« is well known, and since the publication of Jean Rychner's *La Chanson de geste, Essai sur l'art épique des jongleurs*[1] much study has been done on the use to which individual *jongleurs* have put the traditional material. Like the early lyric, the *chanson de geste* seems to rest on an strong tradition to which jongleur and listener make systematic reference. This »dialogue« between the poem and its tradition appears in the numerous variants offered by the manuscripts which have preserved the texts. We can also discover it by comparing multiple treatments of particular elements in various poems. In today's talk I should like to present the findings of some work I have done recently and to outline the tentative conclusions and, more important, the questions which those findings suggest.

---

[1] Publications Romanes et Françaises, 53 (Geneva: Droz, and Lille: Giard, 1955). I shall use the following sigla for the texts used in this study.

    A: *Ami et Amile, Chanson de geste,* publiée par Peter F. Dembowski. Classiques Français du Moyen Age (Paris: Champion, 1969).

    R: *La Chanson de Roland,* publiée d'après le manuscrit d'Oxford et traduite par Joseph Bédier. Edition définitive (Paris: Piazza, 1937).

  CL: *Le Couronnement de Louis, Chanson de geste,* publiée d'après tous les manuscrits connus par E. Langlois. Société des Anciens Textes Français (Paris: Firmin Didot, 1888).

 MG: *Les Deux rédactions en vers du Moniage Guillaume, Chansons de geste du XIIe siècle,* publiées d'après tous les manuscrits connus par Wilhelm Cloetta, 2 vols. Société des Anciens Textes Français (Paris: Firmin Didot, 1906–1911). Reference made to the second redaction only.

The preliminary nature of this study should be emphasized. I have tried to accumulate a fairly large body of information, but I do not claim to have taken note of all the journeys in these four poems, nor is it certain that an exhaustive documentation would represent a measurable advance.

Many aspects of the *chanson de geste* are repetitious. As Rychner put it, at a certain distance the entire genre seems stereotyped (p. 126). I shall limit myself primarily to the motif, a term whose meaning I shall leave imprecise by taking it to be a fairly small element of the narrative, often between ten and twenty lines long, but capable of compression to a single line or amplification to a hundred lines or more. As the term implies, the motif is an element which appears repeatedly. This repetition bears on content as well as on choice of expression. Rychner has composed an illustrative list of motifs with references to numerous examples (pp. 128–30). These motifs range from the highly structured (or stereotyped), like single lance combat, to one as »loose« as that of a character perceiving from the window of a castle the approach of another. (This last motif, apparently, is not even associated with any fixed formulas; see p. 139). Somewhere in between these extremes would be the lament for a dead hero, a motif whose structure Paul Zumthor has studied in two articles.[2]

The structure analyzed by Zumthor is essentially a series of interrelated networks. The motif is associated with a network of details, and each detail is associated in turn with a network of major lexical items. The details occur regularly, but not necessarily in every single realization of the motif. The detail may be expressed in a single hemistich, in a complete line, in a cluster of lines. The order in which the details occur is somewhat fixed: a link to the narration appears at the beginning of the motif and an apostrophe to the fallen hero often appears in the middle of either praise spoken of him or the expression of internal grief.

Since the lament is after all an expression of emotion, one has no trouble seeing it as a lyrical element, and Zumthor even sees the possibility that the lament could have been a set piece derived from a previously existing independent genre. The occurrences which Zumthor studies make considerable use of repetition, amplification, and variation so that a kind of verbal modulation corresponds to the sentiment expressed. Other occurrences, lacking this modulation, Zumthor qualifies as either narrative or harbinger *(annonciateurs)* occurrences.

---

[2] »Étude typologique des *planctus* contenus dans la *Chanson de Roland*«, in *La Technique littéraire des chansons de geste*, Actes du Colloque de Liège (septembre 1957), Bibliothèque de la Faculté de Philosophie et Lettres de l'Université de Liège, Fasc. CL (Paris: Les Belles Lettres, 1959), pp. 219–34; and »Les *Planctus* épiques«, *Romania* 84 (1963), 61–69.

The journey is neither lyrical nor neatly defined. On the one hand no emotional content sets it up for lyrical treatment. And on the other, it can be military, as in a sortie against opposing troops (A 368–73), it can be the carrying of a message the length of a country or simply through the streets of a town, a pilgrimage, any displacement in time and space. Further, in the number of details clustered about both the preparatory activities and those which characterize arrival it becomes difficult to determine exactly where to identify the limits of this motif. On this point it is symptomatic to note that Rychner lists as motifs both greetings and taking leave but not journeys whereas I see greetings and leave-taking as details among those forming the network which defines the motif of the journey.

Since neither emotional content nor distinct narrative boundaries seem to characterize the journey as a tidy unit, the credentials of this motif as »unstereotyped« are fairly good. For this reason the journey represents a good control for the evidence found in the rigid motif of lance attack (the regularity of the structure of this motif encourages one to think of formulas as a series of ready-made beads strung end to end, and I hope that my paper will show why I think otherwise) or for the lyrical one of the lament, the first being more »stereotyped« than the »typical« passage in the *chanson de geste,* and the second representing of necessity a pause in the unfolding of the plot. The interplay of norm and variation in the motif of the journey will, hopefully, give an insight into the use of convention in the genre as a whole.

Two aspects of my terminology may need some explanation. The first, »narrative detail«, is not particularly difficult in itself. I use the term as referring to any item of content abstracted from the particular formulation it receives in the text. A narrative detail, or simply detail, may be large or small; there may be one or more in a given formula, depending largely on our point of view. A formula generally expresses one essential detail, but we can fix our attention on other, secondary ones. The formula *monte el cheval* expresses the essential detail of mounting (the horse is simply understood), but we can equally well take the formula to use two details, »mounting« and »horse«. We shall see below a series of examples which give the detail, »at a given point in time«, first as a secondary detail and then as the essential detail of a formula (see n. 4).

Just as the comparison of texts shows elements regularly expressed in approximately ten to twenty lines, it also shows elements which regularly appear as the essential detail of a formula, that is, expressed in one or two hemistichs. These elements too can be compressed (and become secondary details in a formula) or amplified (expanded to a number of formulas). There being less copywork involved with these elements than with motifs, there are naturally more repertories of details published than of motifs.

The second, and perhaps more difficult, aspect of my terminology is that I define the formula as a metrical unit of syntax. Whether the individual poem is written in decasyllables or dodecasyllables does not seem to matter; the heavy reinforcement of the caesura (after the fourth syllable in the decasyllable, and after the sixth in the dodecasyllable) by the syntax of the line, and, to an even greater degree, the syntactic break at the end of the line are so characteristic of epic versification in Old French that the difference between a four- and a six-syllable first hemistich is insignificant. What is significant is the extraordinary coincidence of meter and syntax, so much so that the syllable count is in fact as much a grammatical rule in the language of the *chanson de geste* as is the agreement of nouns and adjectives. This particular rule of epic grammar seems to me the essential aspect of formulaic language; the formula has in metric language roughly the same place as the clause has in ordinary prose. Every line is therefore entirely formulaic, composed of either one two-hemistich formula or two one-hemistich formulas. I have divided the first examples in my paper at the hemistich in order to emphasize the syntactic importance of meter.

By abstracting the content from the particular formulation it may receive in a given passage, we discover an even greater degree of repetition in the *chanson de geste* than is evident in formula lists based on near-identity of wording. Conversely, this repetition underscores variety – variety of expression, variety of combination, variety of implication – and it is this verbal modulation, this scheme of variations on themes which I should like to examine.

To illustrate this verbal modulation, I have chosen, from the details which form the network of the journey, five details, each of which illustrates a different way in which the network of formulas expressing a given detail may be formed.

The first, the detail of mounting on horseback, is marked essentially by one lexical item, the verb *monter*. One way of analyzing these formulas is by the construction of the predicate. The verb may figure in an absolute construction (R 2851, MG 3177, MG 1110, R 3679). The circumstance of place may be specified by the prepositions en[3] or sor followed by either the animal on which the man has mounted (A 290, R 2841, R 1801, R 2811, R 2816, CL 603, CL 1800, R 2765, R 3943) or the saddle (A 1114, A 582; in these two cases the second hemistich specifies the animal). Under special circumstances the character mounting figures as the direct object of the verb; in A 2517 Ami is suffering from leprosy, and his being lifted to the horse's back reveals both his own weakness and his two followers' devotion; in R 3943 Charlemagne and his followers honor Thierry for having defended the emperor's cause; in MG 3178 the Saracens unceremoniously raise their prisoner Guillaume on to a pack horse.

Examples:

Monte el cheval	quant la selle fu mise	A	290
Muntet el ceval	vient a sa gent puignant	R	2841
Montent es selles	des destriers arrabis	A	1114
Montent es selles	des destriers sejornez	A	582
Es destrers muntent	tuit li barun de l'ost	R	1801
Puis sunt muntet	par grant vertut chevalchent	R	2851
Puis sunt muntez	es chevals e es muls	R	2811
Puis est munted	en un sun destrer brun	R	2816
A tant en monte	sor l'alferant destrier	CL	603
A cest mot montent	la pute gent grifaigne	MG	3177
A icest mot	est Guillaumes montés	MG	1110
Il est montez	sor un mul aragon	CL	1800
Muntet li reis	e si hume trestuz	R	3679
Li dui message	es chevals sunt muntet	R	2765
Et lor seignor	dant Ami il monterent	A	2517
Munter l'unt fait	en une mule d'Arabe	R	3943
Guillaume lievent	sour un soumier aufaigne	MG	3178
Li frans Alelmes	mist pié en son estrier	CL	1858

In order to emphasize the variety of systems to which every formula belongs, I have grouped the formulas for this detail, not by the construction of the predicate as I have just analyzed it, but by certain »superficial« resemblances, primarily rhythmic ones related to word order and syntactic and semantic functions. In the first group monter combines in the first hemistich with a prepositional phrase indicating

---

[3] En + le > el; en + les > es.

place. (The last example in the group is somewhat different from the others because the verb comes at the end instead of the beginning of the hemistich.) The point of resemblance in the second group is that *monter* figures at the end of the first hemistich, preceded by an expression indicating a point in time. Notice that the last two examples in this group do not fit the description I have given. *MG* 1110 expands the expression of time to fill the first hemistich and puts the verb in the second hemistich.[4] And in *CL* 1800 a one-syllable subject pronoun replaces the one-syllable expression of time; this characteristic slippage of grammatical categories underlines the multiplicity of the components of the formula. The examples of the third group show extensive variety of expression. Those of the fourth group show the character mounting as the direct object of the verb *monter*. And the two examples of the fifth group show the exceptional case of expressing this detail without the verb *monter*.

A second detail, »so much that«, always occurs in combination with other details and never occurs as a complete formula in itself. It is expressed by the tool words *tant ... que* and can be constructed in three ways:

1. *tant* + action + *que* + result;
2. action + *tant que* + result;
3. *tant* + action + (ellipse of *que*) result.

Ordinarily the result is some detail expressing either the point of arrival or some point reached during the journey.

Examples:

    Tant chevalchat   qu'en Saraguce fut   *R* 2818
        He rode until he was in Saragossa

    Mont Chevrol puie   tant que il vint en som   *A* 61
        He climbs Mount Chevrol until he reached the summit

    Tant ont tuit troi   esploitié et erré
    De Rome virent   les murs et les piliers   *A* 2477–78
        All three have gone so far
        They saw the walls and pillars of Rome

---

[4] The circumstance of »time at which« seems sufficiently independent of the predicate to function as a formula when it fills a hemistich. On the relation of syntactic independence to the length of the formula, see pp. 9–11 of »Composition stylisée et technique littéraire dans la *Chanson de Roland*«, *Romania* 94 (1973) 1, 1–28.

I should like to emphasize that the expression of this detail is grammatical rather than lexical. Since language grammaticalizes some notions and lexicalizes others, there exists little reason *a priori* why we should not choose a grammatical construction to label a detail, and the detail »so much that« is not unique in this respect. A detail which in the *chanson de geste* is very often the essential detail of a formula is one which can best be labeled »adverbial expression of manner«: *par tel vertu,* »with such vigor/manliness/virtue«; *en guise de baron,* »in the manner of a noble warrior«; *par peine e par ahans,* »with great pain and suffering«. I have given these three formulas in increasing order of semantic weight, a circumstance which in no way changes their being the expression of the same essential detail, »adverbial expression of manner«. Another well-known detail is the filler cliché, often expressed as a relative clause or as a pair of appositions to the name of a person. It could well be that this cliché would be described best in grammatical terms, »qualifier of a person«.

The third detail, »points passed«, is interesting in that one of its characteristic marks is a syntactic pattern.

Key marks:

    1. lexical: *passer* or an occasional synonym
    2. tool words: *par, par mi*
    3. syntactic: accumulation in parallel constructions of
       geographical nouns: place names
       borc »town, fortified place«; *ville, cité*
       terre, manandie, contrée, païs »domain, estate«

Examples:

Passent les terres	et les citez estraingnes	*A*	2044
Passa Torainne	et Poitiers autressi	*A*	1873
Passe les terres	et les grans manandies	*A*	291
Passent les terres	et les amples contrees	*A*	484
Passe Mortiers	et Chomin et Chastel	*A*	57
Passent les villes	et les bors et les terres	*A*	2518
Passent les bors	et les citez traversent	*A*	203
Passe les bos	et les puis et les tertres	*MG*	2085
Par Monbardon	s'en sont outre passé	*A*	2475
Par mi les rues	s'en vait a esperon	*CL*	1801
Par mi les rues	s'en vait tot eslaissiez	*CL*	1859
Le val passerent	adonques quitement	*MG*	971
Le gaut parfont	tot delivrement passent	*MG*	982
Le bos trespasse	et les amples regnés	*MG*	2462

Puis si chevalchent	par mult grant cuntençun		
La Tere Certaine	e les vals et les munz	R	855–56
Puis sunt muntet	par grant vertut chevalchent		
Cez veiez lunges	e cez chemins mult larges	R	2851–52

In the final two examples, taken from *Roland*, the verb *chevalchier* (»to ride«) governs the names of places passed. This use, by extending the sense of the verb, underlines the importance of the syntactic pattern as a sign of the detail of points passed.

The fourth detail, »I could not tell the details of their trip«, is a relatively rigid network combining three fixed elements, [*de* + possessive + *jornees*], an expression signifying »give an account«, and *ne sai*. The variety of word order and of expressions for »give an account« appears directly related to assonance.[5]

Key marks:

   1. *de* + *les/ses/lor* + *jornees*, constructed as object of 2.
   2. verb or expression meaning »give an account«:
      dire, deviser, conter, anoncier, tenir compte.
      Constructed as complement of 3.
   3. *ne sai* »I do not know (how)«; *ne m'en chaut mais* »it is of no importance to me«.

Examples:

De lor jornees	ne sai compe tenir	A	1877
De ses jornees	ne sai conte tenir	CL	1451
De lor jornees	ne vos sai deviser	CL	2276
De ses jornees	ne vos sai anoncier	CL	2053
De lor jornees	ne sai que vos contasse	CL	1448
De ses jornees	ne vous sai aconter	MG	896
De lor journees	ne sai pas conte dire	MG	2994
Ne m'en chaut mais	des jornees conter	A	2476
Ne sai pas dire	trestor lor airrement	MG	926
Que vous diroie?	tant a fait et erré ...	MG	86

---

5 A similar cluster of fixed elements is found in the detail, »did not stop until« (2.3.3), for which Duncan McMillan has compiled an extensive repertory under the rubric »allèrent tout droit à«. See pp. 492–93 of his »Notes sur quelques clichés formulaires dans les chansons de geste de Guillaume d'Orange«, in *Mélanges de linguistique romane et de philologie médiévale offerts à M. Maurice Delbouille* (Gembloux: Duculot, 1964), t. II, pp. 477–93.

I have chosen the fifth detail, »seeking out and greeting a person«, for its lack of fixed expression. Five of the examples use the verb *trover*, and, of these, three construct the first hemistich *Iluec trova*, »There he found«. Two more of the examples use *veoir* (»to see«), and one uses *encontrer* (»to encounter«), so that it would be possible to affirm that the lexical field »to perceive« is the mark of this detail.

Occasional mark: *trover* + person.

Examples:

La a Guillelmes	rei Looïs trové	CL 2217
Iluec trouva	Amile le chatainne	A 517
Iluec trova	Looïs le fill Charle	CL 2385
Iluec trova	le riche rei Galafre	CL 448
Acelin trueve	molt ot de compaignons	CL 1803

Premiers encontre   Guillelme le guerrier   CL 1860
    He encounters first Guillaume the warrior

Ou voit Hardré   vers lui prinst a aler   A   344
    He goes over to where he sees Hardré

But, in a third group of examples, the roles are reversed, and a character at the point of arrival comes to and greets the traveler instead of vice versa.

Depart la presse   de la chevalerie
Gombaus le voit   si li a prins a dire   A   295–96
    He makes his way through the crowd of knights
    Gombaut sees him and has begun to speak to him

E Bramidonie   vient curant cuntre lui   R 2822
    And Bramidonie comes running up to him

As li Alde venue   une bele damisele   R 3708
    Here is Aude come before him, a fair young noblewoman

And one last example will illustrate a greeting, as opposed to seeking out and finding a character.

Par bel' amur   malvais saluz li firent   R 2710
    Out of friendship they gave him evil greetings

As I have already said, I have not given you an exhaustive study of the possibilities. These illustrations claim only to show some of the structures which make variety of expression, of combination, and of implication integral to the formulation of any given detail. The details in the Appendix, »Network of Details in the Motif of the Journey«, are all formulated by similar networks of formulas.

The details forming the motif of the journey divide into three groups, departure, the actual movement in space and time, and arrival. The details of departure and arrival show a curious mirror-image quality in the tradition (although not necessarily in any particular realization of the motif). Departure takes place in the morning (1.1), arrival in the evening (3.1). Mounting (1.2.3) and dismounting (3.4) are regularly represented at their respective ends of the journey. Exit from (1.3.2) and entry to (3.2.2) a city, building, tent, or ship characterize the two ends of trips, as do taking leave of (1.4.1) and greeting (3.3) a character. The same is true of descending stairs at departure (1.3.1) and climbing them (3.2.3) upon arrival.

The trip itself does not receive much attention from *jongleurs*. Its durational aspect is minimized to the advantage of what might be called its »inchoative«, »punctual«, or »perfective« aspects. We find quite a few formulas like *acoille son chemin* (»he takes to the road«), which, expressing the very beginning of the journey, belong to detail 1.3.3, setting out. But the verbs *brochier* and *chevalchier* of detail 2.1 (direct statement of movement) are often constructed with *tant que* (2.3.2), so that the movement is closely linked to its goal and the journey expressed in its »perfective« aspect. And of course the three formulations of detail 2.3, »gap implied in the narration«, imply a »perfective« aspect of the journey, a leap to the arrival.

Detail 2.2, »passing points along the way«, reduces the movement to the series of points enumerated. The difference between the two versions of this detail is really one between a marked and an unmarked version of points passed. Difficulties are points passed which happen to be marked notionally, such as mountains, narrow passes, dangerous rivers. Occasionally the difficulty is stated as such, as in *CL* 2277, *Mongeu trespassent qui molt les a penez*, »They cross through the Great St. Bernard pass, which has caused them much suffering«. But many of the lines I have put in 2.2.2 differ from 2.2.1 only in that the places listed seem more difficult to pass than the others.

Of course no individual realization of the motif uses all these details. The *number* of details is related to the degree of amplification, and the *selection* depends on the nature of the journey. In *CL* 603–06, for example, where Guillaume rides out to a hillock to await single combat with the giant Corsolt, he mounts his horse, takes his shield and lance, and rides out. Obviously he will not dismount or enter the gates of a city at the end of this particular journey. The choice of detail is to some extent dictated by reality.

The esthetic system to which the motif of the journey belongs depends thus on latent repertories whose relation to any particular concrete realization is much the same as that of the grammar and lexicon of a *langue* to the specifix text of a *parole*. The listener/reader decodes the text using the rules of the language. The network of details in the Appendix represents an initial codification of the »grammar« of the motif of the journey. The journey is a pre-verbal notion which convention (or epic »grammar«) associates with a network of details, approximated by those outlined in the Appendix.[6] These details are in turn associated with various lexical items and grammatical constructions, the selection of which represents the initial step of formulating both the detail and motif. The *langue* in which the *chansons de geste* are codified systematically limits its repertories, thereby producing very repetitive texts in which small effects of variation stand out in high relief. The system thus offers the following as possibilities for artistic exploitation.

1. Presence and absence of traditional details, degree of expansion, use of non-standard details.
2. Choice between standard and unusual possibilities of expression, degree of expansion (formulas of one or two hemistichs).
3. The combination of details within a formula or linked by juxtaposed formulas, and diversity of implication as a consequence of variety of combination.

The structure of the journey is too loose, and my documentation too limited to allow any certainty about standard and non-standard details for this particular motif. The networks of formulas examined above point toward norms of sorts for those formulas, but rather flexible ones. We can, however, with the materials at hand, briefly evoke the mechanisms of amplification as well as of combination and implication.

CL 1347 relates an entire journey, albeit a short one, in a single line:

> De ci a Rome ne firent arestage
>> They did not stop between here and Rome

---

[6] For the formula as deriving from a pre-verbal *Gestalt*, see Michael N. Nagler, »Towards a Generative View of the Oral Formula«, *Transactions and Proceedings of the American Philological Association* 98 (1967), 269–311.

The use of detail 2.3.3, »did not stop until«, by itself here suggests that it may enjoy special status in the tradition. Whatever the case may be, the journey usually occupies several lines and is composed of several details:

> Hardrez s'en va, s'a congié demandé,
> Gombaus li donne volontiers et de gré. 312
> Il en avale les mauberins degrez
> Et vint aval, son destrier a trové,
> Par son estrier a Hardrez sus monté,
> Passe les terres et les amples regnés 316
> Et les chastiax, les bors et les citez,
> Jusqu'a Paris ne s'est pas arrestez.
> Il descendi el borc a son ostel,
> La nuit i jut desci qu'a l'ajorner; 320
> *Ami et Amile*, 311–20[7]

In this realization of the motif we have a leave-taking (311–12), descent of stairs (313–14A), mounting the horse (314B–15), points passed (316–17), perseverence right to the goal (318), dismounting (319A), and lodgings for the night (319B–20). Most of these details receive expression more than one line long.

In *MG* 1110–1894 we have a journey amplified to the extent that it becomes a frame for Guillaume's adventures in the robber-infested woods of the val de Sigré. Most of the passage relates things other than the trip, but the evocations of travel scattered through the passage always take the form of the basic details, as you can see.

> A icest mot est Guillaumes montés 1110
> Et vient a l'oste, congié a demandé
> . . .
> Vait s'ent Guillaumes, qui plus ne volt atendre, 1124
> Lor voie aqueillent entre lui et son famle
> . . .
> Tant va li quens entre lui et son famle, 1152
> Qu'en la valee entra sans demorance
> . . .
> A ces paroles acueillent lor cemin.
> En la vile entre ou l'abëie sist 1767
> . . .
> Tant s'esploita que vers la porte vint[8] 1787

---

[7] Hardré goes, he has asked leave / Gombaut grants it gladly / He descends the marble stairs / And he came down, he has found his war horse / By his stirrup Hardré has mounted / He passes the lands and the vast fiefs / And the castles, the fortified places, and the old cities / He has not stopped until reaching Paris / He dismounted in the town at his lodgings / He slept there that night until morning.

[8] At this word Guillaume has mounted / And he comes to his host and has taken

In a motif as loose as the journey, the most important aspect of the code is the combination of details and the diverse effects these combinations may have. In elementary terms, combination refers to something as simple as A 290 (see above, p. 182), which combines the details of mounting and saddling in two formulas in a single line. A more instructive case is the use to which the poems of the Guillaume cycle often put detail 3.2.2, »entry through the gate of a city (or monastery)«. Guillaume has many conversations with gatekeepers, some of whom let him in despite orders they have received from villainous masters (CL 1528–1611), others of whom try to keep him out because they are scared of him. Guillaume manages to pass through the gates of his monastery at the end of his 800 line journey in MG only by battering them down and incidentally crushing the gatekeeper beneath them, in a comic register of course. These combinations are common in the Guillaume cycle.

We can see a very sophisticated use of combination and implication in R 1830–31. I have given with it a similar passage from A 2464–72 to show just how much difference the context can make.

> Halt sunt li pui e tenebrus e grant,   AOI
> Li val parfunt e les ewes curant.[9]
>   R 1830–31

> Li cuens Amis s'en entra en sa voie,   2464
> Celle de Rome que on tient la plus droite.
> Haut sont li pui et les montaingnes roides,
> Li val sont grief qui forment les guerroient.
> Morir i cuident, moult sont en grant desroie.   2468
> A Mongieu vinrent tantost com il le voient,
> Trois jors i furent, belement s'i conroient,
> Et au quart montent, si acoillent lor voie,
>   Or sont en Lombardie.[10]   2472
>   A 2464–72

---

leave of him / Guillaume sets out, who wants to wait no longer / He and his servant take their road / The count and his servant have gone so far / That they entered the valley without delay / With these words they take to the road again / He enters the city where his abbey was located / He continued until he came before the gate.

[9] The mountains are high and dark and vast / The valleys deep, and the waters violent.

[10] Count Ami enters on his way / The road to Rome which is considered the most direct / The summits are high and the mountains precipitous / The valleys are dangerous and make the passage difficult / They nearly die there, they are in great danger / They came to the Great St. Bernard pass as soon as they see it / They stayed there three days, where they were well provisioned / The fourth day they mount and set out / Now they are in Lombardy.

The two passages use the same details of high mountains and treacherous valleys, and in the first case even the formulas are identical. But the text in *A* remains a fairly neutral rendition of the details of dangers overcome; it does not allude to other passages in the poem. The two lines in *R* on the other hand, carry far more weight than merely the evocation of the obstacles to the desperate ride of Charlemagne's army back through the mountain passes to answer the oliphant. This is the third time the poem uses the formula *halt sunt li pui*, and from the very first use, where it introduces a premonition of disaster (814), the formula has been charged with foreboding. The obstacles to this journey take on all the weight of fatality.

Let me point out in guise of conclusion some questions which my research in the journey has raised. First, four texts, incompletely sifted, do not constitute an adequate basis for conclusions. To speak with assurance about the *chanson de geste*, I would have to carry out my research in a much larger corpus. What I have done so far suffices to outline the components of the motif, but the relative values of those parts remain unclear. Further, two sources of variations must be taken into account, the norms set up by individual texts, and a possible evolution in the norms of the genre, the well-known »rigidification« of the genre. Two examples: *R* does not use the detail »I could not tell the details of their trip«, 2.3.1. Is it that *Roland* avoids clichés or that the cliché itself did not belong to the tradition at the time of the composition of the poem? The two examples I have given from *R* to illustrate points passed (856 and 2852) are constructed with the verb *chevalchier* governing the geographical nouns. As I remarked earlier, this construction extends the sense of the verb and stands apart from the other formulations of the same detail. Is it that the tradition had not yet rigidified or that *R* stretches the limits of a rigid genre? I suppose it is best to end on a question.

APPENDIX: Network of Details in the Motif of the Journey

1. Departure

1. Evocation of morning (specification of time of day, waking up, mass): *A* 288, 1876, 2034. *R* 2845–49, 3675. *MG* 59–60, 806–08, 813, 3626.
2. Arming (or disarming, depending on the purpose of the journey).
    1. Armor: *A* 202, 2035. *R* 1796–1800, 2849–50, 3942. *CL* 604–05, 2645. *MG* 65–66, 813, 2063–65 (absence of armor).
    2. Saddle horses: *A* 201, 1859, 2516.
    3. Mount horses: *A* 290, 582, 1114, 2517. *R* 1801, 2811, 2816, 2841, 2851, 3679, 3943. *CL* 603, 1800, 1858. *MG* 1110, 3178.

3. Leave a place.
   1. Descend the stairs of a palace: *A* 313. *R* 2840.
   2. Pass through gates, entry of a tent, or disembark from a boat: *A* 483, 583, 2036.
    R 2766, 2810. *CL* 2381. *MG* 859, 2066.
   3. Region in general, or simply setting out: *A* 45, 333, 906, 1871, 2042, 2460,
    2464–65. *CL* 446, 1446. *MG* 825, 1125, 2062.
4. Take leave of a person.
   1. Ask leave or safe-conduct: *A* 311–12. *R* 2763–64. *CL* 228–36, 249–52, 553,
    1442, 1856. *MG* 827–28, 1111, 2450, 3632.
   2. Accompanied by another for the initial leg of the journey: *A* 584–85, 1860–61,
    2038–39. *CL* 254, 555. *MG* 2451.
   3. Emotion at separation: *A* 586–87, 2040–41. *CL* 1445. *MG* 2459.

2. *Movement in space and time*

1. Stated directly by such verbs as *brochier* »to spur«, *chevauchier* »to ride«, *repairier*
  »to return«: *A* 3297. *R* 1802, 2570, 2689, 2812, 2818, 3944. *MG* 895, 924–25, 945.
2. Stated by implication, passing points in space and time.
   1. Space and time: *A* 57, 70–74, 85–89, 203, 291, 316–17, 484, 2461, 2475, 2518,
    2603. *R* 855–56, 2690–91, 2852. *CL* 1801, 1859. *MG* 971–72, 982, 2085, 2462,
    3000–04.
   2. Difficulties encountered and overcome: *A* 56, 61, 1115, 2045–47, 2466–68.
    R 1830–31. *CL* 1447, 2277. *MG* 927–30, 2081, 2463.
3. Gap implied in the narration, the text skips directly to the arrival.
   1. »I could not tell the details of their trip«: *A* 1877, 2476. *CL* 1448, 1451, 2053,
    2276. *MG* 86, 896, 926, 2994.
   2. So much that: *A* 61–62, 2477–78. *CL* 2215–16, 2646–47. *MG* 86–88, 946–47,
    988–89, 1152–53, 2100–01, 3005–06.
   3. Did not stop until: *A* 204, 292, 318, 334, 342, 485, 516, 908, 1116, 2519, 2604,
    3298. *CL* 447, 1347, 1449, 1452, 2050, 2054, 2278, 2382. *MG* 923.

3. *Arrival*

1. Evocation of evening, night (lodgings): *A* 63, 319, 1875–76, 2462, 3299–3300.
  CL 283–88, 2055. *MG* 3760.
2. Place.
   1. Sees some aspect of point of arrival, or »Here he is at«: *A* 1879–80, 2477–78,
    58, 2050, 2520. *R* 857, 2853–54. *MG* 2473–79.
   2. Enters gates or tent: *A* 2048–49. *R* 2690. *CL* 2279–80, 2384. *MG* 89, 3187.
   3. Stairs and/or hall: *A* 294, 343. *R* 2708–09, 2821, 3707.
3. Seeks out and/or greets a person (or conversely a person seeks out the newcomer):
  A 295–96, 344, 517. *R* 2710, 2822, 3708. *CL* 448, 1803, 1860, 2217, 2385.
  MG 3647–49, 3993–95.
4. Dismount: *A:* 293, 2479, 3301. *R* 2571, 2704–07, 2819–20, 3697, 3945. *CL* 2383.

Antonín Hrubý

Moralphilosophie und Moraltheologie in Hartmanns *Erec*

Selbst dreißig Jahre, nachdem Curtius die Termini Moralphilosophie und Moraltheologie aus dem Vokabular der Germanisten verbannt hatte, zögert man sie zu gebrauchen, um nicht in den Verdacht zu geraten, daß man sich unbedachterweise allzu anspruchsvolle Ziele setzt. Denn ein Versuch, den Geist und das Ethos einer positiven Sittenlehre aus dem Wortgebilde einer Dichtung herauszuschälen, darf gewiß nur im Bewußtsein der »Dürftigkeit des eigenen philologischen Rucksacks« gewagt werden, und – um an ein Wort des großen Baesecke zu erinnern – mit staunendem Respekt »angesichts der Sedimentgebirge mittelalterlicher Theologie«.[1] Doch es wäre ungerecht, die problematisch gewordenen Begriffe Ehrismanns stillschweigend beiseite zu schieben, denn es sollen hier einige Gedanken zur Diskussion gebracht werden, die, falls sie sich bestätigen ließen, die Ausführungen des berühmten Aufsatzes über das »Ritterliche Tugendsystem« in eine neue Perspektive rücken würden.[2] Man wird nämlich, aufgrund des allgemeinen Kontextes des *Erec* – und ohne auf theologische oder dogmatische Spitzfindigkeiten zurückgreifen zu müssen – zu dem Schluß geführt, Hartmann habe, rund fünfzig Jahre vor Thomas von Aquino, eine Sittenlehre vertreten, die auf denselben ethischen Konzepten aufgebaut ist wie die revolutionäre Morallehre des großen Theologen.[3]

---

[1] Georg Baesecke, *Der Vocabularius Sti. Galli in der angelsächsischen Mission*, 1933, Einleitung.

[2] Vgl. Gustav Ehrismann, »Die Grundlagen des ritterlichen Tugendsystems«, *ZfdA* 56 (1919), S. 137–216, und Ernst Robert Curtius, »Das ›Ritterliche Tugendsystem‹«, *DVj* 21 (1943), S. 343–368. Beides wiederabgedruckt in: *Wege der Forschung*, Bd. LVI, 1970, S. 1–84 und S. 116–145.

[3] Das Material, das ich hier besprechen werde, kann allerdings nicht ausreichen, eine solche Hypothese zu unterbauen; die ausgewählten Zitate jedoch vertreten eine Fülle von Belegen, die fast in jedem einschlägigen Satz des *Erec* zu finden sind. Die Frage, in welchem Verhältnis im Hinblick auf die Morallehre der *Erec* zu den

Hartmanns *Erec* scheint für den Versuch, die Grundsätze seiner Moraltheorie zu bestimmen, ein besonders geeignetes Objekt zu sein. Denn wir haben keinen Grund, daran zu zweifeln, daß er, wie Gottfried berichtet, zumindest für einen Teil seiner Zeitgenossen eine besonders verständliche Sprache zu führen verstand und mit kristallner Klarheit die *meine* der Aventiure zu formulieren vermochte. Außerdem sind wir in der glücklichen Lage, in Chrétiens Werk das *buoch* zu besitzen, dessen *sen* zu interpretieren er sich vornahm, so daß wir genau verfolgen können, worauf es dem deutschen Dichter besonders ankam. Schließlich hat uns die gute Fortuna auch noch die *Klage* bewahrt, in der der Autor seine Sittenlehre begrifflich formuliert und moraltheologisch zu begründen versucht.

Man kann sich nur wundern, daß bei solcher Fülle von zeitgenössischem Referenzmaterial der *Erec* in der großen Tugend-Kontroverse relativ wenig Beachtung fand. Vielleicht war daran gerade Hartmanns Klarheit schuld, denn es hat sich früh das Vorurteil gebildet, der deutsche Dichter sei im Vergleich zu seinem imaginativen und schöpferischen Vorbild im Grunde nur ein moralisierender Epigone. Unter dem Moralisten aber verstand man den Didaktiker. Auch Peter Wapnewski sieht in Hartmann den Dichter, dem es »in der *fabula* vor allem um das *docet*« geht. Er unterstreicht jedoch, daß es Hartmann nicht allein um die Vermittlung der höfischen Etikette ging, sondern um den eigentlichen Kern der ritterlichen Ethik.[4] Hugo Kuhn, der als erster die sinnvolle Struktur des deutschen *Erec* und die Funktion der *Joie de la Curt*-Episode herausarbeitete, interpretiert diese »Allegorie der höfischen Freude« ebenfalls vorwiegend auf ihre sozial-ethische Bedeutung hin, doch der letzte Sinn des Romans reicht nach ihm in die religiös-sittliche Sphäre hinüber.[5]

Wir stehen somit im Mittelpunkt unserer Fragestellung: Etikette als normatives System der unreflektierten sittlichen Lebensordnung, Sozial-Ethik als philosophische Reflexion der Norm, und schließlich religiöse Ethik als metaphysisches Fundament der Moral. Zunächst aber gilt es einige terminologische Schwierigkeiten aus dem Wege zu schaffen. Kon-

---

übrigen epischen Werken Hartmanns steht, habe ich im einzelnen nicht überprüft, doch allgemein betrachtet läßt sich erwarten, daß sich das moraltheoretische System Hartmanns in allen seinen Werken als konsistent erweisen wird.

[4] Peter Wapnewski, *Hartmann von Aue*, 1962, S. 41 f.

[5] Hugo Kuhn, »Erec«, *Festschrift für Paul Kluckhohn und Hermann Schneider*, 1948, S. 122–147. Wiederabgedruckt in: *Dichtung und Welt im Mittelalter*, 1969, S. 133 bis 150. Vgl. bes. S. 144–146 des Wiederabdrucks.

zepte wie Moral und Sitte, moralisch, sittlich und ethisch, Ethik und
Ethos, sind nicht nur begrifflich, sondern auch sachlich schwer ausein-
anderzuhalten. Und die Sache wird nicht dadurch erleichtert, daß der
moderne Usus von der scholastischen Terminologie diametral abweicht.
Weil für das moderne Bewußtsein das moralische Verdienst (trotz aller
Unterschiede im einzelnen, auf die es uns hier nicht ankommt) im
Grunde doch in der freiwillentlichen Pflichterfüllung des autonomen
Sittengesetzes liegt, für das 12. Jahrhundert aber, und bis auf den
Aquinaten hin, das moralische Verdienst der menschlichen Handlung
in dem Gnadenakt der göttlichen Rechtfertigung ruhte, bedeutete
»Moral« zu Hartmanns Zeit im eigentlichen Sinne nur die dem Dogma
und dem Mysterium entnommene Lebensregel, die zum Heil der christlichen Seele führte.[6] Eine christliche Ethik in unserem Sinne konnte es
natürlich nicht geben,[7] und es ist nur folgerichtig, wenn die Scholastiker
den Begriff »Ethik« für die Sittenlehren der antiken Autoritäten vor-
behielten. Abaelard hat allerdings als einziger ein Werk verfaßt, das
nicht zufällig den Titel *Ethica* zu tragen scheint. Doch da nach Lottins
Darstellung auch für Abaelard die habituellen Tugenden nur dann Tugenden sind, wenn sie den Menschen zum Verdienst des wahren Glücks,
der *visio Dei, informieren*, handelt es sich auch bei Abaelard keineswegs
um eine in unserem Sinne auf Willens- und Gewissensautonomie be-
gründete Ethik.[8]
Ich werde deshab die Termini Ethik und Moral sowie die entsprechenden Adjektive zu vermeiden suchen. Statt unseres Begriffs Moral in
historisch-sozialem Sinne werde ich den Ausdruck Sittenlehre benützen;
mit dem Begriff Moralphilosophie bezeichne ich die weltlich orientierte,
und mit dem Terminus Moraltheologie die theologische Moraltheorie.
Die in diesem Zusammenhang von Ehrismann gebrauchten und von
Curtius diskreditierten Termini sind übrigens nicht nur treffend und
nützlich, sondern sie scheinen auch sachlich und historisch berechtigt zu
sein. Wenn nämlich die Nachweise Philippe Delhayes stimmen – und es
ist zur Zeit nicht einzusehen, warum sie nicht stimmen sollten – so wurden die Disziplinen der Moralphilosophie und Moraltheologie bereits
im 12. Jahrhundert theoretisch unterschieden, und die Werke der klassischen Philosophen fanden auch im praktischen Unterricht von Gram-

---

6 Nach Alois M. Haas, *Parzivals ›tumpheit‹ bei Wolfram von Eschenbach*, 1964,
   S. 182 f. Vgl. auch Henri de Lubac, *Der geistige Sinn der Schrift*, 1952, passim.
7 Vgl. Alois Dempf, *Ethik des Mittelalters*, 1927, S. 10–12.
8 Vgl. D. Odon Lottin, *Études de morale: histoire et doctrine*, 1961, S. 68–70.

matik und Rhetorik eine größere Beachtung, als Curtius und Ehrismann selbst ahnen konnten.[9]

Für die richtige Formulierung der Frage nach der Laienmoral unserer höfischen Dichter ist das Problem des moralischen Wertes der habituellen Tugenden von Bedeutung, das, wie aus den Arbeiten D. Odo Lottins hervorgeht, vor Thomas Aquinas nicht eindeutig gelöst wurde, obwohl es die Theologen durch das ganze 12. Jahrhundert hindurch eifrig diskutierten. Moralischer Wert bedeutet, wie bereits gesagt, notwendigerweise in erster Linie das übernatürliche Verdienst um das Seelenheil. Die grundlegende Frage jeder mittelalterlichen Moral ist daher die Frage, ob das Konzept der moralischen Tugenden in bezug auf ein weltliches Gut, also auf ein anderes Gut als Gott, überhaupt denkbar sei. Es ist nur allzu begreiflich, daß die absolute Mehrzahl mittelalterlicher Theologen den Tugenden nur dann moralischen Wert zuschrieb, wenn ihnen durch göttliche Gnade übernatürliches Verdienst verliehen wurde. Somit sind aber die sogenannten politischen Tugenden der heidnischen Philosophen wie auch die natürlichen oder erworbenen Tugenden der Christen, die für die weltlichen Sittenlehren der höfischen Dichter in Betracht kämen, aus der mittelalterlichen Moral im strikten Sinne ausgeschlossen. Die Literarhistoriker stehen also vor der Frage, ob es denn denkbar sei, daß die Aristokratie des 12. Jahrhunderts eine weltliche Sittenlehre entwickelt haben könnte, und, im positiven Fall, woher sie die Rechtfertigung einer solchen Sittenlehre schöpfte.

Ehrismanns ideengeschichtliche Erklärung aus Cicero und aus der antiken Ethik kann ebensowenig befriedigen wie Curtius' Vorschlag, die Antwort in Politik und Sozialgeschichte zu suchen. Denn keiner dieser Hinweise kann uns einen Anhaltspunkt dafür bieten, wie der höfische Dichter, dieser Ideologe der herrschenden Aristokratie, mit der für jeden Christen des 12. Jahrhunderts unabwendbaren Frage fertig wurde: *an naturalia fiant gratuita*, ob die durch natürliche Gaben erworbenen Tugenden zu übernatürlichen werden können.

Darauf kann uns nur das Werk der Dichter selbst Antwort geben. Daß aber diese Frage unter den Intellektuellen der Zeit ebenso eifrig diskutiert wurde wie unter den Theologen, darüber legen Dichtungen wie *Parzival*, *Gregorius* und *Der Arme Heinrich* ein sprechendes Zeugnis

---

[9] Vgl. Philippe Delhaye, »L'enseignement de la philosophie morale au XIIe siècle«, *Mediaeval Studies* XI, 1949, S. 77–95. Übersetzung in: *Wege der Forschung* LVI, 1970, S. 301–340. Ehrismann, »Tugendsystem«, *Wege*. S. 5, Anm. 7. Curtius, »Tugendsystem«, *Wege*, S. 125.

ab. Für Hartmann vermeinte man in der Trennung von religiösen und
weltlichen Epen eine unproblematische Lösung gefunden zu haben, die
sogar in seiner berühmten Konversion eine biographische und in den
Moniagen der *Chansons de geste* eine historische Unterstützung fand.
Man braucht dieser Lösung ihre Glaubwürdigkeit nicht abzusprechen,
um dennoch zu fragen, ob ein aufrichtig religiöser Geist wie Hartmann
die weltliche und die religiöse Moral in seinem Leben und Schaffen so
praktisch und pragmatisch hätte voneinander trennen können.

Wir fragen also zunächst, ob Hartmann den natürlichen oder erworbenen Tugenden, den *virtutes* oder Fähigkeiten, durch die man die weltlichen Güter gewinnt, einen moralischen Wert beimißt oder nicht. Der
Erec ist in dieser Hinsicht ein wichtiger Zeuge, denn er gilt als ein frühes
Werk Hartmanns und beruht auf einer Vorlage, die gewiß nicht ohne
Grund als eines der Manifeste der höfischen Weltanschauung gilt. Unter
moralischem Wert verstehen wir in diesem Zusammenhang allerdings
nicht das übernatürliche Verdienst der Moraltheologen, sondern den
eigenständigen sittlichen Wert der Moralphilosophie. Mit anderen Worten, wir fragen, ob für Hartmann der *actus virtutis politicae non sit
indiferens, sed de se bonus*, so wie es später der Aquinate formulieren
sollte.[10] Daß Hartmann die äußeren Güter, Adel, Schönheit, Reichtum,
Ruhm, Macht und gesellschaftliche Anerkennung kannte, braucht nicht
besonders bewiesen zu werden. Ob er sie auch als wahre Güter anerkannte, könnte im Kontext des *Armen Heinrich* und des *Gregorius* als
problematisch erscheinen, im Zusammenhang des *Erec* jedoch, wo so viel
Pomp mit Enidens Schönheit, mit ihrer Kleidung, mit Erecs Geburt,
Reichtum und Ruhm gemacht wird, fällt es uns schwer, daran zu zweifeln. Ausschlaggebend scheint mir für die Beurteilung der Frage der
Umstand zu sein, daß sich Hartmann ohne Bedenken zu der zentralen
Tugend der ritterlichen Sittenlehren bekennt, der *arbeit*. Wenn jemand
die Minne einer Frau erwerben will, so gehört, wie wir aus der *Klage*
wissen, *arbeit* dazu, *denn minne machet niemen frî ze grôzem gemache*
(616 f.).[11] Der Begriff *gemach*, der bekanntlich in der Karnant-Kata-
strophe des *Erec* eine zentrale Rolle spielt, ist der polare Gegensatz von
arbeit, die wiederum die Mutter so mancher anderer, durch Anstrengung, Übung und Beharrlichkeit erworbener Tugend ist.

---

[10] In *II Sent.*, d. 40, q. 1, a. 5. *Sancti Thomae opera omnia*, Impressio Petri Fiacca-
dori, 1852–1873, Bd. 6, S. 750.

[11] Ich ziehe es vor, die *Klage* nach der Ausgabe Fedor Bechs in den Deutschen Classi-
kern des Mittelalters, 5/2, 3. Auflage, 1891, zu zitieren.

Nach Hartmanns Auffassung scheint die *arbeit* sogar einen eigenständigen sittlichen Wert zu besitzen, der nicht von der Erlangung des angestrebten Gutes abhängig ist. In der *Klage* läßt sich nämlich der Körper davon überzeugen, daß es ihm selbst beim Mißerfolg *vil wol tun* würde, einem *alsô schœnen wîbe diensthaft* zu bleiben, weil man durch die Hoffnung auf Erfüllung mehr gewinnt als durch einen Teilerfolg. Man muß sich nämlich, um der Frauen willen, bemühen, richtig und gut zu handeln, und man bewahrt sich dadurch vor jeder Unredlichkeit (1069 bis 1085). Die Katastrophe von Karnant bedeutet für Hartmann also in erster Linie ein moralisches Versagen, denn er erklärt ausdrücklich, daß Erec nach seiner Heirat bemüht war, *alle sîne sache zuo gemache* zu wenden (2931 ff.).[12] Das ist interessant, weil bei Chrétien die Katastrophe nicht durch das *gemach*, sondern durch die *recreantise* ausgelöst wird. Die Vermutung, daß Hartmann hier bewußt anders als Chrétien motivierte, findet in dem Vergleich beider Texte ihre Bestätigung. *Recreantise* kann allerdings auch »Aufgeben des Kampfes«, also etwas Ähnliches wie das deutsche *sich verligen* bedeuten, Chrétiens Erec selbst jedoch versteht es in der geläufigen Bedeutung von Feigheit, denn er hält allein schon den Umstand, daß Enide das Schimpfwort *recreant* wiederholt, für eine tiefe Beleidigung und bezeichnet es als *forfet* und *mesdit* (4891–93).[13]

Im Mittelhochdeutschen gibt es ein Wort, das dem französischen *recreant* haargenau entspricht; es lautet *zage*, und Hartmann hat es in dem ganzen Karnant-Auftritt ängstlich vermieden. Da aber dieses Wort für Hartmann sowie für Chrétien mit dem wichtigen Motiv von Enitens Schuld in Verbindung stand – ein kontroverses Thema, das wir hier tunlichst vermeiden wollen –, konnte es Hartmann nicht völlig aufgeben und versetzte es fünfundsiebzig Zeilen vor die Katastrophe, wo sich Enite eingesteht, daß ihr, trotz der Gefahr, ihren Mann wegen seiner Tapferkeit zu verlieren, *ze manne wære ein degen lieber dan ein arger zage* (2847 f.). Was Hartmanns Enite nur denkt, das spricht Enide bei Chrétien als einen bösen Vorwurf aus: *recreant vos apelent tuit. Cuidiez vos qu'il ne m'an enuit, quant j'oi dire de vos despit?* (2551–53). Es ging darum, zu demonstrieren, daß Hartmann bewußt bemüht war, jedes Mißverständnis in bezug auf Erecs Schuld zu vermeiden. Die Un-

---

12 *Erec* wird nach der Ausgabe von Albert Leitzmann, 4. Auflage, besorgt von Ludwig Wolff, 1967, zitiert.
13 Chrétien de Troyes, *Erec et Enide,* Ausgabe von Mario Roques (Les classiques français du moyen âge), 1963. Im folgenden wird stets nach dieser Ausgabe zitiert.

tugend, die das Verliegen verursachte, ist nicht *recreantise, zagheit,* sondern *gemach,* ein verbales Leitmotiv, das er unabhängig von Chrétien einführte und das in der Verbindung mit *arbeit* als ein polares Motivpaar im *Erec* eine eminente Rolle spielt. Um den Rahmen des Aufsatzes nicht zu sprengen, müssen wir uns die Freude versagen, anhand dieses Motivs auf Schritt und Tritt und bei jeder Wendung des Weges zu verfolgen, wie ein souveräner Meister seiner Zunft es versteht, mit seinen *cristallînen wortelîn* den Sinn der Erzählung durch die sprachliche und formale Struktur seines Werkes zu fixieren. Ich kann hier lediglich auf das Ende der Penefrec-Episode verweisen, denn dies ist genau die Nahtstelle, wo die durch den Ausritt aus Karnant eröffnete Abenteuerfahrt abgeschlossen wird. Hier liest man, daß Erec gleich nach seiner Genesung *wider ûf die vart hügete,* denn *swie guot gemach dâ,* in Penefrec, *wære, im was dâ vil swære.* Erec ist jetzt der echte und wahre Held, der *unvalsche degen,* und er denkt nur noch daran, ganz allein, *âne obedach* und *âne allen gemach* im Walde zu sein, wo ihm Regen und Wind hart zusetzen würden (7239 ff.). Bei Chrétien findet sich statt dessen nur die lakonische Bemerkung, daß Erec und Enide jetzt weiterreisen müßten (5212).

Wir sehen: *arbeit* und *gemach* sind nicht Chrétiens Motive, Hartmann aber bleibt ihnen von einem Ende der Erzählung zum anderen treu. Allerdings ist es denkbar, daß auch für das raffinierte Publikum des literarischen Salons der Gräfin von Champagne der sittliche Wert der Aventiure in ihrem *ungemach* liegen konnte, daß ihm aber in Chrétiens objektiver Gestaltung der *matiere* der *sen* der *conjointure* unmittelbar verständlich war. Hartmann hätte dann auch in dieser Instanz nicht umgestaltet, sondern bloß Chrétiens objektiv dargestellte Sittenlehre reflexiv interpretiert. Diese bei den Kritikern populare Ansicht findet in Hartmanns Text nur teilweise Unterstützung. Gewiß, er hat Chrétiens Gesellschaftsmoral als Didaktiker behandelt und präzisiert, als er in seine Gestaltung der Karnant-Episode die verbalen Motive *schande, êre, vreude, ahte* oder *von den liuten vliehen* einfügte, um auf diese Weise die polare Bedeutungs-Korrelation zur *Joie de la curt* nicht nur strukturell, sondern auch begrifflich zu fixieren, doch in der moralphilosophischen Fundierung der ritterlichen Sittenlehre ging er entschieden seine eigenen Wege.

Chrétien erklärt zum Beispiel, daß für Erec das Turnieren unwichtig geworden sei, weil er seine Frau so sehr und mit einer solchen Art von Liebe liebte, daß er sie zu seiner Freundin und Mätresse machte: *Mes tant l'ama Erec d'amors, que d'armes mes ne li chaloit ... si an fist s'amie et sa drue* (2430 f. und 2435). Diese Sätze, die uns eindeutig auf die höfische Sittenproblematik der *amor fine* und der Ehe hinweisen, übersetzt Hartmann wie folgt: *dô kêrte* (Erec) *allen sînen list an vrouwen Enîten minne. sich vlizzen sîne sinne wie er alle sîne sache wante zuo gemache ... Êrec wente sînen lîp, grôzes gemaches durch sîn wîp* (2929–2933 und 2966 f.). Nicht die Art der Minne steht also bei Hartmann im Mittelpunkt der Motivierung, sondern das moralische Problem, was allerdings nicht bedeutet, daß das Thema der Minne aus seinem Roman ausgeschlossen ist; vielmehr wird es auf einer anderen Ebene behandelt. Wir sind in diesem wichtigen Punkt nicht auf Vermutungen angewiesen, weil uns Hartmann mit seiner üblichen Klarheit verstehen läßt, die Quelle des moralischen Übels liege darin, daß Erec *allen sînen list*, seine ganze Klugheit und sein Wissen, kurz sein ganzes Denken auf die Minne *kêrte*. Früher, als er noch *biderbe unde guot* war, da *stuont sîn muot ritterlîche* (2924 f.), nachdem er aber geheiratet hatte, *vlizzen sich sîne sinne wie er alle sîne sache wante zuo gemache* (2931 ff.). Die moralphilosophisch relevanten Termini sind hier *kêren* und *wenden*, auf die wir noch zurückkommen werden, und *muot* und *sinne*, weil sie Fachbegriffe der scholastischen Psychologie wiedergeben. *muot* bedeutet bei Hartmann in epistemologischen, psychologischen und moraltheoretischen Zusammenhängen entweder *mens* oder *voluntas* oder auch beides; durch *sinne* dagegen wird entweder *rationabilitas* oder *ratio* übersetzt.

Die psychologischen Systeme der Frühscholastik können hier nur summarisch behandelt werden. Sie beruhen durchwegs auf dem augustinischen Grundsatz, daß *anima vero non modo universae moli corporis sui, sed etiam unicuique particulae illius tota simul adest.*[14] Nach ihren Vermögen kann man sie konzeptuell in *anima irrationalis vel vita* und *anima rationalis vel mens* trennen. Die scholastische Systematik ist jedoch nicht einheitlich, weil im Laufe des 12. Jahrhunderts die augustinische Auffassung modifiziert wurde. Neben der platonischen Trichotomie der Seelenpotenzen *concupiscibilitas, irascibilitas* und *rationabilitas*, fand auch die aristotelische Unterteilung in vegetative, sensitive und vernünftige Seele weite Verbreitung. Die beiden ersten Stufen hat der Mensch mit den Pflanzen und Tieren gemein, hingegen die Vernunft den Menschen über alle andere Kreatur hinaushebt. Das platonische wie das

---

[14] Augustinus, *De immortalitate animae*, Cap. 16 (*PL* 32, 1034).

aristotelische Einteilungssystem sind dem Mittelalter durch Chalcidius, Macrobius und Boëthius überliefert worden, und die Versuche, die beiden Systeme zu verschmelzen, führten in der Frühscholastik zu einem weitgehenden Eklektizismus.

Im Hinblick auf Hartmanns Psychologie ist von Bedeutung, daß die Scholastiker zwischen den *potentiae* und *vires* nicht unterschieden und deshalb oft die augustinischen Erkenntniskräfte den drei platonischen Seelenvermögen nach der entsprechenden Stufenfolge des Erkenntnisvorgangs subsumierten. Bei Alcher von Clairvaux liest man zum Beispiel: *Potentiae animae sunt, rationalitas, concupiscibilitas, et irascibilitas, vires sunt, sensus, imaginatio, ratio, memoria, intellectus, intelligentia. Potentiae tamen possunt dici vires, et vires potentiae.*[15] Der Wille, der nach Augustin in allen Seelenfunktionen miteinbeschlossen ist (*voluntas est quippe in omnibus*[16]) wird manchmal der *mens* oder *anima rationalis* zugeordnet: *Et omnis anima rationalis tribus potentiis, scilicet, memoria, consilio, voluntate substitit.*[17]

Zur Erklärung von Hartmanns Morallehre muß ebenfalls erwähnt werden, daß die platonische Triade der Seelenpotenzen als Grundlage für moraltheoretische Spekulationen diente. Bereits Gregor der Große schreibt: *Anima tribus vegetatur naturis. Est enim rationalis ad discernendum, concupiscibilis ad virtutes appetendum, irascibilis ad vitia adversandum.*[18] Dies ist ein allgemein akzeptierter Grundsatz, der bei Alanus wie folgt formuliert wird: *Thesis dicitur proprius status hominis, quem servare dicitur, quando ratione utitur ad considerandum quid bonum, quid malum quid agendum, quid cavendum … sicut per speculationem rationis homo fit homo.*[19] Schließlich sei noch hervorgehoben, daß in der – übrigens sehr uneinheitlichen – frühscholastischen Terminologie der Terminus *anima* entweder im Sinne der antiken Philosophie das geistig-seelische Sein des Menschen bezeichnet, oder im christlichen Sinne nur die unsterbliche Seele bedeutet. In diesem Kontext kann dann, unter dem Einfluß der biblischen und patristischen Tradition, der Ausdruck *cor* sowohl für *anima* als auch für *mens* oder *intelligentia* stehen. Die terminologische Vertauschbarkeit drückt sich deutlich in dem folgenden Satz des Hrabanus Maurus aus: *Cor enim multis speciebus signi-*

---

15 Alcher von Clairvaux, *De spiritu et anima*, Cap. XIII (*PL* 40, 789).
16 Augustinus, *De civitate Dei*, XIV, Cap. 6 (*PL* 41, 409).
17 Alcher von Clairvaux, *De spiritu et anima*, Cap. 12, Anm. 1 (*PL* 40, 788).
18 Gregorius Magnus, *In septem psalmos poenitentiales exposito* (*PL* 79, 551 C).
19 Alanus de Insulis, *Theologicae regulae* (*PL* 210, 673 D).

*ficandis convenienter aptatur. Nam aliquando pro anima ponitur, ali-
quando pro intelligentia, aliquando pro consilio et verbo occulto, aliquando pro intelligentia.*[20]

Die *Klage* eröffnet uns den Zugang zu Hartmanns Morallehre, weil sich
darin seine theoretischen Kenntnisse am deutlichsten widerspiegeln.
Ehrismann befindet sich im Irrtum, wenn er meint, daß Hartmann seine
Ungeschultheit in scholastischer Anthropologie und Psychologie bewies,
als er die Gedanken, die Vernunft, den Willen und den Rat dem Herzen
und nicht der *anima intellectiva* zuschrieb.[21] Die Allegorisierung der
irrationalen Seele oder *vita* als *lîp* und der rationalen oder *mens* als
herze zeugt vielmehr, wie wir eben sahen, von Hartmanns intimer Ver-
trautheit mit der scholastischen Theorie.[22] Ich könnte durch Zitate beweisen, daß er zwischen der Seele und der *anima intellectiva* als deren
Potenz sowie zwischen den seelischen Erkenntnisfähigkeiten und deren
Lokalisierung viel schärfer unterschied als Ehrismann.[23] Doch müssen
wir uns hier auf Stellen mit moraltheoretischen Implikationen beschränken und heben deshalb hervor, daß nach Hartmann – natürlich wiederum in Übereinstimmung mit allgemeinen Ansichten und mit der Theorie – der zum Bösen, zum Laster und zur Trägheit inklinierende Körper
das exekutive Organ der *mens*, des *muotes* ist. Das Herz spricht:

> Stüende der gewalt an mir / diu dinc ze verenden als an dir, / des er leider
> niht entuot / (ichn hân gewaltes wan den muot / und den frîen gedanc), /
> dû müesest under dînen danc / nâch gelobtem worte leben.   (913–919)

Dem Herzen kommen dagegen alle *vires* und *potentiae* der *rationabili-*

---

20 Hrabanus Maurus, *De Universo*, Lib. 6, Cap. 1 (*PL* 111, 169 D). Auf diese Stelle
    verwies bereits A. E. Schönbach, *Über Hartmann von Aue: Drei Bücher Unter-
    suchungen*, 1894, S. 471. Vgl. auch Roswitha Wisniewski, »Hartmanns *Klage*-
    Büchlein«, *Euphorion* 57, S. 359.

21 Ehrismann, »Tugendsystem«, *Wege*, S. 42, Anm. 68.

22 Gegen Ehrismanns Behauptungen wendet sich bereits Wisniewski, »*Klage*-Büchlein«.
    Im Unterschied zu Wisniewski jedoch, die besonders auf die terminologischen
    Parallelen mit der Bibel und Patristik hinweist (S. 358 f.), und Hartmanns Herz-
    Leib Paarung aus allgemeinem Sprachgebrauch und mittelalterlicher Trivialpsycho-
    logie erklärt (S. 361), glaube ich, daß die genauen terminologischen wie auch sach-
    lichen Distinktionen Hartmanns für seine Vertrautheit mit frühscholastischer
    Psychologie und Erkenntnislehre sprechen. Vgl dazu Wolf Gewehr, *Hartmanns
    ›Klage-Büchlein‹ im Lichte der Frühscholastik*, 1975, auf dessen Material sich
    die vorangehende Zusammenfassung der scholastischen Theorie stützt (Gewehr,
    S. 36–66).

23 Vgl. z. B. *Die Klage*, V. 535–580, 888–900, 920–968, 1032–1048.

tas zu, besonders das *consilium* und *ratio;* das bedeutet, wie wir sahen, daß das Herz in genauer Übereinstimmung mit scholastischer Anthropologie und Epistemologie die Fähigkeit besitzt, zwischen Gut und Böse zu unterscheiden. Das Herz spricht wieder:

> sît du mich ze râte erwelet hâst / unde mich des niht erlâst, / sô weist dû wol daz ich dich nie / bœsiu dinc geminnen lie. / ze guoten dingen ich dir riet, / von allem valsche ich dich schiet. (561–566)

Der Rat des Herzens lautet, daß man *reine minne* mit *tugenden unde sinnen* erwerben muß (779–784). *Swer ahte hât ûf minne, der darf wol schœner sinne,* der *ratio,* um zwischen Gut und Böse zu unterscheiden und unterlassen zu können, *swaz anders heizet danne guot.* Minne aber *machet niemen frî ze grôzem gemache,* denn, um des *rehten mannes muot zu minnen,* um also das Gemüt, das Wollen, die Gesinnung, den Sinn, kurz die *mens* des rechten, wirklichen oder auch gerechten Mannes zu besitzen, *dâ gehœret arbeit zuo* (602–617).

Der Wortlaut dieser wenigen Beispiele zeigt wohl nicht bloß eine allgemeine gedankliche, sondern auch eine eingehende terminologische Übereinstimmung mit der scholastischen Theorie. Sie zeigen ebenfalls, welche bedeutende Rolle in Hartmanns Moraltheorie die scholastischen Konzepte *ratio* und *mens, sinne* und *muot* spielen. Welchen hohen moralischen Wert er der *arbeit* zuschreibt, geht aus einer Stelle hervor, wo es fast den Anschein hat, als ob sie Hartmann höher einschätzen würde als die unverdiente Gnadengabe Gottes. Man spricht hier von einem Menschen, *der nie ahte gewan ûf dehein êre, und hât doch heiles mêre dan einer der die sinne hât und dem sîn muot ze tugenden stât. dem hât daz got enteil getân. den sule wir ungenîdet lân* (756–762). Wenn aber ein solcher Mann das Verdienst sich selber zuschreiben wollte, dann *erteile* (man) *im fröude di sint kranc ... wil er dâ von sîn wol gemuot, des gan ich im vil sêre, wan ez ist ein betrogen êre unde ein kintlîcher wân* (768–775). Es handelt sich nicht um einen Konflikt mit der Gnadenlehre der Theologie, denn unter *êre* ist hier natürlich weltliche Anerkennung gemeint: die Stelle beweist aber über jeden Zweifel hinaus, daß Hartmann den erworbenen Tugenden ein hohes moralisches Verdienst zuschrieb, obwohl er mit dem theologischen Konzept der Gratuität der göttlichen Gabe vertraut war. Das geht übrigens auch aus dem bekannten »Krautzauber« der *Klage* hervor, dem zufolge die Tugend der *milte, zuht* und *diemuot* von Gott nicht nach Verdienst, sondern als freie Gnadengabe verliehen wird (1296–1303).

Die in der *Klage* formulierte Moraltheorie Hartmanns kommt auch im
Erec zum Ausdruck und setzt ihn überall von der objektiv-normativen
Sittenlehre Chrétiens entschieden ab. Hartmann schreibt also, um es
noch einmal schärfer zu formulieren, den erworbenen Tugenden ein
natürliches Verdienst zu; es ist aber nicht von dem Wert der angestrebten weltlichen Güter abhängig – seien es Minne, Ehre, Ruhm oder
varnde guot –, sondern von der richtigen Orientierung des Willens, der
Absicht, der Gesinnung, kurz, des *muotes*, die darin besteht, alles zu
unterlassen, *swaz anders heizet danne guot* (611). In diesem Kontext
erscheinen dann die Worte: *sich vlizzen sîne* (Erecs) *sinne wie er alle
sîne sache wante zuo gemache* (2931–2933) wohl nicht als überinter-
pretiert, wenn man sie für den Schlüssel zum Verständnis von Erecs
moralischer Schuld hält. Die korrekte Ausrichtung des *muotes* auf das
Gute ist bei Hartmann immer der Maßstab des Tugendwertes: *Êrec dô
ahten begann, der ritter enwære dehein vrum man, daz er ez vor im ver-
truoc daz sîn getwerc die maget sluoc* (66–69). Bei Chrétien wird dem
Ritter nicht zum Vorwurf gemacht, nicht *vrum*, tüchtig, brav, anstän-
dig, gut, ehrbar zu sein, sondern daß er ein *vilain* sei, ein unhöfischer,
schlecht erzogener Krautjunker. Und das Vergehen ist nicht das Unrecht gegen ein wehrloses Mädchen, sondern die Beleidigung einer *si bele
criature* durch solch eine häßliche Mißgeburt, *une tex fauture* (198–200).
In Übereinstimmung mit Chrétiens höfischer Wertskala wird dem Ritter nach dem Sperberkampf noch einmal vorgeworfen, daß er sich einer
niederträchtigen Gemeinheit *(viltance)* mitschuldig machte, weil er
amüsiert zusah, als der Zwerg, diese häßliche Kröte *(un bot)*, nicht bloß
das Mädchen, sondern auch Erec, den er wohl für einen niedrig gebo-
renen Junker hielt, in den Nacken schlug. Für diesen Irrtum, diese Untat
(mesprison) soll der Ritter jetzt büßen. Dies aber ist auch das einzige
Vergehen *(forfet)*, für das er von Chrétiens Erec verantwortlich gehalten wird (1009–1023).
Bei Hartmann dagegen besitzt die höfische *zuht* nur dann moralischen
Wert, wenn sie für die Anständigkeit, die Sittlichkeit und für den Edel-
mut der Absicht transparent ist. In ausgesprochenem Gegensatz zu
Chrétien erklärt denn auch Hartmanns Erec, daß den Ritter seine
hôchvart, sein *vürgedinge* und *übermuot gevellet* haben; sein Vergehen
liegt darin, daß er Erec im Zweikampf erbarmungslos töten wollte
(967–985). Er sagt auch, daß er den Zwerg bloß für die *unzucht* be-
strafen will, *daz ez die maget hât geslagen* (1043f.), und seine eigene
Beleidigung völlig *ûz der ahte* läßt (1050). Es handelt sich also nicht

um persönliche Rache, sondern um die Gemütsausrichtung auf die Tugend der *iustitia.*

Wir sehen bereits: Man hat es hier mit einer exemplarischen literarischen Gestaltung des in der Moraltheorie oft diskutierten Grundsatzes zu tun, daß das moralische Verdienst nicht in der Handlung selbst, sondern in der Absicht liege. Als Beispiel zitiere ich Abaelard:

> Non enim quae fiunt sed quo animo fiant pensat Deus; nec in opere sed in intentione meritum operantis, vel laus consistit. Saepe quippe idem a diversis agitur: per justitiam unius et per nequitiam alterius; ut si unum reum duo suspendant, ille quidem zelo justitiae, hic antiquae odio inimicitiae; et cum sit suspensionis eadem actio, et utique [uterque] quod bonum est fieri et quod justitia exigit agant, per diversitatem tamen intentionis idem a diversis fit, ab uno male, ab altero bene.[24]

Als ein weiteres Beispiel für den Unterschied zwischen Chrétiens normativer Sittenlehre und Hartmanns Gesinnungsmoral könnte Erecs Einkehr bei seinem zukünftigen Schwiegervater in Tulmein analysiert werden. Ich kann nur darauf hinweisen, daß man Hartmann m. E. falsch liest, wenn man die auffällige Betonung der Etikette, die in diesem Auftritt zu bemerken ist, als pedantische Überspitzung der höfischen Anstandslehre interpretiert. Auch hier kommt es Hartmann darauf an, den Reichtum der Gesinnung gegen den Reichtum des äußeren Gutes auszuspielen: (Koralus) *enphlac niht rîcheite.* Aber: *sîn gebærde was vil hêrlîch, einem edeln manne gelîch* (287–289). Oder: *dar an man mohte schouwen daz er rîches muotes wielt, daz er den gast sô arm enthielt* (313–315). Nach dem spärlichen Abendessen wird diese Gesinnungsmoral sogar noch explizite formuliert: *in gap der reine wille genuoc* (man höre: *bona voluntas,* oder *intentio*) *den man dâ ze hûse vant: wan er ist aller güete ein phant* (393–395).

In diesem Zusammenhang muß kurz darauf hingewiesen werden, daß eine solche Umstellung des Sittlichkeitsbegriffes auf Gesinnungsmoral eine Humanisierung der höfischen Sittenlehre zur Folge hat, wobei es dahingestellt bleiben soll, ob dies von Hartmann beabsichtigt wurde oder nicht. Bei Chrétien wird der Zwerg für seine Tat nicht bestraft, weil er für sie moralisch nicht verantwortlich gemacht werden kann. Er ist eine Mißgeburt, eine häßliche Kröte, die »objektiv« eine niedrigere, tief unter dem höfischen Humanitätsideal liegende Daseinsstufe repräsen-

---

24 Peter Abaelard, *Ethica,* Cap. 3 (*PL* 178, 644 A–B). Zitiert von Lottin, *Études,* S. 69, Anm. 1.

tiert. In seiner Häßlichkeit kann er nicht anders als *plains de felenie* (164) und *molt fel et de pute ere* (171) sein, also tückisch, hinterlistig, boshaft, niederträchtig und von stinkender Gemeinheit. Das Fräulein will ohne Gruß an ihm vorbeigehen, und als sich der, wie Chrétien selbst sagt, schurkische Zwerg, der gar nicht niederträchtiger sein könnte [*Li nains cuiverz* (208), *li nains fu fel tant con nus plus* (218)], in Erecs Weg stellt, stößt er ihn rücksichtslos zur Seite und überhäuft ihn mit Schimpfworten (165–220). Bei Hartmann spricht das Fräulein den Zwerg mit *zühten* an, nennt ihn *gesellen*, betont, daß die Königin *durch ir zuht gebôt*, ihn zu grüßen und daß er *âne schaden* den Namen des Ritters mitteilen könne, weil ihre *vrouwe vrâget wan durch guot* (31–43). Der Zwerg muß wegen Hartmanns Ausrichtung auf Gesinnungsmoral vermenschlicht werden, denn sonst könnte seine Tat nicht als Beleidigung gelten. Man hat aber diesen Auftritt so lange zitiert als Beispiel für Hartmann den Didaktiker, der sein Vorbild an höfischem Anstand übertreffen wollte, bis diese Ansicht zu einer »Wanderstrophe« der Hartmann-Interpretation wurde, obwohl sie offensichtlich darauf beruht, daß man Chrétien überhaupt nicht und Hartmann nur flüchtig las.

Abschließend sollen zwei Stellen kurz besprochen werden, aus denen das theoretische Fundament von Hartmanns Moralphilosophie besonders deutlich zu ersehen ist. Die erste betrifft die Minne. Hartmann sagt uns, daß Erec und Mabonagrin den kräftigen Schlägen des Zweikampfes nur deshalb standzuhalten vermochten, weil ihnen beiden *ir wîp* die *kraft* dazu gaben. Durch feine terminologische Unterschiede versteht Hartmann es jedoch, hier zwei abweichende Minnekonzepte gegeneinander auszuspielen. Bei Mabonagrin, dem Protagonisten der unreflektierten höfischen Minnemoral, verharrt er konsequent bei der traditionellen, ganz sachlich und objektiv ausgerichteten Minneterminologie: Der Anblick der Schönheit seiner Freundin gibt *im niuwe kraft, sô daz er unzagehaft sîne sterke wider gewan* (9176–9178). In Erecs Fall dagegen wird die bereits durch Enitens Abwesenheit bedingte Erinnerung durch psychologische Terminologie auf die moralisch-intentionelle Ebene versetzt. Die Erinnerung an Enitens Minne gibt Erec nicht Kraft und Tapferkeit, sie stärkt vielmehr *sîn herze und ouch die sinne* (was hier, wie in der *Klage*, *mens* und *ratio* bedeutet), so daß er *mit niuwer maht nâch manlîcher tiure vaht* (9182–9187). Wörtlich übersetzt bedeutet aber *maht* »Vermögen«, *potentia*, und *manlîche tiure* »männlicher Wert«.

Die zweite Stelle befindet sich am Ende der Penefrec-Episode und enthält das Lob der beiden Schwestern des Guivreiz, die – wie bereits die allegorisierten Namen Filledâmûr und Genteflûr verraten – die höfischen Tugenden verkörpern. Auch hier vermag Hartmann den Leser verstehen zu lassen, daß der moralische Wert der *zuht* nicht in den gesellschaftlichen Qualitäten selbst, sondern in der *intentio* liegt. Die beiden Damen sind der Inbegriff des Anstandes, *die zuht was in ir huote*, weil man nie *an deheinen andern vrouwen einen vestern willen ... zaller slahte guote* finden konnte (7773–7777). Es handelt sich natürlich wie bei Chrétien um Standesmoral, denn die Trägerinnen des Anstandes sind *vrouwen*, Angehörige des Geburtsadels. Doch die Rechtfertigung des Anspruchs auf die Gleichbedeutung von Geburtsadel und Tugendadel wird entschieden ins Moralische versetzt, weil nur diejenige Dame, die ihren Willen resolut auf alles Gute wendet, mit Recht beanspruchen darf, den Tugendtitel des *guoten wîbes* zu tragen: *die vrouwen hânt ez alsô brâht daz ir von rehte wirt gedâht ... swâ guoter wîbe wirdet wal* (7778–7781). Wir sehen, daß hier Hartmann wiederum, expressis verbis, die Ansicht vertritt, die höfischen Tugend- und Anstands-Normen besäßen nur dann moralischen Wert, wenn der Wille und der *muot*, die *voluntas* und die *mens*, des ausübenden Subjektes von der »intentio« *zaller slahte guote* geleitet wird. In der beharrlichen Ausübung der guten Absicht liegt dann das eigentliche moralische Verdienst: *swâ mite ein wîp gedienen sol daz si gote und der werlde wol von schulden muoz gevallen, des phlâgen si âne gallen* (7782–7785). Wie zu erwarten, fehlt diese Stelle bei Chrétien.

Die letzten Verse verraten bereits, daß Hartmann nicht dem Problem ausweichen konnte, wie denn seine auf dem natürlichen Verdienst der erworbenen Tugenden beruhende Sittenlehre mit der Gnadenlehre der Theologie in Einklang zu bringen sei. Es versteht sich von vornherein, daß die Erwerbung der göttlichen Gnade durch das moralische Verdienst der sozialen Tugenden auf keine Weise präjudiziert werden darf, so daß der letzte Satz nicht bedeuten kann, der tugendhafte Mensch müsse Gott und der Gesellschaft notwendigerweise gefallen; er sagt nur, daß er ihnen verdienterweise gefallen könne. Die Lösung selbst ist allerdings nicht einfach, und ich müßte alle drei Teile des Romans interpretieren, um zu zeigen, wie Hartmann darin die drei Stufen der moralischen Werte, ontologische Gutheit, moralische Tugend und Gottes gnädige Hilfe (nicht Gnade!) gestaltet hat. Statt dessen sei nur nochmals auf den Krautzauber der *Klage* hingewiesen. Gott wird hier als der alleinige Herr der drei Haupttugenden, *milte, zuht und diemuot,* genannt. Andererseits erfahren wir, daß der Mensch diese Tugenden paradoxerweise verdienen muß, um sie als freie Gabe Gottes zu erhalten. Es heißt nämlich in der *Klage,* daß der Mensch die Tugenden zwar *mit schœnem sinne* von Gott gewinnen kann, aber nur dann, wenn es *an sînem heile* steht, denn Gott gibt sie *swem er wil.* Jedoch selbst nachdem der Mensch diese Gabe von Gott erhalten hat, muß er *sælec* sein, den *rehten zouberlist* zu beherrschen, um die drei Kräuter richtig zu *tempern;* und zwar so, wie es für sie bestimmt ist, nach ihrer besonderen Eigenart, oder wie Hartmann sagt: *dar nâch als in gesetzet ist.* Um dies tun zu können, muß der Mensch ein *herze âne haz* besitzen, um darin die weiteren Tugenden, *triuwe, stæte, kiuschheit, schame,* und *manheit* zu verwahren.[25] Über diese Tugenden aber kann der Mensch nur dann verfügen, er kann ihrer nur dann *gewalt* haben, wenn der Körper es sich angelegen sein läßt *(enblanden),* sie zu gewinnen (1335).

Für Hartmanns Moralphilosophie ist es bezeichnend, daß er in diesem zentralen Abschnitt seiner Tugendlehre zwar zwischen den eingeflößten und den erworbenen Tugenden unterscheidet, daß sich seine Unterscheidung jedoch nicht nach den üblichen Kategorien der theologischen Tugenden und der Kardinaltugenden richtet. Von den drei von Gott verliehenen Haupttugenden werden *milte* und *zuht* – soweit man nach dem damaligen Sprachgebrauch schließen kann – primär wohl als gesellschaftliche Tugenden empfunden, doch sie können auch religiös verstanden werden. Die Demut gehört ebenfalls nicht zu der theologischen Trias, *fides, spes, caritas,* sie bildet aber nach der scholastischen Auffassung die Voraussetzung aller Tugenden, der weltlichen sowohl wie der religiösen. Hier liegt der Schlüssel zum Verständnis von Hartmanns

---

25 swer in ze rehte sol begân, / der muoz haben driu krût, / diu tuont in liep unde trût. / der endarftû aber warten / in deheines mannes garten, / ouch vindt sî niemen veile. / ezn stê an sînem heile (1290) / daz er sî von dem gewinne / mit schœnem sinne / der si in sîme gewalte hât, / son hilfet in dehein rât, / erne wese in immer verre (1295). / got der ist der würze herre, / der phliget ir alterseine. / sîn kamer diu ist reine: / dar ûz gît er sî swem er wil: / der hât ouch immer heiles vil. / diu krût sint dir unerkant: / alsô sind sî genant, / milte zuht diemuot. / ezn ist kein krûtzouber sô guot: / swelich sæliger man / diu driu krût tempern kan / dar nâch als in gesetzet ist, / daz ist der rehte zouberlist. / ouch hœrent ander würze derzuo, / ê daz man im rehte tuo, triuwe unde stæte: / swer ir dar zuo niht hæte, / sô müese der list belîben: / ouch muost dû dar zuo trîben / beide kiuscheit unde schame: / dannoch ist ein krûtes name / gewislîchiu manheit: / sô ist daz zouber gar bereit. / und swem alsô gelinget, / daz er sî zesamen bringet, / der sol si schüten in ein vaz, / daz ist ein herze âne haz: / dâ sol er sî inne tragen, / sô wil ich dir daz zwâre sagen, / daz im diu sælde ist bereit / unz er sî bî im treit (1284–1326).

Tugendsystem, das sich weder durch historische Bedeutungsstudien einzelner Termini, noch durch synchronische Wortfelduntersuchungen erschließen läßt. Man würde auch vergeblich versuchen, Hartmanns Tugend-Nomenklatur mit den lateinischen Termini in genauen Einklang zu bringen, weil das Hartmannsche System auf einem von Grund aus anderen Prinzip beruht als die Systeme seiner Zeitgenossen.

Nach der *Klage* werden die fundamentalen Tugenden – wie wir eben sahen – dem Menschen zwar als freie Gabe gespendet, er muß sie aber trotzdem von Gott durch gute Absicht oder Vernunft *(schœner sin)* erwerben (1290–95). Wenn diese Stelle nicht widersinnig ist, und das ist bei Hartmann nicht anzunehmen, so kann er hier nur die ontologische Gutheit im Sinne gehabt haben, die in der Tat eine freiwillige Gabe Gottes ist, obwohl sie auf Grund der *analogia entis* aller Kreatur je nach ihrer Existenzstufe zukommt. Beim Menschen liegt sie vor allem in der Fähigkeit, auch ohne wahre Gnade das Gute kraft seiner Vernunft zu erkennen. Da aber die natürliche Fähigkeit erst durch die Ausrichtung auf ein Gutes zur Tugend wird, darf Hartmann mit Recht sagen, daß wir die uns von Gott freiwillig verliehenen Tugenden durch unsere Vernunft gewinnen müssen; es gelingt ihm sogar, in die präzise Formulierung der Stelle auch das Prädestinationsprinzip mit einzuschließen.[26]

Auf der ontologischen Basis baut der Mensch nach Hartmanns Lehre das natürliche moralische Verdienst auf. Indem er mit der Vernunft das in den Objekten haftende Gute erkennt und seinen *muot* final darauf richtet, erwirbt er durch beharrliches Streben nach diesem Guten eine Reihe von Tugenden, die ihn zum Verrichten des Guten befähigen. Das eigentliche moralische Verdienst liegt im zielbewußten Bemühen des Menschen um das Gute, in der *arbeit.* Hartmanns Auffassung der Tugend als einer durch Übung gewonnenen Fertigkeit ließe sich mit der geläufigen theologischen Definition als *habitus animae optimus* vergleichen. Doch im Unterschied zu den Theologen orientiert das Attribut *optimus* die Tugend nach Hartmann nicht notwendigerweise auf Gott; der Wille kann sich ebensowohl das in den weltlichen Gütern wie Minne, Ruhm, Ehre haftende Gute zum Ziel setzen. Weil aber nach Hartmann die Tugend vor allem in der menschlichen Disposition liegt, die natürliche Fähigkeit auf das ihr zustehende Gute zu richten, brauchen die Grenzen zwischen den theologischen und politischen Tugenden

---

[26] Vgl. Anm. 25, *Klage,* V. 1290–1295.

in seinem System nicht streng gezogen zu werden, denn es wird sich um
eine theologische Tugend handeln, wenn sich der Wille ein *bonum divi-
num* zum Ziele setzt, und um eine politische Tugend, wenn sich die Absicht auf ein natürliches Gut richtet. Man muß, wie Hartmann sagt, die
Tugendkräuter *tempern, darnâch als in gesetzet ist* (1307).

Weil aber ein übernatürliches Gut ohne göttliche Gnade nicht gewonnen werden kann, ist die Frage nach dem Verhältnis zwischen dem
natürlichen und übernatürlichen Verdienst implizite bereits vorgegeben.
Hartmann löst das Problem so, daß er die beiden Verdienste logisch
voneinander trennt und das natürliche Verdienst gewiß nicht als eine
kausale, doch aber recht eindeutig als eine potentielle Voraussetzung der
Gnade postuliert. Das ist der moraltheologische Sinn der Worte, daß ein
tugendhafter Mensch *gote und der werlde wol von schulden muoz
gevallen* (*Erec* 7783 f.), verdienterweise gefallen kann.

In der *Klage* wird diese Auffassung insofern präzisiert, als hier das
Herz ausdrücklich erklärt, das Streben nach weltlichen Gütern – in diesem Falle ist es die Minne – sei besonders deshalb gut, weil es nur *âne
laster ... und âne grôze sünde* geschehen kann (1339–1341); das heißt
also, ohne die weltliche Ehre und das Gebot Gottes zu verletzen. Ein
Mensch, der sich natürliche moralische Verdienste erwirbt, gewinnt
sælekeit, Glück, Vollkommenheit und Heil in dieser Welt, ohne jedoch
Gott zu mißfallen:

> daz ist zer werlte ein sælekeit / und ist gote niht ze leit, / ez ist bêdenthalp
> ein gewin, / got und diu werlt minnet in.   (1343–1346)

Daß das natürliche moralische Verdienst Gottes Gnade zur Folge hätte,
wird zwar nirgends gesagt, doch die Formulierung dieser und vieler
anderer Stellen erlaubt keinen Zweifel daran, daß nach Hartmanns
Ansicht die moralischen Verdienste der erworbenen Tugenden Gottes
Gefallen erwecken, *deo placent*, wie später Thomas sagen wird.[27]

Wenn man sich nach den Modellen umsieht, nach denen Hartmann seine
weltliche Moralphilosophie gestaltet haben könnte, so findet man – so-
fern ich ohne primäre Kenntnis und auf Grund der allerdings sehr er-
schöpfenden Arbeiten Odo Lottins urteilen kann – im 12. Jahrhundert
praktisch keine Anhaltspunkte. Wenn auch die Scholastiker nach dem
Vorbild der antiken Philosophen die Tugend als *habitus mentis opti-*

---

[27] ... sed tamen etiam actus alii, secundum quod sunt boni ex genere vel ex circum-
stantia, Deo placent, non tamen sicut remunerabiles aeterno praemio. In *II Sent.*,
d. 41, q. 1, a. 1, ad 3um. *Opera omnia*, Bd. 6, S. 755.

mus, oder als *habitus bene consituae mentis,* oder auch als *bona voluntas in habitum per animi applicationem versa* definierten, durchwegs also Definitionen, und besonders die letzte, die an Hartmanns Auffassung erinnern, so verstehen sie doch alle unter dem *habitus optimus* die zum übernatürlichen Verdienst des ewigen Lebens führende Tugend. Daß Hartmann solche Definitionen gekannt haben mußte, geht hoffentlich aus unserer Analyse hervor; daß er es aber auch als Theoretiker vermochte, ohne die Stütze eines anerkannten theologischen Systems seine konsequente, weltlich orientierte Moralphilosophie zu entwickeln, bleibt mir unbegreiflich. Dennoch scheint es der Fall gewesen zu sein, weil praktisch alle Theologen, in unzähligen Modifikationen und Variationen, am Ende zu dem augustinischen Schluß gelangen, daß jede wahre Tugend entweder *caritas* oder die Folge der *caritas* sein muß. Die moralphilosophische Auffassung, mit der Hartmann zu seiner Zeit konfrontiert war, läßt sich am deutlichsten mit einem Zitat aus dem um 1150 verfaßten *Ysagoge in theologiam* umschreiben.

> Quidam habitus boni sunt, non tamen virtutes; quia non est Deus in causa, immo rigor vel gloria, ut contemptus pecunie in philosophis et carnis continentia; additur optimus, id est in quo consistit meritum vel ad eternam vitam utilis.[28]

Unter den Theologen des 12. Jahrhunderts finden sich nur zwei, Simon von Tournai und Peter von Poitiers, die einen ähnlichen moralphilosophischen Standpunkt wie Hartmann vertreten. Wie er schreiben sie den politischen Tugenden ein moralisches Verdienst zu, und dies Verdienst ist, wie bei Hartmann, *insufficiens ad salutem.* Bei Simon findet sich noch ein weiterer, an Hartmann erinnernder Gedanke, die Überzeugung nämlich, daß die Tugenden je nach ihrer Orientierung ihre Art verändern, so daß nach dieser Auffassung die natürlichen Tugenden unter dem Einfluß der theologischen Tugenden »katholisch« werden:

> Dicte uirtutes, cum politice sint et nondum catholice, suos fines habent ad quos suis usibus tendunt. Sunt autem fines quatuor: gloria, dignitas, ampliduto, amicitia. Ad dictos fines transeunt politicis uirtutibus, utentes etiam fidei expertes, et tunc in eis uirtutes meriotorie sunt dictorum finium temporalium, sed nullius eterni sine fide et spe et caritate, ex quibus tribus politice uirtutes sortiuntur ut fiant catholice.[29]

---

[28] *Ysagoge in theologiam,* in: A. Landgraf, *Écrits théologiques de l'école d'Abélard: Textes inédits,* 1934, S. 73, Z. 17–20. Zitiert nach Lottin, *Études,* S. 71, Anm. 1.

[29] *Paris Nat. lat. 14886,* f. 33rb – 34ra. Zitiert nach Lottin, *Études,* S. 77, Anm. 2. Der Text ist integral ediert in: D. Odon Lottin, *Psychologie et morale aux XIIe et XIIIe siècles,* Bd. III, 1949, S. 106–109.

Peter von Poitiers und Simon von Tournai scheinen die zwei einzigen
Vorbilder zu sein, an die sich Hartmann hätte anlehnen können. Doch
nach Lottin fanden sie zu ihrer Zeit keinen Widerhall, und selbst dann,
wenn sich eine Bekanntschaft Hartmanns mit diesen Lehren beweisen
ließe, bliebe es unwahrscheinlich, daß durch eine derartige Anregung
seine abgeschlossene und philosophisch wie auch theologisch kompetente
Moraltheorie integral erklärt werden könnte. Das Überraschende an
Hartmanns Moraltheorie ist der Umstand, daß Ansichten wie die sei-
nigen theoretisch erst im 13. Jahrhundert formuliert und zu Systemen
zusammengeschlossen wurden. Hier wäre etwa die Lehre Philipp des
Kanzlers zu nennen;[30] in erster Linie aber natürlich Thomas von
Aquino, mit dessen Moraltheorie Hartmanns Sittenlehre grundsätzlich
übereinstimmt. Thomas aber war der erste große Theologe, der ebenso
resolut wie Hartmann das moralische Verdienst der politischen Tugenden anerkannte und erklärte, daß es das Gefallen Gottes erwecke. Das
Problem des natürlichen moralischen Verdienstes und der Gnade löste
er ebenfalls in demselben Sinne wie Hartmann.

> Et ideo alii dicunt, quod tam in dictis quam in factis contigit aliqua esse
> indifferentia, quae nec bona nec mala sunt; ... ut si aliquis alicui loquatur
> ex quadam civili amicitia, vel etiam aliquod opus amicabile ad ipsum exer-
> ceat. Sed in hoc videtur esse instantia: quia actus virtutis politicae non est
> indifferens, sed de se bonus est, et si sit gratia informatus, erit meritorius ...
> Et ideo aliter secundum alios dicendum est, quod nullus actus a voluntate
> deliberata progrediens potest esse qui non sit bonus vel malus, non tantum
> secundum theologum, sed etiam secundum moralem philosophum; et ulte-
> rius non potest esse actus a deliberata voluntate procedens in habente gra-
> tiam qui non sit meritorius; sed tamen in non habente gratiam potest esse
> aliquis actus deliberatus qui nec meritorius nec demeritorius est, tamen est
> bonus vel malus.[31]

Da ich also vorläufig keine nennenswerten Vorbilder für Hartmanns
System nachweisen kann, bin ich gezwungen zu schließen, daß unser
Dichter ein philosophisch wohl geschulter Theoretiker war und die

---

[30] Triplex est gradus bonitatis in actionibus: primus est boni in genere, secundus boni
moralis, tertius boni gratie ... et hec secundum ordinem se habent. Et similiter
principia horum, Erit ergo natura conuenienter principium actionis boni in genere,
et dico naturam arbitrium; ratio autem recta principium boni moralis; gratia
autem boni gratuiti, aut si immiscet se aliqua gratia in bono morali, hoc erit propter
difficultatem operabilium. *Paris Nat. lat. 16387*, f. 78ra. Bruges Ville 236, f. 68ra.
Zitiert nach Lottin, *Études*, S. 87, Anm. 4.
[31] In *II Sent.*, d. 40, q. 1, a. 5. *Opera omnia*, Bd. 6, S. 750. Zitiert auch von Lottin,
Études, S. 93 und Anm. 2.

Fähigkeit besaß, schon lange vor dem Aquinaten ein moralphiloso-
phisches System aufzubauen, das mit Entschiedenheit eine rational fun-
dierte Ethik in das moraltheologische System des 12. Jahrhunderts
integrierte.

Ich weiß, daß Curtius davor warnte, die Bildung der deutschen Dichter
sowie die der Germanisten zu überschätzen. Ich habe deshalb versucht,
das Ethos, den Sinn und die Logik von Hartmanns Moralphilosophie
aus dem allgemeinverständlichen Kontext seines Werkes zu begreifen.
Die wenigen Parallelen, die ich zu den scholastischen Theoretikern ziehen mußte, waren allgemeiner, fast weltanschaulicher Art. Die Hypothese, daß Hartmann, ein höfischer Dichter des 12. Jahrhunderts, die
Avantgarde des moralphilosophischen Denkens seiner Zeit bildete, wird
also in Hartmanns Text ihre Bestätigung, oder Widerlegung finden.
In diesem Sinne lege ich meine Bemerkungen der Gemeinschaft der
Germanisten zur Überprüfung vor.

Peter Wapnewski

Poor Henry – Poor Job
A Contribution to the Discussion of Hartmann's von Aue so-called »Conversion to an Anti-Courtly Attitude«

1. *Concept*

Hartmann von Aue, carefully arranging his words, thoughts and verses, transparent and clear, guided by the goddess temperance; merely to be considered a talent in comparison to his ingenious colleagues Wolfram and Gottfried; *pater et magister:* this is the way in which the historians of literature describe him, and in doing so they simply round out the picture which was so enthusiastically sketched by his disciple Gottfried. However, there is reason to doubt the truthfulness of this picture. The alleged well-behaved conformist Hartmann is the only one who denounces the exaggerated fiction of the minnesang on grounds of dignity and logic:

> Ir minnesinger, iu muoz ofte misselingen, / daz iu den schaden tuot, daz ist der wân. – (You minnesingers, you are bound to fail often: / it is illusion which causes you damage.)

Hartmann, allegedly so much inclined towards conventions, sweeps aside the ideological trappings of traditional glorifications of the crusades. He motivates his decision to participate with personal bewilderment: it's the death of his master which *beswæret* (depresses) him. Hartmann is not only the first to glorify the heroes of King Arthur in the German language, he is also the first to criticize the isolation of their world of wishful thinking. He also extracts them from such a world and lets them interact socially with their surrounding world. Activity among mankind is king Erec's primary task: *bî den liuten ist sô guot* (it is so good to be with people) – Hugo Kuhn showed this very convincingly.[1] And Iwein does not have to atone for breaking a magic

---

1 *Festschrift Kluckhohn-Schneider*, 1948, p. 122–147; also in: Hugo Kuhn, *Dichtung und Welt im Mittelalter*, 1959, pp. 133–150.

promise, but for a breach of proper social (and sociable) conduct, na-mely the brutal killing of the conquered sovereign Askalon. (And conse-quently the *satisfactio congrua,* the appropriate atonement, takes the form of social help). And also Gregorius is blessed at the end as one who has paid terrible atonement for socially inacceptable behavior: his class and his behavior were prescribed to him by his birth; and breaking out of this class is equal to entry into sin. Finally, the »herre Heinrich« (Lord Henry): his elevation and salvation are manifested in a mar-riage, following the example of the Arthurian model. However, this marriage is such that it must appear scandalous to the social conscious-ness of the feudal era. It is a scandal which Hartmann depicts con-sciously as such.

I want to indicate with these preliminary remarks that Hartmann is not what he has been degraded to by his friends and admirers. He does not conform to given standards, but he breaks these standards and thereby establishes new ones. I have dealt more extensively with this important peculiarity of his elsewhere, and have there spoken of his »gegenhöfische Wendung« (his conversion to an anti-courtly attitude). The following thoughts, too, are to be seen as a contribution to such a (non-conformist) image of Hartmann, as a poet who represents the rebellion against tra-ditional standards.[2]

2. *The Story*

Once upon a time there lived a great lord in the land of Uz – or *ze Swâben* (in Swabia). He was highly respected and honored, loved and admired by this people, and he exercised his power wisely and piously; and his life was visibly blessed. But then misfortune strikes him un-expectedly and like lightning. God lets him fall out of all the happiness of his life, and this happens without any apparent reason: ... he is not aware of having sinned. Leprosy strikes him, he becomes an outcast, and people avoid him. Since he is not only pious, but also righteous, he is incapable of comprehending his misfortune, and he rebels. He curses the day of his birth:

---

[2] See Peter Wapnewski, *Hartmann von Aue,* ⁵1972 (Sammlung Metzler, Bd. 17), *passim.*

Pereat dies in qua natus sum, et nox in qua dicta est: Conceptus est homo!
(Job 3:3) – (Let the day perish in which I was born, and the night that said,
There is a man child conceived.)

verfluochet und verwâzen / wart vil dicke der tac / dâ sîn geburt ane lac. –
(Accursed and reviled, / many a time and oft, / was the day of his birth.)

Finally he bows humbly to his fate and accepts it. In this instant, however, God elevates him more magnificently than ever before, and he
leads a long and happy life: *et mortuus est senex et plenus dierum* (Job
42:16) (And Job died, old and full of days) – he is given *nâch süezem
lanclîbe ... daz êwige rîche* (v. 1514–16) (he is granted the eternal
kingdom after a happy and long life).

3. The Form

The structure of both poems is similar, it is regular. It is a tripartite
structure: the happy Job / the sufferer and the fighter Job / the blessed
Job – der hêrre Heinrîch (the lord Henry) / der arme Heinrîch (the
poor Henry) / der guote hêrre Heinrîch (the blessed lord Henry).
However, if we look at the story of Job in the Old Testament from the
point of view of textual criticism, we see that it consists of many overlapping layers and that the (metrically scanned) central portion is of
different origin than the prose frame.[3] But we are concerned with the
canonized version of the Book of Job as it was known to the Middle
Ages. In their extant form, both poems exhibit the structure of a
triptych.[4]

4. Henry and Job

Three times Hartmann explicitly relates his hero to Job: in verses
120–130 and verses 1356–1370 he equates him with Job, whereas in the
third instance verses 133–148 he contrasts Henry negatively with Job
as the stoic sufferer. But it is this negative quality of Henry which Hartmann characterizes by quoting verbatim the central statement of Job's

---

[3] See *Das Buch der Bücher, Altes Testament,* hg. von Hanns-Martin Lutz, Hermann
Timm, Eike Christian Hirsch, München 1970, pp. 534 ff.
[4] Concerning *Poor Henry,* see Wapnewski, p. 100.

rebellious phase: *Pereat dies in qua natus sum* (Let the day perish in which I was born) – *AH*, vv. 160–162:

> vervluochet und verwâzen / wart vil dicke der tac / dâ sîn geburt ane lac. –
> (Accursed and reviled, / many a time and oft, / was the day of his birth.)

This relationship between Henry and Job, stressed so expressly by the poet, has, of course, been the subject of extensive research, beginning with Schönbach and Wackernagel, continuing with Kraus and Sparnaay to this very day.[5] Most attention caught that passage in which Hartmann interprets the rebellious Henry as an anti-Job, as a type antithetical to Job as the patient sufferer. This interpretation of Hartmann clearly contradicts the text of Job's story. Critics claimed that this is a case of definite misunderstanding. Thus Carl von Kraus, who found additional resemblances to Job in *Der Arme Heinrich,* could arrive at this seemingly logical conclusion: Hartmann couldn't have used the Book of Job as an immediate model, for Henry obviously did not behave any differently from Job. Yet the poet described Henry as a type antithetical to Job. Therefore Hartmann must have used a source which interpreted Job's curse as a lament of Henry, or he must have misunderstood his source. It is the outcry with which Henry damns the day of his birth, and for which the poet reproaches his hero Henry.[6]

5. Job in the Middle Ages

The explanation by von Kraus[7] obviously is due to a misjudgment of the medieval knowledge and understanding of the story of Job. Job[8] was known to the Middle Ages only in the form and to the extent in which he was depicted by the official Bible exegesis. The same applies to other Biblical figures, especially to those of the Old Testament. The medieval understanding of Job was based mainly on the commentaries of Ambrose, St. Augustine and, above all, Gregory the Great. From those commentaries alone the picture of Job was derived, as known to the Middle Ages. What kind of Job was that?

---

[5] See the bibliography, Wapnewski, pp. 103–105.
[6] vv. 160–162. I quote according to the text of Paul-Wolff's edition, Tübingen 1972.
[7] Carl von Kraus, in: *Festgabe für Samuel Singer,* hg. von Harry Maync, Tübingen 1930, pp. 1–19.
[8] I should like to stress that I owe my knowledge concerning Job in the Middle Ages to the study of the Ph. D.-Dissertation of Karl Heinz Glutsch, Karlsruhe 1972.

For medieval theology there was only one perspective from which Job was considered, and that was from the perspective of the New Testament. (And again, the same is true for other figures of the Old Testament). St. James mentions and praises Job in the New Testament (in his letter 5:11):

> Sufferentiam Job audistis, et finem Domini vidistis, quoniam misericors Dominus est et miserator. – (Ye have heard of the endurance of Job, and seen the end of the Lord; that the Lord is full of tender compassion and pitiful.)

This characterization of Job and this characterization of the Lord and his attitude determined the medieval understanding of Job. Job's fate had to be understood from the point of view of its end – and this is the manner in which it was understood all throughout the Middle Ages. Job the rebel, Job the fighter, the bitter Job (thus the Job of the great central portion of his Book!) did not exist as far as the Middle Ages were concerned. For the Middle Ages, Job is the Christian stoicist, the sufferer who has accepted God's will. And in as much as he is a humble sufferer, he is the *typus Christi*, the type of Christ.

6. The Typological Method of Interpretation

One simply had to use the typological method of interpretation in order to deal successfully with those traits in the text of the Old Testament which prevented the desired glorification of Job. The theory of the fourfold meaning of Scripture in the Middle Ages is well known, and therefore requires only a few sketchy remarks.[9] The ecclesiastical exegetes strived to eradicate contradictions and to harmonize the doctrine; and therefore they had to derive from the literal meaning (the *sensus litteralis, sensus historicus*) a »higher« truth. This truth was said to be contained in the *sensus spiritualis*. This spiritual sense revealed itself in different methods. It conformed, for instance, to the moralistic or tropological, or to the mystical method of interpretation. (The allegorical and the anagogical methods have traditionally been subsumed under the mystical method.)

The typological method also belongs to the techniques of allegorical interpretation. This method is the result of an expressly Christian, i.e.

---

[9] See the article of my Marburg colleague Werner Schröder in this volume, pp. 64–85.

Christ-centered view of the world. Its essence is to interpret figures and events of the Old Testament as prefigurations of figures and events of the New Testament (therefore it is called the typological-figural interpretation). They stand to each other in the relationship of *promise* to *fulfillment*. By virtue of such a method of interpretation, the medieval theologians interpreted Job as the type of Christ because of his willingness to suffer, his *gedultecheit* (patience),[10] his acceptance of God's will.

In order to arrive at this interpretation, which was the only valid one in the Middle Ages, the *expositio* of the text had to be flatly manipulated, especially the passage of Job's curse. Not one of the medieval interpretations of Job takes the curse »literally«, they all follow the theological interpretation as developed mainly by Gregory the Great. (In fact, the rebellious Job is known again only since the 18th century, and then not so much among theologians as among poets and philosophers, from Johann Christian Guenther to Heine, Kierkegaard, and Bloch.)[11] In his *Moralia*, Gregory interprets Job's cursing the day of his birth as a curse of Adam and his sin which made man lose his immortality (which will be given back to him by Christ). To curse the day of one's birth is supposed to mean to curse the day of mortality, and thus *nativitas* (birth) becomes *mortalitas* (death). To curse mortality means to overcome it, and this points to Christ who will bring eternity. Twisted this way, the curse finally turns into a pious wish . . ., *dies* (day) becomes *nox* (night), *nox* (night) becomes *diabolus* (the devil).[12] (The dialectics of this discussion even goes so far as to maintain that a day which has passed and is thus not existent any longer, could not be cursed . . .)

7. Hartmann and his Job

Research has shown that the relation between Job and *Der Arme Heinrich* goes far beyond the three afore-mentioned direct references to Job.[13] In fact, there is a wealth of quotations from Job in *Der Arme Heinrich*. Since there can be no doubt that there exists a direct literary dependence between the two texts, it is methodologically not only

---

[10] Henry's and Job's *gedultecheit:* see Glutsch, pp. 143 ff.
[11] See Glutsch, pp. 11–22.
[12] See Glutsch, pp. 93–99.
[13] Kraus *für Singer*, pp. 1 ff.

justified but even mandatory to take seriously also those references which would have to be called vague, if there were not a direct relationship already established. Between these two texts it is especially noteworthy that Henry, after having been saved, is even richer and more powerful than at the beginning – in spite of the fact that he gave away all his possessions. This miracle can be explained only in view of the end of the Book of Job which also contains an increase in his wealth. (It is a miracle indeed, a fairy tale, even though one worked by God, and in that sense understandable.)

The philologist who wants to understand Hartmann's *Armer Heinrich* will first try to investigate the sources. The sources are unknown. There are the two Latin *Predigtmærlein (exempla)*, found and edited by Klapper: the tale of *Henricus pauper* (Poor Henry) and that of *Albertus pauper* (Poor Albert). Both are known only from manuscripts of the 14th century and could be dependent on Hartmann just as well as they could have used the same source from which Hartmann drew his story.

It is of importance here that the two tales agree in saying that the hero has suffered *omnia tanquam (alter) Hiob benigne*,[14] that is, he has patiently suffered just like Job! In view of the undisputed fact that Hartmann refers to the conventional medieval concept of Job as the patient sufferer and that he contrasts his hero to Job when he has him rebel against his fate, the following question arises: is it more likely that the author of those *exempla* knew Hartmann's story and changed Henry back to a traditional Job type – the hero *tanquam Job*, just like Job –, or is it more likely that Hartmann found in his source, which also was the source of the two *exempla*, a Job like hero and deviated from it by turning Henry into a rebel?[15]

8. *The Protesting Henry*

At this point of our investigation, we can state the following thesis: Hartmann owes to his source an image of Henry modelled according to the accepted medieval understanding of Job. But he is not satisfied with Henry's passive submission to his fate. Not because he was a theo-

---

14 Glutsch, p. 134, note 2.
15 Joseph Klapper, *Die Legende vom Armen Heinrich*, Wiss. Beilage zum Bericht der Oberrealschule zu Breslau, Ostern 1914.

logical reformer (which is, by definition, unthinkable in the Middle Ages), but because he wants to bestow on his heroes some responsibility, which can be manifest, for instance, in the possibility of becoming guilty.

In this sense Hartmann makes his hero »human«, by allowing him to rebel against God and against the misfortune imposed on him by God. In much the same way, he also depicts Erec's and Iwein's and Gregory's guilt as self-inflicted – apparently clearly deviating from his respective sources. And he does this in the same way as he asks the minnesinger to renounce *wân* (illusion) in favor of the only important reality: one's relation to God. In such a way Hartmann's own concept of the Arthurian knight might have influenced his representation of Henry.

The structure of the events in Hartmann's Arthurian romances depends on a discrepancy between the hero and his fate, between the hero and his world (surrounding), between the hero and society. The hero is always guilty insofar as he gives in momentarily or temporarily to subjective desire in the conflict between personal wants and extra-personal tasks. (For example Erec in his total absorption in love, Iwein in his obsession with fighting and killing, Gregory as the *werlttôre*, the fool, like Henry). Within such a concept Hartmann could not leave Henry to unquestioned suffering; he could not depict him as the innocent sufferer, suffering because of an inscrutable decree. (His self-accusation, probably due to his source, seems appended and grafted on: see the monologue vv. 383–458.) So Hartmann makes his hero react rebelliously and has him cry out his curse in the *sensus historicus*, which Job was not allowed to have meant »literally« according to the medieval interpretation! This means: Hartmann presents the Middle Ages with the true Job.

His curse of the day of his birth with the words of Job is the main point, the explosive point of the story. Thus Henry would not be the victim of a punitive ethics, but of an ethics centered around suffering, and initially he does not accept it humbly. Therefore God does not punish him, but He tries him, just as He once tried Job. (Cynical and sadistic we would call it, if a man would treat his fellow man in this manner: like playing cat and mouse ...) God does not punish Henry, but he tempts him, that is: He has *beide versuocht* (tempted both), the man and the girl (v. 1385 f.).[16]

---

[16] See Wapnewski, p. 101.

9. Absalom

However, Hartmann not only refers to one figure of the Old Testament, but to two. So far I attempted to make Hartmann's Poor Henry a »true« Job, as in the Old Testament, one who rebelled against God, like Job; who became guilty through such a rebellion (not in the moral, not in the social sense, but) in the theological sense of the word; who became sinful and now must go his own, lonesome path of atonement, like an Arthurian knight, but yet differently, turned towards his inner self; who finally, after his absolution, experiences the process of »re-integration« (Erich Köhler) (again like an Arthurian knight in the form of marriage; for this refer to what we discussed before).

But this attempt to understand Henry as a »rebel taken back« analogous to Job would remain mere assumption, if the poet had not given us an additional indication in a second figure from the Old Testament which is related to the hero. This is Absalom. Lines 84–90 of *Der Arme Heinrich* read:

> an im wart erzeiget / als ouch an Absalône, / daz diu üppige krône / werlt-lîcher süeze / vellet under vüeze / ab ir besten werdekeit ... – (In him was made manifest, as previously in Absalom, that the height of secular sweetness, being transient, falls to the ground, down from the peak of its greatest splendor ...)

Werner Fechter showed in a remarkable essay what Absalom stands for in the (Latin as well as in the Middle High German) Bible exegesis and in the secular literature of the Middle Ages. In the following, I will refer to Fechter's article.[17]

First of all, it must be noted: contrary to Job, Absalom does not constitute a »clear-cut type« for the Middle Ages (Fechter, p. 302). What dominates is his identification with the quality of human, virile beauty; he is the prototype of aesthetic perfection. That is said about him. Or he is used for comparison. Or someone else (as, for instance, Amfortas after having been healed) surpasses him. Usually, we do not find Absalom the beautiful in isolation; he is mentioned as a link of a for-mulized chain, such as: strong like Samson, wise like Salomon, beautiful like Absalom (Fechter, p. 307). It is clear that it is not this particular characteristic which makes Absalom a type for Henry. Which one of his other characteristics would provide a *tertium comparationis*? Absalom

---

[17] Werner Fechter, »Absalon als Vergleichs- und Beispielfigur im mittelhochdeutschen Schrifttum«, *Beitr.* (Tübingen) 83, 1961/62, pp. 302–316.

is also the murderer of his brother (2. Sam. 13:1 ff.), and medieval literature does refer to this fact. Hartmann, however, refrains from doing so. (Incidentally, he refers to Absalom also in *Erec:* Leitzmann vv. 2813 ff.; cf. Fechter, p. 303 – but there he uses him clearly as the prototype of beauty.)

However, it is much more important for medieval literature, and of highest importance for our investigation, to note that Absalom is also used as the model of a rebel: according to Second Samuel 15:1 ff. he rose against his father David and chased him from the city of Jerusalem. He flees on a mule from the site of the decisive battle and his long hair (the symbol of his beauty) gets caught in the branches of a tree, and he is left hanging between heaven and earth. David's general Joab kills him with three spears (against David's will). »Thus the German Middle Ages see also a rebel in Absalom« (Fechter, p. 308). The rebel rising against his own father. If one wants to find an analogy to Job here, one is moving on uncertain ground. But this ground does become more secure considering that medieval literature regards David as a »prefiguration of Christ, as was common theological usage« (Fechter, p. 309). Therefore, according to the Bible, Absalom's death is nothing else but a »punishment for his rebellion«. When Fechter states with resignation: »But Poor Henry is obviously not guilty of the sins of slander, rebellion, disobedience, greed and immodesty« (p. 311), he absolves Henry too rashly of one thing (or two), if we are not mistaken. Rebellion and disobedience have removed Henry from God, at least temporarily.

The medieval literature examined by Fechter confirms that Absalom is the figure of the rebel and slanderer. Philipp of Harvengt comments on David's lament over the dead rebel Absalom:

> . . . per David intellegimus Dominum nostrum Jesum Christum, et per Absalon accipimus genus humanum (*PL* 203, 558 = Fechter, p. 312 f.) – (by David we mean our lord Jesus Christ, and by Absalon we mean mankind.)

Again, David appears as a prefiguration of Christ, thus of God. »In his letters, Emperor Henry the fourth compares himself to the persecuted David, and he compares his son Henry the fifth to the rebellious Absalom« (Fechter, p. 313). (Pursuing such notions, the Latin exegetes could finally arrive at the opinion that Absalom »is a prefiguration of the traitor Judas«, Fechter, p. 313.)

That much is clear: Absalom is for the Middle Ages the prototype of the worldly man, the slave to beauty, caprice and dissipation. Henry is not that type of man. At the most, he is made to such a man *post festum* (afterwards): in his embarrassing selfaccusation which stands in contradiction to everything we learn about him from Hartmann.

10. *Job, Absalom and Henry*

Let us return to our thesis. I hope it has been somewhat confirmed by showing the role which these two figures from the Old Testament play in medieval literature (and thus in the general consciousness). Hartmann uses these two in order to characterize Henry and his wrong behavior. Rebellion belongs to Job's original portrait as confirmed by the Bible. Rebellion is also part of Absalom's being. Job turns against God. Absalom turns against his father. His father is David. David is a prefiguration of Christ for the Middle Ages (thus of God). Therefore, both Job and Absalom turn against God (understood literally or allegorically), that is: against the first and the second hypostasis of divine trinity.

In conclusion, we ask ourselves again, what might have been the sin of Henry, the perfect image of the Christian *cortegiano* (courtier)? Nothing. But it pleased God to try him. This is a temptation for God Himself, since His product is so perfect. Hartmann's text does not maintain this motivation. But the poet lets the subliminal relations still be seen by claiming that Henry had rebelled, but differently from Job. Differently? We know that he did not behave in »a different way« than Job. Just as the great sufferer did originally, Henry rebels against God's inscrutable decree. Not only does he rebel like Job, but also like the other richly gifted *herre* (lord) of the Old Testament, Absalom, whom the poet uses for illustration. Absalom, too, falls deep – even though not because of a trial of God, but because of the initial act of rebellion, just like Lucifer. The reference to Absalom makes it clear, clearer still, what could have become clear already from the mention of Job: Hartmann did not want to depict the sufferer, but the fighter, the rebel (and only subsequently: the sufferer).

The doubling of the typological figure is in itself remarkable. It must be added that Absalom's primary characteristic, for which he is generally known, is his beauty. Beauty is always an expression of high moral qualities for the Middle Ages, and beauty is always a characteristic trait of Arthurian knights. So »herre Heinrich« (lord Henry) approaches even more the type of Hartmann's Arthurian knight: namely by his beauty, dignity and value; and by breaking out of a given order. (The Arthurian knights Erec and Iwein violate the social order, just like the Arthurian-like prince Gregory; Henry violates the basic theological order.) The Arthurian knights, too, rebel: Erec by his defiant departure, Iwein by his flight into insanity, Gregory by making wild accusations (and Parzival through *zwîvel*, his doubts). Henry, too, rebels – like Job. And accepts – like Job. Henry, too, »rebels« – like Absalom: against the father. And »dies« – like Absalom (if only metaphorically). And he passes into a new life through this death: like Job, like Amfortas who resembles Absalom, like the Arthurian knights.[18]

18 At the very end, I give all my thanks to my friend and colleague Joachim Bumke and our colleagues at Stanford University, who translated the text of my paper into English.

Christian J. Gellinek

Iwein's Duel and Laudine's Marriage

Our remarks will most likely bear the stamp of adventure themselves, since this topic focusses on two general aspects in connection with two particular ones found in *Iwein* which seem intertwined in turn.

Fortunately the first aspect, *âventiure*, has stayed well defined ever since G. F. Benecke started our principal MHG Dictionary and Jacob Grimm had her personification gently knock at old Benecke's door. Since that bygone time it has generally been agreed that *âventiure* implies a sort of happenstance, an equivalent of *Begebenheit* (aventura) or of *Ereignis (eventus)*, or in its literarily derived meaning, that of narration and narrative unit, *Erzählung* and *Erzählteile*. Evidently all these meanings have one feature in common: the miraculous, the incomprehensible, the fortuitous, or something which is very much at stake.

The second aspect has been picked out of frustration with the formerly much debated value system, maintained by G. Ehrismann and subsequently crushed by E. R. Curtius. We will not delve into this abstract discussion again from any traditional viewpoint. Instead we presuppose that normally both average and exceptional knight were directed to broadly conduct themselves in a Christian attitude. An honorous Christian knight would have to show tangible lack of *tugent* before his *êre* could be questioned by the court he belonged to or was known at. Our specific problem was what happens if a knight separated himself deliberately from his group and its social orbit in order to seek *âventiure* clandestinely, as Iwein clearly does? If Fr. Maurer succeeded in demonstrating that a knight's *êre* originally grew out of the societal sphere of team spirit *(die Gefolgschaftssphäre)* – an interpretation endorsed by the editor of *Ritterliches Tugendsystem* (1970), G. Eifler –, what happens to a knight that comes across a challenge? What of his sense of values if he accepts it (or extends it) unobserved by and freed from courtly witnesses? Could his socially tested sense of values be totally upheld and stay up to par even under these tempting unprecedented circumstances? Would it not be more than human to suspect and observe a relaxation of his sense of values?

Let us look at two highly individual acts such as killing and marriage in *Iwein* and treat these acts as paradigmatic, by throwing some light on the two general aspects under consideration.

Despite vigorous recent *Iwein* scholarship[1] two traditionally accepted clichés have not been elucidated. Taken into one, they imply that Laudine, the heroine, badly in need of a new defender of her magic Fountain, *marries the murderer*[2] in undue haste because of the power of *minne*. Rarely are these points expressed in one sentence, but we shall see that the two clichés support each other. The areas are interrelated, and we shall try to clarify them by textual criticism.

I. *Iwein's Final Acquittal of the Murder Charge*

When Peter Wapnewski summarizes the prevailing opinion that Iwein *is* the murderer of his opponent Ascalôn, the decisive paragraph is so typical of the majority opinion that it deserves to be quoted:

> »Man wird also tiefer fragen müssen; und es bietet sich nur eine Antwort an, wenn sie auch von der Dichtung *nirgends* expressis verbis formuliert wird: Iwein hat sich des elementarsten Verstoßes gegen die *triuwe* und *erbermde*, gegen das Recht auf Schutz und Schonung schuldig gemacht (p. 66). Der rechtmäßige Herr der Quelle ... – er wird von Iwein gegen alle Regeln des ritterlichen Kampfes erschlagen (p. 66/67). Hartmann aber tut den Vorgang fast unwillig ab, er sieht ihn vom Gesichtspunkt des Moralisten her und sagt das schwerwiegende Wort: *her Îwein jaget in âne zuht* (v. 1056) ...

---

[1] By such critics as: H. Sacker, H. B. Willson, H. Sparnaay, H. Milnes, P. Wapnewski, W. Dittmann, A. T. Hatto, K. Ruh, X. v. Ertzdorff, M. Wehrli, E. Spielmann, Th. C. van Stockum, R. Endres, Th. Cramer. For more precise references see notes *passim*.

[2] The expression »Mörder« rather than »Totschläger« is used by G. Ehrismann, *Geschichte der Deutschen Literatur bis zum Ausgang des Mittelalters*, II, 2, 1 (1927), pp. 173–183; P. Wapnewski, *Hartmann von Aue*, Realienbücher für Germanisten, Sammlung Metzler, second edition (Stuttgart, 1964), pp. 55–72; X. v. Ertzdorff, »Spiel der Interpretation: Der Erzähler in Hartmanns Iwein«, *Festgabe für Friedrich Maurer zum 70. Geburtstag* (Düsseldorf, 1968), pp. 135 ff., 149; and F. Whitehead, »Yvain's Wooing«, *Medieval Miscellany* presented to Eugène Vinaver, ed. by F. Whitehead, A. H. Diverres, and F. E. Sutcliffe (Manchester U. P. N. Y., 1965), 321–336, 327.

Daß die Witwe des so rüde Erschlagenen den *Mörder* heiratet, ist übrigens ein offenbar schwererer Verstoß gegen die *triuwe* als später Iweins Terminversäumnis. ... Er ... bemüht schließlich die irrationale Instanz der *Frau Minne,* der die letzte Verantwortung zufalle.« (p. 67)[3]

The passage contains several problems that bear on our topic. *Triuwe* (approximating *fides*) and *erbermde* (resembling *caritas*) in a knightly duel fought while on *âventiure* (in the absence of witnesses and judges) are highly problematical virtues which Hartmann, the narrator, takes up in the text. Before Iwein can be condemned as a murderer, we must examine whether Ascalôn himself observed the rules of a knightly duel. Furthermore, we have to ascertain whether Iwein's conduct during the duel might not have been justifiable in terms of the twelfth-century tournament rules. And finally, if we do pass judgment, are we entitled to a free and possibly arbitrary choice between different points of view, e.g. those of the narrator, the combatants, or others, such as Laudine in her subsequent judgment?

The first textual basis we have seems to suggest a rather ambiguous attitude on the narrator's part (525–542). The speaker, Kâlogrenant, one of King Arthur's knights, lets the medieval audience know and understand that he entertains a particular notion of *âventiure:*

> Ich heize ein riter und hân den sin / daz ich suochende rîte / einen man der mit mir strîte, / der gewâfent sî als ich. / daz prîset in, und sleht er mich: / gesige aber ich im an, / sô hât man mich vür einen man, / und wirde werder danne ich sî.[4]   (530–537)

Since Kâlogrenant talks to a woodsman who appears more human in outlook (*swer mir niene tuot, / der sol ouch mich ze vriunde hân,* 484 f.) than he himself, the primitive adventure seeker,[5] we are to assume that Hartmann meant to be polemic, and certainly ironic. The gist of this deliberately »corny« definition of *âventiure* reads as follows: »Once I find another knight armored like myself (533), I'll fight him. If he kills me, he will increase his reputation; if on the other hand I succeed in killing him, my reputation will be enhanced.« What he is talking about is the type of the arbitrary fight of the *âventiure* which was recognized.[6] It was not governed by artistic rules like the *turnei* or tournament. Even

---

[3] *Hartmann von Aue,* pp. 55–72. The two German italics are mine.
[4] The quotations are from the critical edition by L. Wolff, *Iwein,* 7th ed. (1968), vol. 1.
[5] H. Sacker, »An Interpretation of Hartmann's *Iwein*«, *Germanic Review* xxxvi (1961), 5–26, 8.
[6] F. Niedner, *Das deutsche Turnier im XII. und XIII. Jahrhundert* (Berlin, 1881), p. 13.

at the *turnei ze ernste,* which was governed by rules and was fought with sharp weapons, death of one or both combatants could easily occur.[7] Therefore we may conclude that Kâlogrenant is not talking about a knightly duel but rather about a duel with sharp weapons that could easily result in a killing. During such a duel the rôle of *erbermde* is unfortunately rather minimal. That is not to say that there ought not be a place or function for *erbermde* after the combat is over. According to the minimal *triuwe* extended in the context of such a duel, a challenge had to be forwarded and accepted so that the other combatant would be forewarned and know that a serious fight *(ze ernste)* was imminent. This is precisely what Ascalôn missed in Kâlogrenant's behavior: *mirn wart von iu niht widerseit*[8] (713). Since Kâlogrenant also wilfully destroyed some of Ascalôn's property, the Lord of the Fountain may say that Kâlogrenant acted *triuwelôs* (712).

At the outset of his duel with his enemy, Iwein entertains a narrow-minded notion of what knightly duels should be, and perhaps of knighthood altogether. The narrator refers back to this simple creed in a subsequent narrative strand while Iwein is awakening from his madness (obviously without being capable of ironizing it as this stage): *ich bejagte swes ich gerte / mit sper und mit swerte* (3525–3526). This narrow notion is still further reduced in size by his selfish initial fear that Arthur might grant Gawein rather than him the privilege of fighting the Lord of the Fountain (918).

Iwein, knowing full well the prowess of that Lord (as every reader will remember), does succeed in provoking a magic storm there; but this time the irate Lord Ascalôn does not wait for the extension of a formal challenge for combat – rather he himself challenges the rude intruder from a distance (1002–1003). Iwein understands the unmistakable sign perfectly well (1004–1005), and is thereby forewarned. Both are now set on hurting the other combatant, for both are mad at each other. In terms of the ensuing fight this means that both realize it will be fought *ze ernste* (1011) with sharp, i.e. deadly weapons.

The issue is once again the damage caused to Ascalôn's property, which Iwein perpetrates because of his own grievance. Thus they are both angry about different matters; but Ascalôn's rage is certainly much less far-fetched than Iwein's, as the insult suffered by his *neve* lies ten years in the past. Still, the beginning of this fight is quite honorable, in spite

---

[7] *Ibid.,* p. 24.
[8] *Widerseit,* I think, means »challenged« here.

of the possibility that it might end fatally: *hie huop sich ein strîten / daz got mit êren möhte sehen, / und solt ein kampf vor im geschehen.* (1020–22) Even in the eyes of God this fight would have found favor in spite of the extraordinary circumstance that it is a sword fight on horseback.[9]

The first significant blow, coming from the front of course, made Ascalôn *halptôt(e)*. Since Ascalôn had challenged Iwein, what has this hit to do with murder? In pursuing his foe Iwein intends either to kill or capture Ascalôn, but Ascalôn harbors exactly these same intentions toward Iwein![10] The portcullis of the trap-door is disengaged by the lord of the castle, as he rides through the gate. In terms of unfinished duelling action this means that Iwein for a second or two finds himself near death. Now it is time for the ironic narrator to invent a second blow of which Chrétien de Troyes knows nothing. By leaning forward at this split-second Iwein avoids the death trap and strikes Ascalôn a second time, from the rear (but also from the front of the trap-door). This one is, however, not a deadly blow, as Wapnewski erroneously assumed. There seemingly is even a textual basis for this error: v. 1968, where Lunete says (for the sake of rhyming in a turned around fashion) *der in dâ jagete unde sluoc.*[11] The first strike was knightly but lethal; the second one unknightly but non-lethal, which again is not so surprising if one considers the awkward conditions under which it is rendered to the foe. Had Iwein realized the immediate danger to life, the second strike would have been conducted in self-defense, eliminating a crime of murder altogether. I entirely agree with K. Ruh when he argued: »Der zweite Schlag unmittelbar vor dem Fallgitter scheidet als Argument für Hartmanns moralische Kritik aus, da er offensichtlich nur der Erklärung dient, daß Iwein dem todbringenden *slegetor* entgeht.«[12] Since the first blow results in Ascalôn's death, it undeniably constitutes a case of manslaughter. On the question whether it could have been justifiable under the circumstances, Hartmann is hard-pressed to introduce different points of view.

Hartmann goes on by ironizing a possible further narration of indi-

---

[9] The formula expressed in 1021 reoccurs in 3046, where the fight is ennobled by *rîterschaft* (3045). Both types could be honorable in the eyes of God.

[10] F. Niedner, p. 13.

[11] Lunete cannot be well informed since she talks from hear-say only. Cf. 1050–1053; 1122 refers to these lines, but not to 1105.

[12] K. Ruh, *Höfische Epik des Mittelalters*, I. Grundlagen der Germanistik, VII (Berlin, 1967), p. 152.

vidual blows as gratuitous, since he assumed it must have been obvious to his audience that neither Iwein nor Ascalôn was a coward (1046), the eventual victor being such a *hövesch man* (1040) that in any case he would not have bragged about his fighting technique. As a matter of fact the decisive blow splitting Ascalôn's helmet (1049) and an area of his brain (1050) in the framework of this particular fight is undoubtedly a »clean« one. The Lord of the Fountain is mortally wounded (1051) by a blow that will eventually take his life, a point well worth remembering in our subsequent discussion. Although this kind of deadly combat on horseback, according to the narrator, finds no disfavor in the eyes of God, it does not find favor in the eyes of Hartmann, who, at another occasion, dubs such fights as having the derogatory character of *dörperheit* (7116–7122), referring to the preference of the narrator for the more noble fighting on foot (after the spears are used up). In keeping with the narrator's own prejudices it must be supposed that, in his eyes, knightly *zuht* was not necessarily part and parcel of a *dörperhaft* horseback combat to begin with if fought outside a regular tournament, as is the case here.

Had Arthur's intention of reaching the Fountain on midsummernight been fulfilled (901), a combat of higher knightly standards might have taken place, as can be surmised from 905: *daz dûhte si rîterlich und guot, / wan dar stuont ir aller muot.* Yet the duel between the two knights is fought on a reduced level, so that it seems quite appropriate to say *âne zuht*, once the flight from this fight has begun. This expression in v. 1056 has nothing to do with the perspective of the moralist (as Wapnewski and Ehrismann and others allege), but carries a meaning such as »unbridled« or »undisciplined«, ironically reminiscent of a characteristic of Keiî (v. 90). Thus Iwein is a *hövesch man* (1040) who fights a *dörperhaft* (7121) *kampf* (1022) or *strît(en)* (1020) with swords on horseback (1019; 1012) in *ernest und zorn* (1011) with sharp weapons (1027) – and the combination of these traits is lacking self-discipline according to v. 1056, to Niedner (p. 24 ff.), and to Benecke-Borchling, *Wörterbuch zu Hartmanns Iwein* ([3]1901), p. 311.

Let us not forget that such a practice occurs again later in the story, i.e. when Iwein and his men kill the greater part of those of their enemies who do not flee in time (3738–3749), while some others are captured (3747). And again the narrator quite succinctly comments: *hie was der strît ergangen / nâch hern Îweines êren* (3748–3749). We have to suppose that this reaction was accepted as inevitable by the audience, whether or not Hartmann wished to distance himself from it in this context. The narrator plants a hint at Iwein's having regained *zuht,* before the *brûtlouft* (2434) gets started, by which time, in his eyes and those of Laudine's courtiers, Iwein at least *wænlich* (2433) enjoys *volle tugent* (2428). How could such an attestation be justified in any way if Iwein had not just been an undisciplined fighter, but an outright murderer? Could Hartmann, the ethicist, the superb rhetorician, the master in the choice of words be accused of vulgar tastelessness, of which *»die leicht getröstete Witwe«* (Ehrismann), the wicked widow, is but one down-dressing corollary?

We would like to know whether this old prejudice does not by any chance indirectly spring from the hostile tongue of Wolfram von Eschenbach? After all, Wolfram's snub at *vroun Luneten rât ... / diu riet ir vruowen: lât genesen / disen man, der den iuwern sluoc: / er mac ergetzen iuch genuoc.* (*Parzival,* V,253,10–14) ranks very prominently in Ehrismann's standard history of German literature read by generations of Germanists, where it graces the very first sentence in regular print of the entire *Iwein* section.

Had Iwein realized that a deviously set portcullis was about to kill him, his second strike would have been conducted in self-defense, for which knightly rules cannot fully apply; just as Ascalôn/Esclados acted in self-defense with their killing scheme while fleeing in *Iwein/Yvain.* Our summary is comparatively simple. Not only does Iwein not kill Ascalôn with his second blow, it fails to make him Iwein's captive as well; rather it makes him Ascalôn's half-prisoner. Therefore the second blow cannot bear any legal or moral consequences one way or the other.[13] Ascalôn, killed by a knightly blow (1049 f.) in an openly challenged combat has *not* been murdered at all.

In respect to a possible guilt in the manslaughter charge Iwein claims: *... nôt / mich twanc ûf ir herren tôt* (1641 f.), which Cramer aptly translates by *»Zwangslage«.* The wife of the late Ascalôn, Laudine, judges in 2044 *er hât ez werende getân* (cf. also 2050 *nôt: »Zwang«*). This remark implies a situation not very short of self-defense; after all, Lord Ascalôn had the same designs on Iwein or any other serious attacker of the fountain (2045).

---

[13] Disagreeing with J. Bumke, *Die romanisch-deutschen Literaturbeziehungen im Mittelalter: Ein Überblick* (Heidelberg, 1967), p. 31, who dubs Ascalôn's killing »unknightly«, as H. Sparnaay, *Hartmann von Aue: Studien zu einer Biographie,* vol. II (Halle, 1938), p. 48, had.

On the question of whether this manslaughter could have been justifiable, given the tenuous circumstances under which it occurred, we find divergent opinions in the text. Lunete's judgment must of course be dismissed as biased, since for her from the beginning *vil starke ranc dar nâch ir muot / daz er herre wurde dâ* (1786 f.). Laudine, an obstinate lady nevertheless given to tempestuously quick changes of mind, reacts at first erratically; prodded by Lunete, she gradually arrives at a reasoned opinion. This gradual change of mind, including her opinion on the slaying of her husband Ascalôn, is the central concern of the narrative union between Laudine and Iwein, who did deliberately kill her first husband.

II. *Laudine's Interpretation of her Husband's Death*

Laudine mourns her slain husband sincerely (1310 ff.). A picture of her husband's excellence, her matching admiration, as well as the confidence she had in him, emerges. Since in her view he was too brave and too strong to have been defeated in a natural combat, she rather suspects unnatural (*wunderlîchen*, 1383) causes, and flatly accuses God of having sided with her enemy (1384): *dâ bistû eine schuldec an!* In her second lament she draws an even more exaggerated account of the most perfect of all knights (1454–1459). Ironically Iwein witnesses this affect monologue by looking up through a window that Lunete had opened to give him a better view of Laudine, thus undercutting the weight of her grief from the intruder's and future husband's point of view. In the whole series of laments, gradually, personal expressions of loss outweigh the initial emphasis on the praise of the dead. At first Hartmann introduces her death wish seriously (1462–1475), although this seriousness grows thinner by the time the narrator has reached 1811–1815. By then her death wish could be seen as an attempt to deny her *senediu nôt* its natural (at least year long) duration and virtually a desire to repress its full length. On the other hand, he definitely ironizes her death wish from the intruder's point of view, by making Iwein almost jump out of his hiding (1480–1482) at the risk of his *own* life. Finally her death wish is reduced to a conceit when she talks about committing suicide unless a knife or a sword should not be handy (1898). He then proceeds to undercut her grief from Iwein's point of view again

(1660–1680), and from Lunete's (1861!), culminating in Laudine's own admission:

> ›nû clag ich gote mîn ungemach, / daz ich nû niht ersterben mac. / daz ich iemer deheinen tac / nâch mînem herren leben sol, / dâ mite enist mir doch niht wol. / und möht ich umben tôt mîn leben / âne houbetsünde gegeben, / des wurd ich schiere gewert, / od ichn vunde mezzer noch swert.‹ (1890–98)

Since she does not die, she must decide, as Lunete forces her to realize, what to do about herself and her property. After she desisted from her grief, but before *vrou Minne* has produced an effect on her, she reaches the conclusion that the slayer of her husband could not have been guilty of manslaughter completely: *ouch stât unschulde dâ bî* (2042), since he did it in self-defense. Therefore, she sees ground for acquitting Iwein vis-à-vis herself (2053). Immediately thereafter *Minne* puts Laudine under her spell too.

The narrator has to approve this internal intellectual acquittal, because he has to get on with his story. Thus, I think, he neither sides with Laudine, nor does he condemn her attitude.[14] After all Hartmann knew in advance that the foundation of the imminent marriage, haste in covering up unseemly conduct, will eventually have to be made up for by intense suffering as an ultimate preparation for atonement. It is interesting to compare the two different points of view: Although Iwein finds himself under the influence of *Minne* earlier than Laudine, *he* realizes that only *Minne* could cover up *ein unbillîche sache*, whereas Laudine, who is not yet under that influence: *sus brâhte siz in ir muote / ze suone und ze guote . . .* (2051 f.) excuses Iwein vis-à-vis herself. We must conclude that Iwein is being excused of manslaughter by Laudine while she is still in the possession of her full faculties. Hartmann takes pain to separate this personal exculpation from the issue of marriage, and does not take an objective stand in the former question.

III. *Vrou Minne's Reconciliatory Interference in the Marriage Arrangement Between Iwein and Laudine*

Iwein being a totally fictitious literary figure is made capable of rationalizing and exculpating his impromptu conduct in the midst of a con-

---

14 I am siding here with K. Ruh, »Zur Interpretation von Hartmanns *Iwein*«, *Philologia Deutsch,* Festschrift zum 70. Geburtstag von Walter Henzen, hg. von W. Kohlschmidt und P. Zinsli (Francke Bern, 1965), p. 46.

flict monologue,[15] where he proposes to the as yet unpersonified *Minne*
that she should decide to overcome his dilemma by doing one of two
things: either *mir den muot beneme von ir* (1652) or *daz si ir râte her ze
mir* (1651). Otherwise he is lost.

Minne is a many-faceted word,[16] but within this context it can only
mean ἔρως or *ardor (furor)*, not *caritas*,[17] rather the lack thereof.[18] The
spirit of *Minne* makes him worry exclusively about her future rather
than about his past conduct as it might relate to it. He does not want
to see his future wife or lover disfigure herself – and yet *Minne* has not
managed to overcome his critical faculties entirely; he does at least
remember the heavy weight of his guilt (1616 f.). Through Iwein's
words, Hartmann makes it quite clear that any future liaison between
them must be *ein unbillîche sache* (1629), which only *vrou Minne* can
make *billîch*, i.e. acceptable in the eyes of society that was not to be
offended.

Before we consider this particular marriage in poeticized legal terms,
we must touch upon the prospective suitor's qualifications. He has all
of those that are required: high birth, youth, personal worth, social
acceptability, and the excellence essential to make him an effective
protector of her reputation (2092–2095). As a propertied widow she
has the right to choose a husband for herself, especially if she holds a
higher social rank than the suitor (Iwein, however, is of royal rank),
and her bridegroom is bound to join her household. Under these circumstances the appropriate form of marriage is that of mutual consent.
I hope to have demonstrated[19] what the requirements of marriage by
consent were, as the poets in this century saw them and will therefore
only briefly summarize the salient points of my conclusions: The marriage by consent is contracted in three stages, which, not unlike separate
phases of a victorious battle, needed not to coincide in time, nor fall in
line in consecutive order. The stages can be described as the inten-

---

[15] The terminology of monologues and dialogues in Hartmann, here used, is based
on the categorizations arrived at by my pupil, Mrs. J. K. Liebmann, »The Narrative Function of Direct Discourse in the Epics of Hartmann von Aue«, Yale diss.
1970. University Microfilm, Ann Arbor, Michigan.

[16] D. Wiercinski, *Minne: Herkunft und Anwendungsschichten eines Wortes,* Niederdeutsche Studien XI (1964); see chart on p. 97.

[17] Disagreeing H. Sparnaay, *Hartmann von Aue,* vol II, (1938), p. 48 f.

[18] H. B. Willson, »Love and Charity in Hartmann's *Iwein*«, *MLR* LVII (1962), 217.

[19] See author, »Marriage by Consent in Literary Sources of Medieval Germany«,
Collectanea Stephan Kuttner, II; Studia Gratiana XII (Bologna, 1967), 555–579.

tional, the pre-contractual and the contractual stage. In the end there
is a symbolic ornamentation rendered by a ceremony with various
contents.

The intentional stage, during which the suitors express themselves, is
here described in three phases. First, Lunete, knowing that Iwein's passion will ensure his agreement (2117), gains her mistress' consent by
naming an obviously satisfactory marriage prospect (2107–2108) and
suggests that she assemble her subjects as advising witnesses (2148–
2152). Secondly, the couple meet before the mediatrix, Lunete. After
some prodding, Iwein requests Laudine's favors on his knees and throws
himself at her mercy for the injury he has done her. She promises him
her favor, defends her haste, and introduces the »vis?« – »volo!« formula: *ich wil iuch gerne: welt ir mich?* (2333).[20] Rather than complete
the formula (which would have been offensive under the circumstances)
Iwein says that he would be a miserable wretch if he refused (2334–
2335. The end of the first stage is Laudine's suggestion that they consult
her followers for the sake of propriety (2362–2369). Signifying their
union, they join hands in a symbolic gesture. The assembly does not dis-
approve, as Lunete had predicted. Earlier, Laudine seemed to fear
opposition (2160 f.). Here Hartmann himself informs us by using the
traditional disclaimer that opposition would not have deterred her;
there is no pre-contractual stage expressed in *Iwein*, for the couple is
married immediately. It is, after all, a hastily arranged marriage in
which Laudine is a kind of war bride. (Interestingly as soon as she *is*
married the threat of war is over.) In keeping with the narrative perspective (no details about pledges or rings at this point), Hartmann includes some details about the contractual stage in the parting scene.
There the character of the union as a marriage by consent is stressed
(2926; 2929; 2945 f.; 2955). That each takes an oath displays the re-
ciprocity of the marriage agreement. Laudine does not get a ring from
Iwein, possibly because, as Gawein says, she is so constant that there
is no need to worry (2890–2893). Even though she casts her husband
off thirteen months later, she is never unfaithful to him. Since Iwein has

---

20 G. Ehrismann, II, 2.1, p. 177 erroneously takes it for a »Verlöbnisformel«; O. Kra-
tins, »Love and Marriage in Three Versions of ›The Knight of the Lion‹«, *Comparative Literature* XVI (1964), p. 37 thinks that v. 2333 contains »the daringly
uncourtly question«. Both authors miss the point. Only E. Spielmann, »Chrétien's
and Hartmann's Treatment of the Conquest of Laudine«, *Comparative Literature*
XVIII (1966), 242–263, *251*, although still a bit vague on this question, comes
close to interpreting it correctly.

asked to leave her, it is fitting that he take the ring which betokens his faithfulness (2950 f.; 2953–2955). As a pledge of her love and his faithfulness the magic ring links them to *vrou Minne's* rôle in bringing about this match.

The marriage by consent is actually concluded on the formula which Hartmann had used in Heinrich's marriage, *Armer Heinrich* 1511–1513. In saying that this marriage was both honorable and virtuous (2415) in the eyes of Laudine's subjects, and by adhering to the *michel vuoge* idea, Hartmann wished again to single out this match as having extraordinary implications, just as the duel with Ascalôn had at its place. We have no justification to belittle Hartmann as an artist. He does, on the one hand, clearly state that Iwein commands by now *volle tugent* (2428) and has completely taken over his predecessor's land and *êre* (2437); and he ironizes yet, on the other, Iwein's qualifications as *wænlich* (2433; cf. 8148), i.e. as *possibly* missing. There cannot be the slightest doubt which quality in particular, although not missing altogether, may not be present in sufficient degree, the *Leitbegriff*-quality in jeopardy throughout all of *Iwein* from line 1 ff. to the very end, namely the »*rehte güete*«. And it must have been obvious to the medieval audience, as it should be discernible to the modern critic, that this powerful ingredient must have been missing from a marriage by consent so hastily achieved. This particular faculty of the soul had not been given a chance to grow that rapidly. Neither party, but particularly not Iwein, had the time to atone in any meaningful way, since *Minne* interfered by acting as *mediatrix ex machina* (1547), and indirectly by using Lunete as her pawn and both suitors as victims. There is *consensus qui fiat nuptias* – or is there? On the legal level there certainly is. But the *rehte güete* presupposes an affectionate volition of two persons. Now because of the interference just described, the *ultima ratio* of this union is none other than her beauty (2341–2357, *vid.* 2355): *iuwer schœne und anders niht*. It is clear that *minne* made him see it in a particular, extremely favorable way. She short-circuits mutual atonement before the union and acts vicariously as *ein rehtiu süenærinne* (2056), so that the mitigating thoughts crossing Laudine's mind and lips in her rationalizing monologue of 2058 ff. are suggested to her by thoughts of *mediatrix minne*. In the course of the following story *minne* is transformed to *vrou Minne*, changing as it were from a benevolent spirit into a womanly figure. *Vrou Minne*, being shrewd, realizes that this union could not truly last without her committing their hearts to a special maneuver which is of course neither legally relevant nor canonically valid. But that is a narrative concern of its own.

Finally we have to decide whether the consensus between Iwein and Laudine lacks a genuine ethical *synallagma* in respect to their wish to join in marriage permanently. Textually Iwein's answer to her *vis*-question reads as follows:

> ›Spræch ich nû, vrouwe, nein ich, / sô wær ich ein unsælec man. / der liebste tac den ich ie gewan, / der ist mir hiute widervarn. / got ruoche mir daz heil bewarn, / daz wir gesellen müezen sîn.‹   (2334–39)

Th. Cramer translates [21] much too mechanically:

> »Wenn ich jetzt, Herrin, nein sagte, dann wäre ich heillos. Heute ist der glücklichste Tag, den ich je erlebt habe. Gott möge uns das Glück erhalten, daß wir uns lieben.«

The whole syntactic unit is introduced by an elliptic conditional. For comparison's sake I have to render this into German: »Würde ich nun sagen, Dame, nein, ich ...« (*Gemeint ist: will euch nicht*) »so wäre ich ein heilloser Mensch« (*einer der durch Duelltötung nur genommen, nicht auch durch sich selbst gegeben hat*). »Der liebste Tag, den ich mir (*gemeint: durch meinen Sieg*) errungen habe, ist mir heute zuteil geworden. Möge es Gott genehmigen, daß mein Glück nicht abreiße, derart, daß wir Geliebte sein (*und bleiben*) dürfen.« (*Wir haben hier eine futurische Nuance im indirekten Aufforderungssatz*, vgl. Paul-Moser-Schröbler, *Mittelhochdeutsche Grammatik*, 20. Auflage, 367, *Sätze, die mit daz eingeleitet werden.*)

Iwein's six-line answer to Laudine's »do you« question, contains four *ichs*, two *mir*, and one *wir* in the last line. Consequently Iwein's answer contains a hidden ambiguity. Even if he had said: »yes, I do«, for the story's sake, he would have *had* to become an *unsælec man*. After all, this reconciliation is attempted after *minne* had dealt Iwein a deadly blow of her own (1546 f.) that quite literally leaves adverse traces in Iwein's linguistic expressiveness. Ethically at least the consensus lacks the ingredients of a complete reconciliation between former slayer and present groom. A balance between marriage law and marriage order had not been completely achieved. Eventually, however, Iwein will atone for that imbalance with intense mental anguish.

---

[21] *Hartmann von Aue: Iwein,* Text der siebenten Ausgabe von G. F. Benecke, K. Lachmann und L. Wolff. Übersetzung und Anmerkungen von Th. Cramer (Berlin, 1968).

I think we may safely assume that Hartmann found himself in agreement with the *Minne* theorem that an interference of *minne* into marital love could drive a human being into madness.

IV. *Summary*

Let us summarize by first comparing our two heroes in respect to the adherence to their group, and whether they feel constrained by the law of the group they belong to. Iwein *libidine dominandi* happens to kill his enemy in a knightly fashion and thereby aggrieves the lady of the Magic Fountain. Ascalôn's fall at the fountain has made the fountain an *âventiure* turning point. The future relation of whatever dimension between widow-maker and widow has irreversibly been set. What the widow is lacking, Iwein *is*. Thus, after much ironic persuasion, Laudine, the *domina* in want of a husband, forces her court to accept her suitor at all cost.[22] The participation in a common *âventiure*, by the one as active offender, the other as passive sufferer, forces a relaxation of the sense of values. This temporary suspense becomes possible because Laudine and Iwein have in common that they both operate outside or at least at the periphery of the law of their respective peer group which does not become part of the *âventiure*. The order within their merging two groups, however, is ultimately restored in their fountainland. This restoration of »law and order« out of a restored sense of values is achieved at the end of *Iwein* by the ultimate joining of the two groups in the spirit of Christian forgiveness.

A final word of caution about marriage law and *minne* order is, however, necessary. The missing link between whatever law and its order, not only as residually seen by the poets, is original or restored power and sophistication. If this discussion has rendered a new insight, it might be summarized as an acknowledgment that Iwein's duel is an involuntary piece of erotic warfare which seems more closely related to his martial marriage than hitherto suspected. In any case, the link between the two, cunning, consists of power and sophistication. Hartmann depicts two events that do not call for inflated moral value judgments. Both Iwein and Laudine really seek social perfection, but they do not achieve it until much later, in the final *âventiure* of *Iwein* when the sense of understanding has again been fully regained.

---

[22] *Iwein,* 2328 f.; compare *Armer Heinrich,* 1502 f. and *König Rother,* 2223 f.

James W. Marchand

Recta Ratio: Wolfram's Ethics, Aesthetics and Theology

I must say that I am very fortunate in speaking at this point in the program, for much of my work has been done for me. I can refer you to
Professor Donahue's words on the *salus infidelium* as a problem of
Christian Germanic poetry;[1] I can refer you to Professor Bosl's remarks
on the class of ministeriales and the trouble they gave to the German
Geburtsadel of *ca.* 1200 and remind you that Wolfram was a knight
(schildes ambet ist min art) and not a ministerialis.[2] I can point to Professor Hrubý's treatment of the heart and to his demonstration that the
heart is the seat of thought in the Middle Ages, a Semitic/Stoic doctrine
reflected in Isidore's *corde sapimus* (XI,1,127) and in the *Liber de nu-
meris' in corde intellectum* (II,7), and to the fact that, for Wolfram's
hero, Parzival, *zwivel* was only in the *heart (herzen nachgebur),* so that
he was not the *vir duplex animo* of James I, who was *inconstans in omnibus viis suis,* but rather the *vir duplex corde* of Ecclesiasticus II,14.[3]
I can remind you of Professor Pickering's proper insistence on the given

---

1 Cf. Gyburc's »Toleranzrede« in *Willehalm* 306, 12 ff. and Abaelard's *Dialogus
   inter Philosophum, Judaeum et Christianum (PL* 178, 1611 ff.). A. M. Landgraf,
   Dogmengeschichte der Frühscholastik, I/1 (Regensburg, 1952), p. 251, cites a text
   attributed to Abaelard on this point. Throughout the paper, I have avoided citing
   well-known secondary literature. As Augustine says in his *De Dialectica,* Chapter 6: »Quis egeat auctoritate in re tam perspicua?«
2 This is a point frequently misunderstood, e.g. by J. Bumke, *Wolfram von Eschenbach* (Stuttgart, 1964), p. 4. Wolfram shows all the signs of the born knight striving
   against the *parvenu* ministeriales. For a view somewhat similar to Wolfram's, see
   J. W. Thompson, *Feudal Germany* (Chicago, 1928), 324 ff., who insists that »the
   formation of the *ministerialis* class is a historical development unique in German
   history and not found elsewhere.«
3 On the heart, see Xenja von Ertzdorff, »Das ›Herz‹ in der lateinisch-theologischen
   und frühen volkssprachigen religiösen Literatur«, *PBB (E)* 84 (1962), 249–302.
   On *duplex corde,* see Augustine, *In Ioannis Evangelium Tractatus,* 7, 7: »Vae
   duplici corde: qui in corde suo partem faciunt diabolo«, which echoes in part
   Wolfram's first few lines.

story and the given hero and point out that Wolfram took a story of
Parzival as the »fastest sword in the East« and turned it into one of the
three divine comedies of the Western World. We can refer to Professor
Wapnewski's text for the concept of God as *cordis speculator,* reflected
so often in Wolfram's text, particularly in the words: *sit got die herzen
speht so wol, owe der brœden werke dol!* And, finally, Professor
Walshe's sensitive appreciation of Wolfram completes our picture of an
author, »dem es ernst war, was zu sagen«. In good medieval fashion,
I can now begin with an adynaton (*Pz* 4,2–7):

> nu lat min eines werden dri, / der ieslicher sunder phlege, / daz miner künste
> widerwege: / darzuo gehorte wilder funt, / ob sie iu gerne tæten kunt, / daz
> ich iu eine künden wil.

For, also in good medieval fashion, I feel that I cannot fail, being, like
Tristan against Morholt, provided with such fine companions.

I

The most salutary development in the study of medieval literature in
the last quarter of a century or so has been the effort to find out more
about the patterns and habits of thought of medieval man. This has
brought with it many new (or renewed) fields and discoveries: topology,
typology, numerical composition, the study of memoria, etymology as a
mode of thought, to name but a few. Also important is the move away
from the procrustean beds of yesteryear with their black-white *Denkschemata:* the *comitatus,* Lachmannian textual criticism, free-prose
versus book-prose, learned *versus* unlearned, where the eternal either/or
(but never both) of *aufgezwungene Methoden* held sway, and into a
more tolerant position where one admits that there is no *alleinselig-
machende Methode,* but the possibility of simultaneous ambiguous readings, of a functioning in several directions at once, championed by such
critics as Empson, and that there is an interpenetration of art, music,
literature and life. In all these attempts to penetrate the medieval mind,
we must use more *Verstehen* and less *Denkschemata,* must employ more
exegesis and less eisagesis, as it were.
One of the areas of the medieval mind least explored from the standpoint of *understanding* is that of theology, and, although much has been
written on Wolfram's religiosity, almost no attempts have been made

to understand him from the standpoint of technical theology.[4] He practically cries out for such treatment, for he takes a position on many of
the questions argued by the theologians of the day: 1. Who raped his
virgin grandmother?[5] 2. What was the shape of the cross?[6] 3. How
many nails were used in nailing Christ to the cross?[7] 4. Was the crown
of thorns on Christ's head on the cross?[8] 5. The blindness of Longinus.[9]
6. The origin of the monsters of the world.[10] 7. The virgin earth as a
type of Mary.[11] 8. Logos and Virgin.[12] 9. The proper mode of presen-

---

[4] For a survey of opinions on Wolfram's religiosity, see M. Schumacher, *Kritische
   Bibliographie zu Wolframs Parzival, 1945–1958* (Diss. Frankfurt, 1963), 293–319.
   Many authorities have expressly denied a »theological« component in *Parzival*
   and refuse to consider Wolfram as an independent theological thinker (De Boor).
   The two most recent »survey« authors, Joachim Bumke, *Die Wolfram von Eschen-
   bach Forschung seit 1945* (Munich, 1970), particularly pp. 150–175, and Henry
   Kratz, *Wolfram von Eschenbach's Parzival. An Attempt at a Total Evaluation*
   (Bern, 1973), are both rather negative as to the influence of »theology« on Wolfram.

[5] This interesting little piece of *Volkstheologie*, so revealing of Trevrizent's religion,
   has been treated many times, usually without the author's being aware that it had
   been treated before; cf. J. H. Scholte, »Adam zoon der aarde«, *Neophilologus* 19
   (1933/34), 205. Wolfram's source is undoubtedly one of the forms of the *Joca
   Monachorum*.

[6] Cf. Dieter Kartschoke, »Signum Tau«, *Euphorion* 61 (1967), 245–266. It is interesting to note that Kartschoke, who discussed so much of Wolfram's theology,
   earlier was of the opinion that one could trust Wolfram little in theological matters; see his commentary on *Willehalm* 49, 11. He feels that »Die Vorstellung eines
   erzengel Kerubin ist theologisch absurd.« Nevertheless, Isidore XIV,3,4: »Cherubin
   quoque, id est *angelorum praesidium*, arcendis spiritibus malis super rompheae
   flagrantiam ordinatum est . . .«

[7] Kartschoke, 259 ff. Karl-August Wirth, *Die Entstehung des Drei-Nagel-Crucifixus*
   (Diss. Frankfurt, 1953).

[8] Kartschoke, 259 ff. Kartschoke quotes Wilhelm Grimm to the effect that »unter
   allen deutschen Dichtern des Mittelalters bis zum vierzehnten Jahrhundert Wolfram der einzige ist, der ihrer . . . Erwähnung tut«.

[9] Konrad Burdach, »Der Longinusspeer in eschatologischem Lichte«, in his *Vorspiel*,
   I, 217–252.

[10] 518, 18: »vil würze er se miden hiez, / die menschen fruht verkerten / und sin
   geslähte unerten.« That is, Adam's daughters were warned not to eat certain
   herbs, but they ate them anyway and had misshapen children.

[11] 464, 27: »von megeden sint zwei mensche komen. / got selbe antlitze hat genomen /
   nach der ersten megede fruht.« Cf. Honorius Augustodunensis, *PL* 172, 849: »Haec
   (Mary) idcirco terrae comparatur, quia sicut prius Adam de munda terra formatur,
   ita secundus Adam Christus de munda virgine procreatur.« The equation of Mary-
   earth is based on the typological interpretation of Genesis II,5, where the fructifying waters are the type of the insufflation of the Holy Ghost, etc. See *Aurora
   Petri Rigae*, ed. P. E. Beichner (Notre Dame, 1965), I, p. 37 f. I should perhaps also
   mention that this image forms the basis of the whole prologue of Gonzalo de
   Berceo's *Milagros de Nuestra Señora*, roughly contemporary with Wolfram's
   Parzival.

tation of Christ in pictures.[13] 10. The Good Thief's name and what happened to him.[14] 11.Purgatory, the Harrowing of Hell, salvation of Adam, the 72 languages, tears of baptism, neutral angels, the sword in God's mouth at judgement day.[15] 12. Eve sinned more than Adam.[16] 13. Satan's sins.[17] 14. Cain's sin,[18] etc. etc. But along with these questions, which were certainly not trivial to the theologians of the twelfth century, where one could be censured for offering the attributes of God in the ablative instead of the nominative case,[19] he devotes himself to

---

12 W 31, 8: »Daz wort vil creftecliche vart zer magde fuor (diust immer magt), diu den gebar.« The words *diust immer magt* reflect the dogma of *ante partum, in partu, post partum*.

13 *Pz* 105, 22: »den man noch malet für das lamp, / und ouchz kriuze in sine klan.« Cf. *Lexikon für Theologie und Kirche*, 6, 362: »... das Trullanum, 692, ... veranlaßte weiterhin die Darstellung des Lamms, das den Kreuzstab oder die Kreuzfahne mit dem einen Vorderfuß hält ...«

14 W 68, 26: »Tismas / der helle nie bekorte: / Jesus an im wol horte / daz in sin ruof erkande: / der sele not er wande.« Although the *Evangelium Nicodemi* calls him *Dismas*, he is frequently called *Tismas* in Germany; cf. Herrad of Landsberg's picture of the crucifixion.

15 W 331, 28: »zer kreftechlichen hende, / diu der helle porten brach / und der Adam urloesunge jach.« 73,7: »sit zwuo und sibenzec sprache sint, / er dunket mich der witze ein kint, / swer niht der zungen lat ir lant, / da von die sprachen sind bekant.« On the problem of the 72 languages, see Paolo Rotta, *Filosofia del linguaggio nella patristica e nella scolastica* (Turin, 1909). On the tears of baptism, cf. Hartmut Freytag, *Kommentar zur frühmittelhochdeutschen Summa Theologiae* (Medium Aevum 19; Munich, 1970), 144 f. W 303, 12: »der daz swert in sinem munt / vür treget am urteillichen tage, / da mite der küene und der zage / beide geschumfieret sint.« Cf. Rev. I,16; II,12,16; XIX,15.

16 W 218, 15: »Eve al eine schuldic wart.« I Tim. 2,14: »... et Adam non est seductus: mulier autem seducta est ...« This was common doctrine in the middle ages (cf. Peter Lombard, *PL* 191,698: »Plus enim videtur peccasse mulier, quae voluit usurpare divinitatis aequalitatem ... unde Aug. lib. et cap. eisdem: Apostolus ait: Adam non est seductus.«), so that Deinert's remark on gnostic sources, reported by Kartschoke in his commentary, is unnecessary.

17 *Pz* 463,6: »sie warn doch ane gallen: / ja herre, wa namen sie den *nit*, / da von ir endeloser strit / zer helle enpfaehet suren lon?« Wolfram is here touching on a difficult theological point and one discussed by Aquinas at length (I,59, art. 4; I,63, *passim*), namely, where did Lucifer and his companions get their envy from, since they were incorporeal and since the irascible appetite comes from the body, specifically the gall-bladder? Cf. Aquinas, I,63, art. 2: »Spiritualem autem naturam affici non contingit ad bona quae sunt propria corpori ...«

18 W 51, 30: »sit Abel starp durh bruoders *nit*«. Like all medieval theologians, however, he does not seem to have been able to make up his mind about this: *Pz* 463,25: »durh giteclichen ruom«, 464, 17: »umb krankez guot«.

19 In the case of Gilbert de la Porrée, the Pope ruled: »... that the essence of God should be predicated not in the sense of the ablative case only, but also of the nominative«; cf. R. L. Poole, *Illustrations of the History of Medieval Thought and Learning* (London, 1920), p. 168.

many of the central questions of theology: 1. Predestination *versus* free will.[20] 2. What are God's duties and what are man's? 3. How does one attain grace, and how does one know he has attained it? This paper represents an attempt to explore some of his answers to these questions through an investigation of one aspect of his theological thought.

Recta ratio or right reason is so much a part and parcel of medieval theology that it is scarcely mentioned directly before the speculative theology of the thirteenth century, by such authorities as St. Thomas, St. Bonaventure and Grosseteste. Perhaps the best expression of the theory is by a modern, Vernon J. Bourke:

> There developed the teaching that God as Creator had a divine Plan *(Ratio)* in mind for all things that He created. Each creature was known eternally to God and thus the eternal Idea *(ratio aeterna)* of every distinct thing served as an exemplar or archetype for the existence and functioning of that thing. In this sense there is a »reason« for each human person and this reason is present eternally in the creative mind of God *(in arte Dei)*. ... According to this view a man performs good actions when he functions in accord with the requirements of his ›eternal reason‹ in God's mind.[21]

This theory is seen also in St. Thomas Aquinas, II, II,154 ad 2: »Ratio autem hominis recta est secundum quod regulatur voluntate divina, quae est prima et summa regula.« And II, II,54 ad 2: »... executio iusti operis est effectus rationis rectae ...« It has even led him to say: »God is not offended by us except by what we do against our own good.«[22] Thus, according to *recta ratio* theory each and every thing in the universe was but a thought in the mind of God and each might be judged esthetically, morally and theologically by how close it came to finding its right place, its *recta ratio*, »Omnes enim homines in locis suis ordinantur ... Tu tantum vide quid velis esse: nam quomodo volueris esse, novit artifex ubi te ponat ... Qui creare te noverat, ordinare te non novit? Bonum est ibi ut illuc coneris, ut bono loco ponaris.«[23] It is reflected in many ways in the middle ages: 1. By the point made

---

[20] That is, the question as to whether one can only get to the grail by being called there (786, 5) or whether it is on the basis of his own merits. On the problem, see Anselm, *De concordia praescientiae praedestinationis cum libero arbitrio* (*PL* 158, 507–540), Peter Lombard, *Sententiae* I, xi, 1, 4 (*PL* 192,631), Augustine, *De gratia et libero arbitrio, De praedestinatione Sanctorum.*

[21] Vernon J. Bourke, *History of Ethics* (New York: Doubleday, 1970), p. 130.

[22] Cited by Bourke, p. 145.

[23] Augustine, sermo 125, 5 (*PL* 38,692). Honorius Augustodunensis (*PL* 172,1135) uses the metaphor of the painter arranging his paints (derived from Augustine, see

over and over again that God does nothing in vain, that even the little finger is useful for digging in the ear.[24] 2. That each thing and each time has its place, as the preacher saith.[25] 3. The theory of *proprietates verborum*, the use of the »right« word, etc.[26]

Although, as I mentioned above, expressions of *recta ratio* theology are reasonably unusual in twelfth century theological treatises, where it is taken for granted, the poetry of the day is replete with reflections; cf. the *Annolied*, 3:

> Du sich Lucifer du ze ubile gevienc,   unt Adam diu godis wort ubirgieng,
> duo balch sich is got desti mer,   daz her andere sini werch sach rehte gen:
> den manen unten sunnen   die gebin ihre liht mit wunnen,
> die sterrin bihaltent ire vart,   si geberent vrost unte hizze so starc,
> daz fuir havit ufwert sinin zug,   dunnir unte wint irin vlug.
> di wolken dragint den reginguz,   nidir wendint wazzer irin vluz.
> mit bluomin zierint sich diu lant,   mit loube dekkit sich der walt.
> daz wilt havit den sinin ganc,   scone ist der vugilsanc.
> ein iwelich ding diu e noch hat   di emi got van erist virgap,
> newaere die zwei gescefte,   di her gescuf die bezziste:
> die virkerten sich in diu doleheit,   dannin hubin sich diu leit.[27]

That is, everything has its *recta ratio*, its *lex aeterna (diu e, di emi got van erist virgap)*, and only man fails to follow it.

Thus, in ethics the theory of *recta ratio* is rather simple: »... intentio moralis philosophiae principaliter versatur circa rectitudinem. ... Ille enim recte vivit, qui dirigitur secundum regulas iuris divini.«[28] »... executio iusti operis est effectus rationis rectae ...«[29] It is here the inheritance of a Stoic/peripatetic doctrine, voiced by Cicero (*De legibus* I,12,23):

Lefèvre's note): »Sicut pictor omnes colores diligit, sed quosdam prae aliis eligit, et unumquemque apto loco ponit; ita Deus unumquemque sibi convenienti loco disponit.«

[24] Cf. *Wiener Genesis*, 291 ff. Cf. Eph. 4, 15 f.; I Cor. 12, 21 ff.; Rom. 12, 3 ff. and the commentaries. See especially Honorius, *PL* 172, 874.

[25] Eccl. III and the commentaries.

[26] On the doctrine of the *proprietates verborum*, inherited from the Stoics and peripatetics by the middle ages through such rhetoricians as Quintilian and the author of the *Ad Herennium*, see Heinrich Lausberg, *Handbuch der literarischen Rhetorik*, 2 vols. (Munich, 1960), s. v. »proprius« »aptus«, and E. de Bruyne, *Estudios de estética medieval*, transl. Fr. Armando Suárez, 3 vols. (Madrid, 1958), s. v. »acuerdo« »consonantia« »harmonia« »proporción«.

[27] Friedrich Maurer, *Die religiösen Dichtungen des 11. und 12. Jahrhunderts*, vol. II (Tübingen, 1965), p. 11.

[28] St. Bonaventure, *De reductione artium ad theologiam*, 23 and 24.

[29] Thomas Aquinas, *Summa theologica*, II, II, 54 ad 2.

> Quibus enim ratio a natura data est, iisdem etiam recta ratio data est: ergo etiam lex, quae est recta ratio in iubendo et vetando: si lex, ius quoque. At omnibus ratio. Ius igitur datum est omnibus.[30]

According to Clement of Alexandria and Diogenes Laertius, Zeno was the first to propose *recta ratio* ethics:

> Zeno the Stoic thinks the end to be living according to virtue; and Cleanthes, living agreeably to nature in the right exercise of reason, which he held to consist of the selection of things in accordance with nature.[31] – Cicero, *De legibus* II,8: Quam ob rem lex vera atque princeps apta ad iubendum et ad vetandum ratio est recta summi Iovis.[32]

This theory of natural law, derived from God, was taken over by the early fathers of the Church and handed on, through Augustine and Jerome, to the middle ages.[33]

In esthetics, *recta ratio* led to a sort of exemplarism: that horse is esthetically most pleasing who possesses the most *equitudo* »horseness«, and the scholastics liked to argue such questions as the *tabulitas* of a table and the *Socrateitas* of Socrates: »The beauty of that which is exactly what it should be and integrally satisfies its definition.«[34] »Most medieval philosophers also knew about the theory of ideal forms ... As a theory it also carried the implication that a good horse will act in conformity with the archetypal ›horseness‹ – and the good man will act in accord with ideal ›humanity‹.«[35] The ramification of the theory is seen by the number of words used for »beauty« in the middle ages: consonance, congruity, aptness, proportion, *coaptatio, coadunatio,* harmony, etc.[36] The theory of musical consonance was applied to things in the whole universe: »Quia enim non solum in sonis proportione numerorum relativa coaptatis, verum etiam in rebus quibuslibet rite ordinatis consonantia efficitur ... Consonantia ergo habetur in omni creatura.«[37] And anything which was out of tune with nature was ugly:

---

[30] J. von Arnim, *Stoicorum veterum fragmenta,* vol. III (Leipzig, 1903), no. 317. For more information on the Stoic theory of *recta ratio,* see von Arnim's index under *orthòs lógos.*

[31] *Greek and Roman Philosophy after Aristotle,* ed. by Jason L. Saunders (New York, 1966), p. 111.

[32] Von Arnim, III, no. 318.

[33] Cf. Michel Spanneut, *Le stoïcisme des pères de l'église (Patristica Sorbonensia,* I, Paris, 1957), pp. 250 ff.

[34] E. Gilson, *Les idées et les lettres* (Vrim, 1932), p. 166.

[35] Bourke, *op. cit.,* p. 131.

[36] De Bruyne, *op. cit., passim.*

[37] De Bruyne, II,117, citing Otloh.

»Amica est similitudo, dissimilitudo vero odiosa atque contraria.«[38] This led in literary esthetics to two theories, which we might say are diametrically opposed, one, that there was a correct style and ought always to be followed:

> Non dicat graviter, sed convenientia dicta / Scrutetur, leviter dicat, gravitate relicta, / Ne geminum faciat sensum, dicat manifeste, / Pulchriter inveniat, inventaque narret honeste.[39]

The other, that the style ought to be tailored to fit the material: »In quoque stylo possumus peccare non observando proprietates debiti styli, sed declinando ad proprietates aliorum stylorum.«[40] Gottfried's sentiments are too well known to need mentioning here.[41]

In theology, *recta ratio* had a number of ramifications. It was not enough to know that one was a thought in the mind of God, one needed to seek actively to find his place and to hold to it tenaciously (cf. the quote by Augustine above, note 23). Thus, Aquinas was able, following Augustine, to define sin itself as a transgression against *recta ratio:* »Superbia nominatur ex hoc quod aliquis per voluntatem tendit supra id quod est ... Habet autem hoc *ratio recta*, ut voluntas uniuscuiusque feratur in id quod est proportionatum sibi. Et ideo manifestum est quod superbia importat aliquid quod aversatur *rationi rectae*. Hoc autem facit rationem peccati ...«[42] Augustine: »Ergo peccatum est factum vel dictum vel concupitum aliquid contra aeternam legem. Lex vero aeterna est vel ratio divina, vel voluntas Dei ordinem naturalem conservari jubens, perturbari vetans ...«[43] What to do? First one ought to put his trust in God. This consisted simply of believing that God *would* offer salvation to any one who fulfilled his commands (of relinquishing all *dubitatio, zwivel*). He would refuse no one who came to Him in the right way: *Facienti quod in se est Deus non denegat gratiam.*[44] That is,

---

[38] De Bruyne, I,36, citing Boethius.
[39] From the *Debemus cunctis proponere*, ed. Ch. Fierville, *Notices et extraits des manuscrits*, no. 31, p. 135, lines 87 ff.
[40] Geoffroi de Vinsauf, cited by de Bruyne, II, p. 51.
[41] See my »Tristan's *Schwertleite*: Gottfried's Aesthetics and Literary Criticism«, *Husbanding the Golden Grain: Studies in Honor of Henry W. Nordmeyer* (Ann Arbor, 1973), 187–204.
[42] *Summa theologica*, II, II,162 a. 1.
[43] *Contra Faustum*, 22, chap. 27 (*PL* 42, 418).
[44] Landgraf, 249–302, has an excellent discussion of the doctrine of grace and especially the doctrine of *facere quod in se est*. See also Heiko Oberman, *The Harvest of Medieval Theology* (Grand Rapids, 1967), 131–145.

God would perform his *recta ratio,* man should perform his: (Cyril of
Jerusalem, cat. 1,4; my translation) »It is proper to God to lend grace,
it is up to you willingly to accept and to preserve it.« Udo of Bamberg,
Summa (cited Landgraf, p. 249): »Item, super illum locum Exodi, ubi
dicitur Moyses occurrisse Domino, ait Gregorius: occurrit Dominus sibi
occurrentibus.« Origen (Landgraf, p. 249): »Si obtulerimus, que ex
nobis sunt, consequemur ea, que Dei sunt.« Anselm (Landgraf, 250):
»Videtur enim mihi, quod nullum hominem reiiciat Deus ad se sub hoc
nomine accedentem ... Ita est, si accedit, sicut oportet ... Si homo facit,
quod in se est, Deus dat gratiam.« As can be seen from this last quotation, the answer to the problem of what to do was simply to find oneself,
to follow the dictates of one's own conscience: Radulphus Ardens
(Landgraf, p. 251): »Est ergo, acsi dicat Dominus: Facite quod pertinet
ad vos, quia facio, quod pertinet ad me. Ego facio, quod amicus,
animam meam pro vobis ponendo; facite et vos, quod amici, me dili-
gendo et mandata mea faciendo.« Remigius (Landgraf, 250): »Ille fecit,
quod Suum erat pro omnibus moriens, ... et fecit, quod ad Se per-
tinebat ... Ille tamen, quod Suum erat, fecit.« Stephen Langton (Landgraf, 251): »Facite, quod vestrum est, quia Deus faciet, quod suum est.«
The mode of *facere quod in se est* was to follow one's own conscience,
by *synderesis,* for God had put in each person a *scintilla conscientiae*
which would guide him in the right way.[45]

Perhaps the most beautiful »theological« expression of the theme of
obtaining salvation by *facere quod in se est,* or doing one's thing, is the
twelfth century Mary story of the *Jongleur de Notre Dame.*

> A minstrel, tired of the world, enters the monastery of Clairvaux. He finds
> it extremely difficult to live as a monk and can perform his tasks only with
> great effort. It is particularly in praying that he finds difficulty. Once he
> finds himself in front of a statue of the Virgin Mary at the time of prayer.
> Not knowing what to do, he decides to honor Her in the only way he
> knows, by performing his juggler's tricks before Her. He does this day
> after day, until he is finally discovered by one of his fellows. The abbot,
> having been informed of this state of affairs, decides to observe the deed,
> prior to punishing this strange monk. As the »juggler« finishes his act,
> however, and sinks exhausted to the floor, the statue of Our Lady descends

---

[45] Cf. O. Lottin, »Syndérèse et conscience aux XIIe et XIIIe siècles«, *Psychologie et
morale aux XIIe et XIIIe siècles,* vol. II (Louvain, 1948), pp. 103–350. This doctrine, carrying with it as it did the name of St. Jerome (cf. his *In Ezekielem* I,1;
PL 25,22), was of great importance to the theologians of the 12th and 13th
centuries.

from the pedestal, and, taking a white cloth, wipes the perspiration from the minstrel's face and ministers unto him. The juggler is accorded all honor, for he has brought glory to the cloister.[46]

As is frequently the case, we have found that here again theology finds its finest expression in literature. Let us see if Wolfram, first and foremost a poet, might not, like Dante, be somewhat of a theologian as well.

II

Recta ratio in Wolfram's ethics. The theory of *recta ratio* dominates Wolfram's ethics, as a glance at his use of *reht*, one of his most frequent words, will show. If a woman does right by her womanhood, she does not need to be beautiful:

> Dem gliche ich rechten wibes muot: / diu ir wipheit rehte tuot, / dane sol ich varwe prüeven niht, / noch herzen dach, daz man siht. / ist sie inrehalp der brust bewart, / so ist werder pris niht verschart. (3,19–24)

Even God has his *reht* and performs according to it: 7,10 »der git unde nimt, uf reht in beder der gezimt«, 471,25 »was daz sin reht, er nam se wider«. *reht tuon* is used over and over again for performance in accordance with the *recta ratio* of even objects: 254,30 »hastu vrage ir reht getan«, 612,2 »ob der schilt sin reht sol han«, 634,5 »ob ir der zuht ir reht nu tuot«, 3,20 »diu ir wipheit rehte tuot«.

In the case of Wolfram, this *reht* is usually synonymous with *art* »lineage, inborn quality«.[47] This is so strong that the poet himself feels he should be admired by the ladies for doing right by his *art*, the office of shield, rather than his poetry:

> schildes ambet ist min art. / swa min ellen si gespart, / swelchiu mich minnet umbe sanc, / so dunket mich ir witze kranc. / ob ich guotes wibes minne

---

46 See H. Waechter, »Der Springer unserer Lieben Frau«, *Romanische Forschungen* 9 (1880), 223–288, for an edition, retelling and treatment of this 12th century work.

47 Julius Schwietering, »Natur und *art*«, *ZfdA* 91 (1961/62), 108–137. It should be noted that the same ambiguity is attached to Latin *genus* ›birth, descent, origin; kind, sort, class, character‹. It should be noted also that English *kind* formerly had roughly the same meanings that I attribute to Wolfram's *art* (cf. *NED*, vol. V, p. 697 f.): »birth, descent, origin; the station, place, or property belonging to one by birth; one's native place or position; that to which one has a natural right; birthright, heritage; the character or quality derived from birth or native constitution; natural disposition, nature.« Queen Arnive's explanation echoes Gen. I, 11 ff.: »the fruit tree yielding fruit after his kind, etc.«

ger, / mag ich mit schilde und ouch mit sper / verdienen niht ir minne solt, /
al dar nach si sie mir holt.   (115,11–18)

Queen Arnive explains that this *art* is carried from generation to
generation, »ein muoter ir fruht gebirt: / diu fruht siner muoter muoter
wirt / ... da git ein fruht die andern fruht.« (659,23 ff.) In fact, much
of the motivation for his characters is because of their *art*: young Parzival has to cry when he hears the birds' song (that is his *art*, when spring-
time comes); Gahmuret must love, that is his *art*; Schionatulander even
depends on this concept to get him the love of Sigune in *Titurel* (58):
»Ducisse uz Katelangen! la mich geniezen: / ich hœre sagen, du sist erboren von der art die nie kunde verdriezen, / sine wæren helfec mit ir
lone.«

The ability to recognize virtue is emphasized in the phrase *rehte spehen:*
29,3 »sie kunde ouch liehte varwe spehen«, 364,1 »kunnet ir dan ritters
fuore spehen, / ir müezt im rehter dinge jehen«, and we have already
noticed the concept of God as *cordis speculator*. Gawan is not angry
at Orgeluse for her mistreatment of him, but for the fact that she did
not see that he was a knight, because of his *art*:

> so næhert ir dem prise. / ich pin doch wol so wise: / ob der schilt sin reht
> sol han, / an dem hat ir missetan. / des schildes ambet ist so hoch, / daz er
> von spotte ie sich gezoch, / swer riterschaft ze rehte pflac. / frouwe, ob ich so
> sprechen mac, / swer mich derbi hat gesehen, / der muoz mir riterschefte
> jehen. / eteswenne irs anders jahet, / sit ir mich erest sahet.   (612,3–14)

For Wolfram there is a time for everything; he will not tell us about the
Grail until it is time: 241,4: »diu werden iu von mir genant, / her nach
so des wirdet zit«, and Parzival recognizes that his first visit to the
Grail came at the wrong time: 783,15 »done wasez et dennoch niht min
heil.« Two other words which come close to the notion of *recta ratio* are
fuoge »propriety« and *unfuoge* »impropriety«: 343 f. (on Meljacanz)
»er tregt der unfuoge kranz ... was sin ellen ane fuoge ... unrehtiu
minne im daz gebot«, 171 (Gurnemanz to Parzival): »gebt rehter maze
ir orden! ... nu lat der unfuoge ir strit!«

III

Recta ratio in Wolfram's aesthetics. Just a glance at Wolfram's uses
of *schoene* will show that it is closely connected with *art* and *reht*, as
Heckel, pp. 92 ff., already saw: »Manche Belegstellen des vorhergehen-

den Kapitels haben schon gezeigt, daß *hohiu art* und *schœne* eng zu-
sammengehören. Die äußere Erscheinung des Menschen ist eben der
zunächst allein sichtbare Ausdruck seines Blutserbes ...« Cf. 164,15
(knights to Gurnemanz concerning Parzival) »an im liget der sælden
spehe / mit reiner süezen hohen art«, 146,6 »dich brahte zer werlde ein
reine wip. / o wol der muoter, diu dich gebar.« In typical medieval
fashion, Wolfram has his heroes now fashioned by God, now by fortune, and emphasizes often that God was in a good mood when he
created this or that one; cf. 148,26 »got was an einer süezen zuht, / do'r
Parzivalen worhte.« As pointed out above, beauty was more than skin
deep to Wolfram, so that it often becomes an almost ethical concept;
cf. 3,11 »manec wibes schœne an lobe ist breit: / ist da daz herze conterfeit, / die lobe ich als ich solde / daz safer ime golde.« Cundrie sees Parzival's external beauty, but condemns his inner faults and compares his
real beauty with hers:

> gunert si iuwer liehter schin / und iuwer manlichen lide. / hete ich suone oder
> vride, / diu wærn iu beidiu tiure. / ich dunke iuch ungehiure, / und bin
> gehiurer doch dann ir.   (315,20–25)

As an aside, we may notice how important the proper gesture is to
Wolfram. Gahmuret rides into town with his leg over the pommel,
»profiling« for the ladies (63,13); Parzival, after learning how to act
from Gurnemanz, is somewhat *salopp* in the Grail castle with Repanse
de Schoye's robe: (228,9) »man truog im einen mantel dar: / den legt'
an sich der wol gevar / mit offener snüere, / ez was im ein lobs gefüere.«
We have mentioned above the *Bogengleichnis* passage and Wolfram's
literary aesthetics: to tell the story right and with everything at the
right time, »dem maere rehte tuon« (826,21).

IV

1. *God's duty toward man.* Wolfram lived in an age which was dominated by feudalism. Given this fact and his own statement as to his
knighthood and his love of knighthood, it was to be expected that he
would be prone to metaphors from the realm of knightly activities and
feudalism, as was indeed his whole age. Wolfram is unusual in the number and importance of metaphors drawn from knighthood. For him, the
lady of one's desire is the feudal liege, she must preserve *triuwe* »fealty«
towards him, as he must preserve it towards her. He serves her, as the

vassal does the lord, for her reward, for her aid and comfort. If she is
a proper lady, she possesses ample stores of such goods to bestow, »diu
ist helfe und rates riche« (640,20).

This little excursus on the lady as liege has already shown us many of
the characteristics of the medieval feudal contract:[48] fealty, which
bound both the vassal and the liege, service, and the *auxilium et consilium* »helfe unde rat« owed on both sides.[49] Wolfram's picture of God
as a liege lord who possesses *auxilium* is best shown by the lines following Parzival's leave-taking from Kahenis and his daughters:

> er sprach, »waz ob got helfe phliget / diu minem truren an gesiget? / wart
> ab er ie ritter holt, / gediende ie ritter sinen solt, / ode mac schilt unde
> swert / siner helfe sin so wert / und rehtiu manliche wer, / daz sin helfe
> mich vor sorgen ner, / ist hiute sin helflicher tac, / so helfe er, ob er helfen
> mac!«   (451,13–22)

In his *zwivel* after being scorned by Sigune and Cundrie, he makes the
formal *défi* required of the vassal wishing to declare himself free of duty
towards a lord:[50]

> Der Waleis sprach »we waz ist got? / wær der gewaldec, sölhen spot / het
> er uns peden niht gegeben, / kunde got mit kreften leben. / ich was im diens
> undertan, / sit ich genaden mich versan. / nu wil ich im dienst widersagen: /
> hat er haz, den wil ich tragen.«   (332,1–8)

He even accuses God of the sin of *unmilte*, of not being generous:

> »des gihe ich dem ze schanden, / der aller helfe hat gewalt, / ist sin helfe
> helfe balt, / daz er mir denne hilfet niht, / so vil man im der hilfe giht.«
> (461,22–26)

Much of this reminds us also of Schionatulander's importuning of Sigune
in *Titurel*, where he serves to reap the reward of her *helfe:* (57) »Sigune
helferiche! / nu hilf mir, werdiu maget, uz den sorgen! so tuostu helfec-
liche«, (72) »so daz min dienst nach diner helfe ringe. / ich wart in dine

---

48 See Marc Bloch, *Feudal Society* (Chicago, 1961), part IV, and F. L. Ganshof, *Feudalism* (New York, 1961), *passim*, for studies on the feudal contract.
49 Wolfgang Mohr, »Hilfe und Rat in Wolframs Parzival«, *Festschrift für Jost Trier*
(Meisenheim, 1954), 173–197. Mohr's careful study has helped us to understand the
Wortfeld of *helfen-dienen*, but he failed to recognize that *helfe unde rat* are exact
equivalents of the *auxilium et consilium*, the *servitia* sworn to in the feudal contract (Ganshof, 87ff.), which, as is often overlooked, went both ways (Bloch, 227ff.).
In spite of the number of studies of Wolfram and knighthood, there is still much
to be done, particularly with reference to medieval usage.
50 On the practice of the *défi*, see Bloch, p. 228. It is important to realize that Parzival has made an open declaration of cancellation of covenant with God.

helfe erboren: nu hilf so daz mir an dir gelinge!« Thus, God is presented also as the liege, and one must serve Him for his *auxilium,* »der mensche sol beliben mit dienste gein des helfe groz«. What are God's duties? He will always fulfil his side of the bargain, will always reward service:

> der waren buoche mære / kund ich lesen unde schriben, / wie der mensche sol beliben / mit dienste gein des helfe groz, / den der stæten helfe nie verdroz / für der sele senken.   (462,12–17)

In fact, God can do nothing else but offer his *auxilium:* (461,28) »so schult ir got getruwen wol: / er hilfet iu, wand er helfen sol.« (462) »got selbe ein triuwe ist«, »got heizt und ist ein warheit, / . . . ern kan an nieman wenken.« All one needs to do is to call on Him in need:

> er lac, und liez es walten / den, der helfe hat behalten / und den der helfe nie verdroz, / swer in sinem kumber groz / helfe an in versuochen kan, / der wise herzehafte man, / swa dem kumber wirt bekant, / der ruofet an die hohsten hant: / wan diu tregt helfe riche / und hilfet im helfecliche.
> (568,1–10)

Kahenis assures Parzival of God's fealty to man: (448,10) »wa wart ie hoher triuwe schin, / denne die got durch uns begienc, / den man durh uns anz kriuze hienc?« (113,20) »der sit durch uns vil scharpfen tot / ame kriuze mennischliche emphienc / und sine triuwe an uns begienc.« Troughout all these ideas of God, the concept of *helfe* is central, as it is one of the central concepts of Wolfram's work as a whole: the *helfe* of vassal and lord, of the liege lady, of God in *Parzival;* the *helfe* of Signune in *Titurel;* the saint as the *helfære* in *Willehalm.* The *recta ratio* of God is *helfe* (*Willehalm* 103,1): »got ist helfe wol geslaht.«[51]
In understanding Wolfram's view of God's duty toward man, it is important to note his insistence on the family tie between us and God, as expressed best in *Willehalm* (1,16):[52]

> din kint und din künne / bin ich bescheidenliche, / ich arm und du vil riche. / din mennischeit mir sippe git, / diner gotheit mich ane strit / der pater noster nennet, / zeinem kinde erkennet.

The same thought is found in many places in *Parzival* also: (465,3) »sit er uns sippe lougent nicht, / den ieslich engel ob im siht.«
As any good medieval theologian knew, however, grace could not be

---

51 For the meaning of *geslaht* here, see Schwietering, *op. cit.,* 120 f.
52 On the importance of the family tie to feudalism and the surrogate family within feudalism, see Bloch, 123–144; Ganshof, passim.

attained by desire alone and service alone, God had to take a hand in turning the sinner to God.[53] For the *miles Dei,* in contradistinction to the ordinary knight, has a right to expect *helfe* from God: (Augustine, Sermo 105) »Adjuvat certantes, qui certamen indixit: non te sic spectat Deus in agone certantem, ut populus solet athletam, clamore enim populus monet athletam, adjuvare non novit. Coronam parare potest qui indicit certamen, vires autem subministrare non postest. Deus autem quando spectat certantes suos, adjuvat eos certantes, et invocantes ...« Thus, God finds it necessary to help Parzival find the right way. One of the most important steps in his final conversion is his last visit to Signe while she is alive, and this is marked by Wolfram with the pregnant words: (435,12) »sin wolte got do ruochen.«

2. *Man's duty toward God.* We have seen that, in Wolfram's view, God goes more than half way in keeping His covenant with man, whom He redeemed on the cross: (*Willehalm* 322,7) »von der durchslagenen zeswen hant, / diu vür diu helleclichen phant / am kriuze ir bluot durch uns vergoz. / die selben hant noch nie verdroz, / swerz mit einvaldem dienste erholt, / si teilet den endelosen solt.« But the Knight of God must ever strive for the victory, must remember his covenant with God; cf. Chrysostom, *de Martyribus* 3: »Delicatus es miles, si putas te posse sine pugna vincere, sine certamine triumphare. Exsere vires, fortiter dimica atroci et in praelio isto concerta. Considera pactum, conditionem attende, militiam nosce: pactum, quod spopondisti; conditionem, qua accessisti; militiam cui nomen dedisti.« And the best way for the Christian to carry out this struggle is to *facere quod in se est,* for *facienti quod in se est Deus non denegat gratiam.*

But what is Parzival? What is his *recta ratio?* He has a double dose of *minnetriuwe,* for Titurel tells us (*Titurel* 4,4): »ja muoz al min geslähte immer ware minn mit triwen erben«, and we hear also of Mazadan's progeny that they never wavered in *triuwe* to Lady *Minne:* (585,17) »Mazadanes nachkomen, / von den ist dicke sit vernomen, / daz ir enkein iuch [Frou Minne] nie verliez.« Because of this, he possesses one quality that his uncle, Anfortas, did not have, that of proper love, for (468,5) »werdet ir erfundn an rehter e, / iu mac zer helle werden we, / diu not sol schiere ein ende han, / und werdet von banden alda verlan / mit der gotes helfe al sunder twal.« Thus, Parzival's proper love for his wife is one of the properties which leads him to the grail. The other

---

[53] Cf. Landgraf, 264–302, and *passim.*

property which he possesses and which he inherited is knighthood. On his father's side he has inherited *minne* and knighthood:

> er ist erborn von Anschouwe. / diu minne wirt sin frouwe: / so wirt aber er an strite ein schur, / den vinden herter nachgebur, / wizzen sol der sun min, / sin an der hiez Gandin: / der lac an riterschefte tot. / des vater leit dieselben not.   (56,1–8)

Both his father and his uncle died in knighthood. On his mother's side he has inherited knighthood and a claim to the grailship through Titurel and Frimutel, the latter of whom also gave his life in knightly deeds. Just as Anfortas (477,20) »beidiu ist unde was / von *art* des grales herre«, so is Parzival. Recognizing this fact about himself, Parzival tells Trevrizent that he ought to be named to the grail because of his deeds of knighthood:

> mac riterschaft des libes pris / unt doch der sele pardis / bejagen mit schilt und ouch mit sper, / so was ie riterschaft min ger. / ich streit ie swa ich striten vant, / so daz min werlichiu hant / sich næhert dem prise. / ist got an strite wise / der sol mich dar benennen, / daz sie mich da bekennen: / min hant da strites niht verbirt.   (472,1–11)

That is, his *recta ratio* is knighthood, he thinks he should gain the grail by being a perfect knight.

After leaving his mother's brother, Trevrizent, who has instructed him as the mother's brother is supposed to in the Germanic system of kinship,[54] Parzival remains faithful to God, as a true *miles Dei:*

> der getoufte wol getruwete gote, / sit er von Trevrizende schiet, / der im so herzenliche riet, / er solte helfe an in gern, / der in sorge fröude kunde wern.
> (741,26–30)

He has found his *riterliche fuore,* which his mother kept from him in Soltane, and we hear of many battles he fights, even being treated later to a list of them. His most difficult battle, however, is with his own self in the person of his half-brother, Feirefiz, who is careful to point out: (752,15) »mit dir selben hastu hie gestriten.« Once he has overcome his own *zwivel,* personified in the pied figure of his brother, he is

---

[54] That Trevrizent owes Parzival upbringing and instruction according to the Germanic kinship system is often ignored. For a discussion of this system, a so-called Crow type, see Clair Hayden Bell, »The Sister's Son in Medieval German Epic«, *University of California Publications in Modern Philology,* 10,2 (1922), 67–182. Much work remains to be done on the Germanic kinship system, particularly as it applies to Wolfram's *Parzival.*

called to the grail.[55] Cundrie, who comes to tell him the good news, knows well that it is because of God's grace,[56] but she misunderstands the manner of Parzival's gaining of the grail, as can be seen by the acyrologia: (782,29) »du hast der sele ruowe erstriten.« Trevrizent also expresses his amazement at this turn of events: (798,2) »grœzer wunder selten ie geschach, / sit ir ab got erzürnet hat, / daz sin endelosiu Trinitat / iwers willen werschaft worden ist«, words which sound blasphemous even to our ears, and which are in direct contradiction of what Parzival has said earlier, perhaps to correct the impression left by Cundrie: (786,5) »daz den gral ze keinen ziten / niemen möhte erstriten / *wan der von gote ist dar benant.*« We can perhaps understand the reason for the confusion when we see that the same word, *erstriten* »gain by fighting«, is used, also in an acyrologia, to express the manner in which St. Willehalm, the patron saint of knights, gained the highest prize:

> du hast und hetest werdekeit, / helfære, do din kiusche erstreit / mit diemuot vor der hœhsten hant / daz si dir helfe tet erkant.   (*Willeh.* 4,3–6)

How can one force God by fighting to grant him help, how can one humbly strive? The answer is, it seems to me, quite simple: if one's *recta ratio* is fighting. In his enigmatic way, Wolfram is telling us that no one can gain the grail by fighting, but that he can gain it by fighting, where the first *fighting* means »struggling« (i.e. with God) and the second means »being a knight« (i.e. fulfilling one's mission). Had Parzival been a juggler, Wolfram could have said: »No one can gain the grail by fighting, but he *can* gain it by juggling (if that is what he is born to do).« It is not that Parzival has taken the grail by force; he has merely been the best knight that one could be, has found his *recta ratio,* and, like the *jongleur de Notre Dame,* his reward, for *facienti quod in se est Deus non denegat gratiam,* »er hilft iu, wand er helfen sol, ... der stæten lon nach dienste git«.

---

[55] The symbolic nature of his battle with Feirefiz is emphasized by the latter's speech (752,7) after the battle and his words: »mit dir selben hastu hie gestriten.«

[56] 781,3: »owol dich, Gahmuretes suon! / got wil genade an dir nu tuon.«

Maurice O'C. Walshe

The Graal Castle and the Cave of Lovers

Petrus W. Tax, in the appendix to the second edition of his well-known *Tristan* book (1971),[1] quotes an anonymous reviewer as saying: »Um zu einem ganzheitlichen Thesen-Wurf zu gelangen, hätte es wohl eines energischen Beiseiteschiebens von Sekundärliteraturbergen bedurft.« My purpose here is more modest – and more specific – than a total »Thesenwurf«, and I shall refer here only very selectively to the secondary literature, for which further reference should be made to the works of Picozzi[2] and Bumke[3] for *Tristan* and *Parzival* respectively. I would merely point out that the »secondary literature« on *Tristan* and *Parzival* begins in the thirteenth century, with Wolfram's and Gottfried's reactions to each other. And it is this aspect in particular that I propose to discuss. Wolfram's first critic known to us was certainly Gottfried, and almost equally certainly Gottfried's first discernible critic was Wolfram. *We* may interpret *Parzival* and *Tristan* how we will, but it is of absorbing interest to try to see how the two great rivals interpreted each other, the more so because I believe the works themselves underwent profound modification as a direct result of the confrontation. We know that in the eighteenth century Goethe and Schiller at first approached each other with suspicion and feelings of rivalry, out of which there developed a friendship which was immensely fruitful for both. This clearly did not happen with Wolfram and Gottfried. Whether they were personally acquainted is unknown but improbable, even though K. K. Klein once thought they had actually lived together

---

1 Petrus W. Tax, *Wort, Sinnbild, Zahl im Tristanroman*, 2nd ed., 1971, p. 226.
2 Rosemary Picozzi, *A History of Tristan Scholarship* (Kanadische Studien zur deutschen Sprache und Literatur 5), 1971.
3 J. Bumke, *Die Wolfram von Eschenbach Forschung seit 1945: Bericht und Bibliographie*, 1970. See now also H. Kratz, *Wolfram's Parzival: An Attempt at a Total Assessment*, 1973.

in the same house and only parted company later.[4] This is a possibly
interesting but quite profitless speculation. I want to suggest, however,
that their rivalry and continuing mutual antagonism did have a profoundly fructifying effect on both. Though I have a very little to say
(and most of that not particularly original) on the interpretation of
their works as I see it, it is on their interpretation of each other, and its
effects, that I wish to concentrate.

Perhaps at this point I should declare an interest. It is a fact, I think,
that most modern readers find themselves temperamentally drawn to
either Wolfram or Gottfried, perhaps to an extent which renders it
difficult for them to do justice to the other. I must confess that I am
attracted to Wolfram in this way, and it may therefore be, or at least
seem, that I am sometimes less than fair to Gottfried. It is also a fact
that there is even less agreement on the fundamental interpretation of
Tristan than of *Parzival* – partly at least because of the former's unfinished state –, and so even with the greatest impartiality it is probably
objectively more difficult to be »fair to Gottfried«. But for the sake
of propriety let my temperamental bias against Gottfried be noted and,
if need be, discounted. Part of my object in this paper is concerned with
some aspects of the interpretation of *Tristan*; I seek herein not so much
to establish my own interpretation as to attempt to establish what
Wolfram thought of it. If I find myself partly in agreement with Wolfram, then at least I can escape the charge that my interpretation is not
sufficiently *mittelaltergemäß*.

I take as my starting-point the article by Werner Betz.[5] Betz refers to
the great trial of Cathari in 1212 in Straßburg, which ended with almost 80 executions, and suggests that this event may have frightened
Gottfried into abandoning his poem before completion. In fact, if we
are to believe Norman,[6] it is not so sure that Gottfried was still alive in
1212. This, however, is not the point I am concerned with. I will say
nothing of Gottfried's possible relations to the Cathari, about which
in any case we know nothing concrete. But the chief point of Betz's
article is his interpretation of a passage in the allegory of the *Minne-*

---

4 K. K. Klein, »Das Freundschaftsgleichnis im *Parzival*prolog«. In *Ammann-Fest-
   gabe*, 1953.
5 W. Betz, »Gottfried von Straßburg als Kritiker höfischer Kultur und Advokat religiöser erotischer Emanzipation«, in *Festschrift für Konstantin Reichardt*, 1969.
6 F. Norman, »Meinung und Gegenmeinung: die literarische Fehde zwischen Gottfried von Straßburg und Wolfram von Eschenbach«, in *Miscellanea di studi in
   onore di Bonaventura Tecchi*, 1969.

grotte. Referring to the Cathar teaching as revealed at the trial, that what happens below the waist is not sinful, Betz writes: »Seine Minnegrotte ist, in der Übertragung der Allegorie des Kirchengebäudes, ein Sakralisierungsversuch der Liebesvereinigung. Es gipfelt die ganze Beschreibung – und das scheint bisher noch nicht beachtet worden zu sein – in einer Allegorie des Liebesaktes.«[7] At the very end of the allegorical description of the grotto (16985 ff.), we are told how the bronze door of the grotto is locked, and how it can be opened. Within there is a *valle*, which can be opened from without by a *heftelin.* According to Betz, these terms are ambiguous: beside their ostensible meaning, they can also denote the vagina and the male organ. These meanings are attested in the Fastnachtspiele.

The *valle*, we are told, is of gold. This is perhaps not very surprising in the context, but why then is the *heftelin* of tin? This certainly requires *some* explanation, whether Betz has hit on the right one or not. Gottfried himself says: »daz zin daz ist diu guote andaht«, while of the gold he says: »daz golt daz is diu linge«, i.e. success or good fortune. He goes on:

> sin andaht mac ein ieclich man / nach sinem willen leiten, / smalen oder breiten, / kürzen oder lengen, / vrien oder twengen / sus oder so, her oder hin / mit lihter arbeit alse zin / und ist da lützel schaden an; / swer aber mit rehter güete kan / ze minnen wesen gedanchaft, / den treit binamen dirre haft / von zine, dem swachen dinge, / ze guldiner linge / und ze lieber aventiure.   (17044–57)

I cannot help thinking that Betz has found the only possible interpretation of these lines when he says: »Die ›Andacht‹, die jeglicher Mann mit dem geschmeidigen ›Stab aus Zinn‹ nach seinem ›Willen‹ (auch dies ein Wort aus der erotischen Sphäre) leiten kann und dabei ›die gute Andacht‹ – das ist das biegsame Zinn – kann ›smalen oder breiten, kürzen oder lengen, vrien oder twengen sus oder so, her oder hin‹ – das kann hier doch wohl nicht anders verstanden werden als eine vom männlichen Genitale her gesehene psychologisch-physiologische Schilderung des Liebesaktes.«[8] Betz concludes with a quotation from Denis de Rougemont: »Die im Mythos verherrlichte leidenschaftliche Liebe ist zum Zeitpunkt ihres Auftretens im 12. Jahrhundert eine Religion in der vollen Bedeutung des Wortes gewesen, und zwar eine historisch bestimmbare christliche Häresie.«[9] Betz does not entirely agree

---

[7] Betz, p. 170 f.   [8] Betz, p. 172.   [9] Quoted by Betz, p. 173.

with de Rougemont here, and nor do I. But it may nevertheless not be much of an exaggeration in regard to Gottfried's poetic intention, which is not necessarily the same thing as his personal »existential« view. And it may well be that it was in some such light that Wolfram regarded the matter – with grave disapproval.

The literary feud between Gottfried and Wolfram has been much discussed, and the results have been admirably summed up in Frederick Norman's posthumous article of 1969.[10] I assume with Norman that there was indeed a real and bitter feud between the two writers, and that, though we cannot be sure of the chronological details, each work came out in instalments which quickly became known to the author of the other. The first parts of *Parzival* to come out were, in some form, Books 3–6 and possibly part of 9, though later insertions were almost certainly made.[11] As regards *Tristan*, there is no such clear evidence, but something comparable may well have happened. Norman is rightly sceptical about a number of the passages alleged to refer to this feud, but is in no doubt that Gottfried's scathing attack on the *vindære wilder mære* in fact refers to Wolfram. To put it briefly, each was outraged at the other. Gottfried's objections to Wolfram were at least partly aesthetic, while Wolfram's were moral. Gottfried felt towards Wolfram a little as Walther did towards Neidhart, that this new way of writing simply should not be tolerated in polite circles. But, and this is a point that Norman emphasises, Wolfram was in Gottfried's eyes a deadly menace. And Gottfried was vulnerable on several grounds. In the first place he was a humourless man,[12] seemingly of a jealous nature, and did not suffer rivals gladly. Walther as a lyric poet was less of a direct rival, Veldeke was dead and his reference to Hartmann has been considered a trifle patronising, while as regards his build-up of Bligger von Steinach we have no firm evidence to go on, though Norman's suggestion that this is a disguised form of self-praise has much plausibility. The impressive quality of Wolfram's writing was something he could

---

10 See note 6.

11 Refs. in Bumke, p. 86 ff., 180 ff. Cf. esp. Werner Schröder, *DVj* 31 (1957), 264–302.

12 The nearest approach to a joke in *Tristan* is the rather cruel humour of the seneschal's discomfiture 11309–365. Much funnier than this is the unconscious humour of Isolt's painful working out of the equation »Tantris = Tristan« 10092–10122. Unless a medieval audience was much slower on the uptake than we are, Gottfried has misjudged his effect here. I think he occasionally did so, as I have attempted to show in this paper. Klein (note 4) seems to think likewise. Cf. also W. Schröder (note 11), p. 289 f.

not ignore however much he disliked it. But he was also vulnerable to charges of immorality, whether or not we go further and consider that he exposed himself – rightly or wrongly – to possible accusations of heresy. This brings us to the problem of mysticism – or what has been termed such – in Wolfram's and Gottfried's works, and here we may be touching on something fundamental, though difficult.

At this point it might be helpful for a moment to consider the two poets from the standpoint of Jungian typology. In Wolfram's case there can be little doubt that he belongs to what Jung calls the extravert intuitive type, of which he is an outstanding representative.[13] I would suggest that Gottfried was his polar opposite, the introvert sensorial type. One feature of this type according to Jung is a kind of »negative intuition«, which sniffs out everything ambiguous, inferior and negative in others. Such characters are strongly inclined to jealousy and suspicion, and this seems to me to be borne out by Gottfried's attitude to Wolfram. The hated rival had to be devalued at all costs, and his claims to recognition invalidated. But I want to suggest that this effort at devaluation and annihilation of his rival was a positive spur to Gottfried – he had at all costs to outdo Wolfram, to beat him at his own game, or rather at the game as he *ought* to be playing it, according to Gottfried's own rules. And the great artist in Gottfried responded to the challenge presented by his own somewhat ignoble feelings. The outcome was not merely negative, but profoundly positive. But first, a brief word on »mysticism«.

I shall not say much about this subject, though much has been written about it in connection with both poets.[14] Of *Parzival* it is perhaps enough to say here that it is clearly a religious work with, at least, what might be loosely called a mystical aura about it. As Hermann Schneider puts it: »die durchgehende Idee des verlorenen und wiedergefundenen Gottes ist der Kitt, der die losen Bestandteile des Aventiurenromans aneinanderbindet«.[15] Now, when we pose the *Gretchenfrage* to Gottfried, the answer is less clear. He uses the language of mysticism, as Wolfram does not, but what he means by it is another matter. Anyway, we can safely say that the sexual union of Tristan and Isolt, even if it were not adulterous, would not constitute a valid case

---

[13] C. G. Jung, *Psychological Types*, English transl., 1946, p. 464 ff.
[14] Cf. Tax, p. 228 ff., Picozzi, p. 129 ff.
[15] H. Schneider, *Heldendichtung, Geistlichendichtung, Ritterdichtung*, 1st ed., 1925, p. 283. I do not agree with Kratz's assessment (note 3).

of the *unio mystica* for either St. Bernard of Clairvaux or Meister Eck-
hart. Gottfried, of course, knew exactly what he was doing, but I don't.
It would no doubt have been much easier to judge if he had finished the
poem. It may be, as Tax thinks, that Tristan and Isolt were to go
through a process of purification leading to their salvation,[16] but Betz's
discovery, which I accept, makes this even more difficult to believe than
before. But whatever Gottfried precisely intended, he was certainly
playing a tricky game and he knew it. He was sensitive to attacks from
any quarter, but especially from Wolfram. Wolfram had at all costs to
be outtrumped. And this, I suggest, is how he set about it.

In *Parzival*, Book V, Wolfram mentions the castle of *Wildenberg*,[17]
which seems to be the home of the Counts of Durne in the Odenwald,
and it is frequently stated that Munsalvæsche is Wolfram's own French
translation of »Wildenberg«. This is probably true, but in any case if
modern scholars think so, Gottfried might also have thought so, the
more so as he ostentatiously plays on the word *wilde* in his remarks
about Wolfram. Now, when we come to the Lovers' Cave, Gottfried
describes the way thither as follows:

> Sus kerten si driu under in / allez gegen der *wilde* hin / über walt und über
> heide / vil nach zwo tageweide. / da wiste Tristan lange e wol / in einem
> *wilden berge* ein hol, / daz hæter zeinen stunden / von aventiure vunden: /
> do was er da geriten jagen / und hætin sin wec dar getragen. / daz selbe
> hol was wilent e / under der heidenischen e / vor Corineis jaren, / do risen
> da herren waren, / gehouwen in den *wilden berc*.   (16679–93)

Thus we hear of a »wilden berc« twice in a very few lines. I do not
think this is mere chance. I think Gottfried had studied *Parzival* with
some care, and that the name *Wildenberg* fixed itself in his memory
when he thought of the *vindære wilder mære* (a phrase echoed by
Wolfram in 503,1: *ez næht nu wilden mæren*). The wild and trackless
place in which the Cave lies is reminiscent of the remote wilderness in
which Parzival finds the Castle of the Graal, and this is underlined by
Gottfried's interpretation:

> ouch hat ez guote meine / daz diu fossiure als eine / in dirre wüesten wilde
> lac, / daz man dem wol gelichen mac, / daz minne und ir gelegenheit / niht
> uf der straze sint geleit / noch an dekein gevilde: / si loschet in der wilde, /
> zir cluse ist daz geverte / arbeitsam unde herte; / die berge ligent dar umbe /
> in maneger swæren crumbe / verirret hin unde wider; / die stige sint uf
> unde nider / uns marteræren allen / mit velsen so vervallen, / wirn gan

---

[16] Tax, p. 179.   [17] *Parz.* 230,13.

dem pfade vil rehte mite, / verstozen wir an eime trite,[18] / wirn komen
niemer mere / ze guoter widerkere,   (17071–90)

where the emphasis on the risk of going astray reminds us of Anfortas's
warning to Parzival:

›hüet iuch, dâ gênt unkunde wege: / ir muget an der lîten / wol misserîten, /
deiswâr des ich iu doch niht gan‹.   (226,6–9)

Just as Parzival rides straight on without missing the way, so Tristan
and Isolt find their way to the Cave without trouble. But Marke cannot
enter, and we recall that Arthur cannot even find Munsalvæsche.

The Lovers' Cave is substantially Gottfried's own invention, one of his
most notable contributions to the *Tristan* story. It is my suggestion that
this scene was at least partly inspired by, and as an answer to, Wolfram's Munsalvæsche. We can find some confirmation in the so-called
Speisewunder. It has been held by Gottfried Weber and others that this
represents the Eucharist, but Tax,[19] following Eggers, is surely right in
contesting this, although some eucharistic echoes are certainly present.
Let us look at the text. Having installed the lovers in their cave, Gottfried raises a problem, as if forestalling objections from his hearers:

Genuoge nimet hier under / virwitze unde wunder / und habent mit vrage
groze not, / wie sich Tristan unde Isot / die zwene geverten / in dirre wüeste
ernerten.   (16807–12)

His answer is simple: »si sahen beide ein ander an. / da generten si sich
van.« Two points occur to us: first, the fact that the Graal community
receive their food miraculously from the Graal,[20] and secondly, the
fictive scepticism among Wolfram's audience concerning this miracle
(238,18): »esn wurde nie kein bilde, / beginnet maneger sprechen.«
Whereas Wolfram continues tartly: »der wil sich übel rechen«, Gottfried puts the eager questioners aright more urbanely: »des wil ich si
berihten, / ir virwitze beslihten.« But the passage certainly looks like
an imitation of Wolfram.

Wolfram's explanation is tantalisingly brief but makes high-sounding
claims:

wan der grâl was der sælden fruht, / der werlde süeze ein söhl genuht, /
er wac vil nâch gelîche / als man saget von himelrîche.   (238,21–24)

---

[18] Possibly like Lancelot before entering the cart: cf. E. Vinaver, »Les deux pas de
Lancelot«, in *Mélanges pour J. Fourquet*, 1969.
[19] Tax, p. 122.
[20] I prefer this spelling, which is also used by my revered friend Margaret Richey.

His words also, incidentally, have a curiously tentative ring (»vil nâch«, »als man saget«). Like Flegetanis, Wolfram himself refers to these great mysteries with some reluctance, *blûweclîche*. Gottfried, equally characteristically, has no such inhibitions about *his* miracle: he refers to it at some length, and comes back to it again after we had thought he had finished with it.[21] According to him, the lovers need no physical nourishment at all. In one sense this may be a topos, but at the same time we should not fail to note that it represents an even greater miracle than that of the Graal. Clearly, for him, Minne cannot be allowed to lag behind the Graal; whatever the Graal can do, Minne must at all costs be able to do, and more. And if the Graal was almost equal to the kingdom of heaven the realm of Minne where the lovers were was an earthly paradise far surpassing the glories of Arthur's realm.

I have said that Gottfried knew exactly what he was doing, even if I don't. Nevertheless, the point is worth considering whether he did not in this scene allow himself to be carried away. Perhaps in thus attempting to outdo Wolfram he overdid the religious associations and thus created a real problem for himself as well as for us. Could it be that he allowed himself to be led into virtually creating a »religion of love« around the Grotto? It is, after all, *Der Minne benant*, i.e. dedicated to Minne as a church is dedicated to a saint. A small point here, on which however I would not lay much stress, is the reference, still in connection with the miracle of feeding, to »diu gebalsemete minne« (16831). There are, as Tax notes, few references to *balsem* in *Tristan,* and this might just be an echo of Wolfram's reference to the *balsemvaz* that preceded the Graal.

Reverting now to the passage interpreting the dangers that beset those who tread the path leading to the Grotto, we note the words (17085) *uns marteræren allen,* which have led to some discussion of the question whether Tristan and Isolt can be regarded, in Gottfried's view, as »martyrs of love« or *Minneheilige*.[22] But whether we think Gottfried had this intention or not is, for my present purpose, of less importance than whether Wolfram so interpreted the passage. If he did, which I consider highly probable, he may have reacted in a highly significant way, by creating his own image of a *true* martyr of love in the figure of Sigune. The loving development of this striking figure from the nameless *pucele* who makes a fleeting appearance in Chrétien's *Perce-*

---

[21] *Tristan* 16807 ff., 16909 ff.   [22] Cf. Picozzi, p. 131 ff.

val [23] is, of course, one of Wolfram's great achievements which it is unnecessary to enlarge on here. We may simply recall that of her four
appearances in *Parzival* the first, in Book III, is little more than a
»hiving off« of the functional part of her role in Book V (which corresponds to the point where Chrétien placed his lamenting damsel), thus
enabling Parzival to learn his name at an earlier stage than in the
source; her third appearance in Book IX is the prelude to Parzival's
meeting with Trevrizent, and here it is she who is in touch with Munsal-
vaesche, which Parzival still cannot reach, while at the last, after Parzival's mission has been accomplished, he finds her dead beside her lover,
her martyrdom also accomplished. Nowhere does Wolfram refer directly to Gottfried's poem – and though a negative is notoriously difficult
to prove, this is perhaps a deliberate response to Gottfried's treatment
of him –, but in both the second and the third passages we do have
remarkably similar references to Lunete and her advice to Laudine.
We might think that in both these passages Lunete stands in, so to speak,
discreetly for Isolt. This is perhaps confirmed by Wolfram's words
(253,16) about »wîp die man bî wanke siht, / manege, der ich wil
gedagn« – though admittedly this is susceptible of another more personal explanation.
Let us look once again at the *Tristan* passage previously discussed. It
goes on:

> swer aber so sælic mac gesin, / daz er zer wilde kumet hin in, / der selbe
> hat sin arbeit / vil sæleclichen an geleit,   (17091–94)

which, combined with Gottfried's famous reference at an earlier point,
when »Tantris« was Isolt's teacher, to the principle of *moraliteit,* i.e.
»got und der werlt gevallen«, could have been the negative inspiration
of Wolfram's equally famous words at the very end of *Parzival:*

> Swes leben sich so verendet, / daz got niht wirt gepfendet / der sêle durch
> des lîbes schulde, / und der doch der werlde hulde / behalten kan mit werde-
> keit, / daz ist ein nützziu arebeit.   (827,19–24)

But probably the thought is too obvious, and its expression too little
pointed, to make this assumption necessary: the parallel would have
been more striking if Wolfram had written »daz ist ein sæligiu arebeit«.
It is, however, clear that Wolfram approved of Gottfried's *expression*
of »got und der werlt gevallen«, though without agreeing that Gott-

---

[23] *Der Percevalroman,* ed. A. Hilka, 1932, 3431.

fried's characters actually *achieved* this aim. The convergence at one level here merely emphasises the more fundamental divergence.

Be this as it may, one may well imagine that Gottfried's talk of *moraliteit* stuck in Wolfram's throat, and we may well think that his response is to be found in the advice to women in *Parzival* 2,23 ff. His words at 3,11:

> manec wîbes schœne an lobe ist breit: / ist dâ daz herze conterfeit, / die lobe ich als ich solde: / daz safer ime golde

have frequently, and I think rightly, been referred to the *Tristan* passage (12305 ff.): »Wir haben ein bœse conterfeit / in daz vingerlin geleit / und triegen uns da selbe mite«, whether or not we accept that the line »die lobe ich als i'solde« contains a pun on the name of Gottfried's heroine (as I think it does).[24]

It would be possible to pursue our theme further, but let us draw the threads together. Problems of the relative chronology of the two poems need not detain us much. That Wolfram's poem appeared in sections, some of which were reworked, is as nearly certain as such things can be, having regard to our information, and there is no inherent difficulty in assuming a similar state of affairs for *Tristan,* though the evidence is lacking. Only Marold tried to deduce the existence of an *Urtristan* from the manuscript evidence, but his theory, based on a large gap in Ms M, has been shown to be without foundation.[25] But, however obscure the details, internal evidence does make it overwhelmingly probable that Wolfram and Gottfried were in a position to react against each other, and therefore to influence each other, and that is all we need. My aim has been to show that such influence was not merely negative, or comparatively trivial, but on the contrary was profoundly positive and fruitful. They rubbed off on each other in a way that was intensely stimulating to the genius of each.

One of the mysteries about Gottfried is that – with the probable exception of a couple of stanzas – *Tristan* is his only known work. Wolfram and Hartmann are both the authors of several works, and we can venture to say something about their course of development as writers. The author of *Tristan* was no tyro, but of his early efforts we know nothing, and it is likely that he kept them to himself. He appears on the scene, suddenly, with one single highly organised and highly pol-

---

[24] F. Norman, *German Life and Letters* 15 (1961–62), p. 64.
[25] Cf. Picozzi, p. 71 ff.

ished if unfinished work. This, or a part of it, came out *after* a considerable portion of *Parzival*, say Books 3–6 in their earliest form, had become known.[26] So much is clear. Its appearance from Straßburg may have come to Wolfram as something like a bolt from the blue. Wolfram was already familiar with Eilhart's *Tristrant*, as we know, though he probably disliked both its form and its contents. He would scarcely have welcomed an infinitely better work on the same obnoxious theme, even if it had not included a personal attack on him. At any rate when he started working, as W. J. Schröder has pointed out, »der große Mann, mit dem Wolfram rechnen mußte, war Hartmann, nicht Gottfried«.[27] So far from being an old friend with whom he had broken, as K. K. Klein surmised, Gottfried was most likely utterly unknown to Wolfram, and doubtless remained so, personally. We cannot date things very accurately, but it may well be that the date »about 1210«, which has become traditional for the appearance of *Tristan* (and, specifically, the review of poets) is too late. It is based on an assumed date of Reinmar's death »about 1207–8«. All we really know is that Reinmar was probably still alive in 1203, if that is indeed the date of Walther's »Ir sult sprechen willekomen«. Personally, I would put the *Literaturstelle* of *Tristan* tentatively at »ca. 1205«. Hartmann, to whom Gottfried refers as living, wrote no more (as far as we know) after *Iwein* (1202?), and may have died soon after Reinmar. What I am assuming is that the *Minnegrotte* episode, at least as we have it, was penned after Book V of *Parzival*, but that the Sigune episodes of *Parzival* were to some extent at least reworked or developed *after* the *Minnegrotte*. This cannot be proved, but is by no means impossible. Less

[26] Cf. esp. Bodo Mergell, *Tristan und Isolde: Ursprung und Entwicklung der Tristansage des Mittelalters*, 1949; Tax, esp, p. 165 f.; Picozzi, p. 132 ff. Mergell's view that *Tristan* is »complete« as it stands has not found favour and is disproved by the unfinished acrostic, apart from all else. But the last words at 19558 do form the reasonable conclusion of a »section« or »book« (unlike, e.g. the end of Chrétien's *Perceval* or, I think, *Willehalm*). My view is that *Tristan* appeared, as indicated in the text of my paper, in instalments, and 19558 would then be the end of the last instalment that Gottfried was able to complete. Where exactly previous instalments ended, we do not know, but each one was as perfect as Gottfried could make it before it was »released«: whatever drafts for the remaining portion of the work may have existed have simply not been preserved, and were perhaps destroyed on his instructions when he knew he could never finish. This would have been in character, the more so if Gottfried's normal fastidiousness was heightened by Wolfram's rivalry. Wolfram may therefore bear some responsibility for *Tristan's* unfinished condition. Cf. also W. Schröder (note 11), p. 302.

[27] W. J. Schröder, *PBB* (Tübingen) 80 (1958), p. 286.

importantly in itself, but useful as a pointer, is the probability that Wolfram's words »Ez næht nu wilden mæren«, with which Book X opens, postdate the *Literaturstelle*. Wolfram could cheerfully accept and adopt such a description for his account, not of Parzival's but of Gawan's adventures.

I should perhaps add at this point that I do not claim to have *proved* anything. What I *would* claim is to have done approximately what Dr. Rowse has in fact done for his theory about the Dark Lady of the Sonnets [28] – as opposed to what he thinks he has done. He has made out a good plausible case which cannot be disproved, but of course except in his own imagination he has not proved his case, and he can't, at least on the evidence so far produced. I would add further that my two contentions, namely that the Grotto Scene shows evidence of Gottfried's reaction to Wolfram's Munsalvæsche, and that the figure of Sigune (and indeed of Schianatulander) was developed as Wolfram's reaction to Gottfried's real or apparent presentation of Tristan and Isolt as »martyrs of love«, are strictly independent of each other. Though parallel, and in a sense supporting each other, they are essentially two separate hypotheses, each of which, therefore, may independently be right or wrong. Nor do they depend on the validity of Betz's interpretation of the *valle* and the *heftelin*, though this, if right, would lend them further support. [29]

I am not attempting here any detailed interpretation of either *Tristan* as a whole or of the *Minnegrotte* episode. I confess there is much that I, in common with others, find baffling. But it is certainly fair to say that Gottfried cannot possibly, by standard definition, be called a true mystic, however much he may use the language of mysticism. Maybe the union of Tristan and Isolt could be thought of as »analogous« to the *unio mystica*, and it might even be just possible for us moderns to adduce parallels from, say, Tantric yoga to support the view that it represents a valid type of religious experience. But even then, in its own cultural context it could not be other than heretical and blasphemous, if taken seriously. On the other hand, we must bear in mind what was possible at the time in the way of skating on thin ice. Even in terms of sacral kingship, Walther's implied comparison of

---

[28] *The Times*, 29 January 1973.
[29] Of course Wolfram was not excessively prudish, and may not have objected to this aside from its quasi-religious context. Let us not forget Parzival in Book VI, sunk in thoughts about Condwiramurs, »mit ûf gerihtem sper« (284,3).

Philip to the Trinity and his wife to the Virgin Mary [30] seems a trifle strong, and we also have, for instance, Frauenlob's account of the Immaculate Conception in terms reminiscent of a seduction [31] – not to mention Lancelot's worship of the queen in Chrétien's poem, and the like. Yet I think Gottfried goes further than these, and Wolfram at least could not stomach it. Perhaps there were other things he could not stomach. When Tristan and Isolt finally decide to return to Marke's court for the sake of *ere*, Gottfried says (16875 ff.): »sin hæten umbe ein bezzer leben / niht eine bone gegeben / wan eine umbe ir ere«, and one can almost hear Wolfram muttering with Walther: »Waz êren hât frô bône?« I am not proposing to attempt my own analysis of the difficult problem of *ere* in *Tristan*, but I think Wolfram's reaction is not hard to guess.

What I have said so far about Gottfried may seem excessively negative, and I would hate to end on such a note without qualification, though it is true I have sought to show that his poem positively benefited from the unwelcome stimulus provided by *Parzival*. Let me then at least say something to document my appreciation of his great artistry. As I have written elsewhere: »Thomas's invention of the Hall of Statues is a somewhat desperate conceit designed to keep the emotional pressure up at all costs, and Gottfried may have approached this episode without enthusiasm.« [32] Now Mergell in his well-known brilliant but wayward book suggested that Gottfried deliberately broke off where he did, but transferred some elements from this scene to that of the Grotto. [33] Tax does not believe, as I do not, that *Tristan* was deliberately left a torso, but he does take up and develop Mergell's second point, and says: »Denn man darf sich ernstlich fragen, ob der deutsche Dichter wohl Grund hätte, den Bildersaal überhaupt noch zu übernehmen. Sollte Gottfrieds feinem Geschmack diese Szene doch nicht allzu anstößig gewesen sein?« [34] – a sentiment with which I feel in complete agreement.

The contrast, and the conflict, between these two very great German writers of around 1200 is a fascinating, indeed an awe-inspiring spectacle. We might perhaps conclude by considering them in terms of gamesmanship. What game is each one playing? [35] If we pose this question, we may find, I think, that Wolfram at least is not basically playing

---

[30] Walther, 19,5.
[31] *Frauenlobs Marienleich*, ed. L. Pfannmüller, 1913, esp. 10,29.
[32] M. O'C. Walshe, *Medieval German Literature: A Survey*, 1962, p. 192.
[33] See note 26. [34] Tax, p. 166. [35] See also Tax, p. 202.

any »game«. His style may be devious, but his aim is fundamentally
true and straight, a point which he himself makes in characteristic
manner in the »Bogengleichnis«. Whatever we may find to argue about
in attempting to interpret him, he is deeply sincere in his devotion to
the ideals of chivalry and the quest for God's grace symbolised by the
Holy Graal. Some of his theology may possibly be off-beat,[36] nevertheless he is in a real sense a lay counterpart of those French Cistercians
who, shortly after his time and without knowledge of him, were to give
an orthodox but profound, subtle and moving Christian interpretation
to that once pagan theme. Wolfram is certainly playful, but he is not
playing a game. When we come to Gottfried, we are not so sure. Are the
opinions he expresses and implies in *Tristan* his own, or those of his
deliberately assumed literary *persona*? And either way – what do they
mean? To neither of these questions can we return a confident answer.
Even if he *is* expressing his own opinions, which at one level and to
some degree he surely must be, he still seems to be playing a subtle and
elusive game with us, perhaps in self-protection, more probably from
a combination of motives of which self-protection was one. Paradoxic-
ally, it is in one sense almost more to *Tristan* than to *Parzival* that we
might apply Wolfram's famous words (2,5–16):

> Ouch erkante ich nie sô wîsen man, / ern möhte gerne künde hân, / welher
> stiure disiu mære gernt, / und waz si guoter lêre wernt. / dar an si nimmer
> des verzagent, / beidiu si vliehent unde jagent, / si entwîchent unde kêrent, /
> si lasternt unde êrent. / swer mit disen schanzen allen kan, / an dem hât
> witze wol getân, / der sich niht versitzet noch vergêt, / und sich anders wol
> verstêt.[37]

---

[36] See H.-J. Koppitz, *Wolframs Religiosität*, 1958.
[37] Was Wolfram inspired to this play on words by Gottfried? Cf., e.g., *Tristan*
11810 ff.

Hans-Hugo Steinhoff

Artusritter und Gralsheld: Zur Bewertung des höfischen Rittertums im *Prosa-Lancelot*

Auf der Suche nach einem Stoff, mit dessen Hilfe der Erfolg von *My Fair Lady* wiederholt oder übertroffen werden könnte, verfielen die Musical-Autoren Lerner und Loewe auf König Artus und die Liebe zwischen Ginover und Lancelot. Nach einem Roman von Terence H. White[1] entstand *Camelot*,[2] und wenn *Camelot* auch trotz Richard Burton und Julie Andrews nur 873 Aufführungen am Broadway erreichte (gegenüber 2717 von *My Fair Lady*) und die Verfilmung wegen des Mißverhältnisses von Aufwand und Substanz nicht unerheblich zum Ende der Ära Hollywood beigetragen hat, zeugt doch schon der Versuch für ein – aus welchen Motiven auch immer – bis heute lebendiges Interesse an König Artus und Ritter Lancelot. Für den deutschen Betrachter hat das etwas Erstaunliches. Lancelot war schon im Mittelalter keine Zentralfigur der deutschen literarischen Welt. Der mittelhochdeutsche Beitrag zur Lancelot-Epik besteht in den knapp neuneinhalbtausend Versen, die der Schweizer Ulrich von Zatzikhoven darauf verwandte, die Geschichte des gleichermaßen *sige-* und *minnesaeligen* Lanzelet zu erzählen, der in fein abgestufter Folge ritterliche Triumphe, drei Bräute und großes Ansehen am Artushof erringt, für seine vier Königreiche vier Kinder zeugt und schließlich glücklich und gütig im Kreise seiner Enkel lebt.[3] Ernstliche Probleme hat dieser Lanzelet eigentlich nie, nicht

---

[1] *The Once and Future King* (New York: Putnam, 1958).

[2] Frederick Loewe, *Camelot: A new musical.* Book and lyrics by Alan Jay Lerner (New York: Random House, 1961). Premiere am 3. 12. 1960 im Majestic Theatre. – Schallplatten: Columbia, KOL 5620/KOS 2031 (Musical), und Warner Bros., B (S) 1712 (Film).

[3] Ulrich von Zatzikhoven, *Lanzelet,* hg. v. K. A. Hahn (Frankfurt 1845; Nachdruck mit Nachwort und Bibliographie von Frederick Norman, Berlin 1965). – Englische Übersetzung von Kenneth G. T. Webster und Roger Sherman Loomis (New York 1951).

einmal mit seinen vielen Verehrerinnen, denn die frühere wird jeweils elegant aus der Handlung entlassen, ehe die nächste in sie eintritt. Und als es doch einmal zwei nebeneinander gibt, nämlich seine Gemahlin Iblis und eine Dame, die ihn als Turnierbeute gefangen hält, gewinnt Iblis flugs einen Zaubermantel, der allen Kummer von ihr und aus der Erzählung fernhält. Zauberei und wunderbare Abenteuer spielen überhaupt eine große Rolle und machen den Roman zu einem handlungsstarken Stück Unterhaltungsliteratur ohne sonderlichen Tiefgang für ein höfisches Publikum. Die Liebe zu Ginover, die Lancelot berühmt und schließlich musicalreif gemacht hat, spielt bei Ulrich keine Rolle, oder doch fast keine, denn der erwähnte Zaubermantel soll nur einer wahrhaft treuen Frau passen, und Ginover paßt er nicht: sie hat zwar, so erfährt der darob befremdete Artushof zu seiner Beruhigung, nicht wirklich, aber doch in Gedanken gesündigt, und mit wem, fragt sich der mit Lanzelets Qualitäten vertraute Hörer, wenn nicht mit Lanzelet? Ulrich äußert sich jedoch nicht in diesem Sinne, und seine erzählerischen Mittel sind nicht so subtil, daß er einen solchen Gedanken unausgesprochen gelassen hätte.

Es ist verständlich, daß Lanzelet nicht viel Gnade bei den durch so problematische Naturen wie Parzival und Tristan und so beachtliche Helden wie die des *Nibelungenliedes* verwöhnten Germanisten gefunden hat, schade insofern, als die trivialeren Strukturen des *Lanzelet* manches über das Publikumsinteresse der mittelhochdeutschen Blütezeit aussagen, was der hohen höfischen Epik nicht so ohne weiteres abzulesen ist.

Nun gibt es allerdings noch eine zweite, durchaus nicht triviale mittelhochdeutsche Lancelot-Dichtung, aber auch sie ist bis heute nicht recht populär geworden – aus mancherlei Gründen. Es handelt sich zwar um den ältesten deutschen Prosaroman, aber eben doch nur um Prosa aus einer Zeit, in der Literatur sonst stets metrisch und reimweis geordnet daherkommt. Der *Prosa-Lancelot* ist denn auch erst relativ spät als ein Werk des 13. Jahrhunderts erkannt worden, und entsprechend spät begann die – bis heute nicht abgeschlossene – Edition.[4] Vor allem aber:

---

4 *Lancelot.* Nach der Heidelberger Pergamenthandschrift Pal. germ. 147 hg. v. Reinhold Kluge, Bd. I, Deutsche Texte des Mittelalters, 42 (Berlin 1948); Bd. II, Deutsche Texte des Mittelalters, 47 (Berlin 1963). – Ich zitiere diese Ausgabe mit Band-, Seiten- und Zeilenzahl. – Teilausgabe: *Der Karrenritter: Episode des mhd. Prosa-Lancelot,* hg. v. R. Kluge, Kleine deutsche Prosadenkmäler des Mittelalters, 10 (München 1972). – [Korrekturnote: Inzwischen erschien der abschließende Bd. III, Deutsche Texte des Mittelalters, 63 (Berlin 1974).]

der mittelhochdeutsche *Prosa-Lancelot* ist kein Originalwerk, auch keine schöpferische Neufassung wie die Übertragungen der Romane Chrestiens durch Hartmann und Wolfram, sondern eine im Prinzip wortgetreue Übersetzung der altfranzösischen Vorlage.

So blieb seine Existenz innerhalb der Geschichte der deutschen Literatur des Mittelalters lange unbeachtet, in der er doch immerhin durch vier Jahrhunderte hin sein Publikum gefunden hat. Daß es ein solches gegeben hat, läßt jedenfalls die Überlieferung vermuten. Mit der französischen verglichen ist sie gering, doch gibt es zehn Zeugen aus dem 13. bis 16. Jahrhundert und aus dem gesamten deutschen Sprachgebiet – von Ulrichs *Lanzelet* fünf. Die jüngste dieser Handschriften entstand zu einer Zeit, da der allgemeine Literaturbetrieb längst zum Buchdruck übergegangen war; sie greift noch einmal auf den französischen Text zurück und wird dadurch zur vollständigsten von allen. Den Weg in den Druck hat der deutsche *Prosa-Lancelot* dann aber nicht mehr geschafft. Es gibt anscheinend auch kaum direkte Berührungen mit der mittelhochdeutschen Versepik. Hier wirken offenbar Gattungsschranken, die erst aufgehoben wurden, als Mitte des 15. Jahrhunderts Ulrich Füeterer den Roman zunächst zu einer Kurzfassung zusammenstrich [5] und dann in Verse brachte.

Mit dem Fortschreiten der Textedition wächst das Interesse an der Frage, welche dichterischen Möglichkeiten der *Prosa-Lancelot* in die deutsche Literatur des Mittelalters eingebracht hat. Besonders Kurt Ruh, Uwe Ruberg und Wolfgang Harms, Ernst Soudek und Cynthia Caples haben Entscheidendes zu seinem Verständnis beigetragen. [6] Auf

---

[5] Ulrich Füeterer, *Prosaroman von Lanzelot*, nach der Donaueschinger Handschrift hg. v. Arthur Peter, Bibliothek des Literarischen Vereins, 175 (Tübingen 1885; Nachdruck Hildesheim 1972). Daß Peter nicht schon damals den *Prosa-Lancelot* herausgab, begründet er mit der »großen ausdehnung« dieses Textes (S. II).

[6] Kurt Ruh, »Lancelot«, *DVj* 33 (1959), 269–282; ich zitiere die überarbeitete, mit einem »Nachtrag (1968)« versehene Fassung in *Der arthurische Roman*, hg. v. Kurt Wais, Wege der Forschung, 157 (Darmstadt 1970), 237–255. – »Der Gralsheld in der *Queste del Saint Graal*«, in *Wolfram-Studien*, hg. v. Werner Schröder (Berlin 1970), 240–263.

Uwe Ruberg, »Die Suche im *Prosa-Lancelot*«, *ZfdA*, 92 (1963), 122–157. – *Raum und Zeit im Prosa-Lancelot*, Medium Aevum, 9 (München 1965).

Wolfgang Harms, *Der Kampf mit dem Freund oder Verwandten in der deutschen Literatur bis um 1300*, Medium Aevum, 1 (München 1963), 179–201. – *Homo viator in bivio*, Medium Aevum, 21 (München 1970), 250–286.

Ernst Herbert Soudek, »The Cart-Episode: Evolution of an Arthurian Incident from Chrestien's *Le Chevalier de la Charrette*, through the *Old French Prose Lancelot*, the *Middle High German Prose Lancelot*, to Malory's *Morte Darthur*«,

ihre Ergebnisse stützen sich meine folgenden Überlegungen. Ihr unmittelbarer Anlaß ist die Dissertation von Rudolf Voss,[7] der kürzlich eine neue These zur ideologischen Konzeption des Romans zur Diskussion gestellt hat.

Die äußere und innere Einheit dieser Konzeption bildet seit je eins der Kernprobleme der internationalen *Prosa-Lancelot*-Forschung. Während aber ein einheitlicher Handlungsplan der drei Teile *Lancelot – Gralssuche – König Artus' Tod*[8] trotz mancher Widersprüche und Inkonsequenzen im einzelnen und trotz verschiedener Stil-Lage als gesichert gelten kann,[9] ist die ihm entsprechende innere Einheitlichkeit noch immer umstritten. Der gleiche Lancelot, dessen durch nichts aufzuhaltender Aufstieg vom land- und namenlosen Außenseiter zum strahlenden Helden des Artushofs neben, ja über Artus den ersten Teil beherrscht, muß im zweiten die von ihm erwartete Rolle als Erlöser und Vollender aller Aventiuren an Galaad abtreten – die gleiche durch nichts zu beirrende Liebe zu Ginover, der er seine Erfolge als der Welt bester Ritter zuschreibt, wird ihm als Sünde ausgelegt, der er abzuschwören hat, um wenigstens noch an einem Zipfel das Wunder des Grals zu fassen, und sie wird, wie sie zunächst Lancelot zum Retter des von außen bedrohten Artushofes werden läßt, am Ende zu einer der Ursachen für dessen Untergang.

Diss. Univ. of Michigan, 1969 [*Dissertation Abstracts*, 31 (1970), 1240–41 A]. – »Lancelot und Lanzelet: Zur Verbreitung der Lanzelotsage auf deutschem Sprachgebiet«, *Rice University Studies* 57 (1971), 115–121.
Cynthia Barrett Caples, »Feudal Chivalry in the *Prose Lancelot*«, Diss. Harvard Univ., 1970 [*Dissertation Abstracts*, 32 (1971), 1505 A]. (In dieser Arbeit wird versucht, den »ethical or secular code of the *Lancelot propre*«, des altfranzösischen wie des deutschen, unabhängig von den ihm folgenden Teilen des Romans zu interpretieren [S. 5]. Zentrales Thema sei Lancelots Lehensverlust: »The loss of the fief is the tragedy of the *Lancelot propre* from beginning to end« [S. 59], die Konflikte entstünden aus dem Versuch, dieses Lehen zurückzuerhalten, und auch die Ginover-Liebe sei »a surrogate for neglected feudal services« [S. 88, vgl. S. 68 u.ö.]. Trotz dieser m. E. verfehlten These bietet die Autorin eine Fülle wertvoller Beobachtungen zum feudalhöfischen Rittertum im *Prosa-Lancelot*.)

[7] *Der Prosa-Lancelot*, Deutsche Studien, 12 (Meisenheim 1970). Dazu die Rezensionen von Wolfgang Harms, *Leuvense Bijdragen* 59 (1970), Heft 4, 162–164; Dennis Howard Green, *MLR* 66 (1971), 932–934; Uwe Ruberg, *AfdA* 83 (1972), 172–179.

[8] Zum französischen Zyklus gehören außerdem die *Estoire del Saint Graal* und die *Estoire Merlin*, beide mit großer Wahrscheinlichkeit späte Ergänzungen.

[9] Vgl. den Forschungsbericht bei Voss, S. 14–20, wo allerdings die gegen eine einheitliche Konzeption argumentierende Dissertation von Hans Günther Jantzen noch nicht berücksichtigt ist: *Untersuchungen zur Entstehung des altfranzösischen Prosaromans* (Diss. Heidelberg 1966).

Die Liebe zu Ginover bestimmt Lancelots Sinnen und Trachten vom Augenblick seines Eintritts in die höfische Welt. »›Nu sagent mir‹«, fragt ihn Ginover in der durch Dantes Anspielung berühmt gebliebenen ersten Liebesszene,[10] nachdem sie ihm einen halb unfreiwilligen Bericht seiner bisherigen Taten entlockt hat, »›durch wes willen datent ir alle die guten ritterschafft die ir ie hant gethan?‹ ›Durch uwern willen, frauw‹, sprach er« und fügt etwas später hinzu: »›Ich han uch geminnet, frau, ... von dem tag das ich uch von erst sah‹« (I 293,31–33 und 294,9–10). Das war der Tag seiner Ankunft am Artushof. Wie sehr er sein künftiges Geschick an Ginover orientiert, wurde damals sogleich deutlich, da er es fertig brachte, das Ritterschwert nicht aus der Hand des Königs zu empfangen, sondern von Ginover (I 146): sie, und nicht Artus, ist Ausgangs- und Zielpunkt seines Handelns. Nur auf ihre Bitte hin läßt er sich (zweimal) in die Artusrunde aufnehmen (I 481–82 und 543–44), erst ihre Klage über eine Beleidigung durch Claudas bestimmt ihn dazu, den anzugreifen und das seinem Vater geraubte Königreich zurückzuerobern (II 678–79).

An der Liebe zu Ginover hält Lancelot in allen Wechselfällen fest,[11] weder Trennung noch Versuchung oder Verleumdung können sie gefährden. Es bedarf schon eines Zaubertranks und der Vorspiegelung, er liege bei Ginover, um ihn seine heilsgeschichtliche Aufgabe erfüllen und mit der Tochter des Königs Pelles den Gralshelden zeugen zu lassen (II 293 ff.). Auch die immer aufs neue über ihn verhängten teils vermeintlichen, teils wirklichen Verstoßungen durch Ginover, die seine Existenz bis zum Wahnsinn und zum Selbstmordversuch erschüttern, ändern an dieser Liebe nichts: Lancelot ist, mit der einen Einschränkung, daß er sich allzu leicht täuschen läßt, der ideale Liebende, wie er der beste höfische Ritter ist. Seine Verehrung nimmt gelegentlich fast sakrale Züge an, seine Treue macht ihn zum Asketen und Märtyrer[12] im Dienst seiner weltlichen Göttin. Es erscheint nur folgerichtig, daß ihn lange Zeit nicht einmal die Entdeckung beeindruckt, wegen der Liebe zu Ginover von der Vollendung der Gralsaventiure ausgeschlossen zu sein. Als Ginover sich deswegen anklagt – nicht so sehr um Lancelots willen, sondern weil »›durch myner schonheit willen so vil guts underwegen solt verliben zu geschehen‹« (II 439,3–4) –, verweist er ihr diese Klage:

---

10 Dazu besonders Ruh, »Lancelot«, S. 244 ff.
11 Belege bei Voss, S. 74–80.
12 Vgl. Soudek, Diss., S. 74 f.; ähnlich bereits Ruh, »Lancelot«, S. 250 ff.

>Frauw‹, sprach Lancelot, ›wißent das ir ubel gerett habent, wann ich nye so zu großen eren und hohen sachen were komen, werent ir nit gewest. Ich enhett keyn hercz gehabt zu myner ritterschafft mich sölch hohe sachen anzunemen oder im herczen gehabt. Aber darumb das ich an uch und uwer schonheit gedacht han, das hatt myn hercz in groß hoffart gebracht, so, was sachen ich anfing, bracht ich lichticlichen zu ende . . .‹

(II 439,4–9; vgl. 424,18–22) [13]

Folgerichtig auch, daß Lancelot, wo die ihm zugedachte Funktion als Vater des Gralshelden der Liebe zu Ginover widerstreitet, sich für Ginover entscheidet. Er tut alles, ihr das unfreiwillige Beilager mit der Gralstochter zu verheimlichen (II 435,9–12 u.ö.). Als er ein zweites Mal mit ihr zusammen ist, wieder in dem Glauben, er liege bei Ginover, entdeckt und verstößt sie ihn. Er wird wahnsinnig und einsam bis zur Namenlosigkeit, bis ihn der Gral schließlich heilt. Doch die Buße, die er dann in Gesellschaft der Gralstochter übt, gilt nicht der Liebe zu Ginover, sondern dem ungewollten Treuebruch (II 820/21).

Erst in der *Gralssuche*, als Galaad ihn in der Rolle des besten Ritters abgelöst hat – er besiegt ihn ohne viel Mühe im Zweikampf – und als eine Stimme vom Himmel und ein Eremit ihn zur Reue auffordern, beichtet er seine Liebe als Sünde:

> ›Herre‹, sprach Lanczelot, ›es ist also das ich bin dot mit sunden durch ein frauw die ich lieb hann gehabt all myn leben, das ist die konigin, des konig Artus wip –‹

und auch jetzt wiederholt er noch einmal, in deutlichem Anklang an die vorher zitierte Stelle, was er dieser Liebe verdankt:

> ›– das ist die die mich hat gethan in den großen hoen mût, und das ist die durch der willen ich han gethan die groß biederbkeit, da all die welt von saget, und sie ist die die mich hat thûn komen von armût in rychtûm und von ungemach in all weltlich ere.‹[14]

---

[13] Zu dieser Szene vgl. Erich Köhler, *Ideal und Wirklichkeit in der höfischen Epik*, Beihefte zur Zeitschrift für romanische Philologie, 97 (Tübingen 1956; 2. erg. Aufl. 1970), S. 187 f.

[14] Hs. P, fol. 257ᵛ, zitiert nach Voss, S. 22. Der französische Text lautet: »Sire, fet Lancelot, il est einsi que je sui morz de pechié d'une moie dame que je ai amee toute ma vie, et ce est la reine Guenievre, la fame le roi Artus. Ce est cele qui a plenté m'a doné l'or et l'argent et les riches dons que je ai aucune foiz donez as povres chevaliers. Ce est cele qui m'a mis ou grant boban et en la grant hautece ou je sui. Ce est cele por qui amor j'ai faites les granz proeces dont toz li mondes parole. Ce est cele qui m'a fet venir de povreté en richece et de mesaise a toutes les terriannes beneurtez . . .«. *La Queste del Saint Graal: Roman du XIIIe siècle*, hg. v. Albert Pauphilet, Les classiques français du moyen âge, 33 (Paris 1923), S. 66,8–16.

Wenn so die Ginover-Minne einerseits die Ursache für Lancelots Aufstieg zum besten Ritter der (höfischen) Welt ist, andererseits gerade sie ihn vom dem besten Ritter vorbehaltenen Gralsabenteuer ausschließt, scheint sich ein unversöhnlicher Widerspruch zu ergeben, der auf einen dualistischen Gegensatz zwischen höfischem und geistlichem Rittertum deutet.[15] Das ausdrückliche Verdikt kommt freilich zu Beginn der *Gralssuche* auffallend spät und bleibt blaß neben der Präsentation Lancelots als des vorbildlichen Artushelden im an Umfang und erzählerischem Glanz sehr viel wirkungsmächtigeren eigentlichen *Lancelot*. Rudolf Voss, der diese unterschiedliche Gewichtung stark betont hat, schließt aus ihr, daß im *Prosa-Lancelot* zwei je für sich betrachtet werthaltige Weltanschauungen, die höfische und die geistliche, nebeneinander bestünden, ohne daß die eine der anderen ganz Herr werde. Er gewinnt daraus die reizvolle Möglichkeit, die bewußte Darstellung der Aporie zweier Wertsetzungen als das wahre Thema des *Prosa-Lancelot* ausmachen zu können: »Man darf ... konstatieren, daß im Prosa-Lancelot zwei sich grundsätzlich ausschließende Weltanschauungen gegenüberstehen und daß die Art der Vorbereitung der einen und der Nachwirkung der anderen diese Konfrontation als beabsichtigt ausweist« (S. 23). Der Roman artikuliere die Krisenerfahrung des nachklassischen Rittertums in der nicht aufgehobenen Spannung zwischen emanzipatorischer Weltkultur und beharrlich verbindlicher Religiosität (S. 38 u.ö.). Er wäre in der Darstellung einer Krisenerfahrung um ihrer selbst willen von ganz außerordentlicher Modernität – zu modern, will mir scheinen, von einer im 13. Jahrhundert doch nur schwer vorstellbaren literarischen Autonomie. Wenn man die ›Aporie zweier Wertsetzungen‹ nicht doch für eine unfreiwillige und den Versuch einer Verbindung von höfischem Rittertum und Gralsmystik als gescheitert nehmen will, muß diese Aporie überprüft und muß das Erscheinungsbild Lancelots und seiner Liebe im eigentlichen *Lancelot* neu überdacht werden.

Die Relativierung der Wertvorstellungen feudalhöfischen Rittertums in der *Gralssuche* folgt aus der Spiritualisierung der Gralsthematik. Anders als bei Chrestien und wohl im bewußten Widerspruch zu ihm ist sie (nach dem Vorgang Roberts von Boron[16]) unmißverständlich

---

15 Vgl. z.B. Ferdinand Lot, *Étude sur le Lancelot en Prose* (Paris 1918; 2. erw. Aufl. 1954), S. 409 f.; zuletzt C. B. Caples, S. 201. Gegen dualistische Züge im *Prosa-Lancelot* spricht sich Alexandre Micha aus: »Études sur le Lancelot en prose, II«, *Romania* 82 (1961), 357–378, S. 376 f.

16 Dazu Kurt Ruh, »Joachitische Spiritualität im Werke Roberts von Boron«, in

christlich-kirchlich artikuliert. Der Gral ist ein konkretes Sakralgefäß, nämlich Abendmahlskelch und Blutgefäß Christi, die Beendigung des Gralsabenteuers besteht in der unmittelbaren Schau der eucharistischen Transsubstantiation und – dem einen Auserwählten, dem vollkommenen Ritter Galaad vorbehalten – des göttlichen Mysteriums selbst.[17] In ihr und in ihm erfüllt sich die Geschichte des Rittertums, die als Heilsgeschichte entworfen ist. Ihre Anfänge liegen im Alten Testament, ihr Ziel ist die Auffindung des Grals. Die im eigentlichen *Lancelot* dargestellte Phase dieser Geschichte ist von Erlösungserwartung gekennzeichnet:[18]

> ›wir han alle wol vernůmmen das alle die von der Großen Brytanien des alle tag wartende sind, das der kum der alles das wunder und alle die abenture die da im lande geschehent zu ende bringen soll.‹ (I 92,29–31)

Der ritterliche Messias, der hier erwartet wird, ist nach Meinung der Artusritter Lancelot, in Wahrheit ist es sein Sohn Galaad. Seine Vollkommenheit besteht in der Verbindung der Qualitäten eines perfekten Ritters mit der makellosen Reinheit des Herzens.[19] Sie erwächst einer genealogischen Konstellation, die ihn vor anderen auszeichnet: er entstammt der Vereinigung Lancelots mit einer Jungfrau aus dem Gralsgeschlecht, und in Lancelot begegnen sich bereits der Stamm Davids, des ersten Ritters aus dem Alten Testament, und eine Seitenlinie aus dem Geschlecht Josefs von Arimathia, des ersten Ritters des Neuen.[20] Die Verlängerung des Stammes David über Christus hinaus, die durch einen prophetischen Traum Salomos abgesichert wird (*Queste* 221,3 ff.), macht Galaad zu einer Christus ähnlichen Erlösergestalt.[21]

Diese Konstruktion bestimmt Aufgaben und Erscheinungsbild des rechten Ritters als die eines *miles dei*. Als solcher ist er auch im eigentlichen *Lancelot* präsent, nicht nur prospektiv in den Vorausdeutungen auf die Gralssuche und retrospektiv in Rückwendungen zur Vorgeschichte des Grals, sondern auch im Umkreis des Artusrittertums selbst. Am deutlichsten wohl in der berühmten, für die Theorie des Rittertums folgen-

---

Typologia litterarum: Festschrift für Max Wehrli, hg. v. Stefan Sonderegger (Zürich/Freiburg i. Br. 1969), 167–196, bes. S. 194 ff.

17 Ruh, »Gralsheld«, S. 257 f.

18 Ruberg, *Raum*, S. 127 f.

19 Ruberg, Rezension Voss, S. 175; über Lancelots Herz s. unten. Zur Herz-Metaphorik vgl. auch Horst Koch, *Studien zur epischen Struktur des Lancelot-Prosaromans* (Diss. Köln 1965), S. 37–39.

20 Zur Genealogie vgl. Ruberg, *Raum*, S. 126 f.

21 Ruberg, Rezension Voss, S. 177 f., im Anschluß an Ruh, »Gralsheld«, S. 256 und 262.

reichen[22] Ritterlehre, mit der die Dame vom See den achtzehnjährigen Lancelot in die Welt entläßt. Darin ist »die schrifft« (I 121,3 u.ö.) und nicht wie bei Chrestien (und im *Moriz von Craûn*) die Antike Grundlage des »heiligen orden von der ritterschafft« (124,8). Johann Hyrcan und Judas Makkabäus, sein Bruder Simon und König David sind die vorbildlichen Repräsentanten dieser Ritterschaft »in der alten ee«, Josef von Arimathia und seine Nachkommen in der neuen (123,16–29). Ihre Aufgabe ist der Schutz des Glaubens und der Kirche. Sie müssen »alweg fechten umb den glauben zu stercken und die ee wiedder die philistin und wiedder die ungleubigen lút« (ebd. 13–14):

> Ritterschafft wart gemacht betalliclichen umb die heiligen kirchen zu beschutten und zu beschirmen und darzu zu helffen mit libe und mit gut, wann sie sich nit gerechen mag mit arg, noch mit schwerten fechten mag noch mit wapen.   (120,33–36)

Eine Allegorese der ritterlichen Rüstung nach ihrer »bezeichnung« (121,6) bekräftigt: *schilt, halßberg, helm, glene, schwert* und *roß* sind Zeichen der Verpflichtung zum Schutz der Kirche und ihrer Diener vor Gottes Feinden, den geistlichen, die nicht glauben wollen, und den weltlichen, die rauben und stehlen: »Alsus ist des ritters ampt geistlich und fleischlich zu gottes dienst gemacht« (122,19).

Dieser geistlichen Orientierung korrespondiert das Auftreten ehemals weltlich bewährter Ritter im geistlichen Habit. Einer von ihnen, der »auch zur welt ein gut ritter gewesen und was zu gott vil beßer ritter worden« (I 43,3–4), ist berufen, dem König seine Versäumnisse als Lehnsherr vorzuhalten: es ist eine ritterlich-geistliche Instanz, die über die weltlichen Pflichten des König Artus urteilt. Ein anderer, »der ein edel man was und ußermaßen gut ritter« (I 402,3–4), greift wieder zu den Waffen, als sein Sohn belagert wird und tatkräftiger Hilfe bedarf. Der Angreifer, so wird argumentiert, handelte »als böse als ein heiden, wann er cristen solt syn und uncristlichen thete. ›Darumb‹, sprach er [d.i. der Mönch], ›wil ich uff sie farn als gern und mym sûn helffen, das er sin lant und sin lút behalte, als ich uber mere wolt farn off die heiden‹« (402,19–22). »Da reit er also«, schließt die Episode, »mit sinen geistlichen cleidern mit sym sûne« (402,22–23): der ideale Ritter des *Prosa-Lancelot* denkt und handelt als Kreuzritter, und der Geist des Kreuzzugs spricht aus den zahllosen Kampfschilderungen, die sich näher

---

22 Elspeth Kennedy, »Social and Political Ideas in the French Prose *Lancelot*«, *Medium Aevum* 26 (1957), 90–106.

zu denen der *chanson de geste* stellen als zu den fein ritualisierten Turnierübungen des höfischen Romans.[23] Kreuzfahrtstimmung evoziert der
Aufbruch der Artusrunde zur Gralssuche,[24] und Galaads weißer Schild
mit dem roten Kreuz ist der Schild der Kreuzfahrer, sein Schwert das
Schwert des alttestamentarischen Gottesstreiters David.

Dadurch, daß die *begeben ritter* durchweg ehemalige Artusritter sind,[25]
wird das am Artushof gültige höfische Ideal, so anziehend und werthaltig es sich selber erscheint, relativiert. Das Versagen der Artusritter
bei der Gralssuche kommt im Grund nur für sie selbst überraschend.

Lancelot nimmt in diesem Prozeß der Ablösung einer Wertordnung
durch eine sie überbietende neue eine vermittelnde Zwischenstellung
ein. In den Augen der Artuswelt ist er, wie unermüdlich betont wird,
in exemplarischer Weise vollkommen. »So enwart nie man geborn der
frauwen und rittern als wol freud kund machen als er kunde«, heißt es
schon bei der Beschreibung des Kindes (I 35,35–36), und Gawan hängt
seinen Schild allen Rittern zum Vorbild auf, »das alle ... exempel daran
nemen sollent« (II 659,26–27; vgl. 276,25 ff.). Lancelot besiegt, wenn
er nicht gerade wegen Liebeskummer in Gedanken ist, die Ritter der
Tafelrunde und Artus' mächtigste Gegner, deren der König allein nicht
Herr würde; nicht er bittet, wie es die Regel ist, um Aufnahme in die
Tafelrunde, sondern Artus und Ginover bitten ihn. Artus ist bereit,
sein Reich mit ihm zu teilen, und Ginovers Liebe ist ja nichts anderes als
das Gütesiegel für den besten und würdigsten Ritter in dieser Artuswelt (vgl. I 588,5 ff.). Konflikte mit dem Hof entstehen aus ihr erst im
Schlußteil des Romans in einer veränderten geschichtlichen Situation.

Andererseits ist das Bild Lancelots durchaus nicht frei von Trübungen,
welche die Gebrechlichkeit seiner Vollkommenheit ahnen lassen, nicht
nur im Zusammenhang mit der Ginover-Liebe, die in bedrohliche und
groteske Situationen führt, sondern auch im Bereich ritterlichen Handelns. Als beispielhaft für manche anderen Szenen der Demütigung[26]
kann ein beiläufig erzählter Zwischenfall bei einer Begegnung mit dem
Hof gelten. Es ist Pfingsten, die Artusritter versammeln sich in Camelot,
um den fünfzigsten Geburtstag ihres Königs mit einem großen Turnier
zu feiern. Nur Lancelot fehlt noch und wird sehnlichst erwartet. Als er

---

[23] Vgl. Soudek, Diss., S. 157 f. und 206.
[24] Ruh, »Gralsheld«, S. 246 f.
[25] Weitere Belege bei Ruberg, *Raum*, S. 83.
[26] Belege für Demütigungen Lancelots im Zusammenhang mit ritterlichen Unternehmungen bei Voss, S. 66 f.

endlich naht, reitet Artus ihm mit all seinen Rittern entgegen. Man beginnt zu »jostieren« (II 669,18), Gawan greift den heranreitenden Lancelot an. Aber weil er die Stoßkraft seiner Lanze unterschätzt, Lancelots Roß ermüdet ist und Lancelot selbst, »mit den wapen uberladen«, »sich nit (hůt) vor dem fall« (669,28), kommt der Ankömmling schmählich unter sein eigenes Pferd zu liegen, »so das er keyn macht hett me off zu stan« (670,3). Die feierliche Einholung endet mit einem von niemand gewollten Desaster.

Relativiert wird der Rang Lancelots auch schon vor der *Gralssuche* in den Vorausdeutungen auf Galaad. Galaad und nicht Lancelot nimmt schließlich den hundertfünfzigsten Sitz an der Tafelrunde ein (*Queste* 8,9 ff.) und leitet mit deren Vollendung zur Gralsphase über.

Lancelot, dessen eigentlicher Name Galaad ist (I 1,7 u.ö.), steht zu seinem Sohn in der Position eines Vorläufers.[27] Am Johannestag wurde er zum Ritter geschlagen (I 125,35), zum Vorläufer Johannes wird er ausdrücklich in Beziehung gebracht:

> ›Ich wil [erklärt ihm die Dame vom See], das ir an Sant Johans tag ritter werden. Und got, der von der magt Sancta Maria geborn wart durch syn volck zu erlösen, und also gewerlich als Sant Johans verdienet mit syner arbeit den höchsten lone den ye keyn heilig verdienet; also gewerlich muß gott geben das ir die gnad mußent gewinnen und die gabe, synenthalben alle die ritter zu uberhöhenne die nů leben, mit hoher ritterschafft und mit hubscheit und mit allerhand gut.‹ (I 124,29–34)

Es ist ein Verhältnis typologischer Überbietung.[28] In den Visionen, die auf den Gralshelden vorausdeuten, erscheint Lancelot unter dem Bild

---

27 Ruberg, *Raum*, S. 162 f.; Ruh, »Gralsheld«, S. 248 f.
28 Daran möchte ich auch nach Kenntnis des in vieler Hinsicht klärenden Vortrags von Werner Schröder über »Typologie-Begriff und Typologie-Verständnis in der mediävistischen Literaturwissenschaft«, oben S. 64–85, und daraufhin erneuter Lektüre der Dissertation von Hartmut Hoefer, *Typologie im Mittelalter*, Göppinger Arbeiten zur Germanistik, 54 (Göppingen 1971) festhalten, die grundsätzliche Zweifel an der Existenz von Typologie in außerbiblischen Texten äußern. Der *Prosa-Lancelot* erfüllt sämtliche dort genannten Bedingungen für einen typologisch zu deutenden Sachverhalt mit der einen Einschränkung, daß die typologische Beziehung nicht als solche benannt wird. Aber gerade diese Forderung (»Eine unausgesprochene Evidenz [des typologischen Bezuges] gibt es in der Typologie des Mittelalters nicht. Ihre Eindeutigkeit muß sprachlich vermittelt werden; und das geschieht auch: fehlt das sprachliche Signal, kann man füglich nicht von Typologie reden«, Hoefer, S. 198) gilt so ausschließlich doch nur für exegetische Texte, nicht aber für sämtliche von den Exegeten typologisch gedeuteten Bibelstellen. Der *Prosa-Lancelot* (oder ggf. andere nichtbiblische Texte) befindet sich aber, wenn für ihn vom Interpreten Typologie behauptet wird, in der Position der Bibel und nicht

des Leoparden, Galaad unter dem des mächtigeren Löwen (I 504,8 ff.[29]). Lancelot wird mit achtzehn Jahren zum Ritter geschlagen, Galaad (von seinem Vater) als Sechzehnjähriger. Wie Lancelot sein Schwert von der höfisch ausgezeichneten Ginover erhielt, so erhält Galaad das seine von der heilsgeschichtlich ausgezeichneten Schwester Percevals (*Queste* 227–28). Lancelot genügt seiner den Artusrittern überlegenen Stellung, indem er einen Teil der Erlösungsabenteuer zu vollbringen vermag, alle übrigen aber sind wie die Gralsaventiure Galaad vorbehalten.[30] Zweimal fordern die Bedingungen die Mitwirkung Lancelots *und* Galaads. Das eine Mal sind zwei Särge zu heben, in denen Nachfahren Josefs von Arimathia ruhen, sein Sohn Galaas und sein Neffe Symeu. Den Sarg des Königs Galaas hebt Lancelot ohne sonderliche Anstrengung (I 615 ff.). Derjenige Symeus aber ist von Flammen umgeben, die erst Galaad durchschreiten wird (*Queste* 264,3 ff.). In der zweiten Episode (II 521 ff.) ist der Kopf von Lancelots ermordetem Großvater aus einer kochend heißen Quelle zu bergen und mit dem Rumpf zur Ruhe zu betten. Das gelingt Lancelot zwar, aber die Hitze der Quelle, Sinnbild hitziger Sinnenlust wie die Flammen an Symeus Grab, wird erst Galaad löschen (*Queste* 263,27 ff.).

Mit diesen Doppelaventiuren ist mehr geleistet als die pragmatische Verknüpfung von *Lancelot* und *Gralssuche*. In ihnen manifestieren sich der Rang und die Begrenzung von Lancelots Erlöserfunktion. Mit der Bergung Galaas' zeigt er sich zur Befreiung gefangener Artusritter qualifiziert, die Bergung seines Großvaters ist die größte einem Ritter seiner Zeit überhaupt mögliche Tat – die Heilung der Wunden Symeus, der mit ihnen für seine Sünden büßt, und die Tilgung der Zeichen, die Gott nach dem Mord geschehen ließ, ist ihm nicht gegeben. Manifest wird aber auch die *differentia specifica*, die ihn vom wahren Erlöser trennt: es ist, wie die zur Deutung der geheimnisvollen Erscheinungen berufenen Eremiten ihn wissen lassen, »die hicz böser gelúst« (I 617,1; vgl. schon I 503 ff.): »›ir sint unreyn und unkusch und hant uwer jugend gehandelt in unkuscheit‹« (II 531,7). Galaad läßt diese »hicz« nicht in sein Herz, er bleibt »reyn jungfrauw ... als lang er lebt« (II 531,6). Die »hicz böser gelúst« ist natürlich die Liebe zu Ginover, die nicht

---

in der des Exegeten, der erst das typologische Verhältnis sprachlich signalisieren müßte. – Zu den Grenzen der Anwendbarkeit des Typologie-Begriffs auf den *Prosa-Lancelot* vgl. im übrigen Ruberg, Rezension Voss, S. 176 ff.

[29] Weitere Belege bei Voss, S. 15, Anm. 57.

[30] Vgl. Ruberg, »Suche«, S. 124, und *Raum*, S. 127 f.

keusch bleibt wie das Verhältnis Galaads zu Percevals Schwester, sondern auf Vereinigung zielt. Diese Liebe wird nicht nur und nicht erst im
Urteil der beiden Eremiten problematisiert. Hinweise auf die Bedenk-
lichkeit des Phänomens Minne begleiten das Geschehen des Romans von
Anfang an. Ihre bedrohliche Gewalt veranlaßt den klugen König Claudas zu vorsichtigem Verzicht: »›Ich mynnet vil gern von steter mynne,
wann das myn hercz so sere uberladen wurde das ich must sterben‹«
(I 27,8–9). Lancelots Herz ist stark genug, doch stört eben dies seine
sonst makellose äußere Erscheinung: seine Brust ist überproportioniert,
»das missestunt im allermeist an sim libe« (I 35,21–22). Ginover freilich lobt gerade diese Disharmonie: »›Wer ich gott‹, sprach sie, ›so hett
ich Lanceloten wedder mynner noch me gemacht dann er ist‹« (ebd.
28–29).
Wer einmal in den Bann dieser Minne geraten ist, ist aufs schwerste
gefährdet. Selbst Artus unterliegt ihr, gerät in schmähliche Gefangen-
schaft (I 461,5 ff.) und entfremdet sich (in der Episode mit der Falschen
Ginover, I 532 ff.) seinem ganzen Hofe. Durch die Reaktion der von
ihr Betroffenen erhält sie etwas Vorhöfisch-Zwanghaftes, so daß sich
das Bild der Frau Venus mit ihren Pfeilen einstellen kann.[31] Venus trifft
eine Jungfrau beim Anblick Lancelots »so krefftiglichen das sie [näm-
lich die Jungfrau] sichselber sere erschrackt« (II 238,12–13), bleich wird
und sich dieser Gefühle zu erwehren versucht. Das gelingt nicht, sie wird
sterbenskrank; und da sie die einzige ist, die über ein Mittel verfügt,
den vergifet darniederliegenden Lancelot zu heilen, gerät auch er in
Bedrängnis. Die Jungfrau beklagt, »das er sichselber und ander durch
syner schonheyt willen döt, und we im das er ye so schön wart«
(249,10–11). Lancelot muß zwischen seiner Genesung und der Treue zu
Ginover wählen, und nur weil sein Tod die Artuskönigin genauso treffen würde wie seine Untreue, verspricht er der Jungfrau seine Liebe.
Nach der Heilung bewegt er sie dann zum Verzicht. Sie hat ihn fortan
»›in ander maß lieb … dann frauwen manne pflegen zu han‹«,

> ›wann lieb von frauwen und mannen kömpt gemeynlich von begirlichkeit
> des fleischs, da durch die jungfreuwlichkeit zurstört wird. Das ist myn
> meynung nit, sunder ich wil uch in sölchen maßen lieb han das ich umb
> uwernt willen myn jûngfreuwelicheyt so lang ich leb behalten wille.‹
> (II 255,18–22)

---

31 II 238,12. Soweit Kluges Apparat zur Stelle und die Ausgabe Sommers (s. u.
Anm. 33) ein Urteil zulassen, handelt es sich um einen Zusatz der deutschen Fassung (Sommer V 71, 33–34).

So wird der drohende Konflikt durch den Entschluß abgewendet, geistliche Minne an die Stelle der fleischlichen zu setzen. Die Begegnung
Lancelots mit dieser Jungfrau fällt auf den Johannestag, an dem auch
seine Liebe zu Ginover begann, so daß möglicherweise jene als Kontra-
fakt zu dieser gedacht ist. Die Ginover-Minne beschwört immer aufs
neue Konflikte herauf. Instabilität gehört zu ihrem Wesen,[32] die Tiefe
des Falls antwortet der Höhe ihres vergänglichen Glücks: nachdem
Lancelot wegen des unfreiwilligen Treuebruchs mit der Gralstochter
verstoßen ist,

> da gedacht im der großen freuden die im die konigin zu andern zyten ge-
> macht hett und das er yczo arbeyt, verleugniß und unwillen haben must ...
> Und das er in der welt am meysten solt gelobet syn gewest, des must er nů
> inn sennlichem ungluck syn, ›und muß nu den andern teyl myns lebens in
> truren und weynen verschließen.‹   (II 781,15–23)

Daß die mit der Liebe einhergehende, ihre anspornende Kraft ins genaue Gegenteil verkehrende Gedankenverlorenheit Lancelots nicht mit
psychologisierenden Hinweisen auf Trennungsschmerz und Liebessehn-
sucht erklärt und erledigt werden kann, weiß die Dame vom See, die
Ginover den wahren Grund für seine »affenheit« nennt: »›Er důt da
mit nit wißlich, das weiß ich wol, wann werlich sunde wúrt dick mit
affenheit vollebracht, anders enmöcht der súnde so viel nit sin‹« (I 471,
3–5) – es ist die Sündhaftigkeit weltlicher Liebe, die »affenheit« zur
Voraussetzung und zur Folge hat. Im französischen Text heißt es weiter: »›Mais moult a grant raison de sa folie que raison i troeue & honor.
& se vous folie poes trouer en vos amors, ceste folie est a honerer sor
toutes autres. Car vous ames le seignor & la flor de tot cest monde.‹«[33]
Ginovers Liebe wird vom geistlichen Standpunkt verurteilt, vom höfischen her scheint sie gerechtfertigt. Auch Ginover selbst äußert sich so.
Sie deutet das Intermezzo mit der Falschen Ginover, die ihr den Platz
an der Seite des Königs so erfolgreich streitig macht, daß Artus auch
nach der Aufklärung des Schwindels bei der Falschen bleibt, als Strafe
Gottes für ihren Ehebruch mit Lancelot: »›Vil lieber frunt‹, sprach sie
zu Lancelot, ›ir seht wol das es mir uneben get ... wann ich umb unsern
herren gott verwurckt han mit mym libe‹« (I 534,17–19). Höfisch gesehen weiß sie sich im Recht:

---

[32] Ruberg, *Raum*, S. 179 f.
[33] *The Vulgate Version of the Arthurian Romances*, hg. v. H. Oskar Sommer, 7 Bde.
und Index, Carnegie Institution of Washington Publication, 74 (Washington 1908
bis 1916), III 418, 34–37.

›Mir verwißet auch keyn húbsch man nymer das ich mit uch gethan han,
wuste er als wol die ding wie sie herre sint komen, als sie myn herre weiß:
das mich der starcken mynne krafft darzu bracht das ich uwern willen thun
must, die ir mir mit gewalt in myn hercz sandtet mit großem dienst den ir
mir und myme herren dick datend‹ –

aber dennoch glaubt sie, »›das mich unser herre got plage und das er wil
das ich die súnde laß, und das ich myn furter hút‹« (I 534,24–31).[34]
Es kann kein Zweifel sein, daß die höfische Minne aus der gleichen Perspektive, die das weltliche Rittertum relativiert, verurteilt wird. Aber
während diesem Rittertum als der Basis der *militia dei* und der Vorstufe
des geistlichen ein begrenzter Eigenwert zugestanden bleibt,[35] erweist
sich die Minne als diejenige Macht, die den Weg zur geistlichen Vollkommenheit verstellt. Der Widerspruch zwischen dieser negativen Beurteilung und der positiven Kraft, die Lancelot der Minne für seine
höfischen Erfolge beimißt, löst sich erst in der *Gralssuche*, als Lancelot
erfährt, daß seine Taten in Wahrheit auf ursprünglich guten, durch die
Sünde der Minne nicht vollständig zerstörten Anlagen beruhen:

> ›Und noch dann so hett unser hergot als viel gutes in dich gethan und als
> vil volkomenheit das es nit mocht syn, es múst ettlicher maß da verliben.
> Und von dem das dir gott verließ hastu gethan die grost biederbkeit in
> fremden landen, da von alle die welt sagt.‹[36]

Hätte er all seine Tugenden bewahrt, Jungfräulichkeit, Demut, Geduld, Gerechtigkeit und Nächstenliebe,[37] er wäre nicht blind gewesen,
sondern hätte das Wunder des Grals schauen dürfen.
Diese nachträgliche Aufklärung eines vorher von den Personen der
Handlung anders bewerteten Sachverhalts ist nicht ganz so erstaunlich,
wie es auf den ersten Blick scheinen möchte. Nachträgliche Umdeutung
ist für das Erzählgefüge des *Prosa-Lancelot* in ähnlicher Weise konsti-

---

[34] Auch hier formuliert die französische Fassung den Gegensatz von höfischer und
geistlicher Bewertung der Minne prägnanter: »... nostre sire ne garde mie a la
corteysie del monde. kar cil qui est buens al monde est mals a dieu« (Sommer IV 72,
Anm. 1).

[35] Hierzu besonders Ruberg, »Suche«, S. 153 f. – Auch Galaad bewährt sich in ritterlichen Zweikämpfen.

[36] Hs. P, fol. 267ʳ, zitiert nach Voss, S. 23. In der Vorlage lautet die Stelle: »Et ne-
porec Nostre Sires avoit mis tant de bien en toi qu'il ne pooit estre que de cele
grant plenté n'i eust aucune chose de remanant. De cel remanant que Diex te lessa
as tu fetes les granz proesces par les estranges terres, dont toz li monz parole«
(*Queste* 126, 23–27).

[37] »virginité ... humilité ... souffrance ... droiture ... charité« (*Queste* 123,
26–125,1).

tutiv wie das System der Vorausdeutungen.[38] Rätselhaft scheinende Be-
gebenheiten werden durch die spätere Aufhellung ihrer Bedingungen
erklärt, Zusammenhänge zwischen getrennt berichteten Situationen hergestellt, die Bedeutung einzelner Abenteuer im Rückblick verändert –
so wenn in dem erinnernden Gespräch, in dem Ginover Lancelot zum
Geständnis seiner Liebe führt, seine Erfolge nicht länger als Taten im
Dienste des Artushofs erscheinen, sondern in ihrer Bedeutung als Minnedienst erkannt werden. Auch die Erklärung der »affenheit« Lancelots
durch die Dame vom See berichtigt deren bis dahin geltende Deutung.
Täuschung und Illusion regieren im *Prosa-Lancelot* auf den verschiedensten Wahrnehmungsebenen, angefangen bei der Vorspiegelung des
Sees, in dem Lancelot seine Jugend verbringt und der doch in Wahrheit
»nit anders dann gauckelig« ist (I 21,9), bis zu den immer neuen Irr-
tümern über die Identität einander begegnender Ritter.[39] Lancelot läßt
sich über die Motive von Schutzflehenden täuschen und verhilft der falschen Sache zum Sieg, Artus erliegt den Zauberkünsten Gartissies und
den Vorspiegelungen der Falschen Ginover; er und der ganze Hof täuschen sich über den wahren Charakter der Zuneigung Ginovers zu
Lancelot. Auch deren Liebe ist von Täuschung und Selbsttäuschung bestimmt, sie wird das Opfer von Manipulationen der eifersüchtigen Zau-
berin Morgane. Die Unfähigkeit der Liebenden, sich vor Irrtum und
Irreführung zu schützen, entspricht ihrem Grundirrtum in der Bewertung dieser Liebe, der Ginover Dauer verleihen zu können meint und
der Lancelot eben zu Unrecht jene positive Kraft zuschreibt, die sie nur
aus höfischer Perspektive besitzt. Schließlich bedient sich die göttliche
Vorsehung selbst des Mittels der Täuschung und der Täuschbarkeit
Lancelotts, um ihn den Gralshelden zeugen zu lassen.
Die Wahrheit hinter den Erscheinungen dieser Welt tritt erst mit der
Ankunft Galaads ganz ans Licht, nur Träume, Visionen, Inschriften und
die Belehrungen der berufenen Eremiten deuteten auf sie voraus. Zweimal begegnet Lancelot einem geheimnisvollen, von vier[40] Löwen be-

---

38 Belege für »Vorausdeutungen und Vorausteuerung« bei Ruberg, *Raum*, S. 139–144;
   zu den Rückwendungen ebd. S. 136–138.
39 Dazu Harms, *Kampf*, S. 179 ff.; Harms spricht von der »Ungewißheit«, dem »Zu-
   stand des noch Unerkannten«, »die immer wieder die Situation der Handlung bestimmen« (S. 179). Es gehört zu den Erzählprinzipien des Romans, »viele Situationen des Scheins und des Irreführens vor die Situationen des rechten Erkennens
   zu legen« (*Homo viator*, S. 256).
40 Der mhd. Text spricht von »sehs lewen« (II 535,14 und 587,2); die Stelle ist offensichtlich bereits in der Vorlage verderbt, vgl. Kluges Apparat zu beiden Stellen.

gleiteten weißen Hirsch (II 535,11 ff. und 586,25 ff.), dessen »warheit«
er vergeblich zu erfahren sucht. Sie ist »ein zeichen und ein mirackel,
das von den gnaden gottes kompt« (591,25) und erst Galaad sich entdecken wird: vor seinen Augen verwandeln sich der Hirsch in einen
strahlend schönen Mann, die Löwen in Adler, Löwe, Ochs und Jüng-
ling, es sind Christus und die vier Evangelisten. Niemand hat dies
Wunder vorher gesehen, niemand wird es mehr erblicken (*Queste*
234,10 ff.).
Galaads Ankunft beendet die Zeit der Dunkelheit und des Irrens, mit
ihm beginnt die Epoche der unverhüllten Wahrheit:

> ›Denn so wie der Irrtum und der Wahn flohen durch seine [= Christi] An-
> kunft und die Wahrheit sich nunmehr enthüllte, so seid Ihr (Galaad) von
> unserem Herrn aus allen anderen Rittern erwählt, um ausgeschickt zu wer-
> den in fremde Länder, die schlimmen Abenteuer zu bestehen und zu er-
> kennen, wie es zu diesen gekommen ist‹,

heißt es in der Belehrung über die Funktion, die ihm in der Heilsgeschichte des Rittertums zugedacht ist.[41] Offenbarung, Anschauung des
göttlichen Mysteriums von Angesicht zu Angesicht ist ja das Ziel dieser
Geschichte, die gesamte Gralssuche ist als »Sehnsucht nach Erkenntnis ...
zu verstehen«.[42] Das Problem Lancelots ist das Problem der Erkenntnis
von Wahrheit. Nachdem ihm – *nach* Galaads Erscheinen – Einsicht in
die wahren Bedingungen seiner Existenz gegeben ist, kann er abschwören, bereuen und büßen. So wird er gerettet, der Schluß des Romans
findet ihn als bußfertigen Einsiedler auf der Höhe eines Felsens,[43] von
wo aus seine Seele in den Himmel aufgenommen wird.
Es wäre zu prüfen, ob nicht auch die den Schlußteil, *König Artus' Tod*
beherrschende, mit den Worten Frappiers »willentliche« Blindheit[44]
der Artusritter, der eine fast ebenso willentliche Offenheit Lancelots in
seinem für kurze Zeit wiederaufgenommenen Liebesverhältnis zu
Ginover entspricht, von der Wahrheitsmanifestation der Gralsphase her

---

[41] Übersetzung Ruhs, »Gralsheld«, S. 247. Der Originaltext lautet: »Car tout ausi
come l'error et la folie s'en foï par la venue de lui et la verité fu lors aparanz et
manifestee, autresint vos a Nostre Sires esleu sor toz autres chevaliers por envoier
par les estranges terres por abatre les grevoses aventures et por fere conoistre co-
ment eles sont avenues« (*Queste* 38, 15–19).
[42] Ruberg, »Suche«, S. 148.
[43] Zur Signifikanz der Aufwärtsbewegung im *Prosa-Lancelot* vgl. Ruberg, *Raum*,
S. 51 f.
[44] Jean Frappier, »The Vulgate Cycle«, in *Arthurian Literature in the Middle Ages*,
hg. v. Roger Sherman Loomis, (Oxford 1959), 295–318, S. 311: »A wilful blindness leads the heroes to their perdition.«

zu deuten ist. Es ist die Blindheit nach der Offenbarung, sie führt mit
dramatischer Folgerichtigkeit in den Untergang. Im eigentlichen *Lancelot* ist sie in der Blindheit Artus' gegenüber Ginover und in der Blindheit Ginovers gegenüber den warnenden Vorzeichen angelegt – hätte
Ginover auf sie geachtet, »so wer der groß mortlich stryt underwegen
bliben, der syt was in dem schlechten zu Salebiere. Deshalben konig
Artus und die byderben lut sturben sunder ursach« (II 703,19–21).
Eine Überprüfung dieser Hypothese ist am deutschen Text erst möglich, wenn dessen abschließender dritter Band vorliegt. Im ganzen
stellt sich mir jedenfalls – mit Ruberg und Harms[45] – die Konzeption
des *Prosa-Lancelot* als einheitlich und nicht aporetisch dar. Sie ist bestimmt von dem entschlossenen Willen, dem autonomistischen Legiti-
mationsentwurf Chrestiens mit einem geistlich orientierten Ritterbild
mit deutlich restaurativen Zügen zu begegnen. Dem dient die Spiritualisierung des Gralsujets und die Darstellung der Geschichte des Rittertums als einer Heilsgeschichte, in der das höfische Rittertum seinen Platz
als Vorstufe vor dem ›wahren‹, dem geistlichen findet. Von ihm her
erhält es seine (begrenzte) Legitimation, und von ihm her wird es auch
möglich, das Rittertum (wieder) konkreten kirchlichen Interessen zu
verpflichten, wie sie die Ritterlehre und das Kreuzzugsmotiv erkennen
lassen. Verworfen wird nicht das weltlich-höfische Rittertum, sondern
die Blindheit derer, die seinen bedingten Status zu erkennen sich wei-
gern, und die höfische Minnedoktrin, aus der weltliches Rittertum seine
autonome Legitimation abzuleiten versucht hatte.[46]
Die Spiritualisierung des Gralsujets bedingte den Entwurf eines extrem
spiritualisierten Gralshelden, dessen (mit den Worten Kurt Ruhs)
»schlechthinnige Vollkommenheit« nicht nur der »menschlichen und
damit auch künstlerischen Wirkung ... nicht günstig zu sein« schien,[47]
sondern der in seiner Singularität auch nicht als Identifikationsfigur
taugte.[48] Diese Funktion fiel Lancelot zu, der sich zunächst als im höfischen Sinne vollkommener Ritter präsentiert, in dieser Vollkommenheit
fragwürdig wird und schließlich mit Gottes Gnade den Weg zur *militia
dei* findet. Es dürfte mit der literaturgeschichtlichen Stellung des Romans

---

[45] Vgl. die Anm. 7 genannten Rezensionen zu R. Voss.
[46] Zur Geschichte dieser Legitimationsversuche vgl. das Buch von Erich Köhler (s. o.,
    Anm. 13).
[47] »Gralsheld«, S. 262.
[48] Daß die »Annäherung an den Gral, indem sie nur einen kleinen Kreis Auserwählter
    und in ihrer letzten Tiefe einem einzigen vorbehalten ist«, »in Bereiche radikal
    ungesellschaftlicher Existenz führt«, bemerkt (mit anderen Folgerungen) Voss, S. 88.

zu erklären sein, daß bei der Realisierung dieser *vita sancti saecularis*[49] diejenigen Partien das Übergewicht behalten haben, die dem »Weltkind« Lancelot gewidmet sind.[50] Im Bewußtsein der Nachwelt ist er dadurch der große Liebende geblieben. Unsterblichkeit hat ihm am Ende gerade diejenige Qualität gebracht, der er um seiner unsterblichen Seele willen hatte abschwören müssen.

---

[49] Soudek, S. 183.
[50] Nach einer Formulierung von Harms, Rezension Voss, S. 163.

Ingeborg Glier

Diener zweier Herrinnen:
Zu Ulrichs von Lichtenstein *Frauendienst**

Ulrich von Lichtenstein, der steierische Adelige und Minnesänger, ist eine
der rätselhaftesten Figuren in der deutschen Literatur des 13. Jahrhunderts. Während von Gottfried von Straßburg, Wolfram von Eschenbach
und Hartmann von Aue keine Urkunde zeugt, und während uns Walther von der Vogelweide wie zufällig nur die Reiserechnung eines Pas-
sauer Bischofs historisch belegt, sind wir über Ulrich historisch-biogra-
phisch sehr vielseitig informiert. Doch diese Information stellt nun
ihrerseits mehr Probleme, als sie lösen hilft. Sie läßt sich vorerst in zwei
Gruppen gliedern: zahlreiche Urkunden und historische Nachrichten
auf der einen Seite, auf der anderen ein umfängliches literarisches Werk,
der *Frauendienst,* den Ulrich um 1255 abschließt und dem in Hand-
büchern und Literaturgeschichten immer wieder das zweifelhafte Eti-
kett der ersten deutschen Autobiographie angeheftet wurde.
Versuchen wir zunächst, wenigstens in großen Zügen, ein Bild des historisch bezeugten Ulrich von Lichtenstein zu entwerfen. Geboren wurde
er vermutlich um 1200. 1277 stiftet sein Sohn Otto der Johanneskapelle
in Seckau Glasfenster und Seelenmessen zum Gedächtnis seiner Eltern
Ulrich und Bertha. Ulrichs Todesjahr ist nur ungefähr auf 1275 oder
1276 zu datieren. In der deutschen Geschichte ist dies ein Zeitraum vol-
ler Wirren und tiefgreifender Veränderungen. Er ist charakterisiert
durch den Zerfall der staufischen Reichsmacht, das Interregnum und das
Erstarken der Territorialgewalten allenthalben. Ulrich nimmt an den

---

* Diesen Vortrag habe ich an den Universitäten in Ann Arbor, Cincinnati, Innsbruck,
München, Princeton, Tübingen und in Yale gehalten und erinnere mich dankbar
vieler Anregungen aus Diskussionen und Gesprächen. Er wurde seinerzeit als
›Rede‹ konzipiert und hat zwar manche Variationen durchlaufen, aber selbst für
den Druck konnte ich mich nicht dazu entschließen, ihn in eine ›Schreibe‹ zu verwandeln. Lediglich Anmerkungen und Stellenangaben wurden hinzugefügt. Ich
hoffe, auf das Thema in anderem Zusammenhang noch zurückzukommen.

kleineren und größeren politischen Auseinandersetzungen im Südosten des Reiches bis kurz vor seinem Tode regen Anteil. Kein Mann der ›großen‹, der Reichspolitik, doch in seinem Bereich scheint er es rasch zu Einfluß und Ansehen gebracht zu haben. 1241 z. B. urkundet er als *dapifer*, Truchseß der Steiermark, 1245 auch als Landesrichter in Vertretung des Herzogs. Mehrfach erscheint er in nächster Umgebung seines Landesherren, Herzog Friedrichs II. von Österreich. Nach dessen Tode, 1246 in der Schlacht gegen die Ungarn an der Leitha, laviert Ulrich offenbar recht geschickt zwischen böhmischen, babenbergischen und ungarischen Interessen an den Herzogtümern Österreich und Steiermark. Seit 1260 finden wir ihn ziemlich häufig in der Nähe des neuen Landesherren, König Ottokars von Böhmen. Dieser setzt ihn zwar 1268 nebst anderen steirischen Adeligen für etwa ein halbes Jahr ins Gefängnis. Allein das scheint das Verhältnis nur kurzfristig getrübt zu haben. Noch im hohen Alter amtiert Ulrich auch unter Ottokar als Marschall und Landesrichter der Steiermark.[1] Aus alledem können wir wohl auf eine politische Karriere schließen, die zwar nicht ohne Rückschläge und Zwielichtigkeiten ist, im ganzen aber recht zielstrebig und glanzvoll verläuft. Und noch zu Anfang des 14. Jahrhunderts setzt Ottokar von Steiermark seinem Landsmann Ulrich von Lichtenstein in der *Österreichischen Reimchronik* ein ehrendes, historisch-literarisches Denkmal:

Etlich herren tiwer wac　witzic unde menlich
des landes beswæren.　und volkomen an triwen
ich sag iu, wer si wæren:　was er, er lie sich riwen,
von Liehtenstein her Uolrich　swaz dem lande an lac.　(V. 1968–75)

Stellen wir daneben nun das Bild, das Ulrich in seinem *Frauendienst* zeichnet.[2] Dieses Werk – obschon in Strophen von vier Reimpaaren gegliedert – steht formal in der Tradition des höfischen Epos, enthält aber – im Unterschied zu dieser – die Lieder, den Leich und die Büchlein Ulrichs. Diese Mischung schon gibt Rätsel auf, mit denen wir uns später noch ausführlicher auseinandersetzen wollen. Wenn man einmal summarisch zusammenfaßt, so schildert der *Frauendienst* in der Ich-Form Ulrichs jahrelanges und beharrliches Bemühen um die Neigung zweier Damen der höfischen Gesellschaft. Der ersten dient er 13 Jahre (vgl. Leich), der zweiten, auf deren Ge-

---

1 Zu den historischen Angaben vgl. A. Schönbach, »Zu Ulrich von Lichtenstein«, *ZfdA* 26 (1882), 307–326. Ders., *AfdA* 29 (1904), 277 f. Ders., *ADB* 18 (1883), 620 ff. Weitere Urkunden bei U. Aarburg, »Ulrich von Lichtenstein, Autobiographie und Persönlichkeit«, Frankfurt 1966 (Magisterarbeit, masch.).
2 Zitiert nach: *Ulrich von Lichtenstein*. Mit Anmerkungen von Th. v. Karajan hg. v. K. Lachmann, Berlin 1841.

heiß und in deren Dienst er sein Buch verfaßt, wäre er bis zu diesem Zeitpunkt etwa 22 Jahre verbunden. Schärfere Konturen aber gewinnt nur sein Werben um die erste Dame und damit auch deren Bild. Sie erscheint als eine recht kapriziöse Figur, die ihren Verehrer durch strikte Abweisung, dazwischen immer wieder einmal halbes Entgegenkommen und ausgefallene Wünsche hinlänglich in Atem hält. Ulrich dient ihr in seiner frühesten Jugend schon als Page und gesteht, daß er es damals nicht lassen konnte, aus Liebe gelegentlich heimlich ihr Waschwasser zu trinken. Später, nachdem er zum Ritter geschlagen ist, kämpft er auf zahlreichen Turnieren für sie, dichtet und sendet ihr Lied um Lied – und erreicht, nach seiner Darstellung, selten mehr als allenfalls wohlwollende Kritik für seine Werke, hingegen dezidiertes, manchmal sogar schnippisches Abweisen seines Werbens. Doch Ulrich ist auch zu drastischeren Beweisen seiner Minne bereit. Weil der Dame sein *ungefuoge stênter munt* (22,10) mißfällt, unterzieht er sich tapfer einer Schönheitsoperation, der – wie er schreibt – eine seiner drei *lefsen* (Lippen) zum Opfer fällt. Und als ihm schließlich im Turnier ein Finger schwer verletzt wird, der nicht mehr so recht heilen will, läßt er ihn rigoros abhacken und sendet ihn, wie eine Reliquie gefaßt, mit einem gereimten Büchlein seiner Dame als Zeichen seiner unbezweifelbaren *triuwe*. Als die beiden Höhepunkte dieses ersten Minnedienstes schildert Ulrich jedoch die Venusfahrt und seinen Besuch bei der Dame, beide recht ausführlich.

Ulrich erzählt hier einmal, wie er nach einem Sankt-Georgs-Tag als Frau Venus verkleidet bei Mestre der Adria entsteigt und dann mehrere Wochen lang durch Friaul, Kärnten, Steiermark und Österreich bis nach Böhmen zieht, wobei die einzelnen Wegstationen jeweils genau angegeben werden. Ulrich trägt auf dieser Fahrt weiße Kleider und lange stattliche Zöpfe, nichtsdestotrotz erscheint er zugleich als unermüdlicher Kämpfer – wie auch als Zuschauer – zahlreicher Turniere, die er zum Teil recht eingehend und genau beschreibt. Überall wird Ulrich/Venus ehrenvoll empfangen, oft von der Menge staunend umdrängt; die Einwohner von Wien stehen bei seinem glanzvollen Einzug förmlich kopf. Und nicht ein Wort davon, daß irgendwer an dieser Fahrt etwa Anstoß genommen hätte. Der Hauptakzent der Schilderung liegt jedoch auf den Turnieren: jeder, der bei diesen Kämpfen auf Venus/Ulrich einen Speer versticht, erhält als Preis einen goldenen Ring, der auf die Dame seines Herzens als Schönheits- und Liebeszauber zugleich wirken soll. Die Bilanz, die Ulrich zu Ende seiner Reise durch seinen *kameraere* ziehen läßt (S. 291), ist überaus stattlich: 307 Speere hat er im ganzen selbst verstochen und 271 Ringe an seine Kampfpartner verteilt. Und so wird dieses alles nicht nur zu einer Dokumentation seiner eigenen Rittertüchtigkeit, sondern auch der von zahlreichen anderen Adeligen, die sehr oft namentlich genannt werden.

Zu dem Glanz der Venusfahrt mutet die Schilderung vom Besuch bei der Dame fast wie ein Kontrastbild an. Auf Geheiß seiner Angebeteten soll Ulrich als – Aussätziger verkleidet vor ihrer Burg erscheinen. Mit anderen, die wirklich vom Aussatz befallen sind, muß er milde Gaben teilen und dazu noch mancherlei drastische Unbill erdulden. Und noch in letzter Minute erscheint das Zusammentreffen gefährdet, denn die *linden hendelîn* der

Frauen scheinen das Leintuch, mit dem Ulrich zur Kemenate hinaufgezogen werden soll, aus eigener Kraft nicht bis ans Ziel seiner Wünsche zu bringen. Dreimal hängt er so, hilflos zwischen Himmel und Erde. Doch dann, ans Ziel gelangt, findet er oben nicht nur seine Dame und deren Vertraute, sondern noch weitere acht Frauen und bemerkt lakonisch: *mich dûht der vrowen dâ ze vil* (349,2). Nunmehr räumlich am Ziel, wird ihm aber sehr deutlich gemacht, daß er von seinem geforderten Ziel, der Liebesnacht, unendlich weit entfernt ist. Bitten, Drohungen, alles vergebens. Mit einer ziemlich schnöden List wird ihn die Dame wieder los, und Ulrich ist drauf und dran, sich aus schierer Verzweiflung zu ertränken, so erzählt er. Mit knapper Not und einer List kann ihn sein *geselle,* der ihn begleitet, noch retten. Wozu? – Zu neuem unbeirrbaren Dienst für seine Dame. Diese erscheint im weiteren Verlauf zwar etwas günstiger gestimmt, aber dann begeht sie, so erzählt er, eine nicht näher bezeichnete *missetât* (413,23). Ulrich kündigt ihr seinen Dienst auf, er singt Scheltlieder, die sie ärgern, und dann eine Reihe von *wânwîsen:* nur so zum Lobe höfischerer Damen und der Minne allgemein.

Doch bald erwählt sich Ulrich eine neue Dame, die weniger abweisend erscheint als die erste. Ihr Bild gewinnt aber gerade darüber keine schärferen Konturen. Ihr zu Ehren zieht Ulrich noch einmal, diesmal als König Artus, auf eine große Turnierfahrt, die er wiederum recht eingehend schildert. Und er singt in diesem zweiten Minnedienst eine Reihe von Liedern, deren Grundtenor – ganz im Gegensatz zum ersten – Freude und Erfülltheit ist. Doch die Erzählung verliert mehr und mehr an Eigengewicht; nur zwei konkretere Ereignisse – der Tod Friedrichs II. und Ulrichs Gefangennahme durch zwei seiner Lehensleute – werden etwas ausführlicher berichtet. Sonst gewinnen Zeitklagen und mehr noch Reflexionen, welche die Liedinhalte und -leitworte nur begleiten oder wiederholen, immer breiteren Raum. Erst als auch noch das letzte Lied dergestalt kommentiert ist, schließt Ulrich sein Buch ab.

Es erscheint fast überflüssig zu betonen, daß diese beiden Bilder, das objektiv-historische und das selbsterzählte, vermeintlich autobiographische, sich nicht decken. Zwischen ihnen ist auch nur ein schmaler historisch gesicherter Bezug herzustellen: die Ungarnschlacht an der Leitha, in der Herzog Friedrich II. fällt. Ihr folgen im *Frauendienst* allgemeine Zeitklagen, aber kein Wort von den politischen Konsequenzen, die sie auslöst. Weitere ›objektiv‹ autobiographie-verdächtige Ereignisse, wie Ulrichs Schwertleite und seine Gefangennahme, bezeugt allein der *Frauendienst.* Nun könnte man meinen, daß diese verschiedenen Bilder Ulrichs von Lichtenstein, eben weil sie sich so wenig decken, einander geradezu mustergültig ergänzen. Dann böte sich hier eine für das deutsche Mittelalter einzigartige Gelegenheit, die großen Umrisse einer öffentlich politischen Existenz zumindest für ein paar Jahrzehnte mit ›Privatleben‹

gleichsam aufzufüllen.[3] So verlockend das klingt, es ist aus den verschiedensten Gründen in dieser Weise nicht möglich.

Ein erster, noch relativ oberflächlicher Einwand gegen ein solches Verfahren gründet – mit allen hermeneutischen Schwierigkeiten – auf der historischen Wahrscheinlichkeit. Man muß deshalb noch nicht, wie Wilhelm Scherer, den *Frauendienst* naiv biographisch verstehen und dem späten 19. Jahrhundert gemäß kommentieren: »Und alle diese Tollheiten begeht ein verheirateter Mann und Vater von mehreren Kindern.«[4] Aber nicht der mögliche Konflikt von Ehe und Minnedienst, der überdies für den dichtenden Ulrich keiner ist (vgl. 318,21 ff.), steht hier zur Debatte, sondern die Frage, ob ein Minneleben, wie Ulrich es selbst erzählt, mit einer politischen Karriere, wie historisch dokumentiert, zu vereinen ist. Selbst wenn wir der Gesellschaft, in der Ulrich lebte, andere Toleranzgrenzen zugestehen müssen, als die unsere besitzt, bleibt ein schwer zu lösender Widerspruch zwischen dem minnebesessenen Diener zweier Herrinnen und dem geachteten, überlegten Politiker. Dieser Widerspruch ist weder dadurch aufzuheben, daß man, wie versucht wurde, die Venus- und die Artusfahrt politisch motiviert,[5] noch durch den Hinweis, schließlich hätten Ulrichs Zeitgenossen nichts dabei gefunden und bereitwillig mitgespielt.[6] Wenig scheint auch damit gewonnen, den *Frauendienst* zur reinen Erfindung zu erklären. Dann belastet er zwar die biographischen Fragen nicht mehr, aber es bleibt gerade das Problem, warum dennoch der Anschein der autobiographischen Historie so deutlich angestrebt wird.

Ein zweiter, schwerer wiegender Einwand dagegen, Ulrichs Biographie einfach aus historischen Nachrichten und *Frauendienst* zusammenzusetzen, liegt in der verschiedenen Art ihrer Dokumentation. Eine Reihe von Urkunden und ein literarisches Werk, ihr Aussagewert ist nicht so ohne weiteres gleichzusetzen. Die Urkunden, fragmentarische Wirklichkeit, und der Wahrheitsanspruch, den Ulrich verschiedentlich im

---

3 So u. a. F. Neumann, »Ulrich von Lichtensteins Frauendienst: Eine Untersuchung über das Verhältnis von Dichtung und Leben«, *Zs. f. Deutschk.* 40 (1926), 373–386, bes. 382.

4 *Geschichte der Deutschen Litteratur*, Berlin [8]1899, S. 211.

5 So u. a. in: *Ulrich von Lichtenstein: Narr im hohen Dienst*, nach der Textausgabe von K. Lachmann ausgewählt, übertragen und eingeleitet von W. Zitzenbacher, Graz/Wien 1958, S. 20 f., 29 f.

6 So etwa O. Höfler, »Ulrichs von Liechtenstein Venusfahrt und Artusfahrt«, in: *Festschrift Panzer*, Heidelberg 1950, S. 131–152, bes. 131 ff. (hier begründet aus ›verritterten‹ Brauchtumszusammenhängen).

Frauendienst erhebt,[7] sie liegen auf zwei verschiedenen Ebenen. Die Urkunde gibt mehr oder minder zufällig Fakten an die Hand, aus denen – wie auch immer – historische Zusammenhänge zu rekonstruieren sind. Ein literarisches Werk, wie der *Frauendienst,* hat in diesem Sinne allenfalls mittelbaren Quellenwert, weil es, wenn überhaupt Fakten, diese bereits stilisiert und interpretiert enthält. Diese literarischen Zusammenhänge sind aber zum großen Teil weder einigermaßen objektiv überprüfbar, noch aufs rein Faktische zurückzuführen. Deshalb scheint es müßig zu fragen, ob es denn so, wie es Ulrich schildert, »wirklich gewesen sei«. Ein solcher naiver Historismus oder Biographismus verbietet sich angesichts eines so komplizierten literarischen Gebildes, wie es der *Frauendienst* ist, von selbst. Aber ähnlich wie wir etwa gelernt haben, mittelalterliche Chroniken, Viten usw. nicht nur auf ihren faktischen historischen Informationswert zu befragen, sondern nach ihrem ›Geschichtsbewußtsein‹, müssen wir auch Ulrichs vermeintliche ›Privatchronik‹ zunächst in ihren literarischen Gegebenheiten untersuchen. Erst dann wird sie vielleicht, aber auch nur vielleicht, andere und gewichtigere historische Rückschlüsse erlauben, als wenn wir uns von vornherein wortwörtlich auf ihren Bericht verlassen dürften.

Noch ein weiterer, dritter Einwand erhebt sich gegen die fraglose Ergänzung der historischen Lebensdaten Ulrichs von Lichtenstein aus seinem *Frauendienst,* und dieser Einwand nun hat unmittelbar mit dem Problem des Autobiographischen im Mittelalter zu tun. Ich muß mich hier freilich darauf beschränken, dies aus der Perspektive der volkssprachlichen weltlichen ›Lebensberichte‹ aufzurollen; lateinische und geistliche miteinzubeziehen, würde in diesem Rahmen zu weit führen. Überspitzt und vereinfacht ließe sich das Problem erst einmal so fassen: Während wir in der neueren Zeit oft weder eindeutig noch einmütig entscheiden können, wann autobiographische Aufzeichnungen der sogenannten schönen Literatur zuzurechnen sind – man denke etwa an *Die Entstehung des Doktor Faustus: Roman eines Romans* von Thomas Mann, Max Frischs *Tagebücher* oder Adenauers Memoiren –, stellt sich die Frage im Mittelalter meist umgekehrt: Wann kann Dichtung (auto-)biographisch genannt und verstanden werden? Einer Richtung der älteren germanistischen Forschung etwa, für die die Namen Scherer und Müllenhoff hier stellvertretend stehen mögen, galten Liedgruppen

---

[7] U. a. 3,4; 5,8; 11,12; 13,29 f.; 35,17; 38,11; 40,9; 69,1; 74,26; 77,9; 95,13; 113,2; 186,30; 272,15 f.; 461,16; 547,9; 592,3,27 f.

einzelner Minnesänger als biographisch verdächtig. Und von da war der Weg nicht weit, aus diesen Liedern den Dichtern kleine Minneromanzen anzudichten. Während man seit langem ein solches Verfahren mit Skepsis betrachtet, leugnet jedoch kaum jemand, daß z. B. die Lieder Johannes Hadlaubs, Oswalds von Wolkenstein und Hugos von Montfort autobiographische Elemente enthalten. Aber diese sind meist von literarischen und Lebens-Traditionen so überformt, daß Dichtung und Wahrheit und Stilisierung für uns fast unzugänglich ineinanderfließen.

Das gleiche Problem stellt sich noch schärfer, wenn wir die Werke überblicken, die nun wirklich eine Art zusammenhängender Autobiographie zu geben scheinen. Im 13. und 14. Jahrhundert sind dies neben Ulrichs von Lichtenstein *Frauendienst* vor allem Dantes *Vita nuova*, Guillaume de Machauts *Livre de voir dit,* Jean Froissarts *L'espinette amoureuse* und Juan Ruiz' *Libro de buen amor*. Was ihnen bei manchen Unterschieden im einzelnen zunächst einmal gemeinsam ist, läßt sich in zwei Sätzen zusammenfassen: Formal betrachtet sind diese Werke Ich-Erzählungen (in vierhebigen Reimpaaren, Prosa oder Alexandrinerstrophen), in die mehr oder minder zahlreich eigene Lieder oder Gedichte der Verfasser eingestreut sind. Zum zweiten: was die Autoren berichten, ist nun bezeichnenderweise nicht eine Geschichte ihres Lebens, sondern es sind Geschichten ihrer Liebe. Kein zweiter Themenkreis aber besitzt in der mittelalterlichen europäischen Literatur, wie ich an anderer Stelle zu zeigen versucht habe,[8] so vielfach verzweigte literarische Traditionen, kein zweiter bietet eine solche Fülle von Möglichkeiten zu literarischem Rollenspiel. Oder anders formuliert: es ist in diesem Bereich vielfach unmöglich zu unterscheiden, wieweit solch ein dargestelltes Minneleben literarische Traditionen nur nach- und ausschreibt, wieweit es sie benützt, um ›Erlebtes‹ überhaupt sagbar zu machen, oder in welchem Maße ›Erlebtes‹ seinerseits die Tradition verwandeln kann. Zwischen all diesen Möglichkeiten müssen wir den mittelalterlichen Verfassern von Minne-Autobiographien daher, was Erfindung und Stilisierung anlangt, wohl oder übel einen besonders weiten Spielraum zugestehen. Dies ist klärlich ein Teufelskreis, in dem sie den beklagenswerten Literarhistoriker ziemlich beliebig an der Nase herumführen können.

Nachdem wir den historischen Quellenwert und den autobiographischen

---

[8] I. Glier, *Artes amandi: Untersuchung zu Geschichte, Überlieferung und Typologie der deutschen Minnereden,* München 1971.

Charakter des *Frauendienst* von Ulrich von Lichtenstein grundsätzlich angezweifelt haben, wenden wir uns nun mit geschärfter Skepsis der Forschungskritik zu. Im Hinblick auf die eben angedeuteten Schwierigkeiten ist es nicht weiter verwunderlich, daß die Urteile über den *Frauendienst* besonders extrem ausgefallen sind. In großen Zügen lassen sich etwa drei Forschungspositionen umreißen, zwischen denen aber auch Übergänge festzustellen sind.

Erste These: Der *Frauendienst* ist eine Autobiographie, in der Ulrich vor allem sein Leben im Minnedienst schildert, so unter anderen W. Scherer, G. Ehrismann, H. de Boor, F. Neumann.[9] Daraus ergeben sich Urteile, wie das vorhin von Scherer zitierte, über die Tollheiten des verheirateten Mannes, oder eine Deutung, wie sie W. Brecht Ulrichs Übergang zum zweiten Minnedienst unterlegt: »Nach kurzer zeit kann der von natur mit unvertilgbarem lustbedürfnis ausgestatte sanguiniker die catonische miene und das leben ohne minne nicht mehr aushalten. aus wintersnot und altmachender sorge sieht er keinen anderen ausweg als *wibes güete* (XXIV, str. 4): irgendwo muss es doch noch *guotiu wip* geben!«[10] Mit ähnlichen, unmittelbar psychologisierenden Zitaten ließe sich aus der Lichtenstein-Forschung eine hübsche Blütenlese zusammenstellen. Das müssen wir uns hier jedoch versagen. Wichtiger erscheint mir vielmehr, daß auch die meisten Vertreter der strengeren Autobiographie-These natürlich gemerkt haben, daß Ulrich so manches erzählt, was als Motiv oder Szene in der literarischen Tradition, d. h. im Minnesang und in der höfischen Epik bereits vorgebildet ist. Das aber versuchen sie für die Autobiographie zu retten, indem sie annehmen, Ulrich habe sein privates Liebesleben sehr stark nach literarischen Vorbildern stilisiert, d. h. Literatur gelebt. So etwa, um nur ein Beispiel herauszugreifen, F. Neumann: »Er [Ulrich] fühlte sich als Sonderfall eines von den Dichtern gestalteten Menschenbildes und bleibt in der inneren Haltung des ritterlichen Abenteurers.«[11] Das geht noch um einen

---

[9] U. a. W. Scherer (Anm. 4). K. Knorr, *Über Ulrich von Lichtenstein: Historische und litterarische Untersuchungen*, Straßburg 1875. H. Schneider, *Heldendichtung, Geistlichendichtung, Ritterdichtung*, Heidelberg 1925, S. 429 ff. G. Ehrismann, *Geschichte der deutschen Literatur bis zum Ausgang des Mittelalters*, II,2,2 (Schlußband), München 1935, S. 262 ff. H. de Boor, *Die höfische Literatur: Vorbereitung, Blüte, Ausklang, 1170–1250*, München ⁴1960, S. 337 ff. F. Neumann (Anm. 3). H. Reuschel, in: *Verfasserlexikon* 4, 584 ff. W. Brecht, »Ulrich von Lichtenstein als Lyriker«, *ZfdA* 49 (1908), 1–122. – Formulierungen, die Brücken zwischen den verschiedenen Positionen schlagen, finden sich in der Lichtenstein-Forschung in allen ›Lagern‹ recht häufig.

[10] W. Brecht (Anm. 9), S. 11.   [11] F. Neumann (Anm. 3), S. 385.

beträchtlichen Schritt weiter als die generelle, in der Vereinfachung gleichfalls etwas fragwürdige Annahme, daß die anspruchsvollen ethischen Normen der höfischen Literatur um 1200 im Wechselspiel zu den Normen der Gesellschaft stünden, die diese Literatur trägt. Dieser weitere Schritt aber erscheint gefährlich; denn warum sollte ausgerechnet Ulrich, der einer der produktivsten Minnesänger des 13. Jahrhunderts ist und der in seinen Liedern (wie gereimten Büchlein) so bewußt Konventionen und Normen des klassischen Minnesangs variiert, als einziger – täppisch oder übermütig – literarische Konventionen wort-wörtlich genommen und gelebt haben?

Zweite These: Im *Frauendienst* mischen sich Autobiographisches und Fiktives. Diese These klingt gelegentlich schon bei den Vertretern der ersten an, findet sich aber breiter ausgeführt in einer weiteren Gruppe von Untersuchungen, z. B. bei R. Becker, M. Schlereth, K. L. Schneider, O. Höfler.[12] Gerade die Vertreter der Mischungsthese mußten auf breitester Basis allen möglichen literarischen, historischen, auch brauchtümlichen Beziehungen des *Frauendienst* nachspüren, und sie konnten dabei den Text als Brechung der verschiedensten Traditionen begreifen. Freilich steckt auch in diesem Verfahren neben anderen Fraglichkeiten noch ein besonderes Problem. Denn man sieht sich dabei eben gezwungen, entweder einzelne Textabschnitte oder den gesamten *Frauendienst* Punkt für Punkt gleichsam abzuklopfen und zu entscheiden, ist dieses Ereignis oder jene Szene nun autobiographisch-historisch oder fiktiv oder womöglich sogar beides? Um das nur an einzelnen Beispielen zu zeigen: hat Ulrich sich den Mund nun wirklich operieren lassen, oder erfindet er das nur? Und, wenn ersteres zutrifft, war es dann Minnedienst oder vielleicht doch nur – männliche Eitelkeit?[13] Ähnlich die Schilderung vom dramatischen Besuch bei der ersten Dame, die eingangs skizziert wurde. Motive und Reminiszenzen aus der höfischen Epik *(Tristrant, Moriz von Craon, Iwein)* und fabliauhafte Züge durchsetzen diesen Erzählabschnitt besonders dicht. Spielte sich dieser Besuch nun wirklich so ab, oder wertet Ulrich seine reichen Literaturkenntnisse hier besonders effektvoll aus, oder hat er ein wirkliches, vielleicht harm-

---

12 Z. B. R. Becker, *Wahrheit und Dichtung in Ulrich von Lichtensteins Frauendienst*, Halle 1888. M. Schlereth, »Studien zu Ulrich von Lichtenstein«, Würzburg 1950 (Diss. masch.). K. L. Schneider, »Die Selbstdarstellung des Dichters in Ulrichs von Lichtenstein Frauendienst: Bedeutung und Grenzen des Autobiographischen in der älteren deutschen Dichtung«, in: *Festgabe Pretzel*, Berlin 1963, S. 216–222. Vgl. ferner O. Höfler (Anm. 6), W. Zitzenbacher (Anm. 5).

13 So schon G. Ehrismann (Anm. 9), S. 263.

los bis unerquickliches Rendezvous literarisch aufgepeppt? Antworten auf diese Fragen müssen (ad hoc) subjektiv bleiben oder sich an allgemeiner Wahrscheinlichkeit orientieren. Bestenfalls können sie auf bestimmten Leitvorstellungen beruhen, die sich der Interpret aus dem gesamten Text erarbeitet. Nur an einzelnen Punkten bietet sich in diesem Zusammenhang eine Kontrolle von außen. Für die ausführliche Schilderung des Friesacher Turniers etwa konnte Annemarie Bruder nachweisen, daß fast alle genannten Personen historisch belegt sind.[14] Doch fraglich bleibt immerhin, ob und wann dieses Turnier stattgefunden hat und mit welchem historisch-politischem Hintergrund. Ulrich behauptet auch hier – merkwürdigerweise nicht im Bericht selbst, sondern vorher und nachher –, daß es als Beweis seiner unerschütterlichen Liebe zu verstehen sei. Gerade in diesem Fall klingt das fast wie eine nachträglich aufgesetzte Motivation.

Dritte These: Der *Frauendienst* ist eine reine Erfindung, die vorwiegend aus höfischen literarischen Traditionen lebt. Diese These haben bislang nur wenige entschieden zu vertreten gewagt, sie ist aber derzeit mehr und mehr im Kommen. Und es ist gleichfalls aufschlußreich zu verfolgen, wie eine Reihe von Äußerungen auch aus der älteren Forschung immer wieder dahin zielt. Anlaß dazu gab vor allem der zweite Minnedienst, dessen Erzählung, wie gesagt, erheblich blasser und weniger turbulent ausfällt als die des ersten. W. Brecht etwa urteilt lapidar: »Das erste verhältnis hatte noch leben, wenn auch ungesundes; das zweite ist nur der dichtung wegen da.«[15] Doch weitere Konsequenzen zieht er daraus nicht. Demgegenüber hat etwa K. L. Schneider versucht, das konventionelle literarische Motiv des Frauendienstes, wie es im Minnesang erscheint, als das Primäre zu betonen; diesem sei dann sekundär jedweder Ansatz zu biographischem Bericht rigoros untergeordnet.[16] Am weitesten in diese Richtung geht schließlich A. H. Touber,[17] wenn er die »minnesängerische Entwicklung« als den »Kern von

---

[14] A. Bruder, »Studien zu Ulrich von Liechtensteins ›Frauendienst‹: Das Friesacher Turnier 1224 eine historische Quelle«, Freiburg i. Br. 1923 (Diss. masch.), S. 115 ff.

[15] W. Brecht (Anm. 9), S. 33.

[16] K. L. Schneider (Anm. 12), S. 220.

[17] A. H. Touber, »Der literarische Charakter von Ulrich von Lichtensteins ›Frauendienst‹«, *Neophilologus* 51 (1967), 253–262. Ähnlich vor ihm schon H. Milnes, »Ulrich von Lichtenstein and the Minnesang«, *GLL* 17 (1963/64), 27–43. Er versteht die *Frauendienst*-Erzählung als »a projection and extension of the Minnesang Convention« (S. 29) und betont die humoristischen und parodistischen Tendenzen des Werkes.

Ulrichs *Frauendienst*« betrachtet und fortfährt: »Ihr evident literarischer Charakter wirft ein bedenkliches Licht auf den Wirklichkeitsgehalt des ganzen *Frauendienst*. Es will mir scheinen, daß Ulrich das erfundene *maere* durch die Namen wirklich existierender Ritter und durch die Verwendung geschichtlicher Ereignisse zu würzen versucht hat.«[18] Selbst darin ist immer noch ein Hauch von Autobiographie zu spüren, da angenommen wird, der *Frauendienst* zeichne so etwas wie einen künstlerischen Werdegang nach. Aber die Erzählung erscheint nunmehr als etwas Sekundäres, etwas zu den Liedern Erfundenes. Somit wäre das Dilemma sehr glatt und einfach gelöst. Aber, so wäre auch gegen Touber einzuwenden, wozu dann die historische Würze und wozu der Riesenaufwand der drei langen Turnierschilderungen, wenn es vor allem um die künstlerische Entwicklung des Minnesängers Ulrich von Lichtenstein gegangen sein soll? Wir müssen auf diese Frage noch zurückkommen.

Wenden wir uns nach diesen Streifzügen durch die Forschung nun noch einmal dem Werk, dem *Frauendienst* Ulrichs von Lichtenstein selbst zu. Es steht in der deutschen und wohl auch der europäischen Literatur des 13. Jahrhunderts so ziemlich einzigartig da. Denn der *Frauendienst* ist zwar einerseits ohne die klassische, höfische Literatur kaum denkbar, zum anderen aber sind da ganz spezifische Besonderheiten, die ihn sehr weit aus diesen Zusammenhängen heraustreten lassen. Je nachdem, welchen literarischen Aspekt man stärker betont, erscheint Ulrich entweder als langweiliger Epigone oder als ganz besonders origineller Kopf. Aber wie man es auch betrachtet, sein Werk kann, ja muß beanspruchen, in irgendeiner Hinsicht ein ›erstes‹ zu sein.

Zum einen spannen sich also tausend Fäden zum Minnesang und zum höfischen Roman. Wenn man mit dieser Literatur einigermaßen vertraut ist und dann Ulrichs *Frauendienst* liest, kommt einem sehr vieles ziemlich bekannt vor. An vielen Stellen liest sich der *Frauendienst* fast wie eine Zitaten- oder Motivcollage aus der höfischen Literatur. Ulrich kennt, beherrscht und verwendet sie wie kaum ein anderer in dieser Zeit.[19] Den Anfang seines ersten Minnedienstes zum Beispiel gestaltet er so, daß er eine Reihe von Motiven aus dem Minnesang episch auserzählt (u. a. innere und äußere Vollkommenheit der auserwählten Dame; ihre höhere gesellschaftliche Stellung, die zugleich Distanz be-

---

[18] A. H. Touber (Anm. 17), S. 260.
[19] Vgl. dazu die sehr eingehende und differenzierte Darstellung bei U. Peters, *Untersuchungen zu Ulrich von Lichtenstein und zum Wirklichkeitsgehalt der Minnedichtung*, Göppingen 1971, S. 122 ff.

deutet; Sich-klar-werden über die Minne zu ihr in einem Dialog zwischen *herze* und *lîp*; Minne als Dienst; völliges, überwältigtes Verstummen in Gegenwart der Dame; Kommunikation durch Boten; Abgewiesen-werden usw. usf.). Dies alles ist durchsetzt mit Zügen aus der höfischen Erziehung der Epenhelden (u. a. Aufenthalt bei und Unterweisung durch einen erfahrenen älteren Mann; Initiation als Ritter während eines großen Festes; Sich-auszeichnen in ritterlichem Kampf und Turnieren usw.). Besonders auffällig ist, wie eingehend und detailliert zum Teil die zahlreichen Kämpfe der drei großen Turniere (Friesach, Venus- und Artusfahrt) geschildert werden. Auch dafür bietet die höfische Epik Vorbilder im weitesten Sinne. Nur daß Ulrich hier eben nicht irgendwelche erfundenen Figuren – Erec, Gawan, Parzival – auftreten läßt, sondern in der Hauptsache wohl seine Zeit- und Standesgenossen. So langatmig diese Schilderungen zum Teil heutzutage wirken, für Ulrichs zeitgenössisches Publikum mögen sie aber doch recht reizvoll gewesen sein, weil man sich selbst oder Bekannte in guter ritterlicher Gesellschaft ehrenvoll erwähnt fand. Nur selten läßt Ulrich hier auch kritische Bemerkungen einfließen.

Große Teile des *Frauendienst* – das ist kaum zu bestreiten – sind recht konventionell, ja klischeehaft erzählt, und Ulrich selbst ist sich durchaus bewußt, daß er die Geduld seines Publikums vor allem mit den vielen Kampfschilderungen und Turnieren gelegentlich stark beansprucht, wenn nicht gar überstrapaziert. Aber die Schablonen der Tradition werden gerade im ersten Teil des Werkes doch immer wieder durchbrochen. Das geschieht mehrfach, wenn Ulrich physisches Leid schildert, das ihn trifft oder das er auf sich nimmt (z. B. die Lippenoperation, der verletzte Finger, die Quälerei unter den Aussätzigen usw.). So ausladend variiert Minneleid immer wieder ausgekostet wird, so knapp, distanziert und sachlich erzählt Ulrich an solchen Stellen. Als Beispiel den Verlust des Fingers, der nach einigen Präliminarien – Ulrich bittet einen Freund um den Dienst, der willigt ein – in nur fünf Versen stattfindet:

> dô nam ich sâ daz mezer sîn / und satzt ez ûf den vinger mîn, / und sprach
> ›nu slach dar, biderb man‹. / er sluoc: der vinger der spranc dan. / Diu
> wunde diu bluot krefticlîch. (140,1–5)

Ein ähnliches Beispiel – nur ganz anders im Ton – ist die knappe Beschreibung, wie nach der Schlacht an der Leitha ein Diener den getöteten österreichischen Herzog auf dem verlassenen Schlachtfeld findet. Friedrich II. ist seiner Rüstung und zum Teil seiner Kleidung beraubt, ver-

wundet nur im Gesicht, mit Füßen getreten. Und dann das Bild: wie der
einst so mächtige und glänzende Fürst, leblos, quer über dem Rücken
eines Pferdes hängend und mit einem Mantel bedeckt, Einzug hält in
eine Stadt, in der ihn keiner mehr erkennt (528,13 ff.). Es sind solche
Momente eines intensiven, präzisen und unterkühlten Detailrealismus,
in denen der Erzähler Ulrich von Lichtenstein immer wieder aufhorchen
läßt. Doch Analoges dazu findet sich auch sonst in der Literatur des
13. Jahrhunderts.

Ganz und gar unvereinbar mit den deutschen höfisch-literarischen Traditionen aber sind im *Frauendienst* vor allem zwei Tendenzen: einmal
die Erzählung in der Ich-Form (und damit das vermeintlich Autobiographische) und zum anderen die gemischte Form (d. h. epische Reimpaare mit Lied-, Leich- und Prosa-Einlagen).[20] Ist das nun Ulrichs
ureigenste Erfindung oder lassen sich auch dafür mögliche Vorbilder
finden? Eine Anregung P. Neuburgers[21] aufgreifend, untersuchte
M. Schlereth erstmals gründlicher denkbare Beziehungen zu den provenzalischen Trobadorbiographien, die im ersten Drittel des 13. Jahrhunderts vor allem in Oberitalien in großer Zahl entstehen.[22] Die
Parallelen zum *Frauendienst* sind in der Tat frappierend, und Ulrich
könnte solche Biographien auf seinen Reisen durchaus kennengelernt
haben. Um sie nur kurz zu charakterisieren: sie sind in Prosa abgefaßt
und berichten mehr oder minder ausführlich über Herkunft, Leben, Mä-
zene und Minneverhältnisse der provenzalischen und oberitalienischen
Sänger. Nicht selten enthalten sie anekdotische Elemente, und zum Teil
rekonstruieren sie aus den Liedern der Sänger eine Art Biographie. Wieweit diese Angaben historisch richtig sind, darüber sind die Meinungen
der Forschung fast ebenso geteilt[23] wie bei Ulrichs *Frauendienst*. Ein-
mütiger ist hingegen das Urteil über eine Variante dieser Trobador-

---

[20] Zur ›gemischten Form‹ neuerdings J. Ruben, »Zur ›gemischten Form‹ im ›Frauendienst‹ Ulrichs von Lichtenstein«, Hamburg 1969 (Diss.). Ruben freilich tendiert
wiederum zu einer biographischen und didaktischen Auffassung des Werkes
(S. 161 ff.).

[21] P. Neuburger, *Die Verseinlage in der Prosadichtung der Romantik: Mit einer Einleitung zur Geschichte der Verseinlage*, Leipzig 1924, S. 8 f.

[22] M. Schlereth (Anm. 12), S. 115, 147 ff.

[23] Ausgabe: J. Boutière, A.-H. Schutz, *Biographies des troubadours, Textes proven-
çaux des XIIIᵉ et XIVᵉ siècles*, Paris 1964. – B. Panvini, *Le biografie provenzali:
Valore e attendibilità*, Firenze 1952. – Zur Forschungsdiskussion vgl. ferner (in:
*Der provenzalische Minnesang: Ein Querschnitt durch die neuere Forschungs-
diskussion*, hg. v. R. Baehr, Darmstadt 1967) A. Pillet (S. 43–47) und R. Rohr
(S. 82–84).

biographien: nämlich über die sogenannten ›razos‹, die in Prosa einzelne Lieder oder Strophen erklären oder die Situation beschreiben, aus der diese entstanden sind. Kein Zweifel hier: die ›razos‹ sind aus den Liedern heraus entwickelt und gleichsam deren ›Verlängerung‹ ins Epische oder Didaktische. Wenn man nun annehmen will, Ulrich sei vom Typ dieser Trobadorbiographien zu seinem *Frauendienst* angeregt worden, muß man aber doch drei markante Unterschiede festhalten: 1) Der *Frauendienst* ist mit seinen ca. 19 000 Versen wesentlich umfangreicher als selbst die längste dieser Trobadorbiographien samt ihren ›razos‹. 2) Ulrich verwendet eben nicht Prosa, sondern strophisch gegliederte vierhebige Reimpaare und steht damit, konservativ der einheimischen deutschen Epentradition näher. 3) Schließlich erzählt er nicht in der 3. Person von irgendeinem Sänger oder Dichter, sondern in der 1. Person, in der Ich-Form (angeblich) von sich selbst. Ähnlich wie Dante in der *Vita nuova*, der u. a. an Trobadorbiographien anschließt, wagt Ulrich offenbar den für die Zeit revolutionären Schritt von der Biographie zur Autobiographie. Und damit stellt sich dieses Problem hier nun zum letzten Male.

Ich will abschließend kurz versuchen, dazu eine eigene Hypothese zu entwickeln, die teils auf vorhandenen weiterbaut, aber teils auch ihnen widerspricht. Hugo Kuhn bezeichnet den *Frauendienst* einmal als einen »Liederroman«[24] und zweifelt, wie vorsichtige Formulierungen verraten, gleich anderen an seiner autobiographischen Glaubwürdigkeit. Von ähnlicher Skepsis geleitet, meine auch ich: der *Frauendienst* ist keine Autobiographie. Was aber ist er dann?

Mein Versuch einer Antwort: Ulrich schreibt einen ›Roman zum eigenen literarischen Werk‹. Einen ›Roman zum eigenen Werk‹ freilich nicht in dem Sinne, daß er unbedingt die chronologische Entstehung eines literarischen Werkes nachzeichnet.[25] Sondern: ein zu verschiedenen Zeiten und aus verschiedenen Anlässen entstandenes literarisches Werk lag Ulrich vor, und aus diesem Werk heraus bzw. um dieses Werk herum erfindet er seine Geschichte. Daß so etwas wie der *Frauendienst* daraus werden konnte oder mußte, läßt sich aus der Zusammensetzung dieses Werkes begründen oder ableiten. Dieses bestand einmal – daran ist kaum zu zweifeln – aus Minneliedern, Leich und Büchlein. Ferner möchte ich vermuten, daß auch die drei großen Turnierschilderungen

---

24 H. Kuhn, *Minnesangs Wende*, Tübingen ²1967, S. 148.
25 Wie das A. H. Touber (Anm. 17), S. 260, als »minnesängerische Entwicklung« Ulrichs faßt.

– Friesacher Turnier, Venus- und Artusfahrt, die so viele historisch bezeugte Figuren und Wappenschilderungen enthalten – literarisch vorgeformt waren, ehe Ulrich sie in den *Frauendienst* einarbeitete.[26] Vergleichbare Preisgedichte über Zeitgenossen, einzelne oder Gruppen, sind als selbständiges literarisches Genre nur wenig später gut bezeugt, z. B. bei Konrad von Würzburg, ferner bei Pseudo-Zilies von Seine, dem Niederländer Gelre und Peter Suchenwirt.[27] Vor Ulrich von Lichtenstein sind sie literarisch leider nicht zu belegen. Aber manches scheint, wie W. Mohr ausgeführt hat,[28] darauf hinzuweisen, daß es zur Zeit der klassischen Dichtung um 1200 Ansätze zu solchen Preisgedichten unter nichtliterarischen Gebrauchsformen gab.

Ich bin mir der Problematik bewußt, Ulrich einerseits als den Autor der ersten deutschen Autobiographie zu entthronen und ihn andererseits als den ersten Verfasser literarischer Turnier- und Preisgedichte neu herauszubringen. Schwierigkeiten sehe ich vor allem darin, daß keiner der anderen Preisdichter eine so beherrschende Rolle im eigenen Gedicht spielt und daß Ulrich auch im sozialen Status nicht mit ihnen zu vergleichen ist. Doch mit diesen Schwierigkeiten kann man eben auch andersherum argumentieren: gerade der höhere gesellschaftliche Rang erlaubt noch am ehesten die Rolle im Gedicht, dem dann unter anderem eine gruppenbestätigende, vielleicht auch politische Funktion zukommen könnte. Die Probleme um Friesacher Turnier, Venus- und Artusfahrt gewinnen aber im Zusammenhang meiner Hypothese zu den möglichen historischen, politischen, biographischen und brauchtümlichen Aspekten noch einen entschieden literarischen hinzu. Das bedeutet, daß sie von daher eher auf einer Ebene mit Ulrichs Minneliedern, -leich und -büchlein betrachtet werden können als in der Forschung bisher. Wenn das aber zutrifft, dann ergäbe sich aus den vorliegenden Werken Ulrichs, die den verschiedensten Traditionen angehören, der Plan des *Frauendienst* fast von selbst. Die Trobadorbiographien können dabei sehr wohl

---

[26] Daß Ulrich Turnierlisten oder Ausgabenbücher verwendet habe, wird in der Forschung gelegentlich vermutet. Aber – soweit ich sehe – spielt nur A. Schönbach (Anm. 1), S. 314 f., zumindest mit dem Gedanken, daß Venus- und vielleicht auch Artusfahrt in Gedichtform vorgelegen haben könnten.

[27] H. Rosenfeld, »Nordische Schilddichtung und mittelalterliche Wappendichtung«, *ZfdPh* 61 (1936), 232–269, bes. 248 ff. Hinweis auf systematische Wappenblasonierung in Ulrichs *Frauendienst* mit »ersten Ansätzen einer fachgemäßen Kunstsprache« (vgl. Seiler, *Geschichte der Heraldik*, S. 221) auch bei O. Weber, *Peter Suchenwirt: Studien über sein Wesen und Werk*, Greifswald 1937, S. 167 f.

[28] W. Mohr, »*arme ritter*«, *ZfdA* 97 (1968), 127–134.

eine Art Leitbild gegeben haben.[29] Wollte Ulrich Minnesang, Büchlein und Turniergedichte in einen Erzählzusammenhang binden, dann boten sich dafür sowohl die Ich-Erzählung, wie der gemeinsame thematische Nenner Frauendienst, wie auch die gemischte Form geradezu an. Prosa war dann allerdings nur für die eingelegten Briefe zu verwenden, kaum für die Erzählung selbst (wie in den Trobadorbiographien). Daß diese Erzählung nicht endet, bevor nicht auch das letzte – 58. – Lied umdichtet ist, stützt meine These des ›Romans zum eigenen Werk‹ ebenso wie die Beobachtung, daß im zweiten Teil des *Frauendienst* der verbindende Text zwischen den Liedern fast ausschließlich aus deren Themen und Leitworten herausgesponnen ist. Der Verbindung von hochstilisierter Minnedichtung und historisch gefärbter Turnierdichtung würde ferner Ulrichs besondere Erzählweise entsprechen, die höfische Traditionen mit Detailrealismen und mit Elementen durchsetzt, die vermutlich doch historisch sind. Aber das Neue am *Frauendienst* ist nicht, daß hier einer sehr persönlich von seinem Leben und Werk berichtet, sondern daß er aus den verschiedensten Traditionen und Fakten zu seinem Werk eine Geschichte ›erfindet‹, die streckenweise amüsanter und konkreter ist als dieses selbst, und daß er es so der Mit- und Nachwelt übermittelt.[30] Oder anders: den Anlaß für den *Frauendienst* gaben nicht zwei reale Minneverhältnisse Ulrichs, sondern die beiden Frauenfiguren sind eher Projektionen von Ulrichs Minneliedern, denn sie korrespondieren ziemlich genau bestimmten Liedtypen und -gruppen. Nur Ulrich, der Ich-Erzähler, bleibt in einer merkwürdigen Schwebe von Erfindung und Wirklichkeit; er konkretisiert aber auf seine unverwechselbare Weise die Ich-Rolle des Sängers ähnlich wie wir das auch bei andern

---

[29] Diese Auffassung hat sich seit M. Schlereth (Anm. 12) in der Forschung mehr und mehr durchgesetzt, vgl. J. Ruben (Anm. 20), S. 148 ff., U. Peters (Anm. 19), S. 161 ff. In bezug auf den literarischen Charakter des *Frauendienst* argumentieren U. Peters und ich weitgehend in der gleichen Richtung. Meine Auffassung des Werkes unterscheidet sich aber von ihrer u.a. vor allem darin, daß ich mit meinem Ansatz ›Roman zum eigenen Werk‹ (und der Annahme von Turniergedichten) – unter anderem aus den S. 303 gegebenen Gründen – nach einem breiteren Konzept gesucht habe als ›Minnesängerbiographie‹. Da ich in diesem Zusammenhang versuche, fast ausschließlich innerhalb literarischer Traditionen zu argumentieren, stellt sich mir die Frage nicht, ob Venus- und Artusfahrt auf historische Turnierfeste zu beziehen sind, was U. Peters (S. 195 ff.) durchaus für möglich hält.

[30] Den ›Erfolg‹ bestätigt in mancher Hinsicht die Große Heidelberger Liederhandschrift, die – wie schon oft bemerkt – die Lieder Ulrichs in der gleichen Reihenfolge enthält wie die einzige fast vollständig erhaltene Handschrift des *Frauendienst* (Staatsbibliothek München cgm 44, aus dem 13. Jahrhundert). Im Falle Ulrichs bietet C also in der Tat einen authentischen (und überprüfbaren) Zyklus.

Liederdichtern des 13. Jahrhunderts (u. a. Neidhart, Tannhäuser, Johannes Hadlaub) beobachten können. So erscheint Ulrichs *Frauendienst* als ein ›Roman zum eigenen Werk‹, der die verschiedensten literarischen und außerliterarischen Traditionen in sich hineinreißt und dennoch – oder gerade aus diesem Grunde – zu den meisten quersteht. Er bietet nicht die Lebens- und Liebesbeichte eines skurrilen Sonderlings, den man gelegentlich zwischen Don Quichote und Casanova angesiedelt hat.[31] Vielmehr verrät der *Frauendienst* eine ebenso spielerische wie bewußte Beziehung eines Dichters zum eigenen Werk und zu den literarischen Möglichkeiten seiner Zeit. Und damit demonstriert er eine Art von Autor- und Literaturbewußtsein, das einerseits sehr typisch für Ulrich von Lichtenstein ist, zum anderen aber auch für eine Zeit, die literarisch neue Wege sucht – über die normativen Zwänge einer Klassik hinaus!

---

[31] W. Brecht (Anm. 9), S. 121 f.

Donald B. Sands

The Flemish Reynard: Epic and Non-Epic Affiliations

By a complex historical fluke, really difficult to explain, the two medieval poems which gave Reynard the fox his beast epic format in the vernacular are generally ignored outside the Dutch and Flemish speaking areas. The recently completed *Kindlers Literatur Lexikon* treats the Lübeck *Reynke de vos* of 1498 very well, and also Goethe's *Reineke Fuchs,* which is a High German version of the Lübeck poem. *Kindler,* in fact, covers related beast epic literature well – the Latin *Ecbasis captivi,* the Latin *Ysengrimus,* and the Middle High German *Reinhart Fuchs.* Yet the two Middle Dutch poems – *Van den vos Reinaerde* of circa 1275 (which I shall call *R I*) and its continuation *Reinaerts Historie* of *circa* 1375 (which I shall call *R II*) – are not given separate entries, although each is mentioned in passing in the article on *Reynke de vos* as being somehow seminal to the Lübeck poem.[1]

The two Middle Dutch poems and the Low German *Reynke* remain pretty much academic novelties. They are not part of the corpus of literature with which literate peoples are usually on intimate terms – and one can wonder whether Goethe's *Reineke* might not fall into the same category. I suspect that Goethe's version of Reynard's story is slighted in German language areas because it is overshadowed by other later works, because it is often passed off in the lecture hall as the poet's exercise in writing hexameters, because all too easily it can be equated with the *Kinder- und Haus-Märchen,* with *Struwwelpeter,* with *Max und Moritz.*

In French language areas, the great bulk of verse that goes under the title *Roman de Renart* deflects attention completely from the two Flemish beast epics. In fact, there is justification for the usual French treatment of the two Flemish poems as being mere adaptations of the *Ro-*

---

1 Cf. *Kindlers Literatur Lexikon* (Zürich, Kindler Verlag, 1965–72), II,1785 f.; VII,1323 f.; VII,104–106; VI,225 f.; VII,100 f.

man. Van den vos Reinaerde does use portions of the first and tenth
branches of the *Roman,* but it should be added, in a distinctive way.
Where the Reynard episodes in the *Roman* amount to a loosely strung-
out series of *Tierschwänke,* the episodes in *Van den vos Reinaerde* are
organically linked in extended epic form, each episode having something to do with what follows, each, usually, emerging quite naturally
from what has preceded.

In areas where literature in the English language is paramount, Reynard, in whatever form and of whatever origin, has made a poor showing, even though he was introduced into England in his Flemish version
by Caxton in 1481. But Caxton's *Reynard the Fox,* a close translation
of a clumsily transcribed prose version of *Reinaerts Historie,* is itself
very much in the prose of its time – meaning, it is, aesthetically, no better and no worse than it should be. Suffice it to say no English poet of
any talent ever saw fit to transmute it into verse. If English and American readers encounter Reynard at all, they do so before reaching literary
maturity; for them, *Reynard the Fox* is children's literature.

In Flemish and Dutch speaking areas, Reynard's reputation is very
much alive. With some justification, he is looked on as a figure, in his
beast epic format, peculiar to the Low Countries. I know of one Reynard version, a transmutation of *Van den vos Reinaerde* into Modern
Dutch tetrameters, whose preface says that the poetic achievement of
the original is equal to that of the *Divinia Commedia.* But national and
linguistic pride aside, the bulk of critical literature concerning the beast
epic does rest in the Low Countries and hence, perhaps, away from and
to one side of the great body of Western criticism and literary history.
Few scholars outside of the Low Countries are familiar with such
names as D. C. Tinbergen, Wytze Hellinga, Jan van Mierlo, and
J. W. Muller.

The two Flemish poems plus the Lübeck *Reynke* and Goethe's *Reineke*
are siblings. The latter two, with certain syntactic, lexical, and aesthetic
variations, are essentially duplicates of *R II,* and *R II* essentially a
duplication and then continuation, again in a duplicating fashion, of
R I. In fact, Goethe's *Reineke* can be used as a crib – an *Eselsbrücke* –
in an initial reading of the Leitzmann-Voretzsch edition of *Reynke de
vos,* and this in turn for a reading of the various MSS of *R II* and *R I*
in Hellinga's multiple-text edition of the Middle Dutch poems.[2] The

---

[2] Wytze Gs. Hellinga, ed., *Van den vos Reynaerde, Diplomatisch Uitgegeven naar*

four poems are usually given the genre designation »beast epic« – *Tier-epos* – sometimes also with the attributive »comic«, although, as I shall take pains to indicate later, the comic element functions, if at all, in the later portions of *R II*, chiefly as contrast to heighten the aura of pathos, which, willy-nilly, the figure of Reynard ultimately assumes.

The ascription of *R I* and *R II* to a genre »beast epic« is not necessarily misleading, although the label can be used carelessly. In the backnotes to Robinson's *Chaucer*, it is used in a loose and suggestive manner in the paragraphs treating the sources of the »Nun's Priest's Tale«, which itself is no »beast epic« although it is, in part, a »beast fabliau« – a *Tier-schwank* – after the fashion of the beast fabliaux in certain portions of the *Roman de Renart*.[3] But by an understandable process of elective accretion, three long poems, all earlier than *R I* and *R II* – namely, *Ecbasis captivi*, *Ysengrimus*, and *Reinhart Fuchs* – are also given the label »beast epic« and all differ in certain essentials from the later Flemish poems. It is helpful in any attempt to describe the individuality of *R I* and *R II*, to underscore just how different from them *are* the two Latin poems and the one Middle High German poem. All three, it can be noted, arose in rough geographical proximity – one in Lorraine, another in Ghent, the third in Alsace.

Ecbasis captivi is traditionally called the oldest *Tierepos* of the Middle Ages. It is, however, a fable within a fable, and in the outer fable, it is an allegory, a story, as its title tells us, told *per tropologiam*, told »in a figurative manner«.

> A calf leaves the protection of its herd, encounters a wolf, is brought to the wolf's den in preparation for slaughter, and is rescued by the herd under the leadership of the steer. Here, allegorical equations are easy to establish. The calf is a brother chafing under monastic discipline; he flees his monastery and is caught by the devil (the wolf) only to be rescued by his abbot (the steer) and fellow monks (the herd). Within the allegory, however, is the wolf's tale, told to the hedgehog, explaining how enmity arose between fox and wolf – and the tale is the Aesopic fable of the sick lion whose cure is effected by the fox who prescribes that a wolf's skin be wrapped about the ailing monarch.

As Edwin Zeidel points out in his edition and translation of *Ecbasis*,

---

de Bronnen vóór het Jaar 1500 / I Teksten (Zwolle, W. E. J. Tjeenk, 1952) prints in parallel order not only all surviving MSS of *R I* and *R II*, but the prose redaction of *R II* published in Gouda in 1470 called *Die hysterie van reynaert die vos*.

[3] F. N. Robinson, ed., *The Works of Geoffrey Chaucer*, 2nd ed., (Boston, Houghton Mifflin, 1957), p. 751.

there are grounds for the feeling that the poem, in 1229 Latin hexameters, may not be a beast epic at all.[4] It does contain certain motifs
which figure in *R I* – the fox and wolf are uncle and nephew, the wolf
erects a gallows for the execution of the fox, the fox is warned of danger
by a loyal friend (here, however, not by a badger, but by a panther),
and the animal kingdom is passed off as a feudal hierarchy. But the
didacticism of the price; its everpresent display of monastic erudition
(Professor Zeidel points out it is little less than a Horatian-Virgilian
cento); above all, its allegory should make one hesitate to class it as
an epic of any description. Allegory with its attendant distortion of
reality is, it seems to me, foreign to the epic and foreign, certainly,
to the ethos of the Middle Dutch Reynard poems. The matter invites
speculation.

Allegory has been, particularly among medievalists in this country,
very much in fashion, its most rigorous critical document being perhaps
A Preface to Chaucer by D. W. Robertson, Jr.[5] Provocative as much
allegorical interpretation may be, a point of view restricted to it leads
to certain tyrannies. The Robertsonian view sees most medieval literature as allegorical and sees the medieval audience capable only of allegorical interpretation. Hence, a modern who employs his own aesthetic
psychology cannot truly appreciate medieval art; for true appreciation, he must school his vision to duplicate that of a Londoner under
Richard II, a *Ministeriale* under the Hohenstaufens, a troubadour of
thirteenth century Provence. An appreciation deriving from any form
other than a medieval one is, therefore, false.

One cannot deny the presence of allegorical thinking in the intellectual
history of medieval times; but aesthetic impulses operate on a frequency
relatively independent of chronology – one which intuition guides –
and allegory as a guiding principle in art has a suffocating effect on
intuitive perception. If *R I* and *R II* are found not to be allegorical in
any major sense, a feeling of relief ought to accompany the discovery.
Croce, for example, in the first chapter of his *Breviario di estetica*, says
that by a »juxtaposition of two spiritual facts – a concept or thought
and an image – whereby it is pointed out that *this* image must represent

---

4 Zeydel, Edwin H., trans., *Ecbasis cuiusdam captivi per tropologiam*, Studies in
   Germanic Languages and Literatures, No. 46 (Chapel Hill, Univ. of North Carolina Press, 1964), pp. 12 ff.
5 Princeton Univ. Press, 1962. Robertson's views are most sharply expressed in
   »Chapter IV: Allegory, Humanism, and Literary Theory«.

that concept, the allegorist fails to explain the integral character of the artistic image; but, what is more, deliberately sets up a duality«.[6] Croce goes so far as to say that it is a characteristic of a poor work of art to acquire an »apparent unity from the sheer will of the author, who for such purposes avails himself of some scheme or abstract idea or an extra-aesthetic outburst of passions«.[7] An allegory, he adds, usually appears as a »series of images, which separately seem to be rich in significance, [but] leave us afterwards disappointed ... because we do not see them issue from a state of mind ... They succeed each other and are bunched together without that proper intonation or accent which comes from within.«[8] Goethe says essentially the same in *Maximen und Reflexionen:* allegory uses »das Besondere nur als Beispiel, als Exempel des Allgemeinen«. The true nature of poetry, on the other hand, senses »im Besondern das Allgemeine«, but expresses particulars »ohne ans Allgemeine zu denken oder darauf hinzuweisen«. Whoever grasps such particulars in a vital manner, Goethe concludes, »erhält zugleich das Allgemeine mit, ohne es gewahr zu werden, oder erst spät«.[9]

Again, the outer fable of *Ecbasis* is true allegory and, since the poet goes from concept to image, the particulars of the outer fable somehow lack a firm anchor in reality – our sensually perceived, ultimately tragic reality that gives us for a time a sense of our own unique being, the reality in which we all, sooner or later, founder *(scheitern)*. It is conceivable that an allegorically oriented literary critic could utilize the Robertsonian technique on the two Middle Dutch Reynard epics. He could, for example, attempt to equate Noble the lion with pride, Isengrim with gluttony, Bruin with sloth, and Tibert the cat with envy and indicate they are so to be taken or not at all. If such were done, the impact of both poems would suffer and to date no one, I am relieved to say, has made the attempt.

The firm anchor in reality, evident in *R I* and *R II* and lacking in the allegorical fable of *Ecbasis*, I strongly suspect is a requisite of the epic spirit. One senses it in *Beowulf*, in the *Nibelungenlied*, in *Roland*, in the sagas. Without it, in human terms, there can be no pathos, no tragic

---

[6] Benedetto Croce, *Guide to Aesthetics (Breviario di estetica)*, trans. by Patrick Romanell, The Library of Liberal Arts (Indianapolis, Bobbs-Merrill, 1965), p. 22.
[7] *Loc. cit.*
[8] *Loc. cit.*
[9] Number 636, final paragraph, *Maximen und Reflexionen*. For a discussion of the passage see Günther Müller, ed., *Goethe: Maximen und Reflexionen*, Kröners Taschenausgabe Nr. 186 (Stuttgart, Alfred Kröner, 1949), pp. 273–276.

potential. The epic reality of the Middle Dutch Reynard poems can be overlooked. Both the *R I* and *R II* poets have a keen eye for genre pictures. The two peasant farms which figure prominently in the early part of *R I* are sketched boldly – they suggest the plasticity one associates with van Gogh. But this is representational reality, and this I am not really intending. The characters themselves possess intense psychological reality, and I feel they achieve their intensity just because they parade before us in animal personas, personas that create sufficient aesthetic distance to enable their psychology to appear very real to us. Still, there can be psychological reality without pathos and without tragic potential, two aesthetic features which are associated with what can be called existential reality, a reality which appears when an individual, as a free agent, puts his life in balance – as Reynard does at the end of *R II* and thereby achieves a sort of magnificent dignity, however incongruous it may seem when set beside the ludicrous incidents which follow. But here I am getting ahead of myself.

Any remarks made about the Middle High German *Reinhart Fuchs* must be cautious. It is hard to discover any aspect of it that is not controversial. The earliest MS is fragmentary, the two younger ones questionable. Neither the date nor the name of the poet is certain. Currently, from internal evidence, the year of composition is given as 1182 or sometime thereafter and, while someone by the name of Heinrich probably composed the poem, his by-name *glîchesære* »Gleissner« is still a puzzle. Does the by-name, which probably would be covered fairly well by the English word »deceiver«, refer to the fox or to the poet or to both? Any decision one way or the other is based on supposition.[10] Yet a few general remarks can be made. After a rather discursive start, the poem assumes a sort of cohesion; and by the beginning of the final quarter, a reader senses that it has unity and an unmistakable conclusion. In other words, even though most of its motifs derive from the *Roman de Renart*, it is no loosely strung-out series of *Tierschwänke*.

> Initially, the fox is seen attempting to prey on other animals and coming off very badly. The rooster Schantecler, the raven Dizelin, the cat Dieprecht, and the jackass Baldewin humiliate him. But then he joins forces with Ysengrin on the grounds that his cunning and the wolf's strength will make them

---

[10] For a detailed discussion of the textual problems of *Reinhart Fuchs* see F. Norman, »Heinrich (der Glichezare?)«, in Wolfgang Stammler, ed., *Die deutsche Literatur des Mittelalters: Verfasserlexikon* II (Berlin, Walter de Gruyter, 1936), 267–276.

invincible. As it turns out, the mismatched pair become implacable enemies, and they hold the stage to the very end. Certain aspects are not just comic – they are very funny. Reinhart harrasses the overweight she-wolf Hersant on the grounds that from *minne* derives *hoher muot* and that, after all, is what he is after. The climactic episodes evolve from efforts to cure the sick lion Vrevel. Reinhart succeeds: Vrevel is cured by poltices made from the skins of Reinhart's enemies – the wolf, bear, and cat. Reinhart and his henchmen, here the elephant and the camel, are richly rewarded by the grateful king, and the poem ends rather abruptly with Reinhart poisoning the king for no apparent reason other than sheer vicious perversity.

All this suggests an achievement of a nature similar to that of *R I*. The narrative itself does evolve much along the same lines and the foil patterns apparent in *R I* are also there – Reinhart against Isengrin, king against bear, wolf, and cat. Yet one difference between *Reinhart Fuchs* and *R I* is critical. Heinrich's poem is political satire, although the majority of its topical allusions cannot today be deciphered with any certainty. Further, his poem has an informing idea – and this is made explicit: the ideal of loyalty *(triuwe)* has been eroded by the power of bribery and graft *(miete)*. *R I*, on the other hand, is not a medieval *roman à clef*. Topical allusions may be there; but if they are, they are incidental; and no circumscribed moral theme is evident. If *R I* must be looked on as satire, all one can say is that it pillories the potential depravity of human nature in general.

An explanation of the divergence of *R I* from the earlier Middle High German poem can be made by noting that it started off as a parody of the early Flemish *Heldenepos* as it derived from French sources. That it is parody (as well as other things) is pretty much agreed on by Dutch scholars, but the nature of its parody needs some identification. A salient feature of all parodies is that they retain the form of what is parodied, but radically alter subject matter. (Presumably travesty operates exactly in an opposite manner: it dispenses with the original form, but retains – and distorts – original subject matter.) Whether *R I* is, in any respect, a »critical parody« is debatable, although it probably is a parody of the pre-courtly Flemish epic *Carel ende Elegast*, as I shall point out presently; but, even though comic, *R I* does not reveal literary absurdity in order to ridicule the seriously intended absurdities of another work – one, for example, that has become effete, mannered, stale. (Chaucer's »Sir Thopas« does just this for the romance of fourteenth century England.) Nor is *R I* a »polemic parody« – it does not attack, directly or indirectly, the work of another in order to assert its own superiority.

Rather, it falls into the more genial category »comic parody« – it allows
the well-structured *Heldenepos* to stand as pattern; it dispenses with
early courtly figures and substitutes for them animal personas. The
parodistic transformation is an altogether happy one. *R I* unrolls before
us as a self-assured structure, unlike *Reinhart Fuchs,* whose initial episodes do not cohere to the eventual unity that evolves when Heinrich
finally concentrates on the wolf-fox rivalry. There is a further possibility: the *R I* poet's eye – his aesthetic eye – was on another work
(if it were really on *Carel ende Elegast,* it was on a poem of great com-
petence and appeal) and hence, political elaborations did not come into
his mind. If so, the aesthetic referents of *R I* were not on merely topical
figures of late thirteenth century Flanders, but on the human element
itself. What it thereby lost in timeliness, it made up for in basic human
appeal.

Parodistic features in *R I,* moreover, are not overdone as they are in
certain *branches* of the *Roman de Renart.* There is an offensively de-
corous prologue (to be taken ironically) wherein the poet says he completed Reynard's »*vite*« (in Middle Dutch the word bore the signification »saint's life«) by translating it from »*walschen boeken*« (which he
probably did – namely, from the *Roman de Renart*) and warns *dorpen
ende doren* to leave it alone. He adds that he undertook the task at the
request of »*ene*« (a certain female) »*die in groter hoveschede / gherne
keert hare saken*« (who likes to manage her affairs in great propriety).
This is the stuff of literary parody as is also what follows – the great
legal assembly at Nobel's court, the formal complaints lodged by dig-
nitaries against Reynard, the assumption that a blood feud exists between fox and wolf, the swearing of oaths on the relics of saints, the
note taken of the rooster's genealogical tree, the solemn funeral pro-
cession of Coppe the hen, the heroic defense against Isengrim by the
village priest armed with a *tafelmes,* a table knife. As the narrative gets
well underway, parodistic elements recede, but suggestions of parody
never really disappear. To such can be counted the plot, well into the
poem, to depose the king by use of mercenaries, Reynard's *moniage,*
his plans to make a pilgrimage as expiation. Verbal echoes of epic narration appear here and there. The narrator obtrudes, sometimes with
»*Nu hoort*«, sometimes with »*wildi hooren*«. He boosts credibility by
citing oral and written authority. Perhaps even the addition of a species
name after the animal's proper name – *Grimbeert die das, Coppe die
henne, Tibeert die cater, Brunn die bere* – is parodistic echoing of the

names of epic personages wherein the second element is either a lineage
name or an epithet.[11]

But such features in themselves do not fully account for the epic structure of *R I*, nor for its resulting effectiveness. J. W. Muller mentions
several Middle Dutch works which the *R I* poet echoes in idiom, tone,
and motif – *Loreinen, Walewein, Ferguut, Floris ende Blanchefloer,*
above all perhaps Jacob van Maerlant's *Alexander*.[12] Muller, however,
singles out one poem in particular which the *R I* poet not only echoes,
but probably did use as inspiration for the tight epic structure of his
narrative – namely, the anonymous *Carel ende Elegast*. Muller calls
Maerlant's *Alexander* a *ridderroman*, but *Carel ende Elegast* a *heldenepos*. Its theme is *trouwe (Treue)* which, in ironic fashion, is also the
theme of *R I*.

> It tells how an angel commands Charlemagne to flee his court and become
> an outlaw. The same night, the king meets a vassal Elegast, whom he had
> banished for a minor offense, and agrees, under the assumed name of Adel-
> brecht, to help him pillage the stronghold of his brother-in-law Eggheric.
> There is comedy here – Charlemagne is a woeful failure in breaking and
> entering. By accident, however, Elegast learns that the brother-in-law is
> planning to murder the king the following day and the two would-be
> robbers return to court to give warning. When Eggheric arrives, he is dis-
> armed, undergoes trial by combat with Elegast, and loses his life. Charle-
> magne reveals his identity, rewards Elegast with the vanquished traitor's
> wife and possessions, and realizes finally the wisdom of the angel's injunc-
> tion – »Go out and pillage!«[13]

It is something of a task to make clear just what *R I* might owe to *Carel
ende Elegast*, particularly since the trial scene and several of the
Schwänke in the Flemish Reynard derive so obviously from the *Roman
de Renart*. There is, first of all, the supposition that the Carolingian
matter was popular in thirteenth century Flanders and that *Carel ende
Elegast* itself was particularly favored. There is no concrete proof for
the idea, but the fact that a number of MSS of *Carel ende Elegast* survive supports it, as does the fact that the poem was among the first

---

[11] For details I am indebted to J. W. Muller, *Van den vos Reinaerde*, 2nd ed. (Leiden,
E. J. Brill, 1939), I,30–33.

[12] *Ibid.*, p. 31.

[13] A prose translation of *Carel* by Eric Colledge is in Adriaan J. Barnouw and Eric
Colledge, trans., *Reynard the Fox and Other Medieval Netherlands Secular Litera-
ture*, Bibliotheca Neerlandica (Leyden, Sijthoff / New York, London House and
Maxwell, 1967), pp. 15–35. For a select bibliography of editions and studies see
Kindlers Literatur Lexikon IV,333.

books printed in Flemish – an edition appeared in Delft in 1478 and another in Antwerp around 1496. Then, of course, there are internal similarities. Both *R I* and *Carel* deal with the same motifs – outlawry, theft, treason, trial by combat, vindication of innocence, court intrigue. Yet a further consideration, it seems to me, appears more valid than anything else. The *R I* poet could have merely translated portions of the *Roman de Renart* into his native Middle Dutch, but was artist enough to feel he could revamp the material into a form pleasing both to himself and to his possible audience – and this I feel he did. He used materials out of *walsche boeken* to fill out the structure pattern taken from a *Heldenepos* familiar during his time. In this way, Reynard's *lustige Streiche* were given epic format for the first time.

No commentary on Goethe's *Reineke* I have encountered pays much attention to the pronounced medial break in the narrative. A sort of initial momentum keeps the reader going and he traverses the break between the sixth and the seventh *Gesang* with no perceptible jolt. But a break is there. The first half of *Reineke* is altogether different in structure and ethos from the second. The origin of the break is, of course, not to be sought in Goethe's poem, nor in its original, Gottsched's translation of the Lübeck *Reynke*, nor in the Lübeck poem itself. The medial break signals the end of *R I* and the beginning of *R II*, or rather the beginning of the continuation of *R I* which an anonymous poet one hundred years after the completion of *R I* tacked on to the older poem.

What the *R II* poet does to *R I* itself is minor.[14] He changes none of the motifs or names or longer speeches. His language, to be sure, is one hundred years younger, and occasionally he seems not to understand certain words which, by his time, had become puzzling; only in such instances does he appear to innovate. Throughout his retelling of *R I*, he accords the older poem the piety a lesser artist ought to show the work of a master. He is a poor story teller; but, once on his own, he shows that he possesses linguistic facility – but in moralizing, not story telling. Yet his sheer lack of innovative narrative skill may have kept the three thousand odd lines he added to *R I* from becoming completely stale. He probably recognized his deficiency, for he simply retells most of the major narrative motifs of *R I* all over again, to be sure, with the

---

14 Still the handiest text for comparing *R I* and *R II* is Ernst Martin, ed., *Reinaert: Willems Gedicht Van den vos Reinaerde und die Umarbeitung und Fortsetzung Reinaerts Historie* (Paderborn, Ferdinand Schöningh, 1874). Subsequent quotations from *R II* are made from Martin's text.

exception of the Bruin and Tibert incidents. Occasionally, he does insert encapsulated tales of his own, but they are told miserably. For example, at the very end of his continuation, he has Reynard tell the king the tale of the dog scalded by the cook as he stole a roast. The *R II* poet labors to point out that the thieving dog is like Isengrim and the other dogs who wish to share the roast like Isengrim's henchmen. Then, the point is made – thieves like Isengrim are eventually scalded and their henchmen fall away. The *R I* poet would have told the scalded dog tale with verve and let it go. The *R II* poet tells it as parable replete with massive explication.

Yet certain deserts do accrue to the *R II* poet. He gives Reynard a psychology that he does not possess in *R I*, where he is an Eulenspiegel-prankster with a streak of viciousness. In *R I*, Reynard arouses in us no empathy, although the aesthetic distance created by the technique of giving plausible characters the personas of animals gives him a vividness and impact rare in any work; we do not particularly mind not being let in on how the viciousness in him arose. In *R II*, however, matters change. On the way to Nobel's court for a second time, Reynard again makes confession to Grimbart. For a second time there is the amusing byplay that the badger is priest and the fox penitent. But there is also a world of difference. The second confession is not just a succession of encapsulated *Tierschwänke* meant to amuse an audience – the first confession is just this –, it is an extended and angry outburst on the poet's part on the deplorable baseness of the *zoon politikon* himself. The audience, if it is sufficiently receptive, suffers the shock of realizing that here is not a being with the persona of a fox amusing us with proof of his unregenerate nature, but the poet himself hurling angry reproaches at his public for its deplorable lack of virtue.

There is a Brechtian *Verfremdungseffekt* here. The audience is brought up short. It is given, not a diverting account of the fox's transgressions, but a critique of society at large.[15] Reynard says the initial evil is the persistent will to dominate. No one minds his own business. Everyone can find moral justification for doing anything, however despicable. Worse still, moral justification actually blinds an individual so that he does not realize what he is actually doing. Everywhere individuals profess to live by just principles, but when it comes to selfish advantage,

---

15 Reynard's first confession to Grimbart occurs in *R II* in ll. 1491–1685, the second in ll. 3955–4273.

just principles go by the board – an idea, which, in 1794, Kant labeled man's innate *Hang zum Bösen*. What actually is so arresting about the second confession is the fact that quadruped and biped beastliness is not explained and deplored on theological grounds. The tone is psychological. It is credible in its moral anger and its credibility is enhanced by the fact that the *Erzschelm* himself is analyzing human nature – and one can appropriately recall the proverb »Nur wer Sünder ist, kann auch moralisch sein«. Up to this point Goethe remained scrupulously true to his *Vorlage*. Here, however, the impact of the fox's revelations became too inviting to resist. He makes here the only interpolations of his own in the whole poem. In one spot (seven lines) he reproaches the clergy: »Freilich sollten die geistlichen Herren sich besser betragen.« In another (eight lines) he deplores the ruinous effects of power: »das Schlimmste« he finds is man's *Dünkel*, his presumption, »es könne jeder im Taumel / Seines heftigen Wollens die Welt beherrschen und richten«.[16]

The second »private« confession, moreover, introduces an element into the Reynard story heretofore lacking – namely, pathos. The words that are put into the fox's jaws are not confessional, but recriminatory. They strike a note of passionate concern – concern for what, if it cannot be called social responsibility, certainly deserves the label »individual moral honesty«. Once the reader gets over his surprise at being savagely analyzed, not from a sacerdotal point of view, but from a psychological one (one is tempted to say analyzed *innerhalb der Grenzen der praktischen Vernunft*); once he gets over his Brechtian estrangement and again begins to follow the fortunes of what he had looked upon as the arch-rogue, it is likely that his empathy (his *Einfühlung*) returns immeasurably intensified. Reynard has assumed a personality.

Up to this point I have not brought into discussion the first truly epic treatment of the Reynard material – the Latin poem *Ysengrimus*. Nineteenth and twentieth century scholars whose specialty is medieval Latin accord the poem unqualified praise – praise that often verges on astonishment at the poet's inventiveness and linguistic virtuosity. Albert Schönfelder, whose translation of 1955 makes the poem accessible to those not conversant with the intricacies of medieval Latin,

---

16 Both of Goethe's interpolations are in the »Achter Gesang«, the first in ll. 152–160, the second in ll. 171–177. For a thorough discussion of Goethe's relationship to *Reineke* see Klaus Lazarowicz, *Verkehrte Welt*, Hermaea, Germanistische Forschungen, neue Folge, Bd. 15 (Tübingen, Max Niemeyer, 1963), pp. 257–303.

says that *Ysengrimus* »ist unter den gleichzeitigen Tierepen das künst-
lerisch wertvollste« – and presumably he means that it transcends in
quality not only the epic-like segments of the *Roman de Renart* and the
quasi-epic *Ecbasis*, but also Willem's *Van den vos Reinaerde*.[17] His judgment, even for one acquainted only through a modern translation with
Ysengrimus, is difficult to question. The poem is an astonishingly effective thing, and apparently it suffered no undeserved oblivion in Western
Europe during the thirteenth and fourteenth centuries. There are five
complete contemporary MSS. Large portions are included in four contemporary *Florilegien*. Several contemporary MSS quote it *verbatim*.
It was never used as the direct source of a later beast epic, but this fact
does not deny its influence. Lucien Foulet, in fact, in his *Le Roman de
Renard* derives the whole of the French Reynard tradition from *Ysengrimus*. Although the *R I* poet undeniably drew his narrative motifs
from the initial *branche* of the *Roman de Renart*, he repeatedly echoes
both phrase and motif of *Ysengrimus*. (The *Concordantiën* at the end
of Muller's edition of *R I* lists some seventy-four verbal correspondences
between *Ysengrimus* and the Flemish poem.)[18] Even the *R II* poet,
some two hundred years after the composition of *Ysengrimus*, seems
to have known, and perhaps utilized in part, sections of the Latin
poem. Recently, William Foerste, in a clear re-evaluation of past Reynard scholarship, makes the debt of the *R II* poet to the Latin *Ysengrimus*
clear.[19] He concedes that the later Flemish poet followed *R I* closely,
although he probably had little feel for its parodistic qualities. He con-

---

17 *Isengrimus: Das flämische Tierepos aus dem Lateinischen verdeutscht*, Niederdeutsche Studien, Bd. 3 (Münster/Köln, Böhlau Verlag, 1955), p. VIII. For derivation
of the *Roman de Renart* from *Ysengrimus* see »Chapitre VI, Chronologie des branches de Renard« in: Lucien Foulet, *Le roman de Renard*, Bibliothèque de L'École
des Hautes Études, vol. 211 (Paris, Éduard Champion, 1914); and »Chapitre I,
Introduction« and »Chapitre II, Le roman de Renard« in: John Flinn, *Le roman
de Renard dans la littérature française et dans les littératures étrangères du moyen
âge*, University of Toronto Romance Series, No. 4 (Toronto, University of Toronto
Press, 1963). For a discussion of the literary affiliations of *Ysengrimus* (especially
to the theme of Fortune) see Hans Robert Jauss, *Untersuchungen zur mittelalterlichen Tierdichtung*, Beihefte zur Zeitschrift für Romanische Philologie, Nr. 100
(Tübingen, Max Niemeyer, 1959), pp. 93–113.
18 Cf. D. C. Tinbergen, »Concordantiën«, in J. W. Muller, ed., *Van den vos Reinaerde*
(Leiden, E. J. Brill, 1942), II, *Exegetische Commentaar*, 195–197.
19 »Von Reinaerts Historie zum Reinke de Vos«, *Münstersche Beiträge zur nieder-
deutschen Philologie*, Niederdeutsche Studien, Bd. 6 (Köln/Graz, Böhlau Verlag,
1960), pp. 105–146. For Foerste's discussion of *Ysengrimus* vis-à-vis *R II* see
pp. 119–122.

cedes that the continuation of *R I* – namely, lines 3481 to 7794 of *R II* –
draw not only on the older poem for its motifs, but also from the sixth
branche of the *Roman*. However, he argues very convincingly that the
Ysengrimus poet (his name may well have been *Nivardus,* although
only one MS gives the poet's name as such) and the *R II* poet were
spiritually akin *(geistesverwandt)*. Both were angry moralists, although, unlike the poet of the Low German *Reynke,* not overtly dogmatic moralists. (The Low German poet, particularly in his prose glosses, sees nothing but sinfulness in the world; the *Ysengrimus* and *R II*
poets are less concerned with sin than they are with moral dishonesty
and power lust. The distinction is fine, admittedly; but it gives the Lübeck poem, provided the prose glosses are also read, a doctrinaire tone
– a pose of dogmatic authority – which is somehow foreign to both
Ysengrimus and *R II.*) Even though *Ysengrimus* consistently shows
us the wolf parading as monk, and hence in the end lets the poem seem
primarily an attack on monastic corruption; even though monastic corruption figures into *R II* only occasionally, both poems reveal greed –
greed for power and greed for possessions – as the moral flaw of their
time, and neither poem gives much hope that matters will take a turn
for the better. (In this respect, both poems are abysmally pessimistic
vis-à-vis the Lübeck *Reynke,* where, again especially in the glosses,
clear formulas for regeneration are pretty much in evidence.) Foerste,
moreover, does note that the point of impact of the two poems, however much they coincide, differs in on respect: *Ysengrimus* deplores,
inter alia, the plundering of the poor by the powerful and rich; *R II,*
in contrast, laments the rise to power of *scalke,* political and religious
charletans. The observation leads Foerste to the view that the *R II*
poet, forced by the very fact that he is writing a continuation of *R I,*
presents us with incongruities in Reynard's character. Foerste, quite
reasonably, assumes the Reynard of *R I* to be »selbst der größte *scalk*«
and contrasts him with the Reynard in *Ysengrimus,* where he is the
symbol of the little man, the »Vertreter der Armen«, constantly har-
rassed and brutalized by the physically and politically powerful wolf.
Foerste adds that the *R II* poet's transformation of the fox image from
oppressed to oppressor makes both Isengrim and Bruin into different
characters – they appear, in *R II,* as pathetic dupes, as »bemitleidens-
werte Tölpel«. Foerste, as a clearheaded, factual scholar, notes the inconsistency of character delineation that the *R II* poet's respect for
Ysengrimus has lead him into, and, I am afraid, he regrets the fact.

But here the question can be raised as to whether the »inconsistency« in Reynard's character is, apart from scholarly considerations, actually an aesthetic minus. Frankly, I am convinced that it is quite the opposite. Modern psychological novelists are given the credit of discovering the aesthetic effectiveness of portraying individuals laboring under ambivalence and contradictory character traits. It is quite permissible today for a novelist to portray a reprobate guilty of the most saintly actions. The literature of psychology is explicit on the subject. Attestations are easy to find. One prominent psychopathologist (not Freud) writes that one character trait, good or bad, evokes its opposite – »Gegensätze ... erwecken sich gegenseitig ... Hat man einen Trieb, so steht man in einer Polarität.« The very fact that baseness to an extreme actual quadruped mentality is incapable of exists among bipeds enables man to rise to spiritual achievements no animals could attain – or, again quoting the prominent psychopathologist, »Eine starke seelische Entwicklung nach einer Seite tendiert zum Umschlag in die entgegengesetzte, gerade am stärksten bei reiner, gesteigerter Entwicklung der einen Möglichkeit.«[20] I have pointed out Foerste's reservations concerning the *R II* poet's consistency, and also quoted psychopathological views which neutralize Foerste's strictures, in order to explain the peculiar shock which a reader undergoes if he reads Reynard's second »private« confession with his *aesthetic* sense, not his rational or scholarly one. There will remain, I am afraid, always the nagging question »Did the poet of *Reinaerts Historie* really intend to be as psychologically sophisticated as a modern reader with his aesthetic sense might take him?« An answer, it seems to me, lies without the purlieus of historical scholarship. An answer might be that, in the criticism of an art work as such, the poet ought to be given the credit of being ignorant of the exact nature of what he has created. He can be excused for producing something quite different from what he intended. And now I shall have to say that all this is merely preliminary, preliminary to Reynard's emergence as an existence who achieves epic dignity by making a critical decision or, more specifically, by putting his life in critical balance.

I do not wish to imply that presence of what can be recongnized as

---

[20] The two quotations are from Karl Jaspers, *Psychologie der Weltanschauungen,* 6. Aufl. (Berlin, Springer Verlag, 1971), p. 238 f. A clinical discussion of the polarities in human character may be found in his *Allgemeine Psychopathologie,* 8. unveränderte Aufl. (Berlin, Springer Verlag, 1965), pp. 283 ff.

pathos is a monopoly of the epic. It can be found elsewhere, even in the medieval romance, although, I feel, not frequently. Whether pathos itself is an epic »essence« I hesitate to say, but I suspect it must somehow be present before the atmosphere of the heroic ethic can make an appearance – and the heroic ethic, whatever it may really be, is an essence, not an accident, of epic make-up.

For a late medieval writer, the *R II* poet shows few of the romance features one might expect. He gives us no unmotivated quest, no absurd number of knights pitted against an equally absurd number, no dragons, no delicate vixens in distress, no exotic journey, no exotic landscape. His late medieval mentality shows up primarily in his deficiencies. He just cannot tell a story for the sheer joy of telling it. He seems oblivious to the great narrative matters of the century preceding his – of Charlemagne, of Arthur, of Germanic antiquity. His vocabulary is far richer than that of the *R I* poet and his syntax more complex and, although complex, rarely faulty and overinvolved. He is persistently sententious, and in an erudite fashion. He echoes *Physiologus* and Aesop and also, apparently, Ovid and Virgil, although such echoes are put into the lying jaws of Reynard and hence amount to a subliminal dig at erudition as social pretention. His most original addition to the style of *R I* is the multitude of proverbs he puts in the mouths of his animal characters. *R I* contains, on the average, one proverb in each two hundred lines; the portion added to *R I* by the younger poet contains one proverb for every seventy lines, and these proverbs are, like the displays of erudition, ironic. They appear in sophistical argumentation and hence do not serve truth, but the subversion of it.[21] Finally, the *R II* poet is a moralist, something the *R I* poet is only indirectly. And there is something strangely non-medieval about his moral anger. Perhaps saying that it is rationally oriented is not quite right, but certainly his strictures do not come overtly from a dogma or an authoritatively codified scheme of values. (He tells us an animal is a despicable beast because he lies, not only to others, but, what is worse, to himself – and he lets the matter drop as though there exists no apparatus, theological or speculative, to rectify the situation.) But the *R II* poet's tendency to psychologize is both his weakness as a narrator and his strength as a moralist. It pro-

---

21 For a discussion of the proverb as sophism see my »Reynard the Fox and the Manipulation of the Popular Proverb«, in *Learning and Lore: Studies in Chaucer, Middle English, and Medieval Proverbial Lore*, Harvard English Studies (Cambridge, Mass., Harvard Univ. Press, 1974).

duces segments toward the end of his poem which, if one's subjective sense is properly attuned, create a sense of pathos and invest Reynard with a personality, and it is toward the end of the poem also that Reynard assumes his heroic stature.

The heroic ethic is something quite apart, it seems to me, from the subjects usually discussed when the epic is defined. Such subjects – I should call them epic »accidents« – are literary conventions and they can be trivial. I refer to such items as a beginning in medias res, a descent into the underworld, a proem, an invocation, epithets, similes, catalogues, all of which can be localized in Western epics, all of which also can be found in romances, and all of which can, with some astigmatic distortion, be ferreted out in *R II*, except perhaps a descent into the underworld, although Reynard's visit to the cave of the excrement-encrusted she-ape might so be construed.

In the second volume of Karl Jaspers's *Philosophie* – the one entitled *Existenzerhellung* – he sets up the dichotomy »naturalistic ethic« vis-à-vis »heroic ethic«.[22] The former amounts to a ready acceptance of things as they are. The latter *(die heroische Ethik)* amounts to a stance contrary to things as they are – namely, a freely chosen opposition to them. Such, according to Jaspers, amounts to sort of transcendence, and such, again, leads to consciousness of one's individuality (one's *Selbstsein*), especially when one takes the supreme risk of opposing things as they are: »Um überhaupt ein Selbstbewußtsein zu erringen, muß der Mensch sich gewagt haben.«[23] Those who take the supreme risk experience freedom: »Wer sein Leben bewußt wagt, erlebt eine einzigartige Freiheit ... ein neues Bewußtsein ... das etwa der Krieger ... enthusiastisch ergreift.«[24] Such an ethic is visible in the actions of Gunther and Hagen, in those of the West Saxon *Gefolgschaft* at the Battle of Maldon. Jaspers underscores the condition that such a supreme risk – the acceptance of an »unbedingte Forderung« – must be taken out of *no* motive other than assertion of individuality and adds »Für etwas sterben, um es zu bezeugen, bringt eine Zweckhaftigkeit und damit Unreinheit in das Sterben.«[25]

Twice after the second confession, the *R II* poet lets us see Reynard make a gesture that endangers his life – once when the fox dares face the hostile court and again when he accepts Isengrim's challenge to

---

[22] Berlin, Springer Verlag, 1932, p. 192.
[23] *Psychologie*, p. 120 f.
[24] *Loc. cit.*   [25] *Loc. cit.*

single combat. In his decision to face up to both dangers, Reynard acts as a free agent: he is acting out no accepted code; he is not standing witness to any dogma; he is not constrained by external necessity to make his decisions. In contrast, figures at court are, in Jaspers' words, »sophists« – they possess no inner *Unbedingtheit:* they are moved, one way or another, by base impulses within and without themselves. Nobel is swayed by opinion, the queen by greed, Isengrim by pride, Bruin by envy, all the minor figures (the *Komparsen*) by *ressentiment* – the furtive, corrosive suspicion that they are not getting what they deserve.

Frankly, I doubt very much whether the *R II* poet could explain just why the fox, at the very end of his poem, assumes momentarily the stature of a hero. He does go on with his tale. He lets Reynard lie to a court of law in the most outrageous manner and do so unsuccessfully. He lets Reynard overcome in his combat with Isengrim by means of a cruelly funny ruse suggested to him by Dame Rukenaw the she-ape. Yet, before all this, the *R II* poet shows us Reynard quailing at the prospect of facing overwhelming odds and then settling into an unconditioned decision. He writes –

> Reinaert wart een deel outdaen / van twivel in sinen moet: / nochan dede hi daert him toe stoet, / ende maecte hem inte herte coene.   (4276–79)

> (Reynard was a bit unsettled in spirit by doubt, but he put up a proud front and emboldened his spirit.)

As Reynard then walks into the hostile throng of courtiers, he holds his head erect and stares down the opposition. The little badger beside him, Grimbart, his only loyal friend, is overwhelmed by admiration. He whispers into the ear of his *oom,* his mother's brother, and says:

> die blode endooch tot gheenre ure: / den coenen helpt die aventure. / en dach is beter dan sulc een jaer.   (4285–87)

> (The faint-hearted aren't worth anything at any time. Chance helps those who are bold. For such, one day is better than a year.)

These words ring with admiration. They signal the badger's recognition of the fox's superiority. They may also be the sentiments of the poet himself. He had, during the long foregoing confession, put his contempt for society into the jaws of the fox. Here he may again have done the same – only voiced his feeling in the words of the choric figure Grimbart – his feeling that an individual who, by free choice, can hazard his life is worth a whole pack of elegant courtiers.

Finally, to tie matters up – although, I hope, in not too neat a package – what then *are* the epic affiliations of *R I* and *R II*? *R I*, by itself, and because it is a parody of a *Heldenepos*, shows the tight, self-contained structure of that particular genre. Its atmosphere is also epic: its buffoonery aside, it is legalistic and military, rather than chivalric and courtly. Its main issues turn on *Treue*, not *Minne*. It is not allegory – its grasp of the realities precludes this – nor is it a *roman à clef* – its characters are to be taken as represented, not as cyphers for other characters. *R II*, by itself, although lacking the crisp, impersonal narrative of the earlier poem, introduces pathos, gives Reynard polarity of character (which we all possess), and, for a moment, lets us sense in it a heroic ethic which we associate with other epic works which just do not happen to have animals as their dramatis personae.

Bruno Boesch

Das Gattungsproblem in Wittenwilers *Ring*

Wenn wir in der neueren Dichtung davon ausgehen, daß die Gattungs-
vorstellung, der ein Dichter folgt, für die ästhetische Beurteilung seines
Werks von hoher Bedeutung ist, so fallen Feststellungen dieser Art für
das Mittelalter nicht leicht: die unmittelbaren Vorbilder der spätantik-
christlichen oder volkssprachlichen Literatur sind oft nur erschlossen
oder in ihrem Gattungscharakter selber schon recht komplex.[1] Dennoch
steht wohl fest, daß auch der Dichter der mhd. Epoche eine Gattungs-
vorstellung hatte, bevor er sich an seine Arbeit machte. Dazu zwang ihn
schon seine Quelle, die ihm etwa nahelegte, ob er sich des Reimpaars
oder der Strophe bedienen sollte, ja die ganze Erzählhaltung war schon
mit der ersten Zeile entschieden: das *Nibelungenlied* begann ursprünglich mit dem Satz: *Ez wuohs in Burgonden* ... wie die Kudrun mit:
Ez wuohs in Irlande. Aber mit dem vorangestellten Eingang: *Uns ist in
alten mæren wunders vil geseit* und mit der Einteilung in *aventiuren*
sind gleich zwei Gattungsbegriffe eingeführt: zwischen *mære* und *aventiure* ist die Zwienatur des *Nibelungenliedes,* was seine »Gattung« betrifft, angelegt. Bezeichnungen wie Heldenroman, Artusroman, höfischer Roman, höfische Legende, Beispielerzählung, Minneallegorie,
Minnerede, Reimrede, Reimspruch deuten ebenfalls Kreuzungen an:
jedenfalls sind es solche für uns Literaturhistoriker und es wäre zu fra-

---

1 Allgemein dazu Hugo Kuhn, »Gattungsprobleme der mhd. Literatur«, in: *Dichtung
und Welt im Mittelalter*, Stuttgart 1959, S. 41 ff. *Probleme mhd. Erzählformen:
Marburger Kolloquium 1969*, hg. von Peter F. Ganz und Werner Schröder, Berlin
1972, darin bes. der Aufsatz von Ulrich Wyss, S. 214 ff. Eberhard Lämmert, *Bau-
formen des Erzählens*, Stuttgart 1955. Ders., *Reimsprecherkunst im Spätmittelalter*,
Stuttgart 1970, S. 200, und passim. Hubert Hoffmann, *Die geistigen Bindungen an
Diesseits und Jenseits in der spätmittelalterlichen Didaktik: Vergleichende Untersuchungen zu Gesellschaft, Sittlichkeit und Glauben im ›Schachzabelbuch‹, im ›Ring‹
und in ›Des Teufels Netz‹*, Forschungen zur oberrheinischen Landesgeschichte,
Bd. XXII, Freiburg 1969.

gen, inwieweit sie es auch für mittelalterliche Dichter und Hörer waren.
Trotzdem kann der Literaturhistoriker nicht darauf verzichten, nach
dem, was er in antiker oder neuerer Tradition als »Gattung« zu sehen
gewohnt ist, auch im Blick auf mittelalterliche Gebilde zu fragen, wird
aber zweckmäßigerweise von zeitgenössischen Definitionen der Poetiken
absehen und von den überlieferten Dichtungen ausgehen, wenn ihre
Gattungsnatur auch komplex erscheint. Typische Grundhaltungen des
Gestaltens in der Richtung dessen, was Emil Staiger das Lyrische, das
Epische und das Dramatische genannt hat,[2] wirken in jede Dichtung
hinein, wenn auch Grenzziehungen im mittelalterlichen Zeitraum, der
dem antiken doch recht ferne steht, schwieriger zu legen sind als etwa
in der Klassik des 18. Jhs. Dazu kommt, daß wir mit den drei genannten
Kategorien nicht auskommen, wenn wir nicht noch eine vierte, tragende
Grundhaltung veranschlagen, die in die genannten mehr oder minder
bestimmend hineinwirkt: das Lehrhafte. Wenn Legende und höfischer
Roman sich in der höfischen Legende gewissermaßen treffen, so ist der
tragende Grund der, daß auf beiden Seiten Vorbilder aufgestellt werden, die einem klaren Zweck dienen: Nachfolge zu stiften. Daß der
Zweck der Dichtung für den mittelalterlichen Dichter darin liegt, im
Rahmen bestimmter dichterischer Grundhaltungen, wie die Tradition
sie anbietet, implizit oder explizit dem Hörer oder Leser bei seiner eigenen Lebensbewältigung zu helfen, braucht nicht eigens belegt zu werden.
Dafür gibt es lehrhafte Dichtung im engeren Sinne, die explizit Grundsätze menschlichen Verhaltens lehrt, und es gibt – und das in fast allen
nicht zu dieser Kategorie gehörenden Werken – Lehre i n der Dichtung.
Diese kann sich aus dem Gesamtzusammenhang ergeben, so wie die letzten Zeilen des *Parzival* oder dessen Einteilung sie zusammenfassen, sie
kann aber auch Gestalten der Dichtung selber in den Mund gelegt sein,
wie Gurnemanz oder Trevrizent – diese Lehren sind über das Ohr des
unmittelbaren Empfängers hinaus auch zum Leser gesprochen; sie kann
sich, wie im *Tristan* Gottfrieds, in Exkursen aussprechen, die direkt an
den Leser zur Hebung von dessen Verständnis gerichtet und trotzdem
nur im Zusammenhang des ganzen Werks voll verständlich sind.[3] Das
alles ist hier nur anzudeuten. Dieses gelegentliche Aussteigen des Dichters aus dem Erzählzusammenhang ist natürlich etwas anderes als wenn
er die Lehrhaltung von vornherein einnimmt und im Sinne des *prodesse*

---

[2] Emil Staiger, *Grundbegriffe der Poetik*, Zürich 1946.
[3] Lore Pfeffer, *Zur Funktion der Exkurse im ›Tristan‹ Gottfrieds von Straßburg*,
Göppingen 1971, mit weiterer neuerer Literatur.

et delectare sie mit erzählerischen Mitteln nur beispielhaft ausschmückt. Aber aufs Ganze gesehen liegen die beiden Wege nicht völlig auseinander: aus derselben Grundeinstellung von der Einordnung der Dichtung in einen außerdichterischen gesellschaftlichen und ethischen Rahmen will der Erzähler nicht ausschließlich im epischen Bereich verharren – dasselbe gilt für den Dramatiker im dramatischen – und umgekehrt drängt es den Didaktiker zu Einlagen epischer oder dramatischer Art.

Die Gedankendichtung ist zwar auf derartige Symbiose nicht grundsätzlich angewiesen: das Didaktische kann im Ausdruck des Gedankens sich zu einer derartigen sprachlich-dichterischen Prägnanz kristallisieren, wie etwa bei Walther, daß ein solches Gedicht sich von einem Lehrgedicht, in welchem das Lehrhafte dasselbe Ziel auf formal anspruchsloserem Wege erreicht, doch wesentlich unterscheidet. Es mag in der Schwankdichtung andererseits Dichtungen geben, die rein in ihrem angestammten Element verharren, also ganz schlicht erzählend sind; die Regel ist aber doch die, daß ein moralisches Schwänzchen nicht fehlen darf. Oder, wie im *Meier Helmbrecht,* ist die Erzählung derart zwingend auf ihr Ende hin gemünzt, daß auch ohne die Lehren des Vaters und die Zwischenbemerkungen des Dichters die Tendenz nicht zu überhören wäre. Wer umgekehrt die Lyrik von *Minnesangs Frühling* durchmustert, findet selbst dort Sentenzenhaftes genug, so daß auch in diesen besonders empfindlichen Gebilden die Lehre nicht völlig schweigt, und weder Dichter noch Hörer haben in diesem Grund- und Grenzbereich, in welchem das Lehrhafte sich mit dem Lyrischen, Epischen und Dramatischen verbindet, einen Stilbruch wahrgenommen als eine Versündigung gegen das, was als »Reinheit der Gattung« absolute Geltung zu beanspruchen hätte.

Sie spüren natürlich, worauf ich im Blick auf Wittenwilers *Ring* letztlich hinauswill. Konnte man bei den Beispielen, auf die ich im Vorbeigehen hinwies, kaum darüber im Zweifel sein, daß der *Parzival* primär der erzählenden Dichtung, Walthers Elegie der Gedankendichtung und sein Spruch *Niemen kan mit gerten* der didaktischen zugehörten, so gerät man im *Ring* bei einer so global gestellten Frage in ernsthafte Schwierigkeiten, denn kaum irgendwo sonst sind Lehre und Erzählung mit derartiger Gleichgewichtigkeit in ein Ganzes gezwungen wie hier, wobei ich allerdings damit schon etwas vorausnehme, was zu beweisen wäre: ist der *Ring,* der stilistisch derart auf Kontraste gebaut ist, überhaupt ein Ganzes, und wenn ja, wie kann dann in einer Ganzheit, die im wesentlichen in Kontrasten sich bildet, auch noch so etwas wie ein Gattungsganzes vermutet werden, das offensichtlich von erzählerischen, dramatischen und didaktischen Elementen durchwirkt ist, in dem – wenn auch nur als Einlage – sogar auch Lyrisches zu finden ist.

Zweifelsohne ist der Kontrast das wichtigste stilbildende Element im *Ring*.[4] Gegenüber neueren Versuchen, im Gegenteil die Verbindungslinien, die zwischen Ernst und Komik vermitteln, herauszustellen, ist es unerläßlich, den Stilwillen des Dichters zu fassen, nämlich die beiden Seiten in ihrer Gegensätzlichkeit und in möglichst einseitiger Ausprägung aufeinanderprallen zu lassen, in einer Lust am Gegensatz, wie sie gerade auch für die Denkform des Spätmittelalters, in der das Didaktische seinen Nährboden hat, bezeichnend ist. Ich denke etwa an den Kusaner. Man mag an die Narrenfreiheit des Karnevals denken: auf der einen Seite das gewöhnliche, streng hierarchisch geordnete Leben und – davon durch strenge Zeitgrenzen getrennt – das karnevalistische Treiben: voll von unziemlichen Reden und Gesten sowie der Profanierung all dessen, was dem moralischen Alltag heilig ist.[5] Mit den Farblinien der Handschrift wird das auch optisch verdeutlicht: sie sind für den Leser, vielleicht noch eher für den V o r leser gedacht, der seine Mimik entsprechend einzurichten hat. So muß etwa bei der Schilderung des Hochzeitsessens, die als negative Tischzucht mit der roten Farbe des Ernstes bezeichnet wird, die Komik im Unterton des Vorlesers so temperiert werden, daß man spürt: der Vorleser sucht um Verständnis für die Zulassung derartiger handfester Komik – um der Lehre willen, die man daraus ziehen kann. Umgekehrt soll in den lehrhaften Partien wie der Haushaltlehre, der Tugendlehre, in den Namen der Vortragenden *Übelgsmack* und *Saichinkruog* und in den Zwischenbemerkungen vernehmlich ein Unterton mitschwingen, der daran erinnert, daß es törichte Bauern sind, die als Sprachrohr ernstgemeinter Belehrung benutzt werden. Das mindert zwar die Lehre als solche nicht herab, hält aber die Situation wach und den berechtigten Zweifel, ob mit dem Vortragen der Lehre der Lehrer sie begriffen hat und imstande ist, sie selber zu befolgen. So braucht es kein Irrtum des Schreibers zu sein, wenn die Gebete wie Vaterunser, Ave Maria usw. die grüne und nicht die rote Farbe tragen: einmal sind diese Stücke so bekannt, daß sie nicht eigens im Wortlaut hätten vorgetragen werden müssen, deshalb dürfte die grüne

---

[4] Bruno Boesch, »Zum Stilproblem in Heinrich Wittenwilers Ring«, in: *Philologia Deutsch,* Festschrift zum 70. Geburtstag von Walter Henzen, Bern 1965, S. 63 ff.

[5] Michael Bachtin, *Literatur und Karneval: Zur Romantheorie und Lachkultur,* Reihe Hanser 31, München 1969.

Farbe hier eine Anweisung an den Vorleser oder Leser sein, sie in der laien- oder schülerhaften Diktion eines Bauern herabzuleiern, die veranschaulicht, daß sie zwar gelernt, aber kaum verstanden wurden.[6] Sprachkomik, etwa in der Imitation des Stotterns, taucht ja auch sonst im *Ring,* übrigens erstmals in mhd. Dichtung, auf. Es geht damit auch hier um die Kontrastwirkung zwischen Form und nicht adaequat erfaßtem Gehalt.

Kurz: Lehre und Handlung sind vielfältig miteinander verknüpft, im Sinne gegenseitiger Einmischung, die in erster Linie den Kontrast wachhalten soll.[7] Diese Einmischung kann bis zur Auslöschung des Erzählerischen führen, wenn Vorgänge zuerst ausführlich vorausgeplant werden, die Ausführung selber den Dichter kaum mehr interessiert: es geschieht wie vorgesehen. Das geistige Element, das im Entwerfen liegt, hat mehr Gewicht als der wirkliche Verlauf.[8] Umgekehrt belustigt den Leser beim Hochzeitsessen die Auflösung der Tischzucht in lauter komische, säuische Vorgänge, die wie bei einem Breughelschen Bild in einem kolossalen Gesamtrahmen eingefangen sind: das ist Erzählung und nicht bloß Aufzählung einzelner Regeln. Dabei kann es natürlich nur dann im Handlungsrahmen zu den notwendigen menschlichen Konflikten kommen, wenn sich nicht alle Beteiligten im gleichen Maße töricht benehmen, denn die Übertölpelung des einen durch einen anderen ist eine erzählerische Notwendigkeit, d. h. es muß auch Schlauere geben, wenn das Dörperleben einen gewissen Grad von Glaubwürdigkeit, wie er für die Komik unerläßlich ist, behalten soll. An diese Fälle von Differenzierung der geschilderten menschlichen Typen klammert sich Ulrich Gaier in seinen »Studien zu Neidhart, Wittenwiler und Brant« (Tübingen 1967). Er schiebt den Kontrast zurück und will einen Willen des Dichters zur Harmonisierung erkennen, zur Vermittlung

---

6 Gertraud Wehowsky, »Schmuckformen und Formbruch in der deutschen Reimpaardichtung des Mittelalters«, Diss. Breslau 1936. Elmar Mittler, *Das Recht in Heinrich Wittenwilers ›Ring‹,* Forschungen zur oberrheinischen Landesgeschichte, Bd. XX, Freiburg 1967, S. 26.

7 Dazu Mittler, vgl. Anm. 6, S. 16 ff. Rudolf Voss, »Weltanschauung und poetische Totalität in Heinrich Wittenwilers Ring«, *Beiträge* (Tübingen) 1971, S. 351 ff. Winfried Schlaffke, *Heinrich Wittenweilers Ring: Komposition und Gehalt,* Phil. Studien und Quellen, Heft 50, Berlin 1969. Bernhard Sowinski, »Der Sinn des ›Realismus‹ in Heinrich Wittenwilers *Ring«,* Köln 1960, Diss., S. 78 ff. Ulrich Gaier, »Das Verhältnis von Geistigkeit und Vitalität in Wittenwilers ›Ring‹«, *Deutsche Vierteljahrsschrift* 41 (1967), S. 204 ff.

8 Als Beispiel für viele *Ring* 1486: *Wie schier er do hiet vollepracht / Alles daz er im gedacht!*

zwischen den Gegensätzen, was bei der Konsequenz, mit der Gaier seine Auffassung verficht, zu einer bisher nicht vertretenen neuen Gesamtauffassung des Werkes führt.

Es empfiehlt sich, in diesem Zusammenhang die Einleitung des Dichters heranzuziehen: denn von einer kleinen Stelle im Werkinnern abgesehen[9] äußert sich der Dichter nur hier und im Epilog zum tieferen Sinn seines Werkes und zur Einstellung, die er beim Leser voraussetzt.

> Ein puoch, daz ist »DER RING« genant / Mit einem edeln stain beschlait, / Wan es ze ring umb uns beschait / Der welte lauff und lert auch wol, / Was man tuon und lassen schol. / Chlain vingerli ward nie so guot / Sam ditz, gehabt in rechter huot.   (8–14)

Der Dichter, der in der Initiale den Ring, mit einem Edelstein verziert, emporhält, erscheint in der Tracht des Gelehrten, die Kopfbedeckung findet sich in ähnlicher Form an den Universitäten.[10] Sicher kommt neben dem Ring, der *ze ring umb* über den Lauf der Welt Bescheid gibt, dem Edelstein eine noch größere Bedeutung zu, von ihm geht ja die nachher genannte dreiteilige Lehre aus, wobei die zweitgenannte, die Tugendlehre, am meisten zu beherzigen sei. Möglicherweise ist dieser Ring ein Siegelring, worauf das darunter abgebildete Wappen mit dem Bock hindeuten könnte. Wenn das so ist, kommt dem Ring der Charakter eines Amtskennzeichens zu: mit dem eingelassenen Edelstein als Siegel beglaubigt der Dichter mit seinem Wappen, d. h. seiner Person das, was der Ring beinhalten soll; der Edelstein, als die Verbildlichung des Wesentlichen, das im Rahmen des Weltlaufs mitgeteilt werden soll, verkörpert so etwas wie höchste Kompetenz, die einem Amtssymbol zukommt, und es ist kein Zufall, daß beim Eintreten auf die Handlung das Werk als *taiding* bezeichnet wird (54). *Taiding* heißt eigentlich »auf einen Tag anberaumte Gerichtssitzung« *(tageding)*, dann im weiteren Sinne auch »Beratung, Verhandlung«. Indem gewissermaßen das törichte Verhalten der Menschen auf eine Bühne gestellt und sich im Kontrast zu dem in der Lehre vorgetragenen richtigen Verhalten zu verantworten hat, d. h. Handlung immer auch Verhandlung ist, trifft das Wort *taiding*, die episch-dramatisch-didaktische Struktur der Dichtung gut.

Als eine beinahe amtliche Pedanterie mögen die Farblinien erscheinen, die in der Einleitung erläutert werden und somit wesentlich zum Werk

---

[9] V. 2104–2115.
[10] Mittler, a.a.O., S. 14 ff.

gehören, wobei das *törpelleben* ganz eindeutig nur in seiner gegenbildlichen Funktion zu verstehen ist. *gpaur* ist eine Marke für den Menschen,

> der unrecht lept und läppisch tuo, / Nicht ainer, der aus weisem gfert / Sich
> mit trewer arbait nert; / Wan der ist mir in den augen / Sälich vil, daz schült
> ir glauben.   (44–48)

Der rechtschaffene Bauer wird also aus der Geschichte ausdrücklich ausgeklammert. Wittenwiler fährt dann fort:

> Sechts es aver ichts hie inn, / Das weder nutz noch tagalt pring, / So mügt
> irs haben für ein mär, / Sprach Hainreich Wittenweilär.   (49–52)

Gaier interpretiert *mär* als das, was um seiner selbst willen erzählt
werde, was weder *nutz noch tagalt* bringt und gewissermaßen neutral
aus der Spannung von Lehre und Gegenhandlung entlassen sei.[11] *Mär*
aber hat in diesem Zusammenhang den Wortsinn (das bezeugt schon
Wiessner) »erlogenes Zeug«, also etwas, das in keiner Weise zum Erkenntniswert der Dichtung beiträgt. Wenn es dem Leser nicht möglich
ist – im Sinne des *prodesse et delectare* – Nutzen und damit verbundenes
Vergnügen aus dem Werk zu ziehen, dann mag er es eben für eine *mär*
halten, eine erlogene, nutzlose Geschichte. *Mär* ist der Terminus, mit
welchem seit jeher geistliche Dichter die weltliche Literatur als minderwertig abzutun pflegen. Da das ehrliche Bauernleben ja nicht schlecht
gemacht werden soll, kann *mär* nur abwertend den Leser treffen, in Erwartungen, in welchen er gegenüber dem Buch versagt. Verfehlt scheint
es mir jedenfalls, darin einen Freibrief des Dichters zu sehen, man könne
seine Geschichte auch als eine Erzählung schlechthin, gewissermaßen
»wertfrei« hinnehmen, falls man nicht imstande sei, Nutzen auch aus
dem *tagalt* zu ziehen.

Ein anderes Problem ist allerdings, inwieweit die dem *tagalt* als der
Erheiterung dienende Bauernhandlung über ihre negative Zeigefunktion hinaus dank der dichterischen Gestaltungskraft eine gewisse Realität gewinnt, die den Bezug zur Lehre derart lockert und das Kontrastelement derart abschwächt, daß sich von einer so aufgefaßten bäuerlichen Welt eine vermittelnde Brücke schlagen ließe zu den Lehren, die
der Dichter auf der ernsthaften Gegenseite erteilt hat. Damit wäre mit
dem Stichwort des Kontrastes, zum mindesten in vielen Einzelfällen,
nicht das letzte Wort gesprochen. Gaier verweist im besonderen auf den

---

11 Ulrich Gaier, *Satire: Studien zu Neidhart, Wittenwiler, Brant und zur satirischen
Schreibart*, Tübingen 1967, S. 107 ff.

Nissinger Bürgermeister Strudel, auf die Nissinger selber und auf die eine oder andere Figur unter den Lappenhausern, ganz nachdrücklich aber auf Bertschi Triefnas selbst. Daß eine gewisse Differenzierung in der Zeichnung der Typen auch der Kontrastwirkung zugute kommt, habe ich schon angedeutet, ohne daß dies jetzt im einzelnen belegt werden kann. Ich lege nur Wert auf die Feststellung, daß der Dichter in jedem Falle nur Typen zeichnet. Die Folgerung aus Gaiers Auffassung wäre nämlich die, daß nicht mehr in dem Maße wie bisher von Parodie gesprochen werden könnte, die gerade aus der Unangemessenheit von Lehre, Vorbild und dessen krasser mißverstandener Befolgung entsteht, vielmehr sei es die zu beobachtende, zu erfahrende Welt, die sich eine signaturhafte Maske überstülpe (S. 208), so daß nicht eine gegenbildlich konzipierte Darstellung des Weltlaufs den Leser belehrt, sondern daß die absichtliche Maskierung und Verzerrung einer beobachteten, erfahrenen Welt den belehrenden Effekt erzeugt, indem der Dichter durch Handlungsverlauf und Lehre diese Welt demaskiert. Da dies nicht immer gleich radikal geschehe, sei es auch unmöglich, »daß die Bauernwelt in allen Teilen und Aspekten der Lehre auf dieselbe Weise entgegengesetzt ist« (S. 113). Sehr weit bin ich in der Beurteilung dieser mildernden Umstände von Gaier nicht entfernt, indem ich eine differenzierte Typenzeichnung durchaus anerkenne, aber es ist doch mehr als ein Streit um Worte, wenn ich nicht glauben kann, daß der Dichter eine im Grunde als wirklich erfahrene Welt maskiere, um sie dann zu demaskieren, sondern umgekehrt meine, daß eine primär als Gegenwelt konzipierte Dörperschaft vom Dichter in differenzierter Darstellung feiner kontrastiert und schattiert wird, indem er die Torheit der Bauernwelt nicht nur mit der Weisheit der Lehre, sondern auch mit Anzeichen von Weisheit in der *dörperwelt* selbst konfrontiert: die Weisheit in der Lehre ist immer völlig rein und makellos, die Torheit im Dörperleben aber mannigfach gebrochen, weil oft auch List und Verschlagenheit im positiven Sinne als Weisheit gewertet werden muß,[12] weil Torheit und Weisheit im Leben selbst nur situations- und anwendungsbezogen gesehen werden können. Der Unterschied ist schließlich der, daß Gaier aus seiner Sicht dem Dichter die souveräne Rolle des Satirikers zumißt, dem es darum gehe, unter der Maske einer selber entworfenen Scheinwelt eine wahre Welt zu enthüllen, womit der Kontrast zur vorgetragenen Lehre entschärft wird.

---

[12] So die mit roter Linie gezeichnete Anweisung des Arztes, wie dem Bräutigam Keuschheit vorgetäuscht werden kann: V. 2211–2248.

Ich sehe jedoch die unverkennbaren positiven Beurteilungen, die sich auch für Menschen des Dörperteils finden, nicht von der Grundlage einer positiv gesehenen Schicht der bäuerlichen Welt aus, sondern aus dem Stilwillen des Dichters, der in der Dörperhandlung nicht allein von der alles entwertenden Parodie herkommt, sondern von einem umfassenderen Humor, der sich letztlich allem Menschlichen verhaftet weiß und auch für äußerste Formen von Torheit einen gewissen Grad von Verständnis, vor allem aber Toleranz, aufbringt. Wenn der Dichter die Lehre durch Bauern vortragen läßt, andererseits auch halbwegs vernünftige Leute am Torenleben beteiligt, so sieht er hier aus didaktischen Gründen im einen immer auch das andre: er weiß um die Torheit der Weisen, die Weisheit des Toren. Ich würde solche Haltung nicht realistisch nennen, aber einen erkennbaren Grad von Wirklichkeitsverhaftung, wenn nicht gar -freude darin sehen, über den ein Humorist seiner Grundhaltung nach verfügen muß.[13] Aber er leitet weder einen Vernünftigen zur Torheit noch einen Toren zur Vernunft hin, er zeichnet menschliche Typen. Die Verhaftung des Menschen an das Irrationale der Unvernunft trägt archetypische Züge insofern, als sie nicht bloß instinkthaft ist. Nicht die Tiere verleiten beispielsweise die Menschen zum Animalischen, da sie ja außerhalb der Relation *Wisheit-torheit* stehen, sondern umgekehrt: die Tiere treten, die Menschen nachahmend, im Bauernturnier schließlich zum Kampf an, zu einer Torheit, zu der sie aus ihrer Art heraus gar nicht fähig wären.[14]

Aus dem Bereich der Erfahrungswelt kann schließlich ohne allzu absichtliche Verzerrung das Brauchtum zu seinem Recht kommen, dessen letzte Antriebe sich einer vernünftigen Erklärung entziehen. Die Deutungen der Wissenschaft, die auf Vorzeitliches und Heidnisches verweisen, sind für die Betroffenen völlig irrelevant, weil Brauchtum, solange es echt ist, ohne Reflexion vollzogen wird. Es ist ein typisch menschlicher, kein tierischer Affekt, der den Menschen zeitweise aus der Vernunft entläßt. Auf dieser Ebene können darum auch die dämonischen Kräfte der Unvernunft zum Kriege antreten, die Zwerge und Hexen, Dämonen und Riesen, die archetypische Schichten des Menschseins verbildlichen. Die sind so selbstverständlich da, wie ein Brauch vorhanden ist. Zwar geht das Aufgebot von den Lappenhausern aus: das ändert aber nichts daran, daß auch die Nissinger diese Hilfstruppen, die aus

---

[13] Bruno Boesch, »Phantasie und Wirklichkeitsfreude in Heinrich Wittenwilers ›Ring‹«, *ZfdPh* 68 (1943), S. 139 ff. Ferner Sowinski, Anm. 7.
[14] V. 1199 ff.

Feindschaft zu anderen Gruppen zu ihnen stoßen, akzeptieren und auf
derselben Ebene mit ihnen den Kampf aufnehmen. Eine graduelle bes-
sere Beurteilung der Nissinger und ihrer menschlichen Bundesgenossen,
der Mätzendorfer und Schweizer, läßt sich dabei nicht abstreiten. Die
Mätzendorfer aber beteiligen sich am Kriege, um für längst vergangene
Schmach an ihren Vorfahren Rache zu nehmen,[15] was als eine törichte,
kollektive Racheverpflichtung zu werten ist, wie denn überhaupt einzelne, wie der Bürgermeister Strudel, vor allem deshalb herausgehoben
werden, um den Kontrast zwischen der Vernunft des einzelnen und
deren Wirkungslosigkeit gegenüber der Unvernunft der Masse zum
Ausdruck zu bringen. Wo bleibt die von Gaier beschworene Vernünftig-
keit der Nissinger, als sie am Schluß Bertschi, der sich auf einem Heu-
haufen verschanzt, belagern und als er vor Hunger schließlich Heu frißt,
vor ihm die Flucht ergreifen? Aberglauben, eine höchst lächerliche Angst
vor einem Dämon ergreift sie, obschon ihnen doch Bertschi gut bekannt
ist, und eine völlig falsche Einschätzung der Situation läßt sie den Kopf
verlieren. So sind denn auch die Sieger nichts anderes als lächerliche Ver-
lierer. Die Farbe ist natürlich grün. Gaier, der glaubt, Bertschi mache
bis zum Schluß hin eine stete Entwicklung zur *wîsheit* mit, muß das
ganz anders sehen. Falls hinter dem Spaß eine explizite Lehre stecken
soll (die Farblinie ist jedoch grün), so sieht er die Sache insoweit positiv
für Bertschi, als die Szene zeigen soll, »daß e i n weise gewordener Lappenhauser mehr fertig bringt als eine Überzahl närrisch gebliebener«,[16]
wobei übersehen wird, daß es nicht Lappenhauser, die ja alle den Tod
erlitten laben, sondern Nissinger sind, die die Flucht ergreifen. Die
grüne Farbe mag an dieser Stelle zeigen, daß Wittenwiler in doppelter
Weise den *tagalt* als Kontrast der Lehre hinsetzt: beim Hochzeitsessen,
mit roter Farbe, ist die Gegenhandlung regelrecht gegenbildlich. Man
braucht nur jedes Verhalten ins Gegenteil zu wenden und man ist bei
einer Tischzucht angelangt. Hier, in der eben besprochenen Szene und
den vielen übrigen grünen Partien der Bauernhandlung, bietet die
Handlung selbst keine Möglichkeit solcher unmittelbarer Umkehrung.
Aus der Heuhaufenszene läßt sich nur an wenigen rot bezeichneten
Einzelheiten etwas für die Belagerungstaktik lernen, alles andere ist
vom Unsinn diktiert, ist verkehrte Welt, die nur insofern in die Ge-
samtkonzeption einbezogen ist, als sie den nötigen *tagalt*, das kon-
trastierende Vergnügen zum Nutzen liefert, ohne welches man sich eben

---

[15] V. 9352 ff.   [16] Gaier, a.a.O., S. 184.

die Belehrung nur ungern gefallen läßt. Die Begründung liegt hier einzig im Horazischen Rezept.

Gaiers Fehldeutung wird nur verständlich, wenn man von einer Interpretation ausgeht, wonach der Dichter den Bauerntölpel Bertschi zur Weisheit führen will, daß dieser sich durch das Gedicht hindurch zu einer Art vermittelnder Gestalt entwickelt bis hin zu seiner eigentlichen Selbstfindung. Der Satz in V. 9672 *Des cham er zuo im selber do* bedeutet nichts anderes, als daß Bertschi nach seiner Ohnmacht wieder zu sich kommt. Gaier belastet das Sätzchen aber mit einer beinahe philosophischen Sinngebung, nämlich, daß Bertschi zu sich selber, d.h. zu seinem wahren Wesen gelange. Und das soll endlich heißen, daß in ihm »vollendetes Menschentum« wirklich werde, ja daß er »die gesellschaftlichen und stilistischen Unterschiede abgerechnet, sich durchaus mit den großen Menschengestalten der hochhöfischen Epik vergleichen kann«.[17] Wenn man einfach »abrechnet«, läßt sich vieles vergleichen. Aber: Parzival und Bertschi Triefnas auf e i n e r Ebene, ist das nicht ein bißchen viel? Worin besteht aber nach dem Text dieses Zu-sich-selber-Kommen?

> Des cham er zuo im selber do; / Ein sendes gschrai derhuob er so: / Owe, jämerleicher tag, / Daz ich dich ie gelebet hab! / Des muoss ich iemer leiden pein / Mit chlagen an dem hertzen mein / Und mangen pittern jamer dulden / Nicht anders dann von meinen schulden, / Das ich so weisleich was gelert / Und mich so wenig dar an chert. / Wie chlaine wolt ich es gelauben – / Nu sich ich selber mit den augen: / Wer heut lebt, der stirbet morn! (9672–9684)

Endlich gehen dem schwergeprüften Bertschi die Augen auf: daß er so weisheitsgetreu belehrt worden ist und sich so wenig darum gekümmert hat und nun dem Tod in die Augen sehen muß. Sagen denn diese Verse nicht deutlich genug, daß eine Wandlung zur Weisheit bisher nicht erfolgt ist und erst vollendete Tatsachen ihn zur Besinnung gebracht haben? Nur Gottesfurcht und Liebe allein zählt und so macht sich Bertschi unvermittelt auf, um als Einsiedler im Schwarzwald zu leben. Aber der Schritt zeigt die grüne Farbe. Keinerlei Entwicklung, nein harter Augenschein zwingt ihn zu dieser Erkenntnis, und so ist auch die plötzliche Wandlung zwar einleuchtend, ob sie aber den Narren in ihm ganz auszulöschen vermag, mehr als fraglich. Der Dichter nennt die Worte, die in roter Farbe eine Wahrheit aussprechen, auf Bertschi hin besehen ein

---

[17] Gaier, a.a.O., S. 149.

sendes gschrai und knüpft damit wörtlich an den Eingang an: *Dar umb hab ich der gpauren gschrai / Gemischet unter diesen ler.* (36–37) Wäre nicht dies echte Läuterung, wenn Bertschi zum wahren Bauerntum sich zu bekehren vermöchte, das der Dichter zu Anfang ausdrücklich von dem *törpelleben* ausgenommen hat? Steckt in seinem Entschluß nicht die alte Unangemessenheit des Handelns, die ihn schon im Neidhartturnier hat Schiffbruch erleiden lassen? Daß die Lehre an ihm im Grunde wirkungslos geblieben ist, betonte der Dichter mehrfach z. B. in der Szene, als ihm der Brief Mätzlis, der die Minneallegorie enthält, vom Schreiber Henritze verlesen wird: *So man im den brief gelas, / Do wist er wenich was er sait, / Bis im es Nabelreiber zaigt* (2616–18), also es ihm mit Worten verdeutlicht. Bertschi will nichts anderes, als möglichst unbehelligt ans Ziel seiner Wünsche, zur Hochzeit mit Mätzli gelangen; die Lehren läßt er nolens volens über sich ergehen. So muß der Wunsch, Einsiedler zu werden, ohne daß der Dichter hier etwa eine Belehrung über den Weg vom weltlichen in den geistlichen Stand einschaltet, erst recht unvorbereitet, und ohne Begründung seitens der *wîsheit*, also lächerlich wirken, um so mehr, wenn man aus zeitgenössischer Dichtung, etwa des *Teufels Netz* oder den Schriften des Zürcher Kanonikers Felix Hemmerli zur Genüge weiß, daß die Einsiedler um 1400 eine wahre Landplage gewesen sind und geistliche Verfasser der Zeit nicht die geringste Achtung vor ihnen verraten. Ohne Farblinie bittet der Dichter am Schluß für alle Leser um das ewige Leben: *Das well uns auch der selbig geben, / Der wasser aus dem stain beschert / Hat und auch ze wein bekert!* (9697–99) Das lenkt zurück zum Stein des Eingangs, auf höchste Ebene gerückt. Wasser aus dem Stein, das mag die Lehre sein, die uns Menschen zufließt, aber Gott wandelt daraus den Wein des ewigen Lebens. Der Wunsch nach ewigem Leben, um das Bertschi sich nun bemüht, wird auch auf Leser und Autor übertragen. Aber nur das Endziel allen Lebens ist dasselbe. Vom Einsiedler Bertschi wird gesagt, daß er *in gantzer andacht an gevär* (9695) sich das ewige Leben verdiene. Das Wort *andaht* wird sonst im *Ring*, wenn es um religiöse Andacht geht, nur ironisch verwendet, bezeichnet aber auch das Verlangen nach ganz weltlichen Dingen: *Triefnass andacht die was gross / Gen seines lieben Mätzleins schoss* (5207–08). Die Beichtszene im Bauernturnier gibt Grund zur Annahme, daß Wittenwiler von religiöser Ergriffenheit wenig gehalten hat, anders sind seine ironischen Anspielungen auf mystisches Verhalten nicht zu verstehen. Die Verbrennung des Hus in Konstanz war kein

Einzelfall: das Mißtrauen gegenüber Sektierern in- und außerhalb der
Kirche war zu jener Zeit nach Ausweis der Konstanzer und Basler Kon-
zilsakten groß.

Doch brauchen wir diesen Abstecher in die Geschichte nicht unbedingt.
Der Zeigecharakter der Dörperhandlung ist auch mit der Schlußpartie
nicht aufgehoben und man muß sich hüten, hier noch so etwas wie
menschliche Tragik hineinzulesen. Der Tod in der Bauernhandlung wird
mit leichter Hand verteilt, schon beim Turnier sterben ihrer zwei, und
ein Weib stürzt vor Lachen vom Schaugerüst zu Tod. Die beiden Tur-
niertoten sind später wieder dabei, und in der großen Schlacht fallen
Menschen wie Marionetten. Daß Mätzli im Vergleich mit Bertschi eine
»verderbte Person« gewesen sei und den Tod verdient habe, wie Gaier
will,[18] unterstellt dem Dichter auch noch eine psychologische Charakter-
zeichnung, die in dieser Zeit nicht zu erwarten ist, noch der Dichtung
gerecht wird. Bertschi ist ein Getriebener wie alle andern auch; wenn
»Held«, dann nur Hauptperson eines Hochzeitsschwanks, der in seinem
typischen Verlauf auch in der Hand Wittenwilers zu keinem charakter-
lichen Reifeprozeß geworden ist. Aber natürlich ist der *Ring* dank seiner Ausweitung in weitere stoffliche, ethische und künstlerische Bereiche
auch kein Schwank mehr geblieben wie seine Vorlage. Das bedarf keiner
weiteren Begründung.

Fragt man sich, was für Gattungselemente sich im *Ring* finden, wird
man neben dem Erzählgerüst des Hochzeitsschwanks gleich das Lehrgedicht ins Feld führen. Innerhalb der Minnelehren genießt die Minneallegorie ein Eigenleben und es fehlt nicht an Versuchen, ihr Gattungs-
qualitäten zuzusprechen.[19] Die Ehedebatte kann dem Streitgedicht
zugeordnet werden: in ihr fällt auch erstmals das Wort *sophisterei*
(V. 3000) für die scholastische Spitzfindigkeit, mit der Argumente aus-
getauscht werden. Als Grundelement ist hier aber das Dramatische angesprochen, wie man sich schließlich in einer Reihe von Redeszenen,
auch in der Art wie Raum und Zeit freizügig behandelt werden, an das
Simultanverfahren geistlicher Spiele erinnert fühlen kann. An Endzeit-
visionen könnten Szenen während des Dörperkriegs erinnern. Die Heu-
schoberszene gleicht einem kleinen Satyrspiel, wie überhaupt Einlagen,

---

[18] Gaier, a.a.O., S. 168.

[19] Walter Blank, *Die deutsche Minneallegorie: Gestaltung und Funktion einer spätmittelalterlichen Dichtungsform*, Stuttgart 1970, bes. S. 210 ff. Zur Minnelehre
und -allegorie im *Ring* vgl. Ingeborg Glier, *Artes amandi: Untersuchung zu Geschichte, Überlieferung und Typologie der deutschen Minnereden*, München 1971,
S. 235 ff.

die sprachlich und stilistisch von ihrer Umgebung abgehoben sind, recht
häufig vorkommen: ich erinnere an die Urteile in der Form der Ur-
kundensprache, an den Vortrag des *hofelieds* (1758 ff.), des *Eckenlieds*,
zweier Tanzlieder sowie eines Tagelieds. Daß alle Register der Parodie
gezogen werden, war schon für das Bauernturnier festzustellen. Hier
sind aber nur wenige Spielregeln mit roter Farbe bezeichnet, das Ganze
läuft unter Grün, im Gegensatz zum Hochzeitsessen. Zwar hat das Turnier seine ernsthafte Bedeutung für die Kriegsvorbereitung, sei es in der
Wirklichkeit oder im Rahmen der *Ring*-Handlung (V. 899 f.), aber als
Gegenbild lehrhafter Art zum ritterlichen Turnier soll das Kübelstechen
der Bauern offenbar doch nicht aufgefaßt werden, insbesondere nicht
mit dem Blick auf ein bürgerliches Publikum. So bleibt das Ganze stehen
auf der Stufe des Brauchtums, wie es sich in Kärnten bis in unsere Tage
erhalten hat.[20] Der Vergleich mit dem Rittertum und die Gestalt Neidharts fordern die Parodie heraus. Von den Anklängen an die tirolische
Heldendichtung schließlich kann man nicht behaupten, daß damit die
Gattung als solche Eingang gefunden hätte in den Dörperkrieg des
Ring, jedenfalls erscheinen auch die profilierten Helden nur auf der
unteren Ebene der niederen Mythologie und treten nur durch ihre ge-
waltige Kraft, jedoch nicht durch eine besondere Rolle hervor, die an
ihre Taten in der Heldenepik erinnerte.

Es liegt jedoch auf der Hand, daß der *Ring* nicht alle die Gattungen,
an die wir uns im Laufe der Lektüre erinnert fühlen, als solche in sich
vereinigt; die typischen, auf Gattungen weisenden Gestaltungsweisen
sind nur faßbar als fundamentale Möglichkeiten des Epischen und Dramatischen, wobei die Frage, ob es für das Mittelalter auch das Didaktische als eine weitere dieser Möglichkeiten gibt, zunächst nur einmal gestellt sei. Mit den Leitbildern von Gattungen hingegen, wie sie die Antike oder die neuere Zeit in ihren Poetiken definiert hat, läßt sich im
Mittelalter nicht allzuviel anstellen, aber Möglichkeiten und Rich-
tungen, in welche dichterisches Schaffen drängt, sind natürlich in einem
weiten Sinne zeitlos. Jeder taugliche Versuch, darüber hinaus zu einer
Ganzheit zu gelangen, müßte von einem bestimmten, historischen Beispiel ausgehen und das Folgende daran messen. Diesen Versuch wollen

---

[20] Leopold Kretzenbacher, *Ringreiten, Rolandspiel und Kufenstechen: Sportliches
Reiterbrauchtum von heute als Erbe aus abendländischer Kulturgeschichte,* Buch-
reihe des Landesmuseums für Kärnten, Bd. XX, Klagenfurt 1966, Zu Kübeltur-
nieren in der Schweiz im Spätmittelalter vgl. *Schweizerdeutsches Wörterbuch* XIII,
Sp. 1675, und Bd. VII, Sp. 1412, und die Abbildung bei S. 64 in: W. Schaufel-
berger, *Der Wettkampf in der alten Eidgenossenschaft,* Bern 1972.

wir für den *Ring* gar nicht erst unternehmen, weil es dieses Vorbild nicht gibt, wohl aber müssen die fundamentalen Grundpositionen geprüft werden, die in ihm zusammenwirken. Mit der Didaxe ragt aber ein Element in die Dichtung herein, das von Positionen wissenschaftlicher Betrachtung und ethischer Besinnung ausgeht, und wir haben uns damit abzufinden, daß mit dem Didaktischen ein ganzer Teilbereich von Wissenschaft und sachbezogener, zweckbezogener Darstellung in den Bereich der Literatur hineinreicht, so daß eine Abgrenzung gegen »schöne Literatur« illusorisch wird. Mit dem Didaktischen als einer fundamentalen Möglichkeit des Gestaltens verbinden sich Kategorien außerdichterischer Welterfahrung, die einerseits von der Lehre herkommen, sich aber auch bestimmter formaler Schemata bedienen, wie etwa der Aufreihtechnik,[21] die damit auch Eingang in die Bereiche des Lyrischen, Epischen und Dramatischen finden. Ein Beispiel ist die Ständekritik, die eine Angelegenheit der Lehre ist, sich aber kaum anders als am roten Faden einer Aufzähltechnik bewältigen läßt. Besonders das Drama, als geistliches Spiel, läßt sich vom Didaktischen her zu einer fast endlosen Ausweitung verführen, wobei es sich vom Dramatischen sogar weiter entfernt als der als Erzählung angelegte *Ring*, der in der Ausnützung der didaktischen Möglichkeiten in der Ehedebatte tief in eine dramatische Auseinandersetzung hineinführt. Der Vergleich mit dem Spiel läßt es auch im *Ring* hoffnungslos erscheinen, ihm eine einzige Marke aufzuprägen. Es ließe sich vielleicht die Ehedebatte herauslösen und auf die Bühne stellen, doch der Dörperkrieg ergäbe viel eher den Vorwurf für einen Film, wobei – was heute nichts Ungewöhnliches mehr ist – ein Berichterstatter anhand der erzählenden Zwischenstücke die Brücke des Verständnisses zu schlagen hätte.

Fragt man nach dem Band der geistigen Einheit, so erscheint die epische Handlung bloß als roter Faden, in den alles eingereiht wird, während die Stationen, welche die geistige Einheit garantieren, die am Wege aufgestellten Lehren sind. Nach dem rein äußeren Umfang hat die Lehre ein etwas größeres Gewicht: stellen wir auf die Farblinien ab, was nicht ganz unbedenklich ist, so stehen rund 4170 grünen Zeilen 5520 rote gegenüber. Scheidet man die erzählerischen oder didaktischen Partien nach ihrer dichterischen Gestalt, so wären die rund 650 roten Zeilen der negativen Tischzucht der Erzählung zu übertragen, und wohl noch das eine oder andere dazu, und mit dieser Operation ist ein fast völliges Gleichgewicht von 4870 roten und 4820 grünen Zeilen erreicht. Mehr

---

21 Lämmert, a.a.O., Anm. 1, S. 199 ff.

soll dies nicht besagen als dies: der große Baumeister, der unser Dichter ist, hat die Gewichte zwischen Lehrhaftem und Episch-Dramatischem gut ausgewogen, so daß sich von hierher kein Schwergewicht ergibt; man hat die Lehre oft als enzyklopädisch bezeichnet mit dem Blick auf den *kyklos,* den Kreis oder Ring, und von einem Kompendium des Wissens gesprochen. Das bedarf aber der Einschränkung. Eine Reihe von Wissensgebieten fehlt: so eine Lehre über die Kirche und die Geistlichkeit, über Rechtspraxis, über Berufe überhaupt. Ein Vergleich mit dem *Schachzabelbuch* des Konrad von Ammenhausen oder mit des *Teufels Netz* offenbart da Lücken. Wittenwiler wählt mit dem Blick auf den Stadtbürger, der um diese Zeit ja auch unmittelbar Nachbar von Stadtadligen und Ackerbürgern ist, ganz bewußt aus und stellt, da der Großteil der Lehren vorehelicher Unterricht ist, das Praktische voran. Er lehrt die *bescheidenheit,* das Bescheidwissen, wie es dem Durchschnittsbürger von Nutzen ist und wählt danach aus. Anwendungsbezogene Weisheit hat den Vorrang, obschon knifflige juristische Fragen nicht fehlen, wobei auch die List, wie im Falle des Arztes, der eine Methode zur Vortäuschung der Keuschheit lehrt, durchaus die rote Farbe tragen kann. Es kann natürlich für einen mittelalterlichen Menschen, wenn es um ein Drama leiblichen Lebens im Vollzug einer Hochzeit geht, auch das Wichtigste: die Begattung nicht fehlen. Nur wir modernen Menschen schalten hier (oder schalteten hier) das Licht aus. Im Kontrast dazu triumphiert in den reinen Lehrpartien der Intellekt, aber dichterisch sinnenfällig! Auch von der Gestaltung her läßt sich weder dem Erzählerisch-Dramatischen noch dem Intellektuell-Lehrhaften das Primat zuerkennen: der Dichter bewährt sich auf beiden Ebenen mit einem ungewöhnlichen Können.

Noch weniger ausreichend wäre das Gerüst des Schwanks als eine Kennzeichnung für das Ganze, selbst wenn man darin eine Art von Kontrafaktur zur höfischen Aventiure sehen wollte, wie man dies mit mehr Erfolg beim *Meier Helmbrecht* versucht hat.[22] Der *welte lauf* läßt sich von der Lehre nicht beeindrucken: diese behält ihre blockhafte, auf keinerlei menschliche Schwächen der Erzählung sich relativierend einlassende Geschlossenheit.

Gaier plädiert für eine Satire. Für sie sei die Wirklichkeit nicht ein Mangel gegenüber dem Ideale, sondern eine Bedrohung und Gefährdung des menschlichen Wesens, und die Aufgabe des Satirikers sei es, diese Be-

---

[22] Vgl. 8. Aufl. in der Altdten. Textbibliothek (Tübingen 1968), besorgt von K. Ruh, S. XXIII.

drohung zu schwächen oder zu vernichten.[23] Tut dies der Dichter? Er läßt im Gegenteil der Bedrohung und Zerstörung menschlichen Wesens und Lebens freien Lauf, seine Lehre geht immer wieder erstaunlich an diesen Umständen vorbei. Auch die Kriegslehre – die zwar an richtiger Stelle, unmittelbar vor der Schlacht, von einem besonnenen Mann vorgetragen wird – hat letztlich ganz andere Verhältnisse vor Augen, und man erwartet von ihr auch gar nicht, daß sie das gesetzlose Tun zu zügeln oder gar aufzuhalten vermag. Dies geschieht nur in geistiger Vorwegnahme. Der Plan braucht sich nicht um eine Wirklichkeit zu kümmern, die ja auch gar keine solche ist. Daraus spricht dichterische Skepsis, wenn man das fehlende Bezugnehmen auf das »wirkliche Leben« charakterisieren will, aber kein persönlicher Einsatz des Satirikers. Soweit sich die Dinge selber ad absurdum führen, ist es ein parodistisches Verfahren, unangemessenes Vorhaben der Gestalten am Geschehen selbst zuschanden werden zu lassen.

Aber für das Ganze reicht auch die Parodie nicht aus, weil ja nur die von den Gestalten ins Auge gefaßten Ziele durch Übersteigerung fragwürdig erscheinen, keineswegs aber die Lehren selbst, die an sie herangetragen werden. Ihr Wert bleibt unberührt und wird selbst durch törichtes Tun nicht in den Dreck gezogen oder auch nur ironisiert, wie etwa in Neidharts Dichtung. Zwar wird das Turnierwesen parodiert, doch darin sieht auch der Dichter keinen wichtigen Lehrgehalt; dies gilt, wenn auch nicht in dem Maße, auch für das Minnewesen, und die überspannten Liebesbriefe, das zeigt ihr Stil, dürfte der Dichter trotz der roten Farbe nicht als situationsgerecht aufgefaßt haben im Gegensatz etwa zu der stilistisch in keiner Weise ironisierten Tugendlehre.

Noch weniger durchschlagend ist Wessels Versuch, den *Ring* als Groteske zu fassen, trotz fraglos grotesker Partien.[24] In ihr ist, im Gegensatz zur Parodie, der Bezug zu Vorbild und Lehre völlig gelöst, um so weniger vermag die Groteske eine Form zu decken, in der neben Effekten der Entfremdung die Lehre selber ernst genommen sein will. Endlich fragt man sich, ob nicht letztlich mit der Totalität einer Welterfassung, wie sie dem Epos zugesprochen wird, der Ring zu erfassen sei. Ausgangspunkt könnte nur das in der unmittelbaren Tradition vorausliegende mhd. Heldenepos sein. Wenn man ihm im Gegensatz zum Aventiureroman ein Dasein in festen Ordnungen und Bindungen zuspricht, die

---

[23] Gaier, a.a.O., S. 4.
[24] P. B. Wessels, »Wittenwilers ›Ring‹ als Groteske«, *Wirkendes Wort* 10 (1960), S. 204 ff. Dazu Boesch, Anm. 4, S. 75 f.

Bedeutung der Sippe betont, sagenhafte und mythische Züge hervorhebt, die Abwesenheit des Privaten bucht und was immer man an solchen Allgemeinheiten dem gerade griffbereiten Lexikon entnimmt, der *Ring* kann nach Prüfung dieser und weiterer Ansprüche auch als Epos nicht adaequat erfaßt werden. Hier ist keine totale Welt, auch nicht der Bauern, denn sie ist, zumindest in ihrer Ganzheit, nur unter dem Blickpunkt des Kontrastes erfaßt: diese Welt erscheint gesteigert in einer Art Fieber, in Bedrohung und Auflösung; es ist zwar spezifisch dörperliche Dichtung, aber damit ist für die Gattung überhaupt nichts gesagt. Im Blick auf Epos und Roman fehlt auch der Held und es fehlt der Konflikt. Als Konflikt kann man weder das Bauernturnier und die damit verknüpfte Keilerei bezeichnen noch die Tatsache, daß Eisengrein die Gredul beim Tanz in der Hand kitzelt und damit die Schlägerei und schließlich den Krieg entfacht. Das ist nur folgerichtig im Rahmen des Typischen. Es fehlt schließlich der überschaubare, geordnete Raum und eine auf die Handlung bezogene Zeit, in der sich Zustände entfalten und menschliche Gestalten sich entwickeln könnten. Raum und Zeit sind bald reale, bald irreale Größen, die Bühne des Weltlaufs ist simultan, und der Dichter betreibt eine souveräne Montage, indem er auch die untermenschliche Welt auf ihr unterbringt.[25] Auch die Sprache ist manipuliert, als eine Art von Übersprache, angesiedelt zwischen engster örtlicher Mundart und einer Literatursprache, die sich bairische Modeformen aneignet. Gerade diese so unwirkliche Mischung zeigt, daß es im *Ring* noch keineswegs um ein Empfinden für den geschichtlichen Raum geht, wie man die Erhellung der Sprache und der Dialekte im Zeitalter des Humanismus (etwa bei Rabelais) interpretieren kann.[26] Auch mit bairischer »volkstümlicher« Epik – *Rosengarten, Laurin* – läßt sich im Sinne der Gattungstradition nichts anfangen: hinübergewirkt hat nur der hyperbolische Stil.

Worauf wir bisher immer wieder bei unserer Sichtung der Möglichkeiten verwiesen wurden, ist der in der Einleitung des Referates gegebene Hinweis auf die Berührungen, die das Didaktische vornehmlich mit dem Epischen eingeht. Wittenwiler hat die Positionen von epischen und didaktischen Ansprüchen in extremer Weise polarisiert und ein höchst

---

[25] Das zeigt sich z. B. auch an den Ortsnamen, die z. T. sich noch heute auffinden lassen im mittleren Toggenburg und meist ganz kleine, abgelegene Höfe bezeichnen, neben erfundenen Ortsnamen wie *Lappenhausen, Mätzendorf* und anderen. In der Mitte stehen aus der Wirklichkeit entstellte Namen wie *Fützenswille 6964* aus *Bütschwil.*   [26] Bachtin, a.a.O., S. 11 ff.

eigenartiges Gleichgewicht von gegenseitiger Abstoßung und Anziehung geschaffen. Man sagt leichthin, daß Gegensätze sich anziehen; für Wittenwiler hat dieser hingeworfene Satz seine volle Bedeutung. Überschaut man den Weg, welchen die äußere Handlung nimmt, so führt er von stärker erzählerischen Anfängen im Turnier zu den lebhaften, dramatischen Auseinandersetzungen in der Ehedebatte und schließlich zu den großartig gesteigerten, sich überstürzenden Ereignissen des Dörperkrieges, der in der völligen Zerstörung des Dorfes Lappenhausen und dem Tode seiner Bewohner ein grausames Ende findet. Vom Epischen, das am Anfang, aber auch in Teilen der Hochzeitshandlung, so in dem breiten Gemälde des Essens, noch seine Ruhepunkte hat, geht der Weg hin zum Dramatischen, in einer Steigerung, die das Ende der epischen Handlung erzwingt. Staiger nennt den Weg vom Epischen zum Dramatischen den Weg vom Zeigen zum Beweisen.[27] Der Beweis liegt im Untergang der Lappenhauser: es kommt so wie es kommen mußte. Aber das ist nicht alles. An diesem Weg sind immer wieder Wegweiser aufgestellt, weniger für die Figuren der Dichtung selbst, die ihren vorgezeichneten Weg gehen, wie sie ihn gegenbildlich gehen müssen, sondern als Orientierungshilfen für die Leser oder Hörer, mit denen diese aus dem Zusammenhang der Handlung herausgerufen werden, an denen sie, im Gegensatz zu den Gestalten der Dichtung, nicht ungeschoren vorbeikommen. Diese Tafeln sollen nicht in erster Linie mit der widersprüchlichen Handlung verglichen werden, denn jeder Vergleich muß für das Torenleben katastrophal ausfallen. Diese Tafeln dienen nicht dazu, innerhalb der Bauernwelt eine Zwischenwelt der Weisheit aufzubauen, sondern im Gegenteil der Möglichkeit einer klaren Distanzhaltung: mit ihrer Hilfe hält sich der Leser die Zudringlichkeit einer überbordenden Triebhandlung vom Leibe. Unerbittlich geht diese vom Zeigen zum Beweisen, immer stärker kontrastiert und distanziert sich die Lehre, in deren Schutz sich der Leser gestellt hat. Durch den Einbezug überwirklicher Mächte verliert das Zeigen immer mehr an Gewicht, immer dramatischer gravitiert es zum beweisenden Ende. Im Beweisen triumphiert die Weisheit über die Torheit, und hinter der Weisheit steht die Lehre, die sich in diesem Konflikt geschickt ihre Reinheit hat bewahren können: ungetrübt von den Kompromissen, auf die das Leben, aber wohl auch der ehrliche Leser und ehrliche Dichter auf Schritt und Tritt sich einzulassen versucht sieht. Unterschwellige Anteil-

---

[27] Staiger, a.a.O., S. 227 ff.

nahme des scheinbar unbewegten, nur der Lehre vertrauenden Dichters, wird spürbar: sie verrät sich in Sympathien für einzelne Gestalten, d. h. in der Versöhnlichkeit des humoristischen Stils. So frage ich mich zum Schluß: liegt nicht gerade hier ein besonderer Einschlag des Didaktischen, der mehr bedeutet als nackte Lehre, auf dem Wege vom Zeigen zum Beweisen, und bedient sich das Didaktische gerade hier mit gutem Grund im Blick auf den Leser, der zwischen Skylla und Charybdis sich leicht unsicher fühlen kann, jener Wegweiser und Marksteine der Besonnenheit, die in den großen Lehren aufgerichtet sind, aber nicht weniger auch der unzähligen Randbemerkungen und Sentenzen, die das Geschehen begleiten? Zu dieser »Begleitmusik« gehört auch die feine Differenzierung zwischen Torheit und Anzeichen der Weisheit in der Schilderung der Gestalten. Aber es kommt nicht zum Lehrgedicht als einer übergreifenden Gattung: das Didaktische muß dies ebensowenig notwendig bewirken wie das Epische das Epos, das Dramatische das Drama, das Lyrische das Gedicht. Ein reines Lehrgedicht müßte den Kontrast einebnen, die Handlung als beispielhafte mit dem Beispiel der Lehre in Einklang bringen, statt *nutz* und *tagalt* ständig allen Annäherungen zum Trotz in einen unversöhnlichen Kontrast zu verweisen. Der Dichter mutet mit diesem Verfahren dem Leser ein großes Maß an Selbständigkeit zu und erwartet von ihm auch eigene Entscheidung. Der Leser darf sich im Blick auf das Dörperleben mit gutem Grund weiser finden als die Toren der Handlung, aber er wird auch das Maß an Teilhabe an der Torheit erkennen müssen, das ihn von der Weisheit trennt, denn an die Reinheit der Lehre reicht er nicht heran. Die Freiheit des Lesers ist insofern begrenzt, als sie – wie im Karneval – an die Narrenfreiheit gebunden ist: sie endet mit dem trostlosen Aschermittwoch des Dörperlebens; der Spuk ist vorbei, was bleibt sind die nüchternen Lehren, die der Dichter sorgfältig abgeschirmt hat gegen alles, was ihre Reinheit bedrohte.[28] Diese Lehren wurden ihm nicht durch Abstriche ad usum delphini schmackhaft gemacht, sie sind von einer makellosen Ganzheit und Rundung; ihr anziehender Reiz liegt in einem ästhetischen Moment, in einer Form, welche die Überzeugungskraft des Ethischen in der großartigen Folgerichtigkeit eines schlüssigen Stils zum Ausdruck bringt. Das Normative hat sich ein unwiderlegliches gedankliches Gebäude errichtet, in der Debatte wird Theologie, Ethos und Rechtsdenken in überzeugender Klarheit, durchgegliedert bis ins letzte, dar-

---

[28] Bachtin, a.a.O., S. 37.

geboten, die Debatten werden zu Kunstformen von Theologie und
Jurisprudenz.

Das Didaktische schafft damit auch im Stil einen Kontrast zur episch-
dramatischen Dörperhandlung, trägt also vom sprachlichen Fundament
her bei zur Kontrastform, die das Ganze trägt. Wittenwiler geht letztlich durchaus den Weg, der mittelalterlicher Dichtung vorgezeichnet ist;
auch der starke Einschlag der Torheit-Weisheit-Systematik vermag noch
kein humanistisches Weltbild zu schaffen: die Kunst versieht einen
Dienst am Menschen, und außerhalb des christlichen Weltbildes wird
kein Weg gewiesen. Dichtung, insoweit sie lehrt und sich vom Didaktischen leiten läßt, dient der Selbstverwirklichung des Menschen auf
dem Wege zu den letzten Wahrheiten hin; dabei kann die Welt selbst
in ihrer törichten Extremform nicht aus dem Rahmen ausbrechen, der
ihr von der Weisheit her gesetzt ist. Sie kann ihr bis zum bitteren Ende
entgegenwirken, aber es ist immer ein »Entgegen« und hebt nichts auf,
noch ändert sich etwas an der Lehre am anderen Pol. Die Welt kann nur
sich selbst vernichten, nicht aber als Torheit der Weisheit Entscheidendes
anhaben. Darum kann, ja muß man über die Dörperwelt lachen und sie
ihrem Schicksal überlassen.

Mir scheint von der Grundanlage der Dichtung her und ihren dichterischen Qualitäten so viel für die Einheit des Werkes zu sprechen, daß
sie auch gattungsmäßig nicht einfach ein Konglomerat verschieden-
artiger Ansätze sein kann. Der Entscheid für ein einziges Kennwort
ist zwar nicht gelungen; es ist überhaupt müßig, Kennmarken von oben
her einem Werk überzustülpen: in einem Fall wie dem unsern kommt
nur ein Ausgang von den Fundamenten her in Frage und bei dieser Prüfung war ein erneutes Aufrollen des problematischen Verhältnisses von
Erzählteil und Lehre, von *nutz* und *tagalt,* unumgänglich. Sehen wir
aber das Ganze sich bilden in einem Zusammenwirken fundamentaler
Gestaltungskräfte, in welchem neben den »klassischen« Gestaltungsweisen auch dem Didaktischen eine Rolle, nämlich die einer Wegleitung
zukommt, dann mag das erneute Umgraben doch nicht ganz umsonst
gewesen sein.[29]

---

[29] Im großen und ganzen komme ich beinah zu einem Urteil, das sich von dem kaum
unterscheidet, das schon Günther Müller im Jahre 1927 gefällt hat: »Im Ring ist
nicht eigentlich eine neue Gattungsform für das neue Wollen geschaffen, wie das im
Ackermann trotz allem der Fall ist. Aber der Ringdichter hat die Fülle der weltlich-
didaktischen Unterarten zu einer neuen Großform zusammengeschmiedet.« *Deutsche Dichtung von der Renaissance bis zum Ausgang des Barock,* Handbuch der
Lit'wiss., hg. von O. Walzel, Potsdam 1927, S. 74.

Claiborne W. Thompson

Moral Values in the Icelandic Sagas: Recent Re-evaluations

It is an encouraging sign of the times to see the Icelandic Saga included in a discussion of »The Epic in Medieval Society«. Not long ago it would have seemed curiously out of place to most observers to find the aesthetic and moral values of the Icelandic Sagas treated side-by-side with such things as Chanson de Geste, Middle High German Epic, and Arthurian Romance. Typical of this older view might be the words of Henry Osborn Taylor, who in his classic work on *The Mediaeval Mind* wrote of the sagas:

> These Norse compositions belong to the Middle Ages only in time; for they were uninfluenced either by Christianity or the antique culture, the form-ative elements of mediaeval development.[1]

Even a scholar as »modern« in some respects as W. P. Ker remarked that:

> The Icelandic *Sagas* ... are the last and also the finest expression and record of the spirit and the ideas belonging properly to the Germanic race in its own right, and not derived from Rome or Christendom.[2]

The emphasis in this older conception is thus on the isolated nature of the sagas; though written down in the thirteenth century, they are held to preserve older values, uninfluenced by contemporary foreign cur-rents.

Although one still runs across this point of view occasionally (Peter Hallberg, for example, writes of the sagas' »complete absence of any definite points of contact with other literatures«),[3] it is fair to say that

---

[1] Henry Osborne Taylor, *The Mediaeval Mind*, 4th ed. (London, 1925), vol. 1, p. 167.
[2] W. P. Ker, *Epic and Romance* (London, 1897), Dover reprint New York, 1957, p. 57.
[3] Peter Hallberg, *The Icelandic Saga*, tr. Paul Schach (Lincoln, Nebraska, 1962), p. 1.

it has been largely abandoned in favor of a new conception in which the Icelandic Sagas are seen in their medieval European context. There has been a great deal of stimulating scholarship in recent years exploring the sagas in relation to medieval historiography, Christian hagiography, continental romance, and the like.[4]

Such recent re-thinking has also affected our understanding of the moral values found in the Icelandic Sagas. It is possible to say, in fact, that new approaches to the old questions of saga origins, of saga style or rhetoric, of the historicity of the sagas, and of their literary connections have laid the foundation for a re-interpretation of the sagas' moral import.

As long as the sagas were considered, for example, as objective, historically accurate reports of actual events from the »Saga Age« (ca. 850–1050), there was little interest in exploring saga ethics, since this neutral recording of history would preclude to a large extent the possibility of a moral message. The sagas were, so to speak, beyond good and evil, »absolute prose«;[5] there was no »moral superstructure« in them,[6] a unique situation in an age of such widespread didacticism. But as faith in the historical trustworthiness of the sagas was broken down by historians like Lauritz Weibull[7] and literary scholars like Sigurður Nordal,[8] the corollary view that the sagas are fictional pieces of literature – works of art – began to take hold. Today this is without a doubt the dominant view, and within it there is likely to be more room to accommodate an author's moral viewpoint, a moral superstructure.[9]

---

[4] See for example Lars Lönnroth, *European Sources of Icelandic Saga-Writing* (Stockholm, 1965); Hans Bekker-Nielsen, Thorkil Damsgaard Olsen, and Ole Widding, *Norrøn fortællekunst* (Copenhagen, 1965); E. O. G. Turville-Petre, *Origins of Icelandic Literature* (Oxford, 1953); Ursula Dronke, »Classical Influence on Early Norse Literature«, in *Classical Influences on European Culture A. D. 500–1500*, ed. R. R. Bolgar (Cambridge, 1971), pp. 143–149; Bjarni Einarsson, *Skáldasögur* (Reykjavík, 1961).

[5] Andreas Heusler, »Die Anfänge der isländischen Saga«, *Abh. d. Pr. Ak., Phil.-Hist. Kl.* (Berlin, 1914), p. 44.

[6] Walther Gehl, *Ruhm und Ehre bei den Nordgermanen* (Berlin, 1937), p. 75.

[7] For example in his *Kritiska undersökningar i Nordens historia omkring år 1000* (1911); see also the discussion in *Mediaeval Scandinavia* 5 (1972), pp. 96–138.

[8] As in his classic *Hrafnkatla* (Studia Islandica VII, Reykjavík, 1940). English translation by R. George Thomas (Cardiff, 1958).

[9] Cf. Paul Schach, »Some Forms of Writer Intrusion in the *Íslendingasögur*«, *Scandinavian Studies* 42 (1970), pp. 128–156; Lars Lönnroth, »Rhetorical Persuasion in the Sagas«, *Scandinavian Studies* 42 (1970), pp. 157–189. An influential book on this subject is Wayne Booth's *Rhetoric of Fiction* (Chicago, 1961).

The discrediting of the historical aspect of the sagas has been accompanied by a corresponding loss of faith in their oral origins.[10] Again and again scholars have shown that the sagas are not scribal copies of ancient oral stories but rather products of thirteenth century literary consciousness, pre-meditated works of distinctively individual authors. The effect of this re-thinking on a study of moral values is to remind us that what we encounter in an Icelandic Saga is more likely to be a reflection of thirteenth century concerns than of pagan Germanic culture, for in the thirteenth century Iceland was a part of the Christian community of Western Europe and shared in the learning of the time.[11]

There have appeared in recent years three studies which, despite a number of differences, together constitute a serious re-evaluation of the ethical import of the Icelandic Sagas. The studies date from the years 1969 (Lars Lönnroth), 1970 (T. M. Andersson), and 1971 (Hermann Pálsson), and I should like to consider them in that order.

Lönnroth's major concern is to isolate and describe a charactertype found in the sagas which he calls the »noble heathen«.[12] This person is nominally a pagan and in fact has usually never had direct contact with Christianity, yet in his natural inclinations he appears to embody much that is laudable from a Christian point of view. Characteristic of this type of hero is his mature wisdom, his restraint, his sense of justice and mercy, and often a »half-mystical insight into the workings of nature« – qualities which by themselves are not necessarily or exclusively Christian but which taken together anticipate the new religion. There remains a certain distance between such a pagan hero and the Christian saga-author – without the holy spirit and the institution of the church the noble heathen's virtue was imperfect – but nevertheless the sagas testify to a lively interest in exploring the common ground between tenth century pagans and thirteenth century Christians.

According to Lönnroth, this common ground was extensive indeed. Arguing against the prevalent notion that the Christian and pagan moral codes stood in stark contrast to one another, Lönnroth sees much

---

10 Although the one does not necessarily imply the other, since there can be unhistorical oral tradition. Cf. T. M. Andersson, *The Problem of Icelandic Saga Origins* (New Haven, 1964), pp. 108–109.

11 Cf. Paul Lehmann, »Skandinaviens Anteil an der lateinischen Literatur und Wissenschaft des Mittelalters«, reprinted in *Erforschung des Mittelalters* V, pp. 275–393.

12 Lars Lönnroth, »The Noble Heathen: A Theme in the Sagas«, *Scandinavian Studies* 41 (1969), pp. 1–29.

overlapping. Whereas previous scholars tend to associate the virtues of humility, forgiveness, compassion, and obedience to the Church with the Christian »system«, and worldly honor, the duty of revenge, and loyalty to family with the pagan »system«, Lönnroth believes that given a certain leniency on the part of thirteenth century Icelanders, most of the heroic pagan ideals would be found acceptable to a Christian audience. There are, to be sure, certain aspects of paganism, such as heathen sacrifice and worship, the exposure of children, the practice of sorcery and witchcraft, which are completely unacceptable in Christian eyes (and condemned in the sagas), but otherwise most of the so-called heathen values can be found to be supported in Christian documents of the thirteenth century.

Perhaps the most significant of these documents is the thirteenth century Norwegian didactic treatise called the *King's Mirror (Konungs skuggsjá)*. In this work Lönnroth finds not only an attitude sympathetic to worldly honor, but also a reserved approval of the revenge principle, for example in these passages, which Lönnroth cites:

> Keep your temper calm though not to the point of suffering abuse or bringing upon yourself the reproach of cowardice. Though necessity may force you into strife, be not in a hurry to take revenge; first make sure that your effort will succeed and strike where it ought. Never display a heated temper when you see that you are likely to fail, but be sure to maintain your honor at some later time, unless your opponent should offer a satisfactory atonement.

> When you hear things in the speech of other men which offend you much, be sure to investigate with reasonable care whether the tales be true or false; but if they prove to be true and it is proper for you to seek revenge, take it with reason and moderation and never when heated or irritated.[13]

In this emphasis on moderation (ON *hóf*) Lönnroth finds a key to the understanding of the noble heathens in the Icelandic Sagas.

The concept of *hóf* also plays a central role in T. M. Andersson's article from the following year.[14] As a point of departure Andersson uses a traditional conception of saga ethics, according to which honor in the sagas derives directly from the pagan value system and carries with it the absolute necessity of blood revenge. He is especially concerned with

---

[13] L. Holm-Olsen, *Konungs skuggsjá* (Oslo, 1945), pp. 6, 66. English translation by L. M. Larsen (New York, 1917), pp. 85, 231.

[14] T. M. Andersson, »The Displacement of the Heroic Ideal in the Family Sagas«, *Speculum* XLV (1970), pp. 575–593.

countering Walther Gehl's »neutral« view of the chieftain as an over-
bearing and relentless man *(ójafnaðarmaðr)*. Gehl did not believe that
the sagas implied any negative judgement whatsoever of this charactertype, whereas Andersson demonstrates conclusively that the sagas
usually condemn the *ójafnaðarmaðr* and place a high value on men who
show restraint and diplomacy. (Here Andersson is very close to Lönnroth's notion of the »noble heathen«.) Thus in Andersson's reading of
Hænsa-Þóris saga honorable behavior is defined as »a firm but moderate
attitude and a willingness to go more than halfway in meeting even an
unreasonable opponent« (p. 578). Whereas Gehl found no evidence of
an »Enthusiasmus des Entsagens« in the sagas, Andersson argues convincingly that the ideal heroes are those who are willing to renounce
the demands of pride for the sake of reconciliation. The sagas are thus
against excess and in favor of the virtues of moderation and fore-
bearance.

Up to this point Andersson's views are in basic agreement with those
of Lönnroth, who however documented such virtues in Christian writings of the thirteenth century. In contrast, Andersson is inclined to
minimize the debt to Christianity, viewing the emphasis on moderation
as evidence of a new social consciousness analagous to the Greek notion
of sophrosyne. »What we probably have in the sagas is not so much the
replacement of a pagan ideal with a Christian ideal as the replacement
of a warrior ideal with a social ideal« (p. 592). Rather than seeking
support in a Christian work such as the *Konungs skuggsjá*, Andersson
cites the moral precepts of the Eddic *Hávamál*, which in his novel but
troubling analysis also celebrate the virtue of moderation. »What emerges from this collection of gnomic verse«, he writes (p. 592), »is not a
formulation of self-interest. It seems to me rather that *Hávamál* pro-
pounds the values of the middle way and social accommodation and
it seems to me further that this is very close to the spirit which moves the
authors of the sagas.«

The most recent and most radical of the three studies I have chosen to
sketch is Hermann Pálsson's *Art and Ethics in Hrafnkel's Saga*.[15] Although the book is concerned (as the title indicates) with aesthetic as
well as moral values, exemplified in a specific saga, it bears quite heavily
on general questions of saga ethics. At times Pálsson seems in basic
agreement with Lönnroth and Andersson; certainly they build on com-

---

15 Hermann Pálsson, *Art and Ethics in Hrafnkel's Saga* (Copenhagen, 1971).

mon ground. On the other hand, there are certain interpretations in the book which many would be reluctant to accept.

Pálsson's program is clear from the outset: »The present study is an attempt to interpret *Hrafnkel's saga* in terms of thirteenth century values and attitudes, and it is my hope that the essay will also serve to encourage a fresh approach to saga criticism in general.« (p. 9) It is clear that this approach builds on the kind of modern conception of the Icelandic Saga that underlies the work of Lönnroth and, despite some differences, Andersson as well. Pálsson himself is well aware of this when he writes that »a new picture of these sagas is gradually emerging, and scholars are beginning to realize how much this literature owes to the Christian tradition of medieval Europe« (p. 10). The saga is only a »historical novel« on the surface; »at a deeper level the story has a serious moralistic purpose and must therefore be interpreted in terms of medieval ethics« (p. 15).

Since in his view the morality of a saga »has very little to do with pagan attitudes« (p. 21), Pálsson makes considerable use of medieval Christian theologians and philosophers, as well as the Bible itself. (These include especially Hugh of St. Victor, Augustine, and the books of Job and Ecclesiasticus.) Thus in his chapter on »Freedom and Action« he argues that in the sagas »a moral act involves the agent's will and intention« (p. 49) rather than the pagan concept of fate. Different characters have different degrees of freedom, but the morality of each of them can be judged by the way this freedom is used or abused. Similarly, each character's sense of justice (defined in accordance with Augustine as »the virtue by which each man is given his due«), his sense of compassion, his degree of self-knowledge and avoidance of pride are to be measured against Christian doctrine in order to interpret the morality of a specific act.

Pálsson, in fact, maintains that the sagas show very little sympathy for the heroic attitude, pointing out that mouthpieces of the heroic ethic are very often seen in a bad light, such as the servant-woman who goads Hrafnkel into slaying Eyvind and whose speech, according to Pálsson, »serves to exemplify unacceptable morality, as indeed it must have been understood by the author and his public« (p. 73).

In summarizing Pálsson's general conclusions I can do no better than cite the beginning of his final chapter: »A thematic analysis of the Sagas of Icelanders will show that justice figures more prominently in them than the other cardinal virtues, though prudence and fortitude are by no means rare. In this literature, moderation is always a highly valued trait in people's conduct, and peace is the great social ideal.« (p. 75)

No one can overlook the similarity that these conclusions bear to those of Andersson and Lönnroth, who both found moderation to be a key concept. Where Pálsson differs from the other two is in his absolute rejection of the relevance of pagan values in interpreting saga morality. In a sense, then, Pálsson approaches the sagas from the outside, with ethical standards derived from medieval Christianity.

Now although there would seem to be nothing inherently wrong with this approach, and in fact little fault can be found with the general formulation of the conclusions it produces, it can nevertheless lead Pálsson to some very curious interpretations of specific incidents in the saga he is writing about. His analysis of *Hrafnkel's saga* is in fact so disturbing at times that serious doubt is cast on the method he uses.

By way of example, let us consider the boy Einar who rides Freyfaxi without permission and is slain by Hrafnkel. Pálsson correctly notes that his freedom of action is restricted because of his position and because of the injunction against riding Freyfaxi. Pálsson then goes on (p. 46):

> But it is finally left to Einar himself to take the irrevocable step that leads to his death. He deliberately misuses his freedom of choice when he yields to temptation and rides Freyfaxi. The shepherd's fall is no sudden impulse but a premeditated act, and he is brutally made to pay the ultimate penalty for it.

Pálsson then goes on to criticize what he calls the »romantic« view (e.g. Nordal, Turville-Petre) that Einar is a »pawn of fate«. On the contrary, says Pálsson, Einar's choice is a matter of free will, just as in the story of the Fall in Genesis the tempted person is free to resist according to medieval theology. Pálsson in fact would believe that the story of Einar is based on the biblical account of the Fall.

Now there are several things I find disturbing about this interpretation. By implication, Hrafnkel is given the role of God, Einar is guilty and deserves punishment. This is of course absurd, and later Pálsson speaks of Einar's »real innocence« (p. 63). Furthermore, I find Pálsson's criticism of the »romantic« view to a large extent unjustified, since he fails to make some crucial distinctions in this scene which the »romanticists« do make. Einar does not simply make a deliberate decision to ride Freyfaxi. His decision is to travel by horse instead of on foot, and there is nothing forbidden here, since there are ten or twelve other horses available which he may ride. At this point the saga says:

> But when he came closer, all the mares bolted away from him, and he chased them without success. They had never been so shy before. Only Freyfaxi remained behind; he was as still as if he were anchored to the ground.[16]

Now I suggest that there is something strange going on here, and in Freyfaxi's later actions too, some inexplicable configuration of supernatural or chance events for which the term »fate« is not totally inappropriate.

Another example: Pálsson criticizes as »simplistic« the traditional view of Hrafnkel's behavior at the eviction scene. The saga relates that Sám does not put Hrafnkel to death, as the sons of Thjostar advise, but gives him the choice of either being killed or living on as Sám's subordinate. Hrafnkel chooses life, even though, as the traditional interpretation has it, this is a less heroic mode of behavior, since he must accept dishonor along with life. But Pálsson views it in a different light: »For a Christian this is a simple choice, because it is everyman's duty to save and safeguard his life as long as he can, and Hrafnkel makes the obvious decision.« (p. 44)

Now whether or not saga authors in general attributed Christian modes of behavior to their characters, in this case the saga itself tells us a bit about Hrafnkel's thinking on the subject. When Hrafnkel and his men are seized the saga tells us that:

> He made many offers for himself and his followers, and when these served no purpose pleaded for the lives of his men. »For they have done nothing to offend against you, while it is no discredit to me though you kill me. I am not asking to be spared that, but I do ask to be spared humiliation. There is no credit to you in that.«[17]

What Hrafnkel is talking about is *sœmð*, here translated as »credit« and one of the most important words for »honor« in the sagas. Note that Hrafnkel knows the difference between *sœmð* and *ósœmð*: my death would be no dishonor *to me*, but my humiliation would be dis-

---

16 Pálsson's translation, in his *Hrafnkel's Saga and other Icelandic Stories* (Penguin Books, 1971), p. 40.
17 Translation by Gwyn Jones, in *Eirik the Red and other Icelandic Sagas* (London and New York, 1961), p. 111.

honorable behavior *for you*.[18] He thus specifically contradicts the Christian reasoning which Pálsson would attribute to him.

Pálsson further offers the novel idea that Sám in this scene is morally guilty for his refusal to kill Hrafnkel outright, since »to kill a wicked ruler could be regarded as a kind of duty and even an act of justice, as one great medieval authority, John of Salisbury, has stated: ›It is not merely lawful to slay a tyrant, but it is even right and just. He that taketh the sword is worthy of perishing with the sword.‹« (p. 53)

Now regardless of the danger in employing John's complicated and radical doctrine of tyrranicide as typical of medieval Christian thought on Iceland,[19] it seems to me that the saga author does not see Sám's decision as a question of morality at all. Rather, it strikes me as a matter of practical judgement. Sám made the wrong decision from the point of view of power politics, and when Thorkel Thjostarsson tells him he will regret giving Hrafnkel his life, he is not speaking of ethical precepts but of what his brother Thorgeir later calls »intelligence« or »understanding«.[20] What Sám does in sparing Hrafnkel's life is to prove that he is not a born *goði*, he does not understand the rules of the game he has elected to play.

What these examples (and there are many more) go to show, I think, is that the method of citing bits and pieces of medieval Christian doctrine to illuminate a saga episode is basically misguided. For every interpretation of Pálsson the opposite view could also be supported by passages from the Scriptures or from religious treatises. But most importantly, with Pálsson's approach the saga tends to lose the aspect of a story and become a series of disconnected ethical questions. Perhaps this is the way Pálsson intends it to be; on page 70 of *Art and Ethics* he says

---

18 This is curiously mistranslated in Pálsson's version of the saga (p. 57), where for *en þat er mér engi ósœmð, þótt þér drepið mik* one finds »but you can kill me without any discredit to yourselves«.

19 John's views were by no means accepted doctrine in the thirteenth century, but were the subject of great controversy and repudiated in part by later theologians. There was an equally or more powerful tradition in medieval thought which directly contradicts John's notion, viewing wicked rulers as part of God's plan for the world. See e.g. the introduction to *The Statesman's Book of John of Salisbury*, translated by John Dickinson (New York, 1927).

20 »Er þat nú auðsét, hverr vizkumunr ykkarr hefir orðit« (chapter 10). Pálsson and I differ in our views of the two brothers. For Pálsson Thorkel is »a man of high moral principles« whereas his brother Thorgeir is »guided by a sense of self-preservation and expediency« (p. 55). In my view Thorkel is an immature, irresponsible, but engaging character, while Thorgeir's mature reflection represents the author's moral norm.

that »for the purpose of analysing the meaning of the story, the moral
act must be regarded as a basic constituent element«. The danger with
this approach is that the saga no longer has a point; the whole is no
greater than the sum of the parts.

Traditionally there have been two ways of interpreting the story of
Hrafnkel. In the most common view it is »a story of pride, punishment,
and rehabilitation«.[21] A minority would not view the saga as didactic at
all but merely the story of a despot who regains his power without
undergoing any basic change in character.[22] In Pálsson's treatment we
would seem to have a third interpretation: Hrafnkel falls not once but
twice, since his killing of Eyvind at the end of the saga constitutes the
loss of his newly acquired sense of moral justice.[23] That the saga does not
indicate any divine retribution for this sin, but rather tells us that
»Hrafnkel lived on his farm and kept his honours«, his sons inheriting
his authority when he died, does not speak in favor of this view.

That the moral standards used to interpret an Icelandic Saga should
originate *within* the work can be shown, I think, by citing two external
sources which might be taken to bear on Hrafnkel's murder of Eyvind.
One of these is the *King's Mirror*, already cited in the discussion of
Lönnroth's views. When Hrafnkel, after some six years of waiting,
coolly and efficiently removes Sám's brother Eyvind and avenges himself on Sám, he seems to be following the advice of the *King's Mirror*
to the letter: »be not in a hurry to take revenge; first make sure that
your effort will succeed and strike where it ought«.[24] Here we would
seem to have a thirteenth century document, perhaps the work of a
theologian, which provides us with the proper context in which to interpret Hrafnkel's act.

On the other hand, one does not have to go very far to find another
medieval Christian document which would place Hrafnkel in a completely different light. I refer to the Old Norse translation of Alcuin's
treatise on the virtues and vices, contained in a manuscript from about
1200.[25] In the section »On Patience« one finds the following, not inappropriate to Hrafnkel's situation:

---

[21] T. M. Andersson, »The Displacement . . .«, p. 584.
[22] Pierre Halleux, »Hrafnkel's Character Reinterpreted«, *Scandinavian Studies* 38
    (1966), pp. 36–44.
[23] *Art and Ethics* pp. 56, 79.
[24] *King's Mirror*, tr. L. M. Larsen, p. 85.
[25] George T. Flom, *Codex AM 619 Quarto. Old Norwegian Book of Homilies con-*

> There are some people who patiently tolerate unfair treatment for a while
> in order that they may later take vengeance more easily. They do not have
> true patience. True patience is to tolerate unfair treatment with fortitude
> and not seek vengeance later, but rather forgive in the heart.   (p. 59)

What these conflicting sources seem to point out is that in certain situations there is no »simple choice«; on the contrary, a person of average
moral fibre operating in the secular context could be faced with a dilemma, and it is this dilemma which often is found at the core of an Icelandic saga. It is in this context that the words of Flosi, in *Njál's Saga*,
are best understood:

> There are only two courses open to us, neither of them good: we must either
> abandon the attack, which would cost us our own lives, or we must set fire
> to the house and burn them to death, which is a grave responsibility before
> God, since we are Christian men ourselves. But that is what we must do.[26]

Perhaps in our enthusiasm over the discovery that the Icelandic sagas
are largely fictional works in contact with medieval European historio-
graphic, literary, and religious currents we have run the risk of throwing out the baby with the bath. The sagas are not a series of moral
parables but an imaginative treatment of the past: an attempt by thirteenth century Icelanders to come to terms with both their ancestors
and themselves.

And in their treatments of the past the authors must not be denied the
gift of historical perspective. One of the remarkable things about a
writer like Snorri Sturluson is his sense of the past: his ability to perceive anachronism, his critical use of evidence, and his interest in causa-
tion, three factors which are said to be lacking in the middle ages.[27]
The authors of the thirteenth century were able to explore the passions
of their ancestors in the light of native poetry, for example, as well as
contemporary Christian works. From their antiquarian learning they
knew that these people were in some sense different, that the people
they wrote about believed in the role of fate and in the importance of
worldly reputation, and they were able to use these in their depiction
of moral behavior.[28]

---

taining the *Miracles of Saint Olaf* and Alcuin's *De Virtutibus et Vitiis*, University
of Illinois Studies in Language and Literature, vol. XIV no. 4 (Urbana, 1929).
[26] *Njal's Saga*, tr. Magnús Magnússon and Hermann Pálsson (Penguin Books, 1960),
p. 265.
[27] As alleged by Peter Burke, *The Renaissance Sense of the Past* (London, 1969), p. 1.
[28] Note for example a prose passage in *Fáfnismál*: »þat var trúa þeira í fornescio,

The result is an intersection of ethical concepts such as one finds in the *King's Mirror* or in the following piece of advice, given to Svipdag in the Saga of Hrolf Kraki:

> Covet nothing of your neighbour's; act without arrogance, for that is open to men's blame; but defend yourself should you be attacked, for it is a noble thing to boast little about oneself, yet achieve a great destiny if one is put to the test.[29]

We must also bear in mind that religious-ethical standards are not the only key to behavior in the sagas. There are at least two other yardsticks by which character can be measured: the aesthetic and what for lack of a better term I shall call the pragmatic. While the latter deserves more attention than it has hitherto received, the former has long been recognized and in fact overstressed, as in the following quotation from a standard textbook:

> Probably in no other literature is conduct so carefully examined and appraised; and the basis of the valuation is not moral, but aesthetic ... The heroes and heroines themselves had the aesthetic view of conduct; it was their chief guide, for they had a very undeveloped conception of morality, and none at all of sin.[30]

It should be clear in light of the recent developments I have outlined in this paper that this represents an enormous overstatement, precisely the kind of thing that Pálsson, for example, reacts against so violently. Nevertheless, it is still true that the aesthetic criterion can be useful in understanding some behavior in the sagas. Perhaps Eyvind's defense on the Fljotsdal moor is best understood in this light. The last stand of Gísli Súrsson in the saga of that name is also a case in which the author appreciates aesthetically the behavior of a hero who from a Christian moral viewpoint is not very admirable.

Hrafnkel's slaying of Eyvind, on the other hand, is neither an aesthetic act nor a moral one. Like Sám's decision to spare Hrafnkel's life, it has nothing to do with morals but everything to do with practical judge-

---

at orð feigs mannz mætti mikit, ef hann bǫlvaði óvin sínom með nafni« (*Edda. Die Lieder des Codex Regius*, ed. Hans Kuhn [Heidelberg, 1962], p. 180). In his discussion of the fall of Earl Hakon (in Olaf Tryggvason's saga), Snorri cites skaldic verse which attributes great power to fate (*Heimskringla*, ed. Finnur Jónsson [Copenhagen, 1911], p. 143).

29 English translation by Gwyn Jones, *Eirik the Red and Other Icelandic Sagas* (London and Ney York, 1961), pp. 251–252.

30 E. V. Gordon, *An Introduction to Old Norse*, 2nd ed. revised by A. R. Taylor (Oxford, 1957), p. xxxiii.

ment. The difference between them is that Hrafnkel's course of action is efficient whereas Sám's is unproductive. Instead of the moral contrast good/bad or the aesthetic one beautiful/ugly, we are dealing with a wise/foolish contrast as understood in a pragmatic sense.[31]

The wise/foolish scale of conduct and character is not to be associated exclusively with either the pagan value system or the Christian one. It is found in both the *Hávamál* and the *King's Mirror* in, for example, the contempt which is shown for the foolish person who struts around unaware of his own ignorance. It also must lie behind the frequent strictures against drunkenness in both these works. Overindulging is condemned not so much as a moral issue, like the vice of gluttony, but because it renders one foolish:

> Never get drunk, wherever you are; for it may fall out at any time that you will be summoned to hear a dispute or supervise something, or that you will have important business of your own to look after. Now if such demands should come to a man while he is drunk, he will be found wholly incompetent...[32]

Or as the *Hávamál* express it:

> Less good there lies   than most believe
>   In ale for mortal men;
> For the more he drinks   the less does man
>   Of his mind the mastery hold.[33]

I think, too, that there is an aspect of the pragmatic also lying behind the sagas' criticism of violence and the feud mentality. As was the case with the Icelanders' conversion from paganism to Christianity, the institution of blood revenge was examined in its pragmatic implications as well as its moral ones. Just as Thorgeir goði found it politically unwise for Iceland to risk civil war by attempting to resist the new faith, so some saga characters realize that a social system based on inflexible honor and vengeance is out-of-date, self-defeating, and foolish.

It is in this light that I would interpret, for example, the so-called »epilogue« of *Hen-Thorir's saga,* in which renewed violence is averted through the practical good sense of Thorodd Tungu-Oddsson, who

---

[31] Two or more of these criteria can figure in the evaluation of a specific act. For example, Eyvind's defense on the moor ranks high aesthetically, but his behavior (»I'll not run from men to whom I have done no wrong«) is extremely foolish.
[32] *King's Mirror,* tr. L. M. Larsen, p. 166.
[33] *The Poetic Edda,* tr. H. A. Bellows (New York, 1923), p. 31.

marries the daughter of his father's enemy and then manipulates both
men into accepting the »happy ending« of the saga. Behind Thorodd's
behavior, if I understand it correctly, lies not so much a sense of moral
outrage at the potential bloodshed as the feeling that these grumpy old
men with their silly pride and their petty feuds are behaving like a
bunch of foolish children and have to be tricked into agreeing to what
is individually and socially sensible.

Since, therefore, the sagas depict social interaction in all its complexity
and examine behavior from many points of view, the critic must not
limit his own vision in seeking an interpretive key.

Paul Schach

Some Observations on the Generation-Gap
Theme in the Icelandic Sagas

Þorsteins þáttur stangarhöggs (»The Story of Þorsteinn Staff-Struck«)
is a little gem of Icelandic prose fiction written about 1270 as a pendant
to the final chapters of *Vápnfirðinga saga*. Only twelve pages in length
in the popular *Íslendinga sögur* series,[1] this tale has a simple plot in-
volving three main characters and five secondary figures, all but two
of whom are introduced on the first page of the story.

Þórarinn, once a fierce marauder, is now a blind old man who has small
means but a large collection of weapons. Even in his old age he is difficult to deal with, and the weapons, as Hermann Pálsson has pointed
out, serve to »accentuate his failure to integrate into the peaceful rural
society of which he is a reluctant and useless member«.[2] By contrast,
his only son Þorsteinn is an amiable and even-tempered farmer who
supports his destitute father by doing the work of three men on their
farm Sunudalur. Þorstein's first adversary is an arrogant farm hand
named Þórður, who does not let people forget that he is in the employ
of the district chieftain, Bjarni of Hof. Þórður is characterized as a very
truculent man *(ójafnaðarmaður mikill)* and this designation, Walther
Gehl's protestations to the contrary notwithstanding, is nearly always
a label, a code word if you will, of the utmost opprobrium.[3] Bjarni
himself, the wealthiest and most influential man in the district, is introduced without the conventional thumbnail character sketch, evident-

---

[1] *Íslendinga sögur*, ed. Guðni Jónsson, Íslendingasagnaútgáfan: Reykjavík 1949,
   Vol. X, pp. 63–76. The standard edition is found in *Austfirðinga sögur* (= Íslenzk
   fornrit, Vol. XI), ed. Jón Jóhannesson, Hið íslenzka fornritafélag: Reykjavík
   1950, pp. 69–79.
[2] *Art and Ethics in Hrafnkel's Saga*, Munksgaard: Copenhagen 1971, pp. 76–77.
[3] For a provocative discussion and further bibliography on this question see Theodore M. Andersson, »The Displacement of the Heroic Ideal in the Family Sagas«,
   Speculum 45 (1970), 575–593.

ly because the author assumed that his audience was sufficiently familiar with Bjarni's character from the considerably older *Vápnfirðinga
saga,* in which he plays an important role. In addition to these four
characters, the author also introduces two malicious farm hands before
the modest action of the story begins. They bear the names Þórhallur
and Þorvaldur, and are branded as »great babblers« of all the gossip
they hear about in Bjarni's district.

(If I may be permitted a brief digression at this point, I should like
to emphasize that it was *not* a common practice among saga writers
to borrow character portraits from other stories and to use them
unchanged in their own. On the contrary, some of the most memorable saga characters are largely or entirely confined to one work –
such as the titular hero of *Egils saga Skalla-Grímsson,* Kjartan Ólafsson in *Laxdæla,* and Njáll and Bergþóra and their sons in *Njála.*
When a saga author did borrow characters from elsewhere, he usually
transformed them to suit his own artistic or tendentious purpose.
This transformation could be rather subtle, as in the case of the
ubiquitous Snorri goði, or quite dramatic, as in the case of King
Ólafur Tryggvason or Freydís, the daughter of Eiríkur rauði. The
»standard« portrait of Snorri goði is that created by the compiler of
Eyrbyggja, who refined the harsh features and subdued the glaring
colors of the unlovely picture of Snorri that he found in *Heiðarvíga
saga.* The author of *Gísla saga* rather scotched his sketch of Snorri,[4]
while the author of *Njála* subtly reduced the dimensions and erased
certain features in order thereby to enhance the stature of Njáll.[5]
Of the many portraits of Ólafur Tryggvason, the most remarkable
is that found in *Laxdæla,* whose author seems to have created his own
image of the missionary king by methodically reversing practically
every unflattering character trait attributed to that zealot by Od-
dur munkur.[6] And finally, the courageous Freydís Eiríksdóttir in

---

[4] On this see Paul Schach, »Some Observations on the Helgafell Episode in *Eyrbyggja
saga* and *Gísla saga*«, *Saga og Språk: Studies in Language and Literature,* ed. John
M. Weinstock, Jenkins Publishing Company: Austin, Texas 1972, pp. 113–145.

[5] The author of *Njála* denies Snorri the gift of second sight; conversely, he retouches
the portrait of Earl Hákon, borrowed from the king's sagas, by endowing it with
the very quality of which he deprived Snorri. On this see Einar Ól. Sveinsson,
Njáls Saga: A Literary Masterpiece, ed. and tr. Paul Schach, University of Nebraska
Press: Lincoln, Nebraska 1971, pp. 99 and 158.

[6] Einar Ól. Sveinsson explains this remarkable character transformation as a reflection of the *Laxdæla* author's personality, whereas Rolf Heller regards the gentler

Eiríks saga has practically nothing in common with her heartless namesake in *Grænlendinga saga* except the name.[7] But this is a question that I have treated in detail elsewhere.[8] I mention these few examples only in support of my assertion that the author of *Þorsteins þáttur stangarhöggs* departed from conventional saga practice in assuming that his audience was familiar with a major character from another source.)

As already mentioned, the plot of *Þorsteins þáttur* is very simple. During a horse fight, Þórður deliberately strikes Þorsteinn on the head with his horse prod. Þorsteinn chooses to believe the blow accidental and requests that the matter be kept secret from his father. The author suggests that nothing more would have come of this incident had it not been for the two blabbermouths, who jeeringly give Þorsteinn the nickname Staff-Struck.

This malicious gossip leads to a confrontation between father and son, during which the old marauder expresses disbelief that he could have such a craven son. Stung by his father's harsh taunts, Þorsteinn seeks redress for his injury; but when Þórður merely adds insult to injury, he kills him. Bjarni has Þorsteinn outlawed for homicide, but does nothing to enforce the legal sentence since Þorsteinn is his destitute father's only means of support. Again the two scandalmongers set the creaky plot in motion by wondering out loud how the blot is to be wiped from the honor of their *goði*, since Þorsteinn has defied the court sentence of outlawry. Bjarni thereupon orders them to do so by bringing him Þorstein's head. They go to Sunnudalur and make an attempt on Þorstein's life, but he kills them both. Bjarni initiates no legal action against Þorsteinn. At this point Rannveig, Bjarni's wife, enters the story in the conventional role of the female inciter to vengeance.[9] She warns her husband that his followers are beginn-

---

7 For a perceptive analysis and additional bibliography see Erik Wahlgren, »Fact and Fancy in the Vinland Sagas«, *Old Norse Literature and Mythology: A Symposium*, ed. Edgar C. Polomé, University of Texas Press: Austin and London 1969, pp. 19–80.

8 In a paper entitled »Character Transformation in the Icelandic Sagas« presented before the Scandinavian Section of the Midwest Modern Language Association held on November 2, 1972, in Chicago, Illinois, and in a book review in *Scandinavian Studies* 44 (1972), 555–566. See also »Some Observations on the Helgafell Episode«, pp. 126 ff.

9 The subject of women as »troublemakers« in the sagas is discussed by Richard F. Allen in *Fire and Iron: Critical Approaches to Njáls saga*, University of Pittsburgh Press 1971, pp. 163–171. It is significant that in this *þáttur* the role of the woman servant is just the opposite of the conventional one.

aspects of the king's portrayal in *Laxdæla* as borrowings from *Egils þáttur Síðu-Hallssonar*. The two positions are not incompatible. See Rolf Heller, *Laxdæla saga und Königssagas* (Saga, Heft 5), Max Niemeyer Verlag: Halle (Saale) 1961, pp. 47–52.

ing to doubt his ability to protect them from aggression since he has not
avenged his own servants. Accordingly, Bjarni rides over to Sunudalur
and informs Þorsteinn that they must fight a duel because of the killings.
Þorsteinn is most reluctant to fight, but when Bjarni insists, he requests
permission to speak to his father first.

The second confrontation between father and son adds depth and detail to
the portrait of Þórarinn as a useless relic of the bygone Viking Age. He
harshly upbraids Þorsteinn for having been so foolish as to offend such a
powerful man as Bjarni (although it was he who goaded Þorsteinn into
doing so!) and declares that he himself would not have hesitated to face
the chieftain in his younger days. He concludes his harangue with the cold-
hearted assertion: »It seems better to me to lose you than to have a craven
son.«

Bjarni and Þorsteinn proceed to the top of a hillock together and the duel
begins. After a while Bjarni complains of thirst, and the two walk down
to a creek. As the thirsty man is drinking, Þorsteinn picks up his opponent's
sword and examines it. They return to the hilltop and begin the second
round of their duel. Now Bjarni's shoe thong comes loose, and while he
fastens it, Þorsteinn fetches a new shield for each of them and a better
sword for Bjarni. Again the duel is resumed. But although both shields are
shattered and weighty blows are exchanged, these blows are accompanied
by conciliatory and complimentary comments, and it is clear that neither
wishes to harm the other. Finally Bjarni suggests a different kind of settlement: Þorsteinn is to compensate for the three slain servants by living on
the estate Hof and working for Bjarni.

Now the author completes his portrayal of Þórarinn. Bjarni enters the
house and tells the old man that his son has been slain after putting up a
valiant defense. The old man is obviously pleased to learn of his son's
bravery, and he compliments Bjarni for having been able to overcome
»my son«. Bjarni now offers to compensate for the death of Þorsteinn by
inviting Þórarinn to occupy the seat of honor on his estate for the rest of
his life. Þórarinn first reacts with a diatribe on the unreliability of such
promises made by chieftains to old paupers, but then asks Bjarni to seal
the bargain with a handshake. When Bjarni approaches to do so, the unregenerate Viking attempts to run him through with a concealed sword.
As a punishment for this treachery (of which Þorsteinn has warned Bjarni
in advance), the old codger must live out his days at Sunudalur.

»Þorsteinn accompanied Bjarni to Hof and remained in his service until
his dying day. He was thought to be unequaled in integrity and courage.
Bjarni maintained his reputation and became more popular and more self-
controlled the older he grew. He was a most dependable man, and in the
last years of his life he became a devout Christian. Bjarni went on a pilgrimage, and he died on that journey. He lies buried in a town called Sutri, and
that is a large town, a short distance on this side of Rome.«[10]   (pp. 75–76)

---

10 Both MSS have ›Vateri‹, which seems to be a distortion of ›Sutari‹. In the *Alfræði*

The *þáttur* concludes with a long list of Bjarni's descendants, evidently culled from *ættartölur* (genealogical lists). Among his distinguished descendants are Bishop Magnús (d. 1148) and the sons of Sturla: Þórður, Sighvatur, and Snorri.

Theodore M. Andersson sees in this *þáttur* »not only an illustration but a paradigm of the structure to be found in the family sagas«.[11] He divides the story into six parts as follows:

1) Introduction: the introduction of Þórarinn and Þorsteinn and their adversaries Bjarni, Þórður, Þórhallur, and Þorvaldur.
2) Conflict: Þórður strikes Þorsteinn; Þórhallur and Þorvaldur nickname him Staff-Struck; Þórarinn provokes him to revenge.
3) Climax: Þorsteinn kills Þórður.
4) Revenge: Þórhallur and Þorvaldur incite Bjarni; he dispatches them to Þorsteinn and they are killed; Bjarni duels with Þorsteinn.
5) Reconciliation: the duel is indecisive and the men are reconciled.
6) Aftermath: Bjarni goes abroad and dies near Rome; notes on his descendants.

A comparison between the *þáttur* itself and Andersson's outline of it reveals several startling discrepancies. To begin with, Andersson's alignment of characters in part one is strange indeed, in view of what the author himself tells us about them. Through the initial contrastive characterization of father and son he establishes them at the outset as the two chief adversaries of the story. The father is a blind, unsocial (*eigi dældarmaður*), superannuated freebooter (*rauðavíkingur mikill*) whose fine assortment of weapons, as already mentioned, accentuates his uselessness and alienage in a rural society: he has not beaten his swords into plowshares or his spears into pruning hooks. His son, on the other hand, is a paragon of the strong, self-disciplined, hard-working farmer. Father and son are the perfect embodiments of two basically antagonistic, completely incompatible cultures, that of the savage, destructive marauder and that of the peaceful, constructive farmer. What the author thus states subjectively in the initial characterization he demonstrates more objectively in Þórarin's two confrontations with his son and his one confrontation with Bjarni. In view, of the fact that

---

íslenzk (I,17) this city is called *Sutarinn mikli,* and this may account for the clause *ok er þat mikil borg* »and that is a large town«. See Jón Jóhannesson, *Austfirðinga sögur,* p. 78, n. 2.

11 *The Icelandic Family Saga: An Analytic Reading,* Harvard University Press: Cambridge, Massachusetts 1967, p. 4 ff.

these three confrontations make up one-fourth of the entire story, it seems strangs indeed to find Þórarinn relegated to the minor role of inciter along with Þórður, a second-class villain, Bjarni's wife Rannveig, and the two blabbermouths.

In Andersson's outline of the story it is equally startling to find Bjarni listed as one of Þorsteinn's adversaries. We must keep in mind that Þorsteins þáttur was intended as a sequel to Vápnfirðinga saga and as a pendant to the final chapters of that work. In a certain sense the þáttur is a variation on the theme of these last chapters, where Bjarni is depicted as magnanimous, moderate, brave, and eminently reasonable. Despite the fact that Bjarni is a wealthy chieftain and Þorsteinn remains his servant »until his dying day«, the two have the same outlook on life, and they have so many qualities of character in common that they cannot possibly be adversaries, even though, to be sure, for a brief time they are opponents. Like Þorsteinn, Bjarni is a representative of the peaceful rural culture of Iceland during the time of the Commonwealth, and thus he and Þorsteinn are in irreconcilable conflict with Þórarinn, the embodiment of a harsher, more chaotic past.

This interpretation of the þáttur is further confirmed by the manner in which the author takes leave of his three main characters, for the eulogy or final subjective authorial comment is quite as important for the understanding of a saga as the initial characterization. Þórarinn has to remain at Sunudalur in the care of slaves – a useless relic, an armed anachronism, a »miserable old stinker« (allra fretkarla armastur), as Bjarni calls him. His son Þorsteinn, by contrast, becomes Bjarni's alter ego and is regarded as a model of fortitude and integrity. And Bjarni, a paragon of self-discipline and trustworthiness, like many another saga champion, becomes a devout Christian and makes a pilgrimage to Rome before he dies.

Since Andersson's alignment of characters at the beginning of his outline is at variance with the author's clearly stated design, the outline needs little further comment. This þáttur is clearly a little sermon designed to depict in the portraits of Bjarni and Þorsteinn the ideal chieftain and the ideal farmer-thingman, and, at the same time, in the ominous figure of Þórarinn, to warn the Icelanders of the savage Sturlung Age against the perils of a resurgence of the destructive Viking spirit. The external action of the story is trivial, fabricated by the author and designed to contribute to the delineation of the three major characters. Rannveig and the serving woman appear briefly on stage, recite their lines, and make their exits. Þórður, a small-bore villain, and the even less significant two blabbermouths play their brief insolent roles and come to a swift, ignominious end. The high point of the story, as deVries and others have pointed out,[12] is the duel cum dialogue between Bjarni and Þorsteinn, which, together with the three Þórarinn confrontations, comprises half the story. At the end of the *þáttur* Bjarni does not merely go abroad, as Andersson states in his outline; rather, he makes a pilgrimage to Rome, and this, it seems to me, is not insignificant for a proper interpretation of the tale.

Even if the author had not gone to such pains to point up the moral of his story, the meaning of *Þorsteins þáttur stangarhöggs* should be immediately apparent to the perceptive reader since the father-son conflict as here employed is a variant of a basic theme in saga literature, the theme of the unbridgeable gap between representatives of two generations who embody two antagonistic, diametrically opposed, irreconcilably conflicting cultures.

Probably the most sustained treatment of the generation-gap theme in saga literature is the series of confrontations between Þórólfur bægifótur and his son Arnkell goði, which continue throughout a large part of *Eyrbyggja saga*.[13] Þórólfur is introduced in chapter eight as a *víkingur mikill* and *inn mesti ójafnaðarmaður* – the same two labels of opprobrium we found in the introductory descriptions of Þórarinn and Þórður in *Þorsteins þáttur stangarhöggs*. He begins a new career of violence and depredation in Iceland by killing a childless old man and appropriating his lands. The reason for his careful selection of a victim is obvious: an old man is scarcely a dangerous foe for an experienced killer, and the lack of sons made it unlikely that the old man's slaying would be prosecuted or avenged. By contrast, Þórólf's son Arnkell is formally introduced into the story as »a very large and powerful man, a skilful lawyer, and very wise. He was a manly sort of person *(góður drengur)* and superior to all others in the district in popularity and hardihood. He was also a temple priest *(hofgoði)* and had many followers *(þingmenn)*.« It is clear from this contrastive description that there will be serious friction between father and son.

---

12 *Altnordische Literaturgeschichte*, 2nd ed., Walter de Gruyter and Company: Berlin 1967, Vol. II, p. 449, and Hermann Pálsson, *Art and Ethics in Hrafnkel's Saga*, p. 78.
13 Þórólf's major confrontations with his son occur in chapters 30–34. His last hauntings and killings are related in chapter 63.

Like Þórarinn, Þórólfur did not lose his Víking nature with age; on the contrary, as he grew older, »he became mean and violent and altogether indifferent to other peoples' rights (ójafnaðarfullur). Also he and his son got along worse as time passed.« Þórólfur commits a series of crimes against his neighbor, a man named Úlfar, who was an excellent farmer and »so lucky with his livestock that none ever died of starvation or killing diseases«. First Þórólfur steals Úlfar's hay, for which Arnkell eventually makes compensation. Then he sends six slaves to Úlfar's farm to burn him to death in his house. Arnkell detects the fire, puts it out, and has the slaves hanged. Finally Þórólfur has Úlfar murdered, and Arnkell has the assassin killed in just vengeance for farmer Úlfar. Now Þórólfur attempts to recover a valuable forest he once gave Snorri goði as a bribe to prosecute his case against his son Arnkell for the killing of his assassin. When Snorri refuses to return the forest, Þórólfur suggests to his son that »we two could become powerful here in the district with your hardihood and my planning«. But Arnkell realizes that his father merely wants to involve him in further litigation with Snorri, and declines »to reward you for your malice by the spectacle of Snorri and me litigating about it«. Like Þórarinn, Úlfar accuses his son of cowardice (lítilmennska), but Arnkell remains unyielding.

»With that father and son parted. Þórólfur bægifótur went home and felt exceedingly dejected about the turn matters had taken and about being completely thwarted in everything. He arrived home in the evening and spoke with no one. He sat down in the high seat and did not eat anything all evening. He remained sitting there after all the others had gone to bed. And in the morning when they got up, Þórólfur was sitting there and was dead. Then the mistress of the house sent a man to Arnkell to inform him of the passing of Þórólfur. Arnkell rode up to Hvammur with several of his men servants. And when they came there, Arnkell learned for certain that his father was dead, sitting in the seat of honor; but all the people in the house were terrified because they all thought there was something uncanny about his death.« (Ch. 33)

Even in death, however, the old marauder can find no rest in a peaceful community of farmers and dairy husbandmen. Especially during the long winter nights he haunts the neighborhood, killing and maiming people and committing such violence and destruction that no one dare travel about there. In the spring, Arnkell digs up the hideous, undecomposed body and reburies it on a remote promontory, far from human habitation. Here Þórólfur remains quiet – as long as Arnkell is alive. After Arnkel's death, however, his depredations become so terrible that the body is again disinterred, burned, and the ashes scattered to the winds. Thus the author takes leave of his own particular embodiment of the Viking spirit. But even now Þórólf's malevolence does not cease. A cow becomes impregnated by ingesting some of the ashes, and the bull calf she brings forth eventually gores its owner to death.

Because Arnkell has so often bested Snorri goði in legal battles (and for other reasons that need not discussed here), Snorri lets himself be goaded into having Arnkell killed. Arnkell puts up a brave fight, defending himself valiantly against overwhelming odds from (symbolically) an enclosed haystack on his farm. The author's final comment on Arnkell, who incorporates the good qualities of both Þorsteinn and Bjarni, is as follows:

»His death was lamented by all, for he was in every respect one of the best and wisest men in the ancient faith. He was composed, stouthearted, and as daring as anyone; determined, yet with a good hold on himself. He was generally successful in litigation with whomsoever he contended. It was for this reason that he provoked much jealousy, as was shown in this case. The body of Arnkell was now taken and brought to his burial place. Arnkell was placed in a mound by the sea near the promontory Vaðilshöfði, and that mound is as wide around as a large enclosed haystack.« (Ch. 37)

Not all of the uses of the generation-gap theme in the sagas are as sophisticated as the ones from *Þorsteins þáttur* and *Eyrbyggja saga*. As an example of a more primitive, or at least, less artistic treatment of the theme let us look at *Orms þáttur Stórólfssonar*.[14]

Stórólfur, the son of the colonist Hængur, is described as exceedingly strong *(allra manna sterkastr)*, a werewolf, and skilled in magic *(fjölkunnigur)*. He has little love for his son Ormur, partly because he finds him difficult to manage, but Orm's mother loves him dearly. Ormur is powerful, too, but he lacks the superhuman power that the author associates with being a werewolf. He tells us that Ormur »was the strongest man in all Iceland, both in ancient and modern times, among those who were not werewolves«. Starkaður is killed in a fight with his sometime friend Dufþakur, who is also a werewolf, and, the author tells us, »his death was mourned by few people«. Ormur, too, enjoys superhuman help in time of peril, but it derives from a different source. On the point of being overcome by a huge cat, he »promises God and St. Peter to make a pilgrimage to Rome if he can overcome the cat and her son Brusi«. Immediately the monster's strength wanes, and Ormur slays both her and her son. After performing many feats of strength in Scandinavia, Ormur returns home to his farm in Iceland, where, having remained firm in the faith, he dies of old age, highly respected by everyone.

The association of Vikings with werewolves, especially in the dim and distant past, is not unusual in the sagas. The more remote in time and space, the more numerous the characters with superhuman dimensions and powers. In the first chapter of *Egils saga*, for instance, we meet a man named Hallbjörn hálftröll, another named Berðlu-Kári who was a berserker, and Egil's grandfather Kveld-Úlvur, whose very name, »Evening Wolf«, lends weight to the general belief that he was a were-

---

14 *Íslendinga sögur,* Vol. XI, pp. 445–472.

wolf. Egil's father Skalla-Grímur was quite as huge and fierce as Kveld-Úlfur. On one occasion Skalla-Grímur with several companions called on the King of Norway. »There were twelve in the party, all of them very powerful and most were werewolves.« When they arrived at court, the king's steward announced them as follows: »›Some men have arrived here, twelve in all, if they can be called men, for they are more like giants in stature and appearance than human beings.‹«
Although Egill is not a werewolf, his dimensions are no less huge than those of his ancestors. Indeed, he surpasses them in sheer truculence, brutishness, and avarice. His similarity to his father is emphasized in the introductory characterization:

> »As he grew up, it could soon be seen that he would be black haired and very ugly like his father … At an early age he was talkative and clever. He was rather hard to manage when he took part in games with other young men.«   (Ch. 31)

The last sentence in this description is a bit of an understatement, for at the age of seven Egill sinks an axe into the head of a youthful competitor who roughed him up in a ball game. This wanton killing leads to hostilities that cost the lives of nine men – an exemplary beginning of a career of violence and bloodshed. When the news of Egil's first killing reaches his parents, Skalla-Grímur has little to say about it, but his mother Bera declares that he has the makings of a Viking *(víkings-efni)* and that he must have a warship in due time.
After the death of his handsome blond brother Þórólfur in England, Egill becomes the central figure of the story, and at this point the author paints an imposing portrait of the fearsome warrior. King Athelstan is celebrating a glorious victory over the Scots, but Egill is so overwhelmed with grief and rage at the death of his brother that he can neither eat nor drink.

> »He sat down there (in the seat of honor opposite King Athelstan) and cast his shield down before him. He wore his helmet on his head and laid his sword across his knees. He kept drawing his sword halfway out of the sheath and slamming it back in again. He sat upright, but let his head hang low. Egill had coarse features: a broad forehead, bushy eyebrows, and a short and extremely thick nose. His long beard covered much of his face, and his chin and jawbone were terribly broad. His neck was so thick and his shoulders so broad that he stood out from all other men. His expression was harsh and grim when he was angry. He was of great stature, being taller than anyone else. His hair was gray and thick, but he became bald quite young.

As he sat there, as was written above, he alternately pulled one of his eyebrows down to his cheek and the other one up to his hairline. Egil's eyebrows were almost grown together above his black eyes. He refused to drink, although he had been served, but continued to raise and lower his eyebrows.

King Athelstan sat in the high seat. He also laid his sword across his knees, and after they had been sitting thus for a while, the king drew his sword from its sheath, took a large and splendid golden armband from his arm, and drew it onto the point of his sword. He arose from his seat, stepped down onto the floor, and extended the ring across the fire to Egill. Egill arose and stepped forward to the hearth. He thrust the point of his sword through the ring, drew it to him, and returned to his place. The king sat down in the high seat. And when Egill sat down, he drew the ring onto his arm, and then his eyebrows relaxed. He laid aside his sword and helmet, took up the drinking horn that had been given him, and emptied it.« (Ch. 55)

This superb passage needs little discussion. Egill Skalla-Grímsson, Viking par excellence, is the peer of kings, whom he sometimes serves and sometimes defies. He is massive, contentious, cruel, and greedy. Although he owns the estate Borg in Iceland, he is more at home with European royalty than with his Icelandic neighbors. The author states specifically that Egill engaged little in litigation or disputes *hér á landi*. The fundamental differences between Egill and his son Þorsteinn in appearance and temperament are revealed in the following description:

»When Egil's son Þorsteinn was fully grown, he was most handsome in appearance, with light blond hair and shining countenance. He was tall and strong, but nothing like his father in this respect. Þorsteinn was a sensible, peaceful man, and very gentle and composed. Egill loved him little, and Þorsteinn did not have much affection for him either, but his mother Ásgerður and Þorsteinn were very fond of each other.« (Ch. 82)

Whereas Egill consorted with royalty, winning battles for King Athelstan and making life miserable for King Eiríkur blóðöx and Queen Gunnhildur of Norway, Þorsteinn contends with his own peers, his neighboring farmers, about boundary lines and grazing rights and the like, and even here his father has to come to his aid on occasion. Þorstein's conversion and his epitaph conclude his portrait:

»Þorsteinn received baptism when Christianity came to Iceland, and he had a church built at Borg. He was a man firm in the Christian faith and well-mannered. He lived to be an old man and died of illness, and he was buried at Borg by the church that he had had built ... For a long time in that family there were men who were strong and great warriors, but there were some who were gentle and wise *(spakir að viti)*. There was a great discrepancy, for into this family were born the most handsome persons ever to live in Iceland, such as Þorsteinn Egilsson, his nephew Kjartan Ólafsson, and his daughter Helga the Fair ... But the larger number of Mýramenn were very ugly.« (Ch. 90)

Nowhere in saga literature is the generations-gap theme, the confrontation between Viking father and farmer son, more strikingly portrayed than in this story. Egill – huge, brutish, troll-like, avaricious, willful and self-centered, the scourge and the benefactor of kings, a glorious poet and worshiper of Óðinn, god of treachery and deceit; his son Þorsteinn, wise and gentle, firm but patient and moderate, self-controlled, a prosaic farmer with no gift of poetry, and, in the later years of his life, a devout Christian. Although the symbolism is not carried out with perfect consistency, the contrast between the blonde and handsome (and therefore good) individuals and the black and ugly (and therefore evil and ominous) persons, symbolizes clearly the contrast between the two ways of life, the two cultures, embodied by Þorsteinn and Egill.[15] And the author's comment that Egill had more ugly descendants than handsome ones has little meaning unless it is understood within the context of contemporary times – i.e., as a warning to the willful and cruel and avaricious chieftains of Snorri Sturluson's own day. For Snorri, after all, was himself a descendant of Egill, and seems to have inherited traits srom the dark as well as the blonde side of the Mýramenn family.

In *Þórðar saga hreðu* the generation-gap theme takes the form of a series of confrontations between a willful, aggressive father and a reasonable son. Skeggi, the father, is described (Ch. 3) as »a great warrior and duelist *(garpur mikill ok einvígismaður)*«. Before settling in Iceland, he was a freebooter for many years. By chance Skeggi's son Eiður becomes the foster son of his chief adversary, Þórður hreða. Þórður is a formidable fighter, but is much more moderate and self-disciplined than Skeggi. Repeatedly Eiður foils Skeggi's attempts to kill or injure Þórður, and eventually brings about a reconciliation between his father and his foster father.

---

[15] Cf. the statement by Heinrich Hempel in *Thule: Altnordische Dichtung und Prosa*, 2nd ed., Eugen Diederichs Verlag: Düsseldorf-Köln 1963, p. 265: »Im Geschlecht der Myramenn treten fast sinnbildhaft deutlich zwei grundverschiedene Menschentypen und Verhaltensweisen hervor, und ein gut Teil der Handlung vollzieht sich im Widerspiel dieser Charaktere.«

In *Hávarðar saga Ísfirðings,* on the other hand, there is only one minor confrontation between Hávarður and his son Ólafur. But whereas Hávarður is a rather useless superannuated marauder not unlike Þórarinn, Ólafur is exceptionally skillful at finding lost sheep in the mountains and returning them to their owners. Eventually Ólafur is slain by evil, envious neighbors, and the greater part of the saga is a somewhat farcical story of Hávarð's finally successful endeavor to wreak vengeance for the slaying of his son.

It is significant that the figure of the superannuated marauder, the embodiment of the Viking culture of the past, almost always tends toward the ludicrous. Þórarinn, the »miserable stinker«, ends his days in the care of slaves. Þórólfur bægifótur literally vexes himself to death from frustration, and the final function of his ashes is to impregnate a cow. Egill Skalla-Grímsson, glorious poet and warrior, grows deaf and blind in his dotage and is teased and scolded by the women servants. When his remains are disinterred for reburial near a new church, one of those present tests the strength of his huge skull by striking it with an axe. Formidable warrior though he is, Skeggi is consistently outwitted and frustrated by his young son. And Hávarður, as already indicated, is rather a burlesque character throughout most of the story. Yet these portrayals of Vikings, despite their ludicrous traits, for the most part also include ominous, sinister, and menacing features – a warning to contemporaries of the disruptive, destructive, malevolent forces always present as a heritage from the Viking past in the rural civilization of the Icelandic Commonwealth.

No less fascinating than the transition from the savage culture of the Viking Age to the farming community of the Icelandic Commonwealth is the conversion from paganism to Christianity, as recorded by historians and creatively embellished by saga writers. (Space does not permit another digression at this point, but it is instructive and fascinating to read in chronological order the depictions of the conversion from the brief [but not unimaginative] report of Ari Þorgilsson [c. 1130] to the elaborately embellished description that marks the turning point of *Njáls saga.*)

It is difficult to ascertain how much the saga writers of the thirteenth century actually knew about paganism, but some of them at least seem to have assumed that the transition to Christianity was a rapid one. In discussing the concessions made to the pagans at the time of the conversion, for instance, Ari the Learned states in his *Íslendingabók*

(Ch. 5) that »a few years later these heathen practices were abolished like the others«. Concerning the character Þrándur stígandi the author of *Eyrbyggja saga* (Ch. 61) states that he »was thought to be a werewolf while he was still a pagan, but most men lost their troll nature when they were baptized«. Other saga writers, however, indicate that certain pagan practices lingered on, or that certain Christian practices had not yet been adopted. Fasting, for example, seems not to have been widely practiced during the infancy of Christianity in Iceland, for the author of *Laxdæla saga* (Ch. 47) tells us that Kjartan Ólafsson was the first man in Iceland to observe Lent properly and that people marveled that he did not die from fasting. Not infrequently such statements are accompanied by the defensive or apologetic observation that »at that time Christianity was still young«.[16] However that may be, this cultural break is frequently portrayed in terms of the generation-gap motive.

The most abrupt and startling confrontation between a pagan father (or, as in this case, between a *nominally* Christian father) and a Christian son is found in *Heiðarvíga saga*. Snorri goði has just finished preparations for an expedition against Þorsteinn Gíslason to avenge the death of his friend and father-in-law Víga-Styrr. Before setting out to butcher Þorsteinn and one of his sons, Snorri, like Flosi in *Njála* and like many a killer in the Sturlung Age, attends divine services.

> »Snorri ate breakfast early in the morning. Their horses stood saddled. He had three sons. One was named Halldór, another one Guðlaugur – he was the eldest –, and Þórður was the youngest.[17] He was then nine year of age, and he was to go along.
> Guðlaugur was always at home, and Snorri let him decide what kind of work he was to do. He was not especially skilful at physical work. He was well-mannered and diligent at prayer and firm in the Christian faith, and had no quarrels with people. Therefore he was unlike his brothers in temperament, who were given to derision and often made sport of him. Snorri went to church – the one he had had built. The sun was shining from the east, and as he entered, he met Guðlaugur. He had been at prayers, as was his custom, and was about to leave. Snorri asked him whether he did not wish to go along to avenge the slaying of his maternal uncle. Guðlaugur replied that he thought Snorri had enough troops without his help, and

---

16 *Grænlendinga saga*, ch. 6, and *Fóstbræðra saga*, chs. 2 and 9, to mention just three examples. Cf. also *Eiríks saga rauða*, chs. 4 and 6, and *Eyrbyggja saga*, chs. 53 and 54.

17 Guðlaugur munkur is mentioned in the *Ævi Snorra goða*, but is otherwise unknown in Old Icelandic literature.

> that he had never before taken part in the slaughter of men. He said that
> his father should decide, but that he much preferred to remain at home.
> Snorri said that he had never seen such a human countenance as that of his
> son Guðlaugur when he met him in the church. He said that his face was
> as red as blood, and that it was rather awe-inspiring. Several years later
> Guðlaugur went to England, and his father provided him with money. He
> entered a monastery, conducted himself well there, and was regarded as
> an excellent clerk as long as he lived.«   (Ch. 12)

This passage is followed immediately by a description of the brutal
slaying of Þorsteinn and one of his sons, both of them unarmed and
taken by surprise by Snorri and three companions in the wee hours of
a Sunday morning. The brutality is accentuated by Snorri's urging his
nine-year old son Þórður kausi (the Cat) to slay Þorstein's nine-year
old son Sveinn.

> Another one of Þorstein's sons was at home. His name was Sveinn, and
> he was nine years old. He missed his father and wanted him to come in-
> doors. He heard a commotion outside, but didn't know what was happen-
> ing. He went to the door, and his eyes were heavy with sleep.
> Snorri said to his son, Þórður kausi, »Does the cat see the mouse? Let the
> young slay the young.«

Þórður, however, declares that he would rather die protecting Sveinn
than kill him. Reluctantly Snorri lets himself be dissuaded from taking the
boy's life, but he warns his companions that Þorstein's son will eventually do harm to his family.

The most disappointing saga in regard to the use of the generation-gap
theme is *Vatnsdæla,* which covers five generations in the history of a
family without providing a single meaningful confrontation between
father and son. The reason for this is that the author idealizes his »good
guys« to such an extent that they are all »noble heathens«,[18] who keep
busy cleansing the countryside of robbers and witches and various and
sundry other evil doers. At the very end of the saga, however, the author does refer to the transition from paganism to Christianity in his
praise of Þorkell krafla, the representative of the fifth and last generation of the story.

> Þorkell made ready for his death in a Christian manner, as well befitted
> him, for he was a good Christian and observed the faith well. Thereafter
> he died, and his death was a source of great grief for his followers and for
> all who lived in the district, for he was thought to be (as, indeed, he was)
> a most outstanding district chieftain and a man of surpassing good fortune

---

18 On this see Lars Lönnroth, »The Noble Heathen: A Theme in the Sagas«, *Scandinavian Studies* 41 (1969), 1–29.

and most like such men of Vatnsdalur as Þorsteinn and Ingimundur. But Þorkell surpassed them in that he was a man of the true faith and was esteemed as the one who loved the true God above all things.

One of the most sophisticated variants of the pagan father – Christian son theme is found in *Eiríks saga rauða*. After having been banished from Norway and Iceland for manslaughter, Eiríkur founds an Icelandic colony in Greenland. Eirík's son Leifur earns the sobriquet *inn heppni* »The Lucky« for discovering Vinland the Good, for rescuing some ship-wrecked persons at sea, and for propagating the Christian religion in Greenland. Eiríkur, on the other hand, is refused his conjugal rights by his wife Þjóðhildur for refusing to accept the true faith; he suffers a dislocated shoulder and three broken ribs for having committed the pagan practice of burying treasure in the ground; and he is further punished by being denied the sight of the promised land, Vinland the Good, which all of his children but one are privileged to visit. Eirík's alter ego and surrogate, Þórhallur veiðimaður, suffers even worse ignominy than Eiríkur, for he is shipwrecked off the coast of Ireland where he is enslaved, beaten, and eventually killed for having derided Christ and appealed to his »patron«, the god Þór, in time of need. The story ends with a list of the descendants of Eirík's daughter-in-law Guðríður, which includes the names of no less than three bishops. Guðríður herself makes a pilgrimage to Rome and becomes an anchoress.

The most memorable father-son contrast in *Njáls saga* is that between Þráinn Sigfússon and Höskuldur, who becomes Njál's foster-son after Þráinn is slain by the Njállssons. Þráinn is not the most evil villain in the story, but his behavior toward the sons of Njáll was somewhat less than noble, and his death at the hands of Skarphéðinn is well deserved according to the ethical code of pagan Iceland. Skarphéðinn strikes him down with a single blow, and he dies surrounded by seven companions including some of the most loathesome creatures in saga literature.

The contrast between pagan father and Christian son is revealed by the author's initial portrait of Höskuldur and by his description of his death:

> »And so time passed until Höskuldur was fully grown. He became tall and strong and very handsome, with a fine head of hair. He was gentle of speech and generous, well- composed and skilled in arms. He spoke kindly to everyone and was well liked. The Njállssons and Höskuldur never disagreed about anything.« (Ch. 94)

»The weather was fine and the sun had risen. Höskuldur awoke and got dressed. He put on the cloak that Flosi had given him. He picked up his grain basket with one hand and his sword with the other and went out to his grainfield to sow.

Skarphéðinn and the others had agreed that they should all strike him. Skarphéðinn sprang up from behind the fence. When Höskuldur saw him, he started to draw back.

Then Skarphéðinn ran at him, crying, ›Don't bother to take to your heels, Hvítanessgoði!‹

He hewed at him, and the blow struck him on the head and he sank to his knees.

He said, ›May God help me and forgive you.‹«   (Ch. 111)

Njáll is more sorely grieved and distressed than anyone else at the death of Höskuldur. The natural grief for the loss of a dear one is intensified by the painful awareness that it was his own offspring who slew his spiritual son and thus nullified his noble attempt to atone for the death of Þráinn Sigfússon by fostering the slain man's son. Added to this grief is the distress caused by the fact that Njáll, like Óðinn after the slaying of Baldur, is prescient of the disaster that will result from Hös-kuld's death. It is this awful prescience of impending, inevitable disaster that moves Njáll to declare that he would willingly lose all of his sons to have Höskuldur alive. Thus his willingness to sacrifice his own sons, if that were possible, to save the life of his spiritual son Höskuldur is not an »heroic« utterance, like old Þórarin's heartless comments to his »craven« son Þorsteinn, but the Christian expression of the willingness to do penance and of faith in God's mercy. Höskuld's dying words were a prayer of forgiveness for his slayers. The last words of consolation that Njáll speaks to his household as the flames flare up and the house fills with smoke are a sort of response to this prayer: »Take heart and speak no words of despair, for this will be but a passing storm, and it will be long before another one like it comes. Have faith in God's mercy, for he will not let us burn in this world and the next.«[19]

As final examples of the use of the generation-gap theme in the *Íslend-ingasögur* I should like to quote three short character portrayals from *Laxdæla saga*. They are portraits of the warrior Ólafur pái; of his son Kjartan, who was converted to Christianity in Norway before the

---

[19] Concerning the relationship between Njáll and Höskuldur and the replacement of the pagan belief in an inexorable fate by the Christian concept of penance and a belief in a benign providence see Einar Ól. Sveinsson, *Njáls saga*, pp. 166–180 and 193–203.

adoption of that religion in Iceland; and of Bolli, the son of the heroin
Guðrún, who has just returned from Constantinople to visit his mother.
The description of Ólafur occurs just before he identifies himself to the
Irish king Myrkjartan as his grandson:

> »Ólafur walked forward to the prow. He wore a coat of mail and had a
> gilded helmet on his head. He was girt with a sword whose pommel and
> guard were embossed with silver. In his hand he carried a barbed spear
> that was chased and beautifully engraved. Before him he carried *a red
> shield on which a lion was traced in gold.*«   (Ch. 21)

The portrait of Kjartan follows his return from the royal court of Norway. Ólafur and his household are preparing to attend an autumn feast
at Laugar:

> »Kjartan did as his father asked. He brought out the clothes of scarlet that
> King Ólafur had given him at parting, and dressed himself in his finery.
> He girded on the sword *Konungsnaut* (›the king's gift‹). He wore a gilded
> helmet on his head and at his side *a red shield with the Holy Cross embla-
> zoned in gold,* and he carried a spear with a gold-inlaid socket.«   (Ch. 44)

As already mentioned, the author of *Laxdæla* paints his full-length portrait of Bolli inn prúði (»the Proud«) just after his return from Constantinople, where, the author tells us, Bolli was the first *Norðmaðr* to serve
in the imperial guard. Bolli and his retinue set out for Helgafell, where
his mother Guðrún, who was the first woman in Iceland to memorize
the psalter, is living as an anchoress:

> »Bolli rode from the ship with eleven men. His companions all wore scarlet
> and rode in gilded saddles. All of them were elegant, but Bolli surpassed
> them all. He was wearing clothes of gold-embroidered silk that the Byzan-
> tine emperor had given him, and over them a cloak of scarlet. He was girt
> with the sword *Fótbítur,* and the pommel was gold embossed and the hilt
> bound with gold. He wore a gilded helmet on his head, and at his side he
> had *a red shield on which a knight was traced in gold.* He carried a lance
> in his hand, as is the custom in foreign lands. Wherever Bolli and his com-
> panions took lodging for the night, the women paid no attention to any-
> thing except to gaze at them and all their finery. In such courtly dignity
> *(kurteisi)* did Bolli ride through the countryside until he arrived at Helga-
> fell with his retinue. Guðrún was overjoyed to see her son Bolli.«   (Ch. 77)

What is most noteworthy in these three character portraits is the consistent use of appropriate symbolism. The warrior Ólafur pái (»Pea-
cock«) carries a red shield on which a lion is traced. His son Kjartan,
whose death at the hands of his foster brother is not unlike that of Hös-

kuldur in *Njála,* bears a red shield on which the Holy Cross is emblazoned in gold. And Bolli's red shield is decorated with the figure of a knight. Bolli is clearly intended as an embodiment of the cosmopolitan spirit that grew steadily stronger in Iceland as Icelandic chieftains increasingly became enmeshed in the political net spread for them by King Hákon Hákonarson, and as Norwegian adaptations of French romances gradually replaced the more realistic sagas as popular reading in Iceland.

These memorable depictions of Ólafur, Kjartan, and Bolli Bollason bear striking resemblances to portraits found in the kings' sagas. The picture of Ólaf's arms, and especially the shield with a lion traced upon it, recalls the description of King Magnús berfætur in *Morkinskinna* (Ch. 44) and *Heimskringla* (*Magnúss saga berfætts,* Ch. 24). The description of Kjartan's shield, with the Holy Cross emblazoned on it, is almost identical with that of Saint Ólafur in Snorri's *Ólafs saga helga* (Ch. 40). And Bolli's shield is described almost word for word like that of Benedikt, the brother of King Knútur, in *Knytlinga saga:*

> (Bolli) hafði . . . rauðan skjöld á hlið, ok á dreginn riddari með gulli
> (*Laxdæla,* Ch. 77)
> (Benedikt) hafði skjöld rauðan, ok dreginn á riddari með gulli
> (*Knytlinga saga,* Ch. 56)

There can be no doubt, as Rolf Heller has convincingly demonstrated,[20] that the author of *Laxdæla* was strongly influenced by several of the kings' sagas, and not merely in the weapon descriptions discussed above. The more I study *Laxdæla,* the more probable it seems to me that these portrayals of Ólafur, Kjartan, and Bolli are not merely intended to represent three levels or aspects of Icelandic culture, but that the allusive technique of the author is designed to cast an even stronger resplendance upon the characters themselves. If this is so, it suggests that the author of *Laxdæla* wrote his work for a relatively small, highly sophisticated audience, the kind of audience who would readily distinguish between the surface plot and the deeper meaning of stories such as those treated in this paper.[21]

---

20 *Literarisches Schaffen in der Laxdæla Saga* (Saga, Heft 3) VEB Max Niemeyer Verlag: Halle (Saale) 1960; and, *Laxdæla Saga und Königssagas.* See also E. Ó. Sveinsson, *Íslenzk fornrit* V, p. xii and Margaret Arent Madelung, »Snorri Sturluson and Laxdæla: The hero's accoutrements«, *Saga og Språk,* pp. 45–111.

21 Cogent evidence for the literary sophistication of the Icelanders in the thirteenth century is found in the ironic use of prophetic dreams. On this see Paul Schach,

And now a few words by way of summary and conclusion. We began with an analysis and interpretation of *Þorsteins þáttur stangarhöggs*, which we found to be not a paradigm of saga structure, but a thinly disguised sermon written by a Christian author for a Christian audience. The protagonists of the story are an idealized chieftain and an idealized farmer who, together, embody and symbolize the spirit of the free and independent Icelandic Commonwealth as it existed in the nostalgic mind of the author. The chief adversary is Þórarinn, the superannuated, unregenerate marauder, whose uselessness and alienage in a society of free farmers living under laws of their own adoption and adaptation are symbolized by his blindness, his adherence to an out-moded heroic code of honor, and his fine assortment of weapons. The conflict between the protagonists and their adversary seems to have a double function or meaning. It is first of all a portrayal of the transi-tion from the Viking culture of the Age of the Settlement (*ca.* 870–930) to the more peaceful rural life of the Icelandic Commonwealth, during which the raider perfore gave way to the trader and the marauder was replaced by the farmer. The tale is secondly a futile warning to the contentious, avaricious Icelandic chieftains of the Sturlung Age against the resurgence of the rapacious and destructive Viking spirit that final-ly shattered the peace and destroyed the freedom of the Common-wealth.

This interpretation of the *þáttur* is supported by the fact that the theme of the generation-gap occurs in many variations throughout saga liter-ature. Frequently, but not exclusively, the confrontation between re-presentatives of the two generations coincides with a time of cultural change, usually either the transition from the rapacious culture of the Vikings to the less bloody rural civilization of the Commonwealth, or the conversion from paganism to Christianity. The attitude of the author toward his characters is almost never in doubt.[22] Toward a character like Egill Skallagrímsson, who embodies not only the good and bad qualities of the Viking poet, but also the savage and creative characteristics of the Sturlung Age, the attitude of author and audience is ambivalent. But for the most part the representative of the Viking

---

»Symbolic Dreams of Future Renown in Old Icelandic Literature«, *Mosaic* 4 (1971), 51–74.

[22] Cf. Peter Hallberg, *The Icelandic Saga*, University of Nebraska Press: Lincoln 1962, p. 104: »Professional trouble makers such as berserkers and other men of violence arc never favorite characters of a saga.«

culture is branded as an enemy of and a threat to civilized society. The Viking is always on *ójafnaðarmaður*, a truculent and avaricious marauder. In somewhat less harsh and shrill colors saga writers portray their representative pagans when they function as adversaries of Christians.

The use of the generation-gap theme to portray the clash of antagonistic cultures is further evidence that the sagas are not »adaptations of heroic models«, but manifestations of the gradual transvaluation of the heroic ideal that took place in Iceland during the Age of the Commonwealth, largely under the influence of Christianitiy.[23] The theme becomes doubly meaningful when understood within the cultural milieu in which the sagas were composed: the almost incredibly savage, creative Age of the Sturlungs. The Viking Egill Skallagrímsson had descendants who were »the most handsome persons ever to live in Iceland, ... but the larger number of Mýramenn were very ugly«.

---

[23] For statements on the heroic element in the sagas see Theodore M. Andersson, *The Icelandic Family Saga*, pp. 65–93 and »The Displacement of the Heroic Ideal in the Family Sagas«.

Charles J. Donahue

Social Function and Literary Value in *Beowulf*

We are met to discuss the epic in Medieval Society. I offer for your consideration a poem only marginally an epic and one composed in a society only marginally medieval.

Beowulf is a relatively short poem of 3182 lines, much shorter than most poems regarded as epics. In his Gollanz Lecture in 1936, *Beowulf: The Monsters and the Critics*,[1] Tolkien insisted that the poem could not be properly evaluated if the critics approached the poem as an epic. It might be better described, he suggested, as an heroic-elegiac poem in which the first 3136 lines are a prelude to the last forty-six lines which constitute a dirge, »one of the most moving ever written« (p. 33). I believe, however, that Tolkien would readily have granted that the poem, rightly understood, has an ethical and poetic gravity that makes it comparable to many longer and narrative poems that we call epics. The Homeric poems are delightful and were doubtless intended to delight, but they delight by portraying, probably in an idealized form, the value system of the Greek heroic age. Even after the heroic age was passed, Homer was used to teach Greek youth what it meant to be a Greek. In a similar way Vergil performed a social function in propagating the ethos of early imperial Rome. The *Beowulf* poet's obvious social concern for the portrayal and, presumably, propagation of a moral value system by poetic means brings his heroic-elegiac poem, at points, close to epic grandeur. For that reason, I think the poem deserves the attention of our conference. So much for the marginally epic character of the poem.

The question of the marginally medieval character of the poem leads us to our most important reason for considering *Beowulf* here. The only manuscript record of the poem dates from the latter part of the tenth

---

1 Pages cited from the lithographic edition, Oxford University Press, 1958.

century. Most scholars today, however, feel that a person of considerable learning and great poetic power, a northern Englishman, an Anglian, composed the poem, doubtless using earlier plot material derived from Germanic heroic saga, some time late in the seventh century or in the first half of the eighth.

The poet lived at a time when the Angles of Britain were accomplishing a notable work which was to have a decisive effect on the course of European history. They were settling the problem of Christianizing a northern Indo-European warrior society that had never known Roman civilization. The Angles were, to be sure, living in lands where the Romans had once ruled, but by the time the Angles arrived there as conquerors, almost all trace of Roman rule had disappeared. After the Council of Whitby in 664, the Angles were in touch both with the Roman mission established in Canterbury, and with Celtic Christians who had had experience, in Ireland, in Christianizing another northern Indo-European warrior society, that of the Irish Gaels.

Among the Angles, a vital contact between a Germanic warrior society and Christianity was established. Christian, classical and northern barbarian elements were united, not without tension, into a unified culture. It was that culture which English missionaries succeeded in introducing to the still unChristianized *Germani* of Eastern and Northern Europe, thus assuring that the future culture of Europe would be an amalgam of Judeo-Christian, Classical and Northern Barbarian elements. Shortly after the middle of the seventh century, the northern Angles produced a remarkable series of poems based on the historical books of the Old Testament. The poems are composed in a language clearly derived from Old English heroic poetry. The poems were probably the work of monks, but the monks must have been in close contact with heroic poetry and its authors.

The *Beowulf* poet was indubitably acquainted with some of the earlier Christian poems in the English heroic idiom. He aimed, presumably, to compose on a secular theme and to sing praise of the valor of the heroes in days of old, not in the manner of the early heroic lays, but at greater length and with a high seriousness comparable to that of the Biblical poems. He thus brought together Germanic saga and a Germanic heroic ethos with Judeo-Christian and Classical material. He lived during the period when northern barbarian antiquity was being transformed into what became the Northern European Middle Ages. He left us an account of how a Christian, learned in the traditions of his Germanic

ancestors, responded as a Christian to the admiration he felt for the
heroes his ancestors had admired.

The puzzling combination of Christian elements with heroic material
of an indubitably pagan origin has long engaged the attention of scholars and even today there is by no means a consensus on the essential
assumptions for an accurate reading of the poem. Some nineteenth century scholars, particularly those whose imagination had been affected
– and rightly so – by the discoveries of Indo-European comparative lin-
guistics, approached the poem as antiquarians rather than as medievalists or literary critics. Here was a precious relict from some deep and
dark Germanic past. One began interpretation, therefore, by assuming
that numerous passages which could only come from a Christian – references to the »Christian God«, for example, or to the Book of Genesis –
must have been added by some tasteless monk.

In Germany, however, a reaction began before the end of the last century. In the second edition of *Pauls Grundriß* (1901–9) so weighty a
scholar as Brandl objected to arbitrary rejection of Christian passages
and insisted that Christianity had so interpenetrated the poem that any
one who undertook to remove the non-pagan elements from the poem
would find himself compelled to compose a different poem. Brandl
mentioned particularly the exemplary character of the hero. The passage is worth quoting: »The imprint of a Christian graciousness goes to
the very core of Beowulf's character. Beowulf never thought of taking
aggressive military action for the sake of getting booty as the head-
strong Hygelac did. He was concerned only with the protection of his
people from human and diabolical enemies; he is modest and God-
fearing and at the end thanks heaven, in a manner that brings to mind
the Saviour, that he could, at the price of his life, assure the happiness
of his people with treasures« (*Grundriß*, II [1908], 1002).

Following Brandl, Klaeber, in a series of articles appearing in *Anglia*
(1911, 1912) examined traces of Christian influence on the diction of
the poem and the literary reminiscences of Scripture to be found there.
He showed that such elements were numerous and more or less uni-
formly distributed throughout the poem. These articles furnished a
singularly solid philological foundation for the view that the creator
of the *Beowulf* we know was an informed, perhaps even a learned
Christian.

In England, on the other hand, the first decades of the present century
were dominated by advocates of a »pagan« interpretation of the poem.

The most powerful advocate for the older point of view was un-
questionably H. M. Chadwick, who brought his formidable learning to
bear on the problem of *Beowulf,* in his *Origin of the English Nation*
(1907) and *The Heroic Age* (1912).

In the United States, the pagan character of *Beowulf* was insisted upon
by F. B. Gummere in *Germanic Origins* (1892) and in the Introduction
to his translation of *Beowulf* (1909). Perhaps the most influential pro-
pagan voice of all, both in England and America, however, was that of
Henry Bradley in his article »*Beowulf*« for the eleventh edition of the
Encyclopedia Brittanica (1910). He regarded the Christian passages
not only as inappropriate to the poem but as, in themselves, aesthetically inferior.

The second decade of the present century brought about in English
speaking countries a decided change in the preceding views on the
question of religion in *Beowulf.* The first edition of R. W. Chambers'
Beowulf appeared in 1922. Section IV of Chapter III contained a discussion entitled »Are the Christian elements incompatible with the rest
of the poem?« Here the foremost English student of the poem gave
briefly the grounds for his misgivings about the position of Chadwick
and Bradley. He cited in a note on p. 126,[2] Brandl's remarks on the
character of the hero and declared his conviction that »the essentially
Christian character of Beowulf« had been »finally demonstrated by
Klaeber in the last section of his *Die christlichen Elemente im Beowulf*«
(Anglia xxxvi). Chambers' explanation of the Christian elements is that
»a devout but not theologically minded poet, writing battle poetry«
naturally included references to God as »Lord of Hosts or Giver of
Victory« (pp. 126–127). The poem is then »a production of the Germanic world enlightened by the new faith. ... The great merit of *Beowulf* as a historic document is that it shows us a picture of a period in
which the virtues of the heathen ›Heroic Age‹ were tempered by the
gentleness of the new belief: an age warlike, yet Christian: devout, yet
tolerant« (p. 128). In 1922 also, the first edition of Klaeber's *Beowulf*
appeared. The section »The Christian Coloring« supported, with specific reference to passages, his main conclusion: »The general tone of the
poem and its ethical viewpoint« are »predominantly Christian«.

In 1932, Chadwick included, as an »excursus« in Volume I of his ency-
clopedic *Growth of Literature,* a brief essay called »The Written Epic«.

---

[2] Pages cited from the third edition with a supplement by C. L. Wrenn (Cambridge
University Press, 1959). Wrenn left the text of Chambers unaltered.

He regretted a growing tendency in both Homeric and *Beowulf* studies
to abandon the theory that these poems were directly derived from the
lays of presumably illiterate minstrels. He objected particularly to the
notion that the *Beowulf* poet was a learned and broadminded cleric, or
at least had the support of such clerics. He cited the well known letter
written by Alcuin in 797 to Hygbald, Bishop of Iona. Alcuin is sorry to
hear that Hygbald and his monks are listening at table to the songs of
minstrels. »Quid Inieldus cum Christo?« he asks. »Christ reigns in eternity; Inield, that damned pagan, howls in hell« (p. 556). (Inield was a
prince of the Heatho-bards, well known to the *Beowulf* poet.) The
opinion that all pagans were damned, Chadwick goes on to say, was
not an eccentricity of Alcuin's. Indeed, the Venerable Bede shared it,
and so did Bishop Wulframm, who drove the Frisian king Redbad
away from the font when he told him that his pagan Frisian ancestors
were »in Tartarea damnatione« (ibid., note 5). None of these clerics
had any choice in their opinion. That all the unbaptized were damned
was, according to Chadwick, »not an individual opinion but the doctrine of the Church«. Clerics, like Hygbald's monks who patronized
minstrel poetry were not »learned liberal churchmen. ... They seem
rather to be regarded as slack and pleasure-loving«. In short, »the
learned ›liberal churchman‹ of the eighth century seems to us as much
of an anachronism as the literary epic« (p. 557). Such was the gage
which Chadwick threw down to Chambers, Klaeber, and any other
scholar who based his interpretation of the poem on the assumed existence of Christians learned, orthodox, and, at the same time, capable of
approving of a poem wherein pagan ancestors were celebrated and held
up for approval, admiration, and imitation.

In 1936, in the Gollanz lecture mentioned at the beginning of this paper, Tolkien developed a new hypothesis about the relation between the
Christian and the non-Christian elements in the poem. The Christianity
of the poem is not simply a coloring added to the pagan material. It is
one terminus of a contrast which is the basic life of the poem. The other
element is not exactly paganism but the military virtues which were
part of Germanic pagan society. »In the poem I think we may observe
not confusion, a half-hearted or a muddled business, but a fusion that
has occurred *at a given point* of contact between old and new, a product of thought and deep emotion. One of the most potent elements in
that fusion is the Northern courage: the theory of courage, which is the
great contribution of early Northern literature« (p. 20). Such Northern

courage is embodied in the archetypal myth of the Doom of the Gods
(p. 21). Gods and men fight together against the monsters and are defeated. The poet was therefore right in centering his story on battles between his hero and monsters, while more realistic heroic sagas were put
on the periphery of his poem in allusions or in accounts of the performance of scops within the main action of the poem. (Many critics, admirers
of ordinary realistic heroic poetry, had censured the poet for making
the monsters his main theme.) Throughout the poem, as he celebrates
the valor of the men of old, the poet's point of view is secular. He is
»still concerned primarily with *man on earth*« and »an ancient theme:
that each man and all men, and all their works shall die« (p. 23). This
is »a theme no Christian need despise«. The Christian thinks in terms
of beatitude, the transcendence of time, but the poet, still relatively
close to pagan days, »could view from without, but still feel immediately and from within, the old dogma: despair of the event, combined
with faith in the value of doomed resistance. He was still dealing with
the great temporal tragedy and not yet writing an allegorical homily in
verse. . . . The dragon wields a physical fire, and covets gold, not souls;
he is slain with iron in his belly« (pp. 23–24).
In keeping with the secular character of the poem, »the specifically
Christian elements were suppressed« (p. 22). The Judeo-Christian God,
however, *Wealdend, Dryhten,* is frequently mentioned and becomes
part of the action of the poem. Tolkien regards »the passages in *Beowulf*
concerning giants and their war with God, together with the two mentions of Cain (an ancestor of the giants in general and Grendel in particular) are specially important« because they are indications of the point
where »new Scripture and old tradition touched and ignited« (p. 27).
The poem then is »an historical poem about the pagan past. . . . It is a
poem by a learned man writing of old times, who, looking back on the
heroism and sorrow, feels in them something permanent and something
symbolical«. His learning included »a knowledge of Christian poetry,
especially that of the Caedmon School and especially *Genesis*. He
also possessed »considerable learning in native lays and traditions«
(p. 27–28).
Tolkien saw clearly that the poem must be interpreted in terms of both
the Christian elements and the non-Christian elements. It is precisely
the relationship between the two that give the poem its peculiar power.
Older critics were wrong when they tried to extract the pagan core, the
poetic heart of the poem, from the bungling additions of Christian

scribes. More recent critics are also wrong when they try to find the
»thoroughgoing Christian interpretation«[3] called for by the advocates
of Christian allegorical interpretation.

Concerned primarily with a »criticism that is directed to the understanding of a poem as a poem« (p. 3) Tolkien made only an indirect
reply to Chadwick's insistence that there were no »liberal« Christians
in the seventh and eighth centuries and that a poem celebrating the virtues of the men of old must be the work of a lax Christian, who would
not heed the clergy's teaching that all pagans were damned. Tolkien's
indirect comment is as follows:

> Almost we might say that this poem was (in one direction) inspired by the
> debate that had long been held and continued after, and that it was one of
> the chief contributions to the controversy: shall we or shall we not consign
> the heathen ancestors to perdition? What good will it do posterity to read
> the battles of Hector? *Quid Hinieldus cum Christo?* The author of *Beowulf*
> showed forth the permanent value of that *pietas* which treasures the mem-
> ory of man's struggles in the dark past, man fallen and not yet saved, dis-
> graced but not dethroned. It would seem to have been part of the English
> temper in its strong sense of tradition, dependent doubtless on dynasties,
> noble houses, and their code of honour, and strengthened, it may be, by the
> more inquisitive and less severe Celtic learning, that it should, at least in
> some quarters and despite grave and Gallic voices, preserve much from the
> northern past to blend with southern learning, and new faith. (p. 24)

The paragraph is full of interesting suggestions but is not an adequate
reply to Chadwick. Tolkien was correct in remarking that the problem
of the perdition of heathen ancestors is a matter of debate in the Western
Church. There is no firmly established dogma on the point. In the
seventh and eighth centuries, however, the Western Church on the
Continent more or less unanimously agreed that the thirteenth canon
of the Council of Orange (529) meant that all who died unbaptized
were damned.[4] Had the clergy responsible for the instruction of the
Beowulf poet followed the Continental view of heathen ancestors, it is
unlikely that even a strong sense of tradition derived from wholly
secular sources would have enabled him to arrive at his vision of an
heroic Germanic past peopled by men admirable for their stern fortitude and other virtues.

---

[3] The phrase is used by Bernard F. Huppe in his *Doctrine and Poetry* (State University of New York, 1959), p. 231.

[4] The Latin text of the canon with some indication of later theological opinion on
it will be found in *Traditio*, 21 (1965) 63, n. 26.

This consideration led me many years ago to consider the attitude to-wards pagan ancestors in Ireland, which, according to Tolkien, was under the tutelage of a clergy less severe than those of the Continent.[5] There is ample evidence in Hiberno-Latin ecclesiastic texts and in Old Irish sagas, gnomic poetry, and legal texts. At the time the *Beowulf* poet lived, many Irish clerics – not all – and many Irish poets were con-vinced that the Gaelic past had been populated by kings and sages who had knowledge of the true God and of the fundamental principles of equity, although they were unacquainted with Judaism or Christianity. This image of good pre-Christian theists was derived apparently from St. Paul, particularly Romans 1:14–16 and 2:19–32. The Pauline ma-terial was interpreted in a pre-Augustinian »liberal« fashion, derived possibly from such Christian thinkers as Origen, Irenaeus of Lyons, or Eusebius (see *Trad.* 21, 59–63). It is very probable that through one of many available channels Irish ecclesiastical influence reached the *Beo-wulf* poet and accounted for his image of monotheistic, virtuous, and admirable pre-Christian *Germani.* In Ireland is to be found the answer to Chadwick's historical objection to finding a »liberal« Christianity in *Beowulf.*

We are here concerned, however, primarily not with the history of theological thinking in the early Middle Ages but with the social func-tions and poetic value of *Beowulf.* On the surface, the poet's view is secular. Like the more ancient heroic poetry it superseded and tran-scended, *Beowulf* supplied striking images of the value of ancient Ger-manic society and consequently contributed to keeping those values alive. They were still clearly needed in the Age of Bede. There is much in the poem calculated to instruct a warrior in his duties. Kings and princes are often reminded of the importance of generosity. Judged by the plain text, the poem is not designed to teach religious doctrine. In the meadhalls of the early eighth century, however, there were leaders of warriors who, like the poet, were serious Christians. Some of them are known to have retired to monasteries in their old age. Such men might have learned from the poem that the heroes of old, like their Christian descendants, were on the side of *Dryhten* and enjoyed the divine protec-tion. Such a doctrine may have helped the more sensitive and serious Christians in the audience to reconcile an admiration for their ancestors with a Christian faith.

---

[5] Cf. *Traditio,* 7 (1951), 263–277. Further material is available in the later article cited above, n. 4.

The poem has a third social function, real, although certainly not intended by the poet. It can serve to instruct scholars as to the kind of thinking and feeling that was characteristic of the change from the older beliefs to Christianity in Western Europe in the early Middle Ages. Tolkien's approach, I believe, is still of the greatest value for scholars who wish to avail themselves of the third social function of *Beowulf*. Tolkien insists that one must keep both old and new in mind. The student of the early Middle Ages who wants to find the light that *Beowulf* can throw on the Germanic transition to Christianity must not confine himself to Christian documents. He must also give his time and attention to the *Hávamál* and the *Voluspá*. From such ancient and pagan material the student will learn much about those pre-Christian virtues which the *Beowulf* poet put in the foreground of his work. A thoroughgoing Christian *Beowulf* would be a contorted *Beowulf*.

John Reidy

The Education of Chaucer's Duke Theseus

One common view, and perhaps the prevailing one, is that *The Knight's Tale* is a successful work of art, giving powerful expression to the theme of the order in the universe and in the chivalric life of a great knight, Duke Theseus of Athens. Theseus is by some critics treated as if he were the representative and mouthpiece of right reason, almost god-like in his stability and wisdom. William Frost, for example, says that at the scene where he interrupts the duel between Palamon and Arcite: »the poem implicitly associates him with the destiny and divine foreknowledge which ... lie behind all human events and situations«,[1] and he quotes a passage including the following:

> »The destinee ministre general / That executeth in the world over al / The purveiaunce that God hath seyn biforn, / So strong it is that, though the world had sworn / The contrarie of a thing by ye or nay, / Yet sometyme it shall fallen on a day / That falleth not eft withinne a thousand yeer / ... This mene I now by myghty Theseus« (A 1663 ff.)[2]

He goes on: »Theseus is the executant of destiny. On the morning of the final tourney he sits in a window of his palace overlooking the crowd and ›arrayed right as he were a god in trone‹ ... As a personality he is appropriately impressive: terrifying in action, philosophical in outlook; richly experienced yet detached in point of view ...«[3] He is »the ideal conquering governor«.[4]

Professor Muscatine, whose fine analysis of the poem is probably the most influential in the field, takes a similar view. The poem expresses

---

[1] William Frost, »An Interpretation of Chaucer's Knight's Tale«, *R. E. S.* XXV (1949), 290–304; reprinted in and cited from Richard J. Schoeck and Jerome Taylor, edd., *Chaucer Criticism: The Canterbury Tales* (Notre Dame, Indiana: University of Notre Dame Press, 1960), p. 106.

[2] All Chaucer quotations are from F. N. Robinson, ed., *The Works of Geoffrey Chaucer* (Boston: Houghton Mifflin Company, 2nd edn., 1957).

[3] *Op. cit.*, pp. 106–7.   [4] *Ibid.*, p. 109.

»the nature of the noble life«,[5] one, that is, of chivalrous pomp, ceremony and order, and Theseus is the dominant figure in a society whose
»life's pattern is itself a reflection, or better, a reproduction, of the order
of the universe«.[6] The speeches of Theseus »show him as representative
of the highest chivalric conceptions of nobility«,[7] and especially his
final speech concords with »the principle of order which Theseus both
invokes and represents throughout the tale« ... »The actions and speeches by the central figure are the normative ones in the poem.«[8]

Professor Huppé, as might be expected, takes a similarly lofty view of
the »sentence« of the tale, which he thinks is the knight's way of teaching a lesson on true chivalry to his son, the squire.[9] And he too has a
high opinion of Theseus:

> »Theseus may have acted somewhat arbitrarily – if generously – in waging
> war against Thebes because of his pity for the sorrowing widows, but he is
> also the great Duke who ended his war with the ›regne of Femenye‹ by
> marrying its queen, and who has demonstrated the greatness of his friend-
> ship by seeking Perotheus ›down in helle‹. His actions now will be the
> enlightened ones of the just and merciful ruler, preserving peace for his
> realm – in short a true minister of God's Providence.«[10]

This great leader sees the folly of Palamon and Arcite, who prefer
»cupiditas« to »caritas«, following Fortune and earthly love which
leads to discord and violence. The wise Theseus finally succeeds in
bringing Palamon to a sense of responsibility, producing a »happy diplomatic marriage through which the divine wisdom of »Juppiter« is justified of her children.[11]

It cannot be denied, however, that such a view of Theseus as a noble
philosophical reprensentative of the divine order and disentangler of
the golden chain of love, cannot be sustained without brushing aside
certain of his actions which strike the modern reader as harsh. The
charges against Theseus have been pressed most strongly by Henry J.
Webb. He calls Theseus's destruction of Thebes an »expression of rage«,

---

[5] Charles Muscatine, »Form, Texture, and Meaning in Chaucer's *Knight's Tale*«,
PMLA LXV (1950), 911–29; reprinted in and cited from Edward Wagenknecht,
ed., *Chaucer: Modern Essays in Criticism* (New York: O.U.P., 1959), p. 69.
[6] *Ibid.*, p. 70,
[7] *Ibid.*, p. 72.
[8] *Ibid.*, p. 73
[9] Bernard F. Huppé, *A Reading of the Canterbury Tales* (New York: State University of New York, 1964), pp. 54–6.
[10] *Ibid.*, p. 66.
[11] See especially pp. 68, 69, 74.

whereas in the *Teseida* of Boccaccio, Chaucer's source for *The Knight's Tale*, it was not Teseo who burnt the city. Webb condemns likewise his subsequent pillage of the countryside, which, though common in medieval warfare, was condemned by several writers, including Honoré Bonet, Christine de Pisan, Deschamps and Gilbert of the Haye. His perpetual imprisonment of his two young captives Webb calls heartless, and also harsh, where Boccaccio's Teseo treated Arcita and Palemone according to their rank. Even with the suppliant ladies from Thebes, Webb points out, Theseus it at first hasty and selfish, and his abrupt departure for Thebes to avenge them shows »impatience«, and a »hot-headed« desire for immediate action. Even his decree before the tournament that no daggers be used – to avoid slaughter in the melee – Webb takes as being perhaps due to the mood of the crowd, and altogether he agrees with Palamon in calling Theseus's conduct »tiraunye«. Nor does Webb allow Theseus any stable wisdom; on the contrary he sums up: »Underneath his veneer of nobility, there was a hint of ignobility; behind the character known for his kindliness stood another who was sometimes cruel, if not actually brutal, a highly emotional person blowing hot one moment, cold the next.«[12]

Clearly Webb's Theseus is ill-qualified to be a spokesman and representative of the divine wisdom and loving providence, and indeed it does seem clear that Muscatine's and Huppé's views are too much conditioned by the later parts of the tale, by Theseus's speech from the throne

---

[12] Henry J. Webb, »A Reinterpretation of Chaucer's Theseus«, *R. E. S.* XXIII (1947), 289–96. With regard to pillaging the countryside, Christine and Gilbert in the passage cited by Webb follow Honoré Bonet's denunciations (*Tree of Battles,* IV,48,102). But Honoré himself points out that though peasants should be spared in war, if they help their king, they can be treated as enemies: »if on both sides war is ... begun by the Councils of the two kings, the soldiery may take spoil from the kingdom at will ... and if sometimes the humble and innocent suffer harm and lose their goods, it cannot be otherwise, for ... all the weeds cannot be uprooted from among the good plants without some of the latter coming to harm, because they are too close and neighbouring one to another.« (IV,48) For evidence that medieval writers were not untouched by the sufferings of non-combatants, see the speech of the *People* in Alain Chartier's *Quadrilogue Invectif* (»Quadrilogue Invective: Parralel Texts of Two Translations ...«, ed. Margaret S. Blayney [Unpublished Oxford University Dissertation, 1965], II, pp. 44–58). Similarly the *Boke of Noblesse* lists the »infinite damages and extorsions done, as mourdre, slaugheter, blood-sheding, depopulacion of contrees, castelles, citees and townes brennyng ... Wherfor it shulde seme that maintenyng of werre is a cursid deede«. But, of course, war is justified to maintain justice and right! (*The Boke of Noblesse,* ed. J. G. Nichols, Roxburghe Club No. 77, 1860, pp. 6 ff.)

at his Parliament, when he points out that Arcite, like all men, had to die, and had indeed died at the height of his honor; that to mourn over-long for him would be perverse; that God had bound the universe to-gether with a chain of love, and that His providence worked out to the good of all.[13]

I propose that by modifying the extremes of such divergent views we can see Theseus as a consistent character, not ignobly harsh at first, though not full of philosophical wisdom either; one whose conduct is governed by what was accepted as an honorable military code, but whom the events of the poem and the failure of his great plan led to a deeper understanding of the nature of events, and to a philosophical articulation of his new insight in Boethian terms.

For an appreciation and understanding of Theseus's actions in the first part of the poem we are indebted to the researches of Maurice H. Keen in his book *The Laws of War in the Late Middle Ages*. He has shown that for the period of the Hundred Years War, and for all the partici-pants in it (i.e. effectively the whole of Western Europe) a law of arms was accepted as binding on all soldiers. It was enforceable in special courts, argued by competent lawyers, and understood to be the same as the Roman *jus gentium*. It dealt with such things as what constituted a state of war, rights of combatants to plunder, ransom contracts, alle-giance, sieges, truces, safe-conducts and questions of a knight's honor. The standards of humanity and Christian charity which it demanded may not seem very impressive; the same may be said of most codes of law. But this code did set and enforce some standards which were prac-tical for a soldier to observe in a campaign.[14] Theseus seems to me to base his conduct on his rights and obligations under this code. He is thus presented to us, at first, as essentially a great and honorable military captain. But this by no means negligible level of probity was recognized by Chaucer as inadequate for a truly Christian ruler. Consequently, Theseus is educated to a wider more universal philosophy by the end of the tale. I have used the term »Christian ruler«; Theseus is of course a pagan Athenian, but if he was to be relevant to Chaucer's age he must be considered according to Christian standards, or at least according to the Christian concept of a noble and righteous heathen.

---

13 Cf. Paul T. Thurston, *Artistic Ambivalence in Chaucer's Knight's Tale* (Gaines-ville: University of Florida Press, 1968); see especially pp. 79 ff.

14 Maurice H. Keen, *The Laws of War in the Late Middle Ages* (London and Toronto: University of Toronto Press, 1965). See especially pp. 1–22, 240–47.

The first example of Theseus' conduct which is legally justified but imperfect by a stricter code is his making war on Thebes. The cause is simple. As he is returning in triumph to Athens from his victory over the Amazons, he meets a group of suppliants who tell him that they are widows of knights slain in the assault on Thebes, and that the Theban king, Creon, will not permit their husbands' bodies to be buried. He is overcome by pity for them, and vows to avenge their injuries on Creon. He immediately sets off with his army for Thebes. Now it is clear that he has a just cause, for he is going to right a wrong, »to avenge an injury« as St. Augustine puts it and as Raymond of Pennaforte repeats – »to redress injury . . . to right or possessions or persons«.[15] And war is apparently necessary – Creon seems determined.[16] It is true that Raymond says that the war should not be moved by hate (or greed), and St. Augustine says that war's purpose is not to chastize sin – only to restore justice,[17] whereas Theseus does seem to wish to punish Creon and make an example of him:

> »That al the peple of Grece sholde speke / How Creon was of Theseus yserved.« (A 962–3)[18]

If his motives were a little mixed, his cause was none the less just.
But there was also a legal aspect for the medieval ruler. All war was assumed to be just war; if it were unjust it was not war but banditry. For a knight to be legally able to kill, plunder and capture there had to be a legal state of war, and Keen makes clear that the legal ground for deciding whether a war was just was, in effect, whether it was waged by the authority of a prince. Some legists argued that only the emperor could wage war, others that independent kings, such as those of France and England, had no practical superiors and so were free to make war. The same right was allowed to great Dukes such as the Duke of Burgundy.[19] Legally, then, Theseus is so entitled, and he does, forthwith. From the point of view of the laws of war, his is a genuine war. From

---

[15] *Ibid.*, p. 66, 67.
[16] Cp. St. Augustine: »Itaque hostem pugnantem necessitas perimat, non voluntas«, quoted in Alfred Vanderpol, *La Doctrine Scolastique du Droit de Guerre* (Paris: A. Pedone, 1919), p. 93, f.n. 2.
[17] Keen, p. 66.
[18] There is no point in multiplying references to demonstrate the universal medieval view that unjust war was merely banditry. The opinion could be taken for granted in an ordinary sermon; cf. *Jacob's Well*, ed. Arthur Brandeis (London: 1900), EETS OS 115, pp. 210–11; cf. pp. 207–8.
[19] Keen, pp. 74–81.

the point of view of a moral theologian however, or a canon lawyer, Theseus neglects several steps which he should take to be morally correct. For instance, he makes no attempt to settle the matter by embassy, endeavouring to obtain an offer from the other side and accepting it if at all possible, as Lupus of Segovia required.[20] In this Chaucer makes a change from his source. Boccaccio's Tesëo marches off indeed towards Thebes, but on arrival sends an embassy to Creon demanding permission to bury the dead bodies, and waits for the negative response before he lines up his troops for battle.[21] The change puts Theseus in a slightly worse light than Tesëo. But one has only to glance at Chaucer's own *Tale of Melibee* to see how far short of ideal is Theseus's legal action. He did not drive from his heart at least two of the three things »that been contrariouse to good conseil; that is to seyn ire ... and hastifness« (B 2311–2); not only does he not call a judicious council properly composed of old wise friends[22] (and neutrals as Christine de Pisan requires)[23] – he calls no council at all. Melibeus's eloquent wife, Dame Prudence, would have warned him off war altogether of course,[24] and he has indeed a good right to his war. There was, though, a higher standard than that of the military captain, and Chaucer himself in his own *Tale of Melibee* articulated it. Theseus, however, knows nothing of this, but makes his decision promptly and declares a legal state of war by displaying his banner:

> »And right anoon, withouten moore abood, / His baner he desplayeth, and forth rood / To Thebes-ward.«   (A 965–7)

As Keen tells us, »the usual sign of such war was the display of the banner of the prince in whose name it was fought. Once his banner was unfurled, he had given a challenge to combat and a state of war legally existed.«[25]
The vivid impressionistic description Chaucer gives of his banner, with the red figure of Mars shining so »That alle the feeldes glyteren up and doun« A 977, suggests a possible parallel with the French king's famous Oriflamme – whose unfurling meant war to the death with no quarter.

---

[20] Vanderpol, p. 94.
[21] Giovanni Boccaccio, *Teseida*, ed. Aurelio Roncaglia (Bari, 1941), II, st. 51–3.
[22] B 2355–8.
[23] William Caxton, trans. *The Book of Fayttes of Armes and of Chyualrye*, ed. A.T.P. Byles (London, 1932), EETS OS 189, p. 13.
[24] See B 2472 ff., 2721 ff., 2845 ff., and *passim*.
[25] Keen, p. 106.

Keen says it was displayed at Crecy and Poitiers,[26] but it was rarely used in wars againts Christian kings. Froissart tells of its use at the battle of Rosebeque (1382) against Philip van Artevelde and the Flemings:

>Shortly afterwards the oriflamme was displayed by sir Peter de Villiers, who bore it. Some say (as they find it written) that it was never before displayed against Christians, and it was a matter of great doubt during the march whether it should be displayed or not. However, the matter having been fully considered, they resolved to display it, because the Flemings followed opinions contrary to that of Pope Clement, and called themselves Urbanists; for which the French said they were rebellious and out of the pale of the church.«[27]

The oriflamme was red, we may note, and Keen quotes Nicolas Upton that »in heraldry red was the colour signifying cruelty and ferocity, as of a prince against his enemies«.[28] It may be that since burial of the dead was one of the corporal works of mercy, a medieval Christian no less than an ancient Greek would have felt that refusal of burial to dead bodies put one beyond the pale of decent society.

Be that as it may, we turn to Theseus' next action. Chaucer describes it very briefly:

>With Creon, which that was of Thebes kyng, / He faught, and slough hym manly as a knyght / In pleyn bataille, and putte the folk to flyght; / And by assaut he wan the citee after / And rente adoun bothe wall and sparre and rafter.« (A 986–90)

After the dead bodies have been buried Theseus remains in camp and »dide with al the contree as hym leste« (A 1004); this laconic statement seems to mean that he ravaged the countryside. These vigorous measures constitute a very black mark for Theseus in Webb's book, as already noted. But once again if we note the actual laws governing warfare in Chaucer's time we can see the rationale of Theseus' actions. And in this connection we should observe that in Chaucer's very much compressed account he makes one significant change from Boccaccio. In the *Teseida* Tesëo kills Creon in battle, and then the Theban troops flee, but not back into their city. Instead they run into the woods and mountains, and the women, children and elderly who are watching the battle from the city,

---

26 Keen, p. 105.
27 Thomas Johnes, trans. *Chronicles of England, France, Spain and the Adjoining Countries,* by Sir John Froissart (2 vols. London: 1862), I,744.
28 Keen, p. 106.

abandon the city and follow the fugitives through the woods. Tesëo does not follow up the pursuit, but goes towards the city, and at his entrance he meets nobody coming in arms against him. So he admires the fine buildings and then gives the city over to pillage, making a careful exception for the temples. Later the suppliant women, having buried their husbands' bodies, burn the city in revenge.[29] Chaucer has none of these details; Creon is killed in open battle and his army put to flight, but Chaucer is careful to say of Theseus that he gained the city »by assaut« – by assault, which most likely means that it was defended or at any rate that the surrender was unconditional. By fourteenth century standards, while in open battle certain restrictions applied, at least in wars between Christians, if a besieged town was taken by assault – by escalade, ambush, or storm – the rule of war that applied was war to the death without quarter; only churches and priests were technically secure, and women and children might be spared. But all men, not merely soldiers, could be killed, women raped, and all goods were forfeit to the conqueror. The spoliation was systematic; not merely was it done in the heat of fighting, but often in cold blood and with planning.[30] The reason for this as Keen explains is that it was considered contumacious to defend a city against a besieging prince who claimed the town as his and demanded surrender.

> »In contemporary eyes there was thus a great difference between the conquest of a town by force of arms, and a victory in the field. To accept a challenge to battle was to accept the judgment of God; it was also to accept one's adversary as of approximately equal standing to oneself. To refuse the summons of a prince who claimed a town as of right was quite another thing; it was an insult to his majesty and punishable as such.«[31]

Chaucer does not tell us of any formal demand for surrender, or any siege with siege engines. But the mere fact that the town was taken »by assaut« implies this. Chaucer's contemporaries knew what happened to a town thus taken. Keen says he can find no legal sanction for such rules but the chronicles make it clear that the practice was »coustume de la guerre«.[32] Later writers like Cajetan and François de Victoria give a rationale for the practice – Cajetan's view seeming to bear out Keen, that a prince can order pillage of a city as a punishment; Victoria insists on a good reason, but this may include keeping up the morale of the

---

[29] *Teseida*, II, st. 70–81.   [30] Keen, pp. 119–22.
[31] *Ibid.*, pp. 123–4.   [32] *Ibid.*, p. 121, f.n. 3.

troops![33] Theseus seems here to be acting plainly according to the military custom of war. A harsh code in our eyes, and in Chaucer's too, I believe, but it does not make Theseus into an inhuman monster. He is no Tamburlaine.

The action of Theseus most difficult to justify by any standard is his perpetual imprisonment of his two Theban captives, Palamon and Arcite. Boccaccio seems to think in terms of an ancient Roman custom. The two are found wounded on the field after the battle, and are carried carefully to Tesëo. He has them attended to, and, learning that they are of Cadmus's line, keeps them for his triumph. They walk in his triumph, and a few days later he sends for them intending to have them killed, but decides that the danger they potentially represent can be avoided by imprisoning them forever; he therefore imprisons them allotting them a room in the palace in accordance with their rank.[34] Not so with Chaucer's Theseus, more a medieval man; he has no Roman-style triumph, but, with no mention of medical care,

> »... he ful soone hem sente / To Atthenes, to dwellen in prisoun / Perpetuelly, – he nolde no raunsoun.   (A 1022–4)

This merciless sentence is condemned strongly by Webb, and Thurston lays special emphasis on it as well – for the universal custom in wars between Christians was that prisoners were ransomed. Thurston cites Coulton on the free-masonry of knighthood, the requirements of *noblesse oblige* among the brotherhood; and Coulton also appeals to the chivalric oath which Malory's King Arthur imposes upon his knights of the Round Table, and which includes the necessity of showing mercy. Thurston concludes:

> »I see no reasonable explanation that will bring Theseus' failure to grant ransom within the realm of chivalric ideals as Chaucer ostensibly represents them in the Knight's description in the *General Prologue*.«[35]

Now we might object that Chaucer's knight had »followed the wars«, and knew better than most what were the acceptable or legal rules of military conduct. But the difficulty remains that by the very laws of war which we have been applying in judging Theseus' conduct, ransoming of captives was in effect universal, and indeed the gaining of ransom money was a great incentive to join in a war. So it seems that Theseus falls short not only of our ideal code of mercy and moderation which

---

[33] Vanderpol, p. 150.   [34] *Teseida*, II, st. 85–99.   [35] *Op. cit.*, p. 81.

the moral theologians like Victoria encourage[36] but of the law of arms. What can be said?

In the first place the refusal to allow a prisoner to ransom himself was not wholly unprecedented. We might refer to King Arthur in the Alliterative *Morte Arthure*, who sends some of his Roman captives to Paris to be imprisoned without ransom. His reason is, however, that it is unworthy of a great king to be avaricious and seek to make money out of war.[37] But in real life there was the case of Jehans de Graili, known as the captal de Buch, captured in Poitou at Soubise and taken to Paris to be imprisoned. The English offered in exchange for him the Count of Saint-Pol and three or four other knights with ransoms set at one hundred thousand francs. But the king of France refused ransom, because such an able captain was quite capable of doing up to twice that amount of damage to his enemy's territory in a week or less. The squire who captured him, Pierres d'Auviller, thought it a great discourtesy to so noble an adversary not to allow him to ransom himself according to his rank. This squire had received from the king twelve hundred francs as a reward for capturing the capital, whereas if he had paid ransom »selonch son estat«, our courteous Pierre would have been entitled to it, and the sum would have been much more than twelve hundred francs. So perhaps Pierre is not to be considered an unbiassed witness. Many other more important and disinterested Frenchmen, however, agreed with Pierre, and urged the king to allow ransom. But, though much entreated, the king would only release him if he swore not to follow his allegiance and fight on against France. He refused, and died after five years of captivity.[38]

Clearly Theseus had at least as much to fear from Palamon and Arcite. John of Lignano argues that in an open war between two states enemy captives may be enslaved, but by Christian practice persons are not sold and do not become slaves.[39] »Nowadays«, says Bonet, »we have abandoned the ancient rules of making serfs of prisoners«; and he approves a moderate ransom.[40] In fact, in spite of the exception above mentioned,

---

[36] Vanderpol, p. 155.

[37] Erik Björkman, ed., *Morte Arthure* (Heidelberg and New York, 1915), 1571 ff.

[38] Baron Kervyn de Lettenhove, ed., *Oeuvres de Froissart* (Brussels, 1869), VIII, 400–2.

[39] Giovanni da Legnano, *Tractatus de Bello, de Represaliis et de Duello*, ed. Thomas Erskine Holland (O.U.P., 1917), p. 270.

[40] G. W. Coopland, tr. *The Tree of Battles of Honoré Bonet* (Cambridge, Mass.: Harvard University Press, 1949), pp. 152–3.

a knight who surrendered could expect to be ransomed. But from the legal point of view there existed a contract between captor and captive. »When a man surrenders and his victor accepts him as a prisoner then he makes a contract with him that he shall be a captive and shall not be killed«; and according to Bartholomew of Saliceto: »A prisoner is not held as a slave. ... but as a pledge for the price of his ransom.«[41] Since ransoms of captives were an important part of the financial incentives to make war, the specifying of who captured whom and what agreement was made were extremely important in law. Courts spent much time hearing litigation on the subject – e.g., who had ransom rights over a prisoner, the one who seized his right arm and took his gauntlet, or he who first put his right hand in the other's.[42] What is clear from the numerous interesting examples cited by Keen is that business considerations predominated in the military mind, and the making of the contract was legally the important act.[43]

Now it is clear that Palamon and Arcite had no contract with Theseus. They had not, in fact, surrendered, but had fought till they fell wounded, and were discovered after the battle nearly dead among a pile of corpses. Furthermore, while in Boccaccio they were wounded in battle, in Chaucer they may very well have been found in the city, since the city was taken by assault. In this case they had no rights; but even if they fell in the battle, Theseus had no obligations to them. They had not taken his right hand and surrendered to him to save their lives; no compact existed between them. Their imprisonment was harsh, perhaps, – they were in strong prison – but Theseus was within his rights, it seems, in treating them so.

It seems to me, moreover, that Theseus has Honoré Bonet on his side. In Book IV c. 46 of his *Tree of Battles*, Honoré raises the question whether a man according to present usage and laws may at will kill his prisoner. He answers clearly not, since the prisoner is out of the battle.

---

[41] See Keen, p. 157. The former citation is from Paris of Pozzo, *De Re Militari*.

[42] *Ibid.*, p. 34.

[43] How much contractual obligations weighed in the minds of men of the time can be seen in Honoré's two questions in his Book IV concerning the rights and wrongs of a prisoner's attempting to escape. For example: »... if the prisoner has sworn to keep prison on the understanding that his master, so far as his ability and possessions allow, gives him drink, food, and a bed in a given place, and is willing to treat for due and reasonable ransom ... then if he escapes he breaks his oath and his faith, notwithstanding his close imprisonment.« (IV, c. 56, pp. 159–60; see also c. 55).

But he concludes, »I say that jurisdiction should belong to the sovereign prince who is carrying on the war, and by no means to a knight or champion who has made a capture and has no jurisdiction whatever in that territory«.[44] However, although Bonet distinguishes between any subordinate and the captain of the war, e.g., Theseus, allowing the Commander more latitude, this need not be conclusive. What does seem conclusive is his earlier treatment, in c. 13 of the same book, of the question: If the Duke of the Battle is taken prisoner, ought one to have mercy on him and pardon him? His conclusion, after arguing each side, is as follows: »... it is my opinion that he who in battle has captured his enemy, especially if it be the duke or marshal of the battle, truly, according to God and theology and the law of the decretals, should have mercy on him, unless by his deliverance there is danger of having greater wars ... And for this reason the good King of Naples made Conradus die by sentence, having him beheaded, for those of the King's council said that if he escaped the war would not be finished and that there would never be peace in the kingdom while this Conradus lived.«[45] Theseus' sentence of life imprisonment is less severe than the death sentence, and obviously Palamon and Arcite, after the death of Creon, could be considered the Dukes of the battle, for they were of the royal Theban line, and the responsibility for carrying on the war rested on them.

Our examination of these actions of Theseus shows him to be not an ideal ruler, just, merciful and magnanimous, a philosopher king; nor on the other hand a brute under a veneer of nobility. He is a great and successful military captain who operated according to his rights and duties under the law of arms, who had a profession, and, in the eyes of medieval Christian Europe, an honorable one. The »honor« of a soldier had of course a certain technical aspect. As Keen sums it up *a propos* of the relation of captor and prisoner: »The man of honour did not mean for a medieval soldier an ideal human being, but a person of a particular social status and calling who kept on the right side of certain technical rules. These rules were general; idealism lay beyond them in the realm of personal choice.«[46] Theseus's character fits his military profession. He does not display much regard for the feelings of others – as his mocking speech about the folly of love to Palamon and Arcite shows us; he is very touchy about his honor, as witness his indignation when he

---

[44] *Op. cit.,* p. 152.   [45] *Ibid.,* p. 134.   [46] Keen, p. 185.

sees the suppliant ladies blocking his way to Athens in their misery and black clothes. He is a quick and decisive man of action, whose hasty judgments can, however, be changed to mercy by a womanly appeal. But Chaucer makes it plain that, though honorable, the military mind and the military stance are not enough for a ruler; and the events of the Tale are designed to bring the self-confident man of action to more acceptable views and attitudes.

Critics have been quick to see the folly of Palamon and Arcite in unwisely succumbing to love, not recognizing the true good, lacking self-knowledge and following the uncertain favours of Fortune. But in hastening to characterize the unhappy young lovers as two minds with but a single track, they have neglected to turn the same standards of judgment on Theseus; I suppose they are too much impressed by his final speech. But Theseus is equally a follower of *Fortuna,* not a spokesman for Providence; he enjoys good fortune, in contrast to the two lovers, but he is equally blind to the true nature of the case. Palamon and Arcite cannot solve the problem of evil and Providence; Theseus is unaware of it. He thinks he can control events himself. As a result he acts rapidly and decisively, and causes much misery. He avenges the suppliant women, but his deeds, guided by an inadequate military code, bring a great deal of unhappiness in their train, as the long plaints of the two lovers eloquently testify. When we first meet him he is »in his mooste pride« (A 895), and when we see him just before the great tournament »Arrayed right as he were a god in trone« (A 2529), we may well remember that such pride goes before a fall.

And consider the plan which he makes for the love dilemma. Finding Palamon and Arcite fighting a duel on a May morning, he stops the fight, and on being informed that they are fighting for the love of Emily (without her cognizance), this man of decisive action arranges that each shall bring one hundred knights and they shall all fight in a tournament one year hence, the winner to have the lady. Such is his penchant for the pride, pomp, and circumstance of glorious war, that at vast expense he will set up lists, temples and stands so that instead of two knights deciding the case by combat, he will have two hundred and two. For Professor Huppé to call this Theseus' »design for peace in a world of confusion«[47] is indeed to approach the language of 1984. One might wonder, if not overcome by Theseus' power and success, whether he is

---

[47] *Op. cit.,* p. 67.

not really less like a representative of dignity and order than one of the
foolish youths in *Princess Ida:*

> »who is longing for the rattle / of a complicated battle.«

And of course his gigantic grandiose scheme turns out a monumental
failure; destiny adroitly checkmates him. The man of action acts, and
nothing is decided. The mountain labors – and lays an egg, or (more
elegantly) the issue is abortive. Arcite's side wins at the tournament, for
Palamon is captured, but by Saturn's arrangements a fury startles Arcite's horse at the moment of his triumph, and he is thrown on his head,
from which he has just removed his helmet. He dies shortly afterwards,
amid great lamentation.
No one can cheer Theseus except his old father Egeus. Chaucer makes
no comment, and it appears on reading that Theseus is sad for Arcite's
death, like Emily and Palamon. But Egeus moralizes that all must die,
that the world is full of woe, since he

> »knew this worldes transmutacioun, / As he hadde seyn it chaunge bothe up
> and doun, / Joye after wo, and wo after gladnesse.«   (A 2839–41)

All this clearly applicable to Theseus's own case. His confident plans
had gone awry and he is in the initial state of Boethian distress.
Theseus, however, can learn from misfortune. We are not shown the
process of his learning, but at the parliament after Arcite's funeral he
makes his famous Boethian speech. Enough has been written on the
nobility of this address, and enough is as good as a feast. Here we need
only point out that Chaucer, skilfully blending four major passages of
the *Consolation of Philosophy,* makes his Theseus show that he has absorbed his lesson well; that there is a divinity which shapes our ends,
that ill fortune, even death, can be seen as good fortune; that it is useless
to cry out on Fortune, rather the path of wisdom is to accept what
Fortune brings – even death of our friends – and make the best of it.
»The contrarie of al this is wilfulnesse« (A 3057).
The education of Theseus seems to me a major theme of the poem. He is
a successful soldier, acting by a code honorable in the world's eyes, and
really so; he is proud, confident, quick, hasty, and usually decisive in
action, but unwittingly he brings great distress on his two prisoners.
His presumed control over events finally fails, and a great disaster
ensues; from it he has the strength of mind to recover, retains his dignity, and increases in wisdom. As a result by more humbly yielding to

destiny he achieves peace with Thebes and married happiness for Emily and Palamon. He not only attests to the kindliness of »Juppiter's« overriding Providence; he is himself an example of its mysterious but beneficent sway.

From this conclusion follow two corollaries. First, we may be able to answer, at least partially, the adverse judgment which Elizabeth Salter pronounces upon *The Knight's Tale* in what seems to me the most sensitive and intelligent treatment of the poem that I know of. The frequency with which Chaucer shifts the tone of the verse from dignity to bathos is hard to account for, and led Paull Baum to consider the work a failure.[48] These »sinkings« afford Miss Salter a wedge with which to split up the unity of the poem. Chaucer, she says, is prepared to abandon consistency: »In passing so swiftly from powerful expression to comment which is trivial, almost flippant, he seems to be using two voices: one reveals for us the pain latent in the narrative, the other, less sensitive, speaks with imperfect comprehension of that pain.«[49] She finds that Chaucer continually raises lofty and eloquent statements about the misery of Palamon and Arcite, and of the human condition in general, and then withdraws into lightness; even Theseus' last speech is really a withdrawal, and does not satisfactorily answer the questionings about the cruelty of the gods, nor the very evident coldness and unconcern which they themselves display in their debate. In short, Chaucer's attempt at a philosophical poem founders precisely because his sympathy with the lover's plight is too strong for wisdom to overcome. His imagination rises to heights of questioning and complaint, e.g. in Palamon's

> »O cruel goddes that governe / This world with byndyng of youre word eterne / ... What is mankynde moore unto you holde / Than is the sheep that rouketh in the folde? / ... What governance is in this prescience / That giltelees tormenteth innocence?   (A 1303–1314)

and Arcite's famous last words:

> What is this world? what asketh men to have? / Now with his love, now in his colde grave / Allone, withouten any compaignye.   (A 2777–2779)

Chaucer in fact cannot control his imaginative sympathy, and it out-

---

[48] Paull F. Baum, *Chaucer: A Critical Appreciation* (Durham, N.C., 1958), pp. 102–4.
[49] Elizabeth Salter, *Chaucer: The Knight's Tale and The Clerk's Tale* (Barron's Educational Series, Inc.: Great Neck, N.Y., 1962), p. 23.

weighs his philosophy; the lovers' questions are answered rationally, perhaps, but not with imaginative conviction. Miss Salter concludes:

> »It is surely a measure of the greatness of Chaucer that his imaginative response to a situation in which innocent creatures confront the wilful use of absolute power was strong enough to disturb the overall balance of his work. As it is, the words of Theseus, ›Why grucchen we, why have we hevynesse . . .‹, intended as a rallying cry towards cheerful recovery, serve also to emphasise the great gulf which lies between the questions asked by the poet's imagination, and the replies he feels able, in *this* instance, to give.«[50]

Now it may be that Chaucer was indeed trying to write in terms of Book V of Boethius's *Consolatio* when he had matured emotionally little beyond Book I. None the less Miss Salter's objection to the cruelty of the gods does receive a partial answer from Professor Huppé: Venus, Diana and Mars have control over man to his doom only when he gives himself over into their power by following Fortune and seeking temporal partial goods.[51] Only a partial answer, however. Palamon and Arcite's love is not the only cause of their unhappiness, and for a convincing vindication of the justice of Providence, the whole blame for their misery must fall on some human blindness and error. Obviously the blame for much of the sorrow in the poem belongs to Theseus. The gods then are absolved of responsibility, or rather God – Juppiter – is absolved, for the astrological gods are mere personifications of the natural laws of the universe. One might agree that this abstract consideration does not wholly discount Miss Salter's complaint that the poem fails through the emotional imbalance which she describes. But certainly if the action of the poem is seen in a different light, with Theseus bearing part of the blame for the evil as well as for the good, the imbalance will seem less pronounced. Furthermore, if my thesis is accepted, that Theseus is lacking to some degree in wisdom and virtue, and has himself to be educated into wisdom by events, then the reader will more clearly see and be more impressed by the importance and weight of the ways of Providence.

The second corollary concerns the theme of the poem. *The Knight's Tale* is not so much a mirror of chivalry as a mirror for magistrates, a *Fürstenspiegel*. We may now see that the education of an enlightened ruler forms part of Chaucer's theme of order and dignity in the conduct of life and

---

[50] *Op. cit.*, p. 36.
[51] Huppé, pp. 62–3.

the governance of a realm. The question of the relationship between the knight as warrior and knight as Christian had been treated in other romances, and the solution had usually been either a naive assumption (for instance in the English Charlemagne romances) that the pagans are wrong and the Christians are right, or an almost equally simplistic rejection of arms in favor of prayer. The greater maturity of Chaucer's view can be seen from a consideration of the career of Guy of Warwick, the hero of a romance of the previous century. Guy at first goes round Europe from tournament to tournament winning the prize and the glory each time. He is a regular pot-hunter, and his motive is the desire for fame – to become the most renowned knight in the world in order to please his love, Felice, daughter of the Earl of Warwick. A churchman would call these motives lust and vain-glory. A higher motive presents itself when he goes to the aid of Duke Segyn of Louvain who is being wrongfully besieged by the German Emperor. Guy supports the right, and ends the war by capturing the emperor and arranging a reconciliation between him and his vassal, Duke Segyn. After this he fights for the highest motive, as a crusader, helping the Eastern Emperor against the infidels who are besieging him at Constantinople, and this campaign also he quickly concludes, this time by cutting off the Sultan's head. Guy's career shows him fighting for better and better reasons, until he returns to England and marries his lady. Yet after only fifteen days he is struck by the thought that God has done much for him, while he has done nothing for God; so he promptly bids farewell to Felice and sets off in disguise as a pilgrim to do penance for having slain so many people and destroyed cities. He does indeed have to fight a few single combats in just causes, for suppliants who have been seeking Guy of Warwick but have not found him; and he does return to England – still in disguise – in time to help the king Athelston against an invading Danish army by killing their champion giant Colbrond. But the king might well have preferred some more permanent, less vagabond, defence force. In Guy then, as in the *Moniage Guillaume* on which it was partly modelled, the knightly life was worldly and the alternative was to renounce it entirely.

Chaucer knew better. He himself may well have felt a mood of war-weariness and desire for peace of the early years of the reign of Richard II. It was in the 1380's that he wrote his *Tale of Melibee*, based ultimately on Albertano of Brescia's peace document, *Liber Consolationis et Consilii*. But although in these same years he wrote *The*

Knight's Tale (1385), and showed his awareness of the darker side of war in the grim atmosphere he conjures up in the description of the temple of Mars, yet still he knew that military power, however harsh in practice, was the *conditio sine qua non* of a kingdom. Theseus remains powerful, and needs power. He arranges a diplomatic marriage to cement the peace between Athens and Thebes, but without military power that peace would not last long. Theseus learns that more is needed for the blessing of peace than fighting ability, that there is more needed for a good orderly kingdom than the code of a knight; but the more does not replace the less. It is for this reason, I believe, that neither Chaucer himself nor the knightly narrator of the Tale ever criticizes Theseus adversely for the crimes of which Webb and others accuse him. The orderly, ceremonial, dignified life-style which Muscatine finds in *The Knight's Tale* is not possible without the sub-stratum of armed might. Theseus must be educated to go beyond it, but cannot do without it. Such is Chaucer's more practical, more mature view of the ideal ruler – one who possesses power, and develops a philosophical mind the better to wield it. In the words of the sub-title of this conference, the two value »systems« do not conflict; they complement each other.

Speakers and Other Invited Participants of the Symposium

Prof. Franz H. Bäuml, Department of Germanic Languages, University of California, Los Angeles, California, USA

Prof. Bruno Boesch, Deutsches Seminar, Universität Freiburg, Freiburg im Breisgau, Germany

Prof. Karl Bosl, Institut für Landesgeschichte, Universität München and Bayerische Akademie der Wissenschaften, München, Germany

Prof. David Crawford, School of Music, The University of Michigan, Ann Arbor, Michigan, USA

Prof. Charles J. Donahue, Department of English, Fordham University, New York, N.Y., USA

Prof. Christian J. Gellinek, Department of Germanic and Slavic Languages and Literatures, University of Florida, Gainesville, Florida, USA

Prof. Ingeborg Glier, Department of Germanic Languages, Yale University, New Haven, Connecticut, USA

Dr. Harlan H. Hatcher, President Emeritus of The University of Michigan, Ann Arbor, Michigan, USA

Prof. Edward A. Heinemann, Department of French, New College, University of Toronto, Toronto, Canada

Prof. Antonín Hrubý, Department of Germanic Languages and Literature, University of Washington, Seattle, Washington, USA

Prof. Hans-Erich Keller, Department of Romance Languages, The Ohio State University, Columbus, Ohio, USA

Prof. Dennis M. Kratz, Department of Classics, The Ohio State University, Columbus, Ohio, USA

Prof. Sherman M. Kuhn, Middle English Dictionary and Department of English Language and Literature, The University of Michigan, Ann Arbor, Michigan, USA

Prof. James W. Marchand, Center for Advanced Study and Department of Germanic Languages and Literatures, University of Illinois, Urbana, Illinois, USA

Prof. Frederick P. Pickering, Department of German, University of Reading, Reading, England

Prof. John Reidy, Middle English Dictionary and Department of English Language and Literature, The University of Michigan, Ann Arbor, Michigan, USA

Prof. Donald B. Sands, Department of English Language and Literature, The University of Michigan, Ann Arbor, Michigan, USA

Prof. Paul Schach, Department of Germanic Languages, The University of Nebraska-Lincoln, Lincoln, Nebraska, USA

Prof. Kenneth L. Schmitz, Department of Philosophy, Trinity College, University of Toronto, Toronto, Canada

Prof. Harald Scholler, Department of Germanic Languages and Literatures, The University of Michigan, Ann Arbor, Michigan, USA

Prof. Werner Schröder, Institut für Ältere Deutsche Philologie, Universität Marburg, Marburg, Germany

Prof. Hans-Hugo Steinhoff, Fachbereich Sprach- und Literaturwissenschaften, Gesamthochschule Paderborn, Paderborn, Germany

Prof. M. Alison Stones, Department of Art History, University of Minnesota, Minneapolis, Minnesota, USA

Prof. Thomas F. Taylor, School of Music, The University of Michigan, Ann Arbor, Michigan, USA

Prof. Claiborne W. Thompson, Department of Germanic Languages and Literatures, The University of Michigan, Ann Arbor, Michigan, USA

Prof. Maurice O'C. Walshe, Institute of Germanic Studies, University of London, London, England

Prof. Peter Wapnewski, Seminar für Deutsche Literatur des Mittelalters, Universität (TH) Karlsruhe, Karlsruhe, Germany

Prof. Stanley N. Werbow, Dean of the College of Humanities, The University of Texas at Austin, Texas, USA